AUG 14 2012

Forest Park Library
St. Louis Community College
5600 Oakland
St. Louis, MO 63110-1393
314-644-9210

D1174066

CONTEMPORARY
Black
Biography

ISSN-1058-1316

CONTEMPORARY

Black

Biography

Profiles from the International Black Community

Volume 94

GALE
CENGAGE Learning·

Detroit • New York • San Francisco • New Haven, Conn • Waterville, Maine • London

Contemporary Black Biography, Volume 94

Kepos Media, Inc.: Derek Jacques, Janice Jorgensen, and Paula Kepos, editors

Project Editor: Margaret Mazurkiewicz

Image Research and Acquisitions: Leitha Etheridge-Sims

Manufacturing: Dorothy Maki, Rita Wimberley

Composition and Prepress: Mary Beth Trimper, Gary Leach

Imaging: John Watkins

© 2012 Gale, Cengage Learning

ALL RIGHTS RESERVED. No part of this work covered by the copyright herein may be reproduced, transmitted, stored, or used in any form or by any means graphic, electronic, or mechanical, including but not limited to photocopying, recording, scanning, digitizing, taping, Web distribution, information networks, or information storage and retrieval systems, except as permitted under Section 107 or 108 of the 1976 United States Copyright Act, without the prior written permission of the publisher.

This publication is a creative work fully protected by all applicable copyright laws, as well as by misappropriation, trade secret, unfair competition, and other applicable laws. The authors and editors of this work have added value to the underlying factual material herein through one or more of the following: unique and original selection, coordination, expression, arrangement, and classification of the information.

For product information and technology assistance, contact us at **Gale Customer Support, 1-800-877-4253.**
For permission to use material from this text or product, submit all requests online at **www.cengage.com/permissions.**
Further permissions questions can be emailed to **permissionrequest@cengage.com**

While every effort has been made to ensure the reliability of the information presented in this publication, Gale, a part of Cengage Learning, does not guarantee the accuracy of the data contained herein. Gale accepts no payment for listing; and inclusion in the publication of any organization, agency, institution, publication, service, or individual does not imply endorsement of the editors or publisher. Errors brought to the attention of the publisher and verified to the satisfaction of the publisher will be corrected in future editions.

EDITORIAL DATA PRIVACY POLICY. Does this publication contain information about you as an individual? If so, for more information about our editorial data privacy policies, please see our Privacy Statement at www.gale.cengage.com.

Gale
27500 Drake Rd.
Farmington Hills, MI, 48331-3535

ISBN-13: 978-1-4144-7174-7
ISBN-10: 1-4144-7174-2

ISSN 1058-1316

This title is also available as an e-book.
ISBN 13: 978-1-4144-7270-6
ISBN-10: 1-4144-7270-6
Contact your Gale sales representative for ordering information.

Printed in Mexico
1 2 3 4 5 6 7 15 14 13 12 11

Advisory Board

Emily M. Belcher
General and Humanities Reference Librarian
Firestone Library, Princeton University

Dr. Alton Hornsby, Jr.
Professor of History
Morehouse College

Dr. Ronald Woods
Professor, African American Studies Program
Eastern Michigan University

Contents

Introduction ix

Cumulative Nationality Index 165

Cumulative Occupation Index 183

Cumulative Subject Index 209

Cumulative Name Index 259

Carmelo Anthony 1

  NBA All-Star forward

Wanda M. Austin...5

  Engineering expert and CEO of The Aerospace
  Corporation

Paris Barclay 8

  Emmy Award–winning director known for his work
  on NYPD Blue, The West Wing, and Glee

Melba Pattillo Beals 12

  One of the "Little Rock Nine" and memoirist

William Holmes Borders 15

  Longtime Baptist pastor and civil rights pioneer

Oliver Leon Brown 18

  Litigant in landmark Brown v. Board of Education
  case

Wyatt Cenac 20

  Irreverent writer and correspondent for The Daily
  Show with Jon Stewart

Susan E. Chapman 23

  Leading global real estate specialist

Linda Clement-Holmes 25

  Senior vice president and chief diversity officer at
  Procter & Gamble

Cecilia Conrad 28

  Esteemed economist and public policy analyst
  serving as dean of Pomona College

LaVerne Council 31

  Corporate vice president and chief information
  officer of Johnson & Johnson

Mia Amber Davis 33

  Plus-size model who fought against "sizism" in
  American culture

Rocky Dawuni 36

  Globally recognized Ghanaian reggae artist
  and activist

DJ Lance Rock 39

  Colorful host of popular children's program
  Yo Gabba Gabba!

Colman Domingo 41

  Veteran stage actor known for his roles in Passing
  Strange and The Scottsboro Boys

Fantasia 45

  Rags-to-riches American Idol winner

D. M. French 49

  Civil-rights era physician who fostered health care
  services in West Africa

Linda Gooden 51

  Information technology guru for defense giant
  Lockheed Martin

Kim C. Goodman 54

  Hardworking senior executive at American Express

Tyree Guyton 56

  Inspiring artist who created Detroit's Heidelberg
  Project

Sharon Haynie 60

  Research chemist focusing on environmentally
  friendly products

Joshua Henry 62

  Rising Broadway star earning acclaim for In the
  Heights, American Idiot, and The Scottsboro Boys

Grant Hill...65

  NBA all-star who battled back after ankle injuries

Wyllstyne D. Hill..69

  Honored IT officer in the missile defense industry

Terrence Howard 71

  Hollywood actor best known for roles in Crash,
  Hustle & Flow

Deborah Jackson..75

  Leading physicist with the National Science
  Foundation

Nikki M. James 78

  Tony Award–winning Book of Mormon star

Joe Johnson 81
    Versatile Atlanta Hawks all-star forward
Sandra K. Johnson 84
    High-achieving IBM engineer and author
Bobby Jones...86
    Grammy-winning singer and host of groundbreaking
        gospel music show
Herb Kemp 89
    Trailblazing advertising executive who promoted
        diversity in marketing
Sean Kingston 92
    Jamaican-American singer and songwriter known
        for hit "Beautiful Girls"
Don Lemon 94
    Candid host of CNN Newsroom
LL Cool J...97
    Rapper and actor starring in NCIS: Los Angeles
Clara Luper 101
    Beloved Oklahoma educator and leader of civil
        rights–era sit-ins
Jerry Manuel 103
    Philosophical former manager of the
        New York Mets
Melodie Mayberry-Stewart................................106
    Innovative information technology executive
Forrest McClendon 109
    Successful Philadelphia-based stage actor
Robert McFerrin Sr. 112
    Baritone who became the first black male to perform
        with the Metropolitan Opera
Patina Miller 115
    Broadway star of smash hit Sister Act
Maya Moore 118
    Record-breaking UConn basketball star drafted
        by the Minnesota Lynx
Euzhan Palcy..121
    Martinican director best known for the anti-apartheid
        film A Dry White Season

Tony Reagins 125
    Hard-working general manager of the Los Angeles
        Angels of Anaheim
Emmett J. Rice 128
    Prominent economist who served on the Federal
        Reserve Board
Joan Robinson-Berry 131
    High-ranking aerospace engineer active in
        promoting diversity in the profession
Sonny Rollins...133
    Legendary jazz tenor saxophonist
Joseph Boulogne, Chevalier de Saint–Georges 137
    Celebrated 18th-century French composer,
        violinist, fencing champion, and military hero
Gil Scott-Heron 140
    Provocative poet and vocalist known for "The
        Revolution Will Not Be Televised"
Margaret Simms 142
    Respected economist and director of the Urban
        Institute's Low-Income Working Families project
Tracey T. Travis 145
    Successful financial officer of apparel and lifestyle
        giant Polo Ralph Lauren
Michael Vick..147
    Star quarterback who reignited football career
        following imprisonment
Derek Walcott 151
    Nobel Prize–winning West Indian playwright and
        poet
Sammy Wanjiru...156
    Tenacious marathoner remembered for 2008
        Olympic gold-medal performance
William Warfield 159
    Incomparable bass-baritone who sang in Showboat,
        Porgy and Bess
Brian Courtney Wilson...162
    Rising contemporary gospel singer

Introduction

Contemporary Black Biography provides informative biographical profiles of the important and influential persons of African heritage who form the international black community: men and women who have changed today's world and are shaping tomorrow's. *Contemporary Black Biography* covers persons of various nationalities in a wide variety of fields, including architecture, art, business, dance, education, fashion, film, industry, journalism, law, literature, medicine, music, politics and government, publishing, religion, science and technology, social issues, sports, television, theater, and others. In addition to in-depth coverage of names found in today's headlines, *Contemporary Black Biography* provides coverage of selected individuals from earlier in this century whose influence continues to impact on contemporary life. *Contemporary Black Biography* also provides coverage of important and influential persons who are not yet household names and are therefore likely to be ignored by other biographical reference series. Each volume also includes listee updates on names previously appearing in *CBB*.

Designed for Quick Research and Interesting Reading

- **Attractive page design** incorporates textual subheads, making it easy to find the information you're looking for.

- **Easy-to-locate data sections** provide quick access to vital personal statistics, career information, major awards, and mailing addresses, when available.

- **Informative biographical essays** trace the subject's personal and professional life with the kind of in-depth analysis you need.

- **To further enhance your appreciation** of the subject, most entries include photographic portraits.

- **Sources for additional information** direct the user to selected books, magazines, and newspapers where more information on the individuals can be obtained.

Helpful Indexes Make It Easy to Find the Information You Need

Contemporary Black Biography includes cumulative Nationality, Occupation, Subject, and Name indexes that make it easy to locate entries in a variety of useful ways.

Available in Electronic Formats

Diskette/Magnetic Tape. Contemporary Black Biography is available for licensing on magnetic tape or diskette in a fielded format. Either the complete database or a custom selection of entries may be ordered. The database is available for internal data processing and nonpublishing purposes only. For more information, call (800) 877-GALE.

On-line. Contemporary Black Biography is available on-line through Mead Data Central's NEXIS Service in the NEXIS, PEOPLE and SPORTS Libraries in the GALBIO file and Gale's Biography Resource Center.

Disclaimer

Contemporary Black Biography uses and lists websites as sources and these websites may become obsolete.

We Welcome Your Suggestions

The editors welcome your comments and suggestions for enhancing and improving *Contemporary Black Biography*. If you would like to suggest persons for inclusion in the series, please submit these names to the editors. Mail comments or suggestions to:

The Editor

Contemporary Black Biography

Gale, Cengage Learning

27500 Drake Rd.

Farmington Hills, MI 48331-3535

Phone: (800) 347-4253

Carmelo Anthony

1984—

Professional basketball player

Anthony, Carmelo, photograph. Nick Lahman/Getty Images.

Carmelo Anthony is a star basketball player who spent his first seven and a half professional seasons with the Denver Nuggets. He was a marquee scorer at the position of small forward from the time he entered the National Basketball Association (NBA) in 2003, but he was met with criticisms about his lack of discipline and his character. He worked to overcome these criticisms and to become a more complete player, and by the time of the 2007–08 season he had by most accounts accomplished this goal. A three-time All-Star, Anthony was unquestionably one of the NBA's best small forwards by decade's end. Frustrated by an inability to lead the Nuggets to an NBA title, Anthony pushed for a trade to a franchise that would have a better shot at building a championship team. Rumors about a pending blockbuster deal shadowed Anthony and the Nuggets for much of the 2010–11 season before the announcement came in February 2011 that he had been traded to the New York Knicks.

Excelled as High-School Player

Anthony was born on May 29, 1984, in Brooklyn, New York, to Carmelo Iriarte and Mary Anthony. His father died when he was two years old, and his mother, who worked as a housekeeper, struggled to support the family as a single mother. When Anthony was eight years of age, the family moved away from housing projects in Red Hook, Brooklyn, to the crime-ridden area in Baltimore, Maryland, later made infamous by the TV drama *The Wire*. "When I was in high school, I'd go to the bus stop and they were filming the show two blocks away from me," he told Jon L. Wertheim in *Sports Illustrated*. "Guns, drugs, violence, even the characters—that was for real. . . . You get out and you're like, Did I really come from that?"

Mary Anthony saw to it that her family's difficult circumstances did not prevent her children from fulfilling their potential. She demanded that Carmelo keep his grades up, even as he began to show signs of becoming a basketball talent in his early teen years. Anthony entered Baltimore's Towson Catholic High School as a talented but undisciplined player. In his sophomore and junior seasons he worked diligently to improve his game, and he grew physically, reaching 6 feet 5 inches by his sophomore year. He was soon identified as a rising star, but inner-city Baltimore

At a Glance . . .

Born on May 29, 1984, in Brooklyn, NY; son of Carmelo Iriarte and Mary Anthony (a housekeeper); married LaLa Vazquez (a television personality), July 10, 2010; children: Kiyan. *Education*: Attended Syracuse University.

Career: Denver Nuggets, professional basketball player, 2003–11; New York Knicks, professional basketball player, 2011—.

Awards: First Team High School All America, *USA Today,* 2002; First Team High School All America, *Parade,* 2002; Most Valuable Player, NCAA Final Four, 2003; All-American Team, *Sporting News,* 2003; All-Rookie Team, NBA, 2004; All-Star Team, NBA, 2007, 2008, and 2010.

Addresses: *Office*—c/o New York Knicks, Madison Square Garden, Two Pennsylvania Plaza, New York, NY 10121-0091. *Web*—http://www.thisismelo.com/.

proved a distracting environment. Backed by his strong-willed mother, he made the decision to leave Towson Catholic and get serious about school and his game. Anthony transferred to Oak Hill Academy, a Baptist boarding school in rural Mouth of Wilson, Virginia.

Oak Hill was a basketball powerhouse known for producing players who went on to successful college and professional careers, but it was also demanding academically. Before Oak Hill would even take Anthony, he had to attend five weeks of summer school while simultaneously practicing and playing for an Amateur Athletic Union (AAU) team. The discipline paid off: Anthony succeeded academically while leading the Oak Hill basketball team to a 32–1 record and a ranking of third in the nation. He averaged 21.7 points and 7.4 rebounds per game. The highlight of his senior season was a victory over Akron, Ohio's St. Vincent–St. Mary, which was led by future NBA phenom LeBron James.

Led Syracuse to NCAA Title

Although some encouraged Anthony to go straight from high school to the NBA—following the example of stars like Kobe Bryant and Kevin Garnett—his mother encouraged him to attend college. Anthony signed with Syracuse University, where coach Jim Boeheim was building a team of young and capable

players. From his very first college basket, a dunk against Memphis, Anthony showed that he was a star-caliber college player. During the regular season he led the Syracuse Orangemen with 22.2 points and 10.0 rebounds per game, while playing 36.4 minutes per game. Then Anthony led his team to six straight victories in the NCAA tournament, culminating in a 20-point, 10-rebound performance as they defeated the University of Kansas 81–78 to take the national championship.

Sporting News summed up Anthony's remarkable season by noting that "Anthony played the college game better than any freshman in NCAA basketball. Ever." Coach Boeheim echoed these sentiments, telling *Sports Illustrated* that Anthony was "the best player I've ever coached," both on and off the court. "There was never a problem with him. In the admissions office they're always looking for that kid who acts like he's from the suburbs, nice and well-mannered, but when it comes to basketball [we] want him to be tough as hell and banging people. Carmelo is all of those things."

Anthony was selected as the third pick in the 2003 NBA draft by the Denver Nuggets, who had won just 17 games in the previous season. He posted spectacular numbers in 2003–04, his rookie season, starting in all 82 regular season games and averaging 21.0 points, 6.1 rebounds, 2.8 assists, and 1.2 steals per game. He helped lift the Nuggets to a 43–39 overall record and into a first round playoff berth against the Minnesota Timberwolves. Although the Timberwolves won the series 4–1, all of Denver recognized that their team had taken huge steps forward. Anthony's season was capped when he came in second to LeBron James in NBA Rookie of the Year voting.

Worked to Become Complete Player

Anthony performed well in his second season in the league as well, averaging 20.8 points and again leading the Nuggets to the playoffs; once again, however, the team lost in the first round. During this time Anthony also began to develop a reputation as a difficult player and someone who associated with questionable people off the court. As part of the 2004 Olympic team, which won the bronze medal, Anthony complained about his lack of playing time and was publicly criticized. He was also involved in a bar fight, and he appeared in a bootleg rap video that warned people in Baltimore against providing eyewitness testimony to police when crimes were committed.

For the 2005–06 season Denver brought in the veteran coach George Karl, known for his unwillingness to sugarcoat his opinions when dealing with star players. In his first conversation with Anthony, Karl let the Nuggets' young star know that he believed him to be

talented but lazy. Anthony felt unfairly judged, and relations between player and coach remained chilly for much of the season. Anthony averaged 26.5 points per game, placing him among the NBA's elite scorers, but once again the Nuggets folded in the first round of the playoffs.

Anthony ultimately acceded to some of Karl's criticisms of his play. He trained heavily in the off-season and worked to diversify his game, scoring from the low-post as well as from the outside and dispelling notions that he was lazy. As part of the 2006 U.S. World Championship team, he put to rest some of the negativity surrounding his 2004 Olympic outing, not only by posting world-class numbers but by showing that he could be a team leader in the broader sense. "He was the leader in effort, performance, and enthusiasm right from the start," Team USA Coach Mike Krzyzewski told Vicki Michaelis in *Sports Illustrated*.

Anthony's new sense of seriousness did not go unnoticed by teammates or fans as the 2006–07 season got underway, and he appeared to have turned a corner in terms of his personal maturity and his versatility as a player. As of December of 2006 he was the NBA's leading scorer. Off the court, he had donated $1.5 million to start the Carmelo Anthony Youth Center in Baltimore, and he had contributed $3 million toward the construction of a new athletic center at Syracuse. Then, on December 16, as part of a notorious on-court fight between the Nuggets and the New York Knicks, Anthony punched the Knicks' Mardy Collins in the face. He was suspended for 15 games, and once again the talk among pundits and fans was of his lack of discipline and his questionable character.

Anthony finished the season as strongly as he had begun it, averaging 28.9 points on the year, second only to the Los Angeles Lakers' Kobe Bryant. Nonetheless, and even though the Nuggets acquired the aging superstar Allen Iverson at mid-season, the team made another early exit from the playoffs. Anthony made his first All-Star Game appearance that year as a replacement, after other players were unable to participate because of injuries. Although he had come into the league as one of its most promising players, and although he had at times played like one of the NBA's elite stars, he did not yet consistently get the respect that the likes of Bryant, LeBron James, or Dwayne Wade did.

Continued to Develop as a Player

His reputation began to change the following year, when Anthony again appeared in the All-Star game, this time as a starter and the second-leading vote getter in the NBA's Western Conference, trailing only Bryant. He was the league's fourth-leading scorer on the season, with 25.7 points per game, and the Nuggets won 50 regular-season games for the first time in decades. Once again, however, the team's season ended with a first-round exit from the playoffs.

Anthony made another strong showing in international competition at the end of that season, helping the U.S. Team to a gold medal in the 2008 Olympics. Coach Karl of the Nuggets, with whom Anthony was now on better terms than before, told Wertheim that Anthony returned from China with a new sense of dedication: "The same way he's gone from a scorer to a basketball player, he's gone from individualist to more a leader."

Indeed, although Anthony's scoring average was down slightly in 2008–09, to 22.8 points per game, the Nuggets had one of their best years in franchise history, going 54–28 during the regular season. Anthony also broke the first-round curse that had plagued him in the playoffs every year since he had entered the league. The Nuggets won their first-round series against the New Orleans Hornets and then beat the Dallas Mavericks in the second round, before falling to Bryant and the Lakers in the conference finals.

The 2009–10 season saw Anthony continuing to post numbers that placed him among the league's best players, averaging 28.2 points per game. He was named a starter in the All-Star Game for the second time, and the Nuggets again posted one of the best regular season records in franchise history. The team did not perform well in the playoffs, however, exiting in the first round as in previous years.

As the 2010–11 season began, Anthony pushed the Nuggets to trade him, and for months, as he continued to play up to his usual standards, the team worked to orchestrate a multiple-team deal that would allow the Nuggets to recoup some of the value still left on their star's contract. As public as the affair was, Anthony attempted to manage his image while trade talks were ongoing, hoping to avoid provoking the levels of anger that LeBron James had touched off upon leaving the Cleveland Cavaliers for the Miami Heat.

Finally, on February 22, 2011, a deal was announced whereby Anthony would go to the New York Knicks in a blockbuster trade involving nine players, future draft picks, and cash. Playing alongside the standout power forward Amar'e Stoudemire, Anthony once again reached the playoffs. With the Knicks, who had not reached the playoffs since 2004, he once again met with disappointment, however, losing in the first round to the Boston Celtics.

Sources

Periodicals

Daily News (New York), February 23, 2011.
Denver Post, April 4, 2004; June 23, 2004.
New York Times, July 27, 2004, p. D7.
Sports Illustrated, April 16, 2003, p. 24; June 23, 2003, p. 86; November 17, 2003, p. 64.; March 27, 2006, p. 50; January 8, 2007, p. 72; October

29, 2007, p. 119; December 7, 2009, p. 74; January 24, 2011.

Sporting News, April 14, 2003, p. 1; November 17, 2003, p. 22.

USA Today, November 1, 2006, p. 1C; February 22, 2011, p. 1C.

Online

"Carmelo Anthony," http://www.thisismelo.com/ (accessed July 25, 2011).

"Carmelo Anthony Info Page," NBA.com, http://www.nba.com/home/playerfile/carmelo_anthony/index.html (accessed July 25, 2011).

Wihlborg, Ulrica, "LaLa Vazquez Weds Carmelo Anthony," *People,* July 10, 2010, http://www.people.com/people/article/0,,20400870,00.html?xid=rss-topheadlines (accessed July 25, 2011).

—Tom Pendergast and Mark Lane

Wanda M. Austin

1953(?)—

Engineer, mathematician, executive

Dr. Wanda M. Austin has played a leading role in space technology and national security for more than three decades. A mathematician and engineer by training, she had risen by 2008 to become president and CEO of The Aerospace Corporation, a little-known research organization founded by the federal government and closely affiliated with it. Military satellites, spy satellites, and advanced communications systems all fall within Aerospace's mandate as a federally funded research and development center (FFRDC) for the U.S. Air Force, the National Reconnaissance Office, and other government agencies with a compelling interest in space technology. "We don't manufacture anything," the company reminded visitors to its website. "Our greatest asset is the technical expertise of our people."

Austin was born about 1953 in New York City, where she was raised. At the Bronx High School of Science, one of the most rigorous and highly regarded public secondary schools in the country, she was initially drawn to literature. After disagreeing with a teacher on the interpretation of a passage, however, she decided that the field was too subjective for her taste. She turned, therefore, to math. After earning a bachelor's degree in that subject in 1975 from Franklin and Marshall College, a liberal-arts institution in Pennsylvania, she went on to grad school at the University of Pittsburgh, where in 1977 she earned two master's degrees, one in mathematics and the other in systems engineering. Intent by that point on a career in aerospace, she then moved to southern California, which has been a center of that industry since the 1930s. There she found work designing missile systems for

Rockwell International, a major military contractor. Her experience as a member of Rockwell's technical staff soon drew the attention of executives at The Aerospace Corporation, and in 1979 she joined its technical staff in the Engineering Analysis and Programming Department. Amid her various duties there, she also found time to complete her education, earning a PhD in systems engineering from the University of Southern California in 1988. Her doctorate focused on the design of a new interface for "human-to-computer" interaction, according to an abstract available online. By using natural language instead of the awkward computer commands typically employed, Austin's design "enable[d] users to build complex models with fewer errors and in less time."

At Aerospace's sprawling headquarters in the Los Angeles suburb of El Segundo, Austin moved steadily up the corporate ladder. After roughly 17 years on the technical staff, she moved into administration in 1996, when she was named general manager of the Electronic Systems Division, a post that gave her supervisory authority over more than 200 employees. The youngest general manager in the company's history, she was also the first African American and the first woman. Several years later she was promoted again, this time to general manager of the Military Satellite Communications Division, known informally as MIL-SATCOM. In her tenure there, noted a biographical profile on the website of NASA (where she has been a committee member), Austin "was responsible for systems engineering support to the Air Force in the

At a Glance . . .

Born in 1953(?) in New York City. *Education*: Franklin and Marshall College, BA, mathematics, 1975; University of Pittsburgh, MS, mathematics, 1977, MS, systems engineering, 1977; University of Southern California, PhD, 1988.

Career: Rockwell International, member of technical staff, 1977–79; The Aerospace Corporation, member of technical staff, 1979–96, general manager (Electronic Systems Division), 1996–98(?), general manager (Military Satellite Communications Division), 1998(?)–2001, senior vice president (Engineering and Technology Group), 2001–03, senior vice president (Special Studies), 2004, senior vice president (National Systems Group), 2004–07, president and CEO, 2008—.

Memberships: National Academy of Engineering; American Institute of Aeronautics and Astronautics; International Academy of Astronautics; U.S. Human Space Flight Plans Committee (NASA).

Awards: WITI Hall of Fame, Women in Technology International, 2007; Black Engineer of the Year, *U.S. Black Engineer and Information Technology*, 2009.

Addresses: *Office*—The Aerospace Corporation, PO Box 92957, Los Angeles, CA 90009.

architecture, acquisition, development, and orbital operation of advanced satellite communications systems."

Austin's next promotion came in June of 2001, when she was named senior vice president of the Engineering and Technology Group (ETG). There she supervised roughly a thousand employees who were engaged in a diverse array of specialized projects. "The challenge" for an administrator in that kind of environment, she told Roger Witherspoon in *U.S. Black Engineer and Information Technology* magazine in 2009, "is trying to get teams to work together. You have contractor[s], engineers, and sometimes three or four layers of suppliers." After serving with ETG for roughly a year and a half (June of 2001 through December of 2003), she worked for several months as senior vice president of Special Studies before being named senior vice president of the company's National Systems Group, where she focused particularly on the interaction between space-based systems and the ground centers that control them. She filled that role until January 1, 2008, when she was named president and CEO.

With nearly 4,000 employees and hundreds of millions of dollars in revenue every year, The Aerospace Corporation has successfully navigated a rapidly changing field since its founding as a nonprofit organization in 1960. While its unique relationship to the federal government has helped shield it at times from adverse economic conditions, it has also brought a number of challenges, particularly for its leadership. The classified nature of its work, for example, has forced it into the unenviable position of keeping its employees' greatest achievements a secret. As a result, many Americans, even residents of southern California, had little idea of the company's significance. Perhaps the most daunting obstacle for Austin, however, has been the growing instability of government funding. While security has long been a priority in the federal budget, the research underpinning much of Aerospace's work has typically proved more vulnerable to budget constraints. One of Austin's primary tasks, therefore, has been to remind lawmakers of the increasingly important role spy satellites have played in the ongoing struggle to keep the nation safe, particularly from international terrorism. "In terms of national security," Austin told Witherspoon in *U.S. Black Engineer and Information Technology*, "we are more and more dependent on space." Many consumer innovations, she added, have also grown out of developments in astronautics; prominent among these has been the global positioning system (GPS), a satellite-based technology used in cars, boats, airplanes, and cellular phones.

Austin, who is in demand throughout the federal government for her advice and expertise, is also a popular speaker at conferences and schools nationwide, including Pennsylvania's Carlow University and two of her alma maters, the University of Pittsburgh and the University of Southern California. A member of the National Academy of Engineering, the International Academy of Astronautics, and the American Institute of Aeronautics and Astronautics, she was inducted into the WITI Hall of Fame by Women in Technology International in 2007. Two years later she was named Black Engineer of the Year by *U.S. Black Engineer and Information Technology*.

Sources

Periodicals

U.S. Black Engineer and Information Technology, Winter 2009.

Online

"A Trusted Partner; A National Resource," The Aerospace Corporation, April 1, 2009, http://www.aero.org/corporation/ (accessed July 30, 2011).

Austin, Wanda Murry, Ph.D., "A Methodology for System Dynamics Modeling Using Natural Language: Abstract (Summary)," University of Southern California, 1988, http://proquest.umi.com.ezproxy.library.

wisc.edu/pqdweb?index=0&did=744987381&
SrchMode=1&sid=1&Fmt=2&VInst=PROD&V
Type=PQD&RQT=309&VName=PQD&TS=1312
055823&clientId=12286 (accessed July 30, 2011).

"Dr. Wanda M. Austin: President and CEO of The
Aerospace Corp.," NASA, http://www.nasa.gov/
offices/hsf/members/austin-bio.html (accessed July
30, 2011).

"Featured Profile: Dr. Wanda M. Austin," Women in
Technology International, 2007, http://www.witi.
com/center/witimuseum/halloffame/247696/Dr.-
Wanda-M.-Austin-Senior-Vice-President-National-
Systems-Group-and-President/CEO-Elect/ (accessed
July 30, 2011).

—R. Anthony Kugler

Paris Barclay

1956—

Television and film director

Barclay, Paris, photograph. Jason LaVeris/FilmMagic/Getty Images.

Paris Barclay's artful, fluid style as a director has made him one of the most sought-after names in the television industry. A two-time Emmy Award winner for *NYPD Blue,* Barclay has also helmed episodes of *ER, The West Wing, Glee, In Treatment,* and *Sons of Anarchy.* He is also openly gay and the first African American to be elected an officer of the Directors Guild of America. "I do think because of my experience living in both worlds, living in an African American household, and also being educated in the white world of Harvard and New York, it gives me a perspective to tell different kinds of stories than are currently being told," Barclay said in a *Los Angeles Times* interview.

Hailed from the Midwest

Barclay was born in Chicago Heights, Illinois, in 1956, the third of seven children. His mother was a social worker, and his father was a foreman at a tile plant. Barclay's athletic prowess led him to La Lumiere School in LaPorte, Indiana, a private single-sex school affiliated with the Roman Catholic church. In an attempt to integrate its student body, the school offered him a scholarship, and he accepted on the condition

that his brother Neil would also come along. months of the time I was there I was completely overwhelmed," Barclay told the *Los Angeles Times.* "I felt I was not as good as these kids with their big families and big houses. It may have been responsible for my excessive overachieving. The best I could do was [study] and work at football." His efforts paid off. La Lumiere began pushing Barclay toward Harvard University in the college-application race, and he was accepted at age 16.

Barclay majored in English at Harvard but spent much of his time writing musicals—16 in all—including two shows at the prestigious Hasty Pudding Theater, Harvard's comedy troupe. After earning his Harvard degree in 1979, he moved to New York City to work in musical theater, but he also took a more stable job as an advertising copywriter. The pressures were great, and Barclay struggled with substance-abuse dependencies for nearly a decade. He managed, however, to find success in both theater and advertising. He won a spot in a musical theater workshop held by the American Society of Composers, Authors and Publishers (ASCAP). There he met famed Broadway musical composer Stephen Sondheim, who called Barclay's work "terrible but not untalented" and

At a Glance . . .

Born on June 30, 1956, in Chicago Heights, IL. *Education*: Harvard University, BA, English, 1979. *Politics*: Democrat.

Career: Has worked as a television director and producer, actor, playwright, music video director, advertising copywriter, and creative director at an advertising agency; *NYPD Blue*, producer, 1997–98, supervising producer, 1998–99; producer or executive producer of *Cold Case*, CBS, 2005–06, *In Treatment*, HBO, 2008—, and *Sons of Anarchy*, FX, 2011—.

Memberships: Director's Guild of America (member, board of directors; vice president, 2011—).

Awards: MTV Video Award for best rap video, 1991, for LL Cool J's "Mama Said Knock You Out"; Emmy Award for outstanding directing for a drama series, 1998 and 1999, for *NYPD Blue*; Founders Award, Project Angel Food, 1998; Director's Guild of America Award for outstanding directorial achievement in dramatic series—night, 1999, for *NYPD Blue*; Stephen F. Kolzak Award, GLAAD, 2001; Robert B. Aldrich Achievement Award, Directors Guild of America, 2007.

Addresses: *Agent*—Paradigm Talent Agency, 360 N. Crescent Dr., North Bldg., Beverly Hills, CA 90210.

advised him to focus on the "black experience." Barclay recalled in the *Los Angeles Times* interview that Sondheim told him that "unfortunately you're writing musicals with white people, which means you're competing with me and everybody else who's white."

Although Barclay thought the comment racist, he did go on to adapt a short story by African-American playwright Richard Wright into a 1985 musical, *Almos' a Man*, which ran at the Soho Rep Theater. Within a few years, however, Barclay had found a new outlet for his creativity, first in writing songs for advertising campaigns, then directing television commercials. That led to music videos, and Barclay scored one notable success when he directed rapper LL Cool J's 1990 hit single "Mama Said Knock You Out," which won the MTV Video Award for best rap video in 1991.

Barclay's videos attracted the attention of a television producer named John Wells, who gave Barclay his first television directing job on the 1992 CBS series *Angel Street*. The Chicago cop drama was short-lived, but Barclay went on to work on many other television series, while Wells gained fame with the hit NBC medical drama *ER*. Wells tapped Barclay to direct a few episodes, and those drew the attention of legendary television producer Steven Bochco, who hired Barclay to direct for *NYPD Blue* in 1997.

Earned Accolades for NYPD Blue

With *NYPD Blue* Barclay established himself as a visionary director. Of Barclay's work on that show, Emmy-winning television director Thomas Carter told the *Los Angeles Times*, "I was blown away by [the quality]. This was extraordinary work for television, both in terms of the performances he got from the actors and the way he translated the story visually." In 1998 Barclay won the first of his two Emmy awards for outstanding directing for a drama series for an episode of *NYPD Blue*. The same year, the Director's Guild of America voted him best director of a dramatic series, also for *NYPD Blue*, and in 1989 he won a second Emmy for the show.

Barclay has made occasional forays into feature films. The Wayans brothers hired him to direct *Don't Be a Menace to South Central While Drinking Your Juice in the Hood*, a 1996 spoof of the urban-drama genre whose title is usually shortened to *Don't Be a Menace*. At the time, Barclay was not completely open about his sexual orientation, and he was disappointed by the homophobic prejudices he encountered, forcing him to take a more prominent role as a gay black man in Hollywood. "I realized I empowered people to make it an issue by not being open about it," he told the *Los Angeles Times*. "So I said, 'From now on I'm not going to do this.' If I'm open about it, it can never be an issue. The people who are homophobic or feel that's important to know, [they] will not ask me for jobs." Since then Barclay has won accolades for his efforts, including the 2001 Stephen F. Kolzak Award from the Gay and Lesbian Alliance Against Defamation (GLAAD), which is the group's highest honor. He is also an active fund-raiser for Project Angel Food, an organization that provides meals to people suffering from HIV/ AIDS, and was awarded with that organization's Founders Award.

Barclay continued to make powerful television through the end of the 1990s but also found himself in some epic behind-the-scenes battles. In 1999 Barclay partnered with Bochco as co-executive producer of *City of Angels*. The hour-long drama, set at a struggling Los Angeles hospital, was considered groundbreaking for its all African-American cast. It ran for two seasons on CBS through most of 2000 but suffered from poor ratings early on. Behind the scenes Barclay and Bochco debated the direction of the show. Barclay wanted to integrate the cast, while Bochco was adamant it remain all black. "Every hospital I've researched in the inner-city has a mixed staff—blacks, whites, Asians, Latinos," Barclay told the *Los Angeles Times*. Barclay resigned from the series in the summer of 2000.

Diversified from Television

Barclay returned to his original love—the musical—with a 2001 adaptation of the book *Dear America: Letters Home from Vietnam. Letters from 'Nam,* as the musical was titled, premiered at the North Shore Music Theatre in Boston, and Barclay and his partner, food-industry executive Christopher Mason, spent several weeks over August and September on the East Coast. They were originally booked on one of the two United Airlines flights that left Boston's Logan Airport on the morning of September 11, 2001, but had revised their travel plans and flown back a day earlier. The near-miss spurred Barclay and Mason to search for a deeper commitment in their lives, and they became foster parents, eventually adopting two youngsters from the Los Angeles County system. "There's 35,000 kids in foster care just in this L.A. County region," Barclay told Neda Ulaby, a journalist for National Public Radio's *Morning Edition.* "Many of them are dark-skinned like myself and not being adopted because of that. And that made me furious."

From 2002 to 2008 Barclay wrote a column for the *Advocate,* "Final Cut," which dealt primarily with issues pertinent to the LGBT community viewed through the prism of the entertainment industry. He often discussed stereotypes, discrimination, and current events, and in 2005 he used the column to pen an open letter to new U.S. Supreme Court Chief Justice John Roberts, a former classmate of his at La Lumiere. Roberts was a year ahead of him, but both were active in drama productions and athletics. In his column Barclay characterized the future Chief Justice as a fair, hardworking student who later made an extra effort to welcome Barclay to Harvard when they were undergraduates. He cited some questionable cases Roberts had ruled upon, but he commended "your pro bono work on a Supreme Court ruling that to this day helps protect gay people from discrimination." Barclay concluded his open letter by urging Roberts to "embrace the true freedom of a lifetime appointment, and decide the cases before you with a deep sense of the equality of all people that our Constitution uses as its touchstone."

For much of the decade Barclay continued to be one of the most sought-after directors in television. He received multiple Emmy nominations, including one for an episode of *The West Wing,* and he also ventured into a producer's role with the CBS police-procedural *Cold Case,* which ran for seven seasons. He served as executive producer and director for the acclaimed HBO series *In Treatment,* which featured Gabriel Byrne as a psychologist, and it earned a steady stream of Emmy nominations after its 2008 premiere, as well as Directors Guild of America honors and even a prestigious Peabody Award. Barclay also found time to work on other projects, including a 2008 movie for MTV, *Pedro,* about the late HIV/AIDS activist Pedro Zamora, and retooled *Letters from 'Nam* into a new musical, *One Red Flower. Order My Steps,* a stage work he directed in Los Angeles, was a moving piece of community theater dealing with HIV/AIDS and black churches.

In a column for the *Advocate* in 2004, Barclay invoked the words of poet-activist Audre Lorde, "Your silence will not protect you," in a discussion of recently published numbers that showed the rate of HIV infections for African Americans was alarmingly high. He admitted that he was both proud and ashamed of the honors he had won from GLAAD and other groups, asserting, "I have failed because I have not been open and honest about being an African-American man who is HIV-positive. I have failed because I have allowed fear to take that bit of information about who I am off the table and, not unlike my brothers (both 'down low' and otherwise), have avoided committing directly to the struggle to turn the tide of AIDS in my own community."

Barclay has been involved in a pair of highly successful television series: he has directed episodes of the hit Fox show *Glee*—one of which was nominated for an Emmy in 2010—and joined the FX network's top-rated original series *Sons of Anarchy* in 2011 as its new executive producer and principal director. He had worked with the show's creator, Kurt Sutter, several years earlier on the FX series *The Shield.* In 2011 Barclay ran for and won a seat as vice president of the Director's Guild of America, making him the first African American ever to serve as an officer on its executive board. He planned to use that post to ensure the diversity of America was adequately reflected on the small screen. In the *Morning Edition* interview with Ulaby, Barclay described being present at meetings with writers and entertainment-industry executives who sometimes questioned a character's racial and sexual identity. "'Isn't it enough that they're just gay?' or, 'Isn't it enough that they're just black?'" Barclay often hears, he told Ulaby. "As if one cross was enough to bear."

Selected works

Television; as director

Angel Street, CBS, 1992.
ER, NBC, 1996–2000.
Sliders, Fox, 1996–97.
NYPD Blue, ABC, 1997–99.
City of Angels, CBS, 2000.
The West Wing, NBC, 2000–02.
Cold Case, CBS, 2003–08.
The Shield, FX, 2003–07.
Monk, USA Network, 2007–08.
In Treatment, HBO, 2008—.
Glee, Fox, 2009—.
Sons of Anarchy, FX, 2011—.

Films; as director

Don't Be a Menace to South Central While Drinking Juice in the Hood (also known as *Don't Be a Menace*), Miramax, 1996.
The Cherokee Kid, HBO, 1996.
The Big Time, TNT, 2002.
Pedro, MTV, 2008.

Stage; as writer and director

Almos' a Man, produced in New York City, 1985.
Letters from 'Nam (adaptation), produced in Boston, 2001; later revised as *One Red Flower,* produced in Arlington, VA, 2004.
Order My Steps, produced in Los Angeles, 2003.

Sources

Periodicals

Advocate, May 25, 2004, p. 60; September 13, 2005, p. 88.

Back Stage West, June 12, 2003, p. 4.
Hollywood Reporter, December 10, 2001, p. 18.
Los Angeles Times, January 31, 1999, p. 4; September 13, 1999, p. 6; July 1, 2000, p. F1.

Online

Hernandez, Greg, "A Chat with Emmy Nominee Paris Barclay," GregInHollywood, August 29, 2010, http://greginhollywood.com/a-chat-with-emmy-nominee-paris-barclay-36250 (accessed August 12, 2011).
Stockwell, Anne, "Love Stories: Paris Barclay and Christopher Mason," *Advocate,* October 8, 2008, http://www.advocate.com/Politics/Marriage_Equality/Love_Stories_Paris_Barclay_and_Christopher_Mason/ (accessed August 12, 2011).
Ulaby, Neda, "Paris Barclay: A TV Insider with an Outsider Instinct," *Morning Edition,* National Public Radio, January 6, 2011, http://www.npr.org/2011/01/06/132079148/paris-barclay-a-tv-insider-with-an-outsider-instinct (accessed August 12, 2011).

—Candace LaBalle and Carol Brennan

Melba Pattillo Beals

1941—

Communications consultant, educator, author

Melba Pattillo Beals made history at the age of 15 as one of the "Little Rock Nine," the group of schoolchildren chosen as the first African-American students in the public school system of Little Rock, Arkansas. The integration of Central High School by the Little Rock Nine in September of 1957 marked the first attempt to test the United States' commitment to ensuring the civil rights granted to African Americans under the 1954 U.S. Supreme Court ruling *Brown v. Board of Education,* which outlawed segregation in public school systems. White citizens of Little Rock, supported by Arkansas Governor Orval Faubus, protested the integration of the school so angrily that President Dwight D. Eisenhower had to call on the U.S. Army to protect the students, marking the first time since Reconstruction that Federal troops had been ordered to protect the civil rights of African Americans. Images of the integration of Central High were broadcast around the world, helping to build public support for the Civil Rights Movement.

Beals went on to a career in journalism, public relations, and academia. She wrote about the ordeal of integrating and attending Central High School in a 1994 memoir, *Warriors Don't Cry.* A follow-up memoir, *White Is a State of Mind* (1999), picks up her story the following year, when Governor Faubus closed the Little Rock public school system and her life was threatened by those opposed to integration, forcing her to relocate to California, where she lived with a white family and continued her education.

Wanted Educational Opportunity

Beals was born Melba Joy Pattillo on December 7, 1941, the daughter of a railroad worker, Howell Pattillo, and a schoolteacher, Lois Pattillo. Lois held a PhD and was one of the first African Americans to graduate from the University of Arkansas in Fayetteville. In addition to their daughter Melba, the Pattillos had a son, Conrad, and the family lived with the children's maternal grandmother, India Peyton.

Beals was a high-achieving student with career ambitions, and her teachers in the segregated schools of Little Rock were committed and capable, but she understood that her educational goals were being actively limited by the disparity in resources committed to all-white Central High School relative to her own all-black school, Horace Mann. In the wake of the *Brown v. Board of Education* ruling of 1954, in which the U.S. Supreme Court overturned the doctrine of separate-but-equal schooling that had been in place in the American South since the Reconstruction era, the National Association for the Advancement of Colored People (NAACP) was pushing school boards to fulfill their charge to provide equal access to education. In 1957 the NAACP and the Little Rock School Board developed a plan to integrate Central High, which boasted top-flight facilities and teachers and was housed in an imposing building many times larger than Horace Mann.

As a resident of the area where Central High was located, and as a good student, Beals was eligible to be

At a Glance . . .

Born Melba Joy Pattillo on December 7, 1941, in Little Rock, AR; daughter of Howell (a railroad worker) and Lois (a schoolteacher) Pattillo; married John Beals, 1961 (divorced, 1971[?]); children: Kellie, Evan, Matthew. *Education*: San Francisco State University, BA; Columbia University Graduate School of Journalism, MA.

Career: KQED (NBC Television Affiliate), news reporter; Media Exposure (public relations and marketing company), owner; Dominican University of California, has served as associate professor, chair of Department of Communications, and emeritus chair of Department of Communications, 2000—.

Awards: Nonfiction Book of the Year, American Library Association, 1995, for *Warriors Don't Cry;* Congressional Gold Medal, United States Congress, 1999.

Addresses: *Office*—Department of Communications, Dominican University of California, 50 Acacia Ave., San Rafael, CA 94901. *Email*—mbeals@dominican.edu.

part of the integration effort; she volunteered and was selected from an original pool of 100 students. She delayed telling her parents that she had been selected for the task, not wanting to upset them, and they ultimately discovered her role in the effort through TV news coverage of the integration plan. Although her mother had helped to integrate the University of Arkansas, the virulence of the opposition to integration at the high-school level was measurably more intense. Her parents feared for her safety and happiness, but Beals only belatedly understood the intensity of the resistance she would face.

Survived Abuse at Central High

When the Little Rock Nine first tried to enter Central High School, they were turned back by angry white protesters and Arkansas National Guard troops deployed on orders from Governor Faubus. President Eisenhower responded by sending in soldiers from the Army's 101st Airborne Division to escort the students as they entered the high school. A soldier named Danny was assigned to guard Beals personally, and he protected her from attacks initiated by fellow students as well as by white adults. She was tripped, spat upon, cut by broken glass, forced under scalding hot showers, and pelted with burning paper. On one occasion, acid was thrown into her eyes. Her eyesight was saved

when Danny rushed her into a bathroom and doused her face with water.

In addition to the physical assaults, Beals and the other black students were regularly subjected to verbal abuse, including racial slurs and death threats. Moreover, she was often treated as if she simply wasn't there. She told *USA Today,* "People would sit all around me and all I wanted them to say was, 'Hello, how are you? What a nice blouse.' Above all else, I was so lonely."

Beals also lost relationships with many of her black friends after they were threatened with physical violence for associating with her. Of the nine African-American students who integrated Central High School, eight remained by the end of the 1957–58 school year. Beals passed the time praying and clinging to the goal of simple survival.

Started New Life in California

Under the pretense of preventing further violence, Governor Faubus closed all of the Little Rock public high schools the following fall. This proved the start of another eye-opening chapter in Beals's life. While waiting to find out whether she would have a school to attend that year, Beals and her family heard that a reward for her murder or capture had been announced. Within 48 hours the NAACP had arranged to get her away from Little Rock and into the home of the McCabes, a family in Santa Rosa, California, where she would be able to continue her education. Beals was surprised to find that the McCabes, members of the NAACP, were white.

Beals came to consider the McCabes a second set of parents, and she quickly understood that not all white people were like those who had belittled and threatened her in Little Rock. Her time in California, although marked by the difficulties inherent in being a newcomer and an African American in a predominantly white area, likewise made her aware of the variety of possible futures that might now be open to her. Her surrogate father, George McCabe, a university professor on a modest salary, had managed to start Sonoma State University, and Beals saw this accomplishment as a demonstration of the range of options open to people who were allowed by law to pursue their dreams. The McCabes also helped Beals navigate the college admissions process and enroll in San Francisco State University, where she took a B.A. in journalism.

Although Beals's life after leaving Arkansas was marked by greater career opportunity and personal freedom, she continued to confront her share of difficulties. A failed marriage and single parenthood left her impoverished and depressed, but she managed to endure and continue her education, taking a master's degree from the prestigious Columbia University

Graduate School of Journalism in New York City.

Beals went on to work as a TV and print-media journalist, and she founded a public-relations and marketing firm. In 1990 she published her first book, *Expose Yourself: Using the Power of Public Relations to Promote Your Business and Yourself.* A guide to the process of attracting and effectively using media attention, *Expose Yourself* drew on her experience of being a national media figure as well as her journalistic and public-relations experiences.

Wrote Memoirs

After numerous false starts and rewrites over the years, Beals finally managed to render her experiences at Central High School into a book-length narrative in the 1990s. *Warriors Don't Cry*, published in 1994, has received critical praise as a personal document of a turbulent period in American history. Writing for the *Washington Post Book World*, Judith Patterson concluded that it was "a plainly written story that reflects the wisdom of the woman telling it almost 40 years after the fact and the crumbling innocence of the young woman who experienced it." Patterson also deemed it "a history lesson, a civics lesson and as true a story of coming of age in America at a certain time and place as one could hope to find."

Beals continued the story of her life in 1999's *White Is a State of Mind,* in which she detailed the personal journey she undertook upon being forced to leave her home and family and become part of a new family and culture in California. *White Is a State of Mind* tells a more personal and less topical story than its predecessor, and perhaps as a result it did not attract the same level of attention from critics.

1999 also saw Beals, along with the other members of the Little Rock Nine, honored at a White House ceremony and presented with Congressional Gold Medals, the highest honor awarded by Congress. In 2000 Beals took a post as an associate professor in the Department of Communications at Dominican University of California. As of 2011 she was chair emeritus of the department.

Selected works

Expose Yourself: Using the Power of Public Relations to Promote Your Business and Yourself, Chronicle Books, 1990.
Warriors Don't Cry: A Searing Memoir of the Battle to Integrate Little Rock's Central High, Pocket Books, 1994.
White Is a State of Mind: A Memoir, Putnam, 1999.

Sources

Books

Bates, Daisy, *The Long Shadow of Little Rock,* University of Arkansas Press, 1986.
Jacoway, Elizabeth, and C. Fred Williams, eds., *Understanding the Little Rock Crisis: An Exercise in Remembrance and Reconciliation,* University of Arkansas Press, 1999.

Periodicals

Booklist, February 15, 2000.
Christian Science Monitor, August 29, 1996, p. 18; June 3, 1999, p. 20; September 18, 2010.
Dallas Morning News, December 11, 1999, p. 1C.
Ebony, March 1999, p. 32.
English Journal, September 1995, pp. 121–22.
Library Journal, February 15, 1999, p. 160.
New York Times, November 10, 1999, p. A16.
New York Times Book Review, June 19, 1994, p. 33.
Scholastic Update, November 18, 1994, pp. 18–21.
USA Today, May 18, 1994, p. 4D.
Washington Post Book World, May 29, 1994, pp. 3, 12.

Online

"Interview with Melba Pattillo Beals," Scholastic.com, http://www2.scholastic.com/browse/article.jsp?id=4799 (accessed July 12, 2011).
Melba Beals, http://melbabeals.com/ (accessed July 12, 2011).

—Paula Pyzik Scott and Mark Lane

William Holmes Borders

1905–1993

Pastor, activist

Borders, William Holmes, photograph. AP Images/HC.

Rev. William Holmes Borders was an early civil rights activist and community builder in Atlanta, Georgia. From his pulpit at the Wheat Street Baptist Church, Borders exhorted his congregation to stand up for their rights but also to pool their resources to create self-sufficient institutions that could effect more rapid change to their lives. "Sometimes the opposition forces you to speak in the language it understands," he told the *New York Times* in a 1964 article about his Atlanta church and a new housing complex it had built with the help of federal loans. "While the American white man is not immune to religion and the spirit, he, in many instances, respects money and the ballot more highly."

Borders was born in 1905 in Macon, Georgia. His father, James Buchanan Borders, was a Baptist minister in the city, and Borders dreamed at an early age of following in his footsteps. As one of six children he was expected to contribute to the family's income at an early age and become relatively self-sufficient, and he began delivering newspapers while still in elementary school. As a young adult he worked as a mail carrier to earn tuition money for Morehouse College in Atlanta,

considered one of the top schools in the South for African Americans with a religious vocation. Borders struggled financially, however, and was forced to drop out during his junior year. He was so crushed by the circumstances that he continued to attend classes anyway, and when the dean of the seminary learned of this he convinced school officials to let Borders finish his degree on schedule with the Class of 1929. Borders reimbursed the school for the tuition costs when he began working.

Took Over Ailing Church

Borders's life was shaped by several years in Chicago, where he had won a scholarship to the Garrett Biblical Institute, just across the city's northern border in Evanston. He married a Spelman graduate, Julia Pate, who would go on to a career as a middle-school English teacher when they returned to Atlanta, where the future Rev. Dr. Martin Luther King Jr. was one of her students. Borders worked toward a bachelor of divinity degree at Garrett, which he earned in 1932, and then completed a master's degree at the University of Chicago in 1936. He was working toward his doctorate in Chicago when Morehouse College offered him a

At a Glance . . .

Born on February 24, 1905, in Macon, GA; died on November 23, 1993, in Atlanta, GA; son of James Buchanan (a minister) and Leila Birdsong Borders; married Julia Pate (a teacher); children: William H. Jr., Juel P. *Education*: Morehouse College, BA, 1929; Garrett-Evangelical Theological Seminary, BD, 1932; University of Chicago, MA, 1936. *Politics*: Republican. *Religion*: Baptist.

Career: Wheat Street Baptist Church, pastor, 1937–89; taught religion and philosophy at Morehouse College.

Memberships: Southern Christian Leadership Conference (cofounder, 1957).

Awards: Honorary doctorate, Morehouse College, 1969.

job teaching philosophy and religion courses. Another opportunity arose when Atlanta's Wheat Street Baptist Church in Atlanta invited him to serve as pastor. Borders accepted both job offers and returned to the South.

The Wheat Street church, located on the Atlanta thoroughfare that would be renamed Auburn Avenue, had been rebuilt in the early 1920s after a fire. Founded in 1869, the Baptist church was situated in the heart of the city's African-American community and was one of the early gathering places for meetings of Atlanta's NAACP chapter. The church was in a financially precarious position, however, and Borders set to work recruiting new members and rectifying its accounting practices. He dubbed it "the Mighty Fortress," and his Sunday sermons soon attracted audiences for their eloquence and acknowledgment that the plight of African Americans in the South was indeed a dire one. In 1941 Borders became the first African-American minister to have a weekly radio show in Atlanta with his "Seven Minutes at the Mike."

Led Early Civil Rights Efforts

During this era Borders was one of a group of highly dedicated, influential African-American religious leaders in Atlanta whose sermons and nascent civil-rights work helped shape the life of Rev. Martin Luther King Jr. Borders was an ally of the senior Reverend King, who pastored the nearby Ebenezer Baptist Church, and their families were close. King Jr., who cited Borders's wife's classes as a great influence, sometimes ducked out of his father's church to hear Borders's sermons at Wheat Street.

Borders and King Sr. put their lives at risk in pressuring municipal authorities for more of a voice in the growing black metropolis in the 1940s and '50s. Borders led one drive for improved hospital facilities for blacks in segregated Atlanta and, through another initiative, forced the Atlanta Police Department to hire its first black officers. In 1943 a sermon-poem that Borders wrote, "I Am Somebody," was widely reprinted in the black press of the era and declaimed by ministers across the country from their pulpits. Written in commemoration of the 80th anniversary of the Emancipation Proclamation, "I Am Somebody" cited scores of heroes to the race, both famous and forgotten. "I am somebody," begins its first stanza. "I am a poet in Langston Hughes. . . . I am a diplomat in Ralph A. Bunche." Later verses affirmed painful realities. "I am a trustee in slavery," went one line. "I protected my master's wives and daughters while he fought to keep the chains about my body. . . . I am a true Christian, for indeed, I practiced the religion of Jesus at points better than my master from whom I learned it."

Throughout the 1950s Borders worked to solve some of the most pressing crises for Atlanta's African-American community. Some of this he did by protest action, like the Atlanta bus boycott he and other ministers launched in late 1956 on the heels of a favorable court decision regarding the Montgomery Bus Boycott a year earlier. In other cases Borders worked to create new opportunities by marshaling the power of his church, which had grown to 5,000 members. It ran a preschool and a credit union and owned a valuable parcel of rural real estate, which it had acquired for $20,000 back in 1947 to use as a farm and summer camp. Neither project materialized, but Wheat Street held on to the land and in 1961 sold it for nearly five times the original amount. Cash in hand, Borders bought a 22-acre parcel that had recently been cleared as part of a federal urban-renewal program near his church, and he arranged newly available federal loans to construct low-income housing units on the site. The Wheat Street Gardens, which opened in 1964 with 496 units, was unprecedented at the time, although Borders's model would be followed by generations of other black church leaders in America. "This is really one aspect of the freedom fight, for Negroes have a tremendous job to do themselves," he told the *New York Times*. "Freedom is not synonymous with marches and sit-ins. They are means of dramatizing grievous wrongs and have now reached diminishing returns."

Chosen to Play Savior

The zenith moment of Borders's career as a religious and civil rights figure in Atlanta came on September 15, 1968, a little over five months following the tragic assassination of Dr. King in Memphis. In the gloomy months that followed that death, Borders and other Atlantans worked together to stage a passion play to

alleviate tensions in the highly charged racial climate in the city. Borders was cast as Jesus Christ in a production of *Behold the Man,* although the idea of a black man portraying the Christian savor was a risky proposition in 1968. "I prayed over it and thought about it," Borders told *Ebony* magazine a few months later. "And I decided to take the opportunity and do the best I could." Staged by the Christian Council of Metropolitan Atlanta, *Behold the Man* featured a multiracial cast of 500 and a choir of 2,000, who sang for an integrated audience of 45,000 at Atlanta-Fulton County Stadium. Borders was in his early sixties by then, and the passion play—a Christian spectacle dating back to medieval times in which ordinary citizens re-created the persecution and death of Christ at the hands of the Romans in 33 CE—required him to lug a heavy crucifix on which he would be nailed. "As big as that cross was, if it fell, and my father's feet and hands were tied down, it could be catastrophic," his son William Jr. told the *Atlanta Journal-Constitution* years later. The event was covered by both *Newsweek* and *Ebony* magazines. "On the purely psychological level, the sight of a black man depicting Christ may have provided, for the integrated audience, a needed insight into the nature of their religion—its universality, its ultimate humanity," noted the *Ebony* article.

Borders remained a staunch supporter of Republican politics well into the 1980s. President Richard M. Nixon appointed him to the president's Committee on Mental Retardation, and he was sent as Nixon's envoy on two trips to Japan in the 1970s. Borders retired from the pulpit of Wheat Street Baptist Church in 1989. He died of heart failure four years later at Southwest Community Hospital on November 23, 1993, at the age of 88. Both his son and daughter, Juel, became physicians. One of his six grandchildren, Lisa Borders, went on to win election to the Atlanta City Council and became that body's president in 2004. The title of Borders's 1943 sermon-poem "I Am Somebody" was later adopted by Rev. Jesse Jackson as the slogan for his Operation PUSH (People United to Save Humanity) and the National Rainbow Coalition. The "Mighty Fortress on Wheat Street" remains a Gothic Revival landmark in Atlanta's Sweet Auburn historical district and continues to be an active, thriving part of the community. The cross street at its corner, formerly Yonge Street, was later renamed William H. Borders Drive.

Sources

Books

Lischer, Richard, *The Preacher King: Martin Luther King, Jr. and the Word That Moved America,* Oxford University Press, 1997, p. 49, http://books. google.com/books?id=xFt5f9MsuMoC&lpg=PA49 &dq="I Am Somebody," 1943&pg=PA49#v=one page&q="I Am Somebody," 1943&f=false.

Religious Leaders of America, Gale, 1999.

Periodicals

Atlanta Journal-Constitution, April 3, 2004, p. B2.
Ebony, November 1962, p. 96; December 1968, pp. 33-40.
New York Times, March 13, 1985.

Online

"Contemporary Heroes and Heroines Day, The African-American Lectionary," http://www.theafri canamericanlectionary.org/PopupCulturalAid.asp? LRID=11 (accessed August 2, 2011).

—Carol Brennan

Oliver Leon Brown

1918–1961(?)

Minister, welder, litigant

While most Americans are familiar with *Oliver L. Brown et al.* v. *Board of Education of Topeka, Kansas* (1954), the landmark Supreme Court ruling that ended racial segregation in public education, the man who gave his name to the case has never been well known. Oliver Leon Brown, a welder who later entered the ministry, was the only male among the 13 Topeka parents who challenged the local school board's adherence to the separate-but-equal doctrine that had been used for decades to justify and legitimize segregation. "At first he didn't want to do it because [of] all the ladies, you know, and he was one man; he just really didn't want to do it," his widow, Leola Montgomery, recalled to Bill Kurtis of *NewsHour with Jim Lehrer* in 2004. "But they prevailed upon him, and he finally consented to be one of the plaintiffs." His decision to do so helped transform American education and U.S. society as a whole.

Born in Topeka on August 2, 1918, Brown grew up in an impoverished but close-knit family. The 10th child of Frank and Lutie Brown, he was raised primarily by his mother, a laundress, and siblings, who began working outside the home as soon as they were able. Though he had plans to become a minister, the harsh economic climate of the Great Depression forced Brown to leave school so that he could devote all his time to the support of his family. Two decades later, however, he returned to high school, earned his degree, and went on to study briefly at Topeka's Washburn University.

During the 1930s Brown worked in a variety of occupations, including semiprofessional boxing. By the middle of the following decade, however, he had found a stable position as a welder for the Santa Fe Railroad, which had a large yard and repair facility in Topeka. With his wife, the former Leola Williams, he had three children and enjoyed a quiet, middle-class life in a racially diverse neighborhood. His children, however, were unable to attend the elementary school their white neighbors attended—a school that was considerably closer and more convenient than the one reserved for African Americans. That issue of convenience bothered Brown deeply, in part because the route to all-black Monroe Elementary took young students across the Santa Fe rail yard, a dirty and dangerous place. The African-American schools in Topeka had a good reputation, with decent facilities and highly trained teachers. "We're not talking about substandard facilities with leaky roofs and outhouses, like they were in the South," Brown's youngest daughter, Cheryl Brown Henderson, told Kurtis, adding, "We aren't talking about a poor education." Her father, however, had had enough. In 1950 he took Linda, his eldest daughter, to the white school nearby, Sumner Elementary, and tried to enroll her. The principal there rebuffed him, arguing that his hands were tied by the school board.

There the matter might have rested, had it not been for several lawyers who were determined to challenge Topeka's segregationist system. One of them, Charles Scott, was Brown's friend. After hearing of the incident at Sumner, Scott persuaded him to join a class-action suit his office was preparing in partnership with the NAACP. Why Brown was chosen as lead plaintiff has

At a Glance . . .

Born on August 2, 1918, in Topeka, KS; died June 20, 1961(?), probably in Missouri; son of Frank Brown and Lutie Brown (a laundress); married Leola Williams; children: three. *Religion:* African Methodist Episcopal. *Education:* Attended Washburn University, 1950s.

Career: Santa Fe Railroad, welder, 1940s–50s; St. Mark's A.M.E. Church (Topeka, KS), assistant pastor, 1950s; minister, 1950s–61.

Awards: Visiting professorship established in his honor, Washburn University and the Brown Foundation for Educational Equity, Excellence and Research, 1999.

never been entirely clear. That he was the only man almost certainly played a role, although the simplicity of his name may have been a factor as well.

Brown v. *Board* moved slowly but steadily through the court system. After hearing arguments in the summer of 1951, a three-judge panel at the local U.S. District Court dismissed the suit. It was then appealed to the Supreme Court, which combined it under Brown's name with four other desegregation cases from around the country. After an initial hearing in 1952, the Court asked both sides for additional information. The plaintiffs, led by NAACP lawyer Thurgood Marshall (1908-1993), focused particularly in this phase on a growing body of research that underscored the damaging effects of segregation on the self-esteem of African-American students. When the Court met again the following year, Marshall argued that these psychological effects violated the Fourteenth Amendment's guarantee of equal protection under the law. On May 17, 1954, the Court, led by Chief Justice Earl Warren (1891-1974), agreed unanimously.

In the wake of the Brown decision, school administrators in Topeka and elsewhere systematically dismantled the framework of segregation. As enrollments were merged, tensions ran high, and African-American students were the frequent targets of verbal abuse. Overt violence was rare, however, and by the end of the 1950s desegregated public schools were the rule throughout the country. Brown, meanwhile, stepped quietly out of the spotlight. By the middle of the decade, he had fulfilled his dream of becoming a minister and was serving as assistant pastor of St. Mark's A.M.E. (African Methodist Episcopal) Church in Topeka. He later moved east to Springfield, Missouri, where he began work with another congregation. In 1961—perhaps on June 20, though the sources are

unclear—he died of natural but uncertain causes; according to what is probably the most widely accepted story, he was driving from Springfield to Topeka when he suffered a heart attack. In the years since his death, several efforts have been made to honor his contribution to the desegregation struggle. Arguably the most prominent of these occurred in 1999, when Washburn University named the first Oliver L. Brown Distinguished Visiting Scholar for Diversity Issues. It did so in conjunction with the Brown Foundation for Educational Equity, Excellence and Research, a Topeka institution founded and led for many years by his daughter Cheryl. He has also been prominently featured in exhibits at the *Brown* v. *Board of Education* National Historic Site, a memorial and museum housed in what was once Monroe Elementary School.

In a 2004 interview with Greg Toppo in *USA Today*, Cheryl Brown Henderson spoke eloquently of her father and of the *Brown* v. *Board* decision. She was careful to note, however, that the situation he and the other plaintiffs had addressed in Topeka paled in comparison to what African-American students and their parents faced in the South. "What happened in Kansas was nothing like what happened in South Carolina or Virginia," she told Toppo. "I can't emphasize that enough."

Sources

Online

"Background Overview & Summary," Brown Foundation for Educational Equity, Excellence and Research, http://brownvboard.org/content/background-overview-summary (accessed September 22, 2011).

Fry, Timothy S., "The Struggle against 'Separate but Equal'—Teaching about *Brown* v. *Topeka*," Washburn University, http://www.washburn.edu/faculty/tfry/Brown APA style.pdf (accessed September 22, 2011).

Kurtis, Bill, "Black, White, and Brown"(transcript), *NewsHour with Jim Lehrer*, May 12, 2004, http://www.pbs.org/newshour/bb/law/jan-june04/brown_05-12.html (accessed September 22, 2011).

Maruca, Mary, "*Brown* v. *Board of Education*: National Historic Site," Western National Parks Association, 2003, http://www.cr.nps.gov/history/online_books/brvb/brown.pdf (accessed September 22, 2011).

Toppo, Greg, "Cheryl Brown Henderson," USAToday, May 16, 2004, http://www.usatoday.com/life/people/2004-05-14-cheryl-brown-henderson_x.htm (accessed September 22, 2011).

—R. Anthony Kugler

Wyatt Cenac

1976—

Comedian

Cenac, Wyatt, photograph. AP Images/Shea Walsh.

Wyatt Cenac is a staff writer and on-air correspondent for *The Daily Show with Jon Stewart,* Comedy Central's irreverent skewering of the day's headlines. Cenac has parried with titular host Jon Stewart since mid-2008 and delivers timely segments on America's shifting political, cultural, and economic landscape. Writing for the Onion A.V. Club, Joel Keller asserted that Cenac "has quickly become one of the show's most reliable correspondents, creating a persona that's nerdy, arrogant, and defensive all at once."

Cenac was born in New York City in 1976, but his family relocated to Dallas, Texas, when he was still a toddler. His high school years were spent at the academically challenging Jesuit College Preparatory School of Dallas, a single-sex Roman Catholic school. One of his friends there was future comic-book writer Brian K. Vaughn, who also went on to write for the hit ABC series *Lost.*

Cenac attended the University of North Carolina at Chapel Hill and moved to Los Angeles to launch his career in the mid-1990s. He spent several years on the stand-up circuit, worked with a sketch comedy troupe

called Cleo's Apartment, and finally landed a steady, well-paying job on the Fox animated series *King of the Hill* in 2005. His performing skills were further honed with the Upright Citizens Brigade Theatre, an improv group. He also worked with The Doomed Planet, a collective that creates unique, web-based content. It was his impersonation of then-candidate Barack Obama discussing possible campaign-poster designs—including one that read "The Black Guy"—that piqued the interest of *Saturday Night Live* producers, who were auditioning comedians to fill a slot for a regular Obama impersonator. Cenac auditioned but lost out to comedian Fred Armisen.

Cenac's online video content, which includes an appearance in the cult-favorite "Yacht Rock" series, brought him to *The Daily Show with Jon Stewart,* which airs five nights a week on Comedy Central. For its coverage of the 2000 and 2004 elections, Stewart and his staff had collected the highly competitive George Foster Peabody Awards for excellence in radio and television broadcasting, and Cenac was hired in June 2008 as the show's "Indecision 2008" segments ramped up before the historic November contest. He

At a Glance . . .

Born on April 19, 1976, in New York, NY. *Education*: Attended University of North Carolina at Chapel Hill.

Career: Performed stand-up comedy in Los Angeles, after 1995; member of sketch comedy troupe Cleo's Apartment; *King of the Hill,* Fox, writer and story editor, 2005–08(?); Upright Citizens Brigade Theatre, member, 2005–08(?); appeared in film *Medicine for Melancholy,* 2008; *The Daily Show with Jon Stewart,* writer and correspondent, 2008—.

Addresses: *Office*—c/o The Daily Show with Jon Stewart, Comedy Central, 345 Hudson St., New York, NY 10014.

moved back to his hometown of New York City and delivered his first on-air segment on July 21, 2008, bewailing the dullness of the primary season. The clip features Cenac's suggestions on how Republican and Democratic Party leaders might borrow from the impenetrable, labyrinthine plot of ABC's *Lost* to attract more interest in the state primary races.

On *The Daily Show* Cenac mostly skirted around the issue of race in America, with that category largely covered by the show's "senior black correspondent," Larry Wilmore. Cenac's deadpan style blended perfectly with the rest of his colleagues and was particularly well suited to such missions as investigating what conservative American pundits described as the coming "nightmare of socialism" should the newly elected Obama administration be able to implement its policies. Cenac visited Sweden to report back on what life is like in a socialist nation, where private and corporate income is heavily taxed but the government provides a raft of social services in exchange. His footage was heavy with appearances from tall, leggy young Swedish women and included a spoof of *MTV's Cribs* in which he visited the unassuming apartment of Sweden's newest pop star, Robyn.

It was Cenac who voiced the memorable Muppet-like puppet that served as a stand-in for former Republican National Committee chair Michael Steele. "It's an amazing opportunity," Cenac told Robert Wilonsky in the *Dallas Observer* about his new high-profile job. "Because there is so much not just to poke fun at and to skewer, but also just to have access to these things. The other day, I got to interview the state senator of Florida. I don't know if I ever would have had the opportunity to talk to a politician face-to-face, even though I am asking nitwit questions."

Before landing *The Daily Show* job, Cenac appeared in a more serious role in a small independent film, *Medicine for Melancholy,* that made the rounds of the 2008 film-festival season. Critics described it as possibly the first African-American "mumblecore" film, a low-key, meandering urban drama with a tenuous romance at its center. Cenac played Micah, who spends a few days roaming San Francisco with Jo' (played by Tracey Heggins, later to be seen in 2011's *Things Fall Apart*), discussing questions of cultural identity, sexual politics, and the rapid gentrification of their city. His character, wrote A. O. Scott in a *New York Times* review, "is acutely aware of—Jo' might say obsessed with—the demographic changes that have accompanied the city's recent boom. He grieves over the attrition of the black population, which he says has shrunk to only 7 percent, and fears that gentrification will destroy his hometown's free, democratic spirit." Scott went on to praise Cenac's feature-film debut, noting that the comedian "calibrates Micah's vacillations between earnestness and guardedness perfectly."

In the spring of 2011 Cenac appeared on his own hour-long special for Comedy Central titled *Wyatt Cenac: Comedy Person.* He has generally resisted the label of "black" comedian, telling AOL Black Voices, as quoted by Jenée Desmond-Harris in The Root, that "Hollywood either doesn't look at a show like [BET's] *Comic View* or if they just think, 'They're over there, they're taken care of.' I don't know what that mindset is, but it seems [they think] they don't need to worry about booking black comedians on *The Tonight Show* or whatever bigger shows there might be, because [we're] taken care of. That's a question worth asking Hollywood at large."

To promote his Comedy Central special, Cenac submitted comments to the weekly "New York Diet" feature in *New York* magazine's food-section blog, Grub Street. He admitted that late-night fare at a Brooklyn joint called Sidecar was one of his favorites, but he recalled that "the last time I was eating the fried chicken, this guy walked up to me and said, 'Way to live up to the stereotype,'" he told *New York* writer Alan Sytsma. "And then he was like, 'It's okay, I can say it. I'm Indian.' To which my response was, 'It's still racist.' He tried to make it okay and to explain it away, and it still didn't take the racism away from it. And at some point he shared that he's a med student, to which it seemed, like, well, way to live up to the stereotype."

Sources

Periodicals

Maclean's, September 20, 2010.
New York, May 13, 2011.
New York Times, January 30, 2009.

Online

Alter, Ethan, "Talking with Wyatt Cenac," Giant, January 29, 2009, http://giantmag.com/the-magazine/ealter/talking-withwyatt-cenac/ (accessed July 17, 2011).

Cenac, Wyatt, "Barack Obama: Campaign Posters," The Doomed Planet, http://www.youtube.com/watch?v=PeNc_T9CqP0 (accessed July 24, 2011).

Desmond-Harris, Jenée, "The Daily Show's Wyatt Cenac Talks Race and Comedy," The Root, May 17, 2011, http://www.theroot.com/buzz/daily-shows-wyat-cenac-talks-race-and-comedy (accessed July 17, 2011).

Keller, Joel, "Interview: Wyatt Cenac," The Onion A.V. Club, May 13, 2011, http://www.avclub.com/articles/wyatt-cenac,56043/ (accessed July 17, 2011).

"The Stockholm Syndrome, Part 2," *The Daily Show with Jon Stewart,* April 22, 2009, http://www.thedailyshow.com/watch/wed-april-22-2009/the-stockholm-syndrome-pt--2 (accessed July 24, 2011).

Wilonsky, Robert, "Tonight on *The Daily Show,* Jesuit Grad Wyatt Cenac Becomes Part of 'The Best F*&#ing News Team Ever,'" *Dallas Observer,* June 25, 2008, http://blogs.dallasobserver.com/unfairpark/2008/06/tonight_jesuit_grad_wyatt_cena.php (accessed July 17, 2011).

"Wyatt Cenac," *The Daily Show with Jon Stewart,* http://www.thedailyshow.com/news-team/wyatt-cenac (accessed July 17, 2011).

—Carol Brennan

Susan E. Chapman

1968—

Business executive

Susan Chapman's job as a specialist in global real estate has taken her around the world and back—so far, she has visited 45 countries, and she is not unpacking her bags just yet. As the head of global real estate operations for the financial services firm American Express, it is her job to manage all of the properties where the company's 65,000 employees work, located in more than 40 countries. Before joining American Express, Chapman, an engineer and urban planner by training, managed one of the largest corporate real estate portfolios in the world for banking giant Citigroup, overseeing nearly 13,000 properties. Twice named one of *Black Enterprise* magazine's "Most Powerful Players under 40," she is among the top female executives in the country, noted for her community service in nurturing the next generation of leaders.

Susan E. Chapman was born in 1968 and grew up in Cincinnati, Ohio, the daughter of an accountant and a nurse. As a young girl, she knew that she wanted to have a high-powered career. "I am not a widget pusher," she told Tom McGhee in the *Denver Post*. She enrolled at Vanderbilt University, intending to pursue a career as an engineer. When she discovered, however, that it would take too long to achieve the kind of responsibility she craved, she switched gears and headed to the University of Massachusetts at Amherst, where she earned a master's degree in urban planning, and then followed with a master's of business administration at the University of Wisconsin, focusing on real estate finance and urban land economics.

Chapman spent the early years of her career in urban planning, working as a development consultant and planner. In 1998, after completing her MBA, she joined the Security Capital Group, a real estate management and development group based in Santa Fe, New Mexico, as an investment banking manager. In 2000 she took a position at the Denver-based firm Level 3 Communications as director of global real estate and procurement. Shuttling between offices in Denver and London, Chapman managed an 11-million-square-foot portfolio of offices and technical facilities in Europe and Asia and oversaw more than $3 billion in real estate acquisitions and sales. The job took Chapman across the globe—she racked up 200,000 flying miles in just two years—and inspired in her a lifelong passion for travel. In 2003, at age 34, she made *Black Enterprise*'s Most Powerful Players under 40 list, alongside stars such as Jay-Z, Halle Berry, and Tiger Woods.

In late 2004 she went to work for the international banking firm Citigroup as global head of operations for Citi Corporate Realty Services, leading the company's mergers and acquisitions, retail branch development, real estate administration, and global business relationship management functions. Chapman's division was responsible for buying, selling, and building properties to support all of Citigroup's businesses worldwide. The job put Chapman in charge of managing one of the largest corporate real estate portfolios in the world, comprising more than 86 million square feet in some 13,000 facilities, with work space for more than 300,000 employees in 96 countries. As the head of

At a Glance . . .

Born in 1968 in Cincinnati, OH. *Education*: Vanderbilt University, BS, engineering; University of Massachusetts–Amherst, MS, regional planning; University of Wisconsin–Madison, MBA, real estate finance and urban land economics.

Career: Industrial Development Center, development consultant, 1990–92; Knox County Metropolitan Planning Commission, planner, 1992–93; Hammer, Siler, George Associates, associate consultant, 1993–95; Security Capital Group, investment banking manager, 1998–2000; Level 3 Communications, director of global real estate and procurement, 2000–04; Citigroup, Inc., global chief administrative officer of Citi Realty Services, 2004–10; American Express, senior vice president of global real estate and workplace enablement, 2010—.

Memberships: Executive Leadership Council; Urban Land Institute; Wisconsin Real Estate Alumni Association; boards of directors for Brotherhood SisterSol, Leadership Education and Development (LEAD), Global Syndicate, and New York University Schack Institute of Real Estate.

Awards: Named to Hot List: Most Powerful Players under 40, *Black Enterprise,* 2003, 2005; named Distinguished Young Business Alumnus, University of Wisconsin Alumni Association, 2007; named Woman of Distinction, Girl Scout Council of Greater New York, 2008; named to 75 Most Powerful Women in Business list, *Black Enterprise,* 2010; Women of Excellence Community Service Award, National Association of Female Executives, 2010.

Addresses: *Office*—American Express Company, 200 Vesey St., New York, NY 10285.

Citi Realty's global projects team, Chapman also led the company's "green" real estate strategies, one aspect of Citigroup's $50 billion commitment to address climate change. As part of that effort, Citigroup was the first company to have more than 100 buildings LEED (Leadership in Energy and Environmental Design) certified—a measurement of a building's sustainability—by the U.S. Green Building Council.

Chapman made another career move in 2010, joining American Express as senior vice president of global real estate and workplace enablement. There, she has led global real estate operations, which encompass 10 million square feet and more than 65,000 employees in 41 countries; she is charged with working across the portfolio to transform the workplace in order to support the company's future growth.

In addition to her professional roles, Chapman also is a dedicated volunteer, committed to mentoring young people in her community, especially girls. "I have been given a gift, and the exposure I have gotten isn't just something for Susan. I have to give back," she told the *Denver Post.* She is a member of the boards of directors of several nonprofits, including Brotherhood SisterSol, Leadership Education and Development (LEAD), and the Global Syndicate, and she is on the advisory board of New York University's Schack Institute of Real Estate. She previously served on the Dean's Advisory Board at the University of Wisconsin School of Business and is a member of the Executive Leadership Council, the University of Wisconsin Real Estate Alumni Association, and the Urban Land Institute.

Chapman has received many awards for her achievements in business. Twice she was named to *Black Enterprise's* Hot List: Most Powerful Players under 40 (in 2003 and 2007), and in 2010 she was included in the magazine's 75 Most Powerful Women in Business. In 2007 she was honored by the University of Wisconsin Alumni Association as a Distinguished Young Business Alumnus. Recognizing her commitment to community service, the Girl Scout Council of New York named Chapman a Woman of Distinction in 2008, and in 2010 she received the Women of Excellence Community Service Award from the National Association of Female Executives.

Sources

Periodicals

Black Enterprise, January 1, 2007.
Denver Post, March 1, 2004.
Women of Color Magazine, Spring 2010.

Online

"Alumni Profile: Susan Chapman," University of Wisconsin School of Business, http://www.bus.wisc.edu/alumni/profiles/susan_chapman.asp (accessed August 15, 2011).
"Black Women in Technology: Top Achievers," The Root, http://www.theroot.com/multimedia/black-women-techies (accessed August 15, 2011).
"Susan E. Chapman," *Network Journal,* http://www.tnj.com/2010/susan-e-chapman (accessed August 15, 2011).

—Deborah A. Ring

Linda Clement-Holmes

1962—

Business executive

Clement-Holmes, Linda, photograph. AP Images/Paul Fox.

Linda Clement-Holmes serves as senior vice president and chief diversity officer at Procter & Gamble (P&G), one of the world's major manufacturers of consumer products. The Cincinnati-based maker of the Olay, Pantene, Pampers, Cover Girl and Tide detergent brands employs more than 125,000 workers worldwide and is one of the most successful companies in the history of American business. Clement-Holmes's mission as chief diversity officer is to bring a greater balance to the P&G workforce. "We're an $80 billion company in a consumer space that is very competitive," she told Arati Menon Carroll in a 2011 interview for the *Economic Times*, part of the *Times of India* newspaper group. "In the last five years our products have got more diverse, our markets are more diverse and our organisation needs to reflect a similar balance."

Clement-Holmes was born in Chicago in 1962 and graduated from Purdue University in Indiana with a dual bachelor of science degree in industrial management and computer science. Her first job was as a communications service representative at Indiana Bell, and she joined Procter & Gamble in January of 1983 as a systems analyst. She was promoted to senior systems analyst two years later and in 1988 became a section manager with P&G's Management Systems Operations and Development group, responsible for the company-designated Future Email Architecture program. She spent much of the 1990s in various management positions inside P&G's technology division. In 1998 she was made director of Technology Services Worldwide in the Global Engineering and Development division, and six years later was promoted to manager of information technology (IT) in P&G's Global Business Services, responsible for infrastructure and governance. In 2007 she advanced to a vice presidency at the company and was put in charge of Global Business Services for P&G in the Middle East, Africa, and Central and Eastern Europe.

Clement-Holmes works at a company that posts annual sales topping the $80 billion mark. Its multiple brands are divided across three sectors: Beauty & Grooming, Household Care, and Health and Well-Being. Familiar household brands like Crest, Swiffer, Downy, Pepto-Bismal, Febreeze, and Iams are produced at P&G factories located on every continent of the world save for Antarctica. The company has long been a leader in

At a Glance . . .

Born on March 31, 1962, in Chicago, IL; daughter of Thestal Tyndal Clement and Fanny Ida (Turner) Clement; married to Theotis Holmes; two sons. *Education*: Purdue University, BSIM, 1982.

Career: Indiana Bell, communications service representative, 1981-82; Procter & Gamble (P&G), systems analyst, 1983-85, senior systems analyst, 1985-88, section manager, 1988-92, associate director for three different P&G divisions, 1993-98, director of Technology Services Worldwide, 1998-2001, and Global Business Services, 2001-04, manager for various P&G divisions, including Global Business Services, 2004-07, promoted to vice president, 2007, became chief diversity officer at P&G and senior vice president for Global Business Services, 2010.

Memberships: National Urban League (board member); Jack & Jill of America; Delta Sigma Theta.

Addresses: *Office*—The Procter & Gamble Company, 1 Procter & Gamble Plaza, Cincinnati, OH 45202-3315.

both marketing—it sponsored the first radio dramas, which evolved into the familiar television soap opera, back in the 1920s—and workplace innovation. As far back as the early 1980s, when Clement-Holmes was hired, P&G was cited by *Black Enterprise* magazine as one of the top 25 companies for African Americans in the workforce. In the mid-1980s, P&G started turning up on *Working Mother* magazine's equally influential list of the best workplaces in America for working women. Married and a mother herself, Clement-Holmes successfully campaigned for onsite childcare at P&G headquarters in downtown Cincinnati back in the late 1990s.

In 2003 Clement-Holmes's new title as Outsourcing Initiative Leader for Global Business Services at P&G gave her enormous responsibilities in overseeing a contract that made headlines in the business press: P&G inked a deal with computer giant Hewlett-Packard's new HP Services division worth some $3 billion. It marked a period when P&G began to outsource some of its information-technology tasks, and Clement-Holmes oversaw this transition. In 2005 she was made a manager with the Information & Decision Solutions (IDS) inside the Global Business Services, responsible for Infrastructure Services & Governance. This placed the entirely of P&G's information-technology support network—from computer hardware to mobile devices for all P&G employees—under her care.

Clement-Holmes became a vice president in 2007 at a time when P&G was determined to capture and hold an increasing share of the growing international market. Vast cultural differences guide consumer behavior in emerging markets for P&G products in India, Latin America, and the Philippines, for example, and because women are usually the makers of those buying decisions, P&G launched an effort to diversify its management ranks across the board. In February of 2010 Clement-Holmes was named P&G's chief diversity officer and senior vice president of Global Business Services.

P&G actually had informal internal "affinity groups" dating back to the 1960s, but in the early 1990s these were formalized. As the new chief diversity officer Clement-Holmes was given oversight of P&G's African American Leadership Network (AALN), Asian Pacific American Leadership Team (APALT), Corporate Women's Leadership Team (CWLT), Gay, Allies, Bisexual, Lesbian and Transgender Employees (GABLE), Hispanic Leadership Team (HLT), Native American Indian Leadership Team (NAILT), and People with Disabilities (PWD) group.

One example of Clement-Holmes's role as P&G's chief diversity officer is the introduction of new FlexiCenters at P&G production sites. In Auburn, Maine, in the summer of 2011 she was on hand for the opening of a new Tambrands packaging facility. The P&G location brought 60 new jobs to the area, with 18 of them designated for employees with one or more disabilities. Those workers occupy the FlexiCenter space, where special-order shipments are customized. "We have to succeed in touching and improving the lives of our employees before we can touch and improve the lives of our consumers," she explained to the *Insight into Diversity* newsletter. "What we have learned is that through diversity, we can generate more ideas and innovations that better meet the needs of our diverse consumers, we can create brand-building that better resonates with individual consumers, and we can establish stronger partnerships with retail customers."

A longtime resident of the Cincinnati area, Clement-Holmes is active in the National Urban League, Jack & Jill of America, and the Delta Sigma Theta sorority.

Related information

Books

"Linda W. Clement-Holmes," The Complete Marquis Who's Who, Marquis Who's Who, 2010, http://ic. galegroup.com/ic/bic1/ReferenceDetailsPage/ReferenceDetailsWindow?displayGroupName=Reference&disableHighlighting=false&prodId=BIC2&ac

tion=e&windowstate=normal&catId=&documentId
=GALE | K2016418208&mode=view

Periodicals

Cincinnati Enquirer, August 24, 1999.

Online

Carroll, Arati Menon, "How P&G India Has Created a Senior Leadership Team That Is 45% Women," Economic Times, April 1, 2011, http://articles. economictimes.indiatimes.com/2011-04-01/news/ 29370514_1_ag-lafley-pampers-p-g (accessed August 10, 2011).

"Insight Q&A: Linda Clement-Holmes," INSIGHT Into Diversity, http://www.insightintodiversity.com/diver sity-issues/past-articles/61-past-articles/623-insight-qaa-linda-clement-holmes.html (accessed August 10, 2011).

"Linda W. Clement-Holmes," Forbes, http://people. forbes.com/profile/linda-w-clement-holmes/1388 64 (accessed August 10, 2011).

"Linda W. Clement-Holmes," Procter & Gamble, www.pg.com/en_US/downloads/...team/.../pg_ execu tive_bio_holmes.pdf (accessed August 15, 2011).

Pohlmeyer, Beth, "Linda Clement-Holmes Named One of Cincinnati's 'Women to Watch'" Information Technology Senior Management Forum, January 30, 2006, http://www.itsmfonline.org/news/releases/ itsmf_2006_01_30.php (accessed August 10, 2011).

Sanders, Brandee, "Top Black Women Techies," The-Root.com, March 21, 2011, http://www.theroot. com/multimedia/black-women-techies (accessed August 10, 2011).

—Carol Brennan

Cecilia Conrad

1955—

Economist

Economist Cecilia Conrad writes about the roles race and gender play in labor markets and in shaping public policy. An expert in the disparities that persist between African Americans and other racial groups in America, she has authored scores of research papers examining various aspects of this gap, and she serves as editor of *The Review of Black Political Economy*. Her resume includes stints at Columbia and Duke universities, but since 2009 Conrad has served as a professor of economics, vice president for academic affairs, and dean of the college at Pomona College in Claremont, California.

Born on January 4, 1955, Conrad is the daughter of dual high achievers. Her father, Emmett, served in the U.S. Army and Air Force in between college years at Stanford University and Meharry Medical College in Nashville. He completed his surgical residency at Homer Phillips Hospital in St. Louis, Missouri, in the mid-1950s. Up until the year Conrad was born, this was the sole medical facility available to African-American patients and doctors in the city. Once his residency was finished, Dr. Conrad relocated his young family to Dallas, Texas, at the request of friends there and became one of the first black surgeons to be granted hospital privileges at the formerly all-white hospitals in the city. Meanwhile, his wife, Eleanor, joined other Dallas women in taking up the desegregation battle on the consumer front. Conrad has said that as a child she sometimes saw her mother on the local evening news for participating in sit-ins and protests. Her father went on to become the first black staff doctor at a Roman Catholic–affiliated hospital in Dal-las, St. Paul, which later became part of the University of Texas Southwestern Medical Center. In 1967 he was the first black to be elected to the board of trustees of the Dallas Independent School District. Both of Conrad's parents would become well-known civic leaders in Dallas. Her father rose to become chief of staff at St. Paul Hospital, and the Dallas Independent School District named a high school in his honor.

When Conrad graduated from Franklin D. Roosevelt High School as valedictorian of the Class of 1972, her classmates voted her "Most Likely to Succeed." She earned her undergraduate degree from Wellesley College in Massachusetts in 1976 and landed a fellowship with the prestigious Bell Labs, the research and development company affiliated with AT&T. She joined the Federal Trade Commission as an economist in 1978, the same year she earned her master's degree from Stanford University. Four years later she was awarded her Ph.D. in economics after completing her dissertation, *The Pioneer Brand Hypothesis and Other Topics: With Asymmetric Information about Product Quality*. "It is frequently suggested that the first brand in a product market enjoys a price advantage over its imitators due to imperfect information about product quality," she wrote in its introduction. "This article considers the effect of this advantage on prices and market shares in a dominant firm price leadership model."

In 1981 Duke University hired Conrad as an assistant professor of economics, and she stayed in North Carolina for four years. From 1985 to 1995 she taught

At a Glance . . .

Born on January 4, 1955; daughter of Emmett James (a surgeon) and Eleanor Nelson Conrad; married Llewellyn Miller (a risk-management consultant), May 26, 1984; children: Conrad Jr. *Education*: Wellesley College, BA, 1976; Stanford University, MA, 1978, PhD, 1982.

Memberships: Phi Beta Kappa; National Economic Association, president, 1993–94; International Association for Feminist Economics, president, 2008–09.

Career: Bell Laboratories, resident fellow, 1976–81; Federal Trade Commission, economist, 1978–79; Duke University, assistant professor of economics, 1981–85; Hunter College, visiting assistant professor, 1984–85; Barnard College/Columbia University, associate professor, 1985–95; joined faculty of Pomona College, 1997, and became associate dean, 2004, then the Stedman-Sumner Professor of Economics, 2007; in 2009 became Pomona College's vice president for academic affairs and dean of the college; affiliated with the Joint Center for Political and Economic Studies; editor of the *Review of Black Political Economy* and associate editor of *Feminist Economics; Black Enterprise* magazine, board of economists, after 1993; U.S. Census Bureau, member of African-American Advisory Committee, 2007—.

Addresses: *Office*—Office of the Dean of Faculty, Pomona College, Alexander Hall, 550 N. College Ave., Claremont, CA 91711.

Conrad began writing about these and other issues for *Black Enterprise* magazine in the early 1990s, also sitting on its board of economists. On the scholarly front, she discussed affirmative action and its impact on an emergent black middle class, for example, and also explored various shifts in public policy and labor law and how these changes affected minorities. In 1997 Conrad joined the faculty of Pomona College in Claremont, California, and was appointed associate dean in 2004. In 2007 she became the school's Stedman-Sumner Professor of Economics, and in mid-2009 she advanced further up the administrative chain when she was named the new vice president for academic affairs and dean of the college.

Conrad also serves as a member of the African-American Advisory Committee of the U.S. Census Bureau. Because of her impressive command of statistical data on blacks and the labor market, she occasionally appears as a news guest. In July of 2011 she was invited by *PBS NewsHour* to comment on recently released figures from the U.S. Bureau of Labor Statistics, which showed that U.S. unemployment rates remained high but that these figures were nearly double for African Americans. This reflected an historic two-to-one unemployment ratio between blacks and whites that had changed only negligibly over several decades, Conrad explained to anchor Jeffrey Brown. "We sometimes talk about the problem of spatial mismatch, that African-Americans remain more segregated than any other population in the country," she said on *PBS NewsHour*. "They are frequently segregated in areas that do not have the jobs, that haven't seen job growth. And they lack the kind of transportation infrastructure to get to where the jobs are."

Conrad's studies include *A Mixed Record: How the Public Workforce System Affects Racial and Ethnic Disparities in the Labor Market* in 2005, and a 2006 paper, *African Americans and High Tech Jobs: Trends and Disparities in 25 Cities*, both published by the Joint Center for Political and Economic Studies.

Sources

Periodicals

Rocky Mountain News, January 21, 1996, p. 2A.

Online

Brown, Jeffrey, "Dismal Unemployment Report Suggests Recovery May Be Stalling," *PBS NewsHour*, July 8, 2011, http://www.pbs.org/newshour/bb/business/july-dec11/jobs_07-08.html (accessed July 17, 2011).
"Cecilia A. Conrad," Active Living Research, http://www.activelivingresearch.org/about/advisorycommittee/conrad (accessed July 17, 2011).
"Cecilia A. Conrad Appointed Dean of Faculty at

at Barnard College of Columbia University. In the late 1980s she had a child with her husband Llewellyn Miller, a fellow Stanford alumnus and a risk-management consultant. Returning to Dallas for a high school reunion, she was fascinated by the fact she was the only mother with an infant at the gathering, although she was in her early 30s. Reconnecting with classmates who had become parents at a much earlier age, Conrad noted they had achieved modest professional success, and she decided to investigate this from a statistical approach. She looked at data and found some kernel of truth in the presumption that teens who are not college-bound have fewer qualms about becoming parents at an early age because they see few career prospects ahead of them. In lower-income jobs, moreover, women who delayed childbearing until their 20s often found themselves out of a job when they could not meet the demands of both work and home.

Scripps College," Scripps College, http://media.scrippscollege.edu/press-releases/staff/cecilia-a-conrad-appointed-dean-of-faculty-at-scripps-college (accessed July 17, 2011).

"Conrad, Emmett James," Texas State Historical Association, http://www.tshaonline.org/handbook/online/articles/fcoem (accessed July 17, 2011).

"Pomona College Vice President and Dean of the College Cecilia Conrad: Is There a Bubble in the Liberal Arts College Market?," Pomona College, September 1, 2009, http://www.pomona.edu/events/convocation/09/conrad-speech.aspx (accessed July 17, 2011).

—Carol Brennan

LaVerne Council

1961(?)—

Business executive

LaVerne Council is corporate vice president and chief information officer (CIO) of the Fortune 500 health-care products company Johnson & Johnson. In this capacity she has been credited with reorganizing the corporation's information technology systems to create efficiencies across the hundreds of individual companies in the Johnson & Johnson fold. She is considered one of the top CIOs in the United States and has received numerous awards and honors related to her professional achievement. Among other charitable activities, Council has demonstrated particular dedication to the March of Dimes, the national charitable organization dedicated to preventing premature births and promoting the health of babies. She has served since 2006 on the March of Dimes's board of trustees, and in 2011 she was appointed the board's chair.

LaVerne Council grew up in comparatively humble circumstances in East Chicago, Indiana. She distinguished herself academically in high school and attended Western Illinois University, where she earned a B.S. with highest honors in 1983. After graduation Council worked for State Farm Insurance in Bloomington, Illinois, before returning to school to study business. She graduated from Illinois State University in 1986 with an M.B.A. in operations management.

Council's early work history included stints with the utilities company Tennessee Valley Authority and the consulting companies Accenture and Mercer Management Consulting. Then, while working for the consulting firm Ernst and Young (which was acquired by CapGemini in 2000), she developed expertise in global supply chain management and the implementation of new technologies, rising to the rank of partner. While at Ernst and Young/Cap Gemini, Council oversaw the accounts of companies in the life sciences industry and led the in-house Supply Chain Strategy Team.

Council next took a position with the multinational computer and technology services company Dell, Inc., where again she focused on the intersection of technology and globalization. She was the first black woman to serve as the company's global vice president for Information Technology, Global Business Solutions, and Development Services. Her duties included taking the lead in developing globalization strategies in Europe and Asia and overseeing global product development centers in India, Russia, and Brazil.

In 2006 Council reached the highest rungs of the corporate ladder, accepting a position as global vice president and chief information officer at the Fortune 500 health-care products company Johnson & Johnson. Johnson & Johnson was a decentralized corporation consisting of hundreds of individual brands and companies, and it had not effectively mobilized its information technology (IT) programs and systems to take advantage of efficiencies and synergies across its many divisions and subsidiaries. Inside the company, IT was seen as a drain on resources, and Johnson & Johnson's CEO, William Weldon, did not believe that it was central to the organization's success.

Council came to the job as the company's youngest-ever top officer and the first to be promoted to that

At a Glance . . .

Born in 1961(?); married Bennie Council; children: Troy. *Education*: Western Illinois University, BS, 1983; Illinois State University, MBA, operations management, 1986. *Politics*: Democrat.

Career: Worked at State Farm Insurance, Tennessee Valley Authority, Accenture, and Mercer Management Consulting; Ernst & Young, partner; Dell, Inc., global vice president for IT, Business Solutions, and Development Services; Johnson & Johnson, corporate vice president and CIO, 2006—.

Memberships: March of Dimes, chair of board of trustees; Liberty Science Center, chair of board; Microsoft CIO Advisory Committee; Executive Leadership Council.

Awards: CIO of the Year, New Jersey Technology Council, 2009; named one of 75 Most Powerful Women in Business, *Black Enterprise,* 2010; honorary doctorate, Drexel University, 2010.

Addresses: *Home*—Mendham, NJ. *Office*—Johnson & Johnson, 1 Johnson & Johnson Plaza, New Brunswick, NJ 08933. *Web*—http://www.jnj.com.

level from the outside. She also brought a conviction that an enhancement of the company's IT initiatives could provide Johnson & Johnson with a competitive advantage. She traveled widely in her early months on the job to build a consensus for change among the numerous heads of individual Johnson & Johnson companies, and she found that many of them were keen to see their IT capabilities enhanced. She also established direct relationships with the companies' technology heads as well as with the leaders of the various working groups within the corporate IT department. Ultimately, Council was able to oversee the centralization of the corporation's IT structure and processes, streamlining relationships among individual companies and major vendors of Johnson & Johnson products. In a speech that she later gave at her alma mater Illinois State University, she said that her work remaking the IT systems saved the company $1 billion in her first four years on the job.

Council's performance as CIO did not go unnoticed outside the company. She was named CIO of the Year by the New Jersey Technology Council in 2009, and she has been named one of the Best CIOs in the United States by *Computerworld*. She has been invited to speak frequently about her work at Johnson & Johnson, and her leadership of the company's IT overhaul was the subject of a case study in the 2010 management book *The Right Fight: How Great Leaders Use Healthy Conflict to Drive Performance*, by Saj-nicole Joni and Damon Beyer.

Council and her husband, Bennie Council, have one son, Troy, who was born prematurely. Her son's challenges led Council to become involved with the charitable organization the March of Dimes, which works to prevent premature birth and infant mortality. In 2005 Council became a member of the group's board of trustees. As part of a delegation from the group, Council visited U.S. President Barack Obama in 2010 to discuss the relationship between premature birth and health-care reform. In 2011 Council became the first African American and the second woman to serve as the group's chair.

Council was named one of the 75 Most Powerful Women in Business by *Black Enterprise* in 2010, and that same year she received an honorary doctorate from Drexel University. As of 2011 she and her family lived in Mendham, New Jersey, near Johnson & Johnson headquarters in New Brunswick.

Sources

Books

Joni, Saj-Nicole, and Damon Beyer, *The Right Fight: How Great Leaders Use Healthy Conflict to Drive Performance, Innovation, and Value,* HarperCollins, 2010.

Periodicals

Computerworld, December 7, 2009; March 9, 2010.
Pantagraph (Bloomington, Illinois), April 1, 2010.

Online

Alleyne, Sonia, "75 Most Powerful Women in Business," *Black Enterprise,* http://www.blackenterprise.com/2010/02/01/75-most-powerful-women-in-business/ (accessed July 13, 2011).

—Mark Lane

Mia Amber Davis

1975–2011

Model

Davis, Mia Amber, photograph. Gustavo Caballero/Getty Images.

Mia Amber Davis was one of the most sought-after plus-size models in the fashion industry for a few years before her untimely death in 2011. Standing almost six feet tall, the television producer wore her weight with confidence and garnered a devoted following for her appearances on the talk-show circuit and reality shows. In 2009 she appeared on CNN's *Campbell Brown* to discuss obesity and health issues in America. "Sizism is the last acceptable prejudice," Davis asserted. "If you see someone who's overweight, automatically they're the reason for America's problems in the health care industry? That's absolutely not true."

Davis was born in 1974 and played basketball at the college level. In 1995 she was hired as an assistant audience coordinator at Harlem's landmark Apollo Theater for the long-running series *Showtime at the Apollo.* That same year, she also found a second steady job as a producer for Ricki Lake's eponymous daytime television talk show, where she remained for the next six years. In 2000 Davis made her feature-film debut in the comedy *Road Trip.* Her character, Rhonda, meets a scrawny college student named Kyle (played by DJ Qualls, who later appeared in *Hustle &*

Flow) in a nightclub, and they have a life-changing overnight encounter at a black fraternity house that is one of the stops of the titular journey. "Like all comedies of this ilk, 'Road Trip' plays on the sexual and racial fears of its teen Caucasian audience," noted Salon's Andrew O'Hehir. "Despite their purported rowdiness, our wandering foursome are both frightened and fascinated by aggressive women, [and] people of color. . . . But it never condescends or tries to preach against sex, drugs or generalized hedonism, and it does a nice job of rewarding the characters it mocks (such as Kyle)."

Davis's appearance in *Road Trip* led to a magazine cover for *Belle,* but she continued to work in television production jobs while pursuing her modeling career. She was involved with three pilots for Telepictures, none of which were picked up, before landing an unusual behind-the-scenes job as a stand-in and photo double for Queen Latifah on the set of a pair of 2006 movies, *Perfect Christmas* and *Life Support.* Davis also worked as a senior booking producer for former *View* co-host Star Jones' new talk show on Court TV/TruTV, which lasted just six months. After that, Davis worked for both the Food Network and as a

At a Glance . . .

Born in 1974; died of a pulmonary embolism on May 10, 2011, in Los Angeles, CA; married Mike Yard (a comedian), 2008.

Career: Inner City Broadcasting, assistant audience coordinator for *Showtime at the Apollo,* 1995–2001; assistant audience coordinator for *Hard Rock Live,* 1996–98; Telepictures, production assistant, 2002–06; Columbia TriStar/Sony, producer for *Ricki Lake,* 1995–2002; stand-in and photo double for Queen Latifah on the films *Perfect Christmas* and *Last Holiday,* 2006; Turner Broadcasting, senior booking producer for Star Jones on Court TV/TruTV, 2007–08; producer for the Food Network and *Divorce Court*; signed as model with plus-sized retailer Ashley Stewart, 2008; *Plus Model,* creative editor-at-large, after 2008. Made television appearances on *The Ananda Lewis Show, The View, Campbell Brown, Rip the Runway, Mo'Nique's F.A.T. Chance, The Tyra Banks Show, Good Day Street Talk,* and *The Janice Dickinson Modeling Agency.*

supervising producer for *Divorce Court,* one of the first reality series in American television.

In 2008 Davis signed on with plus-sized retailer Ashley Stewart to help launch a new bra line, Butterfly, with the help of brand spokesperson Jill Scott, the singer. That led to scores of television appearances: Davis turned up on BET's *Rip the Runway, Mo'Nique's F.A.T. Chance* for Oxygen, and two vastly different shows hosted by former models, *The Tyra Banks Show* and *The Janice Dickinson Modeling Agency.* Davis was also hired by *Plus Model* magazine to serve as creative editor-at-large.

Davis was often invited on talk shows to discuss the emergence of plus-sized fashion models along with the unrealistic expectations many young women of lesser size face when they attempt to break into the industry. Her most famous appearance came in July of 2009 when CNN prime-time host Campbell Brown attempted to moderate a debate between Davis and MeMe Roth, an anti-junk food activist and founder of the National Action against Obesity. Roth made some valid points about the weight-loss industry as a highly profitable sector of American consumerism, then ticked off a list of health hazards related to being overweight. Roth likened it to "smoking, it's a choice," to which Davis responded, "It's not a choice to be overweight. I think that that's insulting, actually." Roth

went on to discuss her own weight issues, mentioning the "discipline" and "motivation" it took to maintain her own body weight. "I work out four times a week," Davis interjected, at which Roth jibed, "You're supposed to be working out every day." Davis held her ground in the debate, asserting, "I'm not here to argue with you. I'm here to say that stop blaming overweight people or obese people for America's problems. It's not our fault."

The back-and-forth between Davis and Roth went on for several more argumentative minutes. Brown, the host, pointedly gave Davis the last word. "Stop blaming overweight people for America's problems," she reiterated for the third time on the seven-and-a-half-minute segment. "I'm proud of the way I look. I'm proud of my body. I'm proud of all my friends and the hard work that we do to maintain our curves. So stop blaming us for America's health care issues because I am not a part of that plan." At that point, Roth interrupted again. "The studies don't back you up. And nine times out of ten, obesity is a result of lifestyle choices," Roth said. Davis responded, "I'm not included in those studies," and their exchange went on to the final 30 seconds, with Davis asserting she was in excellent health, according to her physician.

In an interview earlier that year with Suzette Banzo for *Plus Model,* Davis revealed she had been attending tough "boot-camp" style fitness classes. "I was partially sidelined for a few weeks with a knee injury but I'm still hanging in there," she said. "I strongly encourage everyone to find a fitness regimen and stick with it." Tragically, the outpatient surgery she chose to undergo in May of 2011 to fix that issue, which dated back to her college hoops days, inadvertently resulted in her death at age 36. Davis had arthroscopic knee surgery on the morning of May 9 in Los Angeles. Her husband, comedian Mike Yard, was in New York, and he reported that Davis's sister had phoned, saying Davis was complaining of feeling dizzy; Yard next received word that his wife had died shortly after arriving at Kaiser Permanente Hospital. The autopsy report from the Los Angeles County Coroner's Office attributed Davis's cause of death to a pulmonary embolism, a blood clot that travels from the veins in the legs to the lungs and heart. It is a complication of knee or hip surgery, when the legs remain immobilized during the post-operative period.

The blogosphere erupted in tributes to Davis in the days following her death. *Plus Model* editor Madeline Figueroa-Jones paid homage to her on the magazine's website. "Mia Amber was an angel," Figueroa-Jones wrote, "a compassionate person who always thought about others before herself. She always stopped to speak with anyone who asked for her time, and never felt she was too good to help, encourage or comfort anyone."

Sources

Periodicals

Daily Mail (London), May 11, 2011.

Online

Banzo, Suzette, "Interview with PLUS Model Magazine Cover Model," *Plus Model,* June 1, 2009, http://www.plusmodelmag.com/General/plus-model-magazine-article-detail.asp?article-id=613019358 (accessed July 17, 2011).

Desmond-Harris, Jenée, "Mia Amber Davis Dies at 36," The Root, May 12, 2011, http://www.theroot.com/buzz/mia-amber-davis-dies-36 (accessed July 17, 2011).

Figueroa-Jones, Madeline, "Plus Size Model Mia Amber Davis Passes Away But Leaves Her Legacy Behind," *Plus Model,* May 11, 2011, http://plus-model-mag.com/2011/05/plus-size-industry-icon-mia-amber-davis-passes-away-but-leaves-her-legacy-behind/ (accessed July 17, 2011).

O'Hehir, Andrew, "Road Trip," Salon, May 19, 2000, http://www.salon.com/entertainment/movies/review/2000/05/19/road_trip/index.html?CP=SAL&DN=110 (accessed July 17, 2011).

Brown, Campbell, "Obesity Strains the Budget: Are Overweight People Being Scapegoated?," *Campbell Brown,* CNN, July 29, 2009, available at http://www.youtube.com/watch?v=QSs1aalWUk8 (accessed on July 24, 2011).

—Carol Brennan

Rocky Dawuni

1969—

Reggae singer, songwriter

Dawuni, Rocky, photograph. Frederick M. Brown/Getty Images.

One of the brightest musical stars to emerge from Africa in the 1990s, vocalist and songwriter Rocky Dawuni is well known to reggae fans around the world. A native of Ghana, his ability to blend danceable beats with socially conscious lyrics has prompted several comparisons to Jamaica's Bob Marley, the genre's founding father. Dawuni's activism extends well beyond his lyrics, however. As the founder of a nongovernmental organization called Africa Live!, he has directed the world's attention to a number of serious issues affecting that continent, from HIV and AIDS to a growing shortage of clean water.

Born in 1969, Dawuni grew up on a military base in northern Ghana, a relatively underdeveloped and impoverished region. Under the watchful eye of his father, an army officer who believed strongly in the value of education, Dawuni won entrance to the University of Ghana, where he studied psychology and philosophy. Eventually, however, his attention turned from his classes to the reggae music he had loved since childhood. "In my first year," he recalled in a 2010 press release, "I met these four guys who were students there and musicians. Everyone was saying, "Why are we in

the University if we want to be musicians? Why don't we form a band?" The group that resulted was soon playing at bars and clubs around Accra, Ghana's sprawling capital. With a warm, resonant voice and a knack for writing lyrics, Dawuni was the band's front man. As he gained experience in that role, his confidence rose, and it was not long before he was approaching record producers, both in Ghana and in the United States. Those promotional efforts paid off, and in 1996 Mesa/Bluemoon, an American label, released his first album, *The Movement*. In a review later quoted on the GhanaWeb website, *The Beat* magazine called it "a thoughtful, spiritual and involved debut recording." From it came two hit singles, "Sugar" and "What Goes Around," both of which received considerable airplay on radio stations around the globe. It was the inclusion of "What Goes Around" on a compilation album (1996's *Strictly Underground: Reggae's Next Generation*), however, that probably did the most to introduce Dawuni to American audiences.

The Movement had not been in stores long when Dawuni began planning a follow-up. Released in the spring of 1998, *Crusade* was arguably even more

At a Glance . . .

Born on January 22, 1969, in Ghana; son of Koyatu (an army officer) and Asibi Dawuni; married Cary Sullivan; children: Safiya. *Education:* Attended the University of Ghana, 1990s.

Career: Independent performer, songwriter, and recording artist, 1990s—.

Awards: Reggae Song of the Year ("In Ghana"), Ghana Music Awards, 2000; Reggae Song of the Year ("I'll Try"), Ghana Music Awards, 2002, Image Award nomination (Outstanding World Music Album, for *Hymns for the Rebel Soul*), NAACP, 2011.

Addresses: *Record company*—c/o Aquarian Records ,PO Box 1510, Pacific Palisades, CA 90272. *Web*—http://www.RockyDawuni.com.

successful than its predecessor. Its centerpiece was "In Ghana," a song Dawuni wrote in honor of his homeland's 40th anniversary as an independent nation. Voted Reggae Song of the Year at the 2000 Ghana Music Awards, it proved a crowd favorite at a series of international concerts in 1999 and 2000. On his return from those gigs, Dawuni reentered the studio, completing his third album, *Awakening in Ghana*, in 2001. This, too, produced several hits, among them "I'll Try," another Reggae Song of the Year (2002).

By the early 2000s, Dawuni had settled in southern California, a move that dramatically increased his contacts in the entertainment world. He returned frequently to Ghana, however, in part to organize such music festivals as Rocky Dawuni's Independence Splash. That annual series began about 2000 as part of his efforts to foster national pride and to highlight serious but long-neglected problems; it has since become the focal point of his Africa Live! organization and of his charitable work generally. He has also found time, however, to join a number of other projects, including (RED), which enlists businesses and consumers in the fight against HIV and AIDS in Africa. In the course of the latter initiative, he met with a group of Ghanaians who had tested positive for HIV. "They told me," he recalled in the 2010 press release, "that my involvement has gone a long way in helping to reduce stigmatization [and in] encouraging more compassionate responses to the disease. They said they could feel a sea change. This just confirmed my commitment." He has also worked with the Carter Center, a charity founded by former U.S. President Jimmy Carter and his wife Rosalynn, on an ambitious plan to eradicate

guinea worm, a parasite that has long had a grievous effect on human health across Africa.

Dawuni's recording career, meanwhile, has continued apace. His fourth album, *Book of Changes*, produced another major hit, "Wake the Town" (also known as "Wake Up the Town"), on its release in 2005. Several years later, its sales received a secondary boost when Electronic Arts, a major video-game producer, licensed "Wake the Town" and another track for use in FIFA 2008, a soccer-based game available around the world. Dawuni has since made several similar deals, including one for FIFA 2008's successor, FIFA World Cup 2010. Together they have done much to bring his albums to the attention of gamers, including many young people in Asia, Europe, and the Americas. In that sense, they were in keeping with Dawuni's determination to make his music—and Ghanaian music generally—accessible to cultures in other parts of the world. That goal has also prompted his routine use of melodies and motifs from other musical traditions, including African-American spirituals and North African pop. Included on his fifth album, *Hymns for the Rebel Soul* (2010), for example, was a track called "Jerusalem," the rhythms of which are dominated by so-called "goblet" or "chalice" drums, widely used in the Middle East for centuries. Also on the album was "African Reggae Fever," which was frequently heard during the festivities surrounding the 2010 World Cup, soccer's preeminent event. Held in Africa for the first time in its history, the Cup sparked intense feelings of pride across the continent. That Dawuni's song aptly reflected those sentiments was clear, particularly after the release of a remixed version, "African Soccer Fever."

An indefatigable performer, Dawuni appeared on stages in Europe, Africa, and North America in 2011. One of the most prominent of those gigs was a concert at the Hollywood Bowl in Los Angeles on July 24, where he was joined by a number of prominent R&B stars, including vocalists Stevie Wonder and Sharon Jones.

Sources

Online

"Artist: Rocky Dawuni," GhanaNation.com, http://www.ghananation.com/profile/music/Rocky-Dawuni.asp (accessed September 20, 2011).

Ofori, Oral, "Rocky Dawuni's Dreadlocks Untangled," GhanaMusic.com, April 2, 2010, http://www.ghanamusic.com/music/featured-artiste/rocky-dawuni-dreadlocks-untangled/index.html (accessed September 20, 2011).

"Rocky Dawuni Profile: Detailed Biography," GhanaWeb, http://www.ghanaweb.com/GhanaHomePage/people/person.php?ID=620 (accessed September 20, 2011).

"Rocky," RockyDawuni.com, http://www.rockydawu

ni.com/index.php/pages/about/ (accessed September 20, 2011).

"Walking the Talk: Rocky Dawuni, Humanitarian Reggae Rebel, Unites Ghanaian Roots with Global Soul" RockPaperScissors.biz, May 25, 2010, http://www.rockpaperscissors.biz/index.cfm/fuseaction/current.press_release/project_id/488.cfm (accessed September 20, 2011).

—R. Anthony Kugler

DJ Lance Rock

1965—

Musician, DJ, actor, television host

DJ Lance Rock, photograph. C. Taylor Crothers/Getty Images.

Beloved by legions of kids around the world, DJ Lance Rock sprang into the spotlight in 2007 as the host of *Yo Gabba Gabba!*, a colorful, music-oriented television program for young children and their parents. A native of Missouri, he worked for many years as a musician and DJ before moving into TV. "This is the last thing in the world I ever thought I'd be doing," he told Gail Pennington in the *St. Louis Post-Dispatch* in the show's early days. That he has since proved a good match for its distinctive blend of music, dance, humor, and education is clear. Winner of several awards for children's programming, *Yo Gabba Gabba!* has become a pop-culture phenomenon, with branded merchandise, live performances around the nation, and a devoted fan base.

Born in 1965 on the northern outskirts of St. Louis, Rock's birth name was Lance Robertson. Drawn to music from an early age, he worked at local record stores while a student at Hazelwood East High School in Hazelwood, Missouri, a racially and economically diverse suburb. While he particularly enjoyed electronic dance beats, he told Pennington, "he explored all sides," adding, "Music has been a real anchor in my

life." Following his graduation in 1983, he continued to work in record stores, rising eventually to become manager of Deep Grooves, a St. Louis outlet that specialized in the dance music, or "techno," he loved. His own music career, meanwhile, was developing rapidly. By the early 1990s, he was attracting notice around the city as the leader of a techno band called My Other Self. He also worked as a DJ and dance-party organizer, often in conjunction with his band's gigs. While he did well in these endeavors, it was increasingly clear to him that St. Louis was at best a minor outpost in the world of techno. He decided, therefore, to move to one of its capitals—Los Angeles.

By all accounts a warm and gregarious person, Rock made friends easily in California. Many of his new acquaintances were musicians, and it was not long before he had a new band, known as the Ray Makers (or Raymakers); he also continued to work as a DJ. As he strove to establish himself in southern California's vibrant but competitive music scene, he became friends with Scott Schultz, the leader of a local band called Majestic. It was that contact that paved the way for his involvement in *Yo Gabba Gabba!*, for Schultz eventu-

At a Glance . . .

Born Lance Robertson in 1965 in St. Louis County, MO.

Career: Independent musician and DJ, 1980s—; *Yo Gabba Gabba!*, host, 2007—.

Addresses: *Office*—c/o *Yo Gabba Gabba!*, Nick Jr., 515 Broadway, New York, NY 10036.

ally turned from music to television production. His first project in that field was a new children's program that needed a friendly, energetic, musically gifted host. Schultz and his partners thought immediately of Rock for the role, and the latter's television career was born, though he had virtually no acting experience.

In the weeks that followed, Rock made a number of contributions that significantly altered the show's dynamics and undoubtedly contributed to its ultimate success. His costume, for example, was largely of his own design. Dissatisfied with the original outfit, which he considered unsuited for dancing, he designed for himself a bright orange jumpsuit and a furry hat. Within a few years of the program's debut, the ensemble had become part of pop culture, with imitations an increasingly common sight on the streets at Halloween. That trend brought Rock a burst of publicity in the fall of 2009, when actor Brad Pitt (born 1963) wore a facsimile of the orange jumpsuit to Halloween festivities in Hollywood.

Initially, however, it was not clear that Rock, his outfit, or the show as a whole would be a hit. Networks, wary of spending money on ill-conceived projects, have traditionally preferred proposals from producers with years of television experience, something Rock, Schultz, and their partners all lacked. Executives at international cable network Nickelodeon, however, were deeply impressed with the positive reaction a *Yo Gabba Gabba!* trailer had generated online, and in the mid-2000s they ordered nearly two dozen episodes for their Nick Jr. subsidiary, then known as Noggin. Critics around the world reacted to the show's 2007 debut with enthusiasm. In 2008 alone, it earned a Children's Award for international programming from the British Academy for Film and Television Arts and the first of several Daytime Emmy nominations. As of 2011, however, its most prominent awards in the United States were probably the two it had received from the Television Critics Association, which honored it in 2009 (Outstanding Achievement in Children's Programming) and 2010 (Outstanding Achievement in Youth Programming).

With its bright colors and hummable songs, *Yo Gabba Gabba!* was designed from the start to recall the classic period of the early 1970s, when children's programming came into its own with shows like *Sesame Street* and *The Electric Company*. *Yo Gabba Gabba!*'s debt to *Sesame Street* was particularly clear, given the reliance of both shows on guest appearances by adult stars, often musicians. On the newer program, however, those stars were given a much more prominent role, in part because they made it easy to introduce a broad range of musical styles. Some guests, including the groundbreaking rapper Biz Markie (born 1964), have had recurring roles, while others, like the comedian Jack Black (born 1969), have appeared less frequently but no less memorably. One consequence of those guest spots has been the show's surprising popularity among teenagers and young adults. For a chance to see their favorite stars in a relaxed and informal setting, *Yo Gabba Gabba!* has proved, even teenagers will watch children's programming—and support it financially. As Joanna Weiss of the *Boston Globe* noted in 2008, adult-sized T-shirts featuring the show's characters have sold briskly. She went on to draw an analogy with *Pee-Wee's Playhouse* (1986–91), another children's program that eventually drew a much broader audience.

In the summer of 2011, *Yo Gabba Gabba!* showed little sign of declining popularity. Television ratings remained high, and scores of live performances were sold out across the country. Rock, for his part, seemed to take his growing fame in stride. "It's hard for him to walk even in his own neighborhood," Schultz told Jill Moon of the TheTelegraph.com, "and he's so gracious, because his fans are really small; he's so great to stop and ask them how they're doing."

Sources

Periodicals

Boston Globe, January 29, 2008.
St. Louis (MO) Post-Dispatch, August 19, 2007.

Online

"Coachella beyond the Main Stage: DJ Lance Rock Meets the Parents," LATimes.com, April 2, 2010, http://latimesblogs.latimes.com/music_blog/2010/04/coachella-beyond-the-main-stage-dj-lance-rock-meets-the-parents.html (accessed September 23, 2011).

Moon, Jill, "DJ Lance Rock's It," TheTelegraph.com, March 11, 2010, http://www.thetelegraph.com/articles/lance-37413-louis-rock.html (accessed September 23, 2011).

"NoCo Hall of Fame: DJ Lance Rock," NoCoSTL.com, December 2, 2009, http://nocostl.com/2009/12/noco-hall-of-fame-dj-lance-rock/ (accessed September 23, 2011).

—R. Anthony Kugler

Colman Domingo

1969—

Actor

Philadelphia-born actor Colman Domingo earned his first Tony Award nomination in 2010 for his role as Mr. Bones in the controversial and short-lived Broadway musical *The Scottsboro Boys.* Although it was his first Tony nod, Domingo was no stranger to the stage. He made a name for himself as an actor and director in the San Francisco Bay Area in the 1990s before heading to New York, where he earned acclaim for his performance in the 2007 rock memoir *Passing Strange,* which played on and off Broadway and later was turned into a film by director Spike Lee. Domingo continued to win praise for his one-man show *A Boy and His Soul,* a loving tribute to his hometown and the soul music it nurtured. In 2011 Domingo's second play as writer, *Wild with Happy,* was in development.

Domingo, Colman, photograph. Bruce Glikas/FilmMagic/Getty Images.

Colman Jason Domingo was born on November 28, 1969, in Philadelphia, Pennsylvania, and grew up with his three siblings on the city's west side, raised by his mother and stepfather, Edie and Clarence Bowles. As a boy, Domingo was shy and sensitive and struggled with a speech impediment. "My mother sent me to speech classes, but the other kids still teased me. I was shy. I stooped. Instead of talking, I kept journals. That's where my love of words comes from," he told Celia McGee in the *New York Times.* Later he enrolled at Temple University as a journalism major, intending to become a war correspondent. However, after taking an acting class as an elective, "the teacher told me I had a gift. No one said that to me before," he recalled to McGee.

Found Success on Both Coasts

Soon after graduating from college, at age 21, Domingo headed for San Francisco, where he did some film and television work but concentrated on theater. He became a well-known actor in the Bay Area, appearing in productions at the Berkeley Repertory Theatre, San Jose Repertory Theatre, Shakespeare Santa Cruz, and California Shakespeare Theater, and he made his directorial debut in 1998 with a staging of Molière's *The Precious Damsels* for San Francisco's African-American Shakespeare Company. In 2003 Domingo went to New York and made his Off-Broadway debut in Shakespeare's *Henry V* at the Joseph Papp Public Theatre, and he appeared later that year in Eric Coble's *Bright Ideas* with the Manhattan Class Company.

At a Glance . . .

Born Colman Jason Domingo on November 28, 1969, in Philadelphia, PA; son of Colman Domingo and Edith Bowles. *Education*: Temple University, BA, journalism.

Career: Film, television, and stage actor, 1990s—; made stage directorial debut in 1998 with *The Precious Damsels,* 1998; member of the Lincoln Center Directors Lab; faculty member of the National Theater Institute, Eugene O'Neill Theater Center.

Memberships: Actors' Equity Association.

Awards: Bay Area Critics Award (ensemble), 2007, and OBIE Award (ensemble), 2008, for *Passing Strange;* Connecticut Critics Circle Award, 2009, for *Coming Home;* Gay and Lesbian Alliance against Defamation Media Award, Best Theater Broadway/Off-Broadway, and Lucille Lortel Award, Best Solo Show, both 2009, for *A Boy and His Soul.*

Addresses: *Agent*—Schiowitz Connor Ankrum Wolf, Inc., 1680 Vine St., Ste. 1016, Los Angeles, CA 90028. *Web*—http://www.colmandomingo.com/.

In 2006 Domingo made his Broadway debut in Lisa Kron's play *Well* at the Longacre Theatre. He returned to the West Coast in the fall for the world premiere of a new play called *Passing Strange* at the Berkeley Repertory Theatre. An autobiography of singer-songwriter Stew (Mark Stewart), the play—part rock concert, part cabaret, and part improvisational theater—chronicles the journey of a young black man as he sets out from his home in Los Angeles to Amsterdam and Berlin, with original music and lyrics by Stew. As part of the ensemble cast, Domingo, a newcomer to musical theater, handled several roles, including the closeted choir director Mr. Franklin and the gender-bending performance artist Mr. Venus. Well received by critics, *Passing Strange* won the Bay Area Critics Award for best ensemble.

Passing Strange moved to New York in 2007 for an Off-Broadway run at the Public Theatre, winning the Audelco, Drama Desk, and New York Drama Critics Circle awards for best musical and earning Domingo and the ensemble an OBIE Award. The production transferred to the Belasco Theatre on Broadway the next year. Reviews both on and off Broadway praised *Passing Strange.* Hilton Als in the *New Yorker* described the musical as "brilliant," while *Variety* called it

"delightful," singling out Domingo's performance as Mr. Venus as "industrial-strength." Director Spike Lee filmed the last three performances on Broadway for a documentary that premiered at the Sundance Film Festival in 2009.

Debuted One-Man Show

While Domingo was working on *Passing Strange,* he also was developing his own play, a one-man show called *A Boy and His Soul,* which he wrote and starred in. Conceived while he was bartending in New York's West Village between acting gigs, the musical memoir, a combination of dialogue and song, pays homage to Domingo's family by tracing his upbringing in West Philadelphia during the 1970s and 1980s. The classic soul music of the period—including, the Isley Brothers, Smokey Robinson, Earth Wind & Fire, and Donna Summer—serves as the soundtrack.

Domingo plays 11 different characters during the show, taking on the personas of his mother and stepfather—who were selling their family home as he was writing the play—as well as siblings, aunts, and uncles. "This play became the journey of a boy from West Philadelphia," he told Broadway.com, "raised in one of the great eras of soul music, searching through the archives of his home and the beat of his heart . . . in the music."

A Boy and His Soul premiered in 2005 at a small theater in San Francisco called Thick Description, becoming the best-selling show in the venue's history. After a few years of fine-tuning, during which time Domingo's parents passed away, the production opened Off-Broadway at the Vineyard Theatre in the fall of 2009, enjoying an extended run into November. Writing in the *New York Times,* theater critic Charles Isherwood described Domingo as a "blazingly charismatic performer. . . . He possesses a voice of remarkable range and dexterity." Likewise, Joe Dziemianowicz in the *New York Daily News* praised Domingo as "commanding and endearing, whether he's acting, singing along to the music (he asks you to, as well) or shaking what his mama (and choreographer Ken Roberson) gave him."

Won First Tony Nomination

Domingo returned to Broadway in 2010, first for a month-long run as Billy Flynn in a revival of *Chicago,* and then for a longer stint in the controversial musical *The Scottsboro Boys.* Penned by the legendary songwriting team of John Kander and Fred Ebb, the play tells the true story of nine young black men who were put on death row in the 1930s for allegedly raping two white women on a train while traveling through Scottsboro, Alabama. *The Scottsboro Boys* began life Off-Broadway with a run at the Vineyard Theatre in the spring before heading to the Guthrie Theatre in Min-

neapolis, Minnesota, that summer. The production transferred to the Lyceum Theatre on Broadway in the fall, opening on October 31.

The musical's creators chose to frame the story as a minstrel show, a storytelling device of the late 19th century in which white actors performed in blackface. In a traditional minstrel show the actors arranged themselves in a semicircle, with an interlocutor or narrator in the center and two "end men" on either side. Domingo played end man Mr. Bones, who morphs into a series of other characters, including a white sheriff, lawyer, clerk, and attorney general.

Although *The Scottsboro Boys* received positive reviews—*Entertainment Weekly* declared it the best new musical of the year, while the *New York Times* called the show "adventurous" and "dynamic"—audiences did not respond as enthusiastically, and the musical closed after 49 performances. Still, *The Scottsboro Boys* received 12 Tony Award nominations in 2011, including a nod for Domingo for best performance by an actor in a featured role. The musical lost in all categories, setting a record as the most-nominated show to win no Tony Awards. After *The Scottsboro Boys* closed in December, Domingo rejoined the cast of *Chicago*, reprising his role as Billy Flynn.

In addition to his stage work, Domingo has appeared in a number of films, including *Around the Fire* (1998), *Freedomland* (2006), and Spike Lee's *Miracle at St. Anna* (2008), as well as the Logo television series *The Big Gay Sketch Show*. He is a member of the Lincoln Center Directors Lab and serves on the faculty of the National Theater Institute at the Eugene O'Neill Theater Center. Domingo's second play, *Wild with Happy*, was developed at the Sundance Institute's Theatre Lab in Alberta, Canada, in 2011 and had its first staged reading at TheatreWorks in Silicon Valley.

Selected works

Theater

Blues for an Alabama Sky, TheatreWorks, Palo Alto, CA, 1996.
Journey to the West, Huntington Theatre Company, Boston, 1996; Berkeley Repertory Theatre, Berkeley, CA, 1996–97.
Two Gentlemen of Verona, Shakespeare Santa Cruz, Santa Cruz, CA, 1999.
Romeo and Juliet, Shakespeare Santa Cruz, Santa Cruz, CA, 1999.
Sons of Don Juan, San Jose Repertory Theatre, San Jose, CA, 2000.
A Midsummer Night's Dream, California Shakespeare Theatre, Orinda, CA, 2002.
Haroun and the Sea of Stories, Berkeley Repertory Theatre, Berkeley, CA, 2002–03.
Henry V, Delacorte Theater, New York, 2003.

Bright Ideas, Manhattan Class Company, New York, 2003.
All's Well That Ends Well, California Shakespeare Theatre, Orinda, CA, 2004.
The People's Temple, Berkeley Repertory Theatre, Berkeley, CA, 2005; Guthrie Theatre, Minneapolis, MN, 2006.
(And writer) *A Boy and His Soul,* Thick Description, San Francisco, 2005; Vineyard Theatre, New York, 2009.
Well, Longacre Theatre, New York, 2006; Huntington Theatre Company, Boston, 2007.
Passing Strange, Joseph Papp Public Theatre, New York, 2007; Belasco Theatre, New York, 2008.
Coming Home, Long Wharf Theatre, New Haven, CT, 2009.
The Wiz, New York City Center, New York, 2009.
The Lily's Revenge, Sundance Theater Lab, New York, 2009.
The Scottsboro Boys, Vineyard Theatre, New York, 2010; Guthrie Theatre, Minneapolis, MN, 2010; Lyceum Theatre, New York, 2010.
Chicago, Ambassador Theatre, New York, 2010–11.

Films

Around the Fire, Mill Creek Entertainment, 1998.
King of the Bingo Game (short), PBS Home Video, 1999.
True Crime, Warner Bros., 1999.
Desi's Looking for a New Girl, Water Bearer Films, 2000.
King Phooey!, Velocity Home Entertainment, 2003.
Freedomland, Columbia Pictures, 2006.
Miracle at St. Anna, Touchstone Pictures, 2008.
Passing Strange, 40 Acres & a Mule Filmworks, 2009.

Television

The Big Gay Sketch Show, Logo, 2008–10.

Sources

Periodicals

Entertainment Weekly, November 1, 2010.
New York Daily News, September 25, 2009.
New York Times, February 29, 2008; September 6, 2009; September 25, 2009; October 21, 2010.
New Yorker, June 11, 2007.
Philadelphia Inquirer, October 17, 2009.
Variety, November 1, 2006.

Online

Domingo, Colman, "Finding My Soul at a Greenwich Village Bar," September 9, 2009, http://www.broadway.com/shows/boy-and-his-soul/buzz/1347 90/colman-domingo-finding-my-soul-at-a-green

wich-village-bar/ (accessed August 11, 2011).

Itzkoff, Dave, "'Scottsboro Boys' Sets Record for Tonys Futility," ArtsBeat, *New York Times,* June 13, 2011, http://artsbeat.blogs.nytimes.com/2011/06/13/scottsboro-boys-sets-record-for-tonys-futility/ (accessed August 5, 2011).

Passing Strange, http://www.passingstrangeonline.com/ (accessed August 11, 2011).

—Deborah A. Ring

Fantasia

1984—

Vocalist, actor

Fantasia, photograph. Douglas Mason/Getty Images.

Fantasia owns one of the most dramatic rags-to-riches stories in American pop culture: in 2004 the single mother and high-school dropout, whose reading skills were so weak that she had trouble filling out job applications, won Season Three of television's *American Idol* talent competition. Since then Fantasia has written an autobiography, starred in a television movie about her life, released three albums of varied R&B-to-soul fare, and even took home a Grammy Award in 2011. The *American Idol* win literally saved her life, she has often said. "I would have been dead by now," she told Kevin Chappell in *Ebony*. "I was singing in the choir on Sunday, but running from the church life the other six days of the week."

Showed Singing Skills Early

Fantasia was born in High Point, North Carolina—the furniture-making capital of the United States—on June 30, 1984. Music-making ran through both sides of her family. Her father, Joseph Barrino, sang in gospel quartets beginning in his teenage years but supported his family by working as a truck driver. Her mother, Diane, and maternal grandmother, Addie, were co-pastors of their own church, Mercy Outreach Church of Deliverance. Everybody in the family sang, including Fantasia's two older brothers, Joseph Jr. (called "Tiny") and Rico, and younger brother, Xavier. All were involved in the church and its choir, and Fantasia gained local renown at a young age for a spectacularly commanding voice.

At High Point's Laurin Welborn Middle School, Fantasia made the all-county chorus, but she struggled with self-esteem issues. She was unhappy with her looks, teased by others, and sought male attention as a form of validation. In her ninth-grade year at T. Wingate Andrews High School, she developed a crush on a popular student-athlete. "One day during a game after school, I was flaunting around in an itty-bitty dress," Fantasia recalled in a candid interview with Oprah Winfrey for *O, The Oprah Magazine* in 2007. "I was flirting, and he told me, 'You're going to get something you don't want.' And that's exactly what happened."

After she was raped, "I didn't go to school for a couple of days," she told Winfrey. "My mom came to me and said, 'Something's not right with you. I know that somebody put his hands on you.' That's when I knew I

At a Glance . . .

Born Fantasia Barrino on June 30, 1984, in High Point, NC; daughter of Joseph (a truck driver and singer) and Diane (a minister) Barrino; children: Zion (daughter).

Career: Mercy Outreach Church of Deliverance, choir director; first-place finisher, Season 3 of *American Idol,* Fox, 2004; signed to a contract with 19 Management and J Records, 2004.

Addresses: *Label*—c/o J-Records, LLC, 745 5th Ave., 6th Floor, New York, NY 10151. *Other*—c/o American Idol, P.O. Box 900, Beverly Hills, CA 90213-0900. *Web*— www.fantasiabarrinoofficial.com.

had her support. We turned the guy in, but going back to school was hell; his homeboys would say, 'I'm going to do to you exactly what he did.' They thought it was funny. That's when I quit school." She lived for a time with an older friend, in exchange for child-care duties, and led an aimless life for a few years. Even a menial-wage job was out of her reach, because her reading skills were so poor that she found filling out a standard job application a challenge.

Fantasia has said that both her mother and grandmother were devastated when they learned she was pregnant at age 17—the same age of their first pregnancies—but supported her emotionally and financially. She named her daughter Zion and spent another few itinerant years, shuttling between relatives' homes and living with boyfriends before securing her own place in First Farmington public-housing complex in High Point. Her daughter's father was not part of their lives, and Fantasia wound up in abusive relationships with other men. Desperately unhappy, she tried to focus on giving Zion the best possible future and started by studying for her high school equivalency degree.

Resisted Idol at First

Fantasia had resisted the pull of *American Idol* through its first season and nearly all of the second. When a young gospel-trained contestant from Alabama rose to the finals in the second season, Fantasia finally heeded her friends' recommendations and tuned in to watch Ruben Studdard win *American Idol* on May 21, 2003. "I just cried and cried," she told Winfrey in the 2007 interview. "I was crying because someone had finally gotten something he wanted. I was also a little angry: Why am I sitting here in the ghetto, living on food stamps and a tiny government check? I'll be honest: Those checks just weren't enough, and I had to steal

what I needed—diapers, milk, food. Some of the girls I hung out with dated guys who were drug dealers."

A few months later Fantasia's brother Rico drove her to Atlanta, Georgia, to enter the open-call auditions for Season 3 of *American Idol.* They had to borrow $50 for gas money but were fortunate to have cousins in the city who let them stay overnight. At the Georgia Dome it was a predictably mobbed scene, with 5,000 hopefuls turning up. Fantasia made it inside, and at one point struck up a conversation with a security guard who heard her sing and suggested she remove her lip piercing before auditioning for the judges. The next day, arriving at an appointed early hour, Fantasia was crushed to find the Georgia Dome doors locked and the remaining *Idol* auditioners barred from entry. She and Rico returned to their cousins' place and called their parents with the news. Her father suggested she try again, and they drove back to the Dome. Peeking around the perimeter, Fantasia spotted the security guard from the day before, who came over and asked if she had been in. She said no, and as she recalled in the *Ebony* interview, "he said, 'I got to get you in.' He went and got somebody from Idol, and they got me in. I was one of the last ones to audition."

Fantasia made it through successive rounds and took her general-equivalency degree study materials with her to Los Angeles for the actual taping of the show. Controversy, however, flared as Fantasia advanced to the final rounds of the competition. Some viewers questioned whether Fantasia's status as a single mother and high-school dropout made her a good role model; to others, her confidence on stage came across as arrogance. In one well-publicized incident, singer Elton John leveled charges of racism against the show's organizers when Fantasia and several other African-American contestants were grouped in one round in such a way that one was sure to be eliminated. Fantasia, deciding that a dramatic move was needed, prepared a song that deviated from the standard pop-rock-R&B fare chosen by contestants to showcase their talents. She selected the George Gershwin classic "Summertime" from the 1935 opera *Porgy and Bess,* made famous by Billie Holiday and a jazz standard in the decades since.

Warmed Over Audiences

The effect on audiences was electric. She drove many to tears, and she started to cry herself when it was over. Judge Randy Jackson rose to his feet to applaud her, saying, "That is the single best *Idol* performance of any season I've ever heard." Jackson's famously tough colleague on the judges' panel, Simon Cowell, also delivered high marks. "You prove the point with that performance tonight why we are critical of people who just sing well," Cowell said, visibly moved. "Because there was something magical about what you just did." Fantasia advanced to the final round against Georgia's

Diana DeGarmo and edged out DeGarmo in nation-wide voting on May 26, 2004.

Just nine months after watching Ruben Studdard win, Fantasia had become America's newest celebrity. The *Idol* win came with a lucrative record deal—its biggest lure—but also scores of other opportunities that catapulted Fantasia virtually overnight from Women, Infants and Children (WIC) supplemental-nutrition benefits recipient into the middle class. Her debut album, *Free Yourself,* was released in November of 2004 on the J Records label, with direction from music industry veteran Clive Davis. Unlike earlier releases by *American Idol* winners, Fantasia's was a cutting-edge affair that drew on creative contributions by hip-hop artists and producers such as Missy Elliott and Jermaine Dupri. Her debut single, the gospel-flavored "I Believe," debuted at No. 1 on *Billboard* magazine's Hot 100 singles chart, and another track, "Baby Mama," drew on Fantasia's experiences as a single parent, although it was attacked in more conservative quarters. "If you listen to the words, I'm not telling anybody to go out and have a baby," she told Chappell, the *Ebony* writer, in defense of the song. "I'm talking about how it ain't easy, how it ain't fun, it's hard and it ain't cute."

Both "Free Yourself" and "Summertime" were nominated for Grammy awards in the best female R&B vocal performance categories, and *Free Yourself* lost the best R&B album of the year award to John Legend's *Get Lifted.* While touring and promoting the record, Fantasia also worked on her memoir, *Life Is Not a Fairy Tale,* which was released in September of 2005 and instantly became a *New York Times* bestseller. The television version of her story, in which Fantasia played herself and Viola Davis (later of *The Help*) was cast as her supportive mother, aired on Lifetime Television in August of 2006 and pulled in a record 19 million viewers.

Fantasia's second record, *Fantasia,* was released later in 2006. Its most successful single, "When I See U," became one of the top-selling songs of the entire decade, sat for eight weeks at the No. 1 spot on *Billboard*'s Hot R&B/Hip-Hop Songs for the U.S., and lingered around on that same chart for a year—a feat achieved by only 14 other R&B tracks in the history of the chart. Her next success came on Broadway: in April of 2007 she began appearing in the *The Color Purple,* the musical adaptation of the acclaimed Alice Walker novel of the same name. She earned terrific reviews as Celie, and her six-month run was extended to accommodate high ticket demand. Winfrey, the show's executive producer, then cast Fantasia in the film version of the musical.

Continued Acting and Recording Success

In 2009 Fantasia worked on her next studio release and appeared in the national tour of *The Color Purple.* Some of her life was chronicled in a reality series for VH1, *Fantasia for Real,* which began airing in early 2010. The August release of *Back to Me,* which debuted in the No. 2 slot on the *Billboard 200* chart, was overshadowed by news reports that Fantasia had been rushed to a hospital for what was classified as a suicide attempt by the Charlotte-Mecklenburg Police Department. The incident happened a day after Fantasia was named in court documents filed by the estranged wife of a man she had been dating, but a judge later agreed that Antwaun Cook had indeed been separated from his wife when he became involved with Fantasia. The "suicide attempt" was actually a drug interaction brought on when Fantasia incautiously took both a sleeping aid and aspirin, although she did later say that the pressures of her life sometimes squeezed too close. "I wanted to be so away from all this noise in my world," she confided to reporter Douglas Quenqua in the *New York Times* a few weeks later. "Whether it's 'mommy' or 'Tasia, I need a bill paid,' or 'we need you here at the record company.' No one was taking care of me. It was only what I could do for other people."

Not surprisingly, Fantasia's third album did very well on the charts, and its single "Bittersweet" again dominated the No. 1 spot on the U.S. *Billboard* Adult R&B Chart. The track also gave the singer her long-awaited Grammy Award for best female R&B vocal performance, which she took home on February 13, 2011. That same month, Fantasia's name was announced as the choice to portray gospel great Mahalia Jackson in a major Hollywood biopic slated for 2012 release. On August 1, 2011, Fantasia announced during a concert in Jacksonville, Florida, that she was expecting her second child.

Fantasia's genuinely inspirational story continued to resonate with fans. She told Ed Gordon on the National Public Radio program *News & Notes* that she was habitually mobbed by young women whose lives were not unlike her own in the pre-*Idol* era. "They just want to know, 'What do I do? How do I raise a child when I'm a child myself?' You know? And I found the way. A lot of people stay lost and they stay lost for a long time. I was lost, but I found the way. I found the key and I found the weapon. All of the childish things I had to put to the side."

Selected works

Albums

(As Fantasia) *Free Yourself,* J-Records, 2004.
Fantasia (includes single "When I See U"), J Records, 2006.
Back to Me (includes single "Bittersweet"), J Records, 2010.

Books

Life Is Not a Fairy Tale (memoir), Touchstone Fireside, 2005.

Stage

The Color Purple, Broadway Theatre, 2007–08.

Television

Life Is Not a Fairy Tale (television movie), Lifetime Television, 2006.
Fantasia for Real, VH1, 2010.

Sources

Periodicals

Ebony, July 2005, p. 102.
Essence, September 2004, p. 292.
New York Times, September 3, 2010.

O, The Oprah Magazine, September 2007, p. 318.

Online

"Fantasia Barrino: Summertime," American Idol Requests, http://www.youtube.com/watch?v=FDNyb o2lysk (August 15, 2011).
Gordon, Ed, "American Idol Winner Fantasia Barrino," *News & Notes,* National Public Radio, October 11, 2005, http://www.npr.org/templates/story/story. php?storyId=4953827 (accessed August 12, 2011).
Oh, Eunice, "Manager: Fantasia Took an Overdose of Aspirin and a Sleep Aid," *People,* August 10, 2010, http://www.people.com/people/article/ 0,,20409338,00.html?xid=rss-fullcontent (accessed August 12, 2011).

Other

20/20 (ABC News Transcripts), November 12, 2004.

—James M. Manheim and Carol Brennan

D. M. French

1924–2011

Physician

D. M. French, a pediatric surgeon, was a leading member of the Medical Committee for Human Rights (MCHR), the group of physicians and other medical professionals who provided care for participants in the civil rights movement protests of the 1960s. French participated in the march from Montgomery to Selma, Alabama, in March of 1965 and in a 1966 march across Mississippi, among other events. His participation in the civil rights movement led him to shift his professional focus from surgery to public health. In the late 1960s and early 1970s he went on to help establish, in Boston, Massachusetts, one of the first community health centers in the United States. He then took his concern for community health to West Africa, where he directed a joint project between various national and international agencies to train medical professionals and improve care for the citizens of 20 African nations.

David Marshall French was born in Toledo, Ohio, on May 30, 1924. He spent his childhood there and in Columbus, Ohio, before attending Western Reserve University (now Case Western Reserve University), where he was a pre-medical student prior to being drafted by the U.S. Army after the country's entry into World War II. French was assigned to a segregated Army unit and stationed in Texas, where his job was to pick cotton to be used for military uniforms. French was struck by the fact that German prisoners being held in Texas received more humane treatment than did he and the other African-American soldiers who were actively defending the nation.

After the war ended, French took advantage of a military program that gave him the opportunity to enroll in the Howard University School of Medicine, where he trained under Charles Drew, a prominent black physician who had done important work associated with the development of blood banks. French settled on a specialty in pediatric surgery, graduating in 1948. He practiced medicine in Detroit, Michigan, where he became an active member of the National Association for the Advancement of Colored People (NAACP), which was then at the forefront of the emerging civil rights movement. French and his family later moved to Washington, D.C., where he took a position as a professor of pediatric surgery at Howard and helped to establish departments of pediatric cardiovascular surgery at Freedmen's Hospital (the hospital associated with Howard) and D.C. General Hospital.

When the civil rights movement gained momentum in the 1960s, French was among many black and white physicians who came together as the Medical Committee for Human Rights to address the issue of health care for marchers and protesters in the South. Participants in civil rights events did not have access to medical attention in many of the segregated areas where they were protesting, and the threat of violence from local authorities and white onlookers was ever-present. As part of the Washington, D.C., chapter of the MCHR, French was a lobbyist on behalf of the organization, with contacts in the administration of President Lyndon Johnson. After the March 5, 1965, march from Montgomery to Selma, Alabama, led by Martin Luther King Jr., was halted when state troopers

---

At a Glance . . .

Born David Marshall French on May 30, 1924, in Toledo, OH; died on March 31, 2011, in Charlottesville, VA; son of Joseph and Bertha Dickerson French; married Carolyn Howard French (died in 2009); children: David Jr., Howard, Joseph, James, Lynn, Mary Ann, Bertha, and Dorothy. *Military service:* U.S. Army, World War II. *Education:* Attended Western Reserve University (now Case Western Reserve University); Howard University School of Medicine, MD, 1948; Johns Hopkins School of Hygiene and Public Health (now Johns Hopkins Bloomberg School of Public Health), MPH, 1969.

Career: Howard University, professor of pediatric surgery, 1960s; Medical Committee for Human Rights, founding member and national chairman, 1960s; Boston University Department of Community medicine, chairman, 1969–70s; Roxbury Comprehensive Community Health Center, medical director, 1969–70s; Strengthening Health Delivery Systems, director, 1970s–80s; Helen Keller International, medical director; African Methodist Episcopal Church, medical officer.

---

beat participants, a successful march was completed on March 21, thanks to the protection provided by federal troops whose presence was partly the result of French's communications with the Johnson administration. French was an organizer of the more than 100 members of the MCHR who participated in the march to Selma, and he was in charge of gathering medical supplies for the effort. When an Alabama supplier refused to take an MCHR check, French paid for the supplies with his own money.

French went on to become president of MCHR, and in 1966 he organized committee members to accompany protesters traveling from Memphis, Tennessee, to Jackson, Mississippi, in a march begun by James Meredith, who had become the first African-American student at the University of Mississippi in 1962. Meredith had set out to march the length of Mississippi alone in June of 1966 to protest racial discrimination, when he was shot by a sniper. He was not fatally injured, and within days, thousands of civil rights activists, led by King, Stokely Carmichael, and others, descended on Mississippi to complete his protest. French and his wife reportedly used their van as an ambulance during the 220-mile "March against Fear."

After his participation in the civil rights movement, French attended the prestigious Johns Hopkins School of Public Health, with a view toward continuing to use his medical expertise for the good of underserved communities. After earning his master's degree in 1969, he took a position at Boston University, where he oversaw the establishment of a department of community medicine. In 1970 he helped launch the Roxbury Comprehensive Community Health Center, which served the predominantly poor and African-American Boston neighborhood of Roxbury. The Roxbury clinic was one of the first of its kind in the United States; it became a model for the delivery of health care to the poor.

During the 1970s French turned his attention to West Africa at the urging of Massachusetts Senator Edward Kennedy, and he went on to direct a groundbreaking program for improving health care in 20 African countries. Based in the Ivory Coast, where he lived with his wife and eight children, French established Strengthening Health Delivery Systems, a joint project of the World Health Organization, the U.S. Agency for International Development, the Centers for Disease Control and Prevention, and Boston University. The program involved the training of health-care professionals and the founding of clinics across West Africa. Its success, like that of the Roxbury center, has since been emulated by thousands of community health efforts worldwide.

French retired from full-time work in the mid-1980s, leaving the Ivory Coast to settle in Barboursville, Virginia, where he spent his later years with his wife and family. He continued to make time for public service in retirement, working for Helen Keller International, a group that sponsors public health initiatives in impoverished countries, and for the service and development branch of the African Methodist Episcopal Church. He died at the age of 86 at the University of Virginia Hospital in Charlottesville, of a pulmonary embolism.

Sources

Books

Dittmer, John, *The Good Doctors: The Medical Committee for Human Rights and the Struggle for Social Justice in Health Care*, Bloomsbury, 2009.

Periodicals

New York Beacon, April 21, 2011, p. 9.
New York Times, April 5, 2011.
Pittsburgh Post-Gazette, April 17, 2011, p. B5.

—Mark Lane

Linda Gooden

1953—

Business executive

Gooden, Linda, photograph. Nikki Kahn/The Washington Post/ Getty Images.

Linda Gooden, executive vice president of Lockheed Martin's Information Systems & Global Solutions division, is one of the United States' foremost business executives in the field of information technology (IT). Trained as a software engineer, Gooden wrote programs for missile systems and the Social Security Administration before creating and presiding over a business group within Lockheed Martin (one of the top defense contractors in the world) that sought to win IT contracts from a wide range of federal offices as they began to modernize their operations for the computer age in the 1990s. Gooden's division went from a start-up in the mid-1990s to a dominant IT contractor for the federal government within a decade. By 2010 Lockheed Martin's Information Systems & Global Solutions group, with Gooden presiding, constituted one of the company's four major business areas and accounted for approximately $10 billion in annual revenue.

Gooden grew up in Youngstown, Ohio, the only daughter in a family of five children. Youngstown had been a thriving steel industry town, but the steel mills began to close during Gooden's childhood. Observing the struggles that mill workers without college degrees faced in finding work, Gooden developed an early awareness of the importance of education in adapting to a changing economy.

Upon entering Youngstown State University, Gooden came into contact with an early computer, the IBM 360. "I was mesmerized by the size of the machine," she told *U.S. Black Engineer and Information Technology*. "It took up six normal-sized rooms, though the computing power you have on your wrist today is probably greater than they had in those early machines. But it was clear to me that that was the direction the nation was moving in, and that's where I wanted to be." Gooden earned a B.S. in computer technology from Youngstown State in 1977 and did post-baccalaureate work at San Diego State University. She later earned a B.S. in business administration and an M.B.A. from the University of Maryland.

Gooden began her career as a software engineer at the defense contractor General Dynamics, before taking a job at Martin Marietta, the chemical, aerospace, and electronics company that later merged with Lockheed Corporation to become Lockheed Martin. Gooden designed software for the Peacekeeper Missile, an

At a Glance . . .

Born in 1953, in Youngstown, Ohio. *Education*: Youngstown State University, BS, 1977; San Diego State University, post-baccalaureate studies; University of Maryland, BS, MBA.

Career: General Dynamics, software engineer, 1977(?)–80; Martin Marietta (later Lockheed Martin), software engineer, 1980–94; Lockheed Martin, vice president of Information Technology Group, 1994–2007, executive vice president of Information Systems & Global Solutions, 2007—; appointed by President Barack Obama to the National Security Telecommunications Advisory Committee, 2010.

Memberships: National Security Telecommunications Advisory Committee; University Systems of Maryland, board of regents member; Eisenhower Fellowships, board of trustees member; Armed Forces Communications and Electronics Association, board member; TechAmerica, board member; Automatic Data Processing, Inc., board member.

Awards: Black Engineer of the Year, *U.S. Black Engineer and Information Technology,* 2006; Executive of the Year, Greater Washington Government Contractor Awards, 2007; inductee, Maryland Business Hall of Fame, 2008; named one of the "100 Most Powerful Executives in Corporate America," *Black Enterprise,* 2009 and 2010; named one of the "Top 50 Most Powerful Women in Business," *Fortune,* 2010; inductee, Career Communications Group Hall of Fame, 2011.

Addresses: *Office*—Lockheed Martin Information Systems & Global Solutions, 700 N. Frederick Ave., Gaithersburg, MD 20879.

Intercontinental Ballistic Missile (ICBM) used by the U.S. military beginning in 1986. After being assigned the task of writing and installing software to meet Martin Marietta's human resources needs, she saw an opening for providing similar services to clients outside the company. In 1988 she won her first such contract for the firm, when the U.S. Social Security Administration hired her to modernize its record keeping.

Gooden's success at winning and fulfilling the multistage Social Security Administration contract over a number of years led her to speculate that pursuing civilian contracts in a more concerted manner could reap rewards for the company. She researched the potential market and determined that government agencies would increasingly require information-technology contracts of the kind she was confident that she could provide. She organized a meeting to pitch the creation of an Information Technology group within Lockheed Martin, which she proposed to lead. Her superiors approved her pitch and authorized her to create the new venture in 1994.

"Execution is by far the most exciting part," Gooden later told Nicole Marie Richardson in *Black Enterprise.* "At first I felt fearful about whether or not management would accept my plan, but once the plan was accepted then I was equally fearful of executing the plan." Gooden's research had been accurate; the need for widespread automation in government agencies grew exponentially in the years that followed, and Gooden's IT group prospered. Lockheed budgeted $600,000 to the enterprise in its first year, and the group brought in $24 million in revenues. In 1997 Gooden lobbied to have all of Lockheed Martin's information-technology initiatives consolidated under her leadership, and over the next several years Lockheed Martin Information Technology developed into a dominant player across the civilian and defense contracting industry.

By 2005 Gooden's group was generating $2 billion in yearly revenues and had more than 10,000 employees. In addition to the ongoing modernization of the Social Security system, the group's high-profile projects included the digitization of the FBI's fingerprint database and the Navy's payroll system. Gooden helmed the creation of communications infrastructure for the Pentagon and the integration of the Federal Aviation Administration's national flight-monitoring systems.

In 2007 Lockheed Martin reorganized its operations to create the Information Systems & Global Solutions (IS&GS) business area, and Gooden was named the division's executive vice president. IS&GS fulfilled information-technology contracts meeting a wide range of civil, defense, intelligence, and other governmental needs. It was the largest IT provider for the U.S. government. As of 2010 it employed over 30,000 workers in all 50 states and in approximately 20 foreign countries, and its annual revenues approached $10 billion.

Gooden's success at creating and managing Lockheed Martin's IT business was an achievement that placed her among the top executives in her field. She was named 2006's Black Engineer of the Year by *U.S. Black Engineer and Information Technology* magazine; she won 2007's Executive of the Year award from the Greater Washington Government Contractor Awards; and she was selected for inclusion in the Maryland Business Hall of Fame in 2008. *Black Enterprise* magazine named her one of its "100 Most Powerful Executives in Corporate America" in both

2009 and 2010, and *Fortune* magazine ranked her 33rd on its list of the "Top 50 Most Powerful Women in Business" in 2010. In 2011 Gooden was inducted into the Career Communications Group's Hall of Fame, an honor reserved for top professionals in the fields of science, technology, engineering, and mathematics.

Gooden's civic contributions included memberships on the board of regents of the University Systems of Maryland and the Eisenhower Fellowships board of trustees. She was also a board member of the Armed Forces Communications and Electronics Association, TechAmerica, and Automatic Data Processing, Inc. In 2010 Gooden was appointed by President Barack Obama to the National Security Telecommunications Advisory Committee, a group of 30 business leaders who offer guidance to the government on communications and national security issues.

Sources

Periodicals

Aviation Week & Space Technology, November 5, 2007, p. 10.

Black Enterprise, July 2005; December 2005.

Defense Daily, February 23, 2007; November 13, 2009.

Gazette (Montreal), December 31, 2008, p. B8.

US Black Engineer and Information Technology, February–March 2006, p. 33.

Washington Post, May 1, 2006, p. D01.

Online

"Linda Gooden," Lockheed Martin, http://www.lockheedmartin.com/aboutus/leadership/bios/gooden.html (accessed July 26, 2011).

McCoy, Frank, "President Obama Names Linda Gooden to Top White House Advisory Panel," The Root, December 11, 2010, http://www.theroot.com/buzz/president-obama-appoints-linda-gooden-top-white-house-advisory-panel (accessed July 26, 2011).

"The 100 Most Powerful Executives in Corporate America," *Black Enterprise,* February 25, 2010, http://www.blackenterprise.com/2010/02/25/the-100-most-powerful-executives-in-corporate-america/ (accessed July 26, 2011).

—Mark Lane

Kim C. Goodman

1966—

Business executive

Kim C. Goodman is a senior executive with the American Express Company. As head of its Merchant Services Americas unit, she is responsible for adding new businesses in North and South America to the transaction network, thereby adding to the number of places American Express cardholders can use their card. Before joining AmEx, as the company is popularly known, Goodman spent several years with Dell Computers in senior-level management positions.

Born in 1966, Goodman grew up on Chicago's South Side. Her father worked long hours for a vending machine company, and her mother was a teacher. "Growing up, my goal was to be the first African-American woman on the Supreme Court," Goodman told Deni Connor in an interview that appeared in *Network World.* She won acceptance at prestigious Stanford University near Palo Alto, California. "When I came to college I thought I was going to be a lawyer," she confessed in another interview, this one for a Stanford alumni publication in 2008. "I had a strong interest in political science. . . . At the same time I was also interested in engineering because I had a strong math background and I was a reasonably logical person."

Goodman fast-tracked her way through Stanford, earning both her undergraduate degree in political science and graduate degree in industrial engineering in 1987. She had abandoned the idea of law school, she told Connor in *Network World.* "I changed from law to business because I did a study on what could have the most impact for advancing the African-American com-

munity. My conclusions came down to more participation in the capital system, as well as improved education."

Goodman went to work for Bain & Company, the Boston-based global consulting firm. She worked in its telecom division, then earned her M.B.A. from Harvard Business School in 1992. At Bain she eventually rose to a vice presidency, but she left in 2000 to join Austin, Texas–based Dell, Inc. She was hired in as vice president of business development and executive assistant to chief executive officer Michael Dell, founder of the computer company, and then she was promoted to vice president and general manager of the networking product group. In 2003 she took over as vice president for public-sector marketing and transactional sales—a significant and lucrative field for all computer manufacturers, who actively court contracts to provide computers to schools, health care facilities, and federal, state, and local governments. From 2005 to 2007 Goodman served as vice president for software and peripherals at Dell, a $5-billion-a-year business.

Goodman joined American Express in 2007 in a newly created title of executive vice president for Merchant Services North America. Her duties included bringing new businesses into the American Express fold, which enables cardholders to use their account in more places. "American Express is quite unique in the payments industry because we both work with and 'own' the relationship with the card member and we 'own' the relationship with the merchant," she said in the article that appeared in the Stanford School of Engi-

At a Glance . . .

Born in 1966; married; children: three. *Education*: Stanford University, BA, political science, MS, industrial engineering, both 1987; Harvard Business School, MBA, 1992. *Religion*: Roman Catholic.

Career: Bain & Company, began as consultant, became vice president; Dell, Inc., vice president for business development and executive assistant to the chief executive officer, 2000–01, vice president and general manager, networking product group, 2001–03, vice president for public sector marketing and transactional sales, 2003–05, vice president for software and peripherals, 2005–07; American Express Company, executive vice president for Merchant Services North America, 2007–10, president of Merchant Services Americas, 2010—.

Memberships: National Black MBA Association; Auto-Nation, Inc., board of directors, 2007–10.

Addresses: *Office*—American Express, Inc., Three World Financial Center, New York, NY 10285.

neering newsletter. "And we manage and own a network business that sits between the two. Because American Express manages all of it within one company it gives us access to a huge amount of data across all three pieces of the business of any given transaction." Although American Express charges its merchants a higher fee per transaction, the company has an edge over its behemoth competitor, Visa, by being able to provide businesses with unique data on how to optimize their local market share or predict repeat business.

In her off-duty hours Goodman is active on several fronts. She has spoken at National Black MBA Association events and has a long commitment to the Girl Scouts organization. In the San Francisco Bay area, where she lived for several years, she was a troop leader in East Oakland. "It meant the world to me, not just what I was contributing to them but what they gave back to me," she said in the Stanford alumni newsletter about the young girls who remained with her scouting troop during their formative years.

Goodman and her husband were also active in their Roman Catholic parish community during their time in Austin. The American Express job gives Goodman an office in the 51-story American Express Tower in Lower Manhattan, whose address is Three World Financial Center. Despite the demands of her job, she sticks to a schedule that brings her back to her New Jersey home at a conventional hour for her three children and their bedtimes at least three nights a week, she told *Working Mother* magazine. "I also make a conscious effort," she told the publication, "to be extremely disciplined and highly productive every minute of the day."

Sources

Periodicals

Network World, December 23, 2002, p. 48.

Online

"Kim Goodman," American Express Company and Subsidiaries, http://www.elcinfo.com/downloads/docs/bwls2010/all_bios/Kim_Goodman.pdf (accessed July 17, 2011).

"Kim Goodman," *Working Mother*, October 2010, http://www.workingmother.com/northeast/new-york/2010/10/american-express (accessed July 17, 2011).

"Meet Our Alumni: Kim Goodman (BA '87, Poli Sci, MS '87 IE)," Stanford School of Engineering, January 2008, http://soe.stanford.edu/alumni/pdfs/pdf_goodman.pdf (accessed July 17, 2011).

"Top Black Women Techies," The Root, http://www.theroot.com/multimedia/black-women-techies (accessed July 17, 2011).

—Carol Brennan

Tyree Guyton

1955—

Artist

Guyton, Tyree, photograph. Jeff Kowalsky/AFP/Getty Images.

Tyree Guyton's unique, world-famous Heidelberg Project celebrated its 25th anniversary in 2011. A collection of abandoned houses and discarded objects that sits in a blighted pocket of Detroit's east side, the Heidelberg Project transformed the street after which it was named into a dazzling display of outsider art and has garnered serious international attention from art critics and urban-landscape visionaries. Yet Guyton's site has long been a source of controversy among city administrators and residents despite its ability to attract foreign tourists to the beleaguered city. "I never thought it'd last this long," Guyton told Michael H. Hodges in the *Detroit News* as the quarter-century celebrations were rolled out in the summer of 2011. "It's just unbelievable."

Considered Paintbrush a "Magic Wand"

Guyton was born on August 24, 1955, in Detroit, to George Guyton and Betty Solomon Guyton. He began painting during his difficult childhood, a time when he was reportedly mistreated, ignored, and teased. Only his grandfather, Sam Mackey, nurtured young Guyton's artistic inclinations. "Grandpa was a housepainter," Guyton told *People* magazine. "When I was eight years old, he stuck a paintbrush in my hand. I felt as if I was holding a magic wand."

It was his mother, however, who influenced Guyton's graphic style. "We were poor," he told *People*. "[My mother] had 10 kids and raised them by herself. Clothes, furniture, everything came from a second-hand store or was given to us. On the floor we had squares of linoleum. On the sofa were stripes. On a chair there were polka dots. Nothing matched, but my mother made it work. Today I paint with stripes and polka dots, and it works too."

As a teenager Guyton attended Northern High School. To further his art education he took adult art classes at high schools and colleges in Detroit, including the Center for Creative Studies, the Franklin Adult Education program, and Marygrove College. He also received early encouragement from the Detroit artists Charles and Ali McGee. After serving in the U.S. Army for two years in the early 1970s, Guyton supported himself by working as an inspector for Ford Motor

At a Glance . . .

Born on August 24, 1955, in Detroit, MI; son of George and Betty (Solomon) Guyton; married Karen Smith, July 19, 1987 (divorced, 1994); married Jenenne Whitfield (an art foundation executive), October 2001; children and stepchildren: Carmen, Darren, Sean, Tyree Jr., Towan, Omar, James, Tylisa. *Military service*: U.S. Army, private, 1972. *Education*: Studied art in the Franklin Adult Education program and at the Center for Creative Studies, Wayne County Community College, and Marygrove College; studied with Charles McGee and other artists.

Career: Painter, sculptor, and mixed-media artist. Ford Motor Company, inspector, c. 1979–84; Detroit Fire Department, firefighter, c. 1979–84; instructor, master residence art program, Northern High School; Franklin Adult Education program; and Marygrove College; president, Heidelberg Project (an artwork in progress), Detroit, 1986—.

Awards: David A. Harmond Memorial Scholarship, 1989; Spirit of Detroit Award, 1989; Michiganian of Year Award, 1991; Governor's Arts Award, 1992; Humanity in the Arts Award, Wayne State University, 1992. Kresge Fellow, Kresge Foundation, 2009.

Addresses: *Office*—3600 Heidelberg St., Detroit, MI 48207. *Web*—http://www.heidelberg.org/ and http://tyreeguyton.com/.

Company in suburban Dearborn, serving as a firefighter with the Detroit fire department, and teaching art at his old high school. However, he continued to think about making art, and with the encouragement of his grandfather, he decided to do just that.

Began Transforming Urban Neighborhood

During the 1980s Guyton still lived on Heidelberg Street near his mother's house. Heidelberg is near Mount Elliott Road and Mack Avenue, two major east-side arteries. In the 1920s Heidelberg had been an unusually integrated block, sitting just at the edge of Detroit's historic African-American neighborhood and near thriving pockets of immigrant families. Riots in Detroit during the summer of 1967 decimated the area, along with much of the city, and successive mayoral administrations lavished dwindling financial resources on showpiece projects to lure visitors down-

town, neglecting the neighborhoods. The crack epidemic of the 1980s devastated entire blocks, and Heidelberg was one of them.

Like many Detroiters, Guyton was enraged by the lack of response to the proliferation of crack houses in abandoned structures. Police response was slow and ineffectual, and a backlog of houses deemed uninhabitable and tagged for demolition reached a five-figure number. Guyton had already been making art from found objects, and in the summer of 1986 he gathered discarded objects and nailed them to the outsides of the abandoned houses on his block. With the help of his grandfather and his wife at the time, Karen Smith, Guyton painted the objects he attached to the exteriors of the houses and surrounded them with everything from tires to toilets to tombstones, depending on his theme for the house. He also filled empty lots with rows of drinking fountains and old appliances. The installations were given playful names—the *Fun House*, the *Babydoll House*, the *Polka-Dot Tree*, and *Tire House*.

People magazine arrived to do a story on Guyton in 1988. "See that house over there?," Guyton asked the reporter. "That was a crack house.... After the first three police raids, it opened right up again. After the fourth raid we couldn't stand it anymore. So we went on over and painted the place. Pink, blue, yellow, white and purple dots and stripes and squares all over it. Up there on the roof we stuck a baby doll and that bright blue inner tube, and on the porch we put a doghouse with a watchdog inside.... Now all day long people drive by and stop to stare at the place.... Believe me, in front of an audience like that, nobody's going to sell crack out of that house anymore."

Lost Art to City Bulldozers

Through his work Guyton has challenged the boundaries between art and life, as did the French artist Marcel Duchamp, who took ordinary objects and presented them as art, and the American artist Robert Rauschenberg, who combined painting and common objects in collages or "combines." Guyton's work falls outside what is commonly recognized as art. Part of a group of "outsider" artists—Western artists who draw inspiration from sources outside traditional art—Guyton draws from the lives of the urban poor and makes their experiences and human spirit visible to people who travel from all over the world to see his work. He also shows how fragments of city life can be turned into art. There are also deeper signifiers in Guyton's works. Hodges, writing in the *Detroit News,* discussed one of Guyton's staunchest supporters, Harvard University Graduate School of Design professor John Beardsley, who "links it to the Southern custom of found-object yard art, which itself connects, he said, to the African tradition of decorating graves with objects sanctified by connection to the deceased."

As Guyton began to earn serious critical attention for his art in the late 1980s, the art-world approval and

honors proved an embarrassment to city officials. Guyton's neighbors finally mobilized into collective action and pleaded with the city to step in and put an end to what they considered a nuisance. Without notice, bulldozers arrived one day in 1989 and tore down the *Babydoll House*. Two years later, the same fate befell Guyton's *Tire House* and *Lost and Found*. It was brash, totalitarian move in a city dominated by a powerful, much-loved mayor—Coleman A. Young, the first African-American elected to the office—who had publicly denounced Guyton's Heidelberg Project as an eyesore. In a city where entire blocks were dotted by more than 15,000 rotting, abandoned structures on the demolition list, Mayor Young's move prompted outrage and galvanized support for Guyton in the arts community.

Guyton's neighbors were not among those supporters. One detractor was B. B. Odums, who complained in the *Detroit News* about the constant traffic. "We can't sit on our front porches because cars drive by, looking—as if we're on exhibit," she told Hodges. "And you can count on one hand the number of blacks that come and walk around. It's mostly the suburban people." In the same article, another black resident disagreed. Teresa Woods said that as a child she and her friends would "help nail things up," she told Hodges. She still lived there and asserted it anything but a detraction. "Everyone always comes to my house, and they're like, 'We're going down the street to look around.' They enjoy it."

Remained a Bright Spot in Detroit

Guyton's battle with the city endured for several more years. Mayor Young's successor, Dennis Archer, tried to make peace, but when Guyton began painting his signature single polka dots on abandoned buildings across the east side, he raised the ire of administration officials, and three more Heidelberg structures—*Your World, Happy Feet,* and the *Canfield House*—were demolished in early 1999, despite a strong legal defense mounted by Guyton and his supporters. Archer had once told Guyton that he should start thinking like an entrepreneur, not an artist-provocateur, and Guyton seemed to take those words to heart. Divorced from his wife, he met bank employee Jenenne Whitfield in 1993 when she took a wrong turn onto Heidelberg Street and saw Guyton at work painting. She asked him what it was about and soon developed an appreciation for the artist and his work. She eventually became the executive director of the Heidelberg Project, and the two were married in 2001.

The Heidelberg Project, a nonprofit organization, has an elementary-school arts program, and for many years Guyton taught art classes himself at a nearby recreational center. He and his work were the subject of an illustrated book, *Connecting the Dots, Tyree Guyton's Heidelberg Project,* published by Wayne State University Press in 2007, and a children's picture book in 2011. In 2009 Guyton was the recipient of a generous grant from the Kresge Foundation. He and Whitfield were also raising money for a large-scale project that would turn the Heidelberg Project into a 21st-century urban arts village, with an artists-in-residence program, a gift shop, a playscape for children, and other features that would provide jobs for local residents.

By then, the city's fortunes had plummeted even further and would be brought to near-ruin after the 2008 economic downturn and mortgage crisis, which decimated the tenuously lower-middle-class neighborhoods left inside its borders. At one historic moment, satellite-image data showed that Detroit now had more vacant lots than buildings. In another telling sign of how far Detroit had fallen, Archer's successor, Kwame Kilpatrick, was sentenced to prison in 2008 on charges related to perjury, fraud, and misuse of campaign funds. A culture of waste, corruption, and mismanagement dating back decades had turned Detroit into one of the poorest, and most unlivable urban centers in America, where entire blocks remained without street lights for months and poorly maintained sewer mains broke during subzero-temperature winters and turned streets into veritable ice rinks untraversable by either car or pedestrian. Veteran journalist Jack Lessenberry, writing in his Detroit *Metro Times* column, asserted that "were it not for Guyton, this street, which was bustling three-quarters of a century ago, would be virtually dead.... What the Heidelberg Project is all about is a damning indictment of Detroit—and a triumphal affirmation of hope."

Selected works

Exhibits

Detroit Institute of Arts, 1990.
"Heidelberg 25," Charles H. Wright Museum of African American History, 2011.
Work shown at Detroit Artists Market; Michigan Gallery, Detroit; Le Minotaure, Ann Arbor; Cade Gallery, Detroit; Trobar Gallery, Detroit; Alexa Lee Gallery, Ann Arbor; Ledis Flam Gallery, New York City.

Sources

Books

Connecting the Dots: Tyree Guyton's Heidelberg Project, Wayne State University Press, 2007.

Periodicals

Art News, October 1989, p. 27; May 1992, pp. 19–20.
Crain's Detroit Business, August 2, 2010, p. 3.

Detroit Free Press, July 30, 1994, p. 7B; September 24, 2003; November 29, 2007.

Detroit News, November 24, 1991, pp. 1A, 10A; March 18, 1992; November 29, 1994; August 1, 2011.

Metro Times (Detroit), June 23, 2004.

Newsweek, August 6, 1990, p. 64.

New York Times, July 2, 1990; February 6, 1999.

People, August 15, 1988, pp. 58–60.

Time, August 25, 1997, p. 4.

Wall Street Journal, November 29, 1991, p. B1.

Online

Benfield, Kaid, "Detroit's Powerful Urban Folk Art: The Heidelberg Project," *The Atlantic,* August 2, 2011, http://www.theatlantic.com/life/archive/2011/08/detroits-powerful-urban-folk-art-the-heidelberg-project/242934/ (accessed October 11, 2011).

The Heidelberg Project, http://www.heidelberg.org/ (accessed October 11, 2011).

—Alison Carb Sussman and Carol Brennan

Sharon Haynie

1955—

Biochemist, laboratory research scientist

Biochemist Sharon Haynie is happiest when she is working in the laboratory, where she thrives on the challenge of using science to create products that will make the world a better place. A principal investigator at the DuPont chemical company for more than 25 years, Haynie is a leader in "green chemistry," working to develop sustainable products derived from renewable resources. Her research has led to innovations in medical biotechnology, such as vascular grafts, as well as new, more environmentally friendly chemicals that are found in such everyday products as cosmetics and apparel. Dedicated to mentoring young scientists in her own laboratory, Haynie also is a dedicated volunteer, helping economically disadvantaged youth gain access to careers in the sciences.

Sharon L. Haynie was born on November 6, 1955, and grew up in Baltimore, Maryland. Her interest in science was sparked early on. As an eighth grader in the Baltimore public schools, she and her class participated in a national pilot program to introduce chemistry into the science curriculum at the junior high level. Haynie "fell in love with molecules," she recounted in an interview at the Women Chemists of Color Summit in 2010, and she was determined to pursue a career as a scientist, even though there were few women or minorities in the field at the time. She found a role model in her mother, Inez, who was part of the first cohort of women to become police officers in Baltimore; from her, Haynie learned to have faith in her convictions and the persistence to pursue them even in the face of obstacles.

Haynie enrolled at the University of Pennsylvania as a chemistry major. During her freshman year she had a work-study job in an organic chemistry lab, and it was there that she discovered her passion for laboratory research. "I was in seventh heaven!" she said in an interview on the University of Pennsylvania's alumni website. "I was immediately immersed in the type of intellectual work community that I had only dreamed of." But the job outlook for chemists in the 1970s was bleak, and friends counseled her to go into the more lucrative medical field. "Thankfully," she said, "I'm very stubborn and I knew enough of myself and my passion to resist the lure."

As an undergraduate, Haynie assumed that she would pursue an academic career, becoming a professor at a research university. In her senior year, however, she finished her studies early and took an extended internship at the Proctor & Gamble laboratories in Miami Valley, Ohio. The experience showed her the possibilities of applied research in industry, and she went on to pursue a doctorate in chemistry at the Massachusetts Institute of Technology, completing her degree in 1981.

Initially Haynie planned to join the Peace Corps for a time before beginning her career. When she was not accepted into the program, she switched gears and took a research position with AT&T Bell Laboratories, where she conducted research on polymer degradation. In 1984 she joined the DuPont chemical company, where she has spent her entire career. Since 1992 Haynie has been located at DuPont's central

At a Glance . . .

Born Sharon L. Haynie on November 6, 1955, in Baltimore, MD; daughter of Inez Penn Haynie Dodson. *Education*: University of Pennsylvania, BS, biochemistry, 1976; Massachusetts Institute of Technology, PhD, chemistry, 1981. *Politics*: American Chemical Society; National Academy of Sciences.

Career: AT&T Bell Laboratories, research scientist, 1981–84; DuPont Experimental Station, principal investigator, 1984—; has served as a mentor in the American Chemical Society's Project SEED.

Awards: Presidential Green Chemistry Award for New Innovation, U.S. Environmental Protection Agency, 2003; Percy L. Julian Award, National Organization of Black Chemists and Chemical Engineers, 2008.

Addresses: *Office*—DuPont Central Research and Development, DuPont Experimental Station, PO Box 80328, Wilmington, DE 19880.

research station in Wilmington, Delaware, in the Biochemical Science and Engineering Department.

At DuPont Haynie's work focused on two key processes: biocatalysis, in which natural catalysts such as proteins are used to perform chemical transformations on organic compounds, and metabolic engineering, in which the natural processes of cells are optimized to increase the production of a particular substance. These techniques commonly are used in industry to produce food and beverage products, animal feed, pharmaceuticals, and other organic materials. As part of DuPont's Vascular Graft Program, for example, Haynie worked with a team of researchers to develop a synthetic replacement vein for use in hip and other bone replacements when the patient's own veins could not be grafted. In another project she helped devise a process for creating synthetic molecules that could be used in medical catheters.

Haynie has emerged as a leader in "green chemistry"—that is, the use of environmentally friendly chemical processes to create polymers derived from renewable plants rather than from petrochemicals. She was a senior member of the DuPont team that developed Bio-PDO (bio-based 1,3 propanediol), a renewable chemical compound derived from corn sugar that is an ingredient in such products as antifreeze fluid, carpeting, apparel, resins, and cosmetics. Compared with its petroleum-based counterpart, Bio-PDO requires 40 percent less energy to produce and reduces emissions of greenhouse gases, which contribute to global warming, by 20 percent. In November of 2002 Haynie was named DuPont's "Scientist of the Month" for her work on green technologies, and in 2003 she and her team received the Presidential Green Chemistry Award from the U.S. Environmental Protection Agency for their development of Bio-PDO.

In addition to her work in the laboratory, Haynie is committed to nurturing the next generation of scientists. For more than a decade she has served as a mentor in the American Chemical Society's Project SEED, a summer research program for economically disadvantaged students. The project gives students, who historically have lacked access to scientific careers, the chance to spend a summer conducting hands-on research in academic, industrial, and government laboratories under the direction of experienced scientists such as Haynie. Such training, Haynie believes, is critical for students who are in the earliest stages of their careers.

In 2008 the National Organization of Black Chemists and Chemical Engineers honored Haynie with its prestigious Percy L. Julian Award, named for the African-American scientists whose synthesis of steroids from soy products led to the discovery of cortisone. She was the first woman ever to win the award, which recognized her work in "bio-inspired chemistry."

Sources

Books

Hinckle, Amber S., and Jody A. Kocsis, eds., *Successful Women in Chemistry*, American Chemical Society, 2005.

Periodicals

Science Spectrum, September/October 2006, p. 32.

Online

DuPont, http://www2.dupont.com/DuPont_Home/en_US/index.html (accessed August 12, 2011).

Interview with Sharon L. Haynie at the 240th ACS National Meeting, 2010, http://vimeo.com/16997047 (accessed August 12, 2011).

"Meet Sharon Haynie," University of Pennsylvania, College of Arts and Sciences, http://www.college.upenn.edu/admissions/alumni-haynie.php (accessed August 12, 2011).

"Sharon Haynie," American Chemical Society, http://portal.acs.org/portal/acs/corg/content?_nfpb=true&_pageLabel=PP_ARTICLEMAIN&node_id=1189&content_id=CTP_004440&use_sec=true&sec_url_var=region1&__uuid=0810c253-aa24-47a5-82b2-11a26a9adfec (accessed August 12, 2011).

—Deborah A. Ring

Joshua Henry

1984—

Actor

Henry, Joshua, photograph. Ben Hider/Getty Images.

Just a few years out of drama school, Joshua Henry has a résumé that is the envy of every struggling actor. Fresh off his graduation from the University of Miami, Henry landed his first professional acting gig in a revival of *Godspell*. Within two years he was performing on Broadway, first in the Tony Award–winning musical *In the Heights,* followed by a memorable performance in the Green Day rock musical *American Idiot*. In 2010 Henry scored a breakthrough role that propelled him from the ensemble to leading man, playing the lead in the controversial and short-lived musical *The Scottsboro Boys*. Henry won high marks for his portrayal of Haywood Patterson (whose real-life story inspired the play), earning his first Tony nomination for best leading actor in a musical. In 2011 Henry appeared in *The Gershwins' Porgy and Bess,* a daring adaptation of the classic opera that was expected to take him back to Broadway.

Found Home on the Stage

Joshua Anthony Charlton Henry was born in 1994 in Winnipeg, Canada, and grew up in Miami, Florida, where his parents relocated when he was a toddler. As a teenager, Henry did not think of performing as a career; instead, he planned to become an accountant, like his mother. That changed after Henry was cast as the con man Harold Hill in a production of *The Music Man* when he was a senior in high school. "I had no doubts as soon as I started performing," he told Michael Mellini of BroadwayWorld.com. "I felt so at home." After one performance, a music teacher took him aside and told him, "You can do this for a living," he recalled in an interview with Tom Nondorf of *Playbill*. "I didn't even know musical theater was a profession, or [that] you could perform for a living."

Henry's teacher gave him private voice lessons and encouraged him to audition for the University of Miami, the only school that he applied to. He was accepted and started his training in musical theater the next year. Because he had no background on the stage, however, he had to work even harder to catch up with his classmates. "From 8 a.m. until three in the morning, I was listening to cast recordings, reading plays and finding out all I could about the business," he told Mellini.

At a Glance . . .

Born Joshua Anthony Charlton Henry in 1994 in Winnipeg, Canada. *Education*: University of Miami, BM, 2006.

Career: Stage and film actor, 2006—; founding member of Jaradoa Theater Company.

Memberships: Actors' Equity Association.

Awards: Drama Desk Award for outstanding ensemble performance, 2007, and ACCA Award for outstanding Broadway chorus, Actors' Equity Association, 2008, for *In the Heights*.

Addresses: c/o Actors' Equity Association, 165 West 46th St., New York, NY 10036.

As graduation neared, Henry headed to New York City to perform in the University of Miami's annual Senior Showcase, which is meant to give the young actors a chance to meet casting directors, agents, and managers. Back in Miami, he received a call from casting director Alison Franck, who asked him to audition for an upcoming production of the popular musical *Godspell* at the Paper Mill Playhouse in Milburn, New Jersey. He landed the dual role of Judas and John the Baptist and made his professional debut that fall.

Made Broadway Debut

While he was working on *Godspell,* a fellow cast member suggested that Henry audition for a new musical called *In the Heights*. He won a place in the ensemble cast and understudied the role of Benny for the Off-Broadway run, which opened at the 37 Arts Theatre in February of 2007. The young actor was struck by the show's story, which focuses on the lives of several characters in a Dominican American neighborhood of New York City. "I knew on my first rehearsal that it was the most special thing I'd been involved in; I was sitting there in tears," he told Mellini. Henry followed the show uptown when it transferred to the St. James Theatre the next year, making his Broadway debut in March of 2008. Henry and the cast of *In the Heights* earned a Drama Desk Award for outstanding ensemble performance and the Actors' Equity Association's ACCA Award for outstanding chorus, and the show went on to win four Tony awards, including best musical.

Soon after *In the Heights*'s Tony triumph, Henry departed the cast to join a planned Broadway revival of *Godspell*, reprising his role from the Paper Mill pro-

duction, but the show was canceled for financial reasons. However, Henry was not idle for long; he soon returned to *In the Heights* as a "swing," or understudy, and later that year made his first appearance on the big screen, playing Jennifer Hudson's boyfriend in the first *Sex and the City* movie. In 2009 Henry played the role of the Tin Man in a summer run of *The Wiz* at the New York City Center and helped compose the lyrics and music for the play *Shafrika, the White Girl,* produced by the Jaradoa Theater Company, of which he was a founding member.

That same year, Henry was cast in the ensemble for the Green Day musical *American Idiot,* which opened at the Berkeley Repertory Theatre in California in the fall and then went on to Broadway in April of 2010. Playing an army soldier, he turned in a crowd-pleasing rendition of "Favorite Son," performing in his underwear surrounded by an entourage of female backup singers. "To be almost naked and have six girls around you singing about how sexy you are . . . is like living your life at 100 miles per hour," he told Mellini.

Told Scottsboro Boys' Story

Just two months into *American Idiot*'s Broadway run, Henry decided to leave the show to take advantage of an opportunity to play the lead role in the new musical *The Scottsboro Boys* for its pre-Broadway stint at the Guthrie Theatre in Minneapolis, Minnesota. The last musical penned by the legendary songwriting team of John Kander and Fred Ebb, who died in 2004, and directed by five-time Tony Award winner Susan Stroman, *The Scottsboro Boys* is based on the real-life story of nine young black men who, in the 1930s, were wrongfully accused of raping two white women on a train while traveling through Scottsboro, Alabama, and spent years on death row. Their case eventually made its way to the U.S. Supreme Court, becoming a galvanizing moment for the civil rights movement.

Henry took the role of Haywood Patterson, who learned to read and write while in prison and told the entire story in his 1950 book *Scottsboro Boy.* "It was one of the most challenging and rewarding experiences of my life," he said in an interview with the *Wall Street Journal.* "The role . . . challenged my voice, my body, my emotions. . . . As an actor, you don't all the time get to show that many sides of your versatility. So that was a blessing." Henry had auditioned for the role two years earlier but never received a callback; when the actor playing Patterson dropped out after the show's Off-Broadway debut, Henry stepped into the part at the request of director Stroman.

The musical's creators made the controversial choice to frame the story as a minstrel show, a storytelling device of the late 19th century in which white actors performed in blackface. That decision prompted the Freedom Party, a black progressive group, to organize a

protest outside Broadway's Lyceum Theatre, where the production opened on October 31, 2010. The protesters argued that the show's use of minstrelsy and blackface was racist. Henry, among other cast members, defended the choice: "It was a subversive piece, and a piece that was going to push buttons, stir hearts, but we also knew that it was the truth," he explained to the *Norwalk Hour* in an interview with co-star Forrest McClendon.

The Scottsboro Boys received positive reviews in the press. *Entertainment Weekly* declared the show the best new musical of the year, while the *New York Times* called it "adventurous" and "dynamic." Writing for the *Toronto Globe and Mail,* reviewer J. Kelly Nestruck described Henry's portrayal of Haywood as "tremendous," going on to say that "throughout his incarnation, Haywood remains defiant and tells the truth even when, in a cruel paradox, a lie would set him free. Henry plays him with a quivering, furious integrity, but also enough flawed humanity that he never turns into a symbol." Despite the critical approval, the show was not a hit with audiences, and it lasted only 49 performances. The production seemed to be vindicated when it received 12 Tony Award nominations, including a nod for Henry for best leading actor in a musical. *The Scottsboro Boys,* however, came up empty-handed (Henry lost to Norbert Leo Butz of *Catch Me If You Can*), setting a record as the most-nominated show to win no Tony awards.

After *The Scottsboro Boys* closed in December, Henry rejoined *American Idiot* in March of 2011 for the remainder of its Broadway run. Later that year he teamed with veteran actors Audra McDonald, Norm Lewis, and David Alan Grier for a new adaptation of the classic opera *Porgy and Bess.* Created by director Diane Paulus, playwright Suzan Lori-Parks, and composer Diedre Murray, *The Gershwins' Porgy and Bess* debuted at the American Repertory Theatre in Cambridge, Massachusetts, in the fall. It was slated to begin a Broadway run at the Richard Rodgers Theatre in December of 2011.

Selected works

Theater

Godspell, Paper Mill Playhouse, Milburn, NJ, 2006.
Serenade, Teatro LATEA, New York, 2007.
In the Heights, 37 Arts Theatre A., New York, 2007; Richard Rodgers Theatre, New York, 2008.
The Wiz, New York City Center, New York, 2009.
Shafrika, the White Girl, Vineyard Theatre, New York, 2009.
American Idiot, Berkeley Repertory Theatre, Berke-

ley, CA, 2009; St. James Theatre, New York, 2010–11.
The Scottsboro Boys, Lyceum Theatre, 2010.
The Gershwins' Porgy and Bess, American Repertory Theatre, Cambridge, MA, 2011.

Films

Sex and the City, New Line Cinema/Warner Bros., 2008.

Sources

Periodicals

Entertainment Weekly, November 1, 2010.
Globe and Mail (Toronto), November 15, 2010.
New York Daily News, October 3, 2010.
New York Times, October 21, 2010.
Norwalk Hour, May 7, 2011.
University of Miami Magazine, Winter 2009.

Online

Cohen, Patricia, "'Scottsboro Boys' Is Focus of Protest," ArtsBeat, *New York Times,* November 7, 2010, http://artsbeat.blogs.nytimes.com/2010/11/07/scottsboro-boys-is-focus-of-protest/ (accessed August 5, 2011).
Itzkoff, Dave, "'Scottsboro Boys' Sets Record for Tonys Futility," ArtsBeat, *New York Times,* June 13, 2011, http://artsbeat.blogs.nytimes.com/2011/06/13/scottsboro-boys-sets-record-for-tonys-futility/ (accessed August 5, 2011).
"Joshua Henry Joins A.R.T.'s *Porgy and Bess,* Starring Audra McDonald and Norm Lewis," April 14, 2011, http://www.broadway.com/shows/porgy-and-bess/buzz/156018/joshua-henry-joins-arts-porgy-and-bess-starring-audra-mcdonald-norm-lewis/ (accessed August 7, 2011).
Mellini, Michael, "*The Scottsboro Boys*' Joshua Henry on His Busy Road to Leading Man," October 14, 2010, http://www.broadway.com/shows/scottsboro-boys/buzz/153917/the-scottsboro-boys-joshua-henry-on-his-busy-road-to-leading-man/ (accessed August 7, 2010).
Nondorf, Tom, "The Leading Men: Joshua Henry of *The Scottsboro Boys,*" *Playbill,* November 18, 2010, http://www.playbill.com/celebritybuzz/article/145098-THE-LEADING-MEN-Joshua-Henry-of-The-Scottsboro-Boys (accessed August 7, 2011).
"Tony Nominee Joshua Henry on Playing a Scottsboro Boy," Speakeasy, *Wall Street Journal,* June 12, 2011, http://blogs.wsj.com/speakeasy/2011/06/12/tony-nominee-joshua-henry-on-playing-a-scottsboro-boy/ (accessed August 7, 2011).

—Deborah A. Ring

Grant Hill

1972—

Basketball player

Hill, Grant, photograph. AP Images/Rick Scuteri.

Grant Hill rose to prominence as a star player for the Duke University Blue Devils basketball team in the early 1990s, helping the team win two National Collegiate Athletic Association (NCAA) championships. He began his professional career with the Detroit Pistons, where he quickly became one of the best all-around players in the National Basketball Association (NBA). A series of ankle injuries and surgeries beginning in 2000, however, derailed Hill's career just as he was entering his prime. He missed most of the next four NBA seasons before successfully rehabilitating the injury. Since returning to the court for the 2004–05 season, Hill has reestablished his career on more modest terms, but he remains an immensely popular player because of the strength of character he has demonstrated while playing and battling injuries.

Raised in Relative Affluence

Grant Henry Hill was born on October 5, 1972, in Dallas, Texas. His father, Calvin Hill, was an All-America football player at Yale who went on to play for the Dallas Cowboys, the Washington Redskins, and the Cleveland Browns. Calvin Hill won Rookie of the Year in 1969, appeared in four Pro Bowls, and was the Cowboys' first 1,000-yard rusher. Hill's mother was similarly accomplished. A suitemate of future first lady, senator, and Secretary of State Hillary Rodham Clinton while the two were at Wellesley College, she worked as an attorney and corporate consultant in the nation's capital.

Hill grew up primarily in Reston, Virginia, an affluent suburb of Washington, D.C. He was an only child, and his upbringing was both luxurious and strict. Professional athletes, politicians, and other celebrities were frequent guests at the house, and Hill was often uncomfortable with the way that his father's fame set him apart from his peers. His parents did not allow him to attend dances or parties until he was 16 years old, and he was subject to significant limitations in his use of the phone and his visits outside the neighborhood. He has since expressed his appreciation for his parents' attentiveness and noted its beneficial effects on his development.

Although Hill's parents encouraged him to pursue sports, football was off-limits until the ninth grade. By the time he reached the ninth grade, however, he had

At a Glance . . .

Born Grant Henry Hill on October 5, 1972, in Dallas, TX; son of Calvin (professional football player) and Janet (attorney and consultant) Hill; married Tamia Washington (a jazz singer) in July of 1999; children: Myla, Lael. *Education*: Duke University, BA, 1994.

Career: Basketball player; played in college for Duke University Blue Devils, 1990–94; professional teams include Detroit Pistons, 1994–2000; Orlando Magic, 2000–07; Phoenix Suns, 2007—.

Awards: Henry Iba Corinthian Award for nation's best collegiate defensive player, National Association of Basketball Coaches, 1992; Rookie of the Year, National Basketball Association (NBA), 1995; All-Rookie First Team, NBA, 1995; All-Star, NBA, 1995–98, 2001, 2005; All-NBA First Team, 1997; All-NBA Second Team, 1996, 1998–2000; NBA Sportsmanship Award, 2005, 2008, 2010.

Addresses: *Office*—Phoenix Suns, 201 E. Jefferson St., Phoenix, AZ 85004. *Web*—http://www.granthill.com/.

already begun to excel on the basketball court, and he no longer had any interest in playing football. He led Reston's South Lakes High School to the state finals twice during his four years on the team, and as a senior he scored 30 points per game on average. He was a top college recruit whose initial first choice was nearby Georgetown University, but he did not have a good experience during his on-campus visit, and he ultimately chose Duke University.

Led the Blue Devils and Pistons

Playing as a freshman in the shadow of such notables as Bobby Hurley and Christian Laettner, Hill was nonetheless central to Duke's unparalleled success during his four years at the school. The Blue Devils won the 1991 and 1992 NCAA national championships, and in 1994 Hill once again led the Blue Devils into the NCAA championship game, this time without the presence of Hurley or Laettner. Even though the 1994 Blue Devils lost the NCAA championship to Arkansas, Hill was still named Atlantic Coast Conference Player of the Year.

Overall, in his four years at Duke, Hill averaged 14.9 points and 6 rebounds per game, while helping the Blue Devils to a remarkable 118-23 four-year record, one of the best multiseason showings of any team in college basketball history. Hill also developed, over the course of his Duke career, a reputation for sportsmanship, team play, and personal responsibility that would distinguish him throughout his professional career.

The Detroit Pistons chose Hill as the third pick in the 1994 NBA draft, signing him to an eight-year, $45-million contract. Almost immediately Hill won commercial endorsement contracts from Fila athletic wear, Sprite, Chevrolet, and other major corporations, and his debut in the NBA generated a dizzying amount of press coverage.

Hill topped the voting for the All-Star Game in his rookie season, a vote that was as much a measure of his likability as his exceptional play. "The vote was a clear and unmistakable scream from the basketball public that they want something better," wrote a columnist in the *Washington Post*. "They want someone with a wonderful game who doesn't have to beat his chest every time he dunks.... They want someone who realizes that humility and dignity are as manly as any characteristics a professional athlete can have." At season's end Hill was named co-Rookie of the Year, sharing honors with Jason Kidd of the Dallas Mavericks. Even with Hill's award-winning performance, however, the Pistons managed only a 28-54 season in 1994–95.

One challenge that Hill faced during his early years in the league was the persistence of unrealistic comparisons to Michael Jordan. Although Hill's celebrity and promise compared to Jordan's during this time, he had never been the kind of single-minded scorer that Jordan was. His play-making was more subtle, and he prided himself on his all-around game, rather than his scoring average.

In 1995–96 Hill led the Pistons to the playoffs, but they lost in the first round to the Orlando Magic. Again Hill was the league's top vote-getter for the All-Star game in 1996. He was also chosen to represent the United States on the 1996 Olympic team, known as the Dream Team III. The 1996–97 season seemed to represent another step forward for the Pistons. The team won 54 games in the regular season, and although they again lost in the first round of the playoffs, they promised to remain contenders in the years that followed.

The following two seasons were disappointing, however. Hill continued to perform well, averaging over 21 points per game over the next three seasons and twice making the All-Star team, but the Pistons missed the playoffs. They did not return to the playoffs until the 1999–2000 season, when Hill averaged a career high 25.8 points per game.

Battled Severe Ankle Injuries

The 2000 playoffs proved the start of a long and

arduous chapter in Hill's career, however. After missing the final three games of the regular season due to a foot injury, Hill broke his left ankle in the second playoff game against the Miami Heat and underwent surgery in which screws and a steel plate were inserted to shore up the broken bone. After signing a $93 million contract with the Pistons, he was traded to the Orlando Magic, but he played only four games before his ankle forced him to bow out of the 2000–01 season. Hill had another surgical procedure, involving the grafting of bone from his hip onto his ankle, and he rehabbed in preparation for another in 2001–02. This time, he played 14 games before pain forced him back into the surgical ward, for the removal of bone spurs.

In 2002–03 Hill got off to a promising start, but his ankle increasingly bothered him as the season wore on, and in January, after consultations with doctors, he again had to end his season and prepare for surgery, his fourth in three years. This procedure involved the removal of screws and bone, the insertion of a steel plate, the use of genetically engineered material intended to promote bone growth, and a procedure involving the breaking of his heel to bring his left leg back into alignment. While recovering at home the following week, he developed a staph infection that almost killed him. He remained in the hospital for over six weeks, ultimately had a fifth surgery, and missed the entirety of the 2003–04 season.

Although Hill could have retired during this ordeal and still collected the remainder of his $93 million contract, he returned to the court for the 2004–05 season, playing on what the Sean Deveney in the *Sporting News* called a "Frankenankle." "A lot of people probably just forgot about me or got tired of wondering if I was going to come back," Hill told Deveney. "I have the ankle of an old man, but I feel I am in great condition."

Signed with Phoenix Suns in 2007

Hill's return to regular health was met with celebration by fans, sportswriters, and even opposing players and coaches. The perseverance he had shown in choosing not to rest on his already notable accomplishments and earnings provided a contrast to ubiquitous stories of player arrogance, entitlement, and misbehavior, and it once again seemed to demonstrate that he was a person of sterling character. Hill started and played in 67 games that season, averaging 19.7 points per game. He was voted to the Eastern Conference All-Star Team, and he won the NBA Sportsmanship Award.

Injuries again hampered Hill in 2005–06, and he underwent yet another surgery, this time to treat a sports hernia that had developed as a result of uneven pressure on his feet. He played only 21 games, averaging 15 points per game. The following season, however, marked a more permanent return to health. Hill played 65 games in 2006–07, averaging 14.4 points per game and helping Orlando to its first playoff appearance since 2002–03.

In 2007 Hill signed a two-year contract as a free agent with the Phoenix Suns. He remained healthy over the next several seasons, but his days as one of the league's top scorers were behind him. He won his second NBA Sportsmanship Award in 2008, and he re-signed with the Suns in 2009. In 2010 the team made it through the first two rounds of the playoffs, in no small part due to the contributions Hill was now making as a defensive specialist. Freed of the need to carry his team as a scorer, he could devote his energy to stopping opponents' high scorers. He took home a record-setting third NBA Sportsmanship Award in 2010.

Although retirement would soon become inevitable for Hill, who was 38 during the 2010–11 season, he remained healthy, playing in over 80 games per year in 2008–09, 2009–10, and 2010–11. He was intent on continuing to play as long as he could meaningfully contribute to his team. Rather than dwell on the twists of fate that had forced him to miss what should have been the prime of his career, Hill focused on the personal growth that had occurred as a result of his struggles with injury. "It may have been bad for my career," he told *Sports Illustrated*'s Lee Jenkins in 2010, "but it was good for my development as a human being. In a weird way I'm glad it happened."

Sources

Boston Globe, December 1, 1994, p. 79.
BusinessWeek, February 7, 2006.
Esquire, February 1995, p. 60.
GQ, April 1995, p. 170.
Los Angeles Times, January 5, 1995, p. C1.
New York Times, July 11, 2009.
People, January 23, 1995, p. 74.
Sporting News, December 23, 2002, p. 6; December 6, 2004, p. 36.
Sports Illustrated, February 1, 1993, p. 58; January 22, 1996, p. 59; November 25, 1996, p. 40; February 9, 1998, p. 64; June 28, 2004, p. 22; December 6, 2004, p. 78; October 29, 2007, p. 26; May 24, 2010, p. 64.
Sports Illustrated for Kids, March 1, 2005, p. T4.
Time, February 13, 1995, p. 78.
USA Today, December 6, 1994, p. C1; May 18, 1995, p. B5, C3; January 26, 1996, p. C1; September 29, 2010.
USA Today Weekend, December 18, 1994, p. 4.
Washington Post, February 12, 1995, p. D1.

Online

"Grant Hill Info Page," NBA.com, http://www.nba.com/home/playerfile/grant_hill/index.html (accessed September 22, 2011).

Grant Hill—The Official Website, http://granthill. com/ (accessed September 22, 2011).

—Mark Kram and Mark Lane

Wyllstyne D. Hill

1950—

Engineer

Wyllstyne D. Hill's name regularly turns up on lists of the top-ranking African Americans in engineering and information-technology sciences. As vice president of information technology and chief information officer at Raytheon Missile Systems in Arizona, Hill heads a team of employees building the next generation of high-tech weaponry. She started at the company in 1971 when it was still Hughes Aircraft, the venture founded by aviation pioneer Howard Hughes.

Hill majored in mathematics and took a minor in computer science at Tuskegee University in Alabama. She graduated in 1971 and was hired at Hughes Aircraft as a general clerk, eventually rising to project engineer, then technical manager. During this period the company built the Phoenix long-range air-to-air missile systems and was perfecting the synchronous communication satellite, whose technological descendants enabled satellite television technology and global positioning systems, better known as GPS.

General Motors bought Hughes Aircraft in 1985, then merged it with its Delco Electronics unit to become Hughes Electronics. In the early 1990s Hughes acquired the missile-development and manufacturing division of General Dynamics, another major U.S. defense contractor. General Motors spun off Delco into a newly created Delphi Electronics, then divested the remaining Hughes Aircraft assets to Raytheon, a vacuum-tube maker founded during the 1920s that revolutionized home electronics, especially radio sets. In the 1960s Raytheon bought the Amana Corporation, a maker of refrigerators, and launched the first affordable kitchen microwaves into the consumer market.

Hill was firmly entrenched in the secretive missile-development programs at Hughes and Raytheon. The Patriot surface-to-air missile, known as the MIM-104 Patriot in military parlance, is one of Raytheon's most successful systems, as is the AIM-9 Sidewinder, a heat-seeking missile fired by fighter aircraft in combat. The company also makes the FIM-92 Stinger, a portable surface-to-air missile (SAM) with a stunning five-mile range.

In 1998 Hill became director of missile systems information technology at Raytheon, and a few years later she was promoted to divisional chief information officer, or CIO, and vice president of information technology (IT). Based out of Raytheon's Missile Systems headquarters in Tucson, Arizona, she oversaw 500 employees and more than 10,000 users of Raytheon's information systems.

The list of Raytheon successes that Hill has helped develop reads like a science-fiction novel about warfare of the future. There is the Tomahawk Cruise Missile, which has been in use for decades; the AGM-154 Joint Standoff Weapon (JSOW), which is a missile launched from aircraft or battleships; the Paveway Laser Guided Bomb (LGB); and the Evolved SeaSparrow Missile (ESSM), a rocket-based missile system used to defend warships. The technologies used by these weapons systems are so advanced that the potential for consumer applications has not yet been fully explored.

At a Glance . . .

Born in 1949; married Collier Hill Sr. (a retired law-enforcement official); children: Collier Jr. *Education*: Tuskegee University, BS, 1971; graduate coursework in computer science and systems engineering at the University of Arizona.

Career: Hughes Aircraft Company, began as general clerk, 1971, became project engineer, then technical manager; Raytheon Missile Systems, director of missile systems information technology after 1998, vice president of information technology and chief information officer, 2002—.

Memberships: National Society of Black Engineers, Society of Mathematicians, Society of Women Engineers, Tucson Urban League, Women in Science and Engineering, Women in Technology International.

Awards: Women of Color in Government and Defense Technology Award, National Society of Black Engineers, 2001; Phenomenal Woman of the Year Award, University of Arizona Alumni Association, 2005; Black Engineer of the Year Award for Career Achievement in Industry Award, National Society of Black Engineers, 2007.

Addresses: *Office*—Raytheon Missile Systems,1151 Hermans Rd., Tucson, AZ 85756-9367.

Microwave ovens, satellite television, and GPS devices are just a few of the products that owe their existence to scientists like Hill working in the defense industry. In the first decade of the 21st century, Hill began working with researchers at the University of Arizona on an advanced image-analysis system developed by Raytheon to analyze battlefields; the technology had potential applications in the detection of melanomas and other skin cancers. It featured "an infrastructure akin to a supercomputing facility," she told Ellen Fanning in *Computer World* in 2009. "The volume of data to be managed may approach petabytes within only a couple of years."

Over the course of her long career Hill has been active in several mentoring programs through various professional organizations, including the National Society of Black Engineers, the Society of Women Engineers, and Women in Science and Engineering. In 2001 she won the Women of Color in Government and Defense Technology Award from the magazine *U.S. Black Engineer & Information Technology,* a publication of the National Society of Black Engineers. Six years later she won its Career Achievement in Industry Award. In between those honors she was recognized by the University of Arizona Alumni Association as one of its Phenomenal Women of the Year in 2005. Hill has accumulated credits in graduate coursework in computer science and systems engineering at the school. In 2009 she was a finalist for the inaugural CIO of the Year Awards from the Arizona Technology Council.

Hill is married to Collier Hill, a native of Pine Bluff, Arkansas, who retired as assistant chief of the police in Tucson. Their son Collier Jr. works for IBM.

Sources

Periodicals

U.S. Black Engineer & IT, Winter 2008, p. 24; Spring 2010, p. 32.

Online

Fanning, Ellen, "Premier 100 IT Leader Profile: Wyllstyne Hill," ComputerWorld.com, December 7, 2009, http://www.computerworld.com/s/article/344579/Wyllstyne_Hill_CIO_Raytheon_Missile_Systems (accessed August 19, 2011).

Horrani, Morriah, "Black Engineer of the Year Awards Marks 21st Anniversary," Black Engineer.com, January 30, 2007, http://www.blackengineer.com/artman/publish/article_674.shtml (accessed August 19, 2011).

"Top Black Women Techies," The Root, http://www.theroot.com/multimedia/black-women-techies (accessed August 19, 2011).

—Carol Brennan

Terrence Howard

1969—

Actor, producer

Howard, Terrence, photograph. Frederick M. Brown/Getty Images.

For more than a decade, Terrence Howard paid his dues as a supporting actor in Hollywood, turning in memorable performances on television and in such films as *Mr. Holland's Opus* (1995), *The Best Man* (1999), *Harts War* (2002), and *Ray* (2004). Finally, in 2004 he earned Hollywood's attention for his breakout role in the Oscar-nominated ensemble drama *Crash,* and the following year he scored a critical triumph for his portrayal of Memphis pimp Djay in the film *Hustle & Flow,* for which he received an Academy Award nomination for best actor. Now an in-demand leading man, Howard starred in more than a dozen films over the next few years. In 2008 Howard made his Broadway debut in an all-black production of *Cat on a Hot Tin Roof* alongside James Earl Jones, and he released his first album—fulfilling a lifelong dream—called *Shine Through It.* Howard made a return to the small screen in 2010, joining the cast of the television drama *Law & Order: Los Angeles.*

Trod Rough Road to Stardom

Born Terrence Dashon Howard on March 11, 1969, in Chicago, he was the third child of Tyrone Howard, a building contractor, and his wife, Anita, an aspiring actress. When Howard was an infant, his family relocated to Cleveland, Ohio, where they settled into a comfortable middle-class existence. His life took a disastrous turn, however, on December 21, 1971. Howard and his two brothers were standing in line to see Santa Claus at a Cleveland department store accompanied by their father, a light-skinned man of mixed race. When their mother—a black woman—joined them in line, a white man accused the family of cutting the line. A fight broke out, which according to some witnesses stemmed from a racial slur used against the Howards, and Tyrone Howard fatally stabbed the man. He was convicted of manslaughter and served 11 months in prison. The incident made headlines across the country as the "Santa line slaying."

Howard's father returned from prison a changed man, becoming a militant Muslim and a strict disciplinarian. His parents separated soon after, and Howard and his brothers shuttled between Cleveland, where they lived with their father in the city's housing projects, and Los Angeles, where their mother had gone with the hope of breaking into show business. Howard, a light-skinned,

At a Glance . . .

Born Terrence Dashon Howard on March 11, 1969, in Chicago, IL; son of Tyrone Howard (a contractor) and Anita Hawkins Williams; married Lori McCommas in 1989 (divorced 2001; remarried 2005; divorced 2005); married Michelle Ghent in 2010 (divorced 2011); children: Aubrey, Heaven, Hunter. *Education*: Pratt Institute, 1990–91.

Career: Television, film, and stage actor, 1992—.

Addresses: *Agent*—Creative Artists Agency, 2000 Avenue of the Stars, Los Angeles, CA 90067. *Publicist*—Baker Winokur Ryder Public Relations, 9100 Wilshire Blvd., Ste. 55 West Tower, Beverly Hills, CA 90212.

red-haired, green-eyed child, endured racial taunts from his schoolmates, and at age five, he started carrying a knife to protect himself. Both of his parents remarried, giving him 10 siblings altogether.

After his stepmother pointed a gun at him, Howard left home with his brothers, moving into a dilapidated house that his father had bought for a pittance; it had neither electricity nor running water, and every day, he worried that they would not have enough money to buy kerosene for the small heater they huddled around at night. As a teenager, Howard spent his summers in New York with his maternal great-grandmother, Minnie Gentry, a stage actress who had appeared on Broadway with Sidney Poitier in the 1940s and later became active in the black theater scene. When Howard saw her perform in a one-act play, he was captivated. "She made me believe she was popping green beans in a colander, made me believe that she had a glass in her hand full of Coca-Cola," he recalled in an interview with the Newark, New Jersey, *Star-Ledger*. "And I knew I wanted to be that kind of Houdini."

Paid Dues in Supporting Roles

Howard graduated from Cleveland's Jane Addams High School, and at age 19 he moved to New York, conning his way into the Pratt Institute to study chemical engineering despite his poor high school record. He spent three semesters at Pratt before dropping out to pursue a career in acting. Howard made the rounds of theatrical agents, offering a padded résumé that listed some 20 plays; in fact, Howard had only walked past the theaters where he claimed to have performed. One day, Howard was spotted on a New York street by a casting director, and on his second audition, he landed a guest spot on *The Cosby Show*. When his part ended up on the cutting room floor, he went straight to Bill

Cosby's dressing room and pounded on the door in protest. The show's producers never called him again, and the incident earned the young actor a reputation for being "difficult" that he would not soon shake.

In 1992 Howard was cast in the television movie *The Jacksons: An American Dream*, in which he played Jackie Jackson. That break led to several guest appearances on such television series as *Tall Hopes, Living Single, Coach*, and *Family Matters*. In 1995 he gave a pair of minor but memorable performances in the films *Mr. Holland's Opus* and *Dead Presidents*, and the following year, he gained additional exposure on the UPN series *Sparks*, appearing for three seasons.

Over the next decade, Howard had steady acting work in supporting roles on the big screen, turning out more than a dozen films, including *The Best Man*, a breakout part opposite Taye Diggs; the comedy *Big Momma's House* (2000), with Martin Lawrence; the Mariah Carey flop *Glitter* (2001); and the World War II drama *Hart's War*. In addition, he turned in solid performances in the made-for-television movies *King of the World* (2000), in which he played Cassius Clay, and *Boycott* (2001), a dramatization of the 1955 Montgomery bus boycott, as well as the Showtime series *Street Time*. Still, Howard was frustrated that he was not being offered leading roles—a sign of racial disparities in Hollywood, he believed—and he even considered giving up on acting. "If I was white," he told the *New York Times* in 2001, "I would be huge. No question. But if you're black, you're going to struggle. It doesn't matter how much good work you do. You will struggle."

Became a Leading Man

After more than a decade of struggling in Hollywood, Howard was a standout in that year's *Crash,* an ensemble drama weaving together several interconnected story lines dealing with racism in Los Angeles. In the film, Howard plays Cameron Thayer, a television executive who, during a routine traffic stop, stands by while a racist police officer sexually abuses his wife (played by Thandie Newton), powerless to stop him. In the aftermath of the incident, his home and work life begin to unravel. "That was probably the hardest role I've ever had to play," Howard told *Essence* magazine, speaking of the traffic stop scene. "Never in my life, since I was 14, have I allowed myself to be afraid of someone." Howard earned kudos for his performance, winning an NAACP Image Award for outstanding supporting actor in a motion picture. That same year, he also appeared in the Ray Charles biopic *Ray*, playing musician Gossie McGee.

A year later, Howard scored a critical triumph with *Hustle & Flow,* in which he played Djay, a small-time Memphis pimp who dreams of making it big as a rapper. The first feature film for writer and director

Craig Brewer, the movie took years to come to fruition; although studio executives approved the storyline, they wanted a big-name rapper in the lead role. Producers John Singleton and Stephanie Allain (who had worked with Howard on the 2003 film *Biker Boyz*) agreed to put their homes up as collateral to get financing for the film, with Howard as the lead. *Hustle & Flow* debuted at the Sundance Film Festival, winning the coveted Audience Award—Howard received a standing ovation—and setting off a hot bidding war among the major studios. When Paramount released *Hustle & Flow* that summer, it took in more than $8 million on its opening weekend alone—a good return for a film that had cost only $3.5 million to make.

Howard earned critical acclaim for his performance and his first Academy Award nomination, for best actor (he lost to Philip Seymour Hoffman of *Capote*). However, he later admitted that he had suffered doubts about the role—in fact, he turned down the part several times. "I was afraid that instead of trying to kill a stereotype, they were trying to propagate a stereotype," Howard explained to Phil Hoad in *The Independent*. "Blaxploitation, glorification of pimps, glorification of the gangsta life. I didn't want to participate in anything like that." To prepare for the part, Howard talked with sex workers to better understand their lives and worked with Memphis rapper Al Kapone, who penned the lyrics for the soundtrack, to perfect his rap delivery. Howard raps on several tracks in the film, including "It's Hard Out Here for a Pimp," "Whoop That Trick," and "Hustle & Flow (It Ain't Over)."

Entertainment Weekly critic Owen Gleiberman singled out Howard's portrayal of Djay as "the single most powerful performance I've seen this year," going on to say that the actor "inhabits his character with a casual mastery that makes him a world unto himself; we're in touch with his ambition and sadness, rage and longing, as if they were our own." Todd McCarthy wrote in *Variety* that Howard's "delivery mixes brooding thoughtfulness with emotional immediacy in a manner that recalls a young Brando," while Richard Corliss declared in *Time* that Howard "explodes with coiled energy, intelligence and sexuality. To the simple scheme of Djay's redemption, he lends nuance and magnetic power. Ta-da! A star is born."

Hailed as the "Next Denzel"

On the heels of *Hustle & Flow*, Howard was hailed as the next Denzel Washington, and in 2005 alone, he appeared in seven movies, including the John Singleton action picture *Four Brothers* and Jim Sheridan's *Get Rich or Die Tryin'*, starring the rapper 50 Cent. On television, Howard received positive reviews for his performances in the HBO movie *Lackawanna Blues* and the ABC production of Zora Neale Hurston's novel *Their Eyes Were Watching God* with Halle Berry.

Howard kept up his prolific pace in 2007, starring in the drama *Pride*, in which he portrayed Jim Ellis, who coaches a swim team comprising troubled teens in Philadelphia. That same year, he also had major roles in *The Hunting Party* with Richard Gere, the thriller *Awake* with Jessica Alba, and *The Brave One* with Jody Foster. In 2008 Howard turned to science fiction, playing Lieutenant Colonel James Rhodes in the summer blockbuster *Iron Man*.

The year 2008 marked two more milestones in Howard's career. First, in March, he made his Broadway debut in a revival of the Tennessee Williams classic *Cat on a Hot Tin Roof*. The all-black cast, directed by Debbie Allen, featured Howard as Brick, Anika Noni Rose as Maggie the Cat, James Earl Jones as Big Daddy, and Phylicia Rashad. Reviewing the production in *Variety*, David Ronney praised Howard's portrayal of the alcoholic, sexually frustrated Brick: "Terrence Howard delivers. It's an understated performance that taps all the quiet, sleepy-eyed charisma of his screen work while also accessing the lacerating wound of a man forced to confront emotional questions he'd rather ignore." The show proved to be a hit with audiences, running for 125 performances and earning more than $750,000.

Also that year, Howard released his first album, *Shine Through It*, the culmination of a long-held musical ambition. Howard wrote, produced, and arranged all 11 songs on the album, which offers a mix of jazz, soul, and country inspired by such diverse artists as the Temptations, Duke Ellington, Bob Marley, Curtis Mayfield, and James Taylor.

In 2010 Howard took on a new role as Deputy District Attorney Jonah "Joe" Dekker on NBC's *Law & Order: Los Angeles*, alternating episodes with Alfred Molina. In 2011 Howard played Nelson Mandela in the biographical film *Winnie* with Jennifer Hudson. He was slated to appear in a Jamaican adaptation of Shakespeare's *Macbeth*, titled *Macbett*, and in a drama with Cuba Gooding Jr. about the Tuskegee Airmen during World War II.

Selected works

Films

Who's the Man?, New Line Cinema, 1993.
Dead Presidents, Buena Vista Pictures, 1995.
Lotto Land, In Pictures, 1995.
Mr. Holland's Opus, Buena Vista Pictures, 1995.
Johns, First Look International, 1996.
Sunset Park, TriStar Pictures, 1996.
Double Tap, Paramount Home Video, 1997.
Butter, Live Entertainment, 1998.
The Players Club, New Line Cinema, 1998.
Spark, Film Sales, 1998.
Best Laid Plans, Twentieth Century Fox, 1999.
The Best Man, Universal Pictures, 1999.
Valerie Flake, Bleiberg Entertainment, 1999.

Big Momma's House, Twentieth Century Fox, 2000.
Angel Eyes, Warner Bros., 2001.
Glitter, Twentieth Century Fox, 2001.
Hart's War, MGM, 2002.
Intimate Affairs, Atlas International, 2002.
Biker Boyz, DreamWorks, 2003.
Crash, Lions Gate, 2004.
Ray, Universal Pictures, 2004.
Four Brothers, Paramount, 2005.
Get Rich or Die Tryin', Paramount, 2005.
Hustle & Flow, Paramount, 2005.
The Salon, Polychrome, 2005.
Idlewild, Universal Pictures, 2006.
August Rush, Warner Bros., 2007.
Awake, MGM, 2007.
The Brave One, Warner Bros., 2007.
The Hunting Party, Weinstein, 2007.
Pride, Lions Gate, 2007.
Iron Man, Paramount, 2008.
Fighting, Rogue Pictures, 2009.
The Princess and the Frog (voice), Walt Disney, 2009.

Television

The Jacksons: An American Dream (television movie), ABC, 1992.
Tall Hopes, CBS, 1993.
The O.J. Simpson Story (television movie), FOX, 1995.
Shadow-Ops (television movie), 1995.
Sparks, UPN, 1996.
Mama Flora's Family (television movie), CBS, 1998.
King of the World (television movie), ABC, 2000.
Boycott (television movie), HBO, 2001.
Independent Lens (narrator), PBS, 2002–09.
Street Time, Showtime, 2003.
Lackawanna Blues (television movie), HBO, 2005.

Their Eyes Were Watching God (television movie), ABC, 2005.
Wifey (television movie), BET, 2007.
Law & Order: Los Angeles, NBC, 2010–11.

Albums

Shine Through It, Columbia Records, 2008.

Sources

Periodicals

Boston Globe, July 17, 2005.
Chicago Sun-Times, July 17, 2005.
Entertainment Weekly, July 29, 2005, p. 47.
Essence, August 2005, p. 116.
The Guardian (London), May 18, 2008.
The Independent (London), November 18, 2005, p. 14.
Los Angeles Daily News, February 19, 2006.
Los Angeles Times Magazine, September 1, 2007.
New York Magazine, March 10, 2008.
New York Times, February 18, 2001.
Star-Ledger (Newark, NJ), July 24, 2005, p. 4.
Time, July 4, 2005, p. 76.
Variety, January 26, 2005, p. 20; March 7, 2008.

Online

Keeps, David A., "The Better Man: Terrence Howard," Men's Health, http://www.menshealth.com/celebrity-fitness/better-man-terrence-howard (accessed August 29, 2011).

—Carol Brennan and Deborah A. Ring

Deborah Jackson

1952—

Physicist, research administrator

One of the nation's leading physicists, Deborah Jackson became interested in science when she read Andre Norton's science-fiction novel *Star Rangers* (1953) in junior high school. In the decades since, she has made important contributions to a number of cutting-edge technologies, including superconductors, laser optics, and the radio equipment used in space exploration. A native of the Midwest, she has worked in facilities across the country, from Bell Laboratories in New Jersey to the Jet Propulsion Laboratory (JPL) in California. She has also had a successful career as a research administrator for the federal government.

The daughter of Collins Jackson, a soldier, and Mennie Ethel Jackson, Deborah Jean Jackson was born in 1952 in Topeka, Kansas, a city with a small but vibrant African-American community. Like many military families, the Jacksons moved often, a circumstance that forced Deborah Jackson to change schools several times. Although such shifts often have a negative impact on a student's academic performance, they do not appear to have done so in her case, for she won admission after high school to one of the country's most competitive universities, the Massachusetts Institute of Technology (MIT). Upon earning a bachelor's degree in physics there in 1974, she moved on to graduate work in the same field at Stanford University, earning a master's degree in 1976 and a doctorate four years later. Much of her work as a graduate student was supported by two fellowships, one from the Ford Foundation (1974–76) and the other from the Cooperative Research Fellowship Program (1976–80). The latter, a longstanding initiative of Bell Laboratories, is one of the oldest and most prominent minority-recruitment programs in the sciences.

At Stanford and Bell, Jackson studied a range of phenomena, often using instruments that harnessed the power of X-rays, ultraviolet radiation, or lasers. Her interests shifted somewhat in 1981, when she became a visiting scientist at IBM Corporation's primary research facility in Yorktown Heights, New York. There she focused particularly on optical harmonics, a field that involves in-depth analysis of the properties and behavior of light waves. After two years there, she moved on in 1983 to Hughes Research Laboratories (HRL), a Malibu, California, facility that was then a subsidiary of the Hughes Aircraft Company, a major defense and aerospace contractor. At HRL, as reported in a biographical profile by the African Scientific Institute, "she initiated a photonic device development program aimed at integrating photo-detectors, modulators, diode lasers, and VSLI [Very Large-Scale Integration] circuits on a common chip." What this work represented, in essence, was an effort to adapt a variety of technologies for use in real-world environments outside the lab. The experience she gained as a member of HRL's technical staff eventually drew the attention of the RAND Corporation, another major contractor, and in 1988 she moved to its lab in Santa Monica, California, where she served as a senior member of the technical staff.

In her four-year tenure at RAND (1988–92), Jackson continued to work on photonics, broadly defined as the study of light. Her focus within that field shifted slightly,

At a Glance . . .

Born Deborah Jean Jackson in 1952 in Topeka, KS; daughter of Collins Jackson (a soldier) and Mennie Ethel Jackson. *Education*: Massachusetts Institute of Technology, BS, physics, 1974; Stanford University, MS, physics, 1976, PhD, physics, 1980.

Career: IBM Corporation, visiting scientist, 1981–83; Hughes Research Laboratories, technical-staff member, 1983–88; RAND Corporation, senior technical-staff member, 1988–92; Jet Propulsion Laboratory, senior researcher, 1992–2005; National Science Foundation, program manager, 2006—.

Memberships: National Society of Black Physicists, Sigma Xi.

Awards: Fellowship, Ford Foundation, 1974–76; fellowship, Cooperative Research Fellowship Program (Bell Laboratories), 1976–80.

Addresses: *Office*—National Science Foundation, 4201 Wilson Blvd., Arlington, VA 22230. *Email*—djackson@nsf.gov.

however, as she increasingly incorporated a wider view of the technology involved. Although practical problems still concerned her, she now devoted a considerable portion of her time to the identification of general problems photonics might help solve. She took a similar approach years later, when she moved into research administration. In the meantime, however, she had a long and successful stint (1992–2005) at the Jet Propulsion Laboratory, a joint venture between NASA and the California Institute of Technology. With roots stretching back to the 1930s, the Pasadena, California, facility has played a major role in the success of the nation's space-exploration program. As a senior researcher there, Jackson was involved in two major NASA projects, the Mars Global Surveyor mission, launched in 1996, and Cassini-Huygens, a mission to Saturn launched the following year. In each case she served as cognizant, or lead, engineer for the Ultra Stable Oscillator, a critical piece of communications equipment. The images and data transmitted by that equipment have added immensely to scientists' understanding of the solar system. Astronomers around the world have been particularly pleased with the data Cassini-Huygens sent back after a tour of Saturn's moons, Titan among them. "Cassini catapulted our knowledge of giant, haze-enshrouded Titan into a

whole new realm," noted Enrico Piazza in a mission overview on JPL's website.

Following the launch of the two space probes, Jackson went on to two other projects within JPL. The first involved the design of a new device that used light to encrypt data on high-speed digital networks. That project, for which she served as principal investigator, resulted in the award of a U.S. patent. She then moved to a division of JPL called the Quantum Computing Technologies Group, where she served as lab director. Quantum computing refers to systems that use complex mechanical phenomena to store and manipulate data, thus avoiding the long strings of zeros and ones used by traditional computers.

After 13 years at JPL, Jackson left in 2005 to join the National Science Foundation (NSF), a federal agency that supports research in engineering and the sciences. As a program manager there, her primary role has been an administrative one. As of 2011, Jackson was focused primarily on the management of the NSF's Engineering Research Centers (ERCs), which were created, according to a note on her LinkedIn.com profile, "to invoke a cultural change in the way research is done." ERC researchers, she explained, first "define an engineering system they would like to build, but which can't be realized with current technology. The research at the Centers then focuses on understanding the fundamentals of the system well enough to figure out how to remove the barriers."

A sought-after speaker, Jackson has addressed colleagues at conferences around the world. She has also proven an enthusiastic mentor to those considering careers in science. "For me, what's fascinating about science is being at the cutting edge and not quite knowing the answer," she told Charles Choi in *Science* magazine in 2005. "It's about the challenge of the mystery."

Sources

Periodicals

Science, March 11, 2005.

Online

"Another ASI Fellow: Dr. Deborah Jackson, Ph.D.," African Scientific Institute, http://www.asi-org.net/ASI Fellows Info/Fellows Bio and Pic/Jackson_Deborah.htm (accessed August 19, 2011).

"Deborah Jackson," LinkedIn.com, http://www.linkedin.com/pub/deborah-jackson/4/529/327 (accessed August 19, 2011).

"Deborah J. Jackson," National Science Foundation, http://nsf.gov/staff/staff_bio.jsp?lan=djackson&org=NSF&from_org= (accessed August 19, 2011).

McCoy, Frank, "Top Black Women Techies: Deborah Jackson," TheRoot.com, March 23, 2011, http://www.theroot.com/multimedia/black-women-techies (accessed August 19, 2011).

"Physicists of the African Diaspora: Deborah Jackson," University of Buffalo, http://www.math.buffalo.edu/ mad/physics/jackson_deborah.html (accessed August 19, 2011).

Piazza, Enrico, "Mission Overview: Introduction," Jet Propulsion Laboratory, http://saturn.jpl.nasa.gov/ mission/introduction/ (accessed August 19, 2011).

—R. Anthony Kugler

Nikki M. James

1981–

Actor

Nikki M. James won the Tony Award for best featured actress in a musical in 2011 for her role in the smash Broadway hit *The Book of Mormon.* Coming just nine days after her 30th birthday, James's win was a fitting reward for what had been a near-lifetime of dedication to her craft. "The first time I performed for people was at my kindergarten graduation," she told Andrew Gans in *Playbill.* "I sang 'The Greatest Love of All' at my kindergarten graduation all by myself, all the way through."

James, Nikki M., photograph. AP Images/Jennifer Graylock.

James was born in 1981 in New Jersey to parents of Haitian and Vincentian origin. She grew up in Livingston and credited her parents with helping to make her Broadway dreams a reality. "I think that naive arrogance that I had as a 12-year-old is a testament to my parents always telling me that I was the best at everything I did," she said in an interview with Heather-Louise Ferris on the Daily Actor website. Another crucial ally was her best friend's aunt, who was a Broadway performer in such hits as *Sweeney Todd* and *Les Misérables.* James spent much of her elementary school years learning lyrics to Broadway musicals, making treks into the city to see shows, and appearing in productions at New Jersey's Paper Mill Playhouse.

In middle school, when James learned that a classmate had an agent and headshots and was auditioning for roles in New York, she told her parents, "'I think that I should be doing that,'" she recalled in the *Playbill* interview. They told her to research the matter further at the library, which she did, and then, "I basically did a presentation to my parents," she continued. "I said, 'This is how you do it. You get headshots. You do mailings, and you go on auditions, and the auditions for young actors are usually after school, and if Mommy's willing to take me in and out of the city to go on my auditions, I could probably do it.'" She used her babysitting earnings to pay for her first headshots, mailed them out, landed an agent, and started out doing television commercials. By the time she was a sophomore at Livingston High School she had earned her Actors' Equity union card and was appearing in small roles on daytime drama.

Performed in Broadway, Stratford Productions

James earned a drama degree from New York University's Tisch School of the Arts, although her semesters

At a Glance . . .

Born June 3, 1981, in Summit, NJ. *Education*: New York University, Tisch School of the Arts, BFA, 2003.

Career: Stage actor, 2001—; began career as a teen in television commercials and daytime dramas.

Memberships: Actors' Equity.

Awards: Tony Award for best featured actress in a musical, American Theatre Wing/Broadway League, and Drama Desk Award for outstanding featured actress in a musical, both 2011, both for *The Book of Mormon*.

Addresses: *Office*—Eugene O'Neill Theatre, 230 West 49th St., New York, NY 10038.

there were interrupted by what she assumed was going to be her big break: she made her Broadway debut in a much-hyped new musical, *The Adventures of Tom Sawyer*, which opened in the spring of 2001. "It was a flop, a big flop," she told Gans in the *Playbill* interview. "I thought I was going to be in this big Broadway show, and we closed two-and-a-half weeks after we opened."

In between shows James supported herself with guest appearances in television dramas set in New York City such as *The Jury* and *Law & Order*. Her next chance on Broadway came in the spring of 2005 when she appeared in *All Shook Up*, another misguided attempt to capitalize on theatergoers' apparently insatiable appetite for nostalgia. In this case the book was based on the songs of Elvis Presley, and although critics savaged it the musical managed to eke out a six-month run. A year later James appeared in *Bernarda Alba* at the Mitzi E. Newhouse Theater at Lincoln Center. This was a musical adaptation of Federico García Lorca's 1936 play *The House of Bernarda Alba* and co-starred Phylicia Rashad.

Later in 2006 James starred as Dorothy in a revival of *The Wiz* at the La Jolla Playhouse outside San Diego, California. That led to an offer from that venue's longtime director, Des McAnuff, to appear at the 2008 Stratford Festival in the Ontario town of the same name. McAnuff—a Broadway veteran responsible for *Jersey Boys* and scores of other blockbuster hits—had recently been brought in as Stratford's new director and cast her opposite British actor Gareth Potter in an interracial-dating update of Shakespeare's *Romeo and Juliet*. She also performed in George Bernard Shaw's *Caesar and Cleopatra* alongside the stage veteran Christopher Plummer. "By being generous to every actor with whom he shares the stage, Plummer displays true star quality, particularly in the performance he helps elicit from Nikki M. James as Cleopatra," wrote Richard Ouzounian in a *Variety* review of this Stratford production. The critic noted that James had earned some less-than-favorable reviews as Juliet, "but she's grown a lot as an actress since then and also seems far more comfortable as a Shavian minx than as a Shakespearean heroine."

Honored for Book of Mormon Role

James was involved in the preproduction creative path that took *The Book of Mormon* to Broadway success. Asked to join a group of actors for the workshop phase, she returned regularly over a two-year period to help bring the musical to its February 24, 2011, previews at the Eugene O'Neill Theatre and then a fanfare-heavy opening night one month later. Written by the creators of television's animated *South Park* series, Trey Parker and Matt Stone, the musical featured music by Robert Lopez, who won a pair of Tony Awards back in 2004, for original music and lyrics, for the puppet musical *Avenue Q*.

James was the sole female lead in *The Book of Mormon*, which recounts the story of two young men fulfilling their year-long missionary obligation as members of the Church of Jesus Christ of Latter-day Saints. They are sent to an AIDS-ravaged village in a part of Uganda already decimated by civil war. James played Nabalungi, "this dreamy girl who lives in this really difficult part of the world, and two Mormon boys sweep into town with their message of hope and salvation, and Nabalungi takes that a little literally," James recounted to Gans in the *Playbill* interview. The musical became the surprise hit of 2010–11 season and was nominated for a Tony Award in nearly every category available, including choreography and lighting. "*The Book of Mormon* achieves something like a miracle," declared theater critic Ben Brantley in the *New York Times*. "It both makes fun of and ardently embraces the all-American art form of the inspirational book musical." At the 2011 Tony Awards, *The Book of Mormon* was named best musical, and James walked away with the Tony for outstanding featured actress in a musical.

After her Tony thrill, James returned to the O'Neill Theatre, where *The Book of Mormon* continued to set ticket-sales records. Gans asked about her favorite part in the hit musical. It comes in the first act, she said in the *Playbill* interview. "I get to stand alone on the stage, and it's a really sweet moment, in the craziness that our show is. It's a really sweet, heartfelt, honest moment, and I get to do a down-center ballad—[it's] every five-year-old girl who sings 'The Greatest Love of All' at her kindergarten graduation's dream to get to do this."

Selected works

Theater

The Adventures of Tom Sawyer, 2001.
All Shook Up, 2005.
Bernarda Alba, 2006.
The Wiz, 2006.
Caesar and Cleopatra, 2008.
Romeo and Juliet, 2008.
The Book of Mormon, 2011—.

Sources

Periodicals

New York Times, August 27, 2008; March 24, 2011.
Variety, August 25, 2008, p. 90.

Online

Ferris, Heather-Louise, "*The Book of Mormon*'s Nikki M. James on Her Tony Nomination and 'Terrible' $75 Headshots," Daily Actor.com, May 26, 2011, http://www.dailyactor.com/2011/05/nikki-m-james-on-her-tony-nomination-and-bad-75-head shots/?utm_source=rss&utm_medium=rss&utm_campaign=nikki-m-james-on-her-tony-nomina tion-and-bad-75-headshots (accessed August 20, 2011).
Gans, Andrew, "Diva Talk: Chatting with *Book of Mormon*'s Nikki M. James," Playbill.com, February 25, 2011, http://www.playbill.com/celebritybuzz/article/148048-DIVA-TALK-Chatting-with-Book-of-Mormons-Nikki-M-James (accessed August 20, 2011).

—Carol Brennan

Joe Johnson

1981—

Professional basketball player

Johnson, Joe, photograph. Kevin C. Cox/Getty Images.

Joe Johnson, a National Basketball Association (NBA) All-Star and the Atlanta Hawks' leading scorer, is known for combining the size and strength of a forward with the shooting prowess and the ball-handling skills of a guard. After two years as a standout player at the University of Arkansas, Johnson signed with the Boston Celtics as the 10th player selected in the 2001 NBA draft. During his first professional season he was traded to the Phoenix Suns, and there he developed into a top-flight player, averaging more than 15 points per game in three-and-a-half seasons for what was at the time one of the best teams in the NBA. Upon becoming a free agent in 2005 Johnson inked a five-year, $70 million contract with the Atlanta Hawks. The deal was commensurate with those of the NBA's elite players, and many initially doubted whether Johnson belonged in such company. After his arrival in Atlanta, however, the Hawks went from being one of the worst franchises in the NBA to being consistent playoff contenders, and Johnson became a regular fixture on the NBA's Eastern Conference All-Star Team.

Dreamed of Playing for Arkansas

Joe Marcus Johnson was born on June 29, 1981, in Little Rock, Arkansas. The only child of a single mother, Diane Johnson, with whom he was very close, he began playing basketball in elementary school. He became a star player at Little Rock Central High School, averaging 18.6 points, 7.8 rebounds, 4.2 assists, and 1.8 steals per game in his senior season. Central High's only in-state loss of the season, to crosstown rivals North Little Rock, came when Johnson was sick. Central went on to demolish the same team, with Johnson healthy this time, in the state championship game. "That's a moment that I'll never forget," Johnson told Jeffrey Slatton in the *Arkansas Democrat-Gazette* years later, at a time when he was an established professional player. "Every time I go home I end up talking about [the championship game] in some kind of way."

Throughout his childhood Johnson dreamed of playing for the University of Arkansas, so he passed up offers

At a Glance . . .

Born Joe Marcus Johnson, on June 29, 1981, in Little Rock, AR; son of Diane Johnson. *Education*: Attended University of Arkansas, 1999–2001.

Career: University of Arkansas, basketball player, 1999–2001; Boston Celtics, basketball player, 2001–02; Phoenix Suns, basketball player, 2002–05; Atlanta Hawks, basketball player, 2005—.

Awards: Newcomer of the Year, Southeastern Conference (SEC), 2000; All-SEC second team, SEC, 2000, 2001; All-Rookie second team, National Basketball Association (NBA), 2002; All-Star, NBA, 2007–11.

Addresses: *Office*—Atlanta Hawks,101 Marietta St. NW, Ste. 1900, Atlanta, GA 30303.

from numerous prominent college programs to sign with the Razorbacks and their long-time coach Nolan Richardson. The beginning of his college career was delayed when he struggled to meet academic eligibility requirements. He attended classes part-time during the fall semester while he worked to become eligible, missing crucial fall practices as well as the first 10 games of the season. Upon meeting his academic requirements and joining the team for the spring semester, Johnson delivered on the promise he had shown as a recruit. He averaged 16 points per game, leading Arkansas to a 2000 Southeastern Conference (SEC) Tournament Championship and a berth in the National Collegiate Athletic Association (NCAA) Tournament. He was voted SEC Newcomer of the Year and was named an All-SEC second-team pick.

From the beginning of his college career Johnson, who stood 6'7" but had the outside shot and the ball-handling skills of a guard, stood out for his versatility. As Richardson told Bob Holt in the *Arkansas Democrat-Gazette*, "Joe can beat you by hitting a tough shot, getting a big rebound, making a great pass, getting a steal when you really need it. He can go to the basket and get to the line and hit free throws. He can hit a three." Johnson had the rare ability to play three positions—point guard, shooting guard, or small forward—and to take advantage of any defensive mismatches occasioned by the absence of a comparably versatile player on the opposing team. If a guard was defending Johnson, for instance, he could post up and play like a forward, taking advantage of his size. If a forward was guarding him, he could take advantage of his speed, his outside shot, and his ball-handling skills.

As a result of his formidable array of talents and his strong performance as a freshman, Johnson won 24 of

28 votes for preseason SEC Player of the Year in the lead-up to his sophomore season. During the summer, however, while practicing with the USA Basketball World Championship for Young Men Qualifying Team, he dislocated a tendon in his left ankle and had to undergo surgery. He was able to join the Razorbacks for a portion of their fall practice schedule, and his ankle was close to being fully healed by the time the season started in November, but Richardson later indicated that Johnson did not in fact play at full strength during the 2000–01 season. His performance therefore did not match preseason expectations, but he remained Arkansas's leading player, averaging 14.2 points and 6.6 rebounds per game and again being named to the All-SEC second team. Once again the Razorbacks made it to the NCAA Tournament, but they lost to Georgetown in the first round.

Flourished with the Phoenix Suns

The summer after his sophomore season, with NBA scouts agreeing that Johnson would be a first-round draft pick, he declared his intention to leave Arkansas and begin a professional career. On June 27, 2001, the Boston Celtics indeed chose Johnson in the first round of the draft. The 10th pick overall, Johnson signed a three-year, $4.25 million contract. In his rookie season Johnson played in 48 games for the Celtics, averaging 6.9 points and 2.9 rebounds per game, and he was successfully making the adjustment to the professional game and his new hometown of Boston, when the Celtics abruptly traded him to the Phoenix Suns. Although he showed signs of being dismayed by the trade, his play was solid. In 29 games with the Suns he averaged 9.6 points and 4.1 rebounds per game.

The following year Johnson played in all 82 regular-season games. He averaged almost 10 points per game, made his first appearance in the playoffs, and emerged as one of the most accurate three-point shooters in the NBA. In his third pro season Johnson became a starter for the Suns, and he stepped into his new role with authority, scoring 16.7 points and pulling down 4.7 rebounds per game. The 2004–05 season saw Johnson improve his game even further, averaging 17.1 points and 5.1 rebounds per game and helping the Suns to the best regular-season record in the NBA and a playoff berth. Although the Suns had other stars, including Amar'e Stoudemire and Steve Nash, Johnson was central to their success. His three-point shooting and his tenacious defensive play were particularly valuable to the team.

Johnson was at the peak of his game during the 2005 postseason when, in game two of the Western Conference semifinals against the Dallas Mavericks, he suffered a mild concussion and fractured a bone above his left eye after being fouled and landing face-down on the court. He underwent reconstructive surgery the next

day and returned to the court just over two weeks later, wearing a protective mask, to help the Suns bounce back from their 2-0 deficit in the Western Conference finals against the San Antonio Spurs. In spite of his valiant play, the Suns lost the series 3-1.

Became Atlanta's Marquee Player

During the 2005 off-season Johnson's contract came up for renegotiation, and he was reportedly disappointed in the offer the Suns made him. Despite the team's viable shot at an NBA Championship, he opted to sign with the Atlanta Hawks, one of the NBA's worst teams, for a sum of $70 million over five years. He was widely perceived as having left for selfish reasons, including greed and the desire to be a star on a losing team rather than a role player on a championship team, and many believed that the Hawks had overpaid for him.

Over the next several seasons, however, Johnson began to silence his critics. Stepping into the role of leading scorer, he began to demonstrate an ability to deliver superstar-level statistics, even as he began to be consistently double-teamed by opposing defenders. He averaged 20.2 points per game in 2005–06, 25 points per game in 2006–07, and 21.7 points per game in 2007–08. In 2006, moreover, he was chosen to play on the U.S. national team at the World Championships in Japan.

After winning only 17 games the season prior to his arrival, Atlanta constantly improved, winning 26 games in Johnson's first season with the team and 30 in his second season, before posting 37 wins and the franchise's first playoff appearance since 1999 in 2007–08. Moreover, the Hawks surprised fans and sportswriters by giving their first-round opponents the Boston Celtics a serious challenge, forcing the series to the full seven games before being eliminated.

Johnson got his first All-Star nod in 2007, when commissioner David Stern selected him as a replacement for an injured Jason Kidd, and he became a returning All-Star in the years that followed, making the team again in 2008, 2009, 2010, and 2011. While his scoring statistics remained strong—varying from 18.2 to 21.7 points per game between 2007 and 2011—he was also a team leader, and as defenders regularly doubled up to prevent him from scoring, he

responded by passing to teammates rather than forcing shots. The Hawks established themselves not only as consistent candidates for postseason play, but as contenders for an NBA title. The team advanced beyond the first round of the playoffs in 2009, 2010, and 2011. Johnson, meanwhile, was by this time reaching what promised to be his peak playing years.

Sources

Periodicals

Arkansas Democrat-Gazette, November 19, 2000, p. K8; April 27, 2001, p. C1; July 11, 2001, p. C1; December 20, 2003.
Atlanta Journal-Constitution, August 20, 2005, p. 9E; February 15, 2007, p. 1C; May 11, 2008, p. 3E.
Sporting News, December 22, 2008, p. 52; February 14, 2011, p. 8.
Sports Illustrated, June 6, 2005, p. 52; August 15, 2005, p. 20; October 24, 2005, p. 112; January 29, 2007, p. 26; January 12, 2009, p. 69.

Online

Associated Press, "Johnson Lands Hard after Foul by Stackhouse," ESPN, May 12, 2005, http://sports.espn.go.com/nba/playoffs2005/news/story?id=2058372 (accessed August 20, 2011).
"Joe Johnson Info Page," NBA.com, http://www.nba.com/home/playerfile/joe_johnson/index.html (accessed August 20, 2011).
"Joe Johnson Stats, News, Videos, Highlights, Pictures, Bio," ESPN, http://espn.go.com/nba/player/_/id/1007/joe-johnson (accessed August 20, 2011).
Mannix, Chris, "Masked Man: Sun's Playoff Hopes Riding on Johnson's Return," SI.com, May 28, 2005, http://sportsillustrated.cnn.com/2005/writers/chris_mannix/05/28/suns.spurs/index.html (accessed August 20, 2011).
Smith, Sekou, "Superstar?", *Atlanta Journal-Constitution* Hawks Blog, December 28, 2008, http://www.ajc.com/blogs/content/shared-blogs/ajc/hawks/entries/2008/12/28/superstar.html (accessed August 20, 2011).

—Mark Lane

Sandra K. Johnson

1960(?)—

Engineer, business executive, author

The first African-American woman to earn a Ph.D. in electrical engineering in the United States, Sandra K. Johnson has been at the forefront of technological innovation for more than 20 years. A native of Louisiana, she has spent much of her career with IBM, for whom she has earned a number of patents. Elected in 2002 to the IBM Academy of Technology, an honor reserved for "outstanding technical accomplishments, leadership and contributions to the business," she has also built a successful career as an author, editor, and motivational speaker.

Sandra Kay Johnson was born about 1960 in Lake Charles, a small city in Louisiana's southwestern corner. Her interest in engineering developed in high school, when she attended an academic institute at Southern University and A&M College, a historically black institution in Baton Rouge, the state capital. She returned to Southern after high school, earning a bachelor's degree in electrical engineering in 1982. Two years later she earned a master's degree in the same field at Stanford University in California. She then headed to Houston's Rice University, where she earned a doctorate in 1988.

Johnson's dissertation at Rice focused on ways to improve the performance of computers through the use of the multi-step commands known as algorithms. Her growing expertise in that field quickly drew the attention of IBM, one of the oldest and largest technology companies in the world. She moved steadily up the corporate ladder there, holding an array of posts. These included technical-staff member, chief technol-ogy officer for global small and medium business in the company's Systems and Technology Group, and Linux performance architect. Linux is a programming language that has powered a growing proportion of desktops, laptops, and other consumer hardware since its development in the early 1990s. It is best known, however, for its use in supercomputers, traditionally one of IBM's strengths and arguably Johnson's greatest area of expertise. During the early 1990s, she was part of the design team that built the processor for a unique machine called Deep Blue, which received worldwide attention when it beat champion Garry Kasparov in a six-game chess match (1997). Although Linux was not used for Deep Blue, the programming problems introduced by the machine proved valuable experience for Johnson and others in their implementation of the new language.

As she moved from post to post within IBM, Johnson managed to combine steadily growing administrative responsibilities with a continued dedication to the thorniest technical problems. As of 2011, she had been granted well over a dozen U.S. patents, an achievement that won her designation as a Research Division Master Inventor within IBM. It was neverthe-less clear by that point that the company was turning to her more and more for help outside the lab. An accomplished public speaker, she served also as a business-development executive for IBM's Middle East and Africa division. Based in Dubai on the Persian Gulf, the position required considerable sensitivity to cultural differences and a thorough understanding of the social,

At a Glance . . .

Born Sandra Kay Johnson in 1960(?) in Lake Charles, LA. *Education*: Southern University and A&M College, BS, electrical engineering, 1982; Stanford University, MS, electrical engineering, 1984; Rice University, PhD, electrical engineering, 1988.

Career: IBM, began as technical-staff member, advanced to positions including chief technology officer for global small and medium business, Linux performance architect, senior technical-staff member, and business development executive for the Middle East and Africa; editor and author, 2005—.

Memberships: Association for Computing Machinery, Institute of Electrical and Electronics Engineers, National Society of Black Engineers, Society of Women Engineers.

Awards: Golden Torch Award for Lifetime Achievement in Industry, National Society of Black Engineers, 2000.

Addresses: *Office*—c/o Ma and Pa Productions, 3036 Golden Hind Rd., Chesapeake, VA 23321. *Web*—http://www.SandraKJohnson.com.

political, and historical factors at work in that troubled but fast-growing region.

Amid her duties at IBM, Johnson also gained notice for her work as an author and editor. Her best-known book, co-edited with Gerrit Huizenga and Badari Pulavarty, was *Performance Tuning for Linux Servers*, an important text for schools and data centers around the world. Originally published by IBM Press in 2005, it came within weeks of a more personal volume, *Inspirational Nuggets* (2005), described on her website as "a collection of words of wisdom designed to encourage and inspire people to reach their ultimate potential." Another personal work, *Gregory: The Story of a Lupus Warrior* (2008), was cowritten with her brother Gregory Garland Johnson. It tells the story of his long battle with that chronic and often debilitating disease. He eventually died of the ailment, and Johnson herself was diagnosed with a less virulent form several months later.

As she has often mentioned in her writing, Johnson has had an abiding interest in mentoring since the start of her own career. Many of her efforts in this area have involved inspirational lectures at corporate conferences and community events. At the same time, however, she has shown a particular interest in assisting engineering students at her alma mater, Southern, and other historically black colleges and universities (HBCUs). In 1998, for example, she joined the advisory board to the School of Engineering at Morgan State University, an HBCU in Baltimore, Maryland. She has also met regularly with a group of 11- to 14-year-old girls. "The advice I give them is simple," she noted in comments quoted by Southern in an undated viewbook for prospective students. "Use your minds to the utmost, work hard, and follow your dreams. Don't let anyone tell you you're not good at something [and] find a good support mechanism to help you traverse life's maze."

Sources

Online

"Sandra K. Johnson, Ph.D.," HBCUConnect.com, October 13, 2005, http://hbcuconnect.com/content/22506/sandra-k-johnson-ph-d (accessed August 23, 2011).

"Sandra K. Johnson, Ph.D.," SandraKJohnson.com, http://www.sandrakjohnson.com/dr-johnsons-bio.html (accessed August 23, 2011).

"Sandra K. Johnson, Ph.D.," Southern University and A&M College: Your Formula for Success [viewbook], http://www.subr.edu/supublications/pdfs/ViewbookPart2.pdf (accessed August 23, 2011).

Taft, Darryl K., "IBM and Black History: Innovation Through Diversity," EWeek.com, February 18, 2011, http://mobile.eweek.com/c/a/IT-Management/IBM-and-Black-History-Innovation-Through-Diversity-516090/ (accessed August 23, 2011).

—R. Anthony Kugler

Bobby Jones

1938—

Gospel singer, television host

Jones, Bobby, photograph. Kris Connor/Getty Images.

Bobby Jones is the host of *Bobby Jones Gospel*, the most influential gospel-music television show in history and the longest-running program on cable in the United States. Jones's show, which features live performances by both established and emerging gospel artists along with interview clips and other church-oriented commentary, has aired continuously on Black Entertainment Television (BET) since 1980. It has remained one of the network's highest-rated shows throughout its run, during which time it has consistently served as a career-making venue for gospel artists. Jones has also made a mark as a gospel artist in his own right, winning a Grammy Award as well as numerous awards within the world of gospel music. In 2009 he was inducted into the Gospel Music Association's (GMA) Gospel Music Hall of Fame.

Jones, born in Henry, Tennessee, grew up the impoverished son of sharecroppers. His father was illiterate, and his mother had only an eighth-grade education. Jones's own educational opportunities were limited by the norms of the segregated school systems of the time; his elementary school, for example, only met when farm labor was not in demand. Nevertheless,

Jones demonstrated an early aptitude for reading and mathematics and was promoted beyond his years in school, skipping numerous grades. He entered Tennessee State University in Nashville at the age of 15 and paid his own way by playing piano at a church. He completed a bachelor's degree as well as a master's degree in education at Tennessee State.

Jones worked for many years in education before his gospel career took flight. He taught elementary school in St. Louis, Missouri, and Nashville, Tennessee, and then for eight years he worked as a traveling textbook consultant for McGraw-Hill Publishers, specializing in elementary education. He later took a doctorate in education from Vanderbilt University and taught reading at his alma mater Tennessee State.

While teaching at Tennessee State in the 1970s, Jones began a second career as a singer on the gospel circuit, and he was active in Nashville civil-rights circles and in his Baptist church. Seeing an opportunity to merge the drive for African-American economic independence with an already-established sense of community among Nashville's black churches, Jones helped create the

At a Glance . . .

Born on September 18, 1938, in Henry, TN; son of Jim (a sharecropper) and Augusta (a sharecropper) Jones. *Education*: Tennessee State University, BS; Tennessee State University, MS; Vanderbilt University, PhD. *Religion*: Baptist.

Career: Teacher in St. Louis (MO) Public Schools, 1959–65 and in Nashville (TN) Metropolitan Schools, 1966–68(?); McGraw-Hill Publishers, National Reading Textbook Consultant, 1968(?)–74; Tennessee State University, instructor, 1974–86; Black Entertainment Television (BET) Network, *Bobby Jones Gospel*, host and executive producer, 1980—; BET Network, *Video Gospel*, host and producer, 1989—; The Word Network, *Bobby Jones Presents*, host and producer, 2001—; Gospel Music Channel, *Bobby Jones Next Generation*, co-host, 2008—; The Sheridan Gospel Network (radio), *Bobby Jones Gospel Countdown*, host.

Memberships: 100 Black Men of America, American Diabetes Association, American Heart Association, National Association for the Advancement of Colored People (NAACP), National Black College Alumni Hall of Fame (board of directors), Phi Beta Sigma Fraternity, Tennessee State University Alumni Association.

Awards: Grammy Award, National Academy of Recording Arts and Sciences, 1983, for "I'm So Glad I'm Standing Here Today"; Dove Award, Gospel Music Association, 1984, for *Come Together*; Stellar Award, Central City Productions, 1996, 1998, 2005; Inductee, GMA Gospel Music Hall of Fame, 2009.

Addresses: *Office*—Black Entertainment Television,1 BET Plaza, 1235 W St. NE, Washington, DC 20018. *Web*—http://www.bet.com/shows/bobby-jones-gospel; and http://www.bobbyjonesgospel.com/.

city's first Black Expo, an event combining workshops with concerts and other attractions, in 1976.

The Black Expo attracted the attention of local media executives, and Jones was asked by a local Nashville television station to produce the pilot for a 30-minute gospel show. The show was picked up and became a local hit, running through the end of the decade, when Robert Johnson, founder of the fledgling BET, decided to acquire it for his new cable network. *Bobby Jones*

Gospel, as the show came to be called, first aired on BET in 1980. It was one of the first shows on the network and an anchor of the programming line-up. As BET matured and was able to offer a wider array of programming, *Bobby Jones Gospel* remained one of the cable outlet's most popular shows.

For many years *Bobby Jones Gospel* was the only gospel show broadcast nationally, and it became a crucial venue for artists looking to market their music. Marilyn Batchelor, an executive with MCA Records, told the *New York Times* that "Bobby Jones has done for gospel what Don Cornelius and 'Soul Train' did for R&B. He embraces new acts, he gives them their first shot, and until more outlets take form, he's practically the only game in town." Jones has been credited with being instrumental in the rise in popularity that gospel as a genre enjoyed during the 1980s and 1990s. Among the many artists he has introduced to national television audiences in his more than 30 years on the air are Vanessa Bell Armstrong, Shirley Caesar, Ricky Dillard, Kirk Franklin, Fred Hammond, John P. Kee, Donald Lawrence, Mary Mary, Dorothy Norwood, Dottie Peoples, Albertina Walker, and the Williams Brothers. Dillard told the *Washington Post*, on the occasion of the show's 30th anniversary, that Jones served as a "liaison for our music to the world. We weren't professionals when we began…. Dr. Jones is the main reason gospel is still standing and in the eyes of the world today."

Jones extended his broadcasting reach in 1989, when he launched the BET show *Video Gospel*, which offered the first national outlet for gospel-music videos. In 2001 he began hosting and producing another TV show, the Word Network's *Bobby Jones Presents*, and 2008 saw the debut of yet another TV offering, the Gospel Music Channel's *Bobby Jones Next Generation*. Jones also hosted a radio show, *Bobby Jones Gospel Countdown*, that reached approximately 150 markets across the United States.

In addition to being a host, producer, and promoter of gospel music, Jones remained a performer and recording artist in his own right. With his group New Life he was nominated for a Grammy Award in 1982. He won a Grammy in 1983 for the single "I'm So Glad I'm Standing Here Today," a duet with the country music singer Barbara Mandrell; and the album on which the Mandrell duet appeared, *Come Together*, won a GMA Dove Award in 1984. Jones's other albums include *I'll Never Forget* (1989), *Another Time* (1990), *Bring It to Jesus* (1995), *Just Churchin'* (1998), *Faith Unscripted* (2007), and *The Ambassador* (2007).

Jones likewise performed on each week's installment of *Bobby Jones Gospel*, and he undertook numerous international tours. He sang at the White House for

President Jimmy Carter; he performed for President Ronald Reagan at the Kennedy Center for the Performing Arts; and President George W. Bush honored him, along with four other internationally renowned recording artists, as part of Black Music Month in 2001.

Among his many other side projects over the years, Jones conducted seminars, guest lectures, and gospel-music conferences. He also coauthored two books related to his career in gospel music, 1998's *Touched by God*, a compilation of the religious testimonies of prominent gospel singers, and 2000's *Make a Joyful Noise*, a memoir of his years in the gospel-music world. As of 2011, Jones divided his time between Fort Lauderdale, Florida, and his longtime home base in Nashville.

Sources

Periodicals

Billboard, March 29, 1997, p. 17; August 13, 2005; November 24, 2007.
Chicago Tribune, November 7, 1985, p. 13D.
Nation's Business, February 1995, p. 13.
New York Times, August 19, 2001.
Washington Post, July 7, 1995, p. N13; July 17, 1995, p. D1; October 3, 2010.

Online

Bobby Jones Gospel, June 14, 2011, http://www.bobbyjonesgospel.com/ (accessed August 24, 2011).

—Carol Brennan and Mark Lane

Herb Kemp

1941–2011

Advertising executive, author

Although his name was never widely known among American consumers, advertiser Herb Kemp had a major role in shaping their behavior. A powerful advocate for diversity in advertising for more than 40 years, he persuaded an array of powerful corporate clients that African Americans were consumers they needed to reach. "Black folk are not just dark-skinned white people," he once noted, in a comment quoted on WhatsBlackAboutIt.com, a website he established in later life. "Marketers who consciously establish a relationship with this lucrative yet underserved market, by better understanding the African-American culture, mindset, attitude, behavior and lifestyle, will reap significant long-term rewards from a loyal, influential, increasingly affluent customer base."

Herbert Kemp Jr. was born on June 24, 1941, in Edgefield, South Carolina, a small community best known as the childhood home of U.S. Senator—and onetime segregationist—Strom Thurmond. Soon after Kemp's birth, his family joined a wave of African-American migration northward. Lured by the promise of better jobs and less onerous discrimination, hundreds of thousands of African-American workers and their families abandoned the rural South for industrial cities across the North. The Kemps chose Buffalo, New York, and it was among that city's steel mills and auto plants that Herb spent much of his childhood. Upon graduation from Hutchinson-Technical High School, he entered Maryland's Morgan State College (now University), a historically black institution, on a basketball scholarship. A business major, he drew the attention of Dartmouth College's Tuck School of Business,

which recruited him as part of its first major effort to increase minority enrollment. In 1966 he became the first African- American in the school's history to earn an MBA. That achievement was honored 40 years later, when the school presented him with its Trailblazer Award.

Even before the completion of his education, Kemp was known for his skill in assessing the qualities that set African-American culture apart from the white mainstream. An informal adviser to Tuck administrators in their efforts to increase racial and economic diversity on campus, he also served as a mentor to the African-American students who followed him. One of them, Mel Fallis, later described Kemp's influence to Tuck's Kirk Kardashian. "He was a good man," Fallis recalled. "I felt that he and I had similar backgrounds, having gone to similar schools, and similar cultural experiences. And then being thrust into an all-white Ivy League situation; I could empathize with him a lot. He talked about the nuances, and that was very valuable to me." Administrator John Hennessey concurred, telling Kardashian, "Herb from the start was an attractive personality. He was energetic, imaginative, and he persevered in a very difficult program."

Following his departure from Tuck, Kemp began working for a succession of consumer-products companies as a brand manager, a role that brought him into regular contact with advertising executives. After several years as a manager for Colgate-Palmolive, Pfizer, General Foods, and Chesebrough-Ponds, he moved into advertising himself. As an executive with J. Walter

At a Glance . . .

Born Herbert Kemp Jr. on June 24, 1941, in Edge-field, SC; died on March 5, 2011, in Charleston, SC; married Dolores Cruse; children: Herbert Kemp III, Courtney Kemp Agboh. *Education*: Morgan State College, BA, business administration, 1964(?); Dartmouth College, MBA, 1966.

Career: Colgate-Palmolive, Pfizer, General Foods, and Chesebrough-Ponds, brand manager, beginning mid-1960s; J. Walter Thomson, senior executive, 1970s; Ogilvy & Mather, senior vice president, 1970s–83; Uni-World Group, president, 1983–94; Chisholm Mingo Group, executive vice president, 1994–2005; What's Black About It? LLC, founder and CEO, 2005(?)–11; author, 2005–11.

Awards: Trailblazer Award, Tuck School of Business (Dartmouth College), 2006.

Thompson and Ogilvy & Mather, two of the industry's largest and most prominent firms, he gained additional experience, overseeing campaigns for a wide variety of products in addition to the consumer staples with which he had begun his career. Then, in 1983, he moved on to become president of UniWorld Group, arguably the most prominent of the nation's minority-owned advertising agencies. His first major initiative there was a campaign for Burger King. Its success in drawing African-American consumers quickly prompted similar campaigns by other major corporations. His own client list, meanwhile, continued to grow, eventually including such names as AT&T, General Motors, Kodak, and Texaco. In keeping with the variety of products he advertised, Kemp used a wide range of merchandising techniques. He was particularly reliant, however, on irony and humor, often noting the importance of these in African-American culture. As colleague Carol H. Williams told Frank McCoy of TheRoot.com, Kemp believed strongly that "every day in the African-American experience is a journey and an irony in and of itself."

Kemp remained at UniWorld until 1994, when he left to become executive vice president at another minority-owned agency, the Chisholm Mingo Group (CMG). He worked there for over a decade, a period in which he focused increasingly on the Web and other emerging media. Because of a perception that minorities were not embracing the Internet as enthusiastically as whites, many corporations were slow to develop ads aimed specifically at African-American Web users. Convinced that such an approach was based on mis-

taken assumptions, Kemp noted to his clients and to fellow advertisers that various aspects of online interaction were, in fact, critically important to African Americans around the nation. He pointed, in particular, to chat rooms and networking sites, characterizing them as increasingly equivalent to beauty salons and barbershops, both of which have served African-American communities for decades as informal meeting places and culture centers.

After 11 years at CMG, Kemp left in 2005 to start his own consulting firm, What's Black About It? LLC. The venture was established, according to its website, to help companies construct "an effective marketing program targeting the new diverse America." That aim also prompted a book, *What's Black About It? Insights to Increase Your Share of a Changing African-American Market* (2005). Cowritten with colleague Pepper Miller, it earned high praise from airline administrator William J. Mitchell, who called it, in a brief review written for the book's jacket, "a must-read for every marketing executive."

On March 5, 2011, Kemp died unexpectedly of a heart attack at his home in Charleston, South Carolina. He was 69 years old. According to McCoy on TheRoot.com, Kemp's passing "stunned" advertisers across the nation. Survived by his wife, Dolores Cruse Kemp, and two children, he was eulogized for his tireless efforts to bring African-American consumers to the attention of the nation's leading corporations. "His goal," colleague Samuel J. Chisholm told McCoy, "was to always provide the right voice for African Americans, one that was very respectful of both the people in the ads and the clients."

Sources

Books

(With Pepper Miller) *What's Black About It? Insights to Increase Your Share of a Changing African-American Market*, Paramount Market, 2005.

Online

"Credentials," WhatsBlackAboutIt.com, http://www.whatsblackaboutit.com/credentials.html (accessed August 24, 2011).
"Herbert Kemp Jr., Pioneering Advertising Executive," BuffaloNews.com, March 14, 2011, http://www.buffalonews.com/city/communities/buffalo/article366505.ece (accessed August 24, 2011).
"Herb Kemp, Veteran Advertising and Marketing Executive, Dies at 69," Target Market News, March 8, 2011, http://www.targetmarketnews.com/storyid03081102.htm (accessed August 24, 2011).
Kardashian, Kirk, "Herbert Kemp, Jr. T'66," Tuck School of Business, March 16, 2011, http://www.tuck.dartmouth.edu/news/articles/herbert-kemp-jr-t66/ (accessed August 24, 2011).

McCoy, Frank, "Remembering Black Advertising Pioneer Herb Kemp," TheRoot.com, March 12, 2011, http://www.theroot.com/print/50765 (accessed August 24, 2011).

—R. Anthony Kugler

Sean Kingston

1990—

Vocalist, songwriter

Kingston, Sean, photograph. ChinaFotoPress/Getty Images.

Vocalist and songwriter Sean Kingston burst onto the music scene in 2007 with a number-one hit, "Beautiful Girls." Subsequent singles and several full-length albums have also done well. A teenager at the time of his debut, he is known for mixing the rhythms of reggae and hip-hop with classic soul and doo-wop. Nominated for a 2008 NAACP Image Award as the year's best new artist, he has also drawn attention for his refusal to use off-color language in his lyrics, a relatively unusual stance in the world of pop and hip-hop. "I write my own songs," he explained on his website (SeanKingston.com), "so it's like if I can write a great track without using those words, then that's the style for me."

Born Kisean Anderson on February 3, 1990, in Miami, Florida, Kingston spent much of his childhood in Jamaica, the birthplace of his parents. In a sign of the pride he felt in his heritage, he adopted the name of the Jamaican capital as his surname when he became a performer. Devoted to music from an early age, he drew inspiration from his grandfather, a reggae producer who had worked with Bob Marley, Burning Spear, and other giants of the genre. His home life, however, was difficult. Arrested at the age of 11 for

breaking and entering, he served several weeks in a boot camp for youthful offenders. His family, meanwhile, had legal troubles of its own. Roughly four years after his own incarceration, his mother and sister received brief prison terms, a punishment that affected him deeply. Deprived of parental support, he was driven for a time into homelessness. In a 2008 interview with Pete Lewis published on BluesAndSoul.com, he was forthright about the difficulties he had faced. "While most people around 14/15 have their mom around them, go to school and live a normal life," he reflected, "I was homeless doing lawnmower services—cutting grass and doing whatever I had to do to get money."

By the time Kingston's home life had stabilized, he was determined to make a career in music. Using a friend's computer, he set up an account on MySpace.com, a social-networking site favored by musicians. By combining his own lyrics with beats and melodies he found online, he put together a number of songs, which he recorded and posted on his MySpace page. He then began to contact music executives, urging them to visit his page and listen to his work. Although many never responded, Kingston persisted, particularly in the case

At a Glance . . .

Born Kisean Anderson on February 3, 1990, in Miami, FL; son of Janice Turner (a mortgage broker and music manager).

Career: Songwriter and recording artist, 2007—.

Addresses: *Record company*—c/o Beluga Heights, 845 Highland Ave., Los Angeles, CA 90038. *Web*—http://www.SeanKingston.com.

of J. R. Rotem, a producer known internationally for his work with such stars as Rihanna and Britney Spears. After receiving multiple messages a day for weeks, Rotem relented and visited Kingston's site. Pleased with what he heard there, he invited the young singer to Los Angeles for an audition. Out of that meeting came a contract with Rotem's Beluga Heights label and a distribution deal with Epic Records.

An intense grooming period followed. "Sean Kingston was a rapper when we found him," Rotem recalled in a 2010 interview with Bill Code on HitQuarters.com, "and it was a development process to get him more melodic." Part of that process involved choosing samples of older hits, a technique that allows artists to construct their own work around familiar melodies. After an initial single, "Colors (2007)," Kingston began work on "Beautiful Girls," using samples from "Stand by Me," Ben E. King's 1961 soul hit. Recorded and released in the spring of 2007, "Beautiful Girls" moved rapidly up the charts, eventually hitting number one on *Billboard* magazine's influential Hot 100 list. Two follow-ups, "Me Love" and "Take You There," also did well, reaching the top 10. In the wake of that success, Kingston and Rotem began immediately to prepare a full-length, self-titled debut. Featuring 13 songs in all, including all four of the singles listed above, *Sean Kingston* sold more than half a million copies in the weeks following its release in the summer of 2007. It was also during this period that Kingston began performing on concert stages across the country, most notably as an opening act for pop stars Gwen Stefani and Beyoncé.

Eager to capitalize on the publicity generated by the success of his debut, Kingston quickly returned to the studio to record a second album. Released in the fall of 2009, *Tomorrow* spawned several hits, including "Face Drop" and "Fire Burning." None of these resonated with the public as deeply as "Beautiful Girls," and the album as a whole reached no higher than number 37 on *Billboard*'s list of the nation's most popular records. At the same time, however, Kingston found himself in increasing demand as a songwriter and guest artist. His work in this area included, as of July of 2011, an appearance on a 2010 single ("For My Hood") by rapper Bow Wow and a songwriting credit, shared with three others, for "Whatcha Say" (2009), a number-one hit for Jason Derülo, another Beluga Heights artist.

Kingston's rise to fame was not without occasional controversy. In 2007, for example, he was criticized for using, in "Beautiful Girls," the word "suicidal." Many felt the term was inappropriate, given the song's lighthearted mood and Kingston's popularity among preteens and teenagers; others felt it contradicted his pledge to avoid offensive language. Although a number of radio stations censored the song or refused to play it altogether, the controversy seemed to have little effect on its popularity. Kingston, for his part, was quick to clarify his intentions, explaining that he meant the term to be metaphorical only.

In May of 2011 Kingston made news around the world when he suffered serious injury in a boating accident. While riding down a Miami Beach waterway on a jet ski, he collided with a bridge at high speed. Rescued by onlookers, he suffered a broken jaw, a broken wrist, and water in his lungs. Placed initially in intensive care, he was later released with expectations for a full recovery.

Sources

Online

"Bio," SeanKingston.com, http://www.myspace.com/seankingston (accessed August 24, 2011).

Code, Bill, "Jonathan 'JR' Rotem [interview]," Hit Quarters.com, April 5, 2010, http://www.hitquarters.com/index.php3?page=intrview/opar/intrview_JR_Rotem_Interview.html (accessed August 24, 2011).

Duke, Alan, "Sean Kingston Expected to Fully Recover, Sources Say," CNN, May 31, 2011, http://articles.cnn.com/2011-05-31/entertainment/ent.sean.kingston.crash_1_kisean-anderson-jet-ski-sean-ingston?_s=PM:SHOWBIZ (accessed August 24, 2011).

Jeffries, David, "Sean Kingston: Biography," AllMusic.com, http://allmusic.com/artist/sean-kingston-p903682/biography (accessed August 24, 2011).

Lewis, Pete, "A Beauuutiful Interview with Sean Kingston," BluesAndSoul.com, February 14, 2008, http://www.bluesandsoul.com/feature/242/a_beauuutiful_interview_with_sean_kingst.../ (accessed August 24, 2011).

—R. Anthony Kugler

Don Lemon

1966—

Television news anchor and reporter

Lemon, Don, photograph. Dario Cantatore/Getty Images.

A familiar figure to millions of television viewers, the award-winning news anchor Don Lemon has been on the front-lines of journalism since the late 1980s. A native of Louisiana, he has covered a number of historic events, including the explosion of the Space Shuttle *Columbia* in 2003 and the inauguration of U.S. President Barack Obama six years later. He is arguably best known, however, for the courage with which he has revealed the details of his personal life. Those revelations began in 2010, when, in a famous broadcast on CNN, he told viewers that he had been molested as a child. One of the first news anchors to "come out" as a gay man, he has also been forthright about his sexuality.

Lemon was born on March 1, 1966, in Louisiana's capital of Baton Rouge. He and his two older sisters were raised by their mother, who worked as a legal secretary, and their grandmother in the industrial suburb of Port Allen. "When I think of Port Allen," he wrote in *Transparent*, his 2011 autobiography, "the smells of summer seem to fill my nostrils. Summer is heat—the kind that bakes the grass so that it almost smells like something fresh out of Mother Nature's oven. Summer is sugar. There was a sugar cane syrup plant near my home, and the odor of burnt sugar covered everything. My memories of Port Allen are tinged with that smell."

After high school, Lemon studied at Louisiana State University before transferring to New York City's Brooklyn College, where he majored in broadcast journalism. His career in that field began even before the receipt of his bachelor's degree. As an assistant at New York's WNYW in the mid-1980s, he gained practical experience behind the scenes of a busy newsroom. That post confirmed his desire to become an anchor, a desire he had maintained since childhood. His first opportunity to serve in that capacity came shortly after college, when he landed a job with WBRC in Birmingham, Alabama. In the years that followed, his career traced a trajectory common in the broadcast industry, which has long emphasized larger markets over smaller ones. Because of that emphasis, young and ambitious anchors typically remain at a station only a few years before looking for a job in a larger city. Lemon was repeatedly successful in that effort, moving from Birmingham to St. Louis to Philadelphia to New York. It was the last of these posts that established his national reputation.

At a Glance . . .

Born on March 1, 1966, in Baton Rouge, LA. *Education*: Brooklyn College, BA, broadcast journalism, 1988(?).

Career: WNYW (New York, NY), news assistant, 1980s; WBRC (Birmingham, AL), news anchor, late 1980s; KTVI (St. Louis, MO), anchor and reporter, 1990s; WCAU (Philadelphia, PA), anchor and reporter, 1990s; NBC, national news anchor and reporter, 1990s(?)–2003; WMAQ (Chicago, IL), anchor and reporter, 2003–06; CNN, anchor and reporter, 2006—.

Awards: At least four Emmy Awards, National Academy of Television Arts and Sciences (Chicago/Midwest chapter), 2000s; Edward R. Murrow Award, Radio Television Digital News Association (Region 7), 2000s.

Addresses: CNN Newsroom, CNN, PO Box 105366, Atlanta, GA 30348.

To all appearances, Lemon thrived in New York, a city known for the intense competitiveness of its media. His primary employer there was NBC, for whom he worked on a variety of nationally distributed programs. Although he served primarily as a reporter, he also had recurring anchor spots on *Weekend Today* and on MSNBC, the network's primary cable affiliate. His performance in all those roles soon drew the attention of executives at WMAQ (also known as NBC 5) in Chicago, and in 2003 they hired him as a reporter and as a co-anchor for one of their evening newscasts. His work there brought him several honors, including several Emmy Awards from the Chicago/Midwest chapter of the National Academy of Television Arts and Sciences and an Edward R. Murrow Award from the local branch of the Radio Television Digital News Association. Particularly visible throughout his tenure in Chicago was his ability to handle difficult subjects with poise and sensitivity. That talent helped him stand out from the crowd when, in 2006, CNN announced plans to bring in a new anchor. Hired by the network in September of that year, he was probably best known, as of 2011, as the host of *CNN Newsroom* on weekend evenings. He had also had a number of important assignments, however, as a traveling correspondent. In January of 2009, for example, he went to Washington, D.C., to report from the scene of Obama's inauguration.

One of the most memorable moments of Lemon's career came in September of 2010, when CNN assigned him a relatively routine story about a clergyman in Georgia, Eddie Long, who had been accused of improper relationships with several parishioners, all of them male teenagers. In a studio interview with church members, Lemon suddenly declared that he had been sexually abused as a child by an adult he had trusted. "I never admitted that on television," he remarked, according to the website of the *Daily Mail*, a British newspaper. "I didn't tell my Mom that until I was 30 years old." His disclosure prompted an outpouring of support, for which he expressed gratitude via Twitter.

Less than a year after that episode, Lemon revealed more details of his life in his forthright autobiography. Published in May of 2011, *Transparent* was originally meant to be inspirational rather than candid in tone. As he began to write, however, he realized, in the words of Bill Carter in the *New York Times,* "that he could not hold back the truth of who he was." Central to that truth-telling effort was a discussion of his sexual orientation. Although many of his colleagues were already aware that he was gay, the public was not, and he worried a great deal about its reaction. "I'm scared," he told Carter at the time of the book's release. "I'm talking about something people might shun me for, ostracize me for." As of the summer of 2011, however, it appeared that public opinion was solidly in his favor. CNN had assured him of its support, and reviewers around the country had found much to praise in the book's honesty and lack of pretense. "Mr. Lemon's memoir is a lesson to its reader in the art of coming out and showing up in your own life," wrote a particularly enthusiastic critic, Malcolm Harris of the Huffington Post, an online news source. "*Transparent* and its author are both truly a celebration of being authentically you." Lemon himself echoed those sentiments, albeit much more modestly, in a comment quoted on the book's jacket. Writing *Transparent* "was one of the hardest things I've ever done," he noted there. "And I figure if I am going to write a book about my life, I may as well tell all, so I approached it the same way I do journalism, there are no questions or subjects off limits. I tell family and personal secrets, and it is cathartic and no one can hold anything over me ever again."

Sources

Books

Lemon, Don, *Transparent*, Farrah Gray, 2011.

Periodicals

New York Times, May 15, 2011.

Online

"Anchors and Reporters: Don Lemon," CNN, http://edition.cnn.com/CNN/anchors_reporters/lemon.don.html (accessed September 7, 2011).

"CNN Anchor Reveals Live on Air That He Was Abused as a Child," Mail Online, September 29,

2010, http://www.dailymail.co.uk/news/article-1315952/CNN-anchor-Don-Lemon-reveals-live-air-abused-child.html (accessed September 7, 2011).

Harris, Malcolm, "CNN's Don Lemon: A Lesson in Style, Grace, and Transparency," Huffington Post, June 22, 2011, http://www.huffingtonpost.com/malcolm-harris/cnns-don-lemon-a-lesson-i_b_882042.html (accessed September 7, 2011).

—R. Anthony Kugler

LL Cool J

1968—

Rap musician, actor

LL Cool J, photograph. Jim Spellman/WireImage/Getty Images.

LL Cool J helped lay down the groundwork for rap during the genre's early days in the 1980s and then refine and reinvent it in the decade that followed. The Queens, New York, native holds a special honor in the annals of music history as the first artist to be released on Def Jam, the label founded by Russell Simmons and Rick Rubin, in 1984. He went on to become one of the top-selling rap acts in the 1980s and early '90s, crowned the young prince of the movement while still living with his grandparents in Queens. In 1988 Cool J provided one of the signature songs of an era with the track "Going Back to Cali," then repeated that a few years later with the Grammy-winning "Mama Said Knock You Out." Like his West Coast counterpart Ice Cube, Cool J has gone on to a successful career in television and film. He made his 13th album for Def Jam in 2008 before signing on to a leading role on the CBS police procedural *NCIS: Los Angeles.*

Witnessed Family Shooting

Like the 1983 Run-DMC song, Cool J endured the proverbial "Hard Times" as a youngster. He was born James Todd Smith in 1968, and his parents' marriage was troubled from the start. Finally, his mother left and returned to her parents' home with her toddler, where her estranged husband tracked her down and shot her with a 12-gauge rifle. Cool J's grandfather was also wounded in the incident. "I ran to get towels from the bathroom," Cool J recalled in *Jet.* "When I pushed them into my grandfather's stomach, I could see where his flesh had been ripped apart."

Fortunately, both his mother and grandparent survived, but the next few years of Cool J's life were equally challenging: his mother entered into a relationship with a man who physically abused him. He found solace with his grandparents, who lived in the black middle-class enclave of St. Albans, Queens.

Cool J began writing his first raps at the age of nine, emulating such local heroes as Kurtis Blow and Grandmaster Flash. For his 13th birthday, he convinced his grandfather—a jazz saxophonist who had played professionally—to buy him his own $2,000 set-up, which included a pair of turntables, a sound mixer, and an amplifier. He made his own tapes, which helped him land performing gigs with early-era rap crews like the Blockbuster Gang, Freeze MCs, Extravagant 3, Super

At a Glance . . .

Born James Todd Smith, on January 14, 1968, in St. Albans, Queens, NY; son of James and Ondrea Smith; married Simone, 1995; children: son Najee, daughters Italia, Samaria, Nina Simone.

Career: Signed to Def Jam and released first single "I Need a Beat," 1984; established nonprofit Camp Cool J Foundation, 1992; founder of the companies: P.O.G. (Power of God) 1993, a music label; founded label and music-production company Rock the Bells; founder of clothing line Todd Smith; founded Boomdizzle.com, social networking site and music label, 2008.

Awards: *Village Voice* Album of the Year Award, 1990; MTV Video Award for best rap video, 1991, for "Mama Said Knock You Out"; Grammy Award for best rap solo performance, National Academy of Recording Arts & Sciences, 1992, for "Mama Said Knock You Out"; Grammy Award for best rap solo performance, 1997, for "Hey Lover"; Quincy Jones Award for Outstanding Career Achievement, Soul Train Music Awards, 2003.

Addresses: *Record Label*—Def Jam Records, 652 Broadway, New York, NY 10012.

Beat" was the new company's first record. Cool J was just 16 years old, and the single turned him into a star overnight, selling 100,000 copies and securing Def Jam's future.

Cool J recorded his debut album *Radio for Def Jam*—also the label's first LP release—which brought him national fame. Called "the most engaging and original rap album of the year" by *Village Voice* music critic Robert Christgau, the album was a showcase of bass-driven favorites such as "Rock the Bells" as well as tender ballads, which gave him major crossover appeal. The album went platinum, and Cool J quickly proved to be a powerful live presence as well. He was invited to perform in the 1985 rap film *Krush Groove* to deliver a version of his song "I Can't Live without My Radio." Within the next several years, Cool J would figure prominently in several major rap tours under the Def Jam banner, including the Fresh Fest of 1985 and the Raising Hell Tour a year later, which featured Run-DMC and the Beastie Boys.

With the release of his second album *Bigger and Deffer* (1987), Cool J secured his status as a rap act with genuine crossover appeal. The album's single "I Need Love" became the first rap song to top *Billboard* magazine's R&B chart, and proved that rap could embrace romantic modes, even while *Spin* magazine called *Bigger and Deffer* "arguably the heaviest rock 'n' roll record ever released on a major label." As the album joined *Radio* in platinum-sales territory, Cool J's track "Going Back to Cali" for the film *Less Than Zero* help push that movie's soundtrack to gold sales and earned him his first Grammy Award nomination for best rap performance.

Rocking Brothers, and Grand Wizard Freddy B. He dubbed himself LL Cool J, a shortened version of "Ladies Love Cool James."

Cut Def Jam's First Record

Cool J came to the attention of Rick Rubin and Russell Simmons, two young New Yorkers who had turned Simmons's brother's act, Run-DMC, into rap's first major stars. That act came out of Hollis, which was a slightly tougher part of Queens than adjacent St. Albans. "I met him as a child, and he was just a poet," Russell Simmons told *Jet* magazine about the teen. "He had so much energy and natural charisma." Legend has it that Cool J ventured into downtown Manhattan to Weinstein Hall, the New York University dormitory building where Rubin was still rooming with Adam Horovitz of the Beastie Boys, for their first meeting, and was shocked that Rubin was white. Sitting in the dorm, they made a recording on Rubin and Horovitz's equipment, and then Rubin funded a studio session and took the demo to Simmons, suggesting they start their own label instead of just producing tracks for other up-and-coming artists. Simmons agreed, Def Jam was born, and Cool J's "I Need a

Won Grammy Award

Cool J's success made him a target, and the "I Need Love" ballad was ridiculed by some hard-core artists for its teenybopper vibe. He had a long-running feud with Kool Moe Dee that played out on several records. Critics also deemed Cool J's 1989 release *Walking with a Panther* overly bloated at 18 tracks, but his follow-up to that, *Mama Said Knock You Out,* was almost unanimously judged his best yet. While the album contained some of Cool J's smoothest compositions, such as the memorable "Around the Way Girl"—yet another single—which peaked on multiple charts, it was the bass-thumping, confident drive of "The Boomin' System" and the album's title cut that gave *Mama Said Knock You Out* its appeal. As Cool J stated in an America Online interview, the title song was "a testament to the fact that no matter how rough times get and no matter how tough times get, you should never give up because that was the entire premise of that song. I was at a rough time in my life, and I was inspired by my grandmother to get out there and knock them out!" The song won him his first Grammy Award, for best rap solo performance.

As the 1990s unfolded, Cool J explored careers in film and television, both as a musician and as an actor. On the big screen, he turned in an impressive performance as an undercover cop in the drama *The Hard Way* in 1991, which led to a part in director Barry Levinson's 1992 film *Toys.* For MTV, Cool J took part in two groundbreaking specials, both in 1991. In May he performed acoustic versions of songs such as "Mama Said Knock You Out" and "Jingling Baby" for the popular series *Unplugged,* and was the first rap artist to do so. Shortly thereafter, he appeared in the music network's *History of Rap* documentary, discussing such classic rap acts as Afrika Bambaataa and the Sugarhill Gang, as rap began to gain recognition as a cultural phenomenon. In addition, Cool J took a starring role on the television series *In the House,* which debuted on NBC in 1995 and switched to the UPN network, where it ran until 1999.

Cool J struggled to stay current as rap music evolved, splitting off into new styles developed by artists with increasingly tough, swaggering personas. His 1993 album *14 Shots to the Dome* was memorable and provided the rapper with yet another platinum-seller. *Mr. Smith,* released in 1995, rated as one of the artist's most successful fusions of hard-edged attitude and laid-back eroticism. As *Rolling Stone* critic Cheo H. Coker noted, Mr. Smith did not always "deliver the haymaker punches of *Mama Said Knock You Out,* but it has enough force to prove that the king from Queens is no punk." The hit "Hey Lover" earned him his second Grammy Award for best rap solo performance, while *Mr. Smith* was nominated for best rap album.

Transitioned into Film Roles

Cool J's 2002 album *10* was followed by *The DEFinition* in 2004, which earned him a Grammy nomination in 2005 for best rap album. He remained in high demand in Hollywood, appearing in such films as *Any Given Sunday* in 1999, *Charlie's Angels* a year later, and the hotly anticipated *S.W.A.T.* in 2003. He also turned in a credible performance as a romantic lead opposite Gabrielle Union in *Deliver Us from Eva* that same year, and with Queen Latifah in *Last Holiday* in 2006.

Still with Def Jam, Cool J put out *Todd Smith* in 2006. "Forget that he's nearing 40—the brother from Hollis still has enough youthful arrogance to step behind the microphone and morph into a savage street talker," asserted Michael A. Gonzales in *Vibe.* With the release of *Exit 13* in 2008, there were rumors it was to be his final record, but Cool J explained in interviews that it was merely his last one due in his Def Jam deal. In 2009 he was cast to co-star with Chris O'Donnell in a spin-off of the top-rated Naval Criminal Investigative Service (NCIS) franchise on CBS, *NCIS: Los Angeles.* He has also written an autobiography, *I Make My Own Rules,* a fitness book, and is an active Twitter user, with more than 1.5 million followers of @llcoolj. His latest business venture was Boomdizzle.com, a social networking site and music label he founded in 2008.

Cool J has four children with his wife, Simone, whom he married in the summer of 1995. "I feel really blessed that Simone waited for me to grow up," he told *Jet* in 1997. "I'm glad she endured and stuck by me during the rough times." Their youngest child, Nina, interviewed her father for *Redbook* in 2010, quizzing him about his favorite Miley Cyrus song ("Party in the USA"), his stunt work on *NCIS,* and possible rewards for a solid report card. Her father replied, "I expect you to get all A's," and dismissed the possibility of an iPad as motivational factor for her. "I think it's obvious we grew up in different neighborhoods," he told his daughter. "I would take you out for ice cream."

Selected works

Albums

Radio (includes "I Need a Beat," "Rock the Bells," and "I Can't Live without My Radio"), Def Jam, 1985.
Bigger and Deffer (includes "I Need Love"), Def Jam, 1987.
Walking with a Panther (includes "Going Back to Cali" and "Jingling Baby"), Def Jam, 1989.
Mama Said Knock You Out (includes "Mama Said Knock You Out," "Around the Way Girl," and "The Boomin' System"), Def Jam, 1990.
14 Shots to the Dome, Def Jam, 1993.
Mr. Smith (includes "Hey Lover"), Def Jam, 1995.
All World Greatest Hits, Def Jam, 1996.
Phenomenon, Def Jam, 1997.
G.O.A.T., Def Jam, 2000.
10, Def Jam, 2002.
The DEFinition, Def Jam, 2004.
Todd Smith, Def Jam, 2006.
Exit 13, Def Jam, 2008.

Films

Krush Groove, Warner Bros., 1985.
Wildcats, Warner Bros., 1986.
The Hard Way, Universal, 1991.
Toys, 20th Century-Fox, 1992.
Out-of-Sync, LIVE Entertainment, 1995.
Halloween H20: 20 Years Later, Dimension, 1998.
Any Given Sunday, Warner Bros., 1999.
Deep Blue Sea, Warner Bros., 1999.
In Too Deep, Dimension Films, 1999.
Charlie's Angels, Columbia Pictures, 2000.
Kingdom Come, Fox Searchlight, 2001.
Rollerball, MGM, 2002.
Deliver Us from Eva, USA Films, 2003.
S.W.A.T., 2003.
Edison, Millennium Films, 2005.
Slow Burn, Lions Gate Entertainment, 2005.
Last Holiday, Image Movers, 2006.
The Deal, Muse Entertainment Enterprises, 2008.

Television

In the House, NBC, 1995–96, UPN, 1996–99.
NCIS: Los Angeles, CBS, 2009—.

Books

(With Karen Hunter) *I Make My Own Rules,* St. Martin's Press, 1998.
(With Dave Honig) *LL Cool J's Platinum Workout,* Rodale Press, 2007.

Sources

Books

Charnas, Dan, *The Big Payback: The History of the Business of Hip-Hop,* Penguin, 2010.

Periodicals

Ebony, July 2006, p. 156.
Jet, September 22, 1997, p. 37; September 1, 2008, p. 36.
Redbook, October 2010.
Rolling Stone, February 8, 1996, pp. 49–50.
Vibe, March 1997; May 2006, pp. 135–36.

Online

"LL Cool J," Island Def Jam Records, http://www.islanddefjam.com/artist/home.aspx?artistID=7309 (accessed September 7, 2011).
LL Cool J on Twitter, http://twitter.com/#!/LL COOLJ (accessed September 7, 2011).

—Shaun Fronter, Sara Pendergast
and Carol Brennan

Clara Luper

1923–2011

Activist, educator, radio host

An unassuming hero of the civil-rights movement, Clara Luper had an impact far beyond her home state of Oklahoma. A teacher and youth leader, she led sit-ins in Oklahoma City for six years (1958–64), a groundbreaking campaign that proved instrumental in bringing an end to some of the most restrictive segregation ordinances in the country. An activist to the end of her life, she once ran for the U.S. Senate. "While her accomplishments are too many to list," wrote Oklahoma City mayor Mick Cornett in a statement quoted by CNN, "her legacy is easily defined. She made Oklahoma and the United States of America a better place to live and was a shining example of the distinctly American idea that while we might hail from many cultures, we are one people."

Born Clara Mae Shepard on May 3, 1923, in Okfuskee County, Oklahoma, a rural district east of Oklahoma City, Luper grew up in the nearby town of Hoffman. Her father, Ezell Shepard, was a bricklayer and World War I veteran; her mother was a maid. In her 1979 autobiography, *Behold the Walls*, and in numerous interviews, Luper recalled the impact of segregation on her childhood. Particularly memorable for her was the inadequacy of the books available to African-American schools under the segregationist system; these were typically volumes white schools had discarded. "We'd be reading sometimes on page four and the next page would be ten," she told the blog Stories in America. It was not just in school, however, that she felt the essential injustice of segregation. A particularly traumatic moment in this regard came when her brother was refused treatment in a hospital because of his race.

"That really triggered her," her daughter Marilyn Hildreth told Dennis Hevesi in the *New York Times*.

After graduating from Grayson High School, a rural institution not far from Hoffman, Luper won entrance to Langston University, a predominately African-American school north of Oklahoma City. She focused there on math and history, earning a bachelor's degree in 1944. Six years later, just as the University of Oklahoma was opening its doors to African-American students for the first time, she matriculated there in pursuit of a master's degree in history, which she earned the following year. She then began work as a history teacher in public schools in and around Oklahoma City. That profession sustained her until 1991, when she retired after four decades of service.

Amid her classroom duties, Luper found time for a great deal of volunteer work, often on behalf of the local branch of the NAACP. In the mid-1950s she became adviser to the branch's youth council, and it was that role that propelled her to the front ranks of the burgeoning desegregation movement. In 1957 she took a group of council members to New York City to attend the performance of a play, *Brother President*, she had written about the Rev. Dr. Martin Luther King Jr. (1929-1968). A highlight of the trip for many of the youngsters was the ability to eat in any restaurant they chose, even one filled with whites. Their inability to do so in Oklahoma angered and confounded them, and on their return home they asked Luper what they could do to end segregation. Determined to help them make a statement, she set her sights on a lunch counter inside

At a Glance . . .

Born Clara Mae Shepard on May 3, 1923, in Okfuskee County, OK; died on June 8, 2011, in Oklahoma City, OK; daughter of Ezell Shepard (a bricklayer) and Isabel (or Isabell) Shepard (a maid); married twice (Charles P. Wilson and Bert Luper); children: three. *Religion:* Baptist. *Education:* Langston University, BA, mathematics and history, 1944; University of Oklahoma, MA, history, 1951.

Memberships: NAACP, National Education Association, Zeta Phi Beta.

Career: Oklahoma City Public Schools and other public schools, history teacher, early 1950s–91; civil rights activist, beginning in the 1950s; radio host, 1960–80; candidate for U.S. Senate, 1972.

Awards: Highway named in her honor; State of Oklahoma, 2000; Clara Luper Scholarship Program established in her honor, Oklahoma City University, 2000s(?).

a Katz Drug Store, in part because it was owned by a multi-state chain; if they could persuade one branch to integrate, she reasoned, the other branches might follow.

On August 19, 1958, Luper, three other adults, and 13 members of the youth council entered a Katz Drug in Oklahoma City, sat down at the lunch counter, and ordered soft drinks. Though they were refused service, they remained until closing. They returned several times over the next few weeks, enduring considerable hostility from some white patrons. The store's management, meanwhile, was increasingly worried about the publicity generated by the protests, which occurred less than a month after a Wichita, Kansas, sit-in, widely regarded as the first to target segregation, and more than a year before the more famous sit-ins in Greensboro, North Carolina, and Nashville, Tennessee. Like those other protests, the one in Oklahoma City was successful, and within months every branch of the Katz chain was desegregated. Luper, however, did not stop. Between 1958 and 1964, the year the federal Civil Rights Act brought an official end to legally mandated segregation, she led dozens of sit-ins in Oklahoma and advised activists planning similar events across the South. In the course of her efforts, she was arrested no

less than 26 times.

Luper's involvement in civic affairs did not end with the demise of segregation. By all accounts an eloquent and persuasive speaker, she hosted a radio show on public affairs for 20 years (1960–80). She also had a foray into politics, running in 1972 for a U.S. Senate seat vacated by the retiring Fred R. Harris. Although she won only a small fraction of the vote, she earned wide praise for her determination to challenge the underrepresentation of women and minorities in Congress.

Luper was honored many times in her later years, perhaps most notably by Oklahoma City University, home of the Clara Luper Scholarship Program, and by the Oklahoma legislature, which named a major thoroughfare after her in 2000. Eleven years after the latter honor, on June 8, 2011, she died at her home in Oklahoma City at the age of 88. Surviving her were three children, a number of grandchildren and great-grandchildren, and hundreds of former students, many of whom attended her funeral. At the direction of Mayor Cornett, flags throughout Oklahoma City were flown at half-staff as a sign of grief, remembrance, and gratitude. "Now we have to step up to the plate and accept the responsibility and do what Mom wanted us to do," her son Calvin told the community through a CNN affiliate, "and that would be to carry on her legacy of honesty and do anything else that would make our city and state a great place."

Sources

Periodicals

New York Times, June 11, 2011.

Online

Decker, Stefanie Lee, "Luper, Clara Shepard (1923-2011)," Oklahoma Historical Society, 2011, http://digital.library.okstate.edu/encyclopedia/entries/L/LU005.html (accessed September 7, 2011).
"Oklahoma Civil Rights Activist Clara Luper Dies," CNN, June 9, 2011, http://articles.cnn.com/2011-06-09/us/oklahoma.activist.dies_1_oklahoma-city-civil-rights-oklahoman?_s=PM:US (accessed September 7, 2011).
"Oklahoma Sit-Ins: A Conversation With Clara Luper," Stories in America, July 28, 2005, http://storiesin america.blogspot.com/2005/07/oklahoma-sit-ins-conversation-with.html (accessed September 7, 2011).

—R. Anthony Kugler

Jerry Manuel

1953—

Professional baseball manager

Manuel, Jerry, photograph. Kevin C. Cox/Getty Images.

Jerry Manuel was a Major League Baseball (MLB) manager for the Chicago White Sox from 1998 to 2003 and for the New York Mets from 2008 to 2010. Known for his restrained demeanor, his intelligence, and his ability to communicate and establish relationships with players, Manuel led the White Sox to one postseason appearance and compiled a career record of 704 wins and 683 losses. A Major League player from 1975 to 1982 and a scout, minor-league manager, and assistant coach with the Montreal Expos organization and then with the Florida Marlins, whom he helped to a 1997 World Series, Manuel was fired by the New York Mets in 2010.

Jerry Manuel was born on December 23, 1953, in Hahira, Georgia, to Lorenzo and Mildred Manuel. Manuel's father was employed by the Air Force, and the family relocated because of military transfers twice during his early years, first to Amarillo, Texas, and then to Sacramento, California. Manuel attended segregated schools in both Georgia and Texas, before attending an integrated high school in California, beginning in the ninth grade. "Going to California was actually the first time I had been in relationships with other races of people," he told Adam Rubin in the New York *Daily News*. "It was a tremendous experience, because you never knew what that side of the world was like."

Manuel was a football, baseball, and basketball star at Cordova High School in Rancho Cordova, California, outside of Sacramento. He received scholarship offers to play each of these sports for college teams including Nebraska, Notre Dame, and Oklahoma. He signed a letter of intent to play football for the University of California, Los Angeles (UCLA), before the Detroit Tigers, a Major League Baseball team, selected him as a first-round pick in June of 1972 in the free-agent draft.

Manuel made his Major League debut with the Tigers in 1975 at the age of 21. He appeared in five MLB seasons between 1975 and 1982, playing with Detroit in 1975 and 1976, with the Montreal Expos in 1980 and 1981, and with the San Diego Padres in 1982. He played only sparingly, however, primarily at second base but also at shortstop, amassing only 127 at-bats and a career batting average of .150. He retired as a player in 1984.

At a Glance . . .

Born on December 23, 1953, in Hahira, GA; son of Lorenzo (an Air Force cook) and Mildred; married Renette; four children.

Career: Professional baseball player, coach, and manager. Playing career included positions with the Detroit Tigers, 1975–76; Montreal Expos, 1980–81; and San Diego Padres, 1982; Jacksonville Expos, manager, 1990; Indianapolis Indians, manager, 1991; Montreal Expos, third-base coach, 1991–96; Florida Marlins, bench coach, 1997; Chicago White Sox, manager, 1998–2003; New York Mets, first-base and outfield coach, 2005, bench coach, 2006–08, manager, 2008–10.

Awards: Manager of the Year, Southern League, 1990; Coach, American League All-Star Team, 1999; Major League Manager of the Year, Associated Press, 2000; American League Manager of the Year, Baseball Writers Association of America and *The Sporting News*, 2000.

Addresses: *Office*—c/o The Jerry Manuel Foundation, PO Box 1127, Loomis, CA 95650.

In the years that followed, Manuel worked as a scout for the Chicago White Sox and as a coach in varying capacities and teams in the Montreal Expos organization, with which he was affiliated from 1986 to 1996. Manuel's progress through the organization included a full season as manager of the Expos' Double-A team the Jacksonville Expos, where he won the Southern League's manager of the year award in 1990. In 1991 Manuel was promoted to the position of manager of the organization's Triple-A affiliate the Indianapolis Indians.

During the 1991 season Manuel was called up from the minors to serve as Montreal's third-base coach, and he remained in this position through 1996. For five of his six seasons with the Expos, he served under manager Felipe Alou, a key mentor. In 1997 he took a job as bench coach under another influential manager, Jim Leyland of the Florida Marlins. Manuel later told Ben Shpigel in the *New York Times* that Alou taught him "to recognize the natural rhythms of baseball, and the importance of making correct decisions within those confines," and that Leyland helped him develop the ability to trust his intuition rather than relying on "the data from a computer."

As a top assistant on both ball clubs, Manuel developed a reputation not only for intelligence and a mastery of the game's dynamics but for being able to establish relationships with otherwise difficult young players. With the Marlins, additionally, Manuel developed a reputation for winning. The team won the 1997 World Series, and immediately thereafter, Manuel became a candidate for a Major League managerial position. He interviewed with the Tampa Bay Devil Rays immediately following the World Series. The Rays ultimately chose another Marlins assistant for the job, but in December of 1997, Manuel was hired as manager of the Chicago White Sox.

In six seasons (1998–2003) with the White Sox, Manuel amassed 500 wins and 471 losses. The highlight of his years with the team was the 2000 season, when the Sox posted the best record in the American League, going 95-67 on the season. Although they were swept 3-0 by the Seattle Mariners in their first playoff series, hopes were high that Manuel would lead the team back to the playoffs in the ensuing years. In each of the following three seasons, however, the White Sox missed the playoffs, and in 2003 Manuel was fired.

Manuel interviewed unsuccessfully for managerial openings with the Cincinnati Reds, the Seattle Mariners, and the Kansas City Royals in the years that followed. His return to Major League coaching came in 2005, when the New York Mets' manager Willie Randolph tapped him to serve as first-base and outfield coach. Randolph named Manuel bench coach in 2006, and while serving in this capacity, he became known as a devotee of the teachings and writings of Martin Luther King Jr., Mahatma Gandhi, and Leo Tolstoy, which he saw as applicable to his job with the Mets. "They move men," he told Shpigel of the three iconic figures. "I always wanted to move men, to take them to a level that they've never seen before. Let's see how far you can go is how I feel."

Manuel's second chance at managing a team of his own came at mid-season in 2008, when Randolph was fired. Manuel was named the Mets' interim manager in June of 2008, and the team's performance improved under his leadership. The Mets were 34-35 at the time Manuel took over; as interim manager he led them to a 55-38 record. Although the team missed the playoffs, Manuel was awarded a two-year contract to manage the team.

In Manuel's two full seasons as manager, the Mets were plagued by, as Shpigel put it, "front-office dysfunction, poor fundamentals and an avalanche of injuries." As the Mets struggled, Manuel remained a well-liked figure by fans and sportswriters, with much of the blame for the team's woes going to general manager Omar Minaya. The Mets' records in 2009 (70-92) and 2010 (79-83) nevertheless sealed Manuel's fate. At the end of the 2010 season, the franchise chose not to extend his managerial contract.

Sources

Periodicals

Chicago Tribune, December 5, 1997.

Daily News (New York), June 19, 2008, p. 60; November 15, 2008; October 4, 2010.

New York Times, February 24, 2007, p. D1; June 18, 2008, p. D1; October 4, 2008, p. D4; October 1, 2009, p. B11.

Sacramento Bee, May 3, 2011.

St. Petersburg (FL) Times, October 31, 1997, p. 7C; December 5, 1997, p. 5C.

USA Today, December 5, 1997, p. 1C; November 9, 2000, p. 6C; September 30, 2003, p. 3C.

Online

"Jerry Manuel Statistics and History," Baseball-Reference.com, http://www.baseball-reference.com/players/m/manueje01.shtml (accessed September 7, 2011).

"Managers and Coaches," Mets.com, http://mlb.mlb.com/team/coach_staff_bio.jsp?c_id=nym&coachorstaffid=118262 (accessed September 7, 2011).

—Mark Lane

Melodie Mayberry-Stewart

1948—

Technology executive

Melodie Mayberry-Stewart is a technology executive whose extensive résumé includes top posts in both the private and the public sectors. Born into an impoverished household in Cleveland, Ohio, Mayberry-Stewart attended college and graduate school in sociology and business before rising through the ranks of International Business Machines (IBM) and taking postgraduate degrees including an MBA in finance and a PhD in information systems. She went on to serve as chief information officer (CIO) at prominent hospital systems, to serve as a top technology executive at the Amoco Corporation, to start her own consulting company, and to serve as CIO for the City of Cleveland, Ohio, and the State of New York. As of 2011 she was CEO of the technology holding company TRI Group Holdings.

Became Family's First College Graduate

Melodie Irene Mayberry-Stewart was born on September 4, 1948, in Cleveland, Ohio. Her father was a bus driver, and her mother a day-care worker. The oldest of three children, she grew up in a public-housing development, but her parents instilled in her the habits of a successful person. She was involved in music and sports, and she went to summer camp, where, as one of the only black children, she learned to fend for herself and work hard to be recognized.

Mayberry-Stewart's resolve to overcome her disadvantaged background gained urgency during an outbreak of race riots in her neighborhood in 1964. Civil-rights activists and community members had organized in the area to protest the construction of a school they believed was intended to promote the re-segregation of the city's educational system. A white minister and civil-rights activist, Bruce W. Klunder, lay in front of a bulldozer at the construction site, and the driver ran over him, instantly killing him and sparking outrage among those present. Mayberry-Stewart returned home from school amid the riots, and after violence raged through the night, she and her family had to clear their lawn of tear-gas canisters the next day. "That event set me on a track to not ever want to be in a situation where I felt so frustrated and powerless that the only option was violence," she told Russell Nichols of *Public CIO*. "I did not want to be in a situation where I would feel powerless over my own destiny. You sort of develop a fearless attitude in terms of the challenges you take on."

In 1970 Mayberry-Stewart became the first member of her family to graduate from college, taking a BS in sociology and business administration from Union College in Lincoln, Nebraska. She stayed on in Lincoln to study sociology as a graduate student, but although she completed her course work for a master's degree, she did not end up finishing her dissertation or pursuing sociology professionally. Instead, she took a position as a systems engineer for IBM, setting out on what would become an enormously successful career in the technology industry.

At a Glance . . .

Born Melodie Irene Mayberry-Stewart on September 4, 1948, in Cleveland, OH; divorced; one son. *Politics:* Democrat. *Education:* Union College, BS, 1970; Pepperdine University, MBA, 1983; Claremont Graduate University, MA, 1989, PhD, 1997.

Career: IBM, software engineer, regional marketing and tech support manager, 1976–88; Community Health Corporation, vice president and chief information officer (CIO), 1988–91; St. Thomas Hospital, vice president and CIO, 1991–95; Beth Israel Medical Center, vice president and CIO, 1995–97; Amoco Corporation, general manager of Global IT Shared Services and Delivery, 1997–99; Black Diamond IT Consulting Group, founder and chief executive officer (CEO), 1999–2002; City of Cleveland, Ohio, chief technology officer and CIO, 2002–07; State of New York, CIO and director of Office for Technology, 2007–11; TRI Group, CEO, 2011—.

Memberships: Advisory Council of Center for CIO Leadership, Harriman Research and Technology Development Corporation (board member), National Association of Female Executives, National Black MBA Association (board chair), National Council of Negro Women, Rensselaer Polytechnic Institute Center for Nanotechnology Innovation (board member), SunTrust Banks (board member).

Awards: Premier 100 Leaders in Technology, *Computerworld*, 2009; Top 50 Government CIOs, *Information Week*, 2009; Urban Empowerment Award, Year Up, 2009; Woman of Inspiration Award, ITT Technical Institute, 2009; Lifetime Achievement Award, National Black MBA Association, 2009.

Addresses: *Office*—TRI Group Holdings, 5 Enterprise Ave., Ste. 100, Clifton Park, NY 12065. *Email*—info@trigh.com. *Web*—http://www.trigh.com.

Promoted to Technology Executive Positions

Mayberry-Stewart was the only black female employee in her IBM office, but she was welcomed by her white male coworkers. Her manager became a valuable mentor to whom she turned for counsel not only while she was at IBM but after she left and became an elite executive. She remained with the corporation from 1976 to 1988, rising to the position of regional marketing and tech support manager.

As she advanced in her career, Mayberry-Stewart laid the groundwork for further progress by continuing her education. In 1983 she took an MBA in finance from Pepperdine University's Graziadio School of Business and Management. She also studied at the Claremont Graduate University's Peter F. Drucker School of Executive Management, taking a master's in executive management on the way to becoming, in 1997, the first African-American woman to earn a PhD at the institution.

The next phase of Mayberry-Stewart's career consisted of serving as the top technology executive at a series of companies in the health-care industry. She served as vice president and CIO at Community Health Corporation of California from 1988 to 1991, at St. Thomas Hospital in Tennessee from 1991 to 1995, and at New York City's Beth Israel Medical Center from 1995 to 1997. In 1997 she took her technological expertise to the Amoco Corporation, the oil-industry giant, where she served as general manager of Global IT Shared Services and Delivery, overseeing 1,900 IT workers in 125 countries and presiding over a budget of $424 million.

Transitioned Career into Public Sector

Mayberry-Stewart left Amoco in 1999 to start her own company, Black Diamond IT Consulting Group, which advised executives at nonprofit organizations on strategies for implementing technology. While working with a nonprofit group in her hometown of Cleveland during this time she became acquainted with the city's newly elected (and first-ever female) mayor Jane L. Campbell. The encounter would mark another turning point in Mayberry-Stewart's career: a move into the public sector.

In 2002 Mayor Campbell, who emphasized the use of technology to promote economic development in Cleveland, appointed Mayberry-Stewart the city's first chief technology officer (CTO) and CIO. Cleveland's use of technology under Mayberry-Stewart's leadership won plaudits from a number of national and international organizations, and her performance over five years in this position led to an even more prominent public-sector appointment, when in 2007 New York Governor Eliot Spitzer tapped her to helm the state's Office for Technology.

As the New York State CIO, Mayberry-Stewart was part of the governor's cabinet under Spitzer and his successors David Paterson and Andrew Cuomo. She was in charge of an annual budget of $2 billion and an estimated 5,600 employees; she was responsible for charting the overall direction and distribution of the

state's IT investments; and she worked with federal and municipal government agencies to find ways of improving state services and encouraging economic development through the use of technology.

Assuming her duties just prior to the onset of the financial crisis of 2008 and the ensuing recession, Mayberry-Stewart also presided over significant downsizing and layoffs within the agency, and a big part of her job, as she told Nichols, was that of determining "how to get more out of the technology investments you're trying to make, pooling your resources for one and one to equal three." Under Mayberry-Stewart, the state's Office for Technology pooled its resources with, for example, the Rensselaer Polytechnic Institute (RPI) and IBM, with which it undertook a $100 million partnership to build one of the world's most powerful supercomputers. The state stood to benefit from its access to the supercomputer by leveraging the system's power and speed to address thorny problems related to security, public safety, education, transportation, and health and human services.

Mayberry-Stewart also addressed diversity in the awarding of state technology contracts. During her tenure, the number of minority and women's business enterprises (MWBE) among the total share of technology contracts awarded rose from 1 percent to 21 percent. Another key element of her push to promote diversity in the technology field more broadly was the spearheading of a project to introduce high-speed Internet access to poor and underserved rural and urban areas in the state.

In March of 2011 Mayberry-Stewart resigned as New York State CIO to return to the private sector, and in May of that year she was named the first CEO of the newly formed TRI Group, a holding company whose chief subsidiaries were the IT management and consulting firm TRIGHTec and the software company Vanguard Behavioral Solutions. Mayberry-Stewart had by this time won widespread recognition as one of the top executives in her field and as an inspiring American success story.

Selected writings

Plays

Brother President, 1957.

Books

Behold the Walls, J. Wire, 1979.

Sources

Online

"Class of 2009 Yearbook: The Honorees," *Computerworld*, http://www.computerworld.com/spring/p100/detail/159 (accessed September 7, 2011).

Nichols, Russell, "Melodie Mayberry-Stewart Blazes a Trail as New York State CIO," *Public CIO*, http://www.govtech.com/pcio/Melodie-Mayberry-Stewart-Blazes-a-Trail-as.html (accessed September 7, 2011).

"Profile for Melodie Mayberry-Stewart, Ph.D.," New York State Chief Information Officer/Office For Technology, http://qa.cio.ny.gov/DrMayberry-StewartProfile (accessed September 7, 2011).

Rich, Sarah, "New York State CIO Melodie Mayberry-Stewart Resigns," Public CIO, http://www.govtech.com/pcio/Melodie-Mayberry-Stewart-Resigns.html (accessed September 7, 2011).

"TRI Group Holdings Leadership and Board of Directors," TRI Group Holdings, http://www.trigh.com/leadership (accessed September 7, 2011).

—Mark Lane

Forrest McClendon

1965—

Actor

For actor Forrest McClendon, leaving New York was the best career choice he ever made. After struggling to make it in on the New York stage, competing against so many other eager young actors, McClendon decided to head to Philadelphia, a city with an equally vibrant, though less well-known, theater scene. It proved to be a smart move, and McClendon became a regular on the stage thereafter, turning in strong performances in such productions as *The Threepenny Opera, Julius Caesar, Dreamgirls, The Fantasticks,* and *The Merchant of Venice.* After more than two decades trodding the boards, New York called to McClendon again, and the veteran actor finally made his Broadway debut in the controversial and short-lived musical *The Scottsboro Boys,* in a role that earned him his first Tony Award nomination.

McClendon, Forrest, photograph. Charles Eshelman/Getty Images.

Struggled to Win Stage Roles

Forrest McClendon was born on December 1, 1965, in Norwalk, Connecticut, and grew up in the city's Roodner Court public housing projects. He had his first taste of theater during his childhood, when he went on a field trip to see a local high school production of *Guys and Dolls.* Sitting in the audience, he longed to be onstage. Later, as a student at Norwalk High School, a friend dared him to audition for the spring musical, and he ended up performing all four years. He had his first singing lessons with Lewis Cisto, a music teacher at the high school, and received encouragement and training from local opera singer Betty Jones and church choir director Cassandra Eaton.

He enrolled at the University of Connecticut, initially planning to study engineering. However, theater was his passion, and soon he switched his major to vocal performance, earning a bachelor's degree in 1987. Friends and family warned him that the life of an actor would be difficult, but he persisted. "I did it anyway because I had to, I was hooked and couldn't be anything else but a performer," McClendon recalled in a 1999 interview in the *Philadelphia Tribune.*

McClendon made his way to New York, and in 1993 he made his Off-Broadway debut in a production of Jo Jackson's play *Faith Journey* at Circle Repertory Theatre. As his friends and family had warned, however, he struggled for nearly a decade to keep working.

At a Glance . . .

Born on December 1, 1965, in Norwalk, CT; son of Ruthie Mae Brown. *Education*: University of Connecticut, BA, vocal performance, 1987.

Career: Stage actor, 1993—. Adjunct associate professor, Ira Brind School of Theater, University of the Arts, Philadelphia; artist in residence, Boyer College of Music, Temple University.

Memberships: Actors' Equity Association.

Awards: Central Texas Critics Table Award, B. Iden Payne Award for outstanding lead actor in a play, 2000, for *The America Play*; Barrymore Award for outstanding supporting actor in a musical, 2009, for *Avenue X*.

Addresses: *Agent*—Schiowitz Connor Ankrum Wolf, Inc., 165 West 46th St., Ste. 1210, New York, NY 10036. *Web*—http://www.forrestmcclendon.com/index.html.

"I began to give in and think of my profession as a compromise," he told the *Philadelphia Tribune*. "I bought into the fact that life, for me, because of what I had chosen to do, would be unstable, difficult, and very hard to live." Finally, McClendon decided to abandon New York for Philadelphia, and suddenly his career began to take off. He appeared in *The Threepenny Opera* at Philadelphia's Wilma Theater in 1997–98, and the following year he took a lead role in a production of Jean Genet's *The Maids* at the Walnut Street Theatre.

Debuted on Broadway in Scottsboro Boys

In 2000 he headed to the Zachary Scott Theatre in Austin, Texas, to play the Founding Father in Suzan Lori-Parks's *The America Play*. Robi Polgar in the *Austin Chronicle* called McClendon a "brilliant performer," and the performance earned him the Central Texas Critics Table Award and the B. Iden Payne Award. That same year, he returned to New York to appear in Howard Simon's two-man play *James Baldwin: A Soul on Fire* at the New Federal Theatre.

Over the next decade McClendon was a regular performer in Philadelphia, appearing in productions of *Julius Caesar* (2004) at the People's Light & Theater Company, *Dreamgirls* (2005–06) at the Prince Music Theater, and *The Fantasticks, A Midsummer Night's Dream,* and *The Merchant of Venice* (all in 2008) at the Theater of the Seventh Sister. For his 2009

performance in the musical *Avenue X* at the 11th Hour Theatre Company, he won the Barrymore Award for outstanding supporting actor, and he followed up that year with *Sizwe Banzi Is Dead* with the Lantern Theatre Company.

In 2010 McClendon finally made his Broadway debut in the musical *The Scottsboro Boys*. Penned by John Kander and the late Fred Ebb, the legendary team that created *Chicago* and *Cabaret,* and directed by Susan Stroman of *The Producers* fame, the show is based on the real-life story of nine young black men who were put on death row in the 1930s for allegedly raping two white women on a train while traveling through Scottsboro, Alabama. *The Scottsboro Boys* debuted Off-Broadway with a run at the Vineyard Theatre in the spring of 2010 before heading to the Guthrie Theatre in Minneapolis, Minnesota, that summer. The production transferred to the Lyceum Theatre on Broadway in the fall, opening on October 31.

Won Praise for Controversial Role

The musical's creators made the controversial choice to frame the story as a minstrel show—a storytelling device of the late 19th century in which white actors performed in blackface to lampoon African Americans—but then turned the genre on its head by staging the show with an all-black cast. In a traditional minstrel show, the actors arranged themselves in a semicircle, with an interlocutor or narrator in the center and two "end men" on either side. In one role, McClendon played end man Mr. Tambo. Soon, however, McClendon's Mr. Tambo turns into a series of other characters, including a malicious prison guard, a racist deputy, and the Jewish lawyer, Samuel Leibowitz, who worked for years to free the so-called Scottsboro Boys. In all, McClendon played six different parts, each with its own voice, deportment, and dialect.

Despite a positive critical reception—*Entertainment Weekly* declared the show the best new musical of the year, and the *New York Times* called it "adventurous" and "dynamic"—*The Scottsboro Boys* did not fare as well with audiences and closed after only 49 performances. A group opposing the play protested outside the theater, arguing that the show's use of minstrelsy and blackface was racist. McClendon, among other cast members, defended the production: "In minstrelsy, the most absurd elements are blown up even bigger. It becomes theater of the absurd," he explained to Jane Holahan in the *Lancaster New Era*. "This is the kind of world the Scottsboro Boys found themselves in. It was a circus environment."

The production seemed to be vindicated when it received 12 Tony Award nominations—more than any show except *The Book of Mormon*—including nods for McClendon and co-star Colman Domingo for best performance by an actor in a featured role. However,

The *Scottsboro Boys* came up empty-handed (McClendon and Domingo both lost to John Benjamin Hickey of *The Normal Heart*), setting a record as the most-nominated show to win no Tony Awards. In May of 2011 director Stroman announced that the production would tour theaters on the West Coast in 2012; McClendon had not yet announced whether he would rejoin the cast.

In addition to his work on the stage, McClendon also serves on the faculties of the University of the Arts and Temple University, both in Philadelphia. In 2011 he appeared in the musical *Jacques Brel Is Alive and Well and Living in Paris* at the Two River Theater Company in Red Bank, New Jersey.

Selected works

Theater

Faith Journey, Circle Repertory Theatre, New York, 1993.

The Threepenny Opera, Wilma Theater, Philadelphia, 1997–98.

The Maids, Walnut Street Theatre, Philadelphia, 1999.

The America Play, Zachary Scott Theatre, Austin, TX, 2000.

James Baldwin: A Soul on Fire, New Federal Theatre, New York, 2000.

Lost Boys of Sudan, New Dramatists, New York, 2003.

Julius Caesar, People's Light & Theater Company, Philadelphia, 2004.

The Overwhelming, PlayPenn, Philadelphia, 2005.

Dreamgirls, Prince Music Theater, Philadelphia, 2005–06.

A Christmas Carol, Westport Country Playhouse, Westport, CT, 2006, 2007.

The Picnic, PlayPenn, Philadelphia, 2007.

The Fantasticks, Theater of the Seventh Sister, Philadelphia, 2008.

A Midsummer Night's Dream, Theater of the Seventh Sister, Philadelphia, 2008.

The Merchant of Venice, Theater of the Seventh Sister, Philadelphia, 2008.

Avenue X, 11th Hour Theatre Company, Philadelphia, 2009.

Sizwe Banzi Is Dead, Lantern Theatre Company, Philadelphia, 2009.

The Scottsboro Boys, Guthrie Theatre, Minneapolis, MN, 2010; Vineyard Theatre, New York, 2010; Lyceum Theatre, New York, 2010.

Jacques Brel Is Alive and Well and Living in Paris, Two River Theater Company, Red Bank, NJ, 2011.

Sources

Periodicals

Austin Chronicle, February 18, 2000.
Connecticut Post, May 14, 2011.
Entertainment Weekly, November 1, 2010.
Lancaster New Era, August 17, 2010; November 12, 2010.
New York Times, March 11, 2010; October 31, 2010.
Philadelphia Inquirer, June 12, 2011.
Philadelphia Tribune, January 8, 1999.

Online

Cohen, Patricia, " 'Scottsboro Boys' Is Focus of Protest," ArtsBeat (*New York Times*), November 7, 2010, http://artsbeat.blogs.nytimes.com/2010/11/07/scottsboro-boys-is-focus-of-protest/ (accessed September 8, 2011).

Itzkoff, Dave, "'Scottsboro Boys' Sets Record for Tonys Futility," ArtsBeat (*New York Times*), June 13, 2011, http://artsbeat.blogs.nytimes.com/2011/06/13/scottsboro-boys-sets-record-for-tonys-futility/ (accessed September 8, 2011).

—Deborah A. Ring

Robert McFerrin Sr.

1921–2006

Opera singer

McFerrin, Robert, Sr., photograph. Charles Payne/NY Daily News Archive/Getty Images.

Baritone Robert McFerrin Sr. is remembered as the first black male singer to join the company of the Metropolitan Opera, making his debut in Giuseppe Verdi's *Aida* in January of 1955, only three weeks after African-American contralto Marian Anderson gave her groundbreaking performance to break the color barrier at the Met. McFerrin's operatic career proved short-lived, however, with only a handful of roles during his three years at the Met. He went on to earn greater acclaim as a concert singer and as the singing voice of Sidney Poitier in the 1959 film version of the opera *Porgy and Bess*. He is perhaps best known as the father of Grammy Award–winning jazz vocalist and conductor Bobby McFerrin Jr., with whom he performed in his later years.

Received Vocal Training in High School

He was born Robert Keith McFerrin on March 19, 1921, in Marianna, Arkansas, one of eight children of Melvin McFerrin, an itinerant Baptist preacher, and his wife, Mary. When he was two years old, his family relocated to Memphis, Tennessee, and it was there that McFerrin began singing as a soprano in the gospel choir of his father's congregation. As a teenager, he joined with two of his siblings to form a vocal trio that accompanied their father on the preaching circuit, performing gospel songs, hymns, and traditional black spirituals. The strict Reverend McFerrin forbade his children to sing any secular music.

In 1936 McFerrin's parents, wishing to give him a better education, sent him to live with an aunt and uncle in St. Louis, Missouri. There he attended Sumner High School, the music department of which attracted students from across the Midwest to study under choir director Kenneth Billups. Initially, McFerrin intended to pursue a career as an English teacher. However, when he auditioned for the choir, Billups was so impressed with the young man's baritone voice that he urged him to study classical music and arranged to give him private voice lessons. McFerrin proved a promising student, and Billups helped organize his first recital to raise money to pay his tuition to Fisk University.

McFerrin enrolled at Fisk in 1940 but stayed there for only a year before returning to St. Louis. The following

At a Glance . . .

Born Robert Keith McFerrin on March 19, 1921, in Marianna, AR; died on November 24, 2006, in St. Louis, MO; son of Melvin (a minister) and Mary McKinney McFerrin (a clerical worker); married Sara Copper in 1949 (divorced 1973); married Athena Bush in 1995; children: Bobby Jr., Brenda. *Military service:* U.S. Army, 1943–47. *Education:* Fisk University, 1940–41; Chicago Musical College, 1948.

Career: Metropolitan Opera, baritone singer, 1955–58; private vocal coach, 1958–73; St. Louis Institute of Music Conservatory, artist-in-residence, 1973–89.

Awards: Honorary doctorates from Stowe Teacher's College, St. Louis, 1987, and University of Missouri—St. Louis, 1989; Lifetime Achievement Award, OPERA America, 2003; St. Louis Walk of Fame, 2004.

year, he received a scholarship to attend Chicago Musical College, where he studied under George Graham. In 1942 McFerrin won his first national vocal competition, taking first prize at the Chicagoland Music Festival. His studies were interrupted in 1943 when he was drafted into the U.S. Army during World War II. He returned to Chicago after four years of service and completed his degree in 1948.

Became the Met's First Black Male

After college, McFerrin moved to New York City to pursue a career as a professional singer. There, he became a protégé of Hall Johnson, the noted African-American composer and choir director. In 1949 McFerrin married fellow singer Sara Copper, and the couple had two children, Robert Jr. and Brenda. Sara McFerrin supported the young family as her husband built his career, serving as his accompanist and helping him study operatic roles.

That same year, McFerrin landed his first role on Broadway, a small part in Kurt Weill's musical *Lost in the Stars.* His performance attracted the attention of the Russian conductor and opera impresario Boris Goldovsky, who gave the young singer a scholarship to study at the Tanglewood Opera Theatre in Lenox, Massachusetts. McFerrin made his operatic debut at Tanglewood in Verdi's *Rigoletto* and then joined Goldovsky's touring company. He went on to appear in Verdi's *Aida* (1949) and Charles Gounod's *Faust* (1952) with the National Negro Opera Company and in the world premiere of *Troubled Island* (1949) by

African-American composer William Grant Still with the New York City Center Opera Company. He returned to Broadway in 1951 for a revival of the Marc Connelly musical *Green Pastures,* and the next year appeared in *My Darlin' Aida,* a version of the Verdi opera set in Memphis on the eve of the Civil War.

In 1953, at the urging of his manager, McFerrin entered the Metropolitan Opera's "Auditions of the Air" competition. Concerned about his lack of experience, he worried that "I might win the damn thing and not know what to do," as there were so few roles available for black opera singers. McFerrin did win—the first African American to do so—and he received a scholarship to the Kathryn Turney Long School in New York, where he spent 13 months learning stage deportment, fencing, and other performance skills. He signed a three-year contract with the Met and made his debut there on January 27, 1955, in *Aida,* becoming the first African-American man to become a member of the company.

Continued Career in Hollywood, Concerts

His performance came just three weeks after contralto Marian Anderson had broken the Met's color barrier as the first black singer to appear in a principal role. McFerrin's debut attracted far less publicity than Anderson's, however. In his first role, he was cast as Amonasro, the Ethiopian king and father to Aida—a part that presumably was chosen because it required no duets with white female singers, which might have stirred controversy. In fact, the role was better suited to a taller and stockier performer—McFerrin was a diminutive 5 feet, 7 inches and just 140 pounds—and did not showcase his voice to its best advantage. Adding insult to injury, McFerrin was not permitted to meet the opera's two leading ladies until opening night. As it turned out, McFerrin's Met career proved short-lived, with only 10 performances over three seasons.

He was better received as a concert singer, displaying his mastery of the black spiritual and the German *lieder,*or art song. Reviewing a recital that McFerrin gave at Occidental College in California, *Los Angeles Times* critic Arthur Goldberg praised, "The voice is a handsome one, mellow and vibrant in quality, with voluminous top tones." By 1958 McFerrin saw that his career at the Met was a dead end. "I did not want to continue the uncertainty of my future," he told music scholar Naymond Thomas, according to the *Washington Post.* "I wanted to sing Wotan or Count de Luna or a romantic lead. I guess this would have created too much controversy. Therefore, I simply chose to resign my position on the Met roster and take my chances in Hollywood." For the 1959 Otto Preminger film of George Gershwin's opera *Porgy and Bess,* McFerrin provided the singing voice for Sidney Poitier's Porgy, a role that brought him some mainstream fame.

When the film wrapped, McFerrin and his family decided to stay on in California, where he opened a vocal studio. After he and his wife divorced in 1973, McFerrin returned to St. Louis, where he served as artist-in-residence at the St. Louis Institute of Music Conservatory. In 1989 he suffered a stroke that impaired his speaking but not his singing. The following year, he appeared on his son's album *Medicine Music,* and in 1993 he performed as a soloist with the St. Louis Symphony, with the younger McFerrin as guest conductor. In 2003 OPERA America honored him with a Lifetime Achievement Award. McFerrin died of a heart attack on November 24, 2006, in a hospital in St. Louis, at the age of 85.

Selected works

Operas

Lost in the Stars, Music Box Theatre, New York, 1949.
Rigoletto, Tanglewood Opera Theatre, Lenox, MA 1949.
Aida, National Negro Opera Company, New York, 1949.
Troubled Island, New York City Center Opera Company, New York, 1949.
Green Pastures, Broadway Theatre, New York, 1951.
Faust, National Negro Opera Company, New York, 1952.

My Darlin' Aida, Winter Garden Theatre, New York, 1952.
Aida, Metropolitan Opera House, New York, 1955.

Sources

Periodicals

Los Angeles Times, May 6, 1959.
New York Times, December 2, 1954; January 28, 1955.
Washington Post, November 29, 2006.

Online

Dougan, Michael B., "Robert McFerrin Sr. (1921–2006)," Encyclopedia of Arkansas History and Culture, July 10, 2008, http://encyclopediaofarkansas.net/encyclopedia/entry-detail.aspx?entryID=3266 (accessed September 23, 2011).
Elliott, Debbie, "Robert McFerrin Lent His Voice to Opera History," *All Things Considered,* National Public Radio, December 2, 2006, http://www.npr.org/templates/story/story.php?storyId=6571205 (accessed September 23, 2011)
Jones, Randye, "Robert McFerrin (1921–2006)," Afrocentric Voices in Classical Music, May 22, 2008, http://www.afrovoices.com/mcferrin.html (accessed September 23, 2011).

—Deborah A. Ring

Patina Miller

1984—

Actor

Patina Miller won the opportunity of a lifetime when she was cast as the lead in a hotly anticipated new stage musical, *Sister Act: A Divine Musical Comedy,* for its 2009 premiere in London's West End. The relatively inexperienced stage actor, armed with little more than a drama degree and a handful of roles on her résumé, was chosen to reprise the role played on film by Whoopi Goldberg in the original 1992 comedy *Sister Act.* In the spring of 2011, Miller debuted on Broadway when the musical moved to New York, and won rave reviews

Miller, Patina, photograph. Jason Kempin/Getty Images.

there for her role as the inadvertent nun who leads a convent choir to stardom. Goldberg, one of the producers of the musical, was one of Miller's biggest supporters. "Patina sings like an angel and works like a devil," Goldberg told *Backstage* magazine. "She's fantastic."

Born in November of 1984, Miller was raised in Pageland, South Carolina, in a household with deep roots in the church. Her grandmother had been pastor of her own church, and Miller's mother installed her daughter in their church choir at a young age. "I come from a very musical family," she told Josh Boyd-Rochford in an interview on the website the Fourth Wall. "I grew up wanting to sing." By the time Miller entered middle school, she had spent time at a performing-arts youth camp, telling Boyd-Rochford, "that's where I think I knew I really wanted to do this for a career and not just for fun."

Trained as Performing "Triple Threat"

During her childhood Miller was a fan of *Sister Act*, a PG-rated comedy about a Nevada nightclub singer who by chance witnesses a mob murder and is placed by law-enforcement authorities in a witness-protection program prior to testifying at the trial. Goldberg's character, Deloris, winds up in a Roman Catholic convent under the assumed name of Sister Mary Clarence. When the Mother Superior (in the film, played by British veteran Maggie Smith), learns of her musical chops, she assigns Deloris to work with the convent's rather undistinguished choir. Deloris turns them into a surprising success, but that acclaim imperils her safety. *Sister Act* proved such a hit at the box office that Goldberg reprised the role for a sequel, *Sister Act 2: Back in the Habit* (1993), in which her former "sisters" ask her to help save their school's youth choir.

At a Glance . . .

Born Patina Renea Miller on November 6, 1984, in Pageland, SC. *Education*: Carnegie Mellon University, BFA, 2006.

Career: Stage actor, 2008—. Made television debut on *All My Children,* ABC, 2007.

Addresses: *Office*—Broadway Theatre, 1681 Broadway, New York, NY 10019.

The sequel featured a young Lauryn Hill, before her Grammy-winning success with The Fugees, and for Miller's seventh-grade talent show she sang Hill's showstopper from the movie, "His Eye Is on the Sparrow."

Miller won a place at South Carolina Governor's School for the Arts & Humanities in Greenville, and from there entered Carnegie Mellon University in Pittsburgh on a scholarship. Her voice teachers recalled being stunned by her talent even during the audition process to get into Carnegie Mellon, which has a rigorous theater-training program that ensures graduates are proficient as "triple threats" before they begin their professional careers—able to dance, sing, and act. Before she graduated in 2006, Miller went out for the lead role in *Dreamgirls,* the 2006 film adaptation of the long-running Broadway musical, loosely based on the story of Diana Ross and the Supremes of Motown Records fame. She was one of three finalists, but lost out to a former *American Idol* runner-up, Jennifer Hudson, for the role of Effie White. The role catapulted Hudson to stardom.

Miller won her first job out of college the following year: a part on the ABC daytime drama *All My Children.* She appeared in 30 episodes as Pam Henderson, a television producer and foil to the series' perennial diva Erica Kane (played by Susan Lucci). The soap opera was filmed in Manhattan, which gave Miller a chance to audition for Broadway parts. She was involved in the workshop stage of two big-budget musicals long before their premieres, *The Book of Mormon* and *American Idiot.*

In the summer of 2008 Miller appeared in a revival of the 1960s hippie-era musical *Hair* as part of the Public Theater's annual Shakespeare in the Park festival. She was cast as Dionne, one of the "tribe" of counterculture rebels who converge in New York's Central Park, and a role made famous by Melba Moore in the original 1969 production. As Dionne, Miller delivered the stirring opening lines of the first song in the show, "When the moon is in the seventh house / And Jupiter aligns with Mars / Then peace will guide the planets / And love will steer the stars."

Won Starring Role in Sister Act

Miller and her castmates earned good reviews for *Hair,* but she did not continue with the show as it moved to Broadway in the fall because she had already landed the part of Deloris/Sister Mary Clarence in the London premiere of *Sister Act: A Divine Musical Comedy.* Reprising a role so closely identified with one of Hollywood's most successful African-American comediennes daunted her, she admitted in *Backstage.* "It was the only thing I was nervous about when I first started," she told writer Mark Kennedy. "I told Whoopi. I was like, 'My biggest fear is that people come expecting you and I'm not you.' She told me, 'You're not me. You have an opportunity to create a role for a new stage. Do it your way. It's your moment. Own it.'"

Miller seized that opportunity and earned effusive reviews during her 17-month run at the London Palladium. Critics turned up on opening night with admittedly dour preconceptions about sitting through another ill-advised musical adaptation, but the audience rose for a swift standing ovation at its close, wrote Fiona Mountford in the *Evening Standard,* who singled out Miller for carrying the show. "Her magnificent voice is rich, soaring and, crucially, unflagging," Mountford declared. "She might have been unknown last night, but today all that will have changed." Even *Variety*'s David Benedict conceded that the musical version of *Sister Act* worked. "With its nuns 'n' disco heart on its long, black sleeve and nonstop dynamo discovery Patina Miller in the Whoopi Goldberg role, the cumulative effect is shamelessly and irresistibly entertaining," wrote Benedict. "Miller's powerhouse vocals, pitched somewhere between Gloria Gaynor and Whitney Houston, and her thrillingly fast vibrato act as the show's engine."

Miller was nominated for a Laurence Olivier Award for best actress in a musical or entertainment of 2010, and *Sister Act* wound to a close in London at the end of 2010. She was the sole original London cast member brought to New York for a slightly retooled Great White Way premiere. *Sister Act* opened at the Broadway Theater on April 20, 2011, and again won over even the dourest of critics. In the *New York Times* Charles Isherwood described it as a musical possessing "all the depth of a communion wafer, and possibly a little less bite," but asserted its lead "has a radiant presence and a strong voice with a tangy timbre.... [When] she is slashing away at the sky with her arms, reaching for heavenly inspiration as she exhorts her flock of gawky nuns to shed their inhibitions and let the spirit put their hips in motion, Ms. Miller is a delight to watch."

Miller's breakout performance was nominated for a Tony Award for best performance by an actress in a leading role in a musical, which she lost to Sutton Foster for *Anything Goes.* Her run in *Sister Act* was likely to be followed by a big-screen debut: one thrilling rumor confirmed by soul singer Aretha Franklin herself

was that Miller was one of the frontrunners to play the gospel-R&B star in an upcoming biographical feature film. "I had a lot of people tell me that I couldn't do it," Miller told Boyd-Rochford in the Fourth Wall interview about her dreams for Broadway stardom. "That it was just a dream, but you know what? You can live your dream."

Selected works

Theater

Hair (revival), New York City, 2008.
Sister Act: A Divine Musical Comedy, London, 2009–10, and New York City, 2011—.
Lost in the Stars, New York City Center, 2010.

Sources

Periodicals

Evening Standard (London), June 3, 2009.
Guardian (London), June 3, 2009.
New York Times, April 20, 2011.
Times (London), June 3, 2009.
Variety, June 8, 2009, p. 24.

Online

"All My Children: News Room," Soaps.com, July 18, 2007, http://soaps.sheknows.com/allmychildren/news/id/895/Meet_AMCs_Patina_Renea_Miller/ (accessed August 21, 2011).
Boyd-Rochford, Josh, "Close Up: Patina Miller & Bonnie Hurst," Fourth Wall, May 13, 2009, http://www.fourthwallmagazine.co.uk/2009/05/close-up-over-here-over-there/ (accessed August 21, 2011).
Kennedy, Mark, "Patina Miller Thanks Heaven for 'Sister Act," Backstage.com, April 20, 2011, http://www.backstage.com/bso/content_display/news-and-features/e3i4aad0f1a455a52dd3f4e765d6e003c51 (accessed August 21, 2011).
"Patina Miller Lands Idol's Role," Carnegie Mellon University, http://www.cmu.edu/homepage/creativity/2009/spring/sister-act.shtml (accessed August 21, 2011).

—Carol Brennan

Maya Moore

1989—

Basketball player

Moore, Maya, photograph. AP Images/Tom Olmscheid.

Maya Moore is one of the best women's basketball players in the United States. In high school she led her team to three Georgia 5A championships and a four-year record of 125-3, and she won the Naismith Girl's High School Player of the Year award in both her junior and senior seasons. At the University of Connecticut (UConn), where she played from 2007 to 2011, she emerged as one of the best college women's players of all time. She was the second National Collegiate Athletic Association (NCAA) player in history to be named an All-American four times; she won both the Naismith Women's College Player of the Year Award and the Associated Press (AP) Player of the Year Award twice; and she was the first-ever three-time winner of the Wade Trophy, awarded annually to the best player in NCAA Division I women's basketball. Moore also led the Huskies to four consecutive Final Four appearances, two national championships, and the longest winning streak (90 games) in NCAA basketball history.

The Minnesota Lynx chose Moore as the first pick in the 2011 Women's National Basketball Association (WNBA) draft. Moore was a starter in that year's WNBA All-Star Game, and the Lynx became championship contenders despite having posted one of the league's worst records the season prior to her arrival.

Became a Celebrated High School Athlete

Moore was born on June 11, 1989, in Jefferson City, Missouri, and raised by her mother, Kathryn Moore. Her father, Mike Dabney, was a college basketball player who led Rutgers University to a 1976 Final Four appearance, but he did not actively participate in her upbringing. Moore became interested in basketball at the age of three, when her mother put up a toy hoop in their apartment as a means of helping the high-energy youngster focus her attention. "I put it up as an outlet for all the energy she had," Kathryn Moore told Arash Markazi in *Sports Illustrated*. "I never thought she would slam-dunk that little ball through that hoop for hours."

At the age of eight Moore decided to forego her interest in other sports to pursue basketball exclusively. That same year she found inspiration in the television launch of the new women's professional basketball league, the WNBA. "That's where I got my passion for

At a Glance . . .

Born on June 11, 1989, in Jefferson City, MO; daughter of Mike Dabney and Kathryn Moore. *Religion*: Christian. *Education*: University of Connecticut, BA, 2011.

Career: Professional basketball player, Minnesota Lynx, 2011—.

Awards: Naismith Girl's High School Player of the Year, Atlanta Tipoff Club, 2006, 2007; First-Team All-American, Associated Press (AP), 2007–08, 2008–09, 2009–10, 2010–11; Player of the Year, AP, 2009, 2011; Naismith Women's College Basketball Player of the Year, Atlanta Tipoff Club, 2009, 2011; Wade Trophy, National Association for Girls and Women in Sports and Women's Basketball Coaches Association, 2009, 2010, 2011.

Addresses: *Office*—Minnesota Lynx, 600 First Ave. N, Minneapolis, MN 55403. *Web*—http://www.wnba.com/lynx/.

the game, watching the WNBA on TV," Moore told *Sports Illustrated*'s Kelli Anderson.

Moore's mother pursued work opportunities first in Charlotte, North Carolina, and then in the Atlanta, Georgia, area, with the intent of providing her daughter with opportunities to develop her talent for basketball. At the age of 12 Moore became a born-again Christian, and her faith was to remain a central source of mental strength for her as a player. "Everything you see me involved in flows from my faith," she told Anderson, accounting for the confidence and ability to thrive under pressure that made her not simply a remarkable talent but a champion worthy of comparison to the greatest men's and women's players of her time. Guided by her mother, Moore began researching colleges, crafting a résumé, and corresponding with basketball coaches while still in middle school. As a sophomore in high school, she had narrowed her selection of colleges to the University of Connecticut, the University of Tennessee, Duke University, and the University of Georgia.

Meanwhile Moore became a dominant player for Collins Hill High School in Suwanee, Georgia. She led the team to three consecutive state championships, a 125-3 record over the course of her four years in high school, and a 53-game winning streak. In her junior year she won the Naismith Award for the top high school girls' basketball player in the United States, and

she committed to UConn because she believed that the Huskies' head coach Geno Auriemma, known for his candor and volubility, would not hesitate to criticize her play and thereby help her to reach new levels of excellence. Moore won a second Naismith Award her senior year and was the most celebrated college prospect in the country in 2007.

Led UConn to Record Winning Streak

As high as expectations for Moore's performance were, she exceeded them during her first year at UConn, posting what many sportswriters maintained was the most impressive performance by a freshman in the history of women's NCAA basketball. She became a starter for the Huskies during the eighth game of the season, when guard Kalana Greene tore her anterior cruciate ligament (ACL), and she went on to lead the team in scoring, averaging 17.8 points per game. The team posted a 36-2 record and advanced to the Final Four in the 2008 NCAA Tournament, losing to Stanford University. Moore won Big East Player of the Year honors, an achievement that had never been accomplished by any freshman, male or female, and she was named an All-American by the AP.

Moore's sophomore showing was even more impressive. She set a new UConn single-season scoring record and led the Huskies to an undefeated year and the 2009 national championship. Moore again won Big East Player of the Year honors, and she was named both an All-American and an Academic All-American, earning a 3.74 grade point average. Moore took home the AP, Naismith, and Wade Trophy awards for the best women's college basketball player in the United States.

The Huskies remained undefeated during Moore's junior year as well, repeating as NCAA Champions on the strength of her continued excellence as well as the contributions of senior center Tina Charles, who edged her teammate out for the 2010 Naismith and AP awards. Moore took home her second Wade Trophy in 2010, however, and she was named an All-American for the third consecutive year.

The 2010–11 season presented a new challenge for Moore. Although the Huskies boasted returning players including guards Caroline Doty and Tiffany Hayes and a number of highly touted freshmen, Moore was the team's sole standout player. Nevertheless the Huskies went into the year as a consensus pick to win the national championship, and with Moore performing at the peak of her abilities, the team extended its winning streak to 90, setting an all-time Division I NCAA record, before losing to Stanford (the same team that had delivered its preceding loss over two years earlier) on December 30, 2010. The Huskies did not lose another regular season game, however, and they

reached the NCAA Final Four yet again, for the fourth time in Moore's four years on the team.

Began Pro Career with Minnesota Lynx

During the 2011 NCAA tournament Moore became the seventh woman in Division I history to score 3,000 points in her career. The milestone as well as the team's advance to the Final Four came in a lopsided victory over Duke University. After the game Duke's coach Joanne P. McCallie told Jere Longman in the *New York Times* that Moore was "the greatest women's basketball player alive today."

The Huskies failed to advance to the championship game, falling to Notre Dame in the semifinal contest. Moore continued to amass honors sufficient to secure her standing among the elite athletes of her time, however. She became only the second NCAA athlete to be named an All-American four times; she won her second AP and Naismith player of the year awards; and she became the first player to win the Wade Trophy three times. During her time with UConn, the Huskies' overall record was an unprecedented 150-4. Moore's shooting percentage surpassed 50 percent in each of her four college seasons, and she finished her career as UConn's all-time leading scorer, with 3,036 points.

The Minnesota Lynx made Moore the first selection in the 2011 WNBA draft, and she became the first WNBA player to be offered an endorsement contract with Jordan Brand, the Nike sneaker company associated with the legendary basketball player Michael Jordan and an elite group of current male superstars. As her first professional season got underway, Moore performed as expected, becoming one of the team's leading scorers and rebounders and winning a starting spot in the 2011 WNBA All-Star Game. The Lynx, which had not posted a winning record since 2004, were among the league's top teams during Moore's rookie season.

Sources

Periodicals

New York Times, March 30, 2010, p. B11; December 31, 2010, p. B7; March 30, 2011, p. B11; April 4, 2011, p. D1; April 12, 2011, p. B13; August 8, 2011, p. D6.

Sports Illustrated, January 15, 2007, p. 39; March 19, 2007, p. 26; February 25, 2008, p. 68; November 17, 2008, p. 68; April 19, 2010, p. 26.

Online

"Maya Moore Playerfile," WNBA.com, http://www.wnba.com/playerfile/maya_moore/ (accessed September 8, 2011).

—Mark Lane

Euzhan Palcy

1958—

Filmmaker

Palcy, Euzhan, photograph. Guillaume Collet/Gamma-Rapho/Getty Images.

In the late 1980s filmmaker Euzhan Palcy earned the distinction of becoming the first black woman director to helm a project for a major Hollywood studio. That work was *A Dry White Season,* a cautionary tale of life in South Africa under apartheid that starred Donald Sutherland, Susan Sarandon, and Marlon Brando. Palcy went on to make other feature films, many of which drew on her roots in the French West Indian island of Martinique. "I don't know if I would be a filmmaker, or an artist, if I had not been born there," she reflected in 2000 in an interview with Karani Marcia Leslie for *American Visions.* She cited the island's beautiful topography and harmonious multicultural atmosphere, adding, "It's been the people of Martinique who have had the greatest influence upon my films. The people stress education of all kinds. They stress values—respect for elders, integrity. All of this you see in my movies."

Euzhan Palcy was born on January 13, 1958. She grew up in Martinique's capital, Fort-de-France, as one of six children born to Romauld and Leon Palcy. Her father was an executive at a pineapple-processing facility, and the family went to the cinema once each week, after Sunday church services. The theater showed mostly vintage Hollywood fare, and the stories spurred Palcy's creativity, which her parents encouraged. She wrote plays and short stories, then went on to write and direct a family saga for Martinican television called *La Messagère* (The Messenger) while still in her teens.

Martinique benefited from close economic ties to France, its former colonial master. While residents of other Caribbean islands were agitating for independence from Britain, Spain, the Netherlands, and other nations, *les Martiniquais* became citizens of France as one of France's four *départements d'outre-mer,* or overseas departments. Palcy left the island in the mid-1970s to study at the Sorbonne in Paris, where she earned a master's degree in French literature with a concentration in theater, following that with a postgraduate diploma in art and archeology. In Paris she discovered the work of black filmmakers from around the world, including Senegal's Ousmane Sembène, and went on to earn a third degree, this one a highly technical certification from the Louis Lumière School of Cinema, one of France's national colleges.

At a Glance . . .

Born on January 13, 1958, in Fort-de-France, Martinique; daughter of Leon (a human resources executive) and Romauld Palcy. *Education*: Earned a master's degree in French literature/theater and a diplôme d'Études approfondies (master of advanced studies) in art and archeology, from the University of Paris (Sorbonne); also earned director of photography (DP) certification from the Louis Lumière School of Cinema.

Career: Filmmaker and writer. First short stories published in a Martinique magazine, c. 1975; wrote and directed movie *La Messagère* for television, 1975; Sundance Institute fellow, c. 1986; has also directed the "Infiniti in Black" commercials for luxury-auto nameplate Infiniti.

Awards: Silver Lion for best debut film, Venice Film Festival, 1983, and César Award for best debut, Académie des arts et techniques du cinéma, 1984, both for *Rue Cases-Nègres*; Chevalier de l'Ordre National du Mérite, France, 1994.

Addresses: *Booking agent*—c/o Ada Babino—Nommo Speakers Bureau, 2714 George Ave. NW, Washington, DC 20001. *Web*—http://www.euzhanpalcy.co/.

Praised for Debut Sugar Cane Alley

A 1982 short film Palcy made, *The Devil's Workshop*, helped her land an introduction to the legendary French filmmaker François Truffaut. He helped her secure government arts funding and a crew to make her first feature film, *Rue Cases-Nègres*, the title of which translates into "Black Shack Alley," but *Sugar Cane Alley* was used for its international release. Based on a novel by the black Martinican writer Joseph Zobel, Palcy's debut is set in the 1930s and follows the story of José, whose grandmother M'Man Tine (played by Martinican-French actress Darling Légitimus) cuts sugar cane and works as a laundress to ensure he will have a better life. The gifted adolescent does his part, tutoring a young man named Carmen who also hopes to leave the island's limited economic opportunities for a better life abroad.

Sugar Cane Alley premiered at the 1983 Venice Film Festival, where it won the Silver Lion for best debut film. It also won a similar honor at the 1984 Césars, the French equivalent of the Academy Awards, after garnering numerous good reviews. In the *New York Times*, film critic Vincent Canby called the novice filmmaker "a new writer-director of exceptional abilities." Canby singled out a dramatic turn of events when José is accused of cheating at his new school, and seeks out Carmen for help. "The usually supportive Carmen provides no comfort, though," wrote Canby. "He proudly shows the boy through the mansion, finally winding up in the master bedroom where, lounging on the magnificent bed, he boasts to José about being the lover of the mistress of the house. The audience's shock and disappointment are equal to the boy's." Roger Ebert, the *Chicago Sun-Times* critic, described Palcy's debut as one of those films that seems to "come out of nowhere. The actors will be people we've never seen before, the location will be an unfamiliar one ... and everything will fit together so naturally that we wonder where these people have been all their lives. In a way, the very story of *Sugar Cane Alley* answers that question."

It took six years before those accolades brought another project to Palcy, however. She won a fellowship to Robert Redford's Sundance Institute in 1986, where she met an independent producer named Paula Weinstein, who was looking to bring a story by South African dissident writer André Brink to the screen. "I had wanted to do something about apartheid," Palcy recalled in an interview with *New York Times* writer Samuel G. Freedman about Weinstein's offer. "My dream would've been to follow a black family, in Soweto, for example. But very clearly nobody wanted to put any money into a black film maker making a movie about blacks in South Africa."

Directed A Dry White Season

It took three years to bring *A Dry White Season* to the screen. Palcy met with Brink illicitly in South Africa—a terrifying place for visitors of color in 1987, when the country still operated under a strict set of laws that denied blacks almost all political and legal rights—but the project was helped immensely when veteran actor and staunch liberal Marlon Brando agreed to come out of a nine-year retirement to play a human-rights lawyer.

The story revolves around a white South African man, played by Donald Sutherland, whose faith in the legitimacy of his government is slowly shattered as he tries to aid his black gardener, whose son has disappeared into police custody. "Doing a movie like *A Dry White Season* was a very serious thing on many levels," Palcy said in the *American Visions* interview. "It put lives on the line. To get visas, all of the actors that we cast had to pretend that they were cast for a play in England. So they left South Africa, flew to England, and came back to Zimbabwe, next door, for security reasons. The set was closed. No press was allowed." She also received death threats when the film was released and, predictably, banned in South Africa.

A *Dry White Season* earned excellent reviews, and Brando was nominated for an Academy Award for best supporting actor. *Variety* delivered some of the strongest praise for Palcy and her second feature film. "A wrenching picture about South Africa that makes no expedient compromises with feel-good entertainment values, *A Dry White Season* displays riveting performances and visceral style," its critic asserted. However, Brando criticized some elements of the final cut, and Palcy still felt constrained by her historic first in the Hollywood system. She fielded offers for other projects, but they often came with various ethical entanglements, and so she eventually left Los Angeles and returned to Paris.

Received Tributes for Her Work

Palcy's next film was *Siméon*, a 1992 ghost story filmed in both Martinique and Guadeloupe, another overseas territory of France. She then made a three-part documentary about one of Martinique's greatest historical figures, the writer Aimé Césaire. Her efforts were rewarded by the official French cultural establishment, who bestowed the Chevalier de l'Ordre National du Mérite, or Knight of the National Order of Merit, on her in 1994. In 1998 Palcy made a television movie, *The Ruby Bridges Story*, for Walt Disney. The story retold the real-life ordeal of its titular heroine, who was one of the first black students to attend a previously all-white elementary school in New Orleans during the civil rights struggle. Bridges's tale was made famous by a Norman Rockwell illustration, "The Problem We All Live With," that showed the six-year-old walking to school accompanied by federal marshals.

In 2001 Palcy made a Showtime movie about the infamous 1971 Attica, New York, prison riots, *The Killing Yard*, which starred Morris Chestnut and Alan Alda. Five years later she completed a documentary film about West Indians who fought for the Allied side during World War II, *Parcours de Dissidents* (The Journey of the Dissidents). Her next release was *Les Mariées de l'Isle Bourbon* (The Brides of Bourbon Island), a historical epic about arranged marriages on the Indian Ocean island of Réunion—another long-held French parcel—during the reign of the Bourbon kings. In 2011 Palcy began working on a biographical film about the gospel great Mahalia Jackson with the Grammy-winning singer Fantasia Barrino in the leading role.

In the spring of 2011 Palcy was honored with dual tributes: the Cannes International Film Festival showed *Sugar Cane Alley* as part of its legacy screenings, and she was also feted with a career retrospective at New York's Museum of Modern Art. Her works have often been described as political in tone, but in an interview with B. L. Hazelwood for the Web site Cinespect Palcy asserted, "I am not interested in politics. I find that boring, because it is so fake, too much manipulation. But I am absolutely interested in how those things will affect the human being. I am, therefore, interested in the human being struggling with life, struggling with pressure and death and how they cope with that. Because our history and our stories have been disregarded and overshadowed, I want to talk about those things."

Selected works

Films

La Messagère (television movie), 1975.
The Devil's Workshop (short film), 1982.
Sugar Cane Alley, Nouvelles Éditions de Films, 1983.
A Dry White Season, MGM/UA Communications, 1989.
Siméon, France2 Cinema, 1992.
Aimé Césaire: A Voice for History (documentary), 1994.
The Ruby Bridges Story (television movie), Walt Disney Co., 1998.
The Killing Yard (television movie), Showtime, 2001.
Parcours de Dissidents (documentary), France 3, 2006.
Les Mariées de l'Isle Bourbon, France 3, 2007.

Sources

Periodicals

American Visions, August 2000, p. 40.
Chicago Sun-Times, January 1, 1984.
New York Times, April 22, 1984; September 17, 1989.
People, October 16, 1989, p. 71.

Online

"A Dry White Season (review)," Variety, December 31, 1988, http://www.variety.com/review/VE11177 90593?refcatid=31 (accessed September 8, 2011).
"Filmmaker in Focus: Euzhan Palcy," Museum of Modern Art, http://www.moma.org/visit/calendar/exhibitions/1173 (accessed September 8, 2011).
Hazelwood, B. L., "Q&A with Legendary Filmmaker Euzhan Palcy," Cinespect, May 17, 2011, http://cinespect.com/qa-with-legendary-filmmaker-euzhan-palcy/ (accessed September 8, 2011).
Keaton, Trica Danielle, "The Defiant One: Euzhan Palcy," The Feminist Wire, May 9, 2011, http://www.thefeministwire.com/2011/05/09/the-defiant-one-euzhan-palcy/ (accessed September 8, 2011).
"Martinique's Most Acclaimed Filmmaker, Euzhan Palcy, Continues to Put Her Home Island in the Spotlight," Repeating Islands, May 18, 2011, http://repeatingislands.com/2011/05/18/martinique's-most-acclaimed-filmmaker-euzhan-

palcy-continues-to-put-her-home-island-in-the-spotlight/ (accessed September 8, 2011).

—Carol Brennan

Tony Reagins

1967—

Professional baseball executive

Reagins, Tony, photograph. Rich Pilling/MLB Photos/Getty Images.

Tony Reagins rose through the ranks of professional baseball's Los Angeles Angels of Anaheim organization to become general manager (GM) in 2007. At the time, Reagins was one of only a handful of minority GMs in Major League Baseball (MLB). He oversaw player and coaching staff transactions, along with other personnel and contractual matters during a period when the Angels posted strong regular-season records and won the American League West Division twice. In recognition of his success, Reagins was offered a long-term contract extension in 2009.

Reagins was a standout tailback for Indio High School's football team and expected to play at the college level, but an injury during his senior year derailed his hopes. Danny, meanwhile, had gone on to become a baseball player for College of the Desert (COD), a community college in nearby Palm Desert, California, before attending California State University, Fullerton. Reagins pursued an education from the same two institutions, earning a degree in business administration from COD in 1988 and a degree in marketing from Cal State, Fullerton, in 1991.

Reagins was born on March 11, 1967, in Indio, California. His father Dalter, a janitor, died of cancer when Reagins was four years old, and his mother Polly worked two jobs to support her four children. Reagins's older brother Danny attempted to fill the gap left by their father's death, and Reagins emulated him in many respects. Religion was also a stabilizing force in the single-parent household. Polly Reagins made sure that her children attended Baptist Church services every Sunday, and Reagins remained committed to his faith as an adult.

Reagins's career with the Angels organization began in 1992, when he took an internship with the club, assisting with marketing and sales efforts. Among his other duties as an intern, he helped create promotional events and costumes for mascots. Subsequent years saw Reagins swiftly climb the organizational ladder, assuming positions of increasing responsibility. He was promoted to the post of marketing assistant in 1994, and in 1996 he became a sponsorship services representative. In 1998 Reagins was appointed manager of baseball operations for the club. In this capacity he reported directly to the organization's top executives,

At a Glance . . .

Born on March 11, 1967, in Indio, CA; son of Dalter (a janitor) and Polly (a school aide and housekeeper) Reagins; married Colleen; children: Kennedy, Luke, Seth. *Religion:* Baptist. *Education:* College of the Desert, AA, 1988; California State University, Fullerton, BA, 1991.

Career: Professional baseball administrator. California Angels/Anaheim Angels/Los Angeles Angels of Anaheim, intern, 1992–94; marketing assistant, 1994–96; sponsorship services representative, 1996–98; manager of baseball operations, 1998–2002; director of player development, 2002–07; general manager, 2007—.

Memberships: Boys and Girls Clubs of Coachella Valley (board of directors), Buck O'Neil Scout Association.

Awards: Andrew "Rube" Foster Award, 2008, Negro Leagues Baseball Museum.

Addresses: *Office*—Los Angeles Angels of Anaheim, 2000 Gene Autry Way, Anaheim, CA 92806. *Web*—http://losangeles.angels.mlb.com.

including general manager Bill Bavasi, minor league director Jeff Parker, and scouting director Bob Fontaine.

In 2002 Reagins himself reached the upper echelon of the Angels organization, when he was named director of player development. In this post he was responsible for managing the club's farm system, which consisted of seven minor-league teams spread across the United States as well as a summer-league team and training facility in the Dominican Republic. Reagins held the post through the 2007 season, during which time he won plaudits for helping the Angels' farm system become one of the best in baseball. Renowned for his communications skills, Reagins improved relationships between the club's front office and each of the various minor-league teams. Angels minor-league affiliates made 18 playoff appearances while Reagins oversaw the system, winning three league titles and 15 division titles. Numerous players from the system were called up to play for the Angels, including six alone in 2002, Reagins's first year in the position and the year that the Angels won the World Series.

Reagins's successful tenure as director of player development, along with his ability to communicate effectively with coaches and players across the demographic and cultural spectrum, made him an ideal candidate to

replace outgoing GM Bill Stoneman, who announced his retirement at the end of the 2007 season. Reagins had long since established relationships with many of the Angels' top players and prospects, and he enjoyed a close working relationship with Stoneman, who had led the team to its only World Series title and was considered one of the best general managers in baseball. "In terms of his people skills," Stoneman said of Reagins to Dylan Hernandez in the *Los Angeles Times*, "he's on the top of my chart." Danny Reagins, speaking to Hernandez, similarly extolled his brother's leadership qualities: "I tell him that if he wasn't in baseball, he'd be the mayor of Indio. He has that many friends and family that follow him."

Reagins was named the Angels' GM on October 16, 2007. Among his most noteworthy moves in his first off-season was the acquisition of perennial Gold Glove–winning centerfielder Torii Hunter. The Angels went on to win the American League West Division in 2008, posting the franchise's first-ever 100-win regular season and the best record in the major leagues (100-62). The team failed to make it past their first playoff matchup, however, falling to the Boston Red Sox in the Division Series.

Prior to the 2009 season Reagins secured a new contract with key outfielder Bobby Abreu, and the team went on to post another superlative regular season record and to outdo their previous year's post-season performance. After posting a regular-season record of 97-65, the Angels swept the Boston Red Sox in the Division Series. Their season ended when the New York Yankees beat them four games to two in the American League Championship Series.

After the 2009 season Reagins was offered a contract extension that he and the Angels described as long-term, although details were not disclosed. Having led the team to the brink of an American League pennant, Reagins told Ben Bolch in the *Los Angeles Times* that his goal, given the added job security that his new contract offered him, was to lead the Angels to a World Series victory: "Our expectation is to be the best in baseball.... So I think you have to say that settling for anything less than a world championship is something we don't desire."

Reagins oversaw the acquisition of two-time All-Star Hideki Matsui prior to the 2010 season, but the Angels had a disappointing year, posting their first sub-.500 record (80-82) since 2003 and failing to make the playoffs. At the conclusion of the season club owner Arte Moreno told the press, as reported by Mike DiGiovanna in the *Los Angeles Times*, that the Angels would do "whatever it takes" to get the team back to the level of play fans had come to expect. Sportswriters understood this to mean that Reagins would be given the financial resources to acquire big-name free agents during the off-season, but the team allowed itself to be outbid for players including Carl Crawford and Adrian

Beltre. Reagins maintained that the team could compete with the American League's best teams if the current roster of players performed up to their abilities, but the franchise's future looked considerably more uncertain during the 2011 season than it had at the outset of Reagins's tenure as general manager.

Sources

Periodicals

Los Angeles Times, October 17, 2007; November 7, 2009; January 6, 2011; February 25, 2011.
USA Today, November 6, 2007, p. 1C.

Online

"Angels Executives," Los Angeles Angels of Anaheim, http://losangeles.angels.mlb.com/ana/team/reagins_tony.jsp (accessed September 9, 2011).
"Los Angeles Angels of Anaheim Team History & Encyclopedia," Baseball-Reference.com, http://www.baseball-reference.com/teams/ANA/ (accessed September 9, 2011).
Nelson, Amy K., "Reagins Earned Angels GM Job Through Faith, Hard Work," ESPN.com, February 29, 2008, http://sports.espn.go.com/espn/black-history2008/news/story?id=3269385 (accessed September 9, 2011).

—Mark Lane

Emmett J. Rice

1919–2011

Economist

In 1979 Emmett J. Rice became the second African American ever to serve on the Federal Reserve Board of Governors. The economist, who taught at Cornell University and spent much of the 1960s working with developing nations, was appointed to the Federal Reserve by President Jimmy Carter. He stepped down in 1986, and it would take more than decade before another African-American economist held a seat on the powerful federal agency whose decisions dramatically affect inflation and interest rates. "If there is a case," Rice told *Black Enterprise* writer Frank McCoy in 1994, "for making the government look like America, then there is a case for making the Federal Reserve look like America."

Born in 1919, Rice spent his earliest years in Florence, South Carolina. He was the youngest child of a minister and a mother who taught in her community's segregated schools, which Rice attended. Rice's father, Ulysses, had graduated from Lincoln University in Pennsylvania, and Rice's older brother also attended the historically black college before moving to New York City. While still in his teens, Rice joined his brother in Harlem and graduated from the City College of New York in 1941 with a bachelor's degree in business administration. He earned an M.B.A. from City College a year later, then served with the elite Tuskegee Airmen unit in the U.S. Army Air Force during World War II.

Rice used his G.I. Bill benefits to enroll in the University of California's doctoral program in economics after the war. He chose the field in part because of his experiences as a child during the Great Depression. "There was a lot of suffering," he recalled in an interview with the University of California Black Alumni Oral History Project. "Twenty-five percent of the country was unemployed. I wanted to understand an economy which allowed this to happen. I wanted to see if it was really necessary."

Rice chose the University of California's Berkeley campus in the Bay Area. The school would gain a measure of notoriety during the 1960s as a hotbed of antiwar protests and the black militant movement, but in the late 1940s Rice was happy to live in a community that was already showing a famously tolerant streak. "It was my first experience where I felt almost free," he said in the Oral History Project. "There was a tremendous openness around in those days. It is no longer true, but people did not lock their doors....It was the first living experience—extended over time—where I did not feel the constant pressure of being black."

Berkeley was so progressive, in fact, that some community groups successfully petitioned the city to integrate its fire department. When Rice read the newspaper notice that new applicants were being accepted, he sat for the civil service exam, passed it, then completed the tough physical training program to become Berkeley's first black firefighter. The job allowed him time to study toward his Ph.D., which he earned in 1954 after a year in Mumbai, India, at the Reserve Bank of India as a research associate on a Fulbright fellowship.

Rice was hired by Cornell University in Ithaca, New York, as an assistant professor of economics. "At that

At a Glance . . .

Born Emmett John Rice on December 21, 1919, in Florence, SC; died of congestive heart failure on March 10, 2011, in Camas, WA; son of Ulysses Simpson Rice (a minister) and Sue Pearl Suber Rice (a teacher); married Lois Dickson (an education scholar; divorced); children: Susan, E. John Jr. *Military service:* U.S. Army Air Force, member of Tuskegee Airmen during World War II. *Politics:* Democrat. *Education:* City College of New York, BBA, 1941, MBA, 1942; University of California—Berkeley, PhD, 1954.

Career: Firefighter in Berkeley, CA; Reserve Bank of India, Fulbright fellow research associate, 1952; Cornell University, assistant professor of economics, 1954–60; Federal Reserve Bank of New York, economist, 1960–62; Central Bank of Nigeria, consultant, 1963–64; U.S. Department of Treasury, Office of Developing Nations, began as deputy director, 1964, became acting director; International Bank for Reconstruction and Development of the World Bank, U.S. alternate executive director, 1966–70; Mayor's Economic Development Committee for Washington, executive director, 1970–72; National Bank of Washington, senior vice president, 1972–79; member of the Federal Reserve Board of Governors, 1979–86.

time the government departments were not taking blacks in professional positions," he explained in the University of California interview. "I could not have worked in the treasury at that time. I could not have worked at the Federal Reserve." That barrier was broken by another black economist, Andrew Brimmer, whose background shared similarities to Rice's. Both left the Jim Crow South for a better education, served their country during the war, and were Fulbright fellows in India. Brimmer earned his Ph.D. from Harvard University and went to work at the Federal Reserve Bank of New York in 1957. Three years later, Rice was hired there, too. This was a terrific opportunity for an economist, but Rice had not prepared for it. "That's one of the great horrors of racial discrimination," he recalled in a 1984 *Ebony* article. "It would have been totally unrealistic for me to prepare to go to the Federal Reserve.... It wasn't until 1955 that we had a black person working in any of the federal banks when Andy Brimmer went to New York. There were only about a half dozen of us by 1960."

As an economist, Rice was an expert on developing economies, like India's. He worked with the govern-

ments of newly independent African nations, helping to set up their banking and treasury departments, and spent a year in Lagos, Nigeria. When he returned in 1964 he was offered the post of deputy director of the Office of Developing Nations at the U.S. Department of Treasury, and served as acting director. In 1966 President Lyndon B. Johnson named Rice to serve as alternate executive director for the International Bank for Reconstruction and Development, one of the five institutions that comprise the World Bank. He held that job for four years before accepting an offer from Walter Washington, the mayor of the District of Columbia, to serve as executive director of his Economic Development Committee. After 1972, Rice became a senior vice president with the National Bank of Washington, where he spent the next seven years of his career.

In the spring of 1979 President Carter appointed Rice to a vacant seat on the Federal Reserve Board of Governors, making him only the second African American to serve on the Board—Brimmer had been the first, back in 1966. Rice's tenure coincided with that of the chair of the Federal Reserve Board, Paul A. Volcker, who continuously battled with the new Republican president, Ronald Reagan. Reagan's team of economic experts advocated dramatic policy shifts to stimulate the nation's economy, including the deregulation of the banking industry, which the Federal Reserve in part oversaw.

Rice resigned from the Federal Reserve Board in 1986, midway through what should have been a term set to expire in 1990. "Rice's announcement comes at a delicate time in Fed policy making, with the economy growing at only a lackluster pace despite very rapid growth in the money supply," remarked Robert D. Hershey Jr. in the *New York Times*. "The Fed has largely abandoned its money targets because deregulation and other factors have made them unreliable policy guides."

Rice was in his mid-sixties by then, and spent the remainder of his career on various corporate boards. He moved to Washington State in the late 1990s and died of congestive heart failure at the age of 91 on March 10, 2011. Two years earlier, his daughter Susan, who had served as U.S. assistant secretary of state for African affairs during the second administration of President Bill Clinton, was appointed by President Barack Obama as U.S. Ambassador to the United Nations. She became the first African-American woman to hold that post. Her father, she told *Washington Post* journalist Matt Schudel, "believed segregation had constrained him from being all he could be. The psychological hangover of that took him decades to overcome. His most fervent wish was that we not have that psychological baggage."

Sources

Periodicals

Black Enterprise, July 1994, p. 22.
Ebony, June 1984, pp. 124–28.
New York Times, January 29, 1986; October 3, 1986.

Online

"Education of an Economist: From Fulbright Scholar to the Federal Reserve Board, 1951-1979: Emmett J. Rice," The Bancroft Library, University of California, Berkeley, 1991, http://content.cdlib.org/view?docId=hb9s201041&brand=calisphere&doc.view=entire_text (accessed September 12, 2011).

Schudel, Matt, "Emmett J. Rice, Federal Reserve Governor, Dies at 91," *Washington Post,* March 13, 2011, http://www.washingtonpost.com/local/obituaries/emmett-j-rice-federal-reserve-governor-and-father-of-un-ambassador-dies-at-91/2011/03/11/ABKrzvS_story.html(accessed September 12, 2011).

—Carol Brennan

Joan Robinson-Berry

Engineer

Joan Robinson-Berry is a senior-level executive with the Boeing Company, responsible for its Defense, Space & Security's Small/Diverse Business & Strategic Alliance division. Active in diversity efforts throughout her career both inside Boeing and in the larger community, Robinson-Berry is believed to be the top-ranking African-American woman in the U.S. corporate aerospace field. "She's one of the smartest people I've come across in my 35 years with the Boeing Company," co-worker Liz Riede told *Sammamish Review* writer Christopher Huber. "She operates with passion in everything she does [and] has a tremendous capacity for compassion, which is rare sometimes in an executive."

Raised in eastern Los Angeles County, Robinson-Berry was an admittedly lax student in high school, but took part in numerous extracurricular activities, including the cheerleading squad, marching band, and student government. She entered California Polytechnic State University (Cal Poly), was drawn to her campus's branch of the leading African-American sorority, Delta Sigma Theta, and majored in mechanical and manufacturing engineering. She earned an undergraduate degree at Cal Poly, then went on to West Coast University, which had a top-ranked aerospace program, for her master's degree in engineering. She would later return to school to earn a graduate business degree from the University of California at Riverside.

Robinson-Berry began her career in aerospace at General Dynamics as a design and manufacturing engineer. She started at McDonnell Douglas in 1986, another major Southern California aerospace company that would be acquired by Boeing in 1997. Early on, she was selected for McDonnell Douglas's Corporate fast-track management program, and rose to become director of Technical Workforce Excellence, then director of Engineering Processes, Tools, and Skills for the Space and Communications business unit. At one point, she served as program manager of McDonnell Douglas's MD-80/-90 Twinjet Programs for the Commercial Airplanes business unit.

When McDonnell Douglas became part of Boeing, Robinson-Berry continued her rise through management ranks. By 2003 she was serving as corporate director of External Technical Affairs out of Boeing's Chicago headquarters, a job that required supervising Boeing's multiple government affiliations with the Department of Defense, its Defense Contract Management Agency, the National Aeronautics and Space Administration, the Small Business Administration, and the Department of Veterans Affairs. In 2004 Robinson-Berry became director and deputy leader of Technical Relations at Boeing.

Part of Robinson-Berry's work at Boeing involves recruitment efforts at historically black colleges and universities, and she also speaks to students as part of Gear Up, a Texas program that helps direct teens from disadvantaged neighborhoods into college. "We need to demystify the notion that math is hard," she told one group of teens, according to Kathryn Walson in the McAllen, Texas, *Monitor* newspaper. "It's a formula. Get a tutor. We can do it." She also pointed out that

At a Glance . . .

Born in California; married to Chris Berry; children: three. *Education*: California Polytechnic State University, BS; West Coast University, MS, engineering; University of California—Riverside, MBA.

Career: General Dynamics, design and manufacturing engineer; joined McDonnell Douglas in 1986 and held various engineering and management posts before and after it was acquired by the Boeing Company in 1997, including director of technical workforce excellence, director of engineering processes, tools, and skills for the Space and Communications business unit. Program manager of the MD-80/-90 Twinjet programs for the Commercial Airplanes business unit, corporate director of external technical affairs, and director of Defense, Space & Security's Small/Diverse Business & Strategic Alliance division.

Awards: Boeing Diversity Change Agent Award, Boeing Company, 2008; Executive Leadership Award, Congressional Black Caucus Foundation, 2009; Golden Torch Award, National Society of Black Engineers, 2011.

Memberships: Billion Dollar Roundtable (board of directors, Boeing representative), Delta Sigma Theta, National Society of Black Engineers.

Addresses: *Office*—The Boeing Company, 100 North Riverside Dr., Chicago, IL 60606.

careers in science generally come with higher salaries. "When I got my first paycheck, I was able to pay my family's rent and have some leftover," she said in the same speech. "I have used my own experience to convince young people that math and science are not as hard as they think and that engineers are not nerds," she told writers William Cole and Gary Sanders in the Boeing publication *Frontiers*. "I want to open doors and help people to reach their potential…. If I can become an engineer, so can you."

In 2009 Robinson-Berry was named Boeing's new Director of Strategic Work Placement and Small Busi-

ness Liaison Officer. That same year, she was honored by the Congressional Black Caucus Foundation with its Executive Leadership Award. Boeing had recognized her efforts, too, naming her the 2008 recipient of its Diversity Change Agent Award. She also represents Boeing on the Billion Dollar Roundtable (BDR) board of directors. The BDR was formed in 2001 to distinguish corporations that award at least $1 billion annually to minority- and woman-owned suppliers. In 2011 the National Society of Black Engineers gave Robinson-Berry its Golden Torch Award at that year's convention.

Robinson-Berry is also active with the U.S. federal government's AbilityOne program, which encourages companies like Boeing to increase the number of employees with disabilities. She lives in Washington State—near Boeing's historical base of operations—with her husband Chris Berry, and is the mother of three children. "Boeing is about technology; it's always been about exploring new frontiers, expanding the envelope," she told Huber in the *Sammamish Review*. "I'm part of inspiring change and improving the quality of life for the world. It's just a blessing."

Sources

Periodicals

Ebony, March 2003, p. 10.
Monitor (McAllen, TX), September 30, 2004.

Online

Cole, William, and Gary Sanders, "Joan Robinson-Berry Is Working to Help Young People Reach Their Potential," Frontiers, July 2004, http://www.boeing.com/news/frontiers/archive/2004/july/ts_sf11.html (accessed September 13, 2011).

Huber, Christopher, "Sammamish Woman Honored for Her Excellence in Engineering," Sammamish Review, April 12, 2011, http://sammamishreview.com/2011/04/12/sammamish-woman-honored-for-her-excellence-in-engineering (accessed September 13, 2011).

"Opening Doors: Boeing Director, Joan Robinson-Berry, to Receive Executive Leadership Award," PRLog, September 17, 2009, http://www.prlog.org/10346180-boeing-director-joan-robinsonberry-to-receive-executive-leadership-award.html (accessed September 13, 2011).

—Carol Brennan

Sonny Rollins

1930—

Musician

Rollins, Sonny, photograph. David Redfern/Redferns/Getty Images.

Sonny Rollins is recognized as one of the best tenor saxophonists in jazz history. He rose to prominence in groups led by Miles Davis, Thelonious Monk, Clifford Brown, and Max Roach, before making a name for himself as a bandleader. His albums *Saxophone Colossus* (1956) and *Way Out West* (1957) established him as one of the leading lights of the bebop era, but he continued to develop artistically throughout the decades that followed. He twice dropped from public view to undertake programs of spiritual and physical rejuvenation, and his performances and recordings have shown him continually willing to take artistic risks and place himself entirely in the service of his musical vision. Although his work from the 1970s and 1980s is generally considered weaker than that of the 1950s and 1960s, he returned to form in the 1990s and continued to push himself musically through the first decade of the new century and beyond.

Began Recording Career in 1949

Theodore Walter Rollins was born in New York City on September 7, 1930. His mother, Valborg Rollins, was born on the island of St. Thomas and worked in the United States as a domestic; his father, Walter William Rollins, was from St. Croix and rose to the rank of chief petty officer during his Naval career. Although his father was seldom home during the 1930s and 1940s, Rollins spent summers with him at the naval base in Annapolis, Maryland. Rollins's father played clarinet, his sister piano, and his brother violin. When Rollins was eight, his parents encouraged him to play the piano. "All West Indian parents wanted children who could entertain by playing something at teatime on Sundays," Rollins's sister, Gloria Anderson, told George Goodman in the *Atlantic Monthly*, "but no one wanted them to think of becoming a jazz musician."

Rollins became interested in the saxophone after listening to recordings of Louis Jordan playing with the Tympany Five. Rollins later listened to recordings by Coleman Hawkins and Ben Webster, but his most important musical education came from other musicians. When he was nine years old, his family moved to the Sugar Hill district of Harlem, a prominent African-American neighborhood where Hawkins, Don Redman, Cy Oliver, and a number of other jazz musicians lived. When he was 13 years old, Rollins received his

At a Glance . . .

Born Theodore Walter Rollins on September 7, 1930, in New York, NY; son of Valborg (a domestic worker) and Walter William (a naval officer) Rollins; married Lucille Pearson Rollins Williams. *Religion*: Zen Buddhism.

Career: Saxophonist accompanying such acts as Babs Gonzales, 1949, Miles Davis, 1951–54, Thelonious Monk, 1953, and Clifford Brown/Max Roach Quintet, 1955–56; bandleader and recording artist, 1956—.

Awards: Guggenheim Fellowship, 1972; *Down Beat*, jazz artist and tenor saxophonist of the year, 1997, 2009; Grammy Awards, National Academy of Recording Arts and Sciences, best jazz instrumental album, 2001, for *This Is What I Do*, and best jazz instrumental solo, 2005, for "Why Was I Born?"; National Medal of Arts, National Endowment for the Arts, 2010.

Addresses: *Agent*—Ted Kurland Associates,173 Brighton Ave., Boston, MA 02134-2003. *Web*—http://www.sonnyrollins.com/.

first saxophone, an alto given to him by his mother, who also gave him the 25 cents needed for lessons at the New York Academy of Music. "Twenty-five cents didn't get very much," he told Goodman. "I consider myself largely self-taught, but not well enough. I've always tried to push myself to make up for it."

When Rollins graduated from Benjamin Franklin High School in 1947, he already belonged to the musicians' union and had begun to work as a professional. He made his first recording in 1949 with singer Babs Gonzales, and played on the pianist Bud Powell's *The Amazing Bud Powell, Vol. 1* in the same year. J. J. Johnson's *Mad Bebop*, which came out soon thereafter, featured one of Rollins's own compositions, "Audubon." Remembering these early recordings, Rollins told Bob Belden in *Down Beat*, "I was just so much in heaven to be there just playing with these guys.... I was just trying to represent myself in a good way."

Became Leading Bebop Saxophonist

In 1951 the trumpet player Miles Davis invited Rollins to join his band. Rollins subsequently played on *Miles and Horns*, *Dig*, and *Conception*. His association with Davis led to his first contract with Prestige Records and his debut recording as a bandleader, *Sonny Rollins*

with the Modern Jazz Quartet, an album comprising recordings made between 1951 and 1953. The album was well received, and it established Rollins as one of the top tenor saxophonists in the jazz world.

In 1953 Rollins played with the pianist Thelonious Monk, appearing on the album *Brilliant Corners*. Rollins later said of Monk, as Gene Santoro reported in the *American Scholar*, "His rhythmic and harmonic conceptions were unique. He was a catalyst, a definite hero. He energized Coltrane and myself to do our own thing. Part of it was that he was so dedicated to the music. It's all he cared about."

Like some other top jazz artists of the 1950s, Rollins began to struggle with a heroin addiction during this time. He went from the verge of jazz stardom to living on the streets in the Chicago subway system by 1955. He eventually kicked the habit with help from the Public Service Hospital in Lexington, Kentucky, where he remained for four months.

Having overcome his addiction, Rollins returned to Chicago, got a job as a janitor, and began practicing the saxophone again. He joined the Clifford Brown-Max Roach Quintet in 1955 and played on the albums *Clifford Brown and Max Roach at Basin Street* and *Sonny Rollins Plus Four*, before Brown's sudden death in a 1956 car accident.

Thereafter, Rollins worked primarily as a bandleader in his own right. Prominent releases of this period include *Tenor Madness*, featuring members of Miles Davis's quintet, most notably John Coltrane, whose appearance on the title track marks the only recorded duet between the two tenor giants. Rollins's breakthrough album as a leader, however, was *Saxophone Colossus*, recorded and released in 1956, when he was 26 years old. Featuring the calypso-infused opening track "St. Thomas," one of the most recognized songs in all of recorded jazz, the album is frequently cited as Rollins's masterpiece, and it is widely considered a landmark in the history of the art form.

Took Two Self-Imposed Sabbaticals

Soon thereafter Rollins dropped the piano and trumpet from his quintet, and for the next two years he performed exclusively with bass and drum accompaniment. Another landmark album came in 1957, *Way Out West*, which included such unlikely jazz pieces as "I'm an Old Cowhand" and the title cut. By 1958, Goodman wrote, "Rollins was at the peak of his powers and reaping the rewards."

When Rollins's mother died in 1959, however, he became emotionally distraught. A year later, following a tour in Europe, he went into seclusion for two years, studying musical theory and composition and undertak-

ing a physical-fitness program. His apartment on New York's Lower East Side was too cramped for his needs, so he began practicing the saxophone on the Williamsburg Bridge walkway against a backdrop of cars, boats, and subway trains, his horn drowned out by the noise. The album that announced his return to public life, fittingly titled *The Bridge*, stands among his finest work, in the view of many critics.

During Rollins's absence, the sonic experiments of Ornette Coleman and John Coltrane, generally categorized as free jazz, shook the foundations of the jazz world. Whereas bebop combined complex chord patterns with breakneck pacing, free jazz allowed players to build compositions without the constrictions of traditional structures. Conceptually exciting as the new music was to many of the artists themselves, the public had a harder time connecting with it.

In the fall of 1961 Rollins performed at New York's Jazz Gallery, reentering the quickly evolving scene. Gradually, he hired such Coleman sidemen as trumpeter Don Cherry and drummer Billy Higgins, and he began to play free jazz on albums like *On the Outside* (1963) and *Stuttgart* (1963). Critics were divided on the saxophonist's new direction, and Rollins vacillated between traditional and avant-garde approaches. He toured Germany and Austria, and while he continued to record, he did so less frequently than in the 1950s. In 1965 he toured England, which led to composing the film score for the movie *Alfie*, and in 1966 he recorded *East Broadway Rundown*, his last album before beginning another, lengthier retirement.

While on his six-year hiatus, Rollins visited Japan and became interested in Zen Buddhism. He explored his spirituality and sought to distance himself from the business side of his music career. In 1968 he departed for India. "Taking his horn and little else," Goodman wrote, "he spent four months in the Powaii Ashram in the Bombay suburbs, meditating on his life's mission and practicing hatha yoga."

Resumed Career, Kept Evolving

Rollins returned to the jazz scene in 1972, signing with Milestone Records and releasing *Next Album*. He received a Guggenheim fellowship in 1972 and was elected as the 38th member of the *Down Beat* Hall of Fame in 1973.

His music continued to evolve, this time absorbing pop influences. Goodman noted that "his work for the next two decades left much of his original following behind and failed to draw the critical acclaim of his earlier years." Rollins, however, continued unperturbed. His wife, Lucille, was now managing his career, and he enjoyed his widest popularity to date.

Rollins also began playing in concert halls, as opposed to clubs, in the late 1970s. He told Belden, "Jazz needs some dignity. It needs to be looked at as a serious, important art form. And if you're going to be playing in nightclubs ... you're not going to get that kind of respect for it."

Rollins's work returned to critical favor in the 1990s and early 2000s when he recorded a series of well-received albums, including *Sonny Rollins Plus Three* (1996) and *Global Warming* (1998). *This Is What I Do* (2000) brought him his first Grammy Award. By this time Rollins was one of the few jazz masters from the 1950s who was still alive, and his place among the top tenor saxophonists in jazz history was assured.

Remained in Top Form Despite Age

Rollins and his wife lived primarily in the rural environs of Germantown, New York, in their later decades. He also kept an apartment in Lower Manhattan until the events of September 11, 2001, during which he found himself trapped in his building for a night and a day and then evacuated by bus, carrying only his saxophone. Lucille Rollins arranged for their driver to bring her husband back to Germantown, and then she insisted, despite his disordered state of mind, that he follow through on a performance date scheduled for September 15 in Boston.

"There was something different in the air that night," Rollins told Santoro. I don't know how to describe it, and I don't know what it was. But it was palpable." The concert was recorded and released in 2005 as *Without a Song: The 9/11 Concert*. A song on the album, "Why Was I Born?" brought Rollins his second Grammy Award.

Well into his 70s, Rollins practiced the saxophone for hours every day, often until well after dark, in a cottage on the Germantown property. His wife would leave a porch light on for him, so that when he finished practicing, he could easily make his way in to the house. When Lucille Rollins died in November of 2004, Rollins ceased practicing in the cottage. "I came out here a few times," he told Nate Chinen in the *New York Times*, in an interview that took place at the cottage, "and then I looked, and there was no light on the porch. It just kind of highlighted that, well, there's nobody there now."

Rollins hardly ceased practicing, however. Although he might reasonably have rested on his past accomplishments, he did nothing of the kind. Stanley Crouch, in a 2005 *New Yorker* profile of the tenor legend, reported an anecdote told by the drummer Victor Lewis, who had recently played with Rollins at an outdoor festival in Antibes, France: "Do you know that man stood up there and gave a three-and-a-half-hour concert and did most of the playing? He wasn't coasting or floating, either. He was deep in it, playing his ass off. That's

surreal. Seventy-three years old, out in the hot sun, blowing a saxophone for that long—who can believe that?"

Awarded National Medal of Arts

Rollins's wife's death also brought other challenges. As his manager since the 1970s, Lucille had long dealt with all business matters, leaving him free to concentrate strictly on his music. In her absence, Rollins found himself having to approve legal and promotional decisions and even, after leaving the Milestone label in 2005, releasing his recordings through his own label, Doxy Records.

The first Doxy release was 2006's *Sonny, Please*, recorded immediately after he and his band returned from a Japanese tour. The album was distributed on the Internet before being officially released in 2007. It is generally regarded as an excellent addition to Rollins's late-career work. Other Doxy releases included the compilation of live recordings, *Road Shows, Vol. 1* (2008).

Rollins continued to tour into his ninth decade. Reviewing a New York concert marking the saxophonist's 80th birthday, Chinen wrote in the *Times*, "Any concert by Sonny Rollins, the great unflagging sovereign of the tenor saxophone, bears the promise of a momentous occasion." In 2011 President Barack Obama presented Rollins with the 2010 National Medal of Arts, the highest award given to artists by the U.S. government. While on tour that same year, Rollins explained his continued interest in performing to Jerry Shriver in *USA Today*: "When I got my sax when I was 7 or 8, I would go in my room and play and play. My mother would say, 'It's time to eat dinner,' but I was in the zone. Completely happy. That feeling is still with me."

Selected discography

Sonny Rollins with the Modern Jazz Quartet, Prestige, 1953.
Saxophone Colossus (featuring "St. Thomas"), Prestige, 1956.
Sonny Rollins Plus Four, Prestige, 1956.
Tenor Madness, Prestige, 1956.
A Night at the Village Vanguard, Vol. 1, Blue Note, 1957.
Way Out West (featuring "Way Out West" and "I'm an Old Cowhand"), Contemporary, 1957.
Freedom Suite, Riverside, 1958.
The Bridge, Bluebird, 1962.
Alfie (film score), Impulse!, 1966.
East Broadway Rundown, Impulse!, 1966.
Next Album, Original Jazz Classics, 1972.
Sonny Rollins Plus Three, Milestone, 1996.
Global Warming, Milestone, 1998.
This Is What I Do, Milestone, 2000.
Without a Song: The 9/11 Concert (featuring "Why Was I Born?"), Milestone, 2005.
Sonny, Please, Doxy, 2007.
Road Shows, Vol. 1, Doxy, 2008.

Sources

Books

Blancq, Charles, *Sonny Rollins: The Journey of a Jazzman*, Twayne Publishers, 1983.

Periodicals

American Scholar, Winter 2007.
Atlantic Monthly, July 1999, p. 82.
Billboard, June 10, 2000.
Down Beat, August 1997, p. 18; February 2001, p. 22.
New Yorker, May 9, 2005.
New York Times, October 21, 2006; August 8, 2008; November 29, 2009; September 13, 2010.
Star Tribune, March 23, 2001, p. 22.
USA Today, May 6, 2011.

Online

"Sonny Rollins," AllMusic, http://allmusic.com/artist/sonny-rollins-p7446 (accessed August 23, 2011).

—Ronnie D. Lankford Jr. and Mark Lane

Joseph Boulogne, Chevalier de Saint-Georges

1745(?)–1799

Violinist, composer, conductor, fencing master

Composer, virtuoso violinist, fencing champion, and military hero, Joseph Boulogne Saint-Georges, known as the Chevalier de Saint-Georges, was among the most celebrated men in 18th-century France, famous across Europe and even as far as the Americas. The son of a wealthy French planter and an African slave, Saint-Georges rose into the elite of Parisian society—unheard of for a black man of his time—and distinguished himself as the finest fencer in France as well as a talented violinist, earning the admiration of Queen Marie Antoinette. He was one of the first black musicians to compose in the classical European tradition, penning at least six operas, more than a dozen concertos for violin, and eight symphony concertantes over his career. During the French Revolution Saint-Georges espoused the republican ideals of the revolutionaries, leading a regiment of black soldiers and helping to foil a treasonous plot. Saint-Georges's compositions fell into obscurity after his death in 1799, but in the late 20th century renewed attention to the composer's life and work sparked a renaissance of scholarly studies on the Chevalier.

Broke into Elite French Society

Born Joseph Boulogne Saint-Georges on Christmas Day, 1745 (some sources give 1739 and others 1748 as the year of his birth), in Basse Terre on the French-controlled Caribbean island of Guadeloupe, he was the son of George de Boulogne Saint-Georges, a French plantation owner, and his mistress Nanon, a 16-year-old Senegalese slave who was known across the island for her remarkable beauty. His father, a descendant of the noble house of Bologne in Italy, was a gentleman in the court of French King Louis XV and a patron of the arts in Paris. He took the unusual step of giving his son his surname, thereby acknowledging his paternity; nonetheless, Joseph, as a child of mixed race, was barred from inheriting his father's noble status. Even more unusual, the elder Saint-Georges took his mistress and illegitimate son, together with his legitimate wife and daughter, with him to France in 1748, when he was forced to flee Guadeloupe after he was convicted for killing a man in a duel.

The younger Saint-Georges was settled in a fashionable quarter of Paris, where he was treated as a young member of the French nobility, in spite of his race. He enrolled at the boarding school of the famous swordsman Texier de La Boëssière, where his studies included literature, science, fencing, swordsmanship, and horseback riding. Tall, handsome, and agile, Saint-Georges distinguished himself as a talented fencer, an excellent horseman, and a quick student, and he soon found his way into the elite of French society. At the age of 19, Saint-Georges entered the French military as a Gendarme de la Garde du Roi of Louis XV, earning the title "chevalier." By the time he was 20 years old, he was recognized as the finest fencer in France and, perhaps,

At a Glance . . .

Born Joseph Boulogne on December 25, 1745(?), in Basse Terre, Guadeloupe; died on June 10, 1799, in Paris, France; son of George de Boulogne Saint-Georges (a plantation owner) and Nanon (a slave). *Education*: Studied violin under Jean-Marie Leclair and François-Joseph Gossec. *Military service*: French National Guard, 1791–93.

Career: Concert des Amateurs, violinist, 1769–73, director, 1773–81; Concert de la Loge Olympique, director, 1781–89; Le Cercle de l'Harmonie, director, 1797–99.

in all of Europe, holding his own against the celebrated Italian fencer Giuseppe Gianfaldoni in 1766.

At the same time, Saint-Georges also was showing himself to be a skilled musician. He had begun studying the violin as a boy in Guadeloupe, possibly under a man named Platon, his father's plantation manager. Later, in Paris, he is believed to have taken lessons from Jean-Marie Leclair *l'aîné* (the elder), the composer of some of the best Baroque violin music to come out of France during the 18th century, and later François-Joseph Gossec, a French composer of music for opera, string quartet, and symphony.

In 1769 Gossec, with the backing of wealthy patrons who may have included Saint-Georges's father, formed an orchestra called the Concert des Amateurs to showcase the best performers in Paris. Saint-Georges joined the company as first violin, and in 1772 he made his debut as a soloist, performing two of his own violin concertos. The *Mercure de France* newspaper reported that the performance "received the most rapturous applause, both for its excellent execution and for the composition itself." The following year, when Gossec left the orchestra, the 28-year-old Saint-Georges succeeded him as director.

Became Known as the "Black Mozart"

Word of Saint-Georges's talent soon reached Versailles, and in 1774 Queen Marie Antoinette invited the young virtuoso to play for her. For many years Saint-Georges enjoyed a close relationship with the queen, serving as a sort of musical adviser—although not as her lover, as rumor had it, or as her teacher, as some sources claim. That same year, Saint-Georges's father died in Guadeloupe, leaving him no income and a heap of debts to sort out. To support himself, Saint-Georges signed a six-year agreement in 1775 with the music publisher Bailleux, and he entered a period of prolific composition, primarily for violin, turning out two sets of string quartets—a new genre that was little known in France at the time—a dozen violin concertos, and at least ten symphonies concertante, a form developed by Saint-Georges that blended the symphony and concerto genres.

By the mid-1770s Saint-Georges, nicknamed the "Black Mozart," was the toast of Paris, well known as a composer, conductor, and soloist. Even as his fame grew, however, he was not immune to racial prejudice. By law, he could not marry within his social class, as interracial unions were prohibited; he remained a bachelor for life. In 1775, when Saint-Georges was considered for the prestigious post of director of the Paris Opéra—at the suggestion of Marie Antoinette—two of the company's sopranos petitioned the queen in protest, arguing that "their honor and the delicacy of their conscience made it impossible for them to be subjected to the orders of a mulatto." Saint-Georges was denied the appointment.

When the Concert des Amateurs disbanded in 1781, Saint-Georges founded a new orchestra called the Concert de la Loge Olympique under the sponsorship of the Masonic lodge, of which he was the first African member in France. Working with the Count D'Ogny, he arranged for the commission of Franz Joseph Haydn's six "Paris Symphonies," traveling to Austria to meet the composer—then the most famous in Europe—and conducting the first performance of the work in 1787.

By the end of the 1780s Saint-Georges had abandoned instrumental music in his own compositions, devoting himself entirely to opera. His first dramatic work, *Ernestine,* debuted in 1777 at the Comedie Italienne, followed by *La Partie de chasse* in 1778 and *L'Amant anonyme* in 1780. In 1787 Saint-Georges, still an able athlete, traveled to London to give a fencing exhibition, meeting the Prince of Wales (the future King George IV). Upon his return he mounted his most successful opera, *Le Fille-garçon,* and composed an opera for children, *Aline et Dupré; ou, Le Marchand des marrons.* He completed his final opera, *Guillaume tout coeur,* in 1790.

Embraced the Spirit of Revolution

During his travels in England, Saint-Georges became involved in that country's growing abolitionist movement, and in 1788 he helped found the Société des Amis des Noirs (Society of the Friends of the Blacks) to continue this work in France. The group achieved a measure of success in 1794, when the French Republic abolished slavery, although that victory would be reversed by Napoleon Bonaparte in 1802.

The last decade of Saint-Georges's life was dominated by the French Revolution, which sought to overturn the

absolute monarchy that had ruled France for centuries. Saint-Georges sympathized with the democratic ideals of the revolutionaries, and in 1791, when the French Assembly called for 91,000 volunteers to join the National Guard, he was among the first to enlist. In September of 1792 he was charged with organizing a corps of 1,000 black and mulatto soldiers, the Legion Nationale des Americains et du Midi, which became known as the "Legion Saint-Georges." The following year, Saint-Georges played a key role in thwarting the "Treason of Dumouriez," a plot by a renegade French officer to seize the city of Lille. Saint-Georges was hailed as a hero, but the revolutionaries soon turned against him, and during the "Reign of Terror" under leader Maximilien Robespierre, he was imprisoned for 18 months.

After the revolution Saint-Georges returned briefly to the Caribbean, traveling to the island of Santo Domingo (now Haiti and the Dominican Republic), which was in the throes of its own revolution. He returned to Paris in 1797 and became the director of a new orchestra, the Cercle de l'Harmonie, which performed at the Palais Royale. His orchestra still attracted crowds, but the heyday of his career was long past. By the time of his death of a bladder infection on June 10, 1799, he was alone and penniless. When Napoleon reinstated slavery in 1802, performances of Saint-Georges's works were banned, and many of his scores were destroyed.

Music historians began to revive interest in the life and work of Saint-Georges during the late 20th century, and in 2002 Paris mayor Bertrand Delanoë renamed a street in honor of the composer. Saint-Georges was the subject of a documentary, *Le Mozart Noir: Reviving a Legend,* broadcast on CBC in Canada in 2002, and two biographies published in 2003 and 2006.

Selected works

Operas

Ernestine, 1777.
La Partie de chasse, 1778.
L'Amant anonyme, 1780.
La Fille-garçon, 1787.
Aline et Dupré, ou Le Marchand de marrons, 1788.
Guillaume tout coeur, 1790.

Sources

Books

Banat, Gabriel, *The Chevalier de Saint-Georges: Virtuoso of the Sword and Bow,* Pendragon, 2006.
Guédé, Alain, *Monsieur de Saint-George: Virtuoso, Swordsman, Revolutionary,* translated by Gilda M. Roberts, Picador, 2003.

Periodicals

Guardian, February 12, 2002.
Independent, May 21, 2007.
New York Times, January 6, 2008.

Online

"Le Chevalier de Saint-Georges," Africlassical.com, March 31, 2011, http://chevalierdesaintgeorges. homestead.com/page1.html (accessed July 18, 2011).
Saint-Georges International Festival in Guadeloupe, http://www.festivalinternationalsaintgeorges.org/ en/aboutsg.html (accessed July 18, 2011).

—Deborah A. Ring

Gil Scott-Heron

1949–2011

Lyricist, vocalist, novelist, poet

Scott-Heron, Gil, photograph. Samir Hussein/Getty Images.

A prominent figure in the political turmoil and artistic ferment of the 1970s, lyricist and vocalist Gil Scott-Heron achieved international fame with a distinctive technique that relied not on singing but on speaking. Generally set to a heavy beat and frequently cited as a precursor to rap, the style he called "bluesology" drew heavily on both jazz and R&B. Its focus, almost invariably, was on social injustice. Though he also wrote poetry and at least two novels, he is far better known for his music. Out of the dozens of pieces he recorded, he is probably best remembered for "The Revolution Will Not Be Televised" (1970 and 1971), a sober look at the failure of the mass media to inspire social change. Forty years after its first release, Alec Wilkinson of the *New Yorker* called it "the species of classic that sounds as subversive and intelligent now as it did when it was new."

Born on April 1, 1949, in Chicago, Gilbert Scott-Heron was the son of a professional soccer player from Jamaica and a librarian/English teacher. His parents broke up when he was young, and he spent much of his childhood with his grandmother in Jackson, Tennessee, a small town between Nashville and Memphis. In a 2010 piece called "On Coming from a Broken Home,"

he recalled the trauma of his parents' split and his reliance on his grandmother's quiet strength. Even she, however, was unable to shield him from local racists. By all accounts a sensitive and impressionable child, he had particular difficulty facing the taunts of white classmates. It was eventually decided, therefore, that he would live in New York City with his mother. That move was complete by his mid teens. Already determined by that point to become a writer, he won a scholarship to Fieldston, one of the city's best-known private schools. Following his graduation there, he entered Lincoln University, a predominately African-American institution in Pennsylvania. He had not been there long when he won the 1968 Hughes Creative Writing Award, one of the school's most prominent honors.

It was also at Lincoln that he completed his first novel, *The Vulture*. A bleak story of drug dealers and revolutionaries, it was published in 1970. That year proved an eventful one for him; within months of the book's appearance, he had dropped out of college, published a volume of poetry, *Small Talk at 125th and Lenox*, and released an album of the same name. It was the recording that drew the most attention, proving par-

At a Glance . . .

Born Gilbert Scott-Heron on April 1, 1949, in Chicago, IL; died on May 27, 2011, in New York, NY; son of a professional soccer player and a librarian/ English teacher; children: three. *Education*: Attended Lincoln University, late 1960s.

Career: Independent writer and musician, late 1960s–2011; Federal City College, creative-writing instructor, 1972–76.

Awards: Hughes Creative Writing Award, Lincoln University, 1968.

ticularly popular among intellectuals and political activists in Harlem and other African-American communities. In comments quoted by Katharine Boyle in the *Washington Post*, Cornel West of Princeton University recalled Scott-Heron's ability "to lay bare some unsettling truths with ... artistic sophistication." In communities still grappling with the legacy of segregation, those truths had a powerful effect.

The next few years were arguably Scott-Heron's most creative period. In 1971 he released a second album, *Pieces of a Man,* which contained what is generally considered the definitive rendition of "The Revolution Will Not Be Televised," an early version of which had appeared on *Small Talk.* Although he continued to produce works on paper, publishing a second novel (*The N****r Factory*) in 1972 and teaching in the creative-writing program at Washington's Federal City College (1972–76), it was clear by the middle of the 1970s that he was increasingly focused on music. He recorded prolifically, releasing roughly an album per year for the next decade. Among his most memorable works from this period was 1976's *From South Africa to South Carolina.* Completed with keyboardist Brian Jackson and set to the soulful beats typical of the early disco era, it drew compelling and provocative links between South Africa's apartheid system and lingering racism in the United States. In doing so, it encapsulated the disappointment felt by many African Americans in the wake of the civil-rights era. In the early 1970s, it often seemed that poverty and hopelessness were preventing the realization of the gains made just a few years earlier. Scott-Heron articulated the frustration that caused with a power few could match.

From *South Africa to South Carolina* was followed by a string of strong albums. By about 1984, however, Scott-Heron's output had dropped dramatically. With a few exceptions, among them the well-received *Spirits*

(1994), he withdrew from recording and from public life for more than a decade. While his disappearance from public view had several causes, the most important of them by far, was his crippling addiction to crack cocaine.

Hundreds of thousands of Americans from all races and walks of life succumbed to crack when it appeared in the 1980s. Like many of them, Scott-Heron wrestled for years with his addiction, often relapsing after brief periods of sobriety. As Wilkinson made clear in his powerful *New Yorker* profile, Scott-Heron's friends and colleagues tried their best to save him. Arrested several times, he served a short term in the mid-2000s at Rikers Island, New York's primary jail. That experience, perhaps paradoxically, gave a significant boost to his career, for it was there that he made arrangements for the release of *I'm New Here* (2010), his first major album since *Spirits* and a favorite of critics. In the words of AllMusic.com's Thom Jurek, "*I'm New Here* contains the artful immediacy that distinguishes Scott-Heron's best art. The modern production adds immeasurably to that quality, underscores his continued relevance in reflecting the times, and opens his work to a new generation of listeners while giving older ones a righteous jolt."

In the spring of 2011, Scott-Heron fell sick after a trip to Europe. Admitted to a hospital on his return to New York, he died there on May 27 of undisclosed causes. Surviving him were a son and two daughters. In the wake of his death, many returned to Wilkinson's *New Yorker* piece, which offered vivid glimpses of an immensely talented man laid low by drugs and personal demons. In one of the most poignant of those vignettes, Wilkinson quoted the reaction of a guard at Rikers when informed of Scott-Heron's presence in the facility: "Don't tell me it's *the* Gil Scott-Heron."

Sources

Periodicals

New Yorker, August 9, 2010.
New York Times, May 28, 2011.

Online

Boyle, Katharine, "Gil Scott-Heron Dies at 62," *Washington Post,* May 29, 2011, http://www.washingtonpost.com/blogs/arts-post/post/gil-scott-heron-dies-at-62/2011/05/29/AGh3KNEH_blog.html (accessed September 16, 2011).
Jurek, Thom, "*I'm New Here*: Review," AllMusic.com, http://allmusic.com/album/im-new-here-r1708884/review (accessed September 16, 2011).

—R. Anthony Kugler

Margaret Simms

1946—

Economist

Simms, Margaret, photograph. Terry Ashe/Time & Life Pictures/ Getty Images.

Margaret Simms is one of the top African-American economists in the United States. She took her Ph.D. in economics from Stanford University and worked in academia through the 1970s, teaching at the University of California, Santa Cruz, and Atlanta University (now Clark-Atlanta University). In 1979 she moved to Washington, DC, to take a position as a researcher for the Urban Institute. She has remained a policy researcher and administrator ever since, leaving the Urban Institute for the Joint Center for Political and Economic Studies in 1986. She remained at the Joint Center for 21 years, ascending the ranks of the organization's leadership to serve as interim president, before returning to the Urban Institute as a fellow and director of the Low-Income Working Families project. Simms has published numerous monographs, policy papers, and opinion pieces, and she is a leading expert on economic issues of import to African Americans.

Came of Age as Segregation Ended

Margaret Constance Simms was born in St. Louis, Missouri, on July 30, 1946, the youngest of three children. Her parents and grandparents were all college graduates, and she had an uncle and an aunt who held prestigious positions in academia. The family accordingly valued academic achievement highly, and from an early age Simms understood that she was expected to excel in school and to attend college.

Simms came of age during the transition from segregated to integrated school systems in St. Louis. She attended segregated schools until the fifth grade, when Missouri began to comply with the 1954 *Brown v. Board of Education* decision, and the aftereffects of segregation remained pronounced throughout her years as a student. At Carleton College in Northfield, Minnesota, she was one of only four African Americans in a student body of 1,400.

Simms planned to study chemistry or physics at Carleton, but she found herself drawn to the real-world implications of economics. She participated in a summer program sponsored by the U.S. State Department in 1966, which was designed to prepare students for jobs in the foreign service. The successful completion of the program entitled Simms to a one-year fellowship to attend the graduate school of her choice. She

At a Glance . . .

Born Margaret Constance Simms on July 30, 1946, in St. Louis, MO; daughter of Frederick T. and Margaret E. Simms. *Education*: Carleton College, BA, 1967; Stanford University, MA, 1969; Stanford University, Ph.D., 1974.

Career: University of California, Santa Cruz, acting assistant professor, 1971–72; Atlanta University, assistant professor, 1972–76, associate professor and chair of Department of Economics, 1976–81; Urban Institute, senior research associate, 1979–81, director of minorities and social policy program, 1981–86; Joint Center for Political and Economic Studies, deputy director of research, 1986–91, director of research programs, 1991–97, vice president for research, 1997, senior vice president for research, 2003–05, vice president for governance and economic analysis, 2005–06, interim president, 2006; Urban Institute, institute fellow and director of low-income working families project, 2007—.

Memberships: National Economic Association, 1971—, president, 1978–79; Council of Economic Priorities, board member, 1979–85; Institute for Women's Policy Research, board member, 1991–99, board chair, 1993–98; Partners for Democratic Changes, board member.

Awards: Samuel Z. Westerfield Award, National Economic Association, 2008; honorary doctor of laws degree, Carleton College, 2010.

Addresses: *Office*—Urban Institute, 2100 M Street NW, Washington, DC 20037. *Email*—publicaffairs@urban.org. *Web*—http://www.urban.org.

completed a bachelor of arts degree in economics from Carleton in 1967 and was accepted into the graduate economics program at Stanford University.

Excelled in Academic World

At the beginning of her time at Stanford, Simms was the only African-American student in her program, and one of very few women. Only one African American had previously taken a Ph.D. in the department, and no women had. She described the professors' attitude toward her, in an interview with Paulette I. Olson and Zohren Emami, as one of "benign neglect," and at first she thought that the lack of encouragement she received might be related to her race and/or gender, but after informally surveying her peers, she determined that this was the attitude the faculty adopted toward all of the graduate students.

Simms's first year at Stanford coincided with the assassination of Martin Luther King Jr., and the political turmoil related to that and other events of the time led the faculty of the Economics department to alter the curriculum to address issues of particular contemporary relevance. The establishment of an urban economics concentration in the department interested Simms intensely enough that she decided to forego a career in the foreign service, opting to stay on at Stanford for her Ph.D. She completed a master's degree in 1969 and finished her coursework for a doctoral degree in 1971; she then took a teaching job and worked while finishing her Ph.D. requirements, eventually taking the degree in 1974.

Simms's first job after graduate school was at the University of California, Santa Cruz. Although opportunities for advancement were available to her, the small-town environment and the lack of contact with people her own age led her to apply for jobs in more socially stimulating locations. After spending the 1971–72 academic year at Santa Cruz, she took a position in the Atlanta University School of Business.

Atlanta University (which later merged with Clark College and became Clark-Atlanta University) was a historically black college, and while there Simms was able to find the mentorship and community involvement that had been lacking in her academic career to that date. She connected with the Caucus of Black Economists, a group that had been formed in New York several years previously, and she became involved in Atlanta politics, serving as an economic adviser to Mayor Maynard Jackson.

In 1976 Atlanta University set up a free-standing Economics department, and Simms was tapped to serve as chair. Soon thereafter, she got her first sustained public-policy experience, when she was offered a fellowship from the Brookings Institution, the think tank devoted to promoting democratic ideals, social justice, and international cooperation. She lived in Washington, DC, and worked, as part of the fellowship, for the U.S. Department of Housing and Urban Development, before returning to resume her duties in Atlanta. In 1979 a job offer from the Urban Institute, a think tank devoted to exploring social and economic problems, prompted her to return to Washington, where she has remained ever since, working as a researcher and administrator for public-policy organizations.

Became Recognized Expert in Her Field

As a researcher and administrator, Simms became one of Washington's leading experts on economic issues

that affect the lives of African Americans. At the Urban Institute, she was a senior research associate from 1979 to 1981, before becoming director of the Minorities and Social Policy Program, in which capacity she served until 1986. She left the Urban Institute to take a position as deputy director of research for the Joint Center for Political Studies, a policy organization established in 1970 to provide assistance and training to black elected officials.

As the center developed in the 1980s and 1990s, its mission was broadened to encompass policy research related to employment, economic development, and related issues, and its name was changed to the Joint Center for Political and Economic Studies. Simms rose steadily through the ranks of the organization, reaching the posts of director of research programs in 1991, vice president for research in 1997, and senior vice president for research in 2003. In 2005 Simms was promoted to the position of vice president for governance and economic analysis, and in 2006 she served as interim president of the organization.

This series of promotions corresponded to an increased focus on administrative duties relative to research, and to an ever-widening set of responsibilities, from the management of individual research projects to the management of overall organizational strategy. Although Simms continued to present researched policy papers and commentary, much of the research itself was conducted by her staff. As she told Olson and Emami, "If I were to think about the impact of the things that I have done, I would say that it has been less about my research, and more about my contributions to building institutions."

In addition to building the institutions that employed her, Simms was instrumental in the development of the National Economic Association, the successor organization to the Caucus of Black Economists, and of the academic journal *Review of Black Political Economy*, which she edited from 1983 to 1988. As an outgrowth of her work at the Urban Institute and the Joint Center for Political and Economic Studies, Simms also co-authored, edited, or co-edited policy monographs and books, including *Slipping through the Cracks: The Status of Black Women* (1986), *The Economics of Race and Crime* (1988), *Choice and Circumstance: Racial Differences in Adolescent Sexuality and Fertility* (1989), *Economic Perspectives on Affirmative Action* (1995), and *Job Creation Prospects and Strategies* (1998).

In 2007 Simms returned to the Urban Institute to serve as an institute fellow and director of the Low-Income Working Families project. The Low-Income Working Families project was an initiative devoted to exploring the difficulties faced by the nine million American families classified as the working poor. The challenges faced by this demographic were particularly pressing during the early years of Simms's tenure as director, given the 2008 economic crisis and the resulting rise in unemployment in the United States. These developments meant that Simms was at the forefront of crucial public-policy debates.

Simms posted analyses and commentary based on the findings of her group's research at the Urban Institute website and on the institute's MetroTrends blog, as well as in mainstream periodicals and media outlets including the *Philadelphia Inquirer* and National Public Radio's *Marketplace*. She was also frequently called on by journalists to comment, as one of the leading experts in her field, on issues concerning the economic welfare of African Americans and the working poor.

Selected works

Author

(With Kristin A. Moore and Charles L. Betsey) *Choice and Circumstance: Racial Differences in Adolescent Sexuality and Fertility*, Transaction, 1989.

Editor

(With Julianne M. Malveaux) *Slipping through the Cracks: The Status of Black Women,* Transaction, 1986.
(With Samuel L. Myers Jr.) *The Economics of Race and Crime,* Transaction, 1988.
Economic Perspectives on Affirmative Action, University Press of America, 1995.
(With Wilhelmina A. Leigh) *Job Creation Prospects and Strategies,* University Press of America, 1999.

Sources

Books

Olson, Paulette I., and Zohren Emami, *Engendering Economics: Conversations with Women Economists in the United States*, Psychology Press, 2002.

Periodicals

San Francisco Chronicle, December 24, 2008, p. C1.

Online

"Margaret Simms," National Economic Association, http://www.neaecon.org/msimms.htm (accessed September 18, 2011).
"Margaret Simms," Urban Institute, http://www.urban.org/about/MargaretSimms.cfm (accessed September 18, 2011).

—Mark Lane

Tracey T. Travis

1963(?)—

Business executive

Engineer turned business executive Tracey T. Travis is the chief financial officer of Polo Ralph Lauren, a $5 billion global luxury apparel and lifestyle goods company that is one of the largest retailers in the United States. Since she joined the company in 2005, Polo Ralph Lauren has exceeded industry analysts' growth forecasts, overcoming a dip in consumer spending to post record profits in 2011. In her two decades in corporate finance, Travis has helped guide the operations of some of the nation's top companies, including General Motors and Pepsi. She is considered one of the most powerful women in the corporate world today.

Travis attended the University of Pittsburgh, earning an undergraduate degree in industrial engineering in 1983. She began her career as an engineer at a General Motors engineering plant in Michigan, where she was the only woman, the only African American, and the youngest person in her department—a fact that motivated her to concentrate on demonstrating her abilities. "I was very focused on proving myself and focused on results," she recalled at the Black Women's Economic Summit in 2005. She took advantage of a GM fellowship that allowed her to attend Columbia University, where she studied business administration with a focus on finance and operations management. After completing her master's degree in 1986, she returned to the company as a financial analyst, working on a variety of international product programs in Asia and Latin America.

In 1989 Travis took a job with the Pepsi Bottling Group, and soon she was moving up the management ladder. As the group manager for new products strategy, she led the strategic planning process for the company's non–soft drink products and served as chief financial officer of a $450 million business unit. As market unit general manager, she oversaw sales, production, and distribution of Pepsi products for the Howell, Michigan, market, driving her unit's sales and profit performance to the top three in the country. Travis was promoted in 1995 to chief financial officer of Pepsi's Michigan Business Unit. In 1999 she left Pepsi to become chief financial officer at the Chicago-based company Beverage Cans Americas, the North American division of the American National Can Company, a manufacturer of metal beverage cans for the soft drink and brewing industries.

Travis switched industries in 2001, leaving the beverage business to join the apparel company Limited Brands in Columbus, Ohio, the parent company of six retail chains, including Victoria's Secret and Bath & Body Works. She first served as senior vice president and chief financial officer of the subsidiary Intimate Brands from 2001 to 2002 and then as senior vice president of Limited Brands from 2002 to 2004.

In January of 2005, Travis was named senior vice president and chief financial officer of Polo Ralph Lauren. Based in New York City, the company specializes in high-end clothing for men and women and lifestyle products such as fragrances, home goods (such as bedding and towels), and housewares. Travis is responsible for Polo Ralph Lauren's worldwide corporate finance, overseeing the company's accounting,

At a Glance . . .

Born on June 22, 1963(?). *Education*: University of Pittsburgh, BS, industrial engineering, 1983; Columbia University, MBA, 1986.

Career: General Motors, engineer, 1983–86, financial analyst, 1986–89; Pepsi Bottling Group, business unit chief financial officer, 1989–94, general manager, 1994–99; Beverage Cans Americas, chief financial officer, 1999–2001; Intimate Brands, senior vice president and chief financial officer, 2001–02, Limited Brands, senior vice president, 2002–04; Polo Ralph Lauren, senior vice president and chief financial officer, 2005—.

Memberships: Finance Executives Institute (executive leadership council), Jo-Ann Stores (board of directors), Lincoln Center Theater (board of directors), National Association of Corporate Directors, New York Women's Forum, Polo Ralph Lauren Foundation (board of directors), Ralph Lauren Cancer Center (board of directors), University of Pittsburgh Board of Trustees.

Awards: Top 25 Women in Finance, *Treasury and Risk Management Magazine*, 2005; Top 50 Women in Business, *Black Enterprise*, 2006, 2010; Best CFO Award, *Institutional Investor*, 2008; Distinguished Alumni Award, University of Pittsburgh, 2009; Top 100 African Americans in Corporate America, *Black Enterprise*, 2009.

Addresses: *Office*—Polo Ralph Lauren Corporation, 650 Madison Ave., New York, NY 10022.

financial planning and analysis, tax, business development, and investor relations functions.

By mid-2011 Travis had handled seven merger and acquisitions transactions for the company, refinanced the corporate debt, implemented foreign exchange hedging, and enhanced the firm's internal and external corporate reporting. In 2011 Polo Ralph Lauren was one of the largest retailers in the United States, valued at nearly $5 billion. Despite the economic recession, which hampered sales of luxury goods for a time, the company posted higher than expected profits—$184.1 million in the second quarter of 2011—and its shares rose 13 percent on the year. The company also increased the dividend it pays to shareholders in 2011,

an indication of its positive long-term outlook.

Travis has received many accolades for her accomplishments in business. In 2005 she was named to *Treasury and Risk Management*'s Top 25 Women in Finance, and in 2008 *Institutional Investor* honored her with its Best CFO Award. Three times she has been recognized by *Black Enterprise*—in 2006 and 2010, when she was included in the magazine's Top 50 Women in Business, and in 2009, when she was named to the Top 100 African Americans in Corporate America. Also in 2009, Travis received the Distinguished Alumni Award from the University of Pittsburgh.

She also is active in many business, civic, and cultural organizations. Travis serves on the boards of directors of Jo-Ann Stores Inc., the Lincoln Center Theater in New York, and the Women's Forum of New York, in addition to the Ralph Lauren Center for Cancer Care and Prevention and the Ralph Lauren Foundation. In 2010 she was appointed to the Board of Trustees of her alma mater, the University of Pittsburgh. She is a member of the Executive Leadership Council, Financial Executives International, and the National Association of Corporate Directors.

Sources

Online

"Black Women on Wall Street: Getting to the Top and Staying There," *Network Journal*, September 2005, http://www.tnj.com/archives/2005/september/black-women-on-wall-street (accessed September 14, 2011).

Hill, Robert, "Alumnus, Polo Ralph Lauren Executive Tracey T. Travis Advanced as New Trustee Candidate by Pitt Board's Nominating Committee," University of Pittsburgh, June 15, 2010, http://www.news.pitt.edu/news/alumnus-polo-ralph-lauren-executive-tracey-t-travis-advanced-new-trustee-candidate-pitt-boards- (accessed September 14, 2011).

Timberlake, Cotten, "Polo Ralph Lauren Jumps after Profit Exceeds Estimates," Bloomberg, August 10, 2011, http://www.bloomberg.com/news/2011-08-10/polo-ralph-lauren-jumps-after-profit-exceeds-estimates-2-.html (accessed August 14, 2011).

"Tracey Travis: Executive Profile," *BusinessWeek*, http://investing.businessweek.com/businessweek/research/stocks/people/person.asp?personId=1112153&ticker=RL:US (accessed September 14, 2011).

White, Patricia Lomondo, "Burton M. Lansky, Tracey Travis Named 2009 Distinguished Fellows," *Pitt Chronicle*, February 23, 2009, http://www.chronicle.pitt.edu/?p=2210 (accessed September 14, 2011).

—Deborah A. Ring

Michael Vick

1980—

Football player

Vick, Michael, photograph. Rob Tringali/SportsChrome/Getty Images.

One of the most gifted athletes in the National Football League (NFL), Michael Vick was a superstar quarterback for the Atlanta Falcons from 2001 to 2006. He was the NFL's highest-paid player and a perpetual presence on highlight reels, but his play was as inconsistent as it was spectacular. Then in 2007 his career was abruptly derailed when it emerged that he had for many years operated an illegal and exceptionally cruel dog-fighting business in his home state of Virginia. As the extent of Vick's cruelty toward the dogs that fought in the enterprise came to light, he became one of the most detested figures in professional sports. He was suspended indefinitely without pay by the NFL, sentenced to 23 months in prison, dropped by his sponsors, and forced into bankruptcy.

Vick missed two NFL seasons while serving his sentence in federal prison and then under house arrest in Virginia. In 2009 the Philadelphia Eagles made the extremely controversial move of signing him to a two-year contract. Vick was a backup quarterback in 2009 and saw little playing time. When the Eagles' first-string quarterback suffered an injury early in the 2010 season, however, Vick stepped into the starter's role with aplomb, leading the Eagles to the National Football Conference (NFC) East Division title and posting passing and rushing statistics that placed him among the NFL's top quarterbacks. Likewise, his off-the-field image improved, and he once again became a sought-after product endorser. Questions about whether or not Vick had truly reformed lingered among many in the media and the public, but no one disputed his ability as a player.

Excelled at Football Early

Michael Vick was born on June 26, 1980, to teenaged parents Michael Boddie and Brenda Vick in Newport News, Virginia. (Vick's mother later took Boddie's name.) Vick grew up with his siblings and his mother in the town's Ridley Circle housing project. His father was often absent or working long hours in the Newport News shipyards, but he had been a football player, and he made time to teach his sons the fundamentals of the game in their very early years.

As a child growing up in an urban housing project, Vick saw numerous peers lose their way, but as he told Paul Attner in the *Sporting News*, "Sports kept me off the

At a Glance . . .

Born Michael Dwayne Vick on June 26, 1980, in Newport News, VA; son of Michael Boddie and Brenda Vick; children: Michael Jr., Jada, London. *Education*: Virginia Tech University, 1998–2000.

Career: Atlanta Falcons, quarterback, 2001–06; Philadelphia Eagles, quarterback, 2009—.

Awards: All-American, 1997; *Sporting News* First Team All America, 1999; Big East Offensive Player of the Year, 1999; Archie Griffin Award, 1999; ESPY Award, top college football player, 1999; Gator Bowl MVP, 2000; NFL Pro Bowl, 2002, 2004, 2005, 2010; NFL Comeback Player of the Year, Associated Press, 2010; NFL Comeback Player of the Year, *Sporting News*, 2010.

Addresses: *Office*—Philadelphia Eagles, NovaCare Complex, One NovaCare Way, Philadelphia, PA 19145. *Web*—http://www.philadelphiaeagles.com/index.html; and http://mikevick.ning.com/.

streets. It kept me from getting into what was going on, the bad stuff." Even though Vick excelled at baseball and basketball, by the time he arrived at Warwick High School in 1994, he had given up all other sports to pursue his passion: football.

As a freshman in high school, Vick was promoted to the position of starting quarterback for the varsity team. In his second game as a varsity starter he threw for 433 yards on only 13 completions. Vick's coach Tommy Reamon, a former running back in the NFL, knew that he had a special player. In the off-season he sent the young prodigy to camps and worked with Vick alone. Reamon also gave Vick the freedom to make plays on his own, a freedom that he would later exercise to great effect at the college and pro levels.

Led Virginia Tech to Championship Game

During his high school career Vick threw for 4,846 yards and 43 touchdowns, and he ran for 1,048 yards and 18 touchdowns. One of the most heavily recruited college football prospects in the country, Vick chose Virginia Polytechnic Institute and State University (better known as Virginia Tech), yielding to his high school coach's advice and his own desire to remain close to home.

Virginia Tech Head Coach Frank Beamer redshirted Vick for his first year, which gave the young quarter-

back time to learn the team's offense and adapt to college life. He later told *Sports Illustrated*'s Lars Anderson, "Before I took my first snap, I wanted to be in control of the offense, know where the players were, how to read defenses. These are all things I learned when I sat out."

Physically Vick was unmatched by anyone on the Virginia Tech team, and he easily won the starting quarterback job during spring practice following his redshirt season. He ran a 4.3-second 40-yard dash and recorded a kangaroo-like vertical leap of 40.5 inches. He impressed his coaches and teammates with his ability to improvise and make plays through a combination of instinct and athleticism. In his first college game—a 47-0 defeat of James Madison—he scored a touchdown on a diving somersault into the end zone. The play was broadcast perpetually on sports highlight reels across the country.

Vick's renown grew as the Hokies racked up victory after victory. The team went undefeated during the regular season and played Florida State for the national championship in the Sugar Bowl. Virginia Tech trailed 28-7 early in the game, but Vick made a number of spectacular plays and led his team to a 29-28 lead. Although the Hokies ultimately lost the game 46-29, Vick's impressive performance in front of a captive national audience raised his profile substantially.

On the season Vick threw for 1,840 yards and 12 touchdowns and set a National Collegiate Athletic Association (NCAA) record for passing efficiency by a freshman (180.37). As a rusher, he gained 585 yards and added eight touchdowns. Vick was named to the *Sporting News* All-America team, won Big East Offensive Player of the Year honors, and finished third in the Heisman Trophy voting.

In his sophomore season Vick led his team to a 6-0 start, but then he sprained his ankle against Pittsburgh and neither he nor the team ended up matching the previous season's successes. Virginia Tech would go on to win the Gator Bowl, and Vick would be named the team's most valuable player, but after an injury-riddled season in which defenses were prepared for him, his numbers were down. Nevertheless, NFL scouts forecast Vick as the top pick in the NFL draft, and he declared his intention to play at the professional level.

Became NFL Superstar

The Atlanta Falcons made Vick the first pick overall of the 2001 draft and signed him to a six-year deal worth approximately $62 million. Falcons coach Dan Reeves planned to bring Vick along slowly in his first season, but when starting quarterback Chris Chandler was injured, Vick took over the offense. He started against Dallas and St. Louis and played in five other games. Even though the Falcons saw glimpses of greatness in

his first year, Vick turned the ball over too often and had trouble memorizing Reeves's complicated offense.

In 2002 the Falcons released Chandler and made Vick their starting quarterback. Reeves simplified the playbook, and Vick worked in the off-season to master the offense. He led the Falcons to the playoffs, and pundits began to speak of him as the prototype for the quarterback of the future. Atlanta won its first-round playoff game against a heavily favored Green Bay Packers before losing the following week to the Philadelphia Eagles. Vick was named to the NFC's Pro Bowl team that year.

After fracturing his fibula in the 2003 preseason, Vick sat out the first 11 games of the 2003 season, and the Falcons missed the playoffs. The following season, with Vick at full strength, the Falcons returned to the playoffs, winning against the St. Louis Rams before losing in the divisional championships to Philadelphia. Vick was chosen for the NFC's Pro Bowl team for the second time that season, and when his contract came up for renewal, the Falcons offered him the most lucrative deal in NFL history: $130 million over 10 years.

The Falcons had a disappointing 2005 season, posting a regular-season record of 8-8 and missing the playoffs. Vick continued to win accolades for his performance, however, and was named to his third Pro Bowl. By the end of the 2006 season, Vick had achieved a number of league records, including the record for the most rushing yards by a quarterback in a single season.

Imprisoned for Running Dog-Fighting Operation

Vick's career was abruptly interrupted when, in April of 2007, it emerged that for many years he had bankrolled an interstate dog-fighting and gambling operation, Bad Newz Kennels, based in Virginia. In June of that year a federal grand jury indicted him for his involvement with the enterprise. Vick initially denied the charges, but over the course of the investigation witnesses came forward claiming to have seen Vick executing dogs and handling proceeds from gambling operations. In August of 2007 Vick pleaded guilty to breeding dogs for illegal fighting and for executing a number of dogs that failed to perform.

In the wake of his plea, the NFL suspended Vick without pay, and the Falcons removed him from their roster and initiated court proceedings to recover approximately $20 million in bonus payments they had made to him. Shortly thereafter, Vick's promotional contracts, including an endorsement deal with Nike, were suspended, and he became widely reviled by the public as news spread about the systematic cruelty that he presided over at Bad Newz Kennels. In December of 2007 Vick was sentenced to 23 months' imprison-

ment. With no income and debts far exceeding his assets, he filed for bankruptcy in 2008.

Upon being released from prison in 2009 Vick took on the popular former Indianapolis Colts head coach Tony Dungy as a mentor to help him with the transition to life outside of prison. Dungy became convinced that Vick truly understood the gravity of his misdeeds and was intent on being a better person and football player. Eventually others were similarly converted, including NFL commissioner Roger Goodell, who had suspended Vick in 2007, and top figures in the Philadelphia Eagles organization. In August of 2009 the Eagles took the controversial step of allowing the widely despised Vick a second chance as an NFL quarterback.

Mounted Spectacular Comeback

The Eagles signed Vick to a $1.6 million contract with the option to renew it for a second season at a price tag of $5.2 million—numbers that paled by comparison with his pre-incarceration salary. Vick was cleared to play by the third week of the season, but he spent the year as a backup to Donovan McNabb and saw very little playing time.

The 2010 season saw Vick return to form with a vengeance, however. He took over starting quarterback duties in the season's second week, after Kevin Kolb suffered a concussion. Vick immediately began posting spectacular performances, reestablishing himself as one of the NFL's very best quarterbacks. In his first two games as a starter he passed for five touchdowns and led the Eagles to victory, before being sidelined with a rib injury for three-and-a-half games.

The turning point in Vick's season, and in public opinion regarding his future as an NFL player, came during a November game against the Washington Redskins. Vick posted one of the most impressive performances of any quarterback in recent memory, passing for 333 yards and four touchdowns and rushing for 80 yards and two touchdowns. In the wake of the Redskins game Vick's rebirth as a player became the most compelling and complex sports story of the year. In the *Philadelphia Inquirer* Ashley Fox spoke for many fans and commentators when she wrote after the game, "With his near-flawless play, his speed, and his determination, Vick has put himself back in the limelight and forced the discussion about how we are supposed to feel about him. Do we forgive? Do we forget? Do we cheer?"

Many Eagles fans were doubtless conflicted, but many others cheered as Vick led the team to a 10-6 record and an NFC East Division title. Although he threw a season-ending interception to end the Eagles' season in the first round of the playoffs (they lost 21-16 to the Green Bay Packers), his comeback was the talk of the NFL. He was named the starting quarterback for the

NFC's Pro Bowl team, and he won 2010 NFL Comeback Player of the Year awards from both the *Sporting News* and the Associated Press.

In early 2011 the Eagles signed Vick to a contract extension projected to net him up to $20 million for the following season. Vick had served his sentence and done substantial community service to make amends for his crimes, but some skeptics continued to doubt the degree to which he had changed. Still, in July of 2011, his image was sufficiently rehabilitated that Nike again signed him to an endorsement contract.

Sources

Periodicals

Jet, January 17, 2005.
New York Times, November 6, 2003; December 1, 2003; August 21, 2007; August 28, 2007; December 11, 2007; January 30, 2010.
Philadelphia Inquirer, November 19, 2010; December 29, 2010; January 10, 2011; March 2, 2011; July 2, 2011; July 27, 2011.
Sporting News, April 9, 2001; January 17, 2011.
Sports Illustrated, January 13, 2000; September 2, 2002; December 2, 2002; March 16, 2009; July 13, 2009; October 4, 2010; November 29, 2010; March 28, 2011.

Online

Wilner, Barry, "Vick Wins Comeback Player Award," Huffington Post, February 5, 2011, http://www.huffingtonpost.com/2011/02/05/vick-comeback-player-award_n_819181.html (accessed September 18, 2011).

—Michael J. Wallace, Micah L. Issit,
Paul Burton and Mark Lane

Derek Walcott

1930—

Poet, playwright

Derek Walcott, a multiracial native of the West Indian island of St. Lucia, is the most celebrated and accomplished Caribbean poet in history. A playwright as well as a poet, he achieved considerable critical acclaim by the 1960s, and he produced the volumes of verse containing what many believe to be his strongest work in the 1970s, 1980s, and 1990s. Much of Walcott's poetry derives its originality and tension from his placing of Caribbean landscapes, people, and folkways in dialog with the European poetic and cultural tradition. He has

Walcott, Derek, photograph. Vittorio Zunino Celotto/Getty Images.

given voice to a previously marginalized people without demonizing or abandoning the cultural values that were imposed on them by colonizing governments, and he has done so in a lush and sensuous language that has won him comparisons with Shakespeare and T. S. Eliot, among others. Walcott's status as a major postwar poet was confirmed when he won the 1992 Nobel Prize for literature. Although his output slowed somewhat after he received the award, he continued to write ambitious and accomplished poetry in the following decades.

Influenced by Island Culture and Environment

Walcott and his twin brother, Roderick, were born on January 23, 1930, in Castries, a colonial town on the small eastern Caribbean island of St. Lucia. At the time of Walcott's birth, St. Lucia was part of the British protectorate, but its past as a French colony was evident in the Creole dialect and religious practice of its citizens. Both of Walcott's parents were schoolteachers. His father died when Walcott was only a year old. His mother nurtured her two sons' love of reading and study. She surrounded her children with English literary classics, recited Shakespeare to them, and encouraged them to appreciate poetry and drama.

In those days Castries was a picturesque town with large, ornate Victorian homes nestled among bright tropical gardens. Jervis Anderson noted in the *New Yorker* that Walcott spent little time during his youth admiring the displays of affluence in the city: "His attention was drawn more strongly to the shanties of

At a Glance . . .

Born Derek Alton Walcott on January 23, 1930, in Castries, St. Lucia, West Indies; immigrated to United States, late 1950s; son of Warwick (a civil servant and teacher) and Alix (a teacher) Walcott; married Fay Moston, 1954 (divorced, 1959); married Margaret Ruth Maillard, 1962 (divorced); married Norline Metivier (actress and dancer; divorced); children: one son, three daughters. *Education*: University of the West Indies, BA, 1953.

Career: Poet and playwright, 1940s—; *Public Opinion* (Kingston, Jamaica), feature writer, 1956–57; *Trinidad Guardian* (Port of Spain, Trinidad), feature writer, 1960–62, and drama critic, 1963–68; Little Carib Theatre Workshop (later Trinidad Theatre Workshop), founding director, 1959–76; Boston University, professor of creative writing, 1981–2007; University of Alberta, distinguished scholar in residence, 2009–12.

Awards: Obie Award, *Village Voice*, 1971, for *Dream on Monkey Mountain*; honorary doctorate of letters, University of the West Indies, Mona, Jamaica, 1973; O.B.E. (Officer, Order of British Empire), 1972; Guggenheim fellowship, John Simon Guggenheim Memorial Foundation, 1977; John D. and Catherine T. MacArthur Foundation grant, 1981; *Los Angeles Times* Prize in poetry, 1986, for *Collected Poems, 1948-1984*; Queen Elizabeth II Gold Medal for Poetry, 1988; Nobel Prize for literature, 1992; St. Lucia Cross, 1993; honorary doctorate, University of Essex, 2008; T.S. Eliot Prize for Poetry, Poetry Book Society (UK), 2011, for *White Egrets*.

Addresses: *Publisher*—Farrar, Straus and Giroux, 18 West 18th St., New York, NY 10011. *Email*—fsg.publicity@fsgbooks.com.

In school, Walcott learned English as a second language and became captivated by the works of Great Britain's best poets. At the same time he was well aware that England was the seat of the colonial government that had encouraged slavery during previous centuries. He therefore approached the European canon with an ambivalent attitude that would remain with him through the decades to come.

Gained Renown in Caribbean Literary Circles

Walcott rebelled against the rigid Catholicism of his homeland and sought a more relaxed atmosphere for continued studies elsewhere. In 1950 he departed for the newly established University of the West Indies in Kingston, Jamaica. Islanders from all parts of the Caribbean descended on the University of the West Indies, and their close association helped to forge a sense of region-wide community. Kingston's vibrant arts and literary communities also had a formative impact on the young writer.

Walcott lost little time in making his own contribution to Caribbean arts. His first play, *Henri Christophe: A Chronicle*, was written and produced in St. Lucia while he was still an undergraduate student. Another piece, *Henri Dernier*, played on radio in 1950. He also began to publish poetry, art criticism, and essays in such periodicals as the *Trinidad Guardian* and Jamaica's *Public Opinion*.

After earning his bachelor's degree in 1953, Walcott returned to St. Lucia to teach at St. Mary's College, the high school he had attended. By 1954 he was spending substantial time in Trinidad. His plays *The Sea at Dauphin* and *Ione* premiered there in the mid-fifties, and he became deeply involved with the establishment of a resident theater project on the island.

In 1957 Walcott received a Rockefeller Foundation grant to study theater arts in New York City. There he worked with Off-Broadway directors and companies, appropriating the skills he would need to establish a repertory group in Trinidad. He felt alienated by the racially segregated world of New York theater, however, and sought a different cultural ambiance for his West Indian project.

Walcott returned to Trinidad and founded the Trinidad Theatre Workshop in the capital city of Port of Spain. The group performed some of Walcott's plays and others that explored the myths, rituals, and superstitions of West Indian folk life. The workshop eventually folded, but Walcott found an audience for his plays in New York City at the Off-Broadway Public Theatre. There, in 1971, his most famous drama, *Dream on Monkey Mountain*, drew enthusiastic reviews and an Obie Award as best foreign play of the year.

the poor, in Castries and elsewhere on the island, occupied by fascinating characters, some of whom later appeared in his book-length autobiographical poem, *Another Life*." Of Walcott's early influences, Anderson further wrote, "Beyond the sociology of the land, young Walcott's imagination was transfixed by the sea: its sounds; its fishermen and schooner men; its far horizon of limits and possibilities; the dangerous seductions of its calm and stormy moods; its record of local drownings; its legends of shipwreck and isolation."

Won International Acclaim as a Poet

Poetry proved Walcott's primary route to international literary attention. At first he published primarily in magazines, but in 1962 his verse came to the attention of editors at the British publisher Jonathan Cape. Cape released Walcott's first major collection, *In a Green Night*, in 1962. The volume was well received and established him as a rising talent. Robert Lowell, at that time one of the most famous and accomplished poets in the world, was so impressed that he visited Trinidad to meet Walcott. "I remember sitting on the living-room floor while Lowell showed me some of the poems he was working on," Walcott told the *New Yorker*. "I was so flattered to hear this great writer asking me what I thought of his work. When he returned to New York, he called up Roger Straus and urged him to sign me on as a new writer. I've been with [publisher Farrar, Straus, and Giroux] ever since."

Having found a congenial publisher, Walcott turned out numerous books of verse. His work was hailed for its expressive language and its brave exploration of the question of cultural ancestry. *New York Times* reviewer Michiko Kakutani, for example, saw in Walcott "an old-fashioned love of eloquence, an Elizabethan richness of words and a penchant for complicated, formal rhymes." In the *New York Review of Books*, the prominent poet Joseph Brodsky (later a friend of Walcott's and a Nobel laureate in his own right) called the Caribbean "the place discovered by Columbus, colonized by the British, and immortalized by Walcott."

In the early 1970s Walcott began to spend part of the year in the United States, teaching creative writing at such universities as Columbia, Rutgers, Yale, Harvard, and Princeton. Farrar, Straus and Giroux published volumes of his poetry regularly, including *The Gulf* (1970), *Another Life* (1973), *Sea Grapes* (1976), *The Star-Apple Kingdom* (1979), and *The Fortunate Traveller* (1981). In 1981 Walcott received the fellowship from the John D. and Catherine T. MacArthur Foundation that is commonly known as a "genius grant," a no-strings-attached award intended to provide for the honoree's financial needs for a period of five years.

Collected Poems (1986) showcased over 40 years' worth of Walcott's poetic output and made the case for his status as a truly major postwar poet. This was followed by the collection *The Arkansas Testament* (1987) and *Omeros* (1990), a book-length poem adapting the Homeric epic tradition to Walcott's Caribbean and cosmopolitan poetic vision. *Omeros* is considered by many critics and scholars to be Walcott's masterpiece and the book that sealed his bid for the Nobel Prize in literature.

Awarded the Nobel Prize

Walcott was rumored to be in the running for a Nobel Prize for years before he received it. He tried not to be distracted by the politics of the prize: "Look at some of the great writers who died without winning the Nobel Prize—[James] Joyce, [W. H.] Auden, Graham Greene, Jorge Luis Borges," he told the *New Yorker*. "Why should my chances be any better than theirs?... It got to the point where I learned to put the whole business out of my mind." Walcott kept busy writing and teaching at Boston University, where he began holding a part-time position in 1982, spending part of the year in the States and part of the year at home in St. Lucia.

The Nobel committee announced Walcott's selection on October 8, 1992. The date is doubly significant since 1992 marked the 500th anniversary of Columbus's landing in the Caribbean. From Sweden came the announcement that Walcott had been chosen for his "poetic oeuvre of great luminosity, sustained by historical vision" and his "multi-cultural commitment." In Walcott, the committee stated, "West Indian culture has found its great poet."

Perhaps nowhere was the joy more visible than on St. Lucia, where the weekly newspaper in Castries devoted an entire 40-page issue to its native son. The Nobel Prize came with a cash award of $1.2 million and assured Walcott's stature in the literary world, ratifying the view of many critics and fellow poets that he was among the very best writers in the English language.

Continued to Produce Ambitious Work

Several years passed between Walcott's winning of the Nobel and his next book, 1997's *The Bounty*, which found him in an elegiac mode, memorializing his recently departed friend Brodsky as well as his mother. During this time Walcott also collaborated with the songwriter Paul Simon and the choreographer Mark Morris on the Broadway musical *The Capeman*. The project generated considerable interest ahead of its 1998 premiere, but it was skewered by critics and was a commercial flop. Walcott's first collection of prose, *What the Twilight Says*, a collection of essays on literature and West Indian culture written between 1970 and 1997, also appeared in 1998.

Walcott continued to produce ambitious work well into his 70s. *Tiepolo's Hound* (2000), a book-length poem combining reflections on the painter Camille Pisarro with an autobiographical narrative, and interspersed with reproductions of Walcott's own paintings, was followed by *The Prodigal* (2004), another autobiographical book-length poem. *Selected Poems* (2007) provided an opportunity for reassessing the best of Walcott's work. The notoriously dyspeptic critic William Logan, reviewing the volume in the *New York Times*, opined that "No living poet has written verse more delicately rendered or distinguished than Walcott, though few individual poems seem destined to be

remembered." This verdict on the future fate of Walcott's work was perhaps belied by a profusion of secondary literature on the Walcott corpus, beginning in the late 1990s and continuing through the new decade.

As he approached his 80th birthday, Walcott was in the news for unpleasant reasons, when accusations of sexual harassment dating to his time as a professor at Harvard in the 1980s forced him to withdraw his 2009 candidacy for the position of professor of poetry at Oxford University. It was later discovered that Walcott's competitor for the job, the poet Ruth Padel, had been responsible for publicizing the episode from Walcott's past; Padel resigned after nine days on the job when her role in the scandal was discovered. Walcott later accepted the post of distinguished scholar in residence at Canada's University of Alberta.

The year 2010 saw the publication of *White Egrets*, yet another book of poems that together formed a conceptual whole. Karl Kirchway, reviewing it in the *New York Times*, called *White Egrets* "both visionary, in the best sense of the word, and intensely personal" and maintained that "It is an old man's book, craving one more day of light and warmth; and it is a book of stoic reckoning." The book won the 2011 T.S. Eliot Prize.

Although Walcott's career was unmistakably in its twilight by this time, there was little doubt that his work would continue to generate critical and scholarly interest for the foreseeable future.

Selected writings

Poetry

In a Green Night (includes "A Far Cry from Africa"), J. Cape, 1962.
Selected Poems, Farrar, Straus and Giroux, 1964.
The Gulf, Farrar, Straus and Giroux, 1970.
Another Life, Farrar, Straus and Giroux, 1973.
Sea Grapes, Farrar, Straus and Giroux, 1976.
The Star-Apple Kingdom, Farrar, Straus and Giroux, 1979.
The Fortunate Traveller, Farrar, Straus and Giroux, 1981.
Collected Poems, 1948-1984, Farrar, Straus and Giroux, 1986.
The Arkansas Testament, Farrar, Straus and Giroux, 1987.
Omeros, Farrar, Straus and Giroux, 1990.
The Bounty, Farrar, Straus and Giroux, 1997.
Tiepolo's Hound, Farrar, Straus and Giroux, 2000.
The Prodigal, Farrar, Straus and Giroux, 2004.
Selected Poems, Farrar, Straus and Giroux, 2007.
White Egrets, Farrar, Straus and Giroux, 2010.

Plays

Henri Christophe: A Chronicle, Advocate, 1950.
The Sea at Dauphin, University College of the West Indies, 1954.
Ione: A Play with Music, University College of the West Indies, 1957.
Dream on Monkey Mountain and Other Plays, Farrar, Straus and Giroux, 1970.
The Odyssey: A Stage Version, Farrar, Straus and Giroux, 1993.
(With Paul Simon) *The Capeman: A Musical,* Farrar, Straus and Giroux, 1998.
The Haitian Trilogy (includes *Henri Christophe*, *Drums and Colours*, and *The Haytian Earth*), Farrar, Straus and Giroux, 2001.
Walker and Ghost Dance, Farrar, Straus and Giroux, 2002.

Essays

What the Twilight Says, Farrar, Straus and Giroux, 1998.

Sources

Books

Baer, William, ed., *Conversations with Derek Walcott,* University Press of Mississippi, 1996.
Breslin, Paul, *Nobody's Nation: Reading Derek Walcott,* University of Chicago Press, 2001.
Burnett, Paula, *Derek Walcott: Politics and Poetics,* University Press of Florida, 2000.
Hamner, Robert D., *Derek Walcott,* Twayne, 1981.
King, Bruce, *Derek Walcott: A Caribbean Life,* Oxford University Press, 2000.

Periodicals

Art Journal, Spring 2001.
Ebony, February 1993, p. 46.
Economist, March 20, 2010.
Evening Standard (London), January 25, 2011.
Jet, October 26, 1992, p. 14; December 28, 1992, p. 24.
Newsweek, October 19, 1992, p. 73.
New Yorker, June 26, 1971, p. 30; December 21, 1992, p. 71.
New York Review of Books, November 10, 1983, p. 39.
New York Times, March 21, 1979; August 21, 1979; May 30, 1981; May 2, 1982; January 15, 1986; December 17, 1986; January 30, 1998; May 31, 2009; June 4, 2009.
New York Times Book Review, September 13, 1964; October 11, 1970; May 6, 1973; October 31, 1976; May 13, 1979; January 3, 1982; April 8, 1984; February 2, 1986; December 20, 1987; October 31, 2004; April 8, 2007; April 25, 2010.

New York Times Magazine, May 23, 1982, p. 32.
Publishers Weekly, May 26, 1997; August 31, 1998; February 7, 2000; October 18, 2004.
Research in African Literatures, Spring 2003.
Time, October 19, 1992, p. 65; April 5, 1993, p. 13.

Twentieth Century Literature, Summer 2001; Spring 2007.
World Literature Today, September-October 2010.

—Anne Janette Johnson and Mark Lane

Sammy Wanjiru

1986–2011

Marathon runner

Sammy Wanjiru was a Kenyan distance runner who in a few short years established himself as one of the great marathoners of all time. After setting the half-marathon world record by the age of 18, Wanjiru won the first marathon he entered, the 2007 Fukuoka Marathon in Japan, at the age of 21. Wanjiru then electrified world audiences with a gold-medal-winning performance at the 2008 Beijing Olympics, setting an Olympic record and delivering what is widely considered one of the finest marathon performances ever. Wanjiru went on to set course records while winning both the London and Chicago Marathons in 2009 and to repeat his Chicago victory in 2010, becoming the youngest runner ever to win four major marathons. Wanjiru was considered a favorite to win gold at the 2012 London Olympics, and his goal of setting a new world record in the marathon was well within reach, when in May of 2011 he died under mysterious circumstances during a domestic dispute.

Wanjiru, Sammy, photograph. Jim Prisching/Getty Images.

Trained in Japan

Sammy Wanjiru was born on November 10, 1986, in the high-altitude Nyahururu Laikipia district of Kenya, approximately 120 miles north of the country's capital of Nairobi. Raised by his mother, Hannah, in impoverished circumstances, Wanjiru began running, like many prominent Kenyan distance racers, as a means of transportation. He left school at the age of 12 due to a lack of money, but he was recognized for his prowess as a runner by a local athletic club, which helped him train and participate in the Kenya National Primary Athletics Championships. He placed third in the event's 10,000-meter race at the age of 14, and soon thereafter he was spotted by Sunnichi Kobayashi, a Kenya-based recruiter for Japanese schools.

Japanese running culture is well-known as an incubator for top distance racers, and Kobayashi offered Wanjiru the opportunity to attend Japan's Sendai Ikue High School as an exchange student and to represent the school as a runner. Aware that her son would not be able to obtain an education or the proper training as a runner in Kenya, given her financial constraints, Wanjiru's mother agreed to the arrangement.

Wanjiru had no previous knowledge of Japan, and he initially battled homesickness and culture shock: "I

At a Glance . . .

Born Samuel Kamau Wanjiru in Nyahururu Laikipia district of Kenya on November 10, 1986; died on May 15, 2011, in Nyahururu, Kenya; son of Hannah Wanjiru; married Triza Njeri; children: one daughter.

Career: Marathon runner, 2007–11.

Awards: Gold Medal, 2008 Summer Olympics, men's marathon; World Marathon Majors Champion, 2008–09, 2009–10.

could not get used to the food," he told Joshua Robinson in the *New York Times*. "For me, it was not good. And my family was in Kenya, and I sometimes got the homesickness. It was a very hard year." Ultimately, however, Wanjiru adapted to life in Sendai and learned to speak Japanese fluently. He also quickly made his mark as one of Japan's top junior runners, posting impressive times in the 5,000- and 10,000-meter individual races and anchoring Sendai Ikue High School's national championship team in the long-distance relay event called the *ekiden*.

Excelled on Toyota Kyushu Team

Wanjiru's performance in high school events won him a contract with the Toyota Kyushu corporate racing team upon graduation. He was put on salary by Toyota and given nominal duties in the company's marketing offices, while being expected to train intensively and compete in major races on the team's behalf. He quickly became one of the world's top distance runners. He set a world record in the half-marathon at the age of 18 and then did so for a second time three years later, by which time he had also begun training as a marathon runner. In December of 2007, at the age of 21, more than a decade earlier than marathoners typically reach their prime, Wanjiru won the first marathon he entered, in the Japanese city of Fukuoka, setting a course record with a time of 2:06:39. He followed this performance with a second-place finish in the 2008 London Marathon.

Having established himself as a top runner, Wanjiru became displeased with some of the restrictions placed on him by the Toyota Kyushu team. He had a wife and child in Kenya by this time, but team rules required him to remain in Japan for 180 days out of the year. The team also had extensive control over his racing schedule; he was barred from running in the 2007 New York Marathon, and even after he won the Fukuoka race, the team's coach Koichi Morishita suggested that he should not race in the London Marathon or the 2008 Olympics.

Although he appreciated the training and opportunity Morishita and Toyota had given him, Wanjiru resigned from the team in July of 2008. He explained his resignation to *Running Times* in the following way: "I needed to train more; I needed time to go to Kenya; I wanted to go to Olympics for my country.... In Kenya there are hills and high altitude, that is the part of my training that has been missing."

Made History at 2008 Olympics

On August 1, 2008, Wanjiru vaulted to the ranks of the best marathoners in history at the Beijing Olympics. A runner's ability to post top times in the marathon is generally considered highly dependent on weather conditions. Record-setting performances usually occur when temperatures are cool, with the mid-50s Fahrenheit representing an ideal range and the 70s and 80s representing a range at which runners' times increase by as much as several minutes over the course of the 26.2-mile race. At the start of the Olympic Marathon in Beijing, the temperature was 74° F, and as the temperature reached the 80s, the race course was in full sun. Most of the field felt the effects of the heat, but Wanjiru ran the race as aggressively as if conditions were perfect, beating the existing Olympic record by more than three minutes, with a time of 2:06:32.

Although his time was not a world record, Wanjiru's showing was immediately hailed by numerous commentators in the running world as possibly the greatest marathon performance of all time, given the uncongenial conditions. The win also made him Kenya's first gold medalist in the event—a surprise to many, since runners from Wanjiru's home country have long been among the world's best marathoners. The fact that Wanjiru was only 21 years old at the time of his spectacular Olympic performance, in a sport historically dominated by runners in their 30s who have reached peak form only after years of training, made his achievement all the more remarkable.

In the months after the Olympics Wanjiru let it be known that his goal, in future races, was to beat the world record posted by the Ethiopian runner Haile Gebrselassie. The record stood at 2:04:26 at the time of the Olympics, before Gebrselassie improved on his own mark in the September of 2008 Berlin Marathon, with a time of 2:03:59. Many commentators felt that Wanjiru had the ability to exceed this goal substantially, given favorable weather conditions.

Was World's Top Marathoner, 2008–10

Wanjiru won his next race, the 2009 London Marathon, with a time of 2:05:10. Though still well short of the world record in spite of ideal weather conditions, the time was good enough for a new course record, and

Wanjiru was never seriously threatened by any of the other racers. The fact that Wanjiru spent the end of the race alone without any other runners to push him made it more difficult for him to post a world-record time. He remained confident that he would eventually beat the world record, especially if he found designated pacesetters who could keep up with him.

Wanjiru made another bid for the world record at the October of 2009 Chicago Marathon, but again, he spent the end of the race alone, frustrated at his pacesetters' inability to keep up with him. In the Chicago race, as well, temperatures were in the mid-30s, and Wanjiru ran into a fierce headwind at the end of the race, scuttling his chances for a world record. Once again, though, his time—2:05:41—was good enough for a course record, and the victory made him the 2008–09 World Marathon Majors Champion, a title given to the top runner overall in the Chicago, New York, Boston, London, and Berlin marathons.

Wanjiru encountered obstacles in 2010, including health and personal problems. He was forced to withdraw from the London Marathon due to knee problems and from a race in Italy due to a chest complaint. Three weeks before the October of 2010 Chicago Marathon, a stomach virus interrupted his training schedule, and he entered the race in comparatively poor physical condition. His performance in the race rivaled his famous 2008 Olympic showing, though, as he used sheer physical ability and determination to outlast his primary challenger, Ethiopia's Tsegaye Kebede, with a finishing time of 2:06:24.

That Wanjiru was able to win against the world's best runners without properly training for the race demonstrated, as the 2008 Olympics race had, that he was in a class of his own as a marathoner. His manager Federico Rosa told the *New York Times* that Wanjiru's victory was "the greatest surprise in a race I've ever seen in my life," and Amby Burfoot of *Runner's World* wrote, "In the press room, we were all stunned. People aren't supposed to run 2:06 when they're down and out."

The victory gave Wanjiru his second consecutive World Marathon Majors Championship, but personal troubles followed. In December of 2010 he was arrested for threatening to kill his wife, Triza Njeri, and a personal security guard with an illegally obtained AK-47 assault rifle. Although he and his wife supposedly reconciled and she dropped the charges against him, the couple's marriage was reportedly badly strained by this time, and observers feared that Wanjiru's life was in danger of falling apart.

Died under Mysterious Circumstances

On May 15, 2011, according to police reports, Njeri returned home to find Wanjiru with another woman, and a fight ensued. What happened next is the subject of conflicting accounts. One police spokesperson maintained that Wanjiru committed suicide as a result of the discord with his wife, jumping to his death from the balcony of the bedroom where he had been with the other woman. Another officer told the media that he believed Wanjiru, locked in the bedroom by Njeri, was jumping down from the balcony in an attempt to prevent her from leaving the family compound.

In any event, Wanjiru jumped from the balcony and died as a result of his injuries. He was 24 years old. Thus ended what had been one of the most promising distance-running careers on record. In a mere three years, Wanjiru went from being a relative unknown to being the world's most formidable marathon runner. The international sports world was stunned by Wanjiru's sudden and inexplicable death, but his achievements were likely to be remembered for many years to come.

Sources

Periodicals

Daily Telegraph (UK), May 17, 2011.
New York Times, August 24, 2008, p. SP4; April 25, 2009, p. D2; April 27, 2009, p. D7; October 12, 2009, p. D8; October 11, 2010, p. D8; May 16, 2011; May 17, 2011.
Running Times, May 2010, p. 52.
Times (London), May 17, 2011.

Online

Burfoot, Amby, "And Now There Are Three—Gebrselassie, Bekele, and Wanjiru," *Runner's World*, August 25, 2008, http://racingnews.runnersworld. com/2008/08/feature-story-and-now-there-are-three-gebrselassie-bekele-and-wanjiru.html (accessed September 19, 2011).
———, "Wanjiru: A Marathon Star with a Short—but Blinding—Arc," *Runner's World*, May 15, 2011, http://footloose.runnersworld.com/2011/05/wanjiru-a-marathon-star-with-a-short-but-blinding-arc. html (accessed September 19, 2011).
Vigneron, Peter, "Sammy Wanjiru Dead at Age 24," *Runner's World*, May 15, 2011, http://racingnews. runnersworld.com/2011/05/sammy-wanjiru-dead-at-age-24.html (accessed September 19, 2011).

—Mark Lane

William Warfield

1920–2002

Vocalist, actor, educator

Warfield, William, photograph. Keystone/Getty Images.

A worthy successor to his mentor Paul Robeson (1898-1976), bass-baritone William Warfield was one of the world's leading vocalists for more than 60 years. A major star on Broadway, he was also a familiar figure to fans of Bach, Handel, Mendelssohn, and other classical composers. He is probably best remembered, however, for his stirring portrayal of Porgy in George Gershwin's iconic opera *Porgy and Bess.* "Warfield's voice was deep, powerful and supple," wrote Allan Kozinn in the *New York Times* in 2002, "and he invested all his work—whether folk songs, German art songs or Bach cantatas—with a combination of elegance and warmth that [was] his trademark."

Warfield was born on January 22, 1920, in West Helena, Arkansas, a small community near the Mississippi state line. His father, Robert Elza Warfield, was a sharecropper who left his fields in the early 1920s to become a Baptist minister. The family moved north to Rochester, New York, shortly thereafter, and it was in that city that Warfield spent the bulk of his childhood. Hymns and pageants at his father's church there gave him an early grounding in music, and by the time he

graduated from Washington High School, where he took voice lessons and sang in the choir, his vocal abilities had drawn the attention of many in his neighborhood. His first break came in 1938, when he entered and won a national music competition, the prize for which included a full scholarship to the school of his choice. His selection of the Eastman School of Music was a logical one; one of the most prominent institutions of its kind in the country, it was also very close to his home. He studied there for the next four years, graduating in 1942 with a bachelor's degree in music. He was then drafted for wartime service in the U.S. Army. Assigned initially to a segregated unit, he was transferred to Army Intelligence when his superiors realized that his vocal training at Eastman had required intensive study of German and Italian.

On his discharge from the Army in 1946, Warfield returned to Eastman to begin a master's degree. His studies there were cut short, however, when he began landing roles in theatrical productions, including *Call Me Mister* (1946) and *Set My People Free* (1947). His first major Broadway role came in 1949, when he

At a Glance . . .

Born on January 22, 1920, in West Helena, AR; died on August 25, 2002, in Chicago, IL; son of Robert Elza Warfield (a sharecropper and Baptist minister) and Bertha McCamery Warfield (a homemaker); married Leontyne Price (a vocalist), 1952 (divorced, 1972). *Military service*: U.S. Army, 1942–46. *Education*: Eastman School of Music, BM, 1942, graduate studies, 1946–47(?).

Career: Independent performer, 1930s–2002; University of Illinois at Urbana-Champaign, professor of music, 1975–90; Northwestern University and other institutions, various faculty positions, 1990s–2002(?).

Memberships: National Association of Negro Musicians (president, 1985–90), Schiller Institute (board of directors, 1996–2002).

Awards: Grammy Award for best spoken word or non-musical recording, 1983, for *Copland: A Lincoln Portrait*; inducted into American Classical Music Hall of Fame, 1999; Alumni Achievement Award, Eastman School of Music, 2000; several honorary doctorates.

starred in an opera called *Regina*. Because the success of these shows depended on the unpredictable tastes of the public, a steady, sustainable income was initially out of his reach. To pay his bills, therefore, he developed a nightclub act, a move that led directly to his next break. At a club in Canada, a wealthy businessman emerged from the audience one night with an offer to finance his formal debut as a singer. Held in the spring of 1950 at Town Hall, then one of the most prominent venues in New York City, the event brought Warfield a number of job offers, including one from the Australian Broadcasting Corporation. On his return from Australia several months later, he won the part of Joe—a role Robeson had made famous—in MGM's remake of *Show Boat* (1951). His arresting performance of "Ol' Man River" in that film was widely regarded as a pivotal moment in Hollywood's treatment of African-American themes.

Warfield never lacked for steady work again. His most famous role, one to which he returned many times over the next four decades, began just months after *Show Boat*, when he took the male lead in a traveling production of *Porgy and Bess*. His female counterpart on that tour was soprano Leontyne Price (born 1927), whom he married in 1952; the two eventually divorced. Recordings of their many appearances as

Porgy and Bess quickly attained the status of classics; a 1963 album was especially prized by fans of what Gershwin (1898-1937) famously called his "folk opera."

Well known abroad by the end of the 1950s, Warfield appeared frequently overseas, often in cultural-exchange programs organized by the U.S. State Department. He had a particularly longstanding relationship with Austria's Volksoper, one of the world's leading opera houses. In the United States, meanwhile, he moved increasingly into television. His roles in that medium included two NBC productions (1957 and 1959) of *The Green Pastures*, a dramatic retelling of the Old Testament. Warfield played the part of God, a role known, in the play's dated and frequently inaccurate rendering of African-American speech, as "De Lawd." One of the first major plays to feature an entirely African-American cast when it debuted on Broadway in the 1930s, *The Green Pastures* remained intensely meaningful for African Americans two decades later, when Warfield appeared in it. Well aware of its symbolic significance, he prepared for it with an intensity not often found in television. Very positive reviews resulted, although his part involved no singing at all.

In the early 1980s Warfield took another non-singing role, this time as the narrator on a recording of Aaron Copland's *A Lincoln Portrait*. The album gave his career a significant boost, particularly after it brought him a Grammy Award as the best spoken word or non-musical recording of 1983. Among his other honors were an Alumni Achievement Award from Eastman in 2000 and several honorary doctorates.

Amid his performances, Warfield also found time for a successful career as an educator. His first major post in that field came in 1975, when he became a professor of music at the University of Illinois at Urbana-Champaign. Following his retirement there in 1990, he moved on to faculty positions at Northwestern University and other schools in the Chicago area. His passion, however, remained performance. An indefatigable entertainer who once told an interviewer that he would continue to sing as long as his voice held out, he took gigs until the last weeks of his life. On August 25, 2002, he died in Chicago of complications from a fall he had suffered the previous month. Survived by two brothers and a number of nieces and nephews, he was buried in a Rochester cemetery just blocks from Eastman, his alma mater.

Sources

Periodicals

New York Times, August 27, 2002.

Online

Stevenson, Joseph, "William Warfield: Biography," AllMusic.com, http://www.allmusic.com/artist/william-warfield-q59535/biography (accessed September 21, 2011).

"William Warfield BM 42," Eastman School of Music, January 26, 2000, http://www.esm.rochester.edu/alumni/files/WilliamWarfield.htm (accessed September 21, 2011).

"William Warfield," Schiller Institute, 2001, http://www.schillerinstitute.org/biographys/bio_warfield_new.html (accessed September 21, 2011).

—R. Anthony Kugler

Brian Courtney Wilson

Gospel singer

Wilson, Brian Courtney, photograph. Mark Sullivan/WireImage/ Getty Images.

For more than a decade, contemporary gospel singer Brian Courtney Wilson toiled at an unfulfilling job in sales before deciding to take a leap of faith and quit his job to pursue his lifelong dream of making music. That gamble paid off, and in the summer of 2009 Wilson released his debut album, *Just Love*. The record, which mixes classic rhythm and blues, soul, jazz, and pop to create a new brand of "neo-sacred" or "urban inspirational" music, spent more than a year in the top 15 of the gospel and Christian music charts, fueled by the hit single "All I Need," and earned the singer an NAACP Image Award nomination. Today, Wilson combines a recording and performing career with a thriving church music ministry in Houston, Texas.

Wilson grew up in the Chicagoland suburb of Bellwood and attended Fenwick High School, a private Catholic school in nearby Oak Park. He got his first taste of gospel music at the Rock of Ages Baptist Church, where his father, a school custodian, served as a deacon and his mother, a clerical worker, was a member of the board. During his childhood, Wilson accompanied his father to choir rehearsals in the evenings, and soon he was singing in the chorus himself. He was inspired as much by the camaraderie among the members as by the music, and he was struck by the power of music to bring people together to deal with hardship. "We were just singing to get each other through the week," he explained to Tuala Williams in the Houston-based paper *African-American News and Issues*. "It was a working-class area of Chicago, and these were family men, and they just wanted to inspire each other."

When he enrolled at the University of Illinois, Wilson began singing with the school's African-American chorus, but he never thought of music as a profession. Instead, he took a more practical path, majoring in economics. After graduating from college, Wilson took a job in sales, settling into a 9-to-5 routine, marrying, and starting a family. Spiritually, however, he was adrift—he no longer attended church—he found that his heart was not really in his work. "I was a lost soul," he explained in an interview on the Music World Entertainment website. "God had a plan for my life, but I got off track."

That would change after Wilson and his family relocated to Houston, Texas, where he went to work for Johnson & Johnson as a pharmaceutical sales repre-

At a Glance . . .

Born in Bellwood, IL. *Education*: University of Illinois, BS, economics.

Career: Recording artist, 2009—.

Addresses: *Record company*—Music World Entertainment, 1505 Hadley St., Houston, TX 77002. *Web*—http://musicworldent.com/artists/briancourtneywilson.

sentative. Wilson's territory covered downtown Houston, where Mathew Knowles, a music industry executive who had launched the recording career of daughter Beyoncé, had his studio. Every day, Wilson looked up to see a huge billboard advertising Destiny's Child. He still loved to sing, and he wondered what it would take to make it in the music business himself. Around the same time, Wilson first visited Windsor Village United Methodist Church on the suggestion of a friend. It would turn out to be a life- and career-changing decision.

He found a home at Windsor Village, both spiritually and musically. He began writing inspirational songs that proved to be popular with parishioners and local radio stations, and soon he became minister of music at Windsor Village. His songs caught the attention of the Reverend Rudy Rasmus, who invited Wilson to join the music ministry at St. John United Methodist Church, where he was pastor. Seeing that music was his true calling, Wilson made a leap of faith, giving up the security of his sales job to work for the church full time. One of the worshipers at St. John was Mathew Knowles, an old friend of Pastor Rasmus. After hearing Wilson perform a song that he had written, called "Already Here," Knowles immediately signed the aspiring musician to his Spirit Rising label, an imprint of his company Music World Entertainment.

Wilson headed to Jackson, Mississippi, to record with producer Stan "Stantastic" Jones, drummer for the Williams Brothers, and his debut album, *Just Love,* was released in June of 2009. The record debuted at number two on the *Billboard* Top Gospel Albums chart and number six on the Top Christian Albums chart. The first single, "All I Need," peaked at number six on the Hot Gospel Songs chart, spending more than 80 weeks on the chart. Wilson followed up with the single "Already Here," which rose to number 13. The third single and title track, "Just Love," reached number 14 on the Hot Gospel Songs chart and earned him a Dove Award nomination for Urban Recorded Song of the Year. In all, *Just Love* spent more than 40 weeks at the top of the Christian Music Trade Association's Inspira-

tion Album chart and earned the singer an NAACP Image Award nomination for outstanding gospel album.

The songs on *Just Love* are inspirational and largely autobiographical, drawing on Wilson's own spiritual journey. The album is "about the corrective and redemptive power in your life," the singer told *Black Gospel Blog.* "It tells you to stand up for what's yours and not to be afraid to forgive. Forgiveness, after all, is what 'communion' is all about." He went on to explain, "I want to be a conduit. I want listeners to come away from my project feeling good about themselves, having experienced hope in a new way. I don't want them to be selfish, but rather to extend a helping hand." Dubbed "neo-sacred" or "urban inspirational" by some critics, Wilson's brand of gospel music incorporates a diverse mix of rhythm-and-blues, soul, jazz, pop, and even hip-hop influences. "It is like Frankie Beverly or the late Donny Hathaway leading worship at church," he explained to *Houston Style* magazine. "Stevie Wonder was the MD [music director]. John Mayer and Fred Hammond were in the choir, and Eminem decided to come to church that day. . . . It's fun and filled with truth."

In October of 2010, Wilson released a deluxe edition of *Just Love* featuring five new songs, including "Awesome God" and "This Christmas" (a cover of the Donny Hathaway holiday classic), as well as a 40-minute DVD. That fall, he opened for gospel singer Marvin Sapp on the 25-city "Most Powerful Voices" tour, sponsored by the American Heart Association.

Sources

Periodicals

African-American News & Issues, October 18, 2010.
Essence, July 20, 2010.
Houston Style, June 12, 2009.

Online

"In Conversation: Brian Courtney Wilson," *Black Gospel Blog,* September 21, 2008, http://www.theblackgospelblog.com/2008/09/in-conversation-brian-courtney-wilson.html (accessed September 20, 2011).

Kelley, Frannie, "Brian Courtney Wilson: Everyman Gospel," National Public Radio, October 5, 2010, http://www.npr.org/2010/12/28/130349434/brian-courtney-wilson-everyman-gospel (accessed September 20, 2011).

Music World Entertainment, "Brian Courtney Wilson," http://musicworldent.com/artists/briancourtneywilson (accessed September 20, 2011).

—Deborah A. Ring

Cumulative Nationality Index

Volume numbers appear in **bold**

American

Aaliyah **30**
Aaron, Hank **5**
Aaron, Quinton **82**
Abbott, Robert Sengstacke **27**
Abdul-Jabbar, Kareem **8**
Abdur-Rahim, Shareef **28**
Abele, Julian **55**
Abernathy, Ralph David **1**
Aberra, Amsale **67**
Abu-Jamal, Mumia **15**
Ace, Johnny **36**
Adams, Eula L. **39**
Adams, Floyd, Jr. **12**
Adams, Jenoyne **60**
Adams, Johnny **39**
Adams, Leslie **39**
Adams, Oleta **18**
Adams, Osceola Macarthy **31**
Adams, Sheila J. **25**
Adams, Yolanda **17, 67**
Adams-Campbell, Lucille L. **60**
Adams Earley, Charity **13, 34**
Adams-Ender, Clara **40**
Adderley, Julian "Cannonball" **30**
Adderley, Nat **29**
Adebimpe, Tunde **75**
Adkins, Rod **41**
Adkins, Rutherford H. **21**
Adu, Freddy **67**
Agyeman, Jaramogi Abebe **10, 63**
Ailey, Alvin **8**
Akil, Mara Brock **60, 82**
Akon **68**
Al-Amin, Jamil Abdullah **6**
Albright, Gerald **23**
Alcorn, George Edward, Jr. **59**
Alert, Kool DJ Red **33**
Alexander, Archie Alphonso **14**
Alexander, Clifford **26**
Alexander, Elizabeth **75**
Alexander, Joyce London **18**
Alexander, Khandi **43**
Alexander, Margaret Walker **22**
Alexander, Sadie Tanner Mossell **22**
Alexander, Shaun **58**
Ali, Hana Yasmeen **52**
Ali, Laila **27, 63**
Ali, Muhammad **2, 16, 52**
Ali, Rashied **79**
Ali, Russlynn H. **92**
Ali, Tatyana **73**
Allain, Stephanie **49**

Allen, Betty **83**
Allen, Byron **3, 24**
Allen, Claude **68**
Allen, Debbie **13, 42**
Allen, Dick **85**
Allen, Ethel D. **13**
Allen, Eugene **79**
Allen, Geri **92**
Allen, Lucy **85**
Allen, Marcus **20**
Allen, Ray **82**
Allen, Robert L. **38**
Allen, Samuel W. **38**
Allen, Tina **22, 75**
Allen, Will **74**
Allen-Buillard, Melba **55**
Alonso, Laz **87**
Alston, Charles **33**
Amaker, Norman **63**
Amaker, Tommy **62**
Amaki, Amalia **76**
Amerie **52**
Ames, Wilmer **27**
Ammons, James H. **81**
Amos, Emma **63**
Amos, John **8, 62**
Amos, Wally **9**
Anderson, Anthony **51, 77**
Anderson, Carl **48**
Anderson, Charles Edward **37**
Anderson, Eddie "Rochester" **30**
Anderson, Elmer **25**
Anderson, Fred **87**
Anderson, Jamal **22**
Anderson, Lauren **72**
Anderson, Marian **2, 33**
Anderson, Michael P. **40**
Anderson, Mike **63**
Anderson, Norman B. **45**
Anderson, Reuben V. **81**
Anderson, William G(ilchrist) **57**
Andrews, Benny **22, 59**
Andrews, Bert **13**
Andrews, Raymond **4**
Andrews, Tina **74**
Angelou, Maya **1, 15**
Ansa, Tina McElroy **14**
Anthony, Carmelo **46, 94**
Anthony, Wendell **25**
apl.de.ap **84**
Appiah, Kwame Anthony **67**
Archer, Dennis **7, 36**
Archer, Lee, Jr. **79**
Archibald, Tiny **90**

Archie-Hudson, Marguerite **44**
Ardoin, Alphonse **65**
Arenas, Gilbert **84**
Arkadie, Kevin **17**
Armstrong, Govind **81**
Armstrong, Louis **2**
Armstrong, Robb **15**
Armstrong, Vanessa Bell **24**
Arnez J **53**
Arnold, Tichina **63**
Arnwine, Barbara **28**
Arrington, Richard **24**
Arroyo, Martina **30**
Artest, Ron **52**
Asante, Molefi Kete **3**
Ashanti **37**
Ashe, Arthur **1, 18**
Ashford, Calvin, Jr. **74**
Ashford, Emmett **22**
Ashford, Evelyn **63**
Ashford, Nickolas **21**
Ashley-Ward, Amelia **23**
Ashong, Derrick **86**
Asim, Jabari **71**
Atkins, Cholly **40**
Atkins, Erica **34**
Atkins, Juan **50**
Atkins, Russell **45**
Atkins, Tina **34**
Aubert, Alvin **41**
Auguste, Donna **29**
Austin, Gloria **63**
Austin, Jim **63**
Austin, Junius C. **44**
Austin, Lovie **40**
Austin, Patti **24**
Austin, Wanda M. **94**
Autrey, Wesley **68**
Avant, Clarence **19, 86**
Avant, Nicole A. **90**
Avery, Byllye Y. **66**
Ayers, Roy **16**
Babatunde, Obba **35**
Babyface **10, 31, 82**
Bacon-Bercey, June **38**
Badu, Erykah **22**
Bahati, Wambui **60**
Bailey, Buster **38**
Bailey, Chauncey **68**
Bailey, Clyde **45**
Bailey, DeFord **33**
Bailey, Pearl **14**
Bailey, Philip **63**
Bailey, Radcliffe **19**

Bailey, Xenobia **11**
Baines, Harold **32**
Baiocchi, Regina Harris **41**
Baisden, Michael **25, 66**
Baker, Anita **21, 48**
Baker, Augusta **38**
Baker, Dusty **8, 43, 72**
Baker, Ella **5**
Baker, Gwendolyn Calvert **9**
Baker, Houston A., Jr. **6**
Baker, Josephine **3**
Baker, LaVern **26**
Baker, Matt **76**
Baker, Maxine B. **28**
Baker, Thurbert **22**
Baker, Vernon Joseph **65, 87**
Baldwin, Cynthia A. **74**
Baldwin, James **1**
Ballance, Frank W. **41**
Ballard, Allen Butler, Jr. **40**
Ballard, Hank **41**
Baltimore, Richard Lewis, III **71**
Bambaataa, Afrika **34**
Bambara, Toni Cade **10**
Bandele, Asha **36**
Banks, Ernie **33**
Banks, Jeffrey **17**
Banks, Michelle **59**
Banks, Paula A. **68**
Banks, Tyra **11, 50**
Banks, William **11**
Banneker, Benjamin **93**
Banner, David **55**
Bannister, Edward Mitchell **88**
Baquet, Dean **63**
Baraka, Amiri **1, 38**
Barbee, Lloyd Augustus **71**
Barber, Ronde **41**
Barber, Tiki **57**
Barboza, Anthony **10**
Barclay, Paris **37, 94**
Barden, Donald H. **9, 20, 89**
Barker, Danny **32**
Barkley, Charles **5, 66**
Barlow, Roosevelt **49**
Barnes, Ernie **16, 78**
Barnes, Melody **75**
Barnes, Roosevelt "Booba" **33**
Barnes, Steven **54**
Barnett, Amy Du Bois **46**
Barnett, Etta Moten **56**
Barnett, Marguerite **46**
Barney, Lem **26**
Barnhill, David **30**

Barrax, Gerald William 45
Barrett, Andrew C. 12
Barrett, Jacquelyn 28
Barrino, Fantasia 53, 94
Barrow, Willie T. 85
Barry, Marion S(hepilov, Jr.) 7, 44
Barthé, Earl 78
Barthe, Richmond 15
Basie, Count 23
Basquiat, Jean-Michel 5
Bass, Charlotta Spears 40
Bass, Karen 70
Bassett, Angela 6, 23, 62
Baszile, Jennifer 79
Bates, Daisy 13
Bates, Karen Grigsby 40
Bates, Peg Leg 14
Bath, Patricia E. 37
Batiste, Alvin 66
Battle, Kathleen 70
Baugh, David 23
Baylor, Don 6
Baylor, Elgin 93
Baylor, Helen 36
Beach, Michael 26
Beal, Bernard B. 46
Beals, Jennifer 12
Beals, Melba Pattillo 15, 94
Bearden, Romare 2, 50
Beasley, Jamar 29
Beasley, Phoebe 34
Beatty, Talley 35
Bechet, Sidney 18
Beckford, Tyson 11, 68
Beckham, Barry 41
Belafonte, Harry 4, 65
Belgrave, Cynthia 75
Belgrave, Marcus 77
Bell, Darrin 77
Bell, Derrick 6
Bell, James "Cool Papa" 36
Bell, James A. 50
Bell, James Madison 40
Bell, Michael 40
Bell, Robert Mack 22
Bellamy, Bill 12
Bellamy, Terry 58
Belle, Albert 10
Belle, Regina 1, 51
Belton, Sharon Sayles 9, 16
Benberry, Cuesta 65
Benét, Eric 28, 77
Benham, Robert 78
Ben-Israel, Ben Ami 11
Benjamin, Andre 45
Benjamin, Regina 20, 75
Benjamin, Tritobia Hayes 53
Bennett, Estelle 77
Bennett, George Harold "Hal" 45
Bennett, Gwendolyn B. 59
Bennett, Lerone, Jr. 5, 84
Benson, Angela 34
Bentley, Lamont 53
Berrien, Jacqueline A. 93
Berry, Edwin C. 81
Berry, Halle 4, 19, 57, 91
Berry, Bertice 8, 55
Berry, Chuck 29
Berry, Fred "Rerun" 48
Berry, Mary Frances 7
Berry, Moses 84
Berry, Theodore 31
Berrysmith, Don Reginald 49

Bethune, Mary McLeod 4
Betsch, MaVynee 28
Bettis, Jerome 64
Betts, Keter 85
Betts, R. Dwayne 86
Bevel, James L. 75
Beverly, Frankie 25
Beyoncé 39, 70
Bibb, Eric 49
Bibb, Henry and Mary 54
Bickerstaff, Bernie 21
Big Daddy Kane 79
Biggers, John 20, 33
Biggers, Sanford 62
Billops, Camille 82
bin Wahad, Dhoruba 85
Bing, Dave 3, 59, 78
Birch, Adolpho A., Jr. 85
Birch, Glynn R. 61
Bishop, Sanford D., Jr. 24
Bivins, Michael 72
Black, Albert 51
Black, Barry C. 47
Black, Joe 75
Black, Keith Lanier 18, 84
Black Thought 63
Blackburn, Robert 28
Blackman, Toni 86
Blackmon, Brenda 58
Blackshear, Leonard 52
Blackwell, David 79
Blackwell, Kenneth, Sr. 61
Blackwell, Robert D., Sr. 52
Blackwell, Unita 17
Blacque, Taurean 58
Blade, Brian 88
Blair, Jayson 50
Blair, Paul 36
Blake, Asha 26
Blake, Charles E. 82
Blake, Eubie 29
Blake, James 43
Blakely, Edward J. 88
Blakey, Art 37
Blanchard, Terence 43
Bland, Bobby "Blue" 36
Bland, Eleanor Taylor 39
Blanks, Billy 22
Blanks, Deborah K. 69
Blanton, Dain 29
Blassingame, John Wesley 40
Blaylock, Ronald 86
Blayton, Jesse B., Sr. 55
Bleu, Corbin 65
Blige, Mary J. 20, 34, 60
Blockson, Charles L. 42
Bloomer, George 86
Blow, Charles M. 73
Blow, Kurtis 31
Bluford, Guy 2, 35
Bluitt, Juliann S. 14
B.o.B. 91
Bobb, Robert C. 83
Bobo, Lawrence 60
Bogle, Donald 34
Bogues, Tyrone "Muggsy" 56
Bolden, Buddy 39
Bolden, Charles Frank, Jr. 7, 78
Bolden, Frank E. 44
Bolden, Tonya 32
Bolin, Jane 22, 59
Bolton, Terrell D. 25
Bolton-Holifield, Ruthie 28

Bond, Beverly 53
Bond, J. Max, Jr. 76
Bond, Julian 2, 35
Bonds, Barry 6, 34, 63
Bonds, Bobby 43
Bonds, Margaret 39
Bonet, Lisa 58
Bontemps, Arna 8
Booker, Cory Anthony 68
Booker, Simeon 23
Borders, James 9
Borders, William Holmes 94
Bosh, Chris 85
Bosley, Freeman, Jr. 7
Boston, Kelvin E. 25
Boston, Lloyd 24
Bow Wow 35
Bowe, Riddick 6
Bowen, John W. E., Sr. 89
Bowen, Ruth 83
Bowman, Bertie 71
Bowser, Yvette Lee 17
Boyd, Edward 70
Boyd, Gerald M. 32, 59
Boyd, Gwendolyn 49
Boyd, John W., Jr. 20, 72
Boyd, Melba Joyce 86
Boyd, T. B., III 6
Boykin, Keith 14
Boykin, Otis 92
Boyz II Men 82
Bradford, Mark 89
Bradley, David Henry, Jr. 39
Bradley, Ed 2, 59
Bradley, J. Robert 65
Bradley, Jennette B. 40
Bradley, Thomas 2, 20
Brady, Wayne 32, 71
Brae, C. Michael 61
Braithwaite, William Stanley 52
Bramlett, Joseph 91
Branch, William Blackwell 39
Brand, Elton 31
Brandon, Barbara 3
Brandon, Terrell 16
Brandy 14, 34, 72
Branham, George, III 50
Branson, Herman 87
Brashear, Carl 29
Brashear, Donald 39
Braugher, Andre 13, 58, 91
Braun, Carol Moseley 4, 42
Brawley, Benjamin 44
Braxton, Brad 77
Braxton, Toni 15, 61, 91
Brazile, Donna 25, 70
Bridges, Ruby 77
Bridges, Sheila 36
Bridges, Todd 37
Bridgewater, Dee Dee 32, 92
Bridgforth, Glinda 36
Briggs, Curtis 84
Brimmer, Andrew F. 2, 48
Briscoe, Connie 15
Briscoe, Marlin 37
Britt, Donna 28
Broadbent, Hydeia 36
Brock, Lou 18
Brock, Roslyn McCallister 86
Bromery, Randolph Wilson 85
Bronner, Nathaniel H., Sr. 32
Brooke, Edward W. 8, 88
Brooks, Aaron 33

Brooks, Avery 9
Brooks, Derrick 43
Brooks, Golden 62
Brooks, Gwendolyn 1, 28
Brooks, Hadda 40
Brooks, Mehcad 62
Brooks, Tyrone 59
Broonzy, Big Bill 82
Brower, William 49
Brown, Angela M. 54
Brown, Anne 76
Brown, Anthony G. 72
Brown, Antron 85
Brown, Bobby 58
Brown, Byrd 49
Brown, Byron W. 72
Brown, Cecil M. 46
Brown, Charles 23
Brown, Chris 74
Brown, Chuck 78
Brown, Clarence Gatemouth 59
Brown, Claude 38
Brown, Clifford 86
Brown, Cora 33
Brown, Corrine 24, 90
Brown, Cupcake 63
Brown, Donald 19
Brown, Eddie C. 35
Brown, Elaine 8
Brown, Ernest 80
Brown, Erroll M. 23
Brown, Foxy 25
Brown, George Leslie 62
Brown, Homer S. 47
Brown, James 15, 60
Brown, James 22
Brown, Jamie Foster 91
Brown, Janice Rogers 43
Brown, Jesse 6, 41
Brown, Jesse Leroy 31
Brown, Jim 11
Brown, Joe 29
Brown, Joyce F. 25
Brown, Kwame R. 91
Brown, Lee Patrick 1, 24
Brown, Les 5
Brown, Lloyd Louis 42
Brown, Marie Dutton 12
Brown, Mike 77
Brown, Nappy 73
Brown, Oliver Leon 94
Brown, Oscar, Jr. 53
Brown, Patrick "Sleepy" 50
Brown, Robert 65
Brown, Ron 5
Brown, Ronald K. 91
Brown, Ruth 90
Brown, Sterling Allen 10, 64
Brown, Tony 3
Brown, Uzee 42
Brown, Vivian 27
Brown, Warren 61
Brown, Wesley 23
Brown, Willa 40
Brown, Willard 36
Brown, Willie 7, 85
Brown, Zora Kramer 12
Browne, Roscoe Lee 66
Brownlee, Lawrence 88
Broyard, Anatole 68
Broyard, Bliss 68
Bruce, Blanche Kelso 33
Bruce, Bruce 56

Bruce, Isaac **26**
Brunson, Dorothy **1, 87**
Bryan, Ashley F. **41**
Bryant, Cullen **81**
Bryant, John **26**
Bryant, John R. **45**
Bryant, Kobe **15, 31, 71**
Bryant, Wayne R. **6**
Bryant, William Benson **61**
Buchanan, Ray **32**
Buckley, Gail Lumet **39**
Buckley, Victoria (Vikki) **24**
Bullard, Eugene **12**
Bullins, Ed **25**
Bullock, Steve **22**
Bully-Cummings, Ella **48**
Bumbry, Grace **5**
Bunch, Lonnie G., III **91**
Bunche, Ralph J. **5**
Bunkley, Anita Richmond **39**
Burgess, John **46**
Burgess, Marjorie L. **55**
Burke, Selma **16**
Burke, Solomon **31, 86**
Burke, Yvonne Brathwaite **42**
Burks, Mary Fair **40**
Burleigh, Henry Thacker **56**
Burnett, Charles **16, 68**
Burnim, Mickey L. **48**
Burns, Eddie **44**
Burns, Ursula **60**
Burnside, R. L. **56**
Burrell, Tom **21, 51**
Burris, Chuck **21**
Burris, Roland W. **25, 75**
Burroughs, Margaret Taylor **9**
Burrows, Stephen **31**
Burrus, William Henry "Bill" **45**
Burt-Murray, Angela **59**
Burton, LeVar **8**
Burwell, Bryan **83**
Busby, Jheryl **3, 74**
Bush, Gordon **82**
Bush, Reggie **59, 88**
Butler, George, Jr. **70**
Butler, Jerry **26**
Butler, Leroy, III **17**
Butler, Louis **70**
Butler, Octavia **8, 43, 58**
Butler, Paul D. **17**
Butts, Calvin O., III **9, 90**
Butts, Cassandra **78**
Bynoe, Peter C. B. **40**
Bynum, Juanita **31, 71**
Byrd, Donald **10**
Byrd, Eugene **64**
Byrd, Michelle **19**
Byrd, Robert **11**
Cadoria, Sherian Grace **14**
Caesar, Shirley **19**
Cage, Byron **53**
Cain, Herman **15, 92**
Calabrese, Karyn **89**
Caldwell, Benjamin **46**
Caldwell, Earl **60**
Caldwell, Jim **81**
Caldwell, Kirbyjon **55**
Calhoun, Lillian Scott **87**
Callender, Clive O. **3**
Calloway, Cab **14**
Cameron, James **80**
Camp, Kimberly **19**
Campanella, Roy **25**

Campbell, Bebe Moore **6, 24, 59**
Campbell, Bill **9, 76**
Campbell, Donald J. **66**
Campbell, E. Simms **13**
Campbell, Mary Schmidt **43**
Campbell-Martin, Tisha **8, 42**
Canada, Geoffrey **23**
Canady, Alexa **28**
Cannon, Katie **10**
Cannon, Nick **47, 73**
Cannon, Reuben **50**
Cara, Irene **77**
Carr, Johnnie **69**
Carr, Keela **74**
Cardozo, Francis L. **33**
Carew, Rod **20**
Cargill, Victoria A. **43**
Carr, Kurt **56**
Carr, Leroy **49**
Carroll, Diahann **9**
Carroll, L. Natalie **44**
Carroll, Rocky **74**
Carruthers, George R. **40**
Carson, André **69**
Carson, Benjamin **1, 35, 76**
Carson, Johnnie **85**
Carson, Julia **23, 69**
Carson, Lisa Nicole **21**
Carter, Anson **24**
Carter, Benny **46**
Carter, Betty **19**
Carter, Butch **27**
Carter, Cris **21**
Carter, Joe **30**
Carter, Joye Maureen **41**
Carter, Kenneth **53**
Carter, Majora **77**
Carter, Mandy **11**
Carter, Nell **39**
Carter, Pamela Lynn **67**
Carter, Regina **23**
Carter, Robert L. **51**
Carter, Rubin **26**
Carter, Stephen L. **4**
Carter, Vince **26**
Carter, Warrick L. **27**
Cartey, Wilfred **47**
Cartiér, Xam Wilson **41**
Carver, George Washington **4**
Cary, Lorene **3**
Cary, Mary Ann Shadd **30**
Cash, Rosalind **28**
Cash, Swin **59**
Cashin, Sheryll **63**
CasSelle, Malcolm **11**
Catchings, Tamika **43**
Catlett, Elizabeth **2**
Catto, Octavius V. **83**
Cayton, Horace **26**
Cedric the Entertainer **29, 60**
Cee-Lo **70**
Cenac, Wyatt **94**
Chadiha, Jeffri **57**
Chamberlain, Wilt **18, 47**
Chambers, Julius **3**
Chamillionaire **82**
Chaney, John **67**
Chanticleer, Raven **91**
Chapman, Nathan A., Jr. **21**
Chapman, Susan E. **94**
Chapman, Tracy **26**
Chappell, Emma **18**

Chappelle, Dave **50**
Charles, Ray **16, 48**
Charleston, Oscar **39**
Chase, Debra Martin **49**
Chase, Leah **57**
Chase-Riboud, Barbara **20, 46**
Chatard, Peter **44**
Chavis, Benjamin **6**
Cheadle, Don **19, 52**
Checker, Chubby **28**
Cheeks, Maurice **47**
Chenault, John **40**
Chenault, Kenneth I. **4, 36**
Cherry, Deron **40**
Chesnutt, Charles **29**
Chestnut, J. L., Jr. **73**
Chestnut, Morris **31**
Chideya, Farai **14, 61**
Childress, Alice **15**
Chineworth, Mary Alice **79**
Chinn, May Edward **26**
Chisholm, Daquan **93**
Chisholm, Samuel **32**
Chisholm, Shirley **2, 50**
Christian, Barbara T. **44**
Christian, Spencer **15**
Christian-Green, Donna M. **17**
Christie, Angella **36**
Christie, Ron **83**
Chuck D **9**
Churchwell, Robert, Sr. **76**
Ciara **56**
Ciara, Barbara **69**
Clack, Zoanne **73**
Claiborne, Loretta **34**
Clark, Celeste **15**
Clark, Joe **1**
Clark, Kenneth B. **5, 52**
Clark, Mamie Phipps **79**
Clark, Mattie Moss **61**
Clark, Patrick **14**
Clark, Septima **7**
Clark-Cole, Dorinda **66**
Clarke, Cheryl **32**
Clarke, Hope **14**
Clarke, John Henrik **20**
Clarke, Kenny **27**
Clarke, Yvette **92**
Clark-Sheard, Karen **22**
Clash, Kevin **14, 93**
Clay, Bryan **57, 74**
Clay, William Lacy **8**
Clayton, Constance **1**
Clayton, Eva M. **20**
Clayton, Mayme Agnew **62**
Clayton, Xernona **3, 45**
Claytor, Helen **14, 52**
Cleage, Pearl **17, 64**
Cleaver, Eldridge **5**
Cleaver, Emanuel **4, 45, 68**
Cleaver, Kathleen **29**
Clemente, Rosa **74**
Clement-Holmes, Linda **94**
Clements, George **2**
Clemmons, Reginal G. **41**
Clemons, Clarence **41**
Clemons, Michael "Pinball" **64**
Clendenon, Donn **26, 56**
Cleveland, James **19**
Cliff, Michelle **42**
Clifton, Lucille **14, 64, 91**
Clifton, Nathaniel "Sweetwater" **47**
Clinton, George **9, 93**

Clyburn, James E. **21, 71**
Clyburn, Mignon **78**
Coachman, Alice **18**
Coates, Ta-Nehisi **76**
Cobb, Jewel Plummer **42**
Cobb, W. Montague **39**
Cobb, William Jelani **59**
Cobbs, Price M. **9**
Cochran, Johnnie **11, 39, 52**
Cockrel, Kenneth V., Jr. **79**
Cockrel, Kenneth Vern, Sr. **79**
CoCo Brother **93**
Cohen, Anthony **15**
Cohen, Cathy J. **88**
Colbert, Virgis William **17**
Cole, Johnnetta B. **5, 43**
Cole, Keyshia **63**
Cole, Lorraine **48**
Cole, Nat "King" **17**
Cole, Natalie **17, 60, 84**
Cole, Rebecca **38**
Coleman, Bessie **9**
Coleman, Donald **24, 62**
Coleman, Gary **35, 86**
Coleman, James E., Jr. **79**
Coleman, Ken **57**
Coleman, Leonard S., Jr. **12**
Coleman, Mary **46**
Coleman, Michael B. **28, 79**
Coleman, Ornette **39, 69**
Coleman, Wanda **48**
Coleman, William F., III **61**
Coleman, William T. **76**
Colemon, Johnnie **11**
Coles, Alice **80**
Colescott, Robert **69**
Collins, Albert **12**
Collins, Barbara-Rose **7, 87**
Collins, Bootsy **31**
Collins, Cardiss **10, 80**
Collins, Janet **33, 64**
Collins, Lyn **53**
Collins, Marva **3, 71**
Collins, Patricia Hill **67**
Collins, Paul **61**
Colston, Hal **72**
Colter, Cyrus J. **36**
Coltrane, Alice **70**
Coltrane, John **19**
Coltrane, Ravi **71**
Combs, Sean **17, 43, 92**
Comer, James P. **6**
Common **31, 63**
Compton-Rock, Malaak **86**
Cone, James H. **3, 82**
Coney, PonJola **48**
Connerly, Ward **14**
Conrad, Barbara Smith **90**
Conrad, Cecilia A. **94**
Contee, Cheryl **88**
Conyers, John, Jr. **4**
Conyers, Monica **85**
Conyers, Nathan G. **24, 45**
Cook, Charles "Doc" **44**
Cook, (Will) Mercer **40**
Cook, Samuel DuBois **14**
Cook, Suzan D. Johnson **22**
Cook, Toni **23**
Cook, Will Marion **40**
Cooke, Marcia **60**
Cooke, Marvel **31**
Cooper, Andrew W. **36**
Cooper, Andy "Lefty" **63**

Cooper, Anna Julia 20
Cooper, Barry 33
Cooper, Charles "Chuck" 47
Cooper, Chuck 75
Cooper, Edward S. 6
Cooper, Evern 40
Cooper, Helene 74
Cooper, J. California 12, 85
Cooper, Lisa 73
Cooper, Margaret J. 46
Cooper, Michael 31
Cooper Cafritz, Peggy 43
Cooper-Dyke, Cynthia 17, 89
Copeland, Michael 47
Coppola, Imani Francesca 82
Corbi, Lana 42
Corley, Tony 62
Cornelius, Don 4
Cornish, Sam 50
Cornwell, Edward E., III 70
Correia, De'Jaun 93
Cortez, Jayne 43
Corthron, Kia 43
Cortor, Eldzier 42
Cosby, Bill 7, 26, 59
Cosby, Camille 14, 80
Cose, Ellis 5, 50
Cotter, Joseph Seamon, Sr. 40
Cottrell, Comer 11
Council, LaVerne 94
Counter, S. Allen 74
Cowans, Adger W. 20
Cowboy Troy 54
Cox, Bryan 83
Cox, Donald Lee 93
Cox, Ida 42
Cox, Joseph Mason Andrew 51
Cox, Renée 67
Cox, William E. 68
Craig, Carl 31, 71
Craig-Jones, Ellen Walker 44
Crawford, Carl 90
Crawford, Hank 77
Crawford, Randy 19
Cray, Robert 30
Creagh, Milton 27
Crennel, Romeo 54
Crenshaw, Kimberlé Williams 88
Crew, Rudolph F. 16
Crew, Spencer R. 55
Crichlow, Ernest 75
Crite, Alan Rohan 29
Croal, N'Gai 76
Crocker, Frankie 29
Crockett, George W., Jr. 10, 64
Croom, Sylvester 50
Cross, Dolores E. 23
Crosthwait, David 93
Crothers, Scatman 19
Crouch, Andraé 27
Crouch, Stanley 11, 87
Crowder, Henry 16
Crumpler, Rebecca Lee 89
Cruse, Harold 54
Crutchfield, James N. 55
Cullen, Countee 8
Cullers, Vincent T. 49
Culpepper, Daunte 32, 85
Cummings, Elijah E. 24
Cuney, William Waring 44
Cunningham, Evelyn 23, 85
Cunningham, Randall 23
Currie, Betty 21

Currie, Ulysses 73
Curry, George E. 23
Curry, Mark 17
Curry, Michael 85
Curtis, Christopher Paul 26
Curtis-Hall, Vondie 17
Da Don, Polow 86
Dabiri, John 93
Daemyon, Jerald 64
Dailey, Ulysses Grant 87
Daly, Marie Maynard 37
Dandridge, Dorothy 3
Dandridge, Ray 36
Dandridge, Raymond Garfield 45
D'Angelo 27
Daniels, Lee 36, 76
Daniels-Carter, Valerie 23
Danner, Margaret Esse 49
Danquah, Meri Nana Ama 93
Dantley, Adrian 72
Dara, Olu 35
Darden, Calvin 38
Darden, Christopher 13
Dash, Damon 31
Dash, Julie 4
Dash, Leon 47
Datcher, Michael 60
David, Keith 27
Davidson, Jaye 5
Davidson, Tommy 21
Davis, Allison 12
Davis, Altovise 76
Davis, Angela 5
Davis, Angela J. 88
Davis, Anthony 11
Davis, Arthur Paul 41
Davis, Artur 41
Davis, Belva 61
Davis, Benjamin O., Jr. 2, 43
Davis, Benjamin O., Sr. 4
Davis, Bing 84
Davis, Charles T. 48
Davis, Chuck 33
Davis, Danny K. 24, 79
Davis, Ed 24
Davis, Eisa 68
Davis, Ernie 48
Davis, Erroll B., Jr. 57
Davis, Frank Marshall 47
Davis, Gary 41
Davis, George 36
Davis, Gordon J. 76
Davis, Guy 36
Davis, James E. 50
Davis, Mia Amber 94
Davis, Mike 41
Davis, Miles 4
Davis, Milt 74
Davis, Nolan 45
Davis, Ossie 5, 50
Davis, Piper 19
Davis, Ruth 37
Davis, Shani 58, 84
Davis, Terrell 20
Davis, Thulani 61
Davis, Tyrone 54
Davis, Viola 34, 76
Dawes, Dominique 11
Dawkins, Wayne 20
Dawn, Marpessa 75
Dawson, Andre 85
Dawson, Matel "Mat," Jr. 39
Dawson, Michael C. 63

Dawson, Rosario 72
Dawson, William Levi 39
Day, Leon 39
Days, Drew S., III 10
De' Alexander, Quinton 57
de Lavallade, Carmen 78
de Passe, Suzanne 25
De Priest, Oscar Stanton 80
De Shields, André 72
De Veaux, Alexis 44
Dean, Mark E. 35
Deas, Gerald 85
DeBaptiste, George 32
DeBarge, El 89
DeCarava, Roy 42, 81
Deconge-Watson, Lovenia 55
Dee, Merri 55
Dee, Ruby 8, 50, 68
Deezer D 53
DeFrantz, Anita 37
Deggans, Eric 71
DeJongh, John, Jr. 85
Delaney, Beauford 19
Delaney, Joe 76
Delaney, Joseph 30
Delany, Bessie 12
Delany, Martin R. 27
Delany, Sadie 12
Delany, Samuel R., Jr. 9
Delco, Wilhemina 33
DeLille, Henriette 30
Dellums, Ronald 2, 81
DeLoach, Nora 30
Delsarte, Louis 34
Demby, William 51
Dennard, Brazeal 37
Dennis, Gary C. 91
Dent, Thomas C. 50
DePreist, James 37
Derülo, Jason 93
DeVard, Jerri 61
DeVaughn, Raheem 91
Devers, Gail 7, 87
Devine, Loretta 24
Dickens, Helen Octavia 14, 64
Dickenson, Vic 38
Dickerson, Debra J. 60
Dickerson, Eric 27
Dickerson, Ernest R. 6, 17
Dickey, Eric Jerome 21, 56
Diddley, Bo 39, 72
Diesel, Vin 29
Diggs, Charles C. 21
Diggs, Taye 25, 63
Diggs-Taylor, Anna 20
Dillard, Godfrey J. 45
Dinkins, David 4
Divine, Father 7
Dixon, Bill 87
Dixon, Dean 68
Dixon, Ivan 69
Dixon, Julian C. 24
Dixon, Margaret 14
Dixon, Sharon Pratt 1
Dixon, Sheila 68
Dixon, Willie 4
DJ Jazzy Jeff 32
DJ Lance Rock 94
DMX 28, 64
Dobbs, John Wesley 89
Dobbs, Mattiwilda 34
Doby, Lawrence Eugene, Sr. 16, 41
Dodson, Howard, Jr. 7, 52

Dodson, Owen Vincent 38
Dogan, Matthew Winifred 91
Doley, Harold, Jr. 26
Domingo, Colman 94
Domino, Fats 20
Donald, Arnold Wayne 36
Donaldson, Jeff 46
Donegan, Dorothy 19
Dorrell, Karl 52
Dorsey, Lee 65
Dorsey, Thomas Andrew 15
Dorsey, Thomas J. 90
Dortch, Thomas W., Jr. 45
Dougherty, Mary Pearl 47
Douglas, Aaron 7
Douglas, Derek 88
Douglas, Emory 89
Douglass, Frederick 87
Dourdan, Gary 37
Dove, Rita 6, 78
Dove, Ulysses 5
Downing, George T. 91
Downing, Will 19
Draper, Sharon Mills 16, 43
Dre, Dr. 10, 14, 30
Drew, Alvin, Jr. 67
Drew, Charles Richard 7
Drexler, Clyde 4, 61
Driskell, David C. 7
Driver, David E. 11
Drummond, William J. 40
Du Bois, David Graham 45
Du Bois, W. E. B. 3
du Cille, Michel 74
DuBois, Joshua 88
DuBois, Shirley Graham 21
Ducksworth, Marilyn 12
Dudley, Edward R. 58
Due, Tananarive 30
Duerson, Dave 93
Duggins, George 64
Duke, Bill 3
Duke, George 21
Dukes, Hazel Nell 56
Dumars, Joe 16, 65
Dumas, Henry 41
Dunbar, Paul Laurence 8
Dunbar-Nelson, Alice Ruth Moore 44
Duncan, Michael Clarke 26
Duncan, Tim 20, 91
Duncan, Todd 76
Dungey, Merrin 62
Dungy, Camille 86
Dungy, Tony 17, 42, 59
Dunham, Katherine 4, 59
Dunlap, Ericka 55
Dunn, Jerry 27
Dunn, Warrick 90
Dunner, Leslie B. 45
Dunnigan, Alice Allison 41
Dunston, Georgia Mae 48
Duplechan, Larry 55
Dupri, Jermaine 13, 46
Durant, Kevin 76
Durham, Bobby 73
Durham, James 90
Dutton, Charles S. 4, 22
Dworkin, Aaron P. 52
Dwight, Edward 65
Dye, Jermaine 58
Dyson, Michael Eric 11, 40
Eagleson, William Lewis 90

Early, Gerald 15
Earthquake 55
Easley, Annie J. 61
Easton, Hosea 91
Ebanks, Michelle 60
Eckstine, Billy 28
Edelin, Ramona Hoage 19
Edelman, Marian Wright 5, 42
Edley, Christopher 2, 48
Edley, Christopher F., Jr. 48
Edmonds, Terry 17
Edmonds, Tracey 16, 64
Edmunds, Gladys 48
Edwards, Donna 77
Edwards, Esther Gordy 43
Edwards, Harry 2
Edwards, Herman 51
Edwards, Lena Frances 76
Edwards, Melvin 22
Edwards, Teresa 14
Edwards, Willarda V. 59
El Wilson, Barbara 35
Elder, Larry 25
Elder, Lee 6
Elder, Lonne, III 38
Elders, Joycelyn 6
Eldridge, Roy 37
Elise, Kimberly 32
Ellerbe, Brian 22
Ellington, Duke 5
Ellington, E. David 11
Ellington, Mercedes 34
Elliott, Missy 31, 90
Elliott, Sean 26
Ellis, Charles H., III 79
Ellis, Clarence A. 38
Ellis, Dock 78
Ellis, Jimmy 44
Ellis-Lamkins, Phaedra 88
Ellison, Keith 59
Ellison, Ralph 7
Elmore, Ronn 21
Emanuel, James A. 46
Emeagwali, Dale 31
Ephriam, Mablean 29
Epperson, Sharon 54
Epps, Archie C., III 45
Epps, Mike 60
Epps, Omar 23, 59
Ericsson-Jackson, Aprille 28
Ervin, Anthony 66
Ervin, Clark Kent 82
Erving, Julius 18, 47
Escobar, Damien 56
Escobar, Tourie 56
Esposito, Giancarlo 9
Espy, Mike 6
Estes, Rufus 29
Estes, Simon 28
Estes, Sleepy John 33
Eubanks, Kevin 15
Eugene-Richard, Margie 63
Europe, James Reese 10
Evans, Darryl 22
Evans, Etu 55
Evans, Faith 22
Evans, Harry 25
Evans, Mari 26
Evans, Melvin H. 88
Evans, Warren C. 76
Eve 29
Everett, Francine 23
Everett, Percival 93

Evers, Medgar 3
Evers, Myrlie 8
Ewing, Patrick 17, 73
Fabio, Sarah Webster 48
Fabolous 93
Fabre, Shelton 71
Fair, Ronald L. 47
Faison, Donald 50
Faison, Frankie 55
Faison, George 16
Falana, Lola 42
Falconer, Etta Zuber 59
Fales-Hill, Susan 88
Fargas, Antonio 50
Farley, Christopher John 54
Farmer, Art 38
Farmer, Forest J. 1
Farmer, James 2, 64
Farmer-Paellmann, Deadria 43
Farr, Mel 24
Farrakhan, Louis 2, 15
Farrell, Herman D., Jr. 81
Farris, Isaac Newton, Jr. 63
Fattah, Chaka 11, 70
Faulk, Marshall 35
Fauntroy, Walter E. 11
Fauset, Jessie 7
Favors, Steve 23
Fax, Elton 48
Feelings, Muriel 44
Feelings, Tom 11, 47
Felix, Allyson 48
Felix, Larry R. 64
Feemster, Herbert 72
Fennoy, Ilene 72
Fenty, Adrian 60, 88
Ferguson, Roger W. 25
Ferguson, Ronald F. 75
Ferrell, Rachelle 29
Fetchit, Stepin 32
Fielder, Cecil 2
Fielder, Prince Semien 68
Fields, C. Virginia 25
Fields, Cleo 13
Fields, Evelyn J. 27
Fields, Felicia P. 60
Fields, Julia 45
Fields, Kim 36
50 Cent 46, 83
Files, Lolita 35
Fils-Aimé, Reggie 74
Fine, Sam 60
Finner-Williams, Paris Michele 62
Fishburne, Laurence 4, 22, 70
Fisher, Ada Lois Sipuel 76
Fisher, Ada M. 76
Fisher, Antwone 40
Fisher, Gail 85
Fisher, Miles Mark 91
Fitzgerald, Ella 1, 18
Flack, Roberta 19
Flanagan, Tommy 69
Flavor Flav 67
Fleming, Erik R. 75
Fleming, Raymond 48
Fletcher, Arthur A. 63
Fletcher, Benjamin 90
Fletcher, Bill, Jr. 41
Fletcher, Geoffrey 85
Flo Rida 78
Flood, Curt 10, 93
Flowers, Sylester 50

Flowers, Vonetta 35
Floyd, Elson S. 41
Forbes, Calvin 46
Forbes, James A., Jr. 71
Ford, Barney 90
Ford, Cheryl 45
Ford, Clyde W. 40
Ford, Harold E(ugene) 42
Ford, Harold E(ugene), Jr. 16, 70
Ford, Jack 39
Ford, Johnny 70
Ford, Nick Aaron 44
Ford, T-Model 91
Ford, Wallace 58
Forman, James 7, 51
Forman, James, Jr. 89
Forrest, Leon 44
Forrest, Vernon 40, 79
Forté, John 74
Forte, Linda Diane 54
Fortune, James 92
Foster, Andrew 79
Foster, Ezola 28
Foster, George "Pops" 40
Foster, Henry W., Jr. 26
Foster, Jylla Moore 45
Foster, Marie 48
Foster, William P. 88
Fowler, Reggie 51
Fox, Vivica A. 15, 53
Foxx, Anthony 81
Foxx, Jamie 15, 48
Foxx, Redd 2
Francis, Norman (C.) 60
Francis, Thais 93
Franklin, Aretha 11, 44
Franklin, C. L. 68
Franklin, Hardy R. 9, 87
Franklin, J. E. 44
Franklin, John Hope 5, 77
Franklin, Kirk 15, 49
Franklin, Shirley 34, 80
Franti, Michael 93
Frazer, Jendayi 68
Frazier, E. Franklin 10
Frazier, Joe 19
Frazier, Kevin 58
Frazier, Oscar 58
Frazier, Ryan 89
Frazier, Walt 91
Frazier-Lyde, Jacqui 31
Freelon, Nnenna 32
Freeman, Aaron 52
Freeman, Al, Jr. 11
Freeman, Charles 19
Freeman, Harold P. 23
Freeman, Leonard 27
Freeman, Marianna 23
Freeman, Morgan 2, 20, 62
Freeman, Paul 39
Freeman, Yvette 27
French, Albert 18
French, D. M. 94
Fresh, Doug E. 93
Friday, Jeff 24
Fryer, Roland G. 56
Fudge, Ann (Marie) 11, 55
Fudge, Marcia L. 76
Fulani, Lenora 11
Fuller, A. Oveta 43
Fuller, Arthur 27
Fuller, Blind Boy 86
Fuller, Charles 8

Fuller, Howard L. 37
Fuller, Hoyt 44
Fuller, Meta Vaux Warrick 27
Fuller, S. B. 13
Fuller, Solomon Carter, Jr. 15
Fuller, Thomas O. 90
Fuller, Vivian 33
Funderburg, I. Owen 38
Funnye, Capers C., Jr. 73
Fuqua, Antoine 35
Fuqua, Harvey 90
Futch, Eddie 33
Gaines, Brenda 41
Gaines, Clarence E., Sr. 55
Gaines, Ernest J. 7
Gaines, Grady 38
Gaines, Lloyd 79
Gaiter, Dorothy J. 80
Gaither, Alonzo Smith (Jake) 14
Gaither, Israel L. 65
Gamble, Kenny 85
Gans, Joe 91
Gantt, Harvey 1
Gardere, Jeffrey 76
Gardner, Chris 65
Gardner, Edward G. 45
Garner, Erroll 76
Garnett, Kevin 14, 70
Garrett, James F. 78
Garrett, Joyce Finley 59
Garrison, Zina 2
Garvin, Gerry 78
Gary, Willie E. 12
Gaskins, Eric 64
Gaskins, Rudy 74
Gaspard, Patrick 84
Gaston, Arthur George 3, 38, 59
Gaston, Cito 71
Gaston, Marilyn Hughes 60
Gates, Henry Louis, Jr. 3, 38, 67
Gates, Sylvester James, Jr. 15
Gaye, Marvin 2
Gaye, Nona 56
Gayle, Addison, Jr. 41
Gayle, Helene D. 3, 46
Gaynor, Gloria 36
Gentry, Alvin 23
George, Eddie 80
George, Nelson 12
George, Zelma Watson 42
Gervin, George 80
Ghostface Killah 90
Gibbs, Marla 86
Gibson, Althea 8, 43
Gibson, Bob 33
Gibson, Donald Bernard 40
Gibson, John Trusty 87
Gibson, Johnnie Mae 23
Gibson, Josh 22
Gibson, Kenneth Allen 6
Gibson, Ted 66
Gibson, Truman K., Jr. 60
Gibson, Tyrese 27, 62
Gibson, William F. 6
Giddings, Paula 11
Gidron, Richard D. 68
Gilbert, Christopher 50
Gilbert, John Wesley 91
Giles, Roscoe C. 93
Gill, Gerald 69
Gill, Johnny 51
Gill, Turner 83
Gilles, Ralph 61

Gillespie, Dizzy **1**
Gilliam, Frank **23**
Gilliam, Joe **31**
Gilliam, Sam **16**
Gilliard, Steve **69**
Gilmore, Marshall **46**
Gilpin, Charles Sidney **81**
Ginuwine **35**
Giovanni, Nikki **9, 39, 85**
Gist, Carole **1**
Givens, Adele **62**
Givens, Robin **4, 25, 58**
Givhan, Robin Deneen **72**
Glanville, Douglas Metunwa **82**
Gloster, Hugh Morris, Sr. **90**
Glover, Corey **34**
Glover, Danny **1, 24**
Glover, Donald **85**
Glover, Keith **79**
Glover, Nathaniel, Jr. **12**
Glover, Savion **14**
Goapele **55**
Goines, Donald **19**
Goings, Russell **59**
Goldberg, Whoopi **4, 33, 69**
Golden, Marita **19**
Golden, Thelma **10, 55**
Goldsberry, Ronald **18**
Golson, Benny **37**
Golston, Allan C. **55**
Gomes, Peter J. **15, 93**
Gomez, Jewelle **30**
Gomez-Preston, Cheryl **9**
Gomillion, Charles **90**
Goode, Mal **13**
Goode, W. Wilson **4**
Gooden, Dwight **20**
Gooden, Linda **94**
Gooding, Cuba, Jr. **16, 62**
Goodlett, Carlton B. **91**
Goodman, Al **87**
Goodman, Kim C. **94**
Goodnight, Paul **32**
Gorden, W. C. **71**
Gordon, Bruce S. **41, 53, 82**
Gordon, Carl **87**
Gordon, Dexter **25**
Gordon, Ed **10, 53**
Gordone, Charles **15**
Gordon-Reed, Annette **74**
Gordy, Berry, Jr. **1**
Goss, Carol A. **55**
Goss, Tom **23**
Gossett, Louis, Jr. **7**
Gotti, Irv **39**
Gourdin, Edward O. **93**
Gourdine, Meredith **33**
Gourdine, Simon **11**
Grace, George H. **48**
Graham, Lawrence Otis **12**
Graham, Lorenz **48**
Graham, Stedman **13**
Graham, Trevor **84**
Granderson, Curtis **66**
Granger, Lester B. **75**
Grant, Augustus O. **71**
Grant, Bernie **57**
Grant, Gwendolyn Goldsby **28**
Granville, Evelyn Boyd **36**
Gravely, Samuel L., Jr. **5, 49**
Graves, Butch **77**
Graves, Denyce Antoinette **19, 57**
Graves, Earl G. **1, 35**

Gray, Darius **69**
Gray, F. Gary **14, 49**
Gray, Farrah **59**
Gray, Fred **37**
Gray, Ida **41**
Gray, Macy **29**
Gray, Vincent C. **88**
Gray, William H., III **3**
Gray, Willie **46**
Gray, Yeshimbra "Shimmy" **55**
Greaves, William **38**
Greely, M. Gasby **27**
Green, A. C. **32**
Green, Al **13, 47, 74**
Green, Darrell **39, 74**
Green, Dennis **5, 45**
Green, Grant **56**
Green, Isaac H. **79**
Green, Jonathan **54**
Greene, Jimmy **74**
Greene, Joe **10**
Greene, Maurice **27, 77**
Greene, Petey **65**
Greene, Richard Thaddeus, Sr. **67**
Greenfield, Eloise **9**
Greenhouse, Bunnatine "Bunny" **57**
Greenlee, Sam **48**
Greenwood, Monique **38**
Greer, Hal **92**
Gregory, Ann **63**
Gregory, Dick **1, 54**
Gregory, Frederick **8, 51**
Gregory, Wilton **37**
Grier, David Alan **28**
Grier, Eliza Ann **90**
Grier, Mike **43**
Grier, Pam **9, 31, 86**
Grier, Roosevelt **13**
Griffey, Dick **89**
Griffey, Ken, Jr. **12, 73**
Griffin, Anthony **71**
Griffin, Bessie Blout **43**
Griffin, Johnny **71**
Griffin, LaShell **51**
Griffith, Mark Winston **8**
Griffith, Yolanda **25**
Griffith-Joyner, Florence **28**
Grimké, Archibald H. **9**
Grist, Reri **84**
Grooms, Henry R(andall) **50**
Guillaume, Robert **3, 48**
Guinier, Lani **7, 30**
Gumbel, Bryant **14, 80**
Gumbel, Greg **8**
Gunn, Moses **10**
Gurira, Danai **73**
Guru **84**
Guy, George "Buddy" **31**
Guy, Jasmine **2**
Guy, Rosa **5**
Guy-Sheftall, Beverly **13, 92**
Guyton, Tyree **9, 94**
Gwynn, Tony **18, 83**
Haddon, Dietrick **55**
Hageman, Hans **36**
Hageman, Ivan **36**
Hailey, JoJo **22**
Hailey, K-Ci **22**
Hairston, Jester **88**
Hairston, Sam **88**
Hale, Clara **16**
Hale, Lorraine **8**
Haley, Alex **4**

Haley, George Williford Boyce **21**
Hall, Aaron **57**
Hall, Alvin D. **86**
Hall, Arsenio **58**
Hall, Arthur **39**
Hall, Elliott S. **24**
Hall, Juanita **62**
Hall, Kevan **61**
Hall, Lloyd A. **8**
Halliburton, Warren J. **49**
Ham, Cynthia Parker **58**
Hamblin, Ken **10**
Hamburg, Beatrix **84**
Hamburg, Margaret **78**
Hamer, Fannie Lou **6**
Hamilton, Anthony **61**
Hamilton, Samuel C. **47**
Hamilton, Lisa Gay **71**
Hamilton, Virginia **10**
Hamlin, Larry Leon **49, 62**
Hammond, Fred **23**
Hammonds, Evelynn **69**
Hammons, David **69**
Hampton, Fred **18**
Hampton, Henry **6**
Hampton, Lionel **17, 41**
Hancock, Herbie **20, 67**
Handy, W. C. **8**
Haney, Lee **77**
Hannah, Marc **10**
Hansberry, Lorraine **6**
Hansberry, Tony, II **93**
Hansberry, William Leo **11**
Hansen, Austin **88**
Hardaway, Anfernee (Penny) **13**
Hardaway, Tim **35**
Hardin Armstrong, Lil **39**
Harding, Vincent **67**
Hardison, Bethann **12**
Hardison, Kadeem **22**
Hare, Nathan **44**
Harkless, Necia Desiree **19**
Harmon, Clarence **26**
Harold, Erika **54**
Harper, Ben **34, 62**
Harper, Frances Ellen Watkins **11**
Harper, Hill **32, 65**
Harper, Michael S. **34**
Harper, Rachel M. **92**
Harrell, Andre **9, 30**
Harrington, Oliver W. **9**
Harris, Alice **7**
Harris, Barbara **12**
Harris, Barry **68**
Harris, Bernard A. **90**
Harris, Bill **72**
Harris, Carla A. **67**
Harris, Corey **39, 73**
Harris, E. Lynn **12, 33**
Harris, Eddy L. **18**
Harris, Gary L. **87**
Harris, James **79**
Harris, Jay T. **19**
Harris, Jessica B. **91**
Harris, Kamala D. **64**
Harris, Leslie **6**
Harris, Lyle Ashton **83**
Harris, Marcelite Jordon **16**
Harris, Mary Styles **31**
Harris, Maya Lakshmi **88**
Harris, Monica **18**
Harris, Patricia Roberts **2**
Harris, Richard E. **61**

Harris, Robin **7**
Harris, Sylvia **70**
Harris, Wesley L. **92**
Harris-Lacewell, Melissa **81**
Harrison, Alvin **28**
Harrison, Calvin **28**
Harrison, Charles **72**
Harris-Stewart, Lusia **90**
Harsh, Vivian Gordon **14**
Hart, Alvin Youngblood **61**
Harvard, Beverly **11**
Harvey, Steve **18, 58**
Harvey, William R. **42**
Haskins, Clem **23**
Haskins, James **36, 54**
Hassell, Leroy Rountree, Sr. **41**
Hastie, William H. **8**
Hastings, Alcee L. **16**
Hatcher, Andrew T. **90**
Hatcher, Richard G. **55**
Hatchett, Glenda **32**
Hathaway, Donny **18**
Hathaway, Isaac Scott **33**
Hathaway, Lalah **57, 88**
Hawkins, Augustus F. **68**
Hawkins, Coleman **9**
Hawkins, Connie **91**
Hawkins, Erskine **14**
Hawkins, La-Van **17, 54**
Hawkins, Screamin' Jay **30**
Hawkins, Steven **14**
Hawkins, Tramaine **16**
Hawkins, Walter **87**
Hayden, Carla D. **47**
Hayden, Palmer **13**
Hayden, Robert **12**
Hayes, Bob **77**
Hayes, Cecil N. **46**
Hayes, Dennis **54**
Hayes, Elvin **93**
Hayes, Isaac **20, 58, 73**
Hayes, James C. **10**
Hayes, Roland **4**
Hayes, Teddy **40**
Haygood, Wil **83**
Haynes, George Edmund **8**
Haynes, Marques **22**
Haynes, Roy **87**
Haynes, Trudy **44**
Haynie, Sharon **94**
Haysbert, Dennis **42**
Haysbert, Raymond V., Sr. **87**
Haywood, Gar Anthony **43**
Haywood, Jimmy **58**
Haywood, Margaret A. **24**
Hazel, Darryl B. **50**
Healy, James Augustine **30**
Healy, Michael **90**
Heard, Gar **25**
Heard, Nathan C. **45**
Hearns, Thomas **29**
Hedgeman, Anna Arnold **22**
Height, Dorothy I. **2, 23, 78**
Hemphill, Essex **10**
Hemphill, Jessie Mae **33, 59**
Hemsley, Sherman **19**
Henderson, Cornelius Langston **26**
Henderson, David **53**
Henderson, Fletcher **32**
Henderson, Gordon **5**
Henderson, Henry Fairfax, Jr. **89**
Henderson, Jeff **72**
Henderson, Rickey **28, 78**

Henderson, Stephen E. **45**
Henderson, Thelton E. **68**
Henderson, Wade J. **14**
Henderson, Zelma **71**
Hendrix, Jimi **10**
Hendryx, Nona **56**
Hendy, Francis **47**
Henries, A. Doris Banks **44**
Henry, Aaron **19**
Henry, Clarence "Frogman" **46**
Henry, Joshua **94**
Henry, Troy **85**
Henson, Darrin **33**
Henson, Josiah **90**
Henson, Matthew **2**
Henson, Taraji P. **58, 77**
Herbert, Bob **63**
Hercules, Frank **44**
Herenton, Willie W. **24, 81**
Herman, Alexis M. **15**
Hernandez, Aileen Clarke **13**
Herndon, Alonzo Franklin **89**
Herndon, Angelo **90**
Hernton, Calvin C. **51**
Hickman, Fred **11**
Higginbotham, A. Leon, Jr. **13, 25**
Higginbotham, Jay C. **37**
Higginsen, Vy **65**
Hightower, Dennis F. **13**
Hill, Andrew **66**
Hill, Anita **5, 65**
Hill, Bonnie Guiton **20**
Hill, Calvin **19**
Hill, Donna **32**
Hill, Dulé **29**
Hill, Grant **13, 94**
Hill, Hugh Morgan **83**
Hill, Janet **19**
Hill, Jesse, Jr. **13**
Hill, Lauryn **20, 53**
Hill, Leslie Pinckney **44**
Hill, Marc Lamont **80**
Hill, Oliver W. **24, 63**
Hill, Peter **92**
Hill, Wyllstyne D. **94**
Hillard, Terry **25**
Hillary, Barbara **65**
Hilliard, Asa Grant, III **66**
Hilliard, David **7**
Hilliard, Earl F. **24**
Hilliard, Wendy **53**
Hilson, Keri **84**
Himes, Chester **8**
Hinderas, Natalie **5**
Hine, Darlene Clark **24**
Hines, Earl "Fatha" **39**
Hines, Garrett **35**
Hines, Gregory **1, 42**
Hinton, Milt **30**
Hinton, William Augustus **8**
Hoagland, Everett H. **45**
Hobson, Julius W. **44**
Hobson, Mellody **40**
Hogan, Beverly Wade **50**
Holder, Eric H., Jr. **9, 76**
Holder, Laurence **34**
Holdsclaw, Chamique **24**
Holiday, Billie **1**
Holland, Endesha Ida Mae **3, 57**
Holland, Kimberly N. **62**
Holland, Robert, Jr. **11**
Holland-Dozier-Holland **36**
Holloway, Brenda **65**

Hollowell, Donald L. **57**
Holmes, Amy **69**
Holmes, Clint **57**
Holmes, Hamilton E. **82**
Holmes, Larry **20, 68**
Holmes, Santonio **87**
Holmes, Shannon **70**
Holsey, Lucius Henry **92**
Holstein, Casper **89**
Holt, Lester **66**
Holt, Nora **38**
Holt Baker, Arlene **73**
Holton, Hugh, Jr. **39**
Holyfield, Evander **6**
Honeywood, Varnette P. **54, 88**
Honoré, Russel L. **64**
Hood, James Walker **91**
Hooker, John Lee **30**
hooks, bell **5, 90**
Hooks, Benjamin L. **2, 85**
Hooks, Robert **76**
Hope, John **8**
Hope, Lugenia Burns **89**
Hopkins, Bernard **35, 69**
Hopkins, Donald R. **89**
Hopkins, Lightnin' **83**
Horn, Shirley **32, 56**
Horne, Frank **44**
Horne, Lena **5, 86**
Horsford, Steven **88**
Horton, Andre **33**
Horton, Gladys **92**
Horton, James Oliver **58**
Horton, Suki **33**
Houghton, Israel **92**
House, Son **8**
Houston, Charles Hamilton **4**
Houston, Cissy **20, 83**
Houston, Whitney **7, 28, 83**
Howard, Ayanna **65**
Howard, Desmond **16, 58**
Howard, Juwan **15**
Howard, M. William, Jr. **26**
Howard, Michelle **28**
Howard, Ryan **65**
Howard, Sherri **36**
Howard, Terrence **59, 94**
Howell, Ayinde **91**
Howlin' Wolf **9**
Howroyd, Janice Bryant **42**
Hoyte, Lenon **50**
Hrabowski, Freeman A., III **22**
Hubbard, Arnette Rhinehart **38**
Hubbard, Freddie **75**
Hudlin, Reginald **9, 86**
Hudlin, Warrington **9**
Hudson, Cheryl **15**
Hudson, Ernie **72**
Hudson, Jennifer **63, 83**
Hudson, Wade **15**
Huff, Leon **86**
Huggins, Edie **71**
Huggins, Larry **21**
Huggins, Nathan Irvin **52**
Hughes, Albert **7**
Hughes, Allen **7**
Hughes, Cathy **27**
Hughes, Dora **88**
Hughes, Ebony **57**
Hughes, Langston **4**
Hughley, D. L. **23, 76**
Hull, Akasha Gloria **45**
Humphrey, Bobbi **20**

Humphries, Frederick **20**
Hunt, Darnell **92**
Hunt, Richard **6**
Hunter, Alberta **42**
Hunter, Clementine **45**
Hunter, Torii **43**
Hunter-Gault, Charlayne **6, 31**
Hurston, Zora Neale **3**
Hurt, Byron **61**
Hurt, Mississippi John **84**
Hurtt, Harold **46**
Hutch, Willie **62**
Hutcherson, Hilda Yvonne **54**
Hutchinson, Earl Ofari **24**
Hutson, Jean Blackwell **16**
Hyde, Cowan F. "Bubba" **47**
Hyman, Earle **25, 79**
Hyman, Phyllis **19**
Ice Cube **8, 30, 60**
Iceberg Slim **11**
Ice-T **6, 31**
Iman, Chanel **66**
Ifill, Gwen **28**
Imes, Elmer Samuel **39**
India.Arie **34**
Ingram, James **84**
Ingram, Rex **5**
Innis, Roy **5**
Irvin, Michael **64**
Irvin, Monford Merrill **31**
Irvin, Vernon **65**
Irving, Larry, Jr. **12**
Irvis, K. Leroy **67**
Isaacs, John **76**
Isley, Marvin **87**
Isley, Ronald **25, 56**
Iverson, Allen **24, 46**
Ivey, Phil **72**
Ja Rule **35, 91**
Jackson, Alexine Clement **22**
Jackson, Alphonso R. **48**
Jackson, Brenda **87**
Jackson, Deborah **94**
Jackson, Earl **31**
Jackson, Edison O. **67**
Jackson, Frank G. **76**
Jackson, Fred James **25**
Jackson, George **14**
Jackson, George **19**
Jackson, Hal **41**
Jackson, Isaiah **3**
Jackson, Jamea **64**
Jackson, James A. **90**
Jackson, Janet **6, 30, 68**
Jackson, Jermaine **79**
Jackson, Jesse **1, 27, 72**
Jackson, Jesse, Jr. **14, 45, 81**
Jackson, Joe **78**
Jackson, John **36**
Jackson, Judith D. **57**
Jackson, Lisa **77**
Jackson, Mae **57**
Jackson, Mahalia **5**
Jackson, Mannie **14**
Jackson, Mary **73**
Jackson, Maynard **2, 41**
Jackson, Michael **19, 53, 76**
Jackson, Millie **25**
Jackson, Milt **26**
Jackson, Rampage **83**
Jackson, Randy **40**
Jackson, Reggie **15**
Jackson, Rickey **88**

Jackson, Samuel **8, 63**
Jackson, Sheneska **18**
Jackson, Shirley Ann **12**
Jackson, Tito **81**
Jackson, Tom **70**
Jackson, Vera **40**
Jackson Lee, Sheila **20**
Jacob, John E. **2**
Jacobs, Regina **38**
Jacquet, Illinois **49**
Jaheim **58**
Jakes, Thomas "T. D." **17, 43**
Jamal, Ahmad **69**
Jamerson, James **59**
James, Charles H., III **62**
James, Daniel, Jr. **16**
James, Donna A. **51**
James, Etta **13, 52**
James, G. Larry **74**
James, Juanita **13**
James, LeBron **46, 78**
James, Nikki M. **94**
James, Rick **19**
James, Sharpe **23, 69**
James, Skip **38**
Jamison, Judith **7, 67**
Jarreau, Al **21, 65**
Jarrett, Valerie **73**
Jarrett, Vernon D. **42**
Jarvis, Charlene Drew **21**
Jarvis, Erich **67**
Jarvis, Kristen **85**
Jasper, John J. **91**
Jasper, Kenji **39**
Jay-Z **27, 69**
Jealous, Benjamin **70**
Jefferson, Blind Lemon **81**
Jefferson, Denise **87**
Jefferson, Mildred Fay **89**
Jefferson, William J. **25, 72**
Jeffries, Leonard **8**
Jemison, Mae C. **1, 35**
Jemison, Major L. **48**
Jenifer, Franklyn G. **2**
Jenkins, Beverly **14**
Jenkins, Ella **15**
Jenkins, Ray **17**
Jennings, Lyfe **56, 69**
Jerkins, Rodney **31**
Jeter, Claude **75**
Jeter, Derek **27, 93**
Jimmy Jam **13**
Joe, Yolanda **21**
John, Daymond **23**
Johns, Vernon **38**
Johnson, Angela **52**
Johnson, Anthony M. **92**
Johnson, Avery **62**
Johnson, Beverly **2**
Johnson, Buddy **36**
Johnson, Charles **1, 82**
Johnson, Charles S. **12**
Johnson, Chris **92**
Johnson, Clifford "Connie" **52**
Johnson, Dennis **89**
Johnson, Earvin "Magic" **3, 39**
Johnson, Eddie Bernice **8, 90**
Johnson, Eunice W. **83**
Johnson, Fenton **91**
Johnson, George E. **29**
Johnson, Georgia Douglas **41**
Johnson, Gus **92**
Johnson, Hall **90**

Johnson, Hank, Jr. **80**
Johnson, Harry E. **57**
Johnson, Harvey, Jr. **24, 82**
Johnson, J. J. **37**
Johnson, Jack **8**
Johnson, James Weldon **5**
Johnson, Je'Caryous **63**
Johnson, Jeh C. **76**
Johnson, Jeh Vincent **44**
Johnson, Joe **94**
Johnson, John H. **3, 54**
Johnson, Johnnie **56**
Johnson, Katherine (Coleman Goble) **61**
Johnson, Kevin **70**
Johnson, Keyshawn **91**
Johnson, Larry **28**
Johnson, Leroy R. **89**
Johnson, Levi **48**
Johnson, Lonnie **85**
Johnson, Lonnie G. **32, 93**
Johnson, Mamie "Peanut" **40**
Johnson, Mat **31**
Johnson, Michael **13**
Johnson, Mordecai Wyatt **79**
Johnson, Norma L. Holloway **17**
Johnson, R. M. **36**
Johnson, Rafer **33**
Johnson, Robert **2**
Johnson, Robert L. **3, 39**
Johnson, Robert T. **17**
Johnson, Rodney Van **28**
Johnson, Sandra K. **94**
Johnson, Sheila Crump **48**
Johnson, Shoshana **47**
Johnson, Virginia **9**
Johnson, William **91**
Johnson, William Henry **3**
Johnson-George, Tamara **79**
Jolley, Willie **28**
Jones, Absalom **52**
Jones, Alex **64**
Jones, Bill T. **1, 46, 80**
Jones, Bobby **20, 94**
Jones, Booker T. **84**
Jones, Carl **7**
Jones, Caroline **29**
Jones, Clara Stanton **51**
Jones, Cobi N'Gai **18**
Jones, Cullen **73**
Jones, Deacon **92**
Jones, Donell **29**
Jones, Doris W. **62**
Jones, E. Edward, Sr. **45**
Jones, Ed "Too Tall" **46**
Jones, Edith Mae Irby **65**
Jones, Edward P. **43, 67**
Jones, Elaine R. **7, 45**
Jones, Elvin **14, 68**
Jones, Emil, Jr. **74**
Jones, Etta **35**
Jones, Eugene Kinckle **79**
Jones, Frederick McKinley **68**
Jones, Gayl **37**
Jones, Hank **57, 86**
Jones, Ingrid Saunders **18**
Jones, James Earl **3, 49, 79**
Jones, John **89**
Jones, Jonah **39**
Jones, K. C. **83**
Jones, Lois Mailou **13**
Jones, Lou **64**
Jones, Marion **21, 66**

Jones, Merlakia **34**
Jones, Orlando **30**
Jones, Paul R. **76**
Jones, Quincy **8, 30**
Jones, Randy **35**
Jones, Robert Elijah **90**
Jones, Robert G. **81**
Jones, Sam **85**
Jones, Sarah **39**
Jones, Sharon **86**
Jones, Thad **68**
Jones, Thomas W. **41**
Jones, Van **70**
Jones, Wayne **53**
Jones, William A., Jr. **61**
Joplin, Scott **6**
Jordan, Barbara **4, 78**
Jordan, Eddie **82**
Jordan, Eddie **83**
Jordan, June **7, 35**
Jordan, Michael **6, 21**
Jordan, Montell **23**
Jordan, Vernon E. **3, 35**
Joseph, Kathie-Ann **56**
Josey, E. J. **10**
Joyce, Dru **81**
Joyner, Marjorie Stewart **26**
Joyner, Matilda Sissieretta **15**
Joyner, Tom **19, 90**
Joyner-Kersee, Jackie **5**
Julian, Hubert **90**
Julian, Percy Lavon **6**
July, William **27**
Just, Ernest Everett **3**
Justice, David **18**
Kaigler, Denise **63**
Kaiser, Cecil **42**
Kandi **83**
Kani, Karl **10**
Karenga, Maulana **10, 71**
Karim, Benjamin **61**
Kaufman, Monica **66**
Kay, Ulysses **37**
Kearney, Janis **54**
Kearse, Amalya Lyle **12**
Keckley, Elizabeth **90**
Kee, John P. **43**
Keene, John **73**
Keflezighi, Meb **49**
Keith, Damon J. **16, 74**
Keith, Floyd A. **61**
Kelis **58**
Kelley, Cliff **75**
Kelley, Elijah **65**
Kelley, Malcolm David **59**
Kellogg, Clark **64**
Kelly, Patrick **3**
Kelly, R. **18, 44, 71**
Kem **47**
Kemp, Herb **94**
Kendrick, Erika **57**
Kendricks, Eddie **22**
Kennedy, Adrienne **11**
Kennedy, Florynce **12, 33**
Kennedy, Randall **40**
Kennedy-Overton, Jayne Harris **46**
Kenney, John A., Jr. **48**
Kenoly, Ron **45**
Kenyatta, Robin **54**
Kerry, Leon G. **46**
Keyes, Alan L. **11**
Keys, Alicia **32, 68**
Khan, Chaka **12, 50**

Khanga, Yelena **6**
Kid Cudi **83**
Kidd, Jason **86**
Kidd, Mae Street **39**
Killens, John O. **54**
Killings, Debra **57**
Killingsworth, Cleve, Jr. **54**
Kilpatrick, Carolyn Cheeks **16**
Kilpatrick, Kwame **34, 71**
Kimbro, Dennis **10**
Kimbro, Henry A. **25**
Kimbro, Warren **76**
Kincaid, Bernard **28**
Kincaid, Jamaica **4**
King, Alonzo **38**
King, B. B. **7**
King, Barbara **22**
King, Bernice **4, 81**
King, Colbert I. **69**
King, Coretta Scott **3, 57**
King, Dexter **10**
King, Don **14**
King, Freddie **92**
King, Gayle **19**
King, Martin Luther, III **20**
King, Martin Luther, Jr. **1**
King, Martin Luther, Sr. **89**
King, Preston **28**
King, Reatha Clark **65**
King, Regina **22, 45**
King, Robert Arthur **58**
King, Robert Hillary **84**
King, Teresa **80**
King, Woodie, Jr. **27**
King, Yolanda **6**
King Curtis **92**
Kingston, Sean **94**
Kirby, George **14**
Kirk, Ron **11, 75**
Kitt, Eartha **16, 75**
Kitt, Sandra **23**
Kittles, Rick **51**
Kitwana, Bakari **86**
Klugh, Earl **59**
Knight, Etheridge **37**
Knight, Gladys **16, 66**
Knight, Marie **80**
Knight, Suge **11, 30**
Knowles, Tina **61**
Knowling, Robert E., Jr. **38**
Knox, Simmie **49**
Knuckles, Frankie **42**
Komunyakaa, Yusef **9**
Kong, B. Waine **50**
Kool Moe Dee **37**
Kotto, Yaphet **7**
Kountz, Samuel L. **10**
Kravitz, Lenny **10, 34**
KRS-One **34**
K-Swift **73**
Kunjufu, Jawanza **3, 50**
Kweli, Talib **93**
La Salle, Eriq **12**
LaBelle, Patti **13, 30**
LaChanze **93**
Lacy, Sam **30, 46**
Ladd, Ernie **64**
Ladner, Joyce A. **42**
Lafontant, Jewel Stradford **3, 51**
Lampkin, Daisy **19**
Lampley, Oni Faida **43, 71**
Lane, Charles **3**
Lane, Dick **92**

Lane, Lunsford **93**
Lane, Vincent **5**
Lane, William Henry **90**
Langford, Larry P. **74**
Langhart Cohen, Janet **19, 60**
Lanier, Bob **47**
Lanier, Willie **33**
Lankford, Ray **23**
Larkin, Barry **24**
Larrieux, Amel **63**
Lars, Byron **32**
Larsen, Nella **10**
Laryea, Thomas Davies, III **67**
Lashley, Bobby **63**
Lassiter, Roy **24**
Lateef, Yusef **91**
Lathan, Sanaa **27**
Latimer, Lewis H. **4**
Lattany, Kristin Hunter **88**
Lattimore, Kenny **35**
LaVette, Bettye **85**
Lavizzo-Mourey, Risa **48**
Lawless, Theodore K. **8**
Lawrence, Jacob **4, 28**
Lawrence, Martin **6, 27**
Lawrence, Robert H., Jr. **16**
Lawrence-Lightfoot, Sara **10**
Laws, Hubert **90**
Lawson, James M., Jr. **90**
Lawson, Jennifer **1, 50**
Layton, William **87**
Leadbelly **82**
Leary, Kathryn D. **10**
Leavell, Dorothy R. **17**
Ledisi **73**
Lee, Annie Frances **22**
Lee, Barbara **25**
Lee, Bertram M., Sr. **46**
Lee, Canada **8**
Lee, Consuela **84**
Lee, Debra L. **62**
Lee, Eric P. **79**
Lee, Joe A. **45**
Lee, Joie **1**
Lee, Leslie **85**
Lee, Malcolm D. **75**
Lee, Raphael C. **87**
Lee, Spike **5, 19, 86**
Lee-Smith, Hughie **5, 22**
Leevy, Carrol M. **42**
Leffall, Lasalle, Jr. **3, 64**
Legend, John **67**
Leggs, Kingsley **62**
Leland, Mickey **2**
Lemmons, Kasi **20**
Lemon, Don **94**
Lennox, Betty **31**
LeNoire, Rosetta **37**
Lenox, Adriane **59**
Leon, Kenny **10**
Leonard, Buck **67**
Leonard, Sugar Ray **15**
Leslie, Lisa **16, 73**
Lester, Bill **42, 85**
Lester, Julius **9**
Lesure, James **64**
LeTang, Henry **66**
Letson, Al **39**
Levert, Eddie **70**
Levert, Gerald **22, 59**
Lewis, Ananda **28**
Lewis, Aylwin B. **51, 88**
Lewis, Butch **71**

Lewis, Byron E. 13
Lewis, Carl 4
Lewis, David Levering 9
Lewis, Delano 7
Lewis, Edmonia 10
Lewis, Edward T. 21
Lewis, Emmanuel 36
Lewis, Henry 38
Lewis, John 2, 46, 83
Lewis, Marvin 51, 87
Lewis, Norman 39
Lewis, Oliver 56
Lewis, Ramsey 35, 70
Lewis, Ray 33
Lewis, Reginald F. 6
Lewis, Samella 25
Lewis, Shirley A. R. 14
Lewis, Terry 13
Lewis, Thomas 19
Lewis, William Henry 89
Lewis, William M., Jr. 40
Lewis-Thornton, Rae 32
Ligging, Alfred, III 43
Ligon, Glenn 82
Lil' Kim 28
Lil Wayne 66, 84
Liles, Kevin 42
Lincoln, Abbey 3, 88
Lincoln, C. Eric 38
Lindsey, Tommie 51
Lipscomb, Mance 49
LisaRaye 27
Lister, Marquita 65
Liston, Sonny 33
Little, Benilde 21
Little, Floyd 86
Little, Larry 90
Little, Robert L. 2
Little Milton 36, 54
Little Richard 15
Little Walter 36
Littlepage, Craig 35
LL Cool J 16, 49, 94
Llewellyn, J. Bruce 13, 85
Lloyd, Earl 26
Lloyd, John Henry "Pop" 30
Lloyd, Reginald 64
Locke, Alain 10
Locke, Attica 85
Locke, Eddie 44
Lofton, James 42
Lofton, Kenny 12
Logan, Onnie Lee 14
Logan, Rayford W. 40
Loguen, J. W. 91
Lomax, Louis E. 90
Lomax, Michael L. 58
Long, Eddie L. 29, 89
Long, Huey 79
Long, Loretta 58
Long, Nia 17
Long, Richard Alexander 65
Lopes, Davey 92
Lopes, Lisa "Left Eye" 36
Lorde, Audre 6
Lott, Ronnie 9
Loueke, Lionel 88
Louis, Errol T. 8
Louis, Joe 5
Loury, Glenn 36
Love, Darlene 23, 92
Love, Ed 58
Love, Laura 50

Love, Nat 9
Love, Reggie 77
Lovell, Whitfield 74
Lover, Ed 10
Loving, Alvin, Jr. 35, 53
Loving, Mildred 69
Lowe, Herbert 57
Lowe, Sidney 64
Lowery, Joseph 2
Lowery, Myron 80
Lowry, A. Leon 60
Lucas, John 7
Lucie, Lawrence 80
Lucien, Jon 66
Luckett, Letoya 61
Lucy, William 50
Lucy Foster, Autherine 35
Ludacris 37, 60
Luke, Derek 61
Lumbly, Carl 47
Lumet, Jenny 80
Luna, Donyale 88
Luper, Clara 94
Lyles, Lester Lawrence 31
Lymon, Frankie 22
Lynch, Shola 61
Lyons, Henry 12
Lyttle, Hulda Margaret 14
Mabley, Moms 15
Mabrey, Vicki 26
Mabry, Marcus 70
Mac, Bernie 29, 61, 72
Mackey, Biz 82
Mackey, Nathaniel 75
Madhubuti, Haki 7, 85
Madison, Joseph E. 17
Madison, Paula 37
Madison, Romell 45
Madlib 88
Mahal, Taj 39
Mahorn, Rick 60
Maitreya, Sananda 85
Majette, Denise 41
Major, Clarence 9
Majors, Jeff 41
Malco, Romany 71
Mallett, Conrad, Jr. 16
Mallory, Mark 62
Malone, Annie 13
Malone, Karl 18, 51, 90
Malone, Maurice 32
Malone, Moses 79
Malone Jones, Vivian 59
Malveaux, Floyd 54
Malveaux, Julianne 32, 70
Malveaux, Suzanne 88
Mane, Gucci 91
Manigault, Earl "The Goat" 15
Manigault-Stallworth, Omarosa 69
Manley, Audrey Forbes 16
Mann, Tamela 92
Manning, Frankie 78
Manuel, Jerry 94
Marable, Manning 10
March, William Carrington 56
Mariner, Jonathan 41
Marino, Eugene Antonio 30
Mario 71
Marrow, Queen Esther 24
Marsalis, Branford 34
Marsalis, Delfeayo 41
Marsalis, Ellis 90
Marsalis, Wynton 16, 90

Marsh, Henry, III 32
Marshall, Bella 22
Marshall, Kerry James 59
Marshall, Paule 7, 77
Marshall, Thurgood 1, 44
Martin, Darnell 43, 78
Martin, Helen 31
Martin, Jesse L. 31
Martin, Louis E. 16
Martin, Roberta 58
Martin, Roland S. 49, 84
Martin, Ruby Grant 49
Martin, Sara 38
Mase 24
Mason, Biddy 89
Mason, Felicia 31
Mason, Herman, Jr. 83
Mason, Ronald 27
Massaquoi, Hans J. 30
Massenburg, Kedar 23
Massey, Brandon 40
Massey, Walter E. 5, 45
Massie, Samuel Proctor, Jr. 29
Master P 21
Matejka, Adrian 87
Mathis, Greg 26
Mathis, Johnny 20
Matson, Ollie 93
Matthews, Benjamin 93
Matthews, Mark 59
Matthews Shatteen, Westina 51
Matzeliger, Jan 93
Maupin, John E., Jr. 92
Maxey, Randall 46
Maxis, Theresa 62
Maxwell 20, 81
May, Derrick 41
Mayberry-Stewart, Melodie 94
Mayfield, Curtis 2, 43
Mayhew, Martin R. 76
Mayhew, Richard 39
Maynard, Nancy Hicks 73
Maynard, Robert C. 7
Maynor, Dorothy 19
Mayo, Whitman 32
Mays, Benjamin E. 7
Mays, Leslie A. 41
Mays, William G. 34
Mays, Willie 3
Mayweather, Floyd, Jr. 57
MC Breed 75
M.C. Hammer 20, 80
MC Lyte 34
McAdoo, Bob 75
McAnulty, William E., Jr. 66
McBay, Henry C. 91
McBride, Bryant 18
McBride, Chi 73
McBride, James 35, 87
McCabe, Jewell Jackson 10
McCall, H. Carl 27
McCall, Nathan 8
McCann, Renetta 44
McCarthy, Sandy 64
McCarty, Osceola 16
McCauley, Gina 76
McClellan, George Marion 91
McClendon, Forrest 94
McClendon, Lisa 61
McClinton, Marion Isaac 77
McClurkin, Donnie 25
McCoo, Marilyn 53
McCoy, Elijah 8

McCrary Anthony, Crystal 70
McCray, Nikki 18
McCullough, Geraldine 58, 79
McDaniel, Hattie 5
McDaniel, Randall Cornell 81
McDaniels, Ralph 79
McDonald, Audra 20, 62
McDonald, Erroll 1
McDonald, Gabrielle Kirk 20
McDougall, Gay J. 11, 43
McDuffie, Dwayne 62
McEwen, Mark 5
McFadden, Bernice L. 39
McFarlan, Tyron 60
McFarland, Roland 49
McFerrin, Bobby 68
McFerrin, Robert, Sr. 94
McGee, Charles 10
McGee, James D. 74
McGee, James Madison 46
McGill, Anthony 76
McGlowan, Angela 64, 86
McGrady, Tracy 80
McGriff, Fred 24
McGriff, Jimmy 72
McGruder, Aaron 28, 56
McGruder, Robert 22, 35
McGuire, Raymond J. 57
McHenry, Donald F. 83
McJunkin, George 93
McKay, Claude 6
McKay, Nellie Yvonne 17, 57
McKee, Lonette 12
McKenzie, Vashti M. 29
McKinney, Cynthia 11, 52, 74
McKinney, Nina Mae 40
McKinney-Whetstone, Diane 27
McKinnon, Isaiah 9
McKissack, Leatrice 80
McKissick, Floyd B. 3
McKnight, Brian 18, 34
McLean, Jackie 78
McLendon, John B., Jr. 89
McLeod, Gus 27
McMillan, Rosalynn A. 36
McMillan, Terry 4, 17, 53
McMillan, Tracy 93
McMurray, Georgia L. 36
McNabb, Donovan 29
McNair, Ronald 3, 58
McNair, Steve 22, 47, 79
McNeil, Lori 1
McPhail, Sharon 2
McPherson, David 32
McPherson, James Alan 70
McQueen, Butterfly 6, 54
McRae, Carmen 77
McRae, Hal 84
McTell, Blind Willie 89
McWhorter, John 35
McWorter, Free Frank 91
Meadows, Tim 30
Meek, Carrie 6, 36
Meek, Kendrick 41, 89
Meeks, Gregory 25
Meeks, James T. 92
Mehretu, Julie 85
Mell, Patricia 49
Melton, Frank 81
Melton, Harold D. 79
Memphis Minnie 33
Menard, John Willis 90
Mengestu, Dinaw 66

Mercado-Valdes, Frank 43
Meredith, James H. 11
Merkerson, S. Epatha 47, 83
Metcalfe, Ralph 26
Method Man 81
Mfume, Kweisi 6, 41
Michaux, Solomon Lightfoot 91
Micheaux, Oscar 7
Michele, Michael 31
Mickelbury, Penny 28
Miles, Buddy 69
Millender-McDonald, Juanita 21, 61
Miller, Bebe 3
Miller, Cheryl 10, 74
Miller, Dorie 29
Miller, Larry G. 72
Miller, Marcus 84
Miller, Omar Benson 93
Miller, Patina 94
Miller, Reggie 33
Miller, Warren F., Jr. 53
Miller, Wentworth 75
Miller-Travis, Vernice 64
Millines Dziko, Trish 28
Millner, Denene 76
Mills, Florence 22
Mills, Joseph C. 51
Mills, Sam 33
Mills, Stephanie 36
Mills, Steve 47
Milner, Ron 39
Milton, DeLisha 31
Minaj, Nicki 86
Mingo, Frank 32
Mingus, Charles 15
Minoso, Minnie 89
Minor, DeWayne 32
Mitchell, Arthur 2, 47
Mitchell, Arthur Wergs 91
Mitchell, Brian Stokes 21
Mitchell, Clarence M., Jr. 88
Mitchell, Corinne 8
Mitchell, Elvis 67
Mitchell, Kel 66
Mitchell, Leona 42
Mitchell, Loften 31
Mitchell, Nicole 66
Mitchell, Parren J. 42, 66
Mitchell, Russ 21, 73
Mitchell, Sam 82
Mitchell, Shireen 89
Mitchell, Stephanie 36
Mo', Keb' 36
Mohammed, Nazr 64
Mohammed, W. Deen 27
Mokae, Zakes 80
Monáe, Janelle 86
Monica 21
Mo'Nique 35, 84
Monk, Art 38, 73
Monk, Thelonious 1
Monroe, Bryan 71
Monroe, Earl 89
Monroe, Mary 35
Montgomery, Isaiah T. 91
Montgomery, Tim 41
Montgomery, Wes 88
Moody, James 83
Moody-Adams, Michele 76
Moon, Warren 8, 66
Mooney, Paul 37
Moore, Barbara C. 49
Moore, Chante 26

Moore, Dorothy Rudd 46
Moore, Gwendolynne S. 55
Moore, Harry T. 29
Moore, Jessica Care 30
Moore, Johnny B. 38
Moore, Juanita 83
Moore, LeRoi 72
Moore, Maya 94
Moore, Melba 21
Moore, Minyon 45
Moore, Shemar 21
Moore, Undine Smith 28
Moore, Wes 86
Moorer, Michael 19
Moose, Charles 40
Moran, Jason 89
Morgan, Garrett 1
Morgan, Gertrude 63
Morgan, Irene 65
Morgan, Joe Leonard 9
Morgan, Rose 11
Morgan, Tracy 61
Morial, Ernest "Dutch" 26
Morial, Marc H. 20, 51
Morón, Alonzo G. 91
Morris, Garrett 31
Morris, Greg 28
Morris, Raheem 77
Morrison, Sam 50
Morrison, Toni 2, 15, 86
Morrison, Vanessa 84
Morton, Azie Taylor 48
Morton, Ferdinand Q. 90
Morton, Frederick A., Jr. 93
Morton, Jelly Roll 29
Morton, Joe 18
Mos Def 30
Moses, Edwin 8
Moses, Gilbert 12
Moses, Robert Parris 11
Mosley, Shane 32
Mosley, Walter 5, 25, 68
Moss, Carlton 17
Moss, J. 64
Moss, Otis, Jr. 72
Moss, Otis, III 72
Moss, Preacher 63
Moss, Randy 23, 90
Mossell, Gertrude Bustill 40
Mossell, Nathan Francis 91
Moten, Etta 18
Motley, Archibald, Jr. 30
Motley, Constance Baker 10, 55
Motley, Marion 26
Moton, Robert Russa 83
Mourning, Alonzo 17, 44
Moutoussamy-Ashe, Jeanne 7
Mowry, Jess 7
Mowry, Tamera 79
Mowry, Tia 78
Moyo, Karega Kofi 36
Moyo, Yvette Jackson 36
Muhammad, Ava 31
Muhammad, Elijah 4
Muhammad, Jabir Herbert 72
Muhammad, Khallid Abdul 10, 31
Mullen, Harryette 34
Mullen, Nicole C. 45
Murphy, Eddie 4, 20, 61
Murphy, John H. 42
Murphy, Laura M. 43
Murray, Albert L. 33
Murray, Cecil 12, 47

Murray, Eddie 12
Murray, Lenda 10
Murray, Pauli 38
Murray, Tai 47
Murrell, Sylvia Marilyn 49
Muse, Clarence Edouard 21
Musiq 37, 84
Mya 35
Myers, Walter Dean 8, 70
Myles, Kim 69
Nabrit, Samuel Milton 47
Nagin, Ray 42, 57, 88
Nail, John E. 92
Nance, Cynthia 71
Nanula, Richard D. 20
Napoleon, Benny N. 23
Nas 33
Nash, Diane 72
Nash, Joe 55
Nash, Johnny 40
Nash, Niecy 66
Nash, Shannon King 84
Nate Dogg 92
Naylor, Gloria 10, 42
Ndegeocello, Meshell 15, 83
Neal, Elise 29
Neal, Larry 38
Neal, Mark Anthony 74
Neal, Raful 44
Neals, Otto 73
Nelly 32, 90
Nelson, Jill 6, 54
Nelson, Sophia A. 93
Nelson, Stanley 92
Nelson Meigs, Andrea 48
Neville, Aaron 21
Neville, Arthel 53
Newcombe, Don 24
Newkirk, Pamela 69
Newman, David 76
Newman, Lester C. 51
Newsome, Ozzie 26
Newton, Huey 2
Ne-Yo 65
Ngaujah, Sahr 86
Nicholas, Denise 82
Nicholas, Fayard 20, 57
Nicholas, Harold 20
Nichols, Nichelle 11
Nissel, Angela 42
Nix, Robert N. C., Jr. 51
N'Namdi, George R. 17
Noble, Gil 76
Noble, Ronald 46
Norman, Christina 47
Norman, Jessye 5
Norman, Maidie 20
Norman, Pat 10
Norris, Michele 83
Norton, Eleanor Holmes 7, 93
Norton, Meredith 72
Notorious B.I.G. 20
Nottage, Lynn 66
Nugent, Richard Bruce 39
Nunn, Annetta 43
Nutter, Michael 69
Obadele, Imari 84
Obama, Barack 49, 74, 91
Obama, Michelle 61, 90
O'Brien, Soledad 88
Odetta 37, 74
Odom, Lamar 81
Oglesby, Zena 12

Ogletree, Charles, Jr. 12, 47
O'Grady, Lorraine 73
Ojikutu, Bayo 66
Ojikutu, Bisola 65
Ol' Dirty Bastard 52
Olden, Georg(e) 44
O'Leary, Hazel 6
Oliver, Jerry 37
Oliver, Joe "King" 42
Oliver, John J., Jr. 48
Oliver, Kimberly 60
Oliver, Pam 54
O'Neal, Rodney 88
O'Neal, Ron 46
O'Neal, Shaquille 8, 30
O'Neal, Stanley 38, 67
O'Neil, Buck 19, 59
Onyewu, Oguchi 60
Orange, James 74
Orlandersmith, Dael 42
Orman, Roscoe 55
Ormes, Jackie 73
Osborne, Jeffrey 26
Osborne, Na'taki 54
Otis, Clarence, Jr. 55
Otis, Clyde 67
Ouattara, Morou 74
Owens, Helen 48
Owens, Jack 38
Owens, Jesse 2
Owens, Major 6
Owens, Terrell 53
Pace, Betty 59
Pace, Orlando 21
Packer, Daniel 56
Packer, Will 71
Packer, Z. Z. 64
Page, Alan 7
Page, Clarence 4
Page, Greg 78
Page, Inman 82
Paige, Rod 29
Paige, Satchel 7
Painter, Nell Irvin 24, 88
Palmer, Keke 68
Palmer, Rissi 65
Palmer, Violet 59
Parham, Marjorie B. 71
Parish, Robert 43
Parker, Barrington D. 92
Parker, Candace 74
Parker, Charlie 20
Parker, Jim 64
Parker, Kellis E. 30
Parker, Maceo 72
Parker, Nicole Ari 52
Parker, Pat 19
Parker, Ray, Jr. 85
Parker, Star 70
Parks, Bernard C. 17
Parks, Gordon 1, 35, 58
Parks, Henry Green, Jr. 89
Parks, Rosa 1, 35, 56
Parks, Suzan-Lori 34, 85
Parr, Russ 51
Parsons, James 14
Parsons, Richard Dean 11, 33
Paterson, Basil A. 69
Paterson, David A. 59
Patrick, Deval 12, 61
Patterson, Floyd 19, 58
Patterson, Frederick Douglass 12
Patterson, Gilbert Earl 41

Patterson, J. O., Jr. 80
Patterson, Louise 25
Patterson, Mary Jane 54
Patton, Antwan 45
Patton, Paula 62
Paul, Chris 84
Payne, Allen 13
Payne, Donald M. 2, 57
Payne, Ethel L. 28
Payne, Freda 58
Payne, Les 89
Payne, Ulice 42
Payne, William D. 60
Payton, Benjamin F. 23
Payton, John 48
Payton, Philip A., Jr. 88
Payton, Walter 11, 25
Peck, Carolyn 23
Peete, Calvin 11
Peete, Holly Robinson 20
Peete, Rodney 60
Pena, Paul 58
Pendergrass, Teddy 22, 83
Peoples, Dottie 22
Perez, Anna 1
Perkins, Edward 5
Perkins, James, Jr. 55
Perkins, Marion 38
Perkins, Pinetop 70
Perkins, Tony 24
Perren, Freddie 60
Perrineau, Harold, Jr. 51
Perrot, Kim 23
Perry, Herman 89
Perry, James 83
Perry, Laval 64
Perry, Lowell 30
Perry, Tyler 40, 54
Perry, Warren 56
Person, Waverly 9, 51
Peters, Margaret 43
Peters, Matilda 43
Petersen, Frank E. 31
Peterson, James 38
Peterson, James 81
Peterson, Jesse Lee 81
Peterson, Karen Carter 90
Peterson, Marvin "Hannibal" 27
Petry, Ann 19
Phifer, Mekhi 25
Phillips, Charles E., Jr. 57
Phillips, Helen L. 63
Phillips, Joseph C. 73
Phillips, Teresa L. 42
Phipps, Wintley 59
Pickens, James, Jr. 59
Pickett, Bill 11
Pickett, Cecil 39
Pierce, Elijah 84
Pierce, Harold 75
Pierce, Paul 71
Pierce, Wendell 90
Pierre, Percy Anthony 46
Pincham, R. Eugene, Sr. 69
Pinchback, P. B. S. 9
Pinckney, Bill 42
Pinckney, Sandra 56
Pindell, Howardena 55
Pinder, Jefferson 77
Pinderhughes, John 47
Pinkett, Randal 61
Pinkett Smith, Jada 10, 41
Pinkney, Fayette 80

Pinkney, Jerry 15
Pinkston, W. Randall 24
Pinn, Vivian Winona 49
Piper, Adrian 71
Pippen, Scottie 15, 89
Pippin, Horace 9
Pitts, Byron 71
Pitts, Derrick 77
Pitts, Robb 84
Pitts, Leonard, Jr. 54, 85
Player, Willa B. 43
Pleasant, Mary Ellen 9
Pleasure P 84
Plessy, Homer Adolph 31
P.M. Dawn 54
Poindexter, Hildrus A. 87
Poitier, Sidney 11, 36
Poitier, Sydney Tamiia 65
Polite, Carlene Hatcher 82
Pollard, Fritz 53
Pollard, William L. 91
Pope.L, William 72
Porter, James A. 11
Porter, Terry 75
Potter, Myrtle 40
Pough, Terrell 58
Pounder, CCH 72
Poussaint, Alvin F. 5, 67
Poussaint, Renee 78
Powell, Adam Clayton, Jr. 3
Powell, Benny 87
Powell, Bud 24
Powell, Colin 1, 28, 75
Powell, Debra A. 23
Powell, Kevin 31, 74
Powell, Maxine 8
Powell, Michael 32
Powell, Mike 7
Powell, Renee 34
Powell, William J. 82
Power, Will 83
Pratt, Awadagin 31
Pratt, Geronimo 18
Pratt, Kyla 57
Preer, Evelyn 82
Premice, Josephine 41
Pressley, Condace L. 41
Preston, Billy 39, 59
Price, Florence 37
Price, Frederick K. C. 21
Price, Glenda 22
Price, Hugh B. 9, 54
Price, Kelly 23
Price, Leontyne 1
Price, Richard 51
Pride, Charley 26
Primus, Pearl 6
Prince 18, 65
Prince, Richard E. 71
Prince, Ron 64
Prince, Tayshaun 68
Prince-Bythewood, Gina 31, 77
Pritchard, Robert Starling 21
Procope, Ernesta 23
Procope, John Levy 56
Prophet, Nancy Elizabeth 42
Prothrow-Stith, Deborah 10
Pryce, Trevor 89
Pryor, Rain 65
Pryor, Richard 3, 24, 56
Puckett, Kirby 4, 58
Pugh, Charles 81
Purdie, Bernard 77

Purnell, Silas 59
Puryear, Martin 42
Putney, Martha S. 75
Quarles, Benjamin Arthur 18
Quarles, Norma 25
Quarterman, Lloyd Albert 4
Queen Latifah 1, 16, 58
?uestlove 74
Quigless, Helen G. 49
Quince, Peggy A. 69
Quivers, Robin 61
Rabb, Maurice F., Jr. 58
Radcliffe, Ted 74
Ragin, Derek Lee 84
Rahman, Aishah 37
Raines, Franklin Delano 14
Rainey, Ma 33
Ralph, Sheryl Lee 18
Ramsey, Charles H. 21, 69
Rand, A. Barry 6
Randall, Alice 38
Randall, Dudley 8, 55
Randle, John 87
Randle, Theresa 16
Randolph, A. Philip 3
Randolph, Linda A. 52
Randolph, Willie 53
Rangel, Charles B. 3, 52, 85
Ransome, James E. 88
Raoul, Kwame 55
Rapier, James T. 82
Rashad, Ahmad 18
Rashad, Phylicia 21
Raspberry, William 2
Raven 44
Rawlings-Blake, Stephanie 93
Rawlinson, Johnnie B. 79
Rawls, Lou 17, 57
Ray, Charlotte E. 60
Ray, Gene Anthony 47
Ray J 86
Razaf, Andy 19
Reagins, Tony 94
Reagon, Bernice Johnson 7
Reagon, Toshi 76
Reason, J. Paul 19
Record, Eugene 60
Redd, Dana 93
Reddick, Lance 52
Reddick, Lawrence Dunbar 20
Redding, Ann Holmes 77
Redding, J. Saunders 26
Redding, Louis L. 26
Redding, Otis 16
Redman 81
Redman, Joshua 30
Redmond, Eugene 23
Redwood, John Henry 78
Reed, A. C. 36
Reed, Ishmael 8
Reed, Jimmy 38
Reed, Kasim 82
Reed, Willis, Jr. 86
Reed Hall, Alaina 83
Reems, Ernestine Cleveland 27
Reese, Della 6, 20
Reese, Milous J., Jr. 51
Reese, Pokey 28
Reese, Tracy 54
Reeves, Dianne 32
Reeves, Gregory 49
Reeves, Martha 85
Reeves, Rachel J. 23

Reeves, Triette Lipsey 27
Reid, Antonio "L.A." 28
Reid, Irvin D. 20
Reid, Senghor 55
Reid, Tim 56
Reid, Vernon 34
Reverend Ike 79
Reynolds, Harold 77
Reynolds, Star Jones 10, 27, 61
Rhames, Ving 14, 50
Rhimes, Shonda Lynn 67
Rhoden, Dwight 40
Rhoden, William C. 67
Rhodes, Jewell Parker 84
Rhodes, Ray 14
Rhone, Sylvia 2
Rhymes, Busta 31
Ribbs, Willy T. 2
Ribeau, Sidney 70
Ribeiro, Alfonso 17
Rice, Condoleezza 3, 28, 72
Rice, Constance LaMay 60
Rice, Emmett J. 94
Rice, Jerry 5, 55, 89
Rice, Jim 75
Rice, Linda Johnson 9, 41
Rice, Louise Allen 54
Rice, Norm 8
Rice, Susan E. 74
Richard, Dawn 92
Richard, J. R. 87
Richards, Beah 30
Richards, Hilda 49
Richards, Sanya 66
Richardson, Desmond 39
Richardson, Donna 39
Richardson, Julieanna 81
Richardson, LaTanya 71
Richardson, Laura 81
Richardson, Nolan 9
Richardson, Rupert 67
Richardson, Salli 68
Richie, Leroy C. 18
Richie, Lionel 27, 65
Richmond, Cedric 93
Richmond, Mitch 19
Rideau, Iris 46
Ridley, John 69
Riggs, Marlon 5, 44
Riles, Wilson C. 79
Riley, Boots 89
Riley, Helen Caldwell Day 13
Riley, Rochelle 50
Rillieux, Norbert 92
Ringgold, Faith 4, 81
Riperton, Minnie 32
Rivers, Doc 25, 81
Rivers, Eugene F., III 81
Roach, Max 21, 63
Roberts, Darryl 70
Roberts, Deborah 35
Roberts, Kimberly Rivers 72
Roberts, Lillian 83
Roberts, Marcus 19
Roberts, Mike 57
Roberts, Robin 16, 54
Roberts, Roy S. 14
Robertson, Gil L., IV 85
Robertson, Oscar 26
Robeson, Eslanda Goode 13
Robeson, Paul 2
Robinson, Aminah 50
Robinson, Bill "Bojangles" 11

Robinson, Bishop L. 66
Robinson, Cleo Parker 38
Robinson, David 24, 90
Robinson, Eddie G. 10
Robinson, Eugene 77
Robinson, Fatima 34
Robinson, Fenton 38
Robinson, Frank 9, 87
Robinson, Jackie 6
Robinson, LaVaughn 69
Robinson, Malcolm S. 44
Robinson, Matt 69
Robinson, Max 3
Robinson, Patrick 19, 71
Robinson, Rachel 16
Robinson, Randall 7, 46
Robinson, Reginald R. 53
Robinson, Sharon 22
Robinson, Shaun 36
Robinson, Smokey 3, 49
Robinson, Spottswood W., III 22
Robinson, Sugar Ray 18
Robinson, Sylvia 79
Robinson, Will 51, 69
Robinson-Berry, Joan 94
Roble, Abdi 71
Roby, Kimberla Lawson 86
Roche, Joyce M. 17
Rochon, Lela 16
Rochon, Stephen W. 78
Rock, Chris 3, 22, 66
Rock, The 29, 66
Rodgers, Johnathan 6, 51
Rodgers, Rod 36
Rodman, Dennis 12, 44
Rodriguez, Jimmy 47
Rodriguez, Cheryl 64
Rogers, Alan G. 72
Rogers, Desirée 88
Rogers, Jimmy 38
Rogers, Joe 27
Rogers, Joel Augustus 30
Rogers, John W., Jr. 5, 52
Roker, Al 12, 49
Roker, Roxie 68
Rolle, Esther 13, 21
Rollins, Charlemae Hill 27
Rollins, Howard E., Jr. 16
Rollins, Jimmy 70
Rollins, Sonny 37, 94
Rose, Anika Noni 70
Rose, Derrick 82
Ross, Charles 27
Ross, Diana 8, 27
Ross, Don 27
Ross, Isaiah "Doc" 40
Ross, Rick 79
Ross, Tracee Ellis 35
Ross-Lee, Barbara 67
Roundtree, Dovey 80
Roundtree, Richard 27
Rouse, Cecilia 93
Rowan, Carl T. 1, 30
Rowell, Victoria 13, 68
Roxanne Shante 33
Roy, Kenny 51
Rubin, Chanda 37
Rucker, Darius 34, 74
Rudolph, Maya 46
Rudolph, Wilma 4
Ruffin, Josephine St. Pierre 75
Ruffins, Kermit 85
Ruley, Ellis 38

Run 31, 73, 75
RuPaul 17, 91
Rush, Bobby 26, 76
Rush, Bobby 78
Rush, Otis 38
Rushen, Patrice 12
Rushing, Jimmy 37
Russell, Bill 8
Russell, Brenda 52
Russell, Herman Jerome 17
Russell, Nipsey 66
Russell-McCloud, Patricia A. 17
Rust, Art, Jr. 83
Rustin, Bayard 4
RZA 80
Saar, Alison 16
Saar, Betye 80
Sabathia, CC 74
St. Jacques, Raymond 8
Saint James, Synthia 12
St. John, Kristoff 25
St. Julien, Marlon 29
St. Patrick, Mathew 48
Saldana, Zoe 72
Sallee, Charles 38
Salter, Nikkole 73
Salters, Lisa 71
Samara, Noah 15
Sample, Joe 51
Sampson, Charles 13
Sanchez, Sonia 17, 51
Sanders, Angelia 86
Sanders, Barry 1, 53
Sanders, Bob 72
Sanders, Deion 4, 31
Sanders, Joseph R., Jr. 11
Sanders, Malika 48
Sanders, Pharoah 64
Sanders, Satch 77
Sands, Diana 87
Sanford, Isabel 53
Santamaria, Mongo 81
Santiago-Hudson, Ruben 85
Sapp, Marvin 74
Sapp, Warren 38
Sapphire 14
Satcher, David 7, 57
Savage, Augusta 12
Sawyer, Eugene 81
Sayers, Gale 28
Sayles Belton, Sharon 9, 16
Sbraga, Kevin 88
Scantlebury-White, Velma 64
Schmoke, Kurt 1, 48
Schuyler, George Samuel 40
Schuyler, Philippa 50
Scott, C(ornelius) A(dolphus) 29
Scott, David 41
Scott, George 55
Scott, Harold Russell, Jr. 61
Scott, Hazel 66
Scott, Jill 29, 83
Scott, John T. 65
Scott, "Little" Jimmy 48
Scott, Milton 51
Scott, Robert C. 23
Scott, Stuart 34
Scott, Tim 87
Scott, Wendell Oliver, Sr. 19
Scott-Heron, Gil 94
Scurry, Briana 27
Seals, Son 56
Sears, Leah Ward 5, 79

Sears, Stephanie 53
Sebree, Charles 40
Seele, Pernessa 46
Sengstacke, John 18
Senna, Danzy 93
Sermon, Erick 81
Serrano, Andres 3
Sewell, Terri 93
Shabazz, Attallah 6
Shabazz, Betty 7, 26
Shabazz, Ilyasah 36
Shadd, Abraham D. 81
Shakur, Afeni 67
Shakur, Assata 6
Shakur, Tupac 14
Shakur, Yusef 85
Shange, Ntozake 8, 89
Shank, Suzanne F. 77
Shannon, Randy 82
Sharper, Darren 32
Sharpton, Al 21
Shavers, Cheryl 31
Shaw, Bernard 2, 28
Shaw, William J. 30
Sheard, Kierra "Kiki" 61
Sheffield, Gary 16
Shell, Art 1, 66
Shelton, Paula Young 86
Shepherd, Sherri 55
Sherrod, Clayton 17
Sherrod, Shirley 87
Shider, Garry 87
Shinhoster, Earl 32
Shipp, E. R. 15
Shippen, John 43
Shirley, George 33
Shockley, Ann Allen 84
Short, Bobby 52
Short, Columbus 79
Shorter, Wayne 75
Showers, Reggie 30
Shropshire, Thomas B. 49
Shuttlesworth, Fred 47
Sidibe, Gabourey 84
Sifford, Charlie 4, 49
Sigur, Wanda 44
Silas, Paul 24
Silver, Horace 26
Simmons, Bob 29
Simmons, E. Denise 79
Simmons, Gary 58
Simmons, Henry 55
Simmons, Jamal 72
Simmons, Kimora Lee 51, 83
Simmons, Russell 1, 30
Simmons, Ruth J. 13, 38
Simms, Margaret 94
Simone, Nina 15, 41
Simpson, Carole 6, 30
Simpson, Lorna 4, 36
Simpson, O. J. 15
Simpson, Valerie 21
Simpson-Hoffman, N'kenge 52
Sims, Howard "Sandman" 48
Sims, Lowery Stokes 27
Sims, Naomi 29, 79
Sinbad 1, 16
Singletary, Mike 4, 76
Singleton, John 2, 30
Sinkford, Jeanne C. 13
Sir Mix-A-Lot 82
Sisqo 30
Sissle, Noble 29

Sister Souljah 11
Sizemore, Barbara A. 26
Skinner, Kiron K. 65
Sklarek, Norma Merrick 25
Slater, Rodney E. 15
Slaughter, John Brooks 53
Sledge, Percy 39
Sleet, Moneta, Jr. 5
Slice, Kimbo 73
Slick Rick 93
Slim Thug 86
Slocumb, Jonathan 52
Slyde, Jimmy 70
Smalls, Robert 82
Smaltz, Audrey 12
Smiley, Rickey 59
Smiley, Tavis 20, 68
Smith, Anna Deavere 6, 44
Smith, B(arbara) 11
Smith, Barbara 28
Smith, Bessie 3
Smith, Bruce 80
Smith, Bruce W. 53
Smith, Cladys "Jabbo" 32
Smith, Clarence O. 21
Smith, Damu 54
Smith, Danyel 40
Smith, DeMaurice 92
Smith, Dr. Lonnie 49
Smith, Emmitt 7, 87
Smith, Greg 28
Smith, Hilton 29
Smith, Ian 62
Smith, Jaden 82
Smith, Jane E. 24
Smith, Jessie Carney 35
Smith, John L. 22
Smith, Joshua 10
Smith, Kemba 70
Smith, Lonnie Liston 49
Smith, Lovie 66
Smith, Malcolm A. 75
Smith, Mamie 32
Smith, Marie F. 70
Smith, Marvin 46
Smith, Mary Carter 26
Smith, Morgan 46
Smith, Myrna 92
Smith, Nate 49
Smith, Ozzie 77
Smith, Princella 86
Smith, Randy 81
Smith, Rick 72
Smith, Roger Guenveur 12
Smith, Stephen A. 69
Smith, Stuff 37
Smith, Tasha 73
Smith, Trixie 34
Smith, Tubby 18, 83
Smith, Vincent D. 48
Smith, Will 8, 18, 53
Smith, Willi 8
Smith, Willow 92
Smyre, Calvin 90
Smythe Haith, Mabel 61
Sneed, Paula A. 18
Snipes, Wesley 3, 24, 67
Snoop Dogg 35, 84
Snow, Samuel 71
Snowden, Frank M., Jr. 67
Solomon, Jimmie Lee 38
Somi 85
Sommore 61

Songz, Trey **88**
Southern, Eileen **56**
Southgate, Martha **58**
Sowell, Thomas **2**
Sparks, Jordin **66**
Spaulding, Charles Clinton **9**
Spearman, Leonard H. O., Sr. **81**
Spears, Warren **52**
Spector, Ronnie **77**
Speech **82**
Spencer, Anne **27**
Spencer, Michael G. **87**
Spigner, Archie **81**
Spikes, Dolores **18**
Spiller, Bill **64**
Sprewell, Latrell **23**
Spriggs, William **67**
Stackhouse, Jerry **30**
Staley, Dawn **57**
Stallings, George A., Jr. **6**
Stampley, Micah **54**
Stanford, John **20**
Stanford, Olivia Lee Dilworth **49**
Stanton, Alysa **78**
Stanton, Robert **20**
Staples, Brent **8**
Staples, Mavis **50, 88**
Staples, "Pops" **32**
Stargell, Willie **29**
Staton, Candi **27**
Staton, Dakota **62**
Staupers, Mabel K. **7**
Stearnes, Norman "Turkey" **31**
Steave-Dickerson, Kia **57**
Steele, Claude Mason **13**
Steele, Lawrence **28**
Steele, Michael **38, 73, 91**
Steele, Shelby **13, 82**
Steinberg, Martha Jean "The
    Queen" **28**
Stephens, Charlotte Andrews **14**
Stew **69**
Steward, David L. **36**
Steward, Emanuel **18**
Stewart, Alison **13**
Stewart, Ella **39**
Stewart, James "Bubba," Jr. **60**
Stewart, Kordell **21**
Stewart, Maria W. Miller **19**
Stewart, Nzingha **89**
Stewart, Paul Wilbur **12**
Stewart, Tonea Harris **78**
Sticky Fingaz **86**
Still, William Grant **37**
Stingley, Darryl **69**
Stinson, Denise L. **59**
Stith, Charles R. **73**
Stith, Tom **93**
Stokes, Carl **10, 73**
Stokes, Louis **3**
Stone, Angie **31**
Stone, Chuck **9**
Stone, Sly **85**
Stone, Toni **15**
Stoney, Michael **50**
Stoudemire, Amaré **59**
Stout, Juanita Kidd **24**
Stout, Renee **63**
Stoute, Steve **38**
Strahan, Michael **35, 81**
Strautmanis, Michael **87**
Strawberry, Darryl **22**
Strayhorn, Billy **31**

Street, John F. **24**
Streeter, Sarah **45**
Stringer, C. Vivian **13, 66**
Stringer, Korey **35**
Stringer, Vickie **58**
Strong, Barrett **89**
Studdard, Ruben **46**
Sudarkasa, Niara **4**
Sudduth, Jimmy Lee **65**
Sugarhill Gang, The **79**
Sullivan, Jazmine **81**
Sullivan, Leon H. **3, 30**
Sullivan, Louis **8**
Sullivan, Maxine **37**
Summer, Donna **25**
Sun Ra **60**
Sundiata, Sekou **66**
Sutphen, Mona **77**
Sutton, Percy E. **42, 82**
Swann, Lynn **28**
Sweat, Keith **19**
Sweet, Ossian **68**
Swoopes, Sheryl **12, 56**
Swygert, H. Patrick **22**
Sykes, Roosevelt **20**
Sykes, Wanda **48, 81**
Syler, Rene **53**
Tademy, Lalita **36**
Tait, Michael **57**
Talbert, David E. **34, 93**
Talbert, Mary B. **77**
Talley, André Leon **56**
Tamar-kali **63**
Tamia **24, 55**
Tampa Red **63**
Tancil, Gladys Quander **59**
Tanksley, Ann **37**
Tanner, Henry Ossawa **1**
Tate, Eleanora E. **20, 55**
Tate, Larenz **15**
Tatum, Art **28**
Tatum, Beverly Daniel **42, 84**
Tatum, Elinor R. **78**
Tatum, Jack **87**
Tatum, Wilbert **76**
Taulbert, Clifton Lemoure **19**
Taylor, Billy **23, 92**
Taylor, Bo **72**
Taylor, Cecil **70**
Taylor, Charles **20**
Taylor, Ephren W., II **61**
Taylor, Gardner C. **76**
Taylor, Helen (Lavon Hollingshed)
    30
Taylor, Jason **70**
Taylor, Jermain **60**
Taylor, Koko **40, 80**
Taylor, Kristin Clark **8**
Taylor, Lawrence **25**
Taylor, Marshall Walter "Major" **62**
Taylor, Meshach **4**
Taylor, Mildred D. **26**
Taylor, Natalie **47**
Taylor, Recy **92**
Taylor, Regina **9, 46**
Taylor, Robert Robinson **80**
Taylor, Ron **35**
Taylor, Susan C. **62**
Taylor, Susan L. **10, 86**
Taylor, Susie King **13**
Teasley, Lisa **92**
Teer, Barbara Ann **81**
Terrell, Dorothy A. **24**

Terrell, Mary Church **9**
Terrell, Tammi **32**
Terrell-Kearney, Kim **83**
Terry, Clark **39**
Terry, Sonny **88**
Tharpe, Rosetta **65**
The-Dream **74**
Thigpen, Lynne **17, 41**
Thomas, Alma **14**
Thomas, Arthur Ray **52**
Thomas, Clarence **2, 39, 65**
Thomas, Claudia Lynn **64**
Thomas, Debi **26**
Thomas, Derrick **25**
Thomas, Emmitt **71**
Thomas, Frank **12, 51**
Thomas, Franklin A. **5, 49**
Thomas, Irma **29**
Thomas, Isiah **7, 26, 65**
Thomas, Jefferson **88**
Thomas, Michael **69**
Thomas, Mickalene **61**
Thomas, Rozonda **34, 78**
Thomas, Rufus **20**
Thomas, Sean Patrick **35**
Thomas, Thurman **75**
Thomas, Trisha R. **65**
Thomas, Vivien **9**
Thomas-Graham, Pamela **29**
Thompson, Bennie G. **26**
Thompson, Cynthia Bramlett **50**
Thompson, Don **56**
Thompson, John Douglas **81**
Thompson, John W. **26**
Thompson, Kenan **52**
Thompson, Larry D. **39**
Thompson, Tazewell **13**
Thompson, Tina **25, 75**
Thompson, William C. **35**
Thoms, Tracie **61**
Thornton, Big Mama **33**
Thornton, Yvonne S. **69**
Thrash, Dox **35**
Thrower, Willie **35**
Thurman, Howard **3**
Thurman, Wallace **16**
Thurmond, Nate **88**
Thurston, Baratunde **79**
Thurston, Stephen J. **49**
Till, Emmett **7**
Tillard, Conrad **47**
Tillis, Frederick **40**
Tillman, Dorothy **76**
Tillman, George, Jr. **20**
Timbaland **32**
Tinsley, Boyd **50**
Tirico, Mike **68**
Tisdale, Wayman **50**
Tobias, Channing H. **79**
Tobin, Patricia **75**
Todman, Terence A. **55**
Tolbert, Terence **74**
Toler, Burl **80**
Tolliver, Mose **60**
Tolliver, William **9**
Tolson, Melvin **37**
Tolton, Augustine **62**
Tomlinson, LaDainian **65**
Tonex **54**
Toney, James **89**
Tooks, Lance **62**
Toomer, Jean **6**
Toote, Gloria E. A. **64**

Torres, Gina **52**
Torry, Guy **31**
Touré, Askia (Muhammad Abu Bakr
    el) **47**
Touré, Faya Ora Rose **56**
Toussaint, Allen **60**
Towns, Edolphus **19, 75**
Townsend, Robert **4, 23**
T-Pain **73**
Travis, Tracey T. **94**
Tresvant, Ralph **57**
Tribbett, Tye **81**
Tribble, Israel, Jr. **8**
Trotter, Donne E. **28**
Trotter, Lloyd G. **56**
Trotter, Monroe **9**
Troupe, Quincy **83**
Trouppe, Quincy Thomas, Sr. **84**
True, Rachel **82**
Trueheart, William E. **49**
Tubbs Jones, Stephanie **24, 72**
Tubman, Harriet **9**
Tucker, C. Delores **12, 56**
Tucker, Chris **13, 23, 62**
Tucker, Cynthia **15, 61**
Tucker, Rosina **14**
Tuckson, Reed V. **71**
Tunie, Tamara **63**
Tunnell, Emlen **54**
Turnbull, Charles Wesley **62**
Turnbull, Walter **13, 60**
Turner, Big Joe **92**
Turner, Henry McNeal **5**
Turner, Ike **68**
Turner, Tina **6, 27**
Tyler, Aisha N. **36**
Tyner, McCoy **92**
Tyree, Omar Rashad **21**
Tyson, Andre **40**
Tyson, Asha **39**
Tyson, Cicely **7, 51**
Tyson, Mike **28, 44, 93**
Tyson, Neil deGrasse **15, 65**
Uggams, Leslie **23**
Ulmer, James **79**
Underwood, Blair **7, 27, 76**
Union, Gabrielle **31, 92**
Unseld, Wes **23**
Upshaw, Gene **18, 47, 72**
Usher **23, 56**
Usry, James L. **23**
Ussery, Terdema, II **29**
Utendahl, John **23**
Valentino, Bobby **62**
Van Lierop, Robert **53**
Van Peebles, Mario **2, 51**
Van Peebles, Melvin **7**
Vance, Courtney B. **15, 60**
VanDerZee, James **6**
Vandross, Luther **13, 48, 59**
Vanzant, Iyanla **17, 47**
Vaughan, Sarah **13**
Vaughn, Countess **53**
Vaughn, Gladys Gary **47**
Vaughn, Mo **16**
Vaughn, Viola **70**
Vaughns, Cleopatra **46**
Vega, Marta Moreno **61**
Velez-Rodriguez, Argelia **56**
Verdelle, A. J. **26**
Vereen, Ben **4**
Verrett, Shirley **66, 91**
Vick, Michael **39, 65, 94**

Villarosa, Clara **85**
Vincent, Marjorie Judith **2**
Vincent, Troy **91**
Von Lipsey, Roderick K. **11**
Waddles, Charleszetta "Mother" **10, 49**
Wade, Dwyane **61**
Wade-Gayles, Gloria Jean **41**
Wagner, Albert **78**
Wagner, Annice **22**
Wainwright, Joscelyn **46**
Wale **92**
Walker, Albertina **10, 58, 89**
Walker, A'lelia **14**
Walker, Alice **1, 43**
Walker, Arthur, II **87**
Walker, Bernita Ruth **53**
Walker, Cedric "Ricky" **19**
Walker, Cora T. **68**
Walker, Dianne **57**
Walker, George **37**
Walker, Herschel **1, 69**
Walker, Hezekiah **34**
Walker, John T. **50**
Walker, Kara **16, 80**
Walker, Lucius, Jr. **88**
Walker, Madame C. J. **7**
Walker, Maggie Lena **17**
Walker, Margaret **29**
Walker, Rebecca **50**
Walker, T. J. **7**
Walker, Wyatt Tee **80**
Wall, Orindatus S. B. **92**
Wallace, Ben **54**
Wallace, Joaquin **49**
Wallace, Michele Faith **13**
Wallace, Perry E. **47**
Wallace, Phyllis A. **9**
Wallace, Rasheed **56**
Wallace, Sippie **1**
Wallace, William **75**
Waller, Fats **29**
Walters, Ronald **83**
Ward, Andre **62**
Ward, Benjamin **68**
Ward, Douglas Turner **42**
Ward, Hines **84**
Ward, Lloyd **21, 46**
Ware, Andre **37**
Ware, Carl H. **30**
Ware, DeMarcus **92**
Warfield, Marsha **2**
Warfield, William **94**
Warner, Malcolm-Jamal **22, 36**
Warren, Michael **27**
Warwick, Dionne **18**
Washington, Alonzo **29**
Washington, Booker T. **4**
Washington, Denzel **1, 16, 93**
Washington, Dinah **22**
Washington, Ebonya **79**
Washington, Elsie B. **78**
Washington, Fredi **10**
Washington, Gene **63**
Washington, Grover, Jr. **17, 44**
Washington, Harold **6**
Washington, Harriet A. **69**
Washington, Hayma **86**
Washington, Isaiah **62**
Washington, James, Jr. **38**
Washington, James Melvin **50**
Washington, Kenny **50**
Washington, Kerry **46**

Washington, Laura S. **18**
Washington, MaliVai **8**
Washington, Mary T. **57**
Washington, Patrice Clarke **12**
Washington, Pauletta Pearson **86**
Washington, Regynald G. **44**
Washington, Val **12**
Washington, Walter **45**
Wasow, Omar **15**
Waters, Benny **26**
Waters, Ethel **7**
Waters, Maxine **3, 67**
Waters, Muddy **34**
Watkins, Donald **35**
Watkins, Joe **86**
Watkins, Levi, Jr. **9**
Watkins, Perry **12**
Watkins, Shirley R. **17**
Watkins, Tionne "T-Boz" **34**
Watkins, Walter C. **24**
Watley, Jody **54**
Watson, Bob **25**
Watson, Carlos **50**
Watson, Diane **41**
Watson, Johnny "Guitar" **18**
Watt, Melvin **26**
Wattleton, Faye **9**
Watts, J. C., Jr. **14, 38**
Watts, Reggie **52**
Watts, Rolonda **9**
Wayans, Damien **78**
Wayans, Damon **8, 41**
Wayans, Keenen Ivory **18**
Wayans, Kim **80**
Wayans, Marlon **29, 82**
Wayans, Shawn **29**
Weathers, Carl **10**
Weaver, Afaa Michael **37**
Weaver, Robert C. **8, 46**
Webb, Veronica **10**
Webb, Wellington **3, 81**
Webber, Chris **15, 30, 59**
Webster, Katie **29**
Wedgeworth, Robert W. **42**
Weeks, Thomas, III **70**
Weems, Carrie Mae **63**
Weems, Renita J. **44**
Wein, Joyce **62**
Welburn, Edward T. **50**
Welch, Elisabeth **52**
Wells, Henrietta Bell **69**
Wells, James Lesesne **10**
Wells, Mary **28**
Wells, Vernon **91**
Wells-Barnett, Ida B. **8**
Welsing, Frances Cress **5**
Wesley, Dorothy Porter **19**
Wesley, Richard **73**
Wesley, Valerie Wilson **18**
West, Allen **89**
West, Cornel **5, 33, 80**
West, Dorothy **12, 54**
West, James E. **87**
West, Kanye **52, 93**
West, Togo D., Jr. **16**
Westbrook, Kelvin **50**
Westbrook, Peter **20**
Westbrooks, Bobby **51**
Whack, Rita Coburn **36**
Whalum, Kirk **37, 64**
Wharton, Clifton R., Jr. **7**
Wharton, Clifton Reginald, Sr. **36**
Wheat, Alan **14**

Whitaker, Forest **2, 49, 67**
Whitaker, Mark **21, 47**
Whitaker, Pernell **10, 89**
White, Armond **80**
White, Barry **13, 41**
White, Bill **1, 48**
White, Charles **39**
White, Dondi **34**
White, Jesse **22, 75**
White, Jessica **83**
White, John H. **27**
White, Josh **86**
White, Josh, Jr. **52**
White, Linda M. **45**
White, Lois Jean **20**
White, Maurice **29**
White, Michael Jai **71**
White, Michael R. **5**
White, Reggie **6, 50**
White, Terri **82**
White, Walter F. **4**
White, Willye **67**
White-Hammond, Gloria **61**
Whitehead, Colson **77**
Whitfield, Fred **23**
Whitfield, LeRoy **84**
Whitfield, Lynn **18**
Whitfield, Mal **60**
Whitfield, Norman **73**
Whitfield, Van **34**
Whitlock, Jason **78**
Wideman, John Edgar **5, 87**
Wilbekin, Emil **63**
Wilbon, Michael **68**
Wilder, L. Douglas **3, 48**
Wiley, Kehinde **62**
Wiley, Ralph **8, 78**
Wilkens, J. Ernest, Jr. **43**
Wilkens, Lenny **11, 88**
Wilkerson, Isabel **71**
Wilkins, David **77**
Wilkins, Dominique **74**
Wilkins, Ray **47**
Wilkins, Roger **2, 84**
Wilkins, Roy **4**
Wilkins, Thomas Alphonso **71**
will.i.am **64**
Williams, Ann Claire **82**
Williams, Anthony **21**
Williams, Armstrong **29**
Williams, Bert **18**
Williams, Billy **86**
Williams, Billy Dee **8**
Williams, Clarence **33**
Williams, Clarence **70**
Williams, Clarence, III **26**
Williams, Claude **80**
Williams, Daniel Hale **2**
Williams, David Rudyard **50**
Williams, Deniece **36**
Williams, Deron **92**
Williams, Doug **22**
Williams, Dudley **60**
Williams, Eddie N. **44**
Williams, Evelyn **10**
Williams, Fannie Barrier **27**
Williams, Frederick (B.) **63**
Williams, George Washington **18**
Williams, Gregory **11**
Williams, Hosea Lorenzo **15, 31**
Williams, J. Mayo **83**
Williams, Joe **5, 25**
Williams, John A. **27**

Williams, Juan **35, 80**
Williams, Ken **68**
Williams, Lauryn **58**
Williams, Lindsey **75**
Williams, Maggie **7, 71**
Williams, Malinda **57**
Williams, Marco **53**
Williams, Mary Lou **15**
Williams, Michael L. **86**
Williams, Michelle **73**
Williams, Montel **4, 57**
Williams, Nat D. **91**
Williams, Natalie **31**
Williams, O. S. **13**
Williams, Patricia **11, 54**
Williams, Paul R. **9**
Williams, Pharrell **47, 82**
Williams, Preston Warren, II **64**
Williams, Rhonda Y. **86**
Williams, Ricky **85**
Williams, Robert F. **11**
Williams, Ronald A. **57**
Williams, Russell, II **70**
Williams, Samm-Art **21**
Williams, Saul **31**
Williams, Serena **20, 41, 73**
Williams, Sherley Anne **25**
Williams, Stanley "Tookie" **29, 57**
Williams, Stevie **71**
Williams, Ted **91**
Williams, Terrie M. **35**
Williams, Tony **67**
Williams, Vanessa A. **32, 66**
Williams, Vanessa L. **4, 17**
Williams, Venus **17, 34, 62**
Williams, Walter E. **4**
Williams, Wendy **62**
Williams, William T. **11**
Williams, Willie L. **4**
Williamson, Fred **67**
Williamson, Mykelti **22**
Williamson, Sonny Boy **84**
Willie, Louis, Jr. **68**
Willingham, Tyrone **43**
Willis, Bill **68**
Willis, Deborah **85**
Willis, Dontrelle **55**
Wills, Harry **80**
Wills, Maury **73**
Wilson, August **7, 33, 55**
Wilson, Brian Courtney **94**
Wilson, Cassandra **16**
Wilson, Chandra **57**
Wilson, Charlie **31, 77**
Wilson, Debra **38**
Wilson, Donald E. **88**
Wilson, Dorien **55**
Wilson, Ellis **39**
Wilson, Flip **21**
Wilson, Frederica **92**
Wilson, Gerald **49**
Wilson, Jackie **60**
Wilson, Jimmy **45**
Wilson, Margaret Bush **79**
Wilson, Mary **28**
Wilson, Nancy **10**
Wilson, Natalie **38**
Wilson, Phill **9**
Wilson, Stephanie **72**
Wilson, Sunnie **7, 55**
Wilson, Tracey Scott **777**
Wilson, William Julius **20**
Winans, Angie **36**

Winans, BeBe 14
Winans, CeCe 14, 43
Winans, David 77
Winans, Debbie 36
Winans, Marvin L. 17
Winans, Ronald 54
Winans, Vickie 24
Winfield, Dave 5, 91
Winfield, Paul 2, 45
Winfrey, Oprah 2, 15, 61
Winkfield, Jimmy 42
Winslow, Kellen 83
Wisdom, Kimberlydawn 57
Withers, Bill 61
Withers, Ernest C. 68, 88
Withers-Mendes, Elisabeth 64
Witherspoon, John 38
Witt, Edwin T. 26
Wolfe, Ann 82
Wolfe, George C. 6, 43
Womack, Bobby 60, 92
Wonder, Stevie 11, 53
Woodard, Alfre 9
Woodard, Lynette 67
Woodruff, Hale 9
Woodruff, John 68
Woods, Abraham, Jr. 74
Woods, Georgie 57
Woods, Granville T. 5
Woods, Jacqueline 52
Woods, Mattiebelle 63
Woods, Scott 55
Woods, Sylvia 34
Woods, Teri 69
Woods, Tiger 14, 31, 81
Woodson, Ali Ollie 89
Woodson, Carter G. 2
Woodson, Mike 78
Woodson, Robert L. 10
Woodson, Rod 79
Worrill, Conrad 12
Worthy, James 49
Worthy, Kym 84
Wright, Antoinette 60
Wright, Bruce McMarion 3, 52
Wright, Charles H. 35
Wright, Deborah C. 25
Wright, Jeffrey 54
Wright, Jeremiah A., Jr. 45, 69
Wright, Lewin 43
Wright, Louis Tompkins 4
Wright, Nathan, Jr. 56
Wright, Rayfield 70
Wright, Richard 5
Wright, Timothy 74
Wyatt, Addie L. 56
Wynn, Albert R. 25, 77
X, Malcolm 1
X, Marvin 45
Xuma, Madie Hall 59
Xzibit 78
Yancy, Dorothy Cowser 42
Yarbrough, Camille 40
Yarbrough, Cedric 51
Yette, Samuel F. 63
Yoba, Malik 11
York, Dwight D. 71
York, Vincent 40
Young, Al 82
Young, Andrew 3, 48
Young, Charles 77
Young, Coleman 1, 20
Young, Donald, Jr. 57

Young, Jean Childs 14
Young, Jimmy 54
Young, Lee 72
Young, Lester 37
Young, Roger Arliner 29
Young, Whitney M., Jr. 4
Young Jeezy 63
Youngblood, Johnny Ray 8
Youngblood, Shay 32
Zane 71
Zollar, Alfred 40
Zollar, Jawole Willa Jo 28
Zook, Kristal Brent 62

Angolan
Bonga, Kuenda 13
dos Santos, José Eduardo 43
Neto, António Agostinho 43
Roberto, Holden 65
Savimbi, Jonas 2, 34

Antiguan
McGuire, George Alexander 80
Spencer, Winston Baldwin 68
Williams, Denise 40

Aruban
Williams, David Rudyard 50

Australian
Freeman, Cathy 29
Mundine, Anthony 56
Rose, Lionel 56

Austrian
Kodjoe, Boris 34, 89

Bahamian
Christie, Perry Gladstone 53
Ferguson, Amos 81
Ingraham, Hubert A. 19
Pindling, Lynden 81
Spence, Joseph 49

Barbadian
Adams, Grantley 82
Arthur, Owen 33
Brathwaite, Kamau 36
Clarke, Austin C. 32
Foster, Cecil 32
Fresh, Doug E. 93
Grandmaster Flash 33, 60
Kamau, Kwadwo Agymah 28
Lamming, George 35
Rihanna 65

Belizean
Barrow, Dean 69
Jones, Marion 21, 66

Beninese
Gantin, Bernardin 70
Hounsou, Djimon 19, 45
Joachim, Paulin 34
Kerekou, Ahmed (Mathieu) 1
Kidjo, Angelique 50
Loueke, Lionel 88
Soglo, Nicéphore 15
Yayi, Boni T. 84

Bermudian
Cameron, Earl 44
Gordon, Pamela 17

Smith, Jennifer 21
Bissau-Guinean
Sanhá Malam Bacai 84
Vieira, João Bernardo 14, 84

Botswanan
Masire, Quett 5
Mogae, Festus Gontebanye 19, 79

Brazilian
Brown, Carlinhos 81
Caymmi, Dorival 72
da Silva, Benedita 5
dos Santos, Manuel Francisco 65
Gil, Gilberto 53
Jorge, Seu 73
Machado de Assis 74
Mello, Breno 73
Moura, Paulo 87
Nascimento, Abdias do 93
Nascimento, Milton 2, 64
Pelé 6
Pitta, Celso 17
Querino, Manuel Raimundo 84
Ronaldinho 69
Silva, Marina 80

British
Abbott, Diane 9
Adjaye, David 38, 78
Akinnuoye-Agbaje, Adewale 56
Akomfrah, John 37
Amos, Valerie 41
Anderson, Ho Che 54
Anthony, Trey 63
Appiah, Kwame Anthony 67
Armah, Esther 87
Armatrading, Joan 32
Bailey Rae, Corinne 83
Barnes, John 53
Bassey, Shirley 25
Berry, James 41
Blackwood, Maureen 37
Boateng, Ozwald 35
Boateng, Paul Yaw 56
Breeze, Jean "Binta" 37
Brown, Melanie 73
Campbell, Naomi 1, 31
Carby, Hazel 27
Christie, Linford 8
Coleridge-Taylor, Samuel 75
Crooks, Garth 53
D'Aguiar, Fred 50
Danjah, Terror 91
David, Craig 31, 53
Davidson, Jaye 5
DeGale, James 74
Edwards, Trevor 54
Ejiofor, Chiwetel 67
Elba, Idris 49, 89
Emmanuel, Alphonsia 38
Equiano, Olaudah 78
Estelle 75
Evans, Diana 72
Fenton, Kevin 87
Ferdinand, Rio 82
Garrett, Sean 57
Gladwell, Malcolm 62
Griffin, Angela 80
Hall, Stuart 78
Hamilton, Lewis 66
Harewood, David 52
Harris, Naomie 55

Haye, David 82
Henriques, Julian 37
Henry, Lenny 9, 52
Holmes, Kelly 47
Ibrahim, Mo 67
Ince, Paul 83
Jamelia 51
James, David 84
Jean-Baptiste, Marianne 17, 46
Jordan, Ronny 26
Kay, Jackie 37
King, Oona 27
Kwei-Armah, Kwame 84
Lester, Adrian 46
Lewis, Denise 33
Lewis, Lennox 27
Lewis, Leona 75
Lindo, Delroy 18, 45
Markham, E. A. 37
Mbatha-Raw, Gugu 89
McGrath, Pat 72
McKinney Hammond, Michelle 51
McQueen, Steve 84
Miller, Wentworth 75
Morris, William "Bill" 51
Newton, Thandie 26
Okonedo, Sophie 67
Oyelowo, David 82
Pitt, David Thomas 10
Rascal, Dizzee 82
Regis, Cyrille 51
Sade 15, 92
Scantlebury, Janna 47
Seacole, Mary 54
Seal 14, 75
Siji 56
Slash 75
Slick Rick 93
Smith, Anjela Lauren 44
Smith, Richard 51
Smith, Zadie 51
Stoutt, H. Lavity 83
Stuart, Moira 82
Taylor, John (David Beckett) 16
Thomason, Marsha 47
Walker, Eamonn 37
Williams, Roy 89

Burkinabé
Compaore, Blaise 87
Somé, Malidoma Patrice 10

Burundian
Ndadaye, Melchior 7
Nkurunziza, Pierre 78
Ntaryamira, Cyprien 8

Cameroonian
Ahidjo, Ahmadou 81
Bebey, Francis 45
Beti, Mongo 36
Biya, Chantal 89
Biya, Paul 28
Eto'o, Samuel 73
Kotto, Yaphet 7
Milla, Roger 2
Njawe, Pius 87
Oyono, Ferdinand 38

Canadian
Auguste, Arnold A. 47
Augustine, Jean 53
Bannister, Edward Mitchell 88

Bell, Ralph S. 5
Best, Carrie 80
Boyd, Suzanne 52
Brand, Dionne 32
Brathwaite, Fred 35
Brown, Rosemary 62
Brown, Sean 52
Carnegie, Herbert 25
Chanté, Keshia 50
Chong, Rae Dawn 62
Clarke, Austin 32
Clarke, George 32
Cools, Anne 64
Cooper, Afua 53
Cox, Deborah 28
Croal, N'Gai 76
Curling, Alvin 34
Dixon, George 52
Doig, Jason 45
Drake 86
Elliot, Lorris 37
Fiona, Melanie 84
Foster, Cecil 32
Fox, Rick 27
Fuhr, Grant 1, 49
Grand-Pierre, Jean-Luc 46
Hammond, Lenn 34
Harris, Claire 34
Henry, Joshua 94
Iginla, Jarome 35
Isaac, Julius 34
James, Vanessa 84
Jean, Michaëlle; 70
Jenkins, Fergie 46
Johnson, Ben 1
K'naan 76
Laraque, Georges 48
Lewis, Daurene 72
Mayers, Jamal 39
McKegney, Tony 3
Mollel, Tololwa 38
Neale, Haydain 52
O'Ree, Willie 5
Peterson, Oscar 52
Philip, Marlene Nourbese 32
Reuben, Gloria 15
Richards, Lloyd 2
Rodrigues, Percy 68
Sadlier, Rosemary 62
Salvador, Bryce 51
Scarlett, Millicent 49
Senior, Olive 37
Sparks, Corinne Etta 53
Vanity 67
Verna, Gelsy 70
Weekes, Kevin 67
Williams, Denise 40

Cape Verdean
Evora, Cesaria 12
Pereira, Aristides 30

Caymanian
Ebanks, Selita 67

Chadian
Déby, Idriss 30
Habré, Hissène 6

Colombian
Pomare, Eleo 72

Congolese
Kabila, Joseph 30
Kintaudi, Leon 62

Kolosoy, Wendo 73
Lumumba, Patrice 33
Mudimbe, V. Y. 61
Nkunda, Laurent 75

Costa Rican
McDonald, Erroll 1

Cuban
Ferrer, Ibrahim 41
Güines, Tata 69
León, Tania 13
Maceo, Antonio 82
Minoso, Minnie 89
Portuondo, Omara 53
Quirot, Ana 13
Rodríguez, Arsenio 87
Santamaria, Mongo 81
Valdés, Chucho 89
Velez-Rodriguez, Argelia 56

Dominican (from Dominica)
Charles, Mary Eugenia 10, 55
Charles, Pierre 52
Skerrit, Roosevelt 72

Dominican (from Dominican Republic)
Martinez, Pedro 81
Ortiz, David 52, 82
Sosa, Sammy 21, 44
Virgil, Ozzie 48

Dutch
Ali, Ayaan Hirsi 58, 92
Liberia-Peters, Maria Philomena 12

Eritrean
Keflezighi, Meb 49

Ethiopian
Aberra, Amsale 67
Afro, Teddy 78
Astatke, Mulatu 81
Bekele, Kenenisa 75
Dibaba, Tirunesh 73
Gabre-Medhin, Tsegaye 64
Gebrselassie, Haile 70
Gerima, Haile 38, 80
Haile Selassie 7
Kebede, Liya 59
Meles Zenawi 3
Mengistu, Haile Mariam 65
Samuelsson, Marcus 53

Filipino
apl.de.ap 84

French
Baker, Josephine 3
Baldwin, James 1
Baugé, Grégory 86
Bebey, Francis 45
Bonaly, Surya 7
Boulogne, Joseph, Chevalier de
    Saint-Georges 94
Chase-Riboud, Barbara 20, 46
Dieudonné 67
Fanon, Frantz 44
Henry, Thierry 66
James, Vanessa 84
Kanouté, Fred 68
Noah, Yannick 4, 60
Parker, Tony 75

Tanner, Henry Ossawa 1

Gabonese
Bongo, Ali Ben 80
Bongo, Omar 1, 79

Gambian
Jammeh, Yahya 23
Peters, Lenrie 43

German
Massaquoi, Hans J. 30
Watts, Andre 42

Ghanaian
Adu, Freddy 67
Aidoo, Ama Ata 38
Ali, Mohammed Naseehu 60
Annan, Kofi Atta 15, 48
Appiah, Kwame Anthony 67
Armah, Ayi Kwei 49
Atta Mills, John 75
Awoonor, Kofi 37
Bartels, Peggielene 80
Danquah, Meri Nana Ama 93
Dawuni, Rocky 94
DuBois, Shirley Graham 21
Gyan, Asamoah 87
Jawara, Dawda Kairaba 11
Kufuor, John Agyekum 54, 82
Mensah, John 87
Mensah, Thomas 48
Nkrumah, Kwame 3
Rawlings, Jerry 9
Rawlings, Nana Konadu Agyeman
    13
Yeboah, Emmanuel Ofosu 53

Grenadian
Bishop, Maurice 39
Gairy, Eric Matthew 83
Isaac, Julius 34
Mitchell, Keith 82

Guinean
Camara, Moussa Dadis 76
Conté, Lansana 7, 76
Diallo, Amadou 27
Niane, Katoucha 70
Touré, Sekou 6

Guyanese
Amos, Valerie 41
Beaton, Norman 14
Burnham, Forbes 66
Carter, Martin 49
Dabydeen, David 48
D'Aguiar, Fred 50
Damas, Léon-Gontran 46
Dathorne, O. R. 52
Griffith, Patrick A. 64
Jagan, Cheddi 16
Lefel, Edith 41
van Sertima, Ivan 25

Haitian
Aristide, Jean-Bertrand 6, 45
Auguste, Rose-Anne 13
Beauvais, Garcelle 29
Beauvoir, Max 74
Charlemagne, Manno 11
Christophe, Henri 9
Danticat, Edwidge 15, 68
Delice, Ronald 48
Delice, Rony 48

Jean, Wyclef 20, 86
Jean-Juste, Gérard 78
Jean-Louis, Jimmy 76
Laferriere, Dany 33
Laraque, Paul 67
Laroche, Joseph Philippe Lemercier
    85
Magloire, Paul Eugène 68
Manigat, Mirlande 90
Martelly, Michel 90
Pascal-Trouillot, Ertha 3
Peck, Raoul 32
Pierre, Andre 17
Pierre-Louis, Michèle 75
Préval, René 87
Siméus, Dumas M. 25
Verna, Gelsy 70

Irish
Adebari, Rotimi 83
Mumba, Samantha 29

Italian
Esposito, Giancarlo 9

Ivorian
Bedie, Henri Konan 21
Blondy, Alpha 30
Dadié, Bernard 34
De Bankolé, Isaach 78
Drogba, Didier 78
Gbagbo, Laurent 43, 90
Guéï, Robert 66
Houphouët-Boigny, Félix 4, 64
Ouattara 43
Ouattara, Alassane 90
Ouattara, Morou 74

Jamaican
Ashley, Maurice 15, 47
Banton, Buju 93
Barnes, John 53
Barnes, Lloyd 77
Barrett, Lindsay 43
Beenie Man 32
Belafonte, Harry 4
Bennett, Louise 69
Berry, James 41
Bolt, Usain 73
Burning Spear 79
Channer, Colin 36
Cliff, Jimmy 28, 92
Cliff, Michelle 42
Cooper, Afua 53
Cox, Renée 67
Curling, Alvin 34
Dunbar, Sly 34
Ellis, Alton 74
Ewing, Patrick 17, 73
Fagan, Garth 18
Fenton, Kevin 87
Figueroa, John J. 40
Ford, Vincent 75
Garvey, Marcus 1
Golding, Bruce 78
Goodison, Lorna 71
Graham, Trevor 84
Griffiths, Marcia 29
Hamilton, Tanya 93
Hammond, Lenn 34
Hearne, John Edgar Caulwell 45
Heavy D 58
Isaacs, Gregory 89
James, Marlon 85

Johnson, Ben **1**
Johnson, Linton Kwesi **37**
Joseph, Kathie-Ann **56**
Kingston, Sean **94**
Kong, B. Waine **50**
Manley, Edna **26**
Manley, Ruth **34**
Marley, Bob **5**
Marley, Rita **32, 70**
Marley, Ziggy **41**
McKay, Claude **6**
McKenzie, Jaunel **73**
Minott, Sugar **86**
Moody, Ronald **30**
Morrison, Keith **13**
Mowatt, Judy **38**
Palmer, Everard **37**
Patterson, Orlando **4**
Patterson, P. J. **6, 20**
Perry, Ruth **19**
Ranglin, Ernest **78**
Reece, E. Albert **63**
Rhoden, Wayne **70**
Rhone, Trevor **80**
Rogers, Joel Augustus **30**
Senior, Olive **37**
Shaggy **31**
Shakespeare, Robbie **34**
Simpson-Miller, Portia **62**
Sinclair, Madge **78**
Steely **80**
Taylor, Karin **34**
Tosh, Peter **9**
White, Willard **53**
Yabby You **83**

Kenyan
Cheruiyot, Robert **69**
Juma, Calestous **57**
Kariuki, J. M. **67**
Kenyatta, Jomo **5**
Kibaki, Mwai **60**
Kobia, Samuel **43**
Loroupe, Tegla **59**
Maathai, Wangari **43**
Mazrui, Ali A. **12**
Moi, Daniel Arap **1, 35**
Mutu, Wangechi **44**
Mwangi, Meja **40**
Ngilu, Charity **58**
Ngugi wa Thiong'o **29, 61**
Odinga, Raila **67**
Otunga, Maurice Michael **55**
Tergat, Paul **59**
Wambugu, Florence **42**
Wanjiru, Sammy **94**

Korean
Ward, Hines **84**

Lesothoian
Mofolo, Thomas **37**

Liberian
Conneh, Sekou Damate, Jr. **51**
Cooper, Lisa **73**
Fuller, Solomon Carter, Jr. **15**
Gbowee, Leymah **76**
Keith, Rachel Boone **63**
Perry, Ruth **15**
Sawyer, Amos **2**
Sirleaf, Ellen Johnson **71**
Taylor, Charles **20**

Weah, George **58**

Malawian
Banda, Hastings Kamuzu **6, 54**
Kayira, Legson **40**
Muluzi, Bakili **14, 76**

Malian
Keita, Salif **83**
Souleymane, Mahamane **78**
Touré, Amadou Toumani **18**

Martinican
Césaire, Aimé **48, 69**
Palcy, Euzhan **94**

Mozambican
Chissano, Joaquim **7, 55, 67**
Couto, Mia **45**
Diogo, Luisa Dias **63**
Guebuza, Armando **81**
Machel, Graca Simbine **16**
Machel, Samora Moises **8**
Mutola, Maria **12**

Namibian
Mbuende, Kaire **12**
Nujoma, Samuel **10**

Nigerian
Abacha, Sani **11, 70**
Abani, Chris **77**
Abiola, Moshood **70**
Abubakar, Abdulsalami **66**
Achebe, Chinua **6**
Ade, King Sunny **41**
Adichie, Chimamanda Ngozi **64**
Ake, Claude **30**
Akinola, Peter Jasper **65**
Akunyili, Dora Nkem **58**
Amadi, Elechi **40**
Arinze, Francis **19**
Azikiwe, Nnamdi **13**
Babangida, Ibrahim **4**
Bandele, Biyi **68**
Clark-Bekedermo, J. P. **44**
Darego, Agbani **52**
Ekwensi, Cyprian **37**
Emeagwali, Philip **30**
Emecheta, Buchi **30**
Fela **1, 42**
Jonathan, Goodluck **83**
Kuti, Femi **47**
Lawal, Kase L. **45**
Obasanjo, Olusegun **5, 22**
Obasanjo, Stella **32, 56**
Ogunlesi, Adebayo O. **37**
Okara, Gabriel **37**
Okosuns, Sonny **71**
Olajuwon, Hakeem **2, 72**
Olatunji, Babatunde **36**
Olojede, Dele **59**
Olopade, Olufunmilayo Falusi **58**
Onwueme, Tess Osonye **23**
Onwurah, Ngozi **38**
Rotimi, Ola **1**
Sade **15, 92**
Saro-Wiwa, Kenule **39**
Siji **56**
Sowande, Fela **39**
Soyinka, Wole **4, 93**
Tutuola, Amos **30**
Ukpabio, Helen **86**
Wiwa, Ken **67**

Yar'Adua, Umaru **69, 89**

Nigerien
Tandja, Mamadou **33, 78**

Norwegian
Brown, Anne **76**

Panamanian
Bailey, Preston **64**
Williams, Juan **35, 80**

Peruvian
Baca, Susana **80**

Polish
Bridgetower, George **78**

Puerto Rican
Schomburg, Arthur Alfonso **9**

Rhodesian
Brutus, Dennis **38**

Russian
Khanga, Yelena **6**

Rwandan
Bizimungu, Pasteur **19**
Habyarimana, Juvenal **8**
Ilibagiza, Immaculée **66**
Kagame, Paul **54**
Mushikiwabo, Louise **88**
Rusesabagina, Paul **60**

St. Kitts and Nevis
Douglas, Denzil Llewellyn **53**

Saint Lucian
Compton, John **65**

Saudi
Amoudi, Mohammed al- **88**
Kalbani, Adil **77**

Senegalese
Acogny, Germaine **55**
Akon **76**
Ba, Mariama **30**
Boye, Madior **30**
Diop, Birago **53**
Diop, Cheikh Anta **4**
Diouf, Abdou **3**
Maal, Baaba **66**
Mbaye, Mariétou **31**
Mboup, Souleymane **10**
Ndiaye, Iba **74**
N'Dour, Youssou **1, 53, 79**
Sané, Pierre Gabriel **21**
Sembène, Ousmane **13, 62**
Senghor, Augustin Diamancoune **66**
Senghor, Léopold Sédar **12, 66**
Sy, Oumou **65**
Wade, Abdoulaye **66**

Sierra Leonean
Beah, Ishmael **69**
Cheney-Coker, Syl **43**
Jones, Monty **66**
Kabbah, Ahmad Tejan **23**
Koroma, Ernest Bai **84**
Sankoh, Foday **74**

Somali
Ahmed, Sharif **80**
Ali, Ayaan Hirsi **58, 92**
Ali Mahdi Mohamed **5**

Dirie, Waris **56**
Farah, Nuruddin **27**
Iman **4, 33, 87**
K'naan **76**
Roble, Abdi **71**

South African
Abrahams, Peter **39**
Adams, Paul **50**
Biko, Steven **4**
Brutus, Dennis **38**
Buthelezi, Mangosuthu Gatsha **9**
Butler, Jonathan **28**
Chweneyagae, Presley **63**
Dandala, Mvume **77**
Dube, Lucky **77**
Grae, Jean **51**
Hani, Chris **6**
Head, Bessie **28**
Ka Dinizulu, Mcwayizeni **29**
Kente, Gibson **52**
Khumalo, Leleti **51**
Kuzwayo, Ellen **68**
LaGuma, Alex **30**
Luthuli, Albert **13**
Mabuza, Lindiwe **18**
Mabuza-Suttle, Felicia **43**
Mahlasela, Vusi **65**
Makeba, Miriam **2, 50, 74**
Mandela, Nelson **1, 14, 77**
Mandela, Winnie **2, 35**
Masekela, Barbara **18**
Masekela, Hugh **1**
Mathabane, Mark **5**
Mbeki, Govan A. **80**
Mbeki, Thabo **14, 73**
Mhlaba, Raymond **55**
Mokae, Zakes **80**
Motlanthe, Kgalema **74**
Mphalele, Es'kia (Ezekiel) **40**
Naki, Hamilton **63**
Ngubane, Ben **33**
Nkoli, Simon **60**
Nkosi, Lewis **46**
Ntshona, Winston **52**
Nyanda, Siphiwe **21**
Nzo, Alfred **15**
Plaatje, Sol. T. **80**
Ramaphosa, Cyril **3**
Ramphele, Mamphela **29**
Sisulu, Albertina **57**
Sisulu, Sheila Violet Makate **24**
Sisulu, Walter **47**
Sono, Jomo **86**
Thugwane, Josia **21**
Tutu, Desmond (Mpilo) **6, 44**
Tutu, Nontombi Naomi **57**
Zuma, Jacob **33, 75**
Zuma, Nkosazana Dlamini **34**

Spanish
Eto'o, Samuel **73**

Sudanese
Bashir, Halima **73**
Bashir, Omar al- **77**
Bol, Manute **1**
Cham, Adongo Agada Akway **77**
Hussein, Lubna **80**
Kiir, Salva **85**
Nour, Nawal M. **56**
Salih, Al-Tayyib **37**

Wek, Alek **18, 63**

Swazi
Mswati III **56**

Swedish
Hendricks, Barbara **3, 67**
Valdés, Bebo **75**

Tanzanian
Kikwete, Jakaya Mrisho **73**
Mkapa, Benjamin W. **16, 77**
Mollel, Tololwa **38**
Mongella, Gertrude **11**
Mwinyi, Ali Hassan **1, 77**
Nyerere, Julius **5**
Ongala, Remmy **9, 91**
Rugambwa, Laurean **20**

Togolese
Eyadéma, Gnassingbé **7, 52**
Gnassingbé, Faure **67**
Soglo, Nicéphore **15**

Trinidadian
Anthony, Michael **29**
Auguste, Arnold A. **47**
Brand, Dionne **32**
Carmichael, Stokely **5, 26**
Cartey, Wilfred **47**
Dymally, Mervyn **42**
Francis, Thais **93**
Guy, Rosa **5**
Harris, Claire **34**
Hendy, Francis **47**
Hercules, Frank **44**
Hill, Errol **40**
Holder, Geoffrey **78**
Julian, Hubert **90**
Lushington, Augustus Nathaniel **56**
Nakhid, David **25**
Nunez, Elizabeth **62**
Primus, Pearl **6**
Rudder, David **79**
Shorty, Ras, I **47**
Toussaint, Lorraine **32**

Williams, Eric Eustace 65

Tunisian
Memmi, Albert **37**

Ugandan
Amin, Idi **42**
Arac de Nyeko, Monica **66**
Atim, Julian **66**
Atyam, Angelina **55**
Museveni, Yoweri **4**
Mutebi, Ronald **25**
Obote, Milton **63**
Okaalet, Peter **58**
Sentamu, John **58**

Upper Voltan
Sankara, Thomas **17**

West Indian
Césaire, Aimé **48, 69**
Coombs, Orde M. **44**
Innis, Roy **5**
Kincaid, Jamaica **4**
Knight, Gwendolyn **63**
Pitt, David Thomas **10**

Rojas, Don **33**
Staupers, Mabel K. **7**
Taylor, Susan L. **10, 86**
Walcott, Derek **5, 94**

Zairean
Kabila, Laurent **20**
Mobutu Sese Seko **1, 56**
Mutombo, Dikembe **7**

Zambian
Chiluba, Frederick **56, 80**
Kaunda, Kenneth **2**
Moyo, Dambisa **76**
Mwanawasa, Levy **72**
Zulu, Princess Kasune **54**

Zimbabwean
Chideya, Farai **14**
Marechera, Dambudzo **39**
Moyo, Lovemore **76**
Mugabe, Robert **10, 71**
Mukoko, Jestina **75**
Muzorewa, Abel **85**
Nkomo, Joshua **4, 65**
Tsvangirai, Morgan **26, 72**
Vera, Yvonne **32**

Cumulative Occupation Index

*Volume numbers appear in **bold***

Art and design

Abele, Julian **55**
Aberra, Amsale **67**
Adjaye, David **38, 78**
Allen, Tina **22, 75**
Alston, Charles **33**
Amaki, Amalia **76**
Amos, Emma **63**
Anderson, Ho Che **54**
Andrews, Benny **22, 59**
Andrews, Bert **13**
Armstrong, Robb **15**
Ashford, Calvin, Jr. **74**
Bailey, Preston **64**
Bailey, Radcliffe **19**
Bailey, Xenobia **11**
Baker, Matt **76**
Bannister, Edward Mitchell **88**
Barboza, Anthony **10**
Barnes, Ernie **16, 78**
Barthé, Earl **78**
Barthe, Richmond **15**
Basquiat, Jean-Michel **5**
Bearden, Romare **2, 50**
Beasley, Phoebe **34**
Bell, Darrin **77**
Benberry, Cuesta **65**
Benjamin, Tritobia Hayes **53**
Biggers, John **20, 33**
Biggers, Sanford **62**
Billops, Camille **82**
Blackburn, Robert **28**
Bond, J. Max, Jr. **76**
Bradford, Mark **89**
Brandon, Barbara **3**
Brown, Donald **19**
Brown, Robert **65**
Burke, Selma **16**
Burroughs, Margaret Taylor **9**
Camp, Kimberly **19**
Campbell, E. Simms **13**
Campbell, Mary Schmidt **43**
Catlett, Elizabeth **2**
Chanticleer, Raven **91**
Chase-Riboud, Barbara **20, 46**
Colescott, Robert **69**
Collins, Paul **61**
Cortor, Eldzier **42**
Cowans, Adger W. **20**
Cox, Renée **67**
Crichlow, Ernest **75**
Crite, Alan Rohan **29**
Davis, Bing **84**

De Veaux, Alexis **44**
DeCarava, Roy **42, 81**
Delaney, Beauford **19**
Delaney, Joseph **30**
Delsarte, Louis **34**
Donaldson, Jeff **46**
Douglas, Aaron **7**
Douglas, Emory **89**
Driskell, David C. **7**
du Cille, Michel **74**
Dwight, Edward **65**
Edwards, Melvin **22**
El Wilson, Barbara **35**
Ewing, Patrick **17, 73**
Fax, Elton **48**
Feelings, Tom **11, 47**
Ferguson, Amos **81**
Fine, Sam **60**
Freeman, Leonard **27**
Fuller, Meta Vaux Warrick **27**
Gantt, Harvey **1**
Garvin, Gerry **78**
Gilles, Ralph **61**
Gilliam, Sam **16**
Golden, Thelma **10, 55**
Goodnight, Paul **32**
Green, Jonathan **54**
Guyton, Tyree **9, 94**
Hammons, David **69**
Hansen, Austin **88**
Harkless, Necia Desiree **19**
Harrington, Oliver W. **9**
Harris, Lyle Ashton **83**
Harrison, Charles **72**
Hathaway, Isaac Scott **33**
Hayden, Palmer **13**
Hayes, Cecil N. **46**
Holder, Geoffrey **78**
Honeywood, Varnette P. **54, 88**
Hope, John **8**
Hudson, Cheryl **15**
Hudson, Wade **15**
Hunt, Richard **6**
Hunter, Clementine **45**
Hutson, Jean Blackwell **16**
Jackson, Earl **31**
Jackson, Mary **73**
Jackson, Vera **40**
John, Daymond **23**
Johnson, Jeh Vincent **44**
Johnson, William Henry **3**
Jones, Lois Mailou **13**
Jones, Paul R. **76**
King, Robert Arthur **58**

Kitt, Sandra **23**
Knight, Gwendolyn **63**
Knox, Simmie **49**
Lawrence, Jacob **4, 28**
Lee, Annie Frances **22**
Lee-Smith, Hughie **5, 22**
Lewis, Edmonia **10**
Lewis, Norman **39**
Lewis, Samella **25**
Ligon, Glenn **82**
Lovell, Whitfield **74**
Loving, Alvin, Jr. **35, 53**
Manley, Edna **26**
Marshall, Kerry James **59**
Mayhew, Richard **39**
McCullough, Geraldine **58, 79**
McDuffie, Dwayne **62**
McGee, Charles **10**
McGruder, Aaron **28, 56**
McQueen, Steve **84**
Mehretu, Julie **85**
Mitchell, Corinne **8**
Moody, Ronald **30**
Morrison, Keith **13**
Motley, Archibald, Jr. **30**
Moutoussamy-Ashe, Jeanne **7**
Mutu, Wangechi **44**
Myles, Kim **69**
Nascimento, Abdias do **93**
Ndiaye, Iba **74**
Neals, Otto **73**
N'Namdi, George R. **17**
Nugent, Richard Bruce **39**
O'Grady, Lorraine **73**
Olden, Georg(e) **44**
Ormes, Jackie **73**
Ouattara **43**
Perkins, Marion **38**
Pierce, Elijah **84**
Pierre, Andre **17**
Pindell, Howardena **55**
Pinder, Jefferson **77**
Pinderhughes, John **47**
Pinkney, Jerry **15**
Piper, Adrian **71**
Pippin, Horace **9**
Pope.L, William **72**
Porter, James A. **11**
Prophet, Nancy Elizabeth **42**
Puryear, Martin **42**
Querino, Manuel Raimundo **84**
Ransome, James E. **88**
Reid, Senghor **55**
Ringgold, Faith **4, 81**

Roble, Abdi **71**
Ruley, Ellis **38**
Saar, Alison **16**
Saar, Betye **80**
Saint James, Synthia **12**
Sallee, Charles **38**
Sanders, Joseph R., Jr. **11**
Savage, Augusta **12**
Scott, John T. **65**
Sebree, Charles **40**
Serrano, Andres **3**
Shabazz, Attallah **6**
Shonibare, Yinka **58**
Simmons, Gary **58**
Simpson, Lorna **4, 36**
Sims, Lowery Stokes **27**
Sklarek, Norma Merrick **25**
Sleet, Moneta, Jr. **5**
Smith, Bruce W. **53**
Smith, Marvin **46**
Smith, Morgan **46**
Smith, Vincent D. **48**
Steave-Dickerson, Kia **57**
Stout, Renee **63**
Sudduth, Jimmy Lee **65**
Tanksley, Ann **37**
Tanner, Henry Ossawa **1**
Taylor, Robert Robinson **80**
Thomas, Alma **14**
Thrash, Dox **35**
Tolliver, Mose **60**
Tolliver, William **9**
Tooks, Lance **62**
VanDerZee, James **6**
Verna, Gelsy **70**
Wagner, Albert **78**
Wainwright, Joscelyn **46**
Walker, A'lelia **14**
Walker, Kara **16, 80**
Washington, Alonzo **29**
Washington, James, Jr. **38**
Weems, Carrie Mae **63**
Wells, James Lesesne **10**
White, Charles **39**
White, Dondi **34**
White, John H. **27**
Wiley, Kehinde **62**
Williams, Billy Dee **8**
Williams, Clarence **70**
Williams, O. S. **13**
Williams, Paul R. **9**
Williams, William T. **11**
Willis, Deborah **85**
Wilson, Ellis **39**

Withers, Ernest C. **68, 88**
Woodruff, Hale **9**

Business

Abbott, Robert Sengstacke **27**
Abiola, Moshood **70**
Adams, Eula L. **39**
Adams, Jenoyne **60**
Adkins, Rod **41**
Akil, Mara Brock **60, 82**
Al-Amin, Jamil Abdullah **6**
Alexander, Archie Alphonso **14**
Allen, Byron **24**
Allen-Buillard, Melba **55**
Ames, Wilmer **27**
Amos, Wally **9**
Amoudi, Mohammed al- **88**
Archer, Lee, Jr. **79**
Armstrong, Govind **81**
Auguste, Donna **29**
Austin, Gloria **63**
Austin, Jim **63**
Austin, Wanda M. **94**
Avant, Clarence **19, 86**
Avant, Nicole A. **90**
Baker, Dusty **8, 43, 72**
Baker, Ella **5**
Baker, Gwendolyn Calvert **9**
Baker, Maxine **28**
Banks, Jeffrey **17**
Banks, Paula A. **68**
Banks, William **11**
Barden, Donald H. **9, 20, 89**
Barrett, Andrew C. **12**
Beal, Bernard B. **46**
Beamon, Bob **30**
Beasley, Phoebe **34**
Bell, James A. **50**
Bing, Dave **3, 59, 78**
Blackshear, Leonard **52**
Blackwell, Robert D., Sr. **52**
Blaylock, Ronald **86**
Blayton, Jesse B., Sr. **55**
Bolden, Frank E. **44**
Borders, James **9**
Boston, Kelvin E. **25**
Boston, Lloyd **24**
Bowen, Ruth **83**
Boyd, Edward **70**
Boyd, Gwendolyn **49**
Boyd, John W., Jr. **20, 72**
Boyd, T. B., III **6**
Bradley, Jennette B. **40**
Brae, C. Michael **61**
Bridges, Shelia **36**
Bridgforth, Glinda **36**
Briggs, Curtis **84**
Brimmer, Andrew F. **2, 48**
Bronner, Nathaniel H., Sr. **32**
Brown, Eddie C. **35**
Brown, Jamie Foster **91**
Brown, Les **5**
Brown, Marie Dutton **12**
Brunson, Dorothy **1, 87**
Bryant, John **26**
Burgess, Marjorie L. **55**
Burns, Ursula **60**
Burrell, Tom **21, 51**
Burroughs, Margaret Taylor **9**
Burrus, William Henry **45**
Burt-Murray, Angela **59**
Butler, George, Jr. **70**
Cain, Herman **15, 92**

Calabrese, Karyn **89**
Caldwell, Earl **60**
Cameron, James **80**
Carter, Pamela Lynn **67**
CasSelle, Malcolm **11**
Chamberlain, Wilt **18, 47**
Chapman, Nathan A., Jr. **21**
Chapman, Susan E. **94**
Chappell, Emma **18**
Chase, Debra Martin **49**
Chase, Leah **57**
Chenault, Kenneth I. **4, 36**
Cherry, Deron **40**
Chisholm, Samuel J. **32**
Clark, Celeste **15**
Clark, Patrick **14**
Clay, William Lacy **8**
Clayton, Xernona **3, 45**
Clement-Holmes, Linda **94**
Clyburn, Mignon **78**
Cobbs, Price M. **9**
Colbert, Virgis William **17**
Coleman, Donald **24, 62**
Coleman, Ken **57**
Compton-Rock, Malaak **86**
Connerly, Ward **14**
Conyers, Nathan G. **24**
Cooper, Barry **33**
Cooper, Evern **40**
Corbi, Lana **42**
Cornelius, Don **4**
Cosby, Camille **14, 80**
Cottrell, Comer **11**
Council, LaVerne **94**
Cox, William E. **68**
Creagh, Milton **27**
Cullers, Vincent T. **49**
Daniels-Carter, Valerie **23**
Darden, Calvin **38**
Dash, Darien **29**
Davis, Belva **61**
Davis, Ed **24**
Davis, Erroll B., Jr. **57**
Dawson, Matel, Jr. **39**
de Passe, Suzanne **25**
Dean, Mark **35**
Dee, Merri **55**
Delany, Bessie **12**
Delany, Martin R. **27**
Delany, Sadie **12**
DeVard, Jerri **61**
Diallo, Amadou **27**
Doley, Harold, Jr. **26**
Donald, Arnold Wayne **36**
Dorsey, Thomas J. **90**
Downing, George T. **91**
Dre, Dr. **10, 14, 30**
Driver, David E. **11**
Ducksworth, Marilyn **12**
Duerson, Dave **93**
Easley, Annie J. **61**
Ebanks, Michelle **60**
Edelin, Ramona Hoage **19**
Edmonds, Tracey **16, 64**
Edmunds, Gladys **48**
Edwards, Trevor **54**
El Wilson, Barbara **35**
Elder, Lee **6**
Ellington, E. David **11**
Evans, Darryl **22**
Evers, Myrlie **8**
Farmer, Forest J. **1**
Farr, Mel **24**

Farrakhan, Louis **15**
Fauntroy, Walter E. **11**
Ferdinand, Rio **82**
50 Cent **46, 83**
Fils-Aimé, Reggie **74**
Fletcher, Alphonse, Jr. **16**
Flowers, Sylester **50**
Ford, Barney **90**
Ford, Harold E(ugene), Jr. **16, 70**
Forte, Linda Diane **54**
Foster, Jylla Moore **45**
Fowler, Reggie **51**
Franklin, Hardy R. **9**
Friday, Jeff **24**
Fryer, Roland G. **56**
Fudge, Ann **11, 55**
Fuller, S. B. **13**
Funderburg, I. Owen **38**
Gaines, Brenda **41**
Gardner, Chris **65**
Gardner, Edward G. **45**
Garrett, James F. **78**
Gaskins, Rudy **74**
Gaston, Arthur George **3, 38, 59**
Gibson, John Trusty **87**
Gibson, Kenneth Allen **6**
Gibson, Ted **66**
Gidron, Richard D. **68**
Gilles, Ralph **61**
Goings, Russell **59**
Goldsberry, Ronald **18**
Golston, Allan C. **55**
Gooden, Linda **94**
Goodman, Kim C. **94**
Gordon, Bruce S. **41, 53, 82**
Gordon, Pamela **17**
Gordy, Berry, Jr. **1**
Goss, Carol A. **55**
Goss, Tom **23**
Grace, George H. **48**
Graham, Stedman **13**
Graves, Butch **77**
Graves, Earl G. **1, 35**
Gray, Farrah **59**
Greely, M. Gasby **27**
Green, Isaac H. **79**
Greene, Richard Thaddeus, Sr. **67**
Greenwood, Monique **38**
Griffith, Mark Winston **8**
Grooms, Henry R(andall) **50**
Hale, Lorraine **8**
Hall, Alvin D. **86**
Ham, Cynthia Parker **58**
Hamer, Fannie Lou **6**
Hamilton, Samuel C. **47**
Handy, W. C. **8**
Hannah, Marc **10**
Hardison, Bethann **12**
Harrell, Andre **9, 30**
Harris, Alice **7**
Harris, Carla A. **67**
Harris, E. Lynn **12, 33**
Harris, Monica **18**
Harris, Richard E. **61**
Harvey, Steve **18, 58**
Harvey, William R. **42**
Hawkins, La-Van **17, 54**
Hayden, Carla D. **47**
Haysbert, Raymond V., Sr. **87**
Hazel, Darryl B. **50**
Henderson, Gordon **5**
Henderson, Henry Fairfax, Jr. **89**
Henry, Lenny **9, 52**

Henry, Troy **85**
Herndon, Alonzo Franklin **89**
Hightower, Dennis F. **13**
Hill, Bonnie Guiton **20**
Hill, Calvin **19**
Hill, Janet **19**
Hill, Jesse, Jr. **13**
Hill, Peter **92**
Hobson, Mellody **40**
Holland, Kimberly N. **62**
Holland, Robert, Jr. **11**
Holmes, Larry **20, 68**
Holstein, Casper **89**
Howell, Ayinde **91**
Howroyd, Janice Bryant **42**
Hudlin, Warrington **9**
Hudson, Cheryl **15**
Hudson, Wade **15**
Huggins, Larry **21**
Hughes, Cathy **27**
Ibrahim, Mo **67**
Ice Cube **8, 30, 60**
Irvin, Vernon **65**
Jackson, George **19**
Jackson, Joe **78**
Jackson, Mannie **14**
Jackson, Michael **19, 53, 76**
Jakes, Thomas "T. D." **17, 43**
James, Charles H., III **62**
James, Donna A. **51**
James, Juanita **13**
Jenkins, Ray **77**
John, Daymond **23**
Johnson, Earvin "Magic" **3, 39**
Johnson, Eunice W. **83**
Johnson, George E. **29**
Johnson, John H. **3, 54**
Johnson, Kevin **70**
Johnson, Robert L. **3, 39**
Johnson, Sheila Crump **48**
Johnson, William **91**
Jolley, Willie **28**
Jones, Carl **7**
Jones, Caroline **29**
Jones, Ingrid Saunders **18**
Jones, John **89**
Jones, Thomas W. **41**
Jones, Wayne **53**
Jordan, Michael **6, 21**
Jordan, Montell **23**
Joyner, Marjorie Stewart **26**
Julian, Percy Lavon **6**
Kaigler, Denise **63**
Keith, Floyd A. **61**
Kelly, Patrick **3**
Kemp, Herb **94**
Kendrick, Erika **57**
Kidd, Mae Street **39**
Killingsworth, Cleve, Jr. **54**
Kimbro, Dennis **10**
King, Dexter **10**
King, Don **14**
Knight, Suge **11, 30**
Knowles, Tina **61**
Knowling, Robert E., Jr. **38**
Lane, Vincent **5**
Langhart Cohen, Janet **19, 60**
Lanier, Willie **33**
Laryea, Thomas Davies, III **67**
Lawal, Kase L. **45**
Lawless, Theodore K. **8**
Lawson, Jennifer **1, 50**
Leary, Kathryn D. **10**

Leavell, Dorothy R. 17
Lee, Annie Frances 22
Lee, Bertram M., Sr. 46
Lee, Debra L. 62
Leonard, Sugar Ray 15
Lewis, Aylwin B. 51, 88
Lewis, Byron E. 13
Lewis, Delano 7
Lewis, Edward T. 21
Lewis, Reginald F. 6
Lewis, William M., Jr. 40
Ligging, Alfred, III 43
Llewellyn, J. Bruce 13, 85
Long, Eddie L. 29, 89
Louis, Errol T. 8
Lucas, John 7
Lucy, William 50
Madison, Paula 37
Malone, Annie 13
March, William Carrington 56
Marshall, Bella 22
Massenburg, Kedar 23
Master P 21
Matthews Shatteen, Westina 51
Matzeliger, Jan 93
Mayberry-Stewart, Melodie 94
Maynard, Robert C. 7
Mays, Leslie A. 41
Mays, William G. 34
McCabe, Jewell Jackson 10
McCann, Renetta 44
McCoy, Elijah 8
McDonald, Erroll 1
McGee, James Madison 46
McGuire, Raymond J. 57
McKissack, Leatrice 80
McLeod, Gus 27
McPherson, David 32
McWorter, Free Frank 91
Miller, Larry G. 72
Millines Dziko, Trish 28
Mills, Steve 47
Mingo, Frank 32
Mitchell, Shireen 89
Monk, Art 38, 73
Monroe, Bryan 71
Montgomery, Isaiah T. 91
Moore, Wes 86
Morgan, Garrett 1
Morgan, Joe Leonard 9
Morgan, Rose 11
Morris, William 51
Moyo, Karega Kofi 36
Moyo, Yvette Jackson 36
Muhammad, Jabir Herbert 72
Nagin, Ray 42, 57, 88
Nail, John E. 92
Nanula, Richard D. 20
Nash, Diane 72
Nelson Meigs, Andrea 48
Nichols, Nichelle 11
Norman, Christina 47
Ogunlesi, Adebayo O. 37
Olojede, Dele 59
O'Neal, Rodney 88
O'Neal, Stanley 38, 67
Otis, Clarence, Jr. 55
Ouattara, Morou 74
Packer, Daniel 56
Parham, Marjorie B. 71
Parks, Henry Green, Jr. 89
Parsons, Richard Dean 11, 33
Payton, Philip A., Jr. 88

Peck, Carolyn 23
Perez, Anna 1
Perkins, James, Jr. 55
Perry, Laval 64
Perry, Lowell 30
Phillips, Charles E., Jr. 57
Pierce, Harold 75
Pinckney, Bill 42
Pinkett, Randal 61
Pleasant, Mary Ellen 9
Potter, Myrtle 40
Powell, Maxine 8
Price, Frederick K. C. 21
Price, Hugh B. 9, 54
Procope, Ernesta 23
Procope, John Levy 56
Queen Latifah 1, 16, 58
Quivers, Robin 61
Rand, A. Barry 6
Reeves, Rachel J. 23
Reid, Antonio "L.A." 28
Rhone, Sylvia 2
Rice, Linda Johnson 9, 41
Rice, Norm 8
Richardson, Donna 39
Richie, Leroy C. 18
Rideau, Iris 46
Roberts, Mike 57
Roberts, Roy S. 14
Robertson, Oscar 26
Robeson, Eslanda Goode 13
Robinson, Jackie 6
Robinson, Rachel 16
Robinson, Randall 7, 46
Roche, Joyce M. 17
Rodgers, Johnathan 6, 51
Rodriguez, Jimmy 47
Rogers, Desirée 88
Rogers, John W., Jr. 5, 52
Rojas, Don 33
Ross, Charles 27
Ross, Diana 8, 27
Russell, Bill 8
Russell, Herman Jerome 17
Russell-McCloud, Patricia 17
Saint James, Synthia 12
Samara, Noah 15
Samuelsson, Marcus 53
Sanders, Angelia 86
Sanders, Dori 8
Sbraga, Kevin 88
Scott, C. A. 29
Scott, Milton 51
Scott, Tim 87
Sengstacke, John 18
Shakur, Afeni 67
Shank, Suzanne F. 77
Shropshire, Thomas B. 49
Siméus, Dumas M. 25
Simmons, Kimora Lee 51, 83
Simmons, Russell 1, 30
Sims, Naomi 29, 79
Sinbad 1, 16
Smith, B(arbara) 11
Smith, Clarence O. 21
Smith, Jane E. 24
Smith, Joshua 10
Smith, Willi 8
Sneed, Paula A. 18
Spaulding, Charles Clinton 9
Staley, Dawn 57
Stanford, Olivia Lee Dilworth 49

Steinberg, Martha Jean "The
    Queen" 28
Steward, David L. 36
Stewart, Ella 39
Stewart, Paul Wilbur 12
Stinson, Denise L. 59
Stringer, Vickie 58
Sullivan, Leon H. 3, 30
Sutton, Percy E. 42, 82
Taylor, Ephren W., II 61
Taylor, Karin 34
Taylor, Kristin Clark 8
Taylor, Natalie 47
Taylor, Susan L. 10, 86
Terrell, Dorothy A. 24
Thomas, Franklin A. 5, 49
Thomas, Jefferson 88
Thomas-Graham, Pamela 29
Thompson, Cynthia Bramlett 50
Thompson, Don 56
Thompson, John W. 26
Tobin, Patricia 75
Travis, Tracey T. 94
Tribble, Israel, Jr. 8
Trotter, Lloyd G. 56
Trotter, Monroe 9
Tuckson, Reed V. 71
Tyson, Asha 39
Ussery, Terdema, II 29
Utendahl, John 23
VanDerZee, James 6
Vaughn, Gladys Gary 47
Vaughns, Cleopatra 46
Villarosa, Clara 85
Walker, A'lelia 14
Walker, Cedric 19
Walker, Madame C. J. 7
Walker, Maggie Lena 17
Walker, T. J. 7
Ward, Lloyd 21, 46
Ware, Carl H. 30
Washington, Alonzo 29
Washington, Mary T. 57
Washington, Regynald G. 44
Washington, Val 12
Wasow, Omar 15
Watkins, Donald 35
Watkins, Walter C., Jr. 24
Wattleton, Faye 9
Wein, Joyce 62
Wek, Alek 18, 63
Welburn, Edward T. 50
Wells-Barnett, Ida B. 8
Westbrook, Kelvin 50
Wharton, Clifton R., Jr. 7
White, Linda M. 45
White, Walter F. 4
Wilkins, Ray 47
Williams, Armstrong 29
Williams, Lindsey 75
Williams, O. S. 13
Williams, Paul R. 9
Williams, Ronald A. 57
Williams, Terrie 35
Williams, Walter E. 4
Williams, Wendy 62
Willie, Louis, Jr. 68
Wilson, Phill 9
Wilson, Sunnie 7, 55
Winfrey, Oprah 2, 15, 61
Woods, Jacqueline 52
Woods, Sylvia 34
Woodson, Robert L. 10

Wright, Antoinette 60
Wright, Charles H. 35
Wright, Deborah C. 25
Wright, Rayfield 70
Yoba, Malik 11
Zollar, Alfred 40

Dance

Acogny, Germaine 55
Adams, Jenoyne 60
Ailey, Alvin 8
Allen, Debbie 13, 42
Anderson, Lauren 72
Atkins, Cholly 40
Babatunde, Obba 35
Baker, Josephine 3
Bates, Peg Leg 14
Beatty, Talley 35
Brown, Ernest 80
Brown, Ronald K. 91
Byrd, Donald 10
Chanticleer, Raven 91
Clarke, Hope 14
Collins, Janet 33, 64
Davis, Chuck 33
de Lavallade, Carmen 78
Dove, Ulysses 5
Dunham, Katherine 4, 59
Ellington, Mercedes 34
Fagan, Garth 18
Falana, Lola 42
Glover, Savion 14
Hall, Arthur 39
Henson, Darrin 33
Hines, Gregory 1, 42
Jamison, Judith 7, 67
Jefferson, Denise 87
Johnson, Virginia 9
Jones, Bill T. 1, 46, 80
Jones, Doris W. 62
King, Alonzo 38
Lane, William Henry 90
LeTang, Henry 66
Manning, Frankie 78
Miller, Bebe 3
Mills, Florence 22
Mitchell, Arthur 2, 47
Moten, Etta 18
Muse, Clarence Edouard 21
Nash, Joe 55
Nicholas, Fayard 20, 57
Nicholas, Harold 20
Nichols, Nichelle 11
Polite, Carlene Hatcher 82
Pomare, Eleo 72
Powell, Maxine 8
Premice, Josephine 41
Primus, Pearl 6
Ray, Gene Anthony 47
Rhoden, Dwight 40
Ribeiro, Alfonso 17
Richardson, Desmond 39
Robinson, Bill "Bojangles" 11
Robinson, Cleo Parker 38
Robinson, Fatima 34
Robinson, LaVaughn 69
Rodgers, Rod 36
Sims, Howard "Sandman" 48
Slyde, Jimmy 70
Spears, Warren 52
Tyson, Andre 40
Vereen, Ben 4
Walker, Dianne 57

Washington, Fredi 10
Williams, Dudley 60
Zollar, Jawole Willa Jo 28

Education
Abani, Chris 77
Achebe, Chinua 6
Adams, Leslie 39
Adams-Ender, Clara 40
Adkins, Rutherford H. 21
Aidoo, Ama Ata 38
Ake, Claude 30
Alexander, Margaret Walker 22
Allen, Robert L. 38
Allen, Samuel W. 38
Allen-Buillard, Melba 55
Alston, Charles 33
Amadi, Elechi 40
Ammons, James H. 81
Anderson, Charles Edward 37
Appiah, Kwame Anthony 67
Archer, Dennis 7
Archie-Hudson, Marguerite 44
Aristide, Jean-Bertrand 6, 45
Asante, Molefi Kete 3
Aubert, Alvin 41
Awoonor, Kofi 37
Bacon-Bercey, June 38
Bahati, Wambui 60
Baiocchi, Regina Harris 41
Baker, Augusta 38
Baker, Gwendolyn Calvert 9
Baker, Houston A., Jr. 6
Baldwin, Cynthia A. 74
Ballard, Allen Butler, Jr. 40
Bambara, Toni Cade 10
Baraka, Amiri 1, 38
Barbee, Lloyd Augustus 71
Barboza, Anthony 10
Barnett, Marguerite 46
Barthé, Earl 78
Bath, Patricia E. 37
Batiste, Alvin 66
Beals, Melba Pattillo 15, 94
Beckham, Barry 41
Belgrave, Marcus 77
Bell, Derrick 6
Benberry, Cuesta 65
Benjamin, Tritobia Hayes 53
Berry, Bertice 8, 55
Berry, Mary Frances 7
Bethune, Mary McLeod 4
Biggers, John 20, 33
Black, Albert 51
Blackwell, David 79
Blakely, Edward J. 88
Blassingame, John Wesley 40
Blockson, Charles L. 42
Bluitt, Juliann S. 14
Bobo, Lawrence 60
Bogle, Donald 34
Bolden, Tonya 32
Bosley, Freeman, Jr. 7
Boyd, Melba Joyce 86
Boyd, T. B., III 6
Bradley, David Henry, Jr. 39
Branch, William Blackwell 39
Brathwaite, Kamau 36
Braun, Carol Moseley 4, 42
Briscoe, Marlin 37
Bromery, Randolph Wilson 85
Brooks, Avery 9
Brown, Claude 38

Brown, Joyce F. 25
Brown, Sterling Allen 10, 64
Brown, Uzee 42
Brown, Wesley 23
Brown, Willa 40
Bruce, Blanche Kelso 33
Brutus, Dennis 38
Bryan, Ashley F. 41
Bunch, Lonnie G., III 91
Burke, Selma 16
Burke, Yvonne Brathwaite 42
Burks, Mary Fair 40
Burnim, Mickey L. 48
Burroughs, Margaret Taylor 9
Burton, LeVar 8
Butler, Paul D. 17
Butts, Calvin O., III 9, 90
Callender, Clive O. 3
Campbell, Bebe Moore 6, 24, 59
Campbell, Mary Schmidt 43
Cannon, Katie 10
Carby, Hazel 27
Cardozo, Francis L. 33
Carnegie, Herbert 25
Carruthers, George R. 40
Carter, Joye Maureen 41
Carter, Kenneth 53
Carter, Warrick L. 27
Cartey, Wilfred 47
Carver, George Washington 4
Cary, Lorene 3
Cary, Mary Ann Shadd 30
Catlett, Elizabeth 2
Cayton, Horace 26
Chaney, John 67
Cheney-Coker, Syl 43
Clark, Joe 1
Clark, Kenneth B. 5, 52
Clark, Septima 7
Clarke, Cheryl 32
Clarke, George 32
Clarke, John Henrik 20
Clayton, Constance 1
Cleaver, Kathleen Neal 29
Clements, George 2
Clemmons, Reginal G. 41
Cobb, Jewel Plummer 42
Cobb, W. Montague 39
Cobb, William Jelani 59
Cobbs, Price M. 9
Cohen, Anthony 15
Cohen, Cathy J. 88
Cole, Johnnetta B. 5, 43
Coleman, William F., III 61
Colescott, Robert 69
Collins, Janet 33, 64
Collins, Marva 3, 71
Collins, Patricia Hill 67
Comer, James P. 6
Coney, PonJola 48
Conrad, Cecilia A. 94
Cook, Mercer 40
Cook, Samuel DuBois 14
Cook, Toni 23
Cooper, Afua 53
Cooper, Anna Julia 20
Cooper, Edward S. 6
Cooper Cafritz, Peggy 43
Copeland, Michael 47
Cortez, Jayne 43
Cosby, Bill 7, 26, 59
Cotter, Joseph Seamon, Sr. 40
Cottrell, Comer 11

Counter, S. Allen 74
Cox, Joseph Mason Andrew 51
Cox, William E. 68
Creagh, Milton 27
Crenshaw, Kimberlé Williams 88
Crew, Rudolph F. 16
Crew, Spencer R. 55
Cross, Dolores E. 23
Cruse, Harold 54
Cullen, Countee 8
Daly, Marie Maynard 37
Dathorne, O. R. 52
Davis, Allison 12
Davis, Angela 5
Davis, Angela J. 88
Davis, Arthur P. 41
Davis, Charles T. 48
Davis, Erroll B., Jr. 57
Davis, George 36
Davis, Milt 74
Dawson, William Levi 39
Days, Drew S., III 10
Deconge-Watson, Lovenia 55
Delany, Sadie 12
Delany, Samuel R., Jr. 9
Delco, Wilhemina R. 33
Delsarte, Louis 34
Dennard, Brazeal 37
Dickens, Helen Octavia 14, 64
Diop, Cheikh Anta 4
Dixon, Margaret 14
Dodson, Howard, Jr. 7, 52
Dodson, Owen Vincent 38
Dogan, Matthew Winifred 91
Donaldson, Jeff 46
Douglas, Aaron 7
Dove, Rita 6, 78
Dove, Ulysses 5
Draper, Sharon Mills 16, 43
Driskell, David C. 7
Drummond, William J. 40
Du Bois, David Graham 45
Dumas, Henry 41
Dunbar-Nelson, Alice Ruth Moore 44
Dunnigan, Alice Allison 41
Dunston, Georgia Mae 48
Dymally, Mervyn 42
Dyson, Michael Eric 11, 40
Early, Gerald 15
Edelin, Ramona Hoage 19
Edelman, Marian Wright 5, 42
Edley, Christopher 2, 48
Edley, Christopher F., Jr. 48
Edwards, Harry 2
Elders, Joycelyn 6
Elliot, Lorris 37
Ellis, Clarence A. 38
Ellison, Ralph 7
Epps, Archie C., III 45
Evans, Mari 26
Everett, Percival 93
Falconer, Etta Zuber 59
Fauset, Jessie 7
Favors, Steve 23
Feelings, Muriel 44
Ferguson, Ronald F. 75
Figueroa, John J. 40
Fleming, Raymond 48
Fletcher, Bill, Jr. 41
Floyd, Elson S. 41
Ford, Jack 39
Forman, James, Jr. 89

Foster, Ezola 28
Foster, Henry W., Jr. 26
Foster, William P. 88
Francis, Norman (C.) 60
Franklin, Hardy R. 9, 87
Franklin, John Hope 5, 77
Franklin, Robert M. 13
Frazier, E. Franklin 10
Freeman, Al, Jr. 11
Fryer, Roland G. 56
Fuller, A. Oveta 43
Fuller, Arthur 27
Fuller, Howard L. 37
Fuller, Solomon Carter, Jr. 15
Futrell, Mary Hatwood 33
Gaines, Ernest J. 7
Gates, Henry Louis, Jr. 3, 38, 67
Gates, Sylvester James, Jr. 15
Gayle, Addison, Jr. 41
George, Zelma Watson 42
Gerima, Haile 38, 80
Gibson, Donald Bernard 40
Giddings, Paula 11
Gilbert, John Wesley 91
Gill, Gerald 69
Gloster, Hugh Morris, Sr. 90
Golden, Marita 19
Gomes, Peter J. 15, 93
Gomez, Jewelle 30
Gomillion, Charles 90
Goodison, Lorna 71
Granville, Evelyn Boyd 36
Greenfield, Eloise 9
Guinier, Lani 7, 30
Guy-Sheftall, Beverly 13, 92
Hageman, Hans and Ivan 36
Hale, Lorraine 8
Hall, Stuart 78
Halliburton, Warren J. 49
Hamburg, Beatrix 84
Hammonds, Evelynn 69
Handy, W. C. 8
Hansberry, William Leo 11
Harding, Vincent 67
Harkless, Necia Desiree 19
Harper, Michael S. 34
Harris, Alice 7
Harris, Barry 68
Harris, Bill 72
Harris, Gary L. 87
Harris, Jay T. 19
Harris, Jessica B. 91
Harris, Patricia Roberts 2
Harris-Lacewell, Melissa 81
Harsh, Vivian Gordon 14
Harvey, William R. 42
Haskins, James 36, 54
Hathaway, Isaac Scott 33
Hayden, Carla D. 47
Hayden, Robert 12
Haynes, George Edmund 8
Henderson, Stephen E. 45
Henries, A. Doris Banks 44
Herenton, Willie W. 24, 81
Hill, Andrew 66
Hill, Anita 5, 65
Hill, Bonnie Guiton 20
Hill, Errol 40
Hill, Leslie Pinckney 44
Hill, Marc Lamont 80
Hilliard, Asa Grant, III 66
Hine, Darlene Clark 24
Hinton, William Augustus 8

Hoagland, Everett H. **45**
Hogan, Beverly Wade **50**
Holland, Endesha Ida Mae **3, 57**
Holt, Nora **38**
Hope, John **8**
Horton, James Oliver **58**
Houston, Charles Hamilton **4**
Hoyte, Lenon **50**
Hrabowski, Freeman A., III **22**
Huggins, Nathan Irvin **52**
Hughes, Ebony **57**
Hull, Akasha Gloria **45**
Humphries, Frederick **20**
Hunt, Darnell **92**
Hunt, Richard **6**
Hutcherson, Hilda Yvonne **54**
Hutson, Jean Blackwell **16**
Imes, Elmer Samuel **39**
Jackson, Edison O. **67**
Jackson, Fred James **25**
Jackson, Vera **40**
Jarrett, Vernon D. **42**
Jarvis, Charlene Drew **21**
Jarvis, Erich **67**
Jefferson, Denise **87**
Jeffries, Leonard **8**
Jenifer, Franklyn G. **2**
Jenkins, Ella **15**
Johns, Vernon **38**
Johnson, Anthony M. **92**
Johnson, Hazel **22**
Johnson, James Weldon **5**
Johnson, Katherine **61**
Johnson, Mordecai Wyatt **79**
Jones, Clara Stanton **51**
Jones, Edward P. **43, 67**
Jones, Gayl **37**
Jones, Ingrid Saunders **18**
Jones, Lois Mailou **13**
Joplin, Scott **6**
Jordan, June **7, 35**
Josey, E. J. **10**
Just, Ernest Everett **3**
Karenga, Maulana **10, 71**
Kay, Ulysses **37**
Keith, Damon J. **16, 74**
Kennedy, Florynce **12, 33**
Kennedy, Randall **40**
Kilpatrick, Carolyn Cheeks **16**
Kimbro, Dennis **10**
King, Preston **28**
King, Reatha Clark **65**
Kittles, Rick **51**
Komunyakaa, Yusef **9**
Kunjufu, Jawanza **3, 50**
Ladner, Joyce A. **42**
Lawrence, Jacob **4, 28**
Lawrence-Lightfoot, Sara **10**
Lee, Annie Frances **22**
Lee, Joe A. **45**
Leevy, Carrol M. **42**
Leffall, Lasalle **3, 64**
Lester, Julius **9**
Lewis, David Levering **9**
Lewis, Norman **39**
Lewis, Samella **25**
Lewis, Shirley A. R. **14**
Lewis, Thomas **19**
Liberia-Peters, Maria Philomena **12**
Lincoln, C. Eric **38**
Lindsey, Tommie **51**
Locke, Alain **10**
Logan, Rayford W. **40**

Lomax, Michael L. **58**
Long, Loretta **58**
Long, Richard Alexander **65**
Lorde, Audre **6**
Loury, Glenn **36**
Loving, Alvin, Jr. **35, 53**
Lowry, A. Leon **60**
Lucy Foster, Autherine **35**
Luper, Clara **94**
Lyttle, Hulda Margaret **14**
Mackey, Nathaniel **75**
Major, Clarence **9**
Malveaux, Floyd **54**
Manley, Audrey Forbes **16**
Marable, Manning **10**
Markham, E. A. **37**
Marsalis, Ellis **90**
Marshall, Paule **7, 77**
Masekela, Barbara **18**
Mason, Herman, Jr. **83**
Mason, Ronald **27**
Massey, Walter E. **5, 45**
Massie, Samuel P., Jr. **29**
Matejka, Adrian **87**
Maupin, John E., Jr. **92**
Mayhew, Richard **39**
Maynard, Robert C. **7**
Maynor, Dorothy **19**
Mayo, Whitman **32**
Mays, Benjamin E. **7**
McBay, Henry C. **91**
McCarty, Osceola **16**
McCullough, Geraldine **58, 79**
McDaniel, Randall Cornell **81**
McKay, Nellie Yvonne **17, 57**
McLendon, John B., Jr. **89**
McMillan, Terry **4, 17, 53**
McMurray, Georgia L. **36**
McPherson, James Alan **70**
McWhorter, John **35**
Mell, Patricia **49**
Memmi, Albert **37**
Meredith, James H. **11**
Millender-McDonald, Juanita **21, 61**
Mitchell, Corinne **8**
Mitchell, Nicole **66**
Mitchell, Sharon **36**
Mofolo, Thomas Mokopu **37**
Mollel, Tololwa **38**
Mongella, Gertrude **11**
Moody-Adams, Michele **76**
Mooney, Paul **37**
Moore, Barbara C. **49**
Moore, Harry T. **29**
Moore, Melba **21**
Morón, Alonzo G. **91**
Morrison, Keith **13**
Morrison, Sam **50**
Morrison, Toni **2, 15, 86**
Moses, Robert Parris **11**
Moton, Robert Russa **83**
Mphalele, Es'kia (Ezekiel) **40**
Mudimbe, V. Y. **61**
Mullen, Harryette **34**
Murray, Pauli **38**
Nabrit, Samuel Milton **47**
Nance, Cynthia **71**
Naylor, Gloria **10, 42**
Neal, Larry **38**
Neal, Mark Anthony **74**
Newkirk, Pamela **69**
Newman, Lester C. **51**
N'Namdi, George R. **17**

Norman, Maidie **20**
Nour, Nawal M. **56**
Obadele, Imari **84**
Ogletree, Charles, Jr. **12, 47**
Ojikutu, Bisola **65**
Oliver, Kimberly **60**
Onwueme, Tess Osonye **23**
Onwurah, Ngozi **38**
Owens, Helen **48**
Page, Alan **7**
Page, Inman **82**
Paige, Rod **29**
Painter, Nell Irvin **24, 88**
Palmer, Everard **37**
Parker, Kellis E. **30**
Patterson, Frederick Douglass **12**
Patterson, Mary Jane **54**
Patterson, Orlando **4**
Payton, Benjamin F. **23**
Perry, Warren **56**
Peters, Margaret **43**
Peters, Matilda **43**
Peterson, James **81**
Pickett, Cecil **39**
Pinckney, Bill **42**
Pindell, Howardena **55**
Piper, Adrian **71**
Player, Willa B. **43**
Pollard, William L. **91**
Porter, James A. **11**
Poussaint, Alvin F. **5, 67**
Powell, Benny **87**
Price, Florence **37**
Price, Glenda **22**
Price, Richard **51**
Primus, Pearl **6**
Prophet, Nancy Elizabeth **42**
Purnell, Silas **59**
Puryear, Martin **42**
Putney, Martha S. **75**
Quarles, Benjamin Arthur **18**
Querino, Manuel Raimundo **84**
Quigless, Helen G. **49**
Rahman, Aishah **37**
Ramphele, Mamphela **29**
Reagon, Bernice Johnson **7**
Reddick, Lawrence Dunbar **20**
Redding, J. Saunders **26**
Redmond, Eugene **23**
Reid, Irvin D. **20**
Rhodes, Jewell Parker **84**
Ribeau, Sidney **70**
Rice, Condoleezza **3, 28, 72**
Rice, Louise Allen **54**
Richards, Hilda **49**
Riles, Wilson C. **79**
Robinson, Sharon **22**
Robinson, Spottswood W., III **22**
Rodriguez, Cheryl **64**
Rogers, Joel Augustus **30**
Rollins, Charlemae Hill **27**
Ross-Lee, Barbara **67**
Rouse, Cecilia **93**
Russell-McCloud, Patricia **17**
Salih, Al-Tayyib **37**
Sallee, Charles Louis, Jr. **38**
Satcher, David **7, 57**
Schomburg, Arthur Alfonso **9**
Sears, Stephanie **53**
Senior, Olive **37**
Shabazz, Betty **7, 26**
Shange, Ntozake **8, 89**
Shelton, Paula Young **86**

Shipp, E. R. **15**
Shirley, George **33**
Shockley, Ann Allen **84**
Simmons, Ruth J. **13, 38**
Sinkford, Jeanne C. **13**
Sisulu, Sheila Violet Makate **24**
Sizemore, Barbara A. **26**
Smith, Anna Deavere **6**
Smith, Barbara **20**
Smith, Jessie Carney **35**
Smith, John L. **22**
Smith, Mary Carter **26**
Smith, Tubby **18, 83**
Snowden, Frank M., Jr. **67**
Southern, Eileen **56**
Sowande, Fela **39**
Spearman, Leonard H. O., Sr. **81**
Spears, Warren **52**
Spikes, Dolores **18**
Spriggs, William **67**
Stanford, John **20**
Steele, Claude Mason **13**
Steele, Shelby **13, 82**
Stephens, Charlotte Andrews **14**
Stewart, Maria W. Miller **19**
Stewart, Tonea Harris **78**
Stone, Chuck **9**
Sudarkasa, Niara **4**
Sullivan, Louis **8**
Swygert, H. Patrick **22**
Talbert, Mary B. **77**
Tancil, Gladys Quander **59**
Tanksley, Ann **37**
Tatum, Beverly Daniel **42, 84**
Taylor, Helen (Lavon Hollingshed) **30**
Taylor, Susie King **13**
Terrell, Mary Church **9**
Thomas, Alma **14**
Thomas, Michael **69**
Thurman, Howard **3**
Tillis, Frederick **40**
Tobias, Channing H. **79**
Toler, Burl **80**
Tolson, Melvin **37**
Tribble, Israel, Jr. **8**
Trueheart, William E. **49**
Tucker, Rosina **14**
Turnbull, Charles Wesley **62**
Turnbull, Walter **13, 60**
Tutu, Desmond **6**
Tutu, Nontombi Naomi **57**
Tutuola, Amos **30**
Tyson, Andre **40**
Tyson, Asha **39**
Tyson, Neil deGrasse **15, 65**
Usry, James L. **23**
van Sertima, Ivan **25**
Vaughn, Viola **70**
Vega, Marta Moreno **61**
Velez-Rodriguez, Argelia **56**
Verna, Gelsy **70**
Wade-Gayles, Gloria Jean **41**
Walcott, Derek **5, 94**
Walker, George **37**
Wallace, Michele Faith **13**
Wallace, Perry E. **47**
Wallace, Phyllis A. **9**
Walters, Ronald **83**
Washington, Booker T. **4**
Watkins, Shirley R. **17**
Wattleton, Faye **9**
Weaver, Afaa Michael **37**

Wedgeworth, Robert W. **42**
Wells, Henrietta Bell **69**
Wells, James Lesesne **10**
Wells-Barnett, Ida B. **8**
Welsing, Frances Cress **5**
Wesley, Dorothy Porter **19**
Wesley, Richard **73**
West, Cornel **5, 33, 80**
Wharton, Clifton R., Jr. **7**
White, Charles **39**
White, Lois Jean **20**
Wilkens, J. Ernest, Jr. **43**
Wilkins, Roger **2, 84**
Williams, David Rudyard **50**
Williams, Fannie Barrier **27**
Williams, Gregory **11**
Williams, Patricia **11, 54**
Williams, Rhonda Y. **86**
Williams, Sherley Anne **25**
Williams, Walter E. **4**
Wilson, Donald E. **88**
Wilson, William Julius **22**
Woodruff, Hale **9**
Woodson, Carter G. **2**
Worrill, Conrad **12**
Wright, Antoinette **60**
Xuma, Madie Hall **59**
Yancy, Dorothy Cowser **42**
Young, Jean Childs **14**
Zook, Kristal Brent **62**

Fashion
Aberra, Amsale **67**
Bailey, Xenobia **11**
Banks, Jeffrey **17**
Banks, Tyra **11, 50**
Barboza, Anthony **10**
Beals, Jennifer **12**
Beckford, Tyson **11, 68**
Boateng, Ozwald **35**
Bond, Beverly **53**
Boyd, Suzanne **52**
Bridges, Sheila **36**
Brown, Joyce F. **25**
Burrows, Stephen **31**
Campbell, Naomi **1, 31**
Chanticleer, Raven **91**
Common **31, 63**
Darego, Agbani **52**
Dash, Damon **31**
Davidson, Jaye **5**
Davis, Mia Amber **94**
De' Alexander, Quinton **57**
Delice, Ronald **48**
Delice, Rony **48**
Dirie, Waris **56**
Ebanks, Selita **67**
Evans, Etu **55**
Gaskins, Eric **64**
Gibson, Ted **66**
Givhan, Robin Deneen **72**
Hall, Kevan **61**
Harold, Erika **54**
Henderson, Gordon **5**
Hendy, Francis **47**
Iman **4, 33, 87**
Iman, Chanel **66**
John, Daymond **23**
Johnson, Beverly **2**
Johnson, Eunice W. **83**
Jones, Carl **7**
Kani, Karl **10**
Kebede, Liya **59**

Keckley, Elizabeth **90**
Kelly, Patrick **3**
Kodjoe, Boris **34, 89**
Lars, Byron **32**
Luna, Donyale **88**
Malone, Maurice **32**
McGrath, Pat **72**
McKenzie, Jaunel **73**
Michele, Michael **31**
Niane, Katoucha **70**
Onwurah, Ngozi **38**
Powell, Maxine **8**
Reese, Tracy **54**
Rhymes, Busta **31**
Robinson, Patrick **19, 71**
Rochon, Lela **16**
Rowell, Victoria **13, 68**
Simmons, Kimora Lee **51, 83**
Sims, Naomi **29, 79**
Smaltz, Audrey **12**
Smith, B(arbara) **11**
Smith, Willi **8**
Smythe Haith, Mabel **61**
Steele, Lawrence **28**
Stoney, Michael **50**
Sy, Oumou **65**
Talley, André Leon **56**
Taylor, Karin **34**
Walker, T. J. **7**
Webb, Veronica **10**
Wek, Alek **18, 63**
White, Jessica **83**
Williams, Serena **20, 41, 73**

Film
Aaliyah **30**
Aaron, Quinton **82**
Adebimpe, Tunde **75**
Akinnuoye-Agbaje, Adewale **56**
Akomfrah, John **37**
Ali, Tatyana **73**
Allain, Stephanie **49**
Allen, Debbie **13, 42**
Alonso, Laz **87**
Amos, John **8, 62**
Anderson, Anthony **51, 77**
Anderson, Eddie "Rochester" **30**
Andrews, Tina **74**
Armah, Esther **87**
Awoonor, Kofi **37**
Babatunde, Obba **35**
Babyface **10, 31, 82**
Baker, Josephine **3**
Banks, Michelle **59**
Banks, Tyra **11, 50**
Barclay, Paris **37, 94**
Barnett, Etta Moten **56**
Bassett, Angela **6, 23, 62**
Beach, Michael **26**
Beals, Jennifer **12**
Beckford, Tyson **11, 68**
Belafonte, Harry **4, 65**
Bellamy, Bill **12**
Bennett, Louise **69**
Bentley, Lamont **53**
Berry, Fred "Rerun" **48**
Berry, Halle **4, 19, 57, 91**
Beyoncé **39, 70**
Billops, Camille **82**
Bivins, Michael **72**
Blackwood, Maureen **37**
Bleu, Corbin **65**
Bogle, Donald **34**

Bonet, Lisa **58**
Brady, Wayne **32, 71**
Brandy **14, 34, 72**
Breeze, Jean "Binta" **37**
Brooks, Golden **62**
Brooks, Hadda **40**
Brown, Chris **74**
Brown, Jim **11**
Brown, Tony **3**
Browne, Roscoe Lee **66**
Burnett, Charles **16, 68**
Byrd, Michelle **19**
Byrd, Robert **11**
Calloway, Cab **14**
Campbell, Naomi **1, 31**
Campbell-Martin, Tisha **8, 42**
Cannon, Nick **47, 73**
Cannon, Reuben **50**
Cara, Irene **77**
Carroll, Diahann **9**
Carroll, Rocky **74**
Carson, Lisa Nicole **21**
Cash, Rosalind **28**
Cedric the Entertainer **29, 60**
Chase, Debra Martin **49**
Cheadle, Don **19, 52**
Chestnut, Morris **31**
Chong, Rae Dawn **62**
Chweneyagae, Presley **63**
Cortez, Jayne **43**
Crothers, Scatman **19**
Curtis-Hall, Vondie **17**
Dandridge, Dorothy **3**
Daniels, Lee **36, 76**
Dash, Julie **4**
David, Keith **27**
Davidson, Jaye **5**
Davidson, Tommy **21**
Davis, Eisa **68**
Davis, Guy **36**
Davis, Ossie **5, 50**
Davis, Sammy, Jr. **18**
Davis, Viola **34, 76**
Dawn, Marpessa **75**
Dawson, Rosario **72**
De Bankolé, Isaach **78**
de Passe, Suzanne **25**
De Shields, André **72**
Dee, Ruby **8, 50, 68**
Devine, Loretta **24**
Dickerson, Ernest **6, 17**
Diesel, Vin **29**
Dieudonné **67**
Diggs, Taye **25, 63**
Dixon, Ivan **69**
DMX **28, 64**
Domingo, Colman **94**
Driskell, David C. **7**
Duke, Bill **3**
Duncan, Michael Clarke **26**
Dunham, Katherine **4, 59**
Dutton, Charles S. **4, 22**
Earthquake **55**
Ejiofor, Chiwetel **67**
Elba, Idris **49, 89**
Elder, Lonne, III **38**
Elise, Kimberly **32**
Emmanuel, Alphonsia **38**
Epps, Omar **23, 59**
Esposito, Giancarlo **9**
Evans, Darryl **22**
Everett, Francine **23**
Faison, Donald **50**

Faison, Frankie **55**
Fetchit, Stepin **32**
Fishburne, Laurence **4, 22, 70**
Fisher, Antwone **40**
Fisher, Gail **85**
Fletcher, Geoffrey **85**
Fox, Rick **27**
Fox, Vivica A. **15, 53**
Foxx, Jamie **15, 48**
Franklin, Carl **11**
Freeman, Al, Jr. **11**
Freeman, Morgan **2, 20, 62**
Freeman, Yvette **27**
Friday, Jeff **24**
Fuller, Charles **8**
Fuqua, Antoine **35**
Gaye, Nona **56**
George, Nelson **12**
Gerima, Haile **38, 80**
Gibbs, Marla **86**
Gibson, Tyrese **27, 62**
Givens, Adele **62**
Givens, Robin **4, 25, 58**
Glover, Danny **1, 24**
Glover, Donald **85**
Glover, Savion **14**
Goldberg, Whoopi **4, 33, 69**
Gooding, Cuba, Jr. **16, 62**
Gordon, Dexter **25**
Gossett, Louis, Jr. **7**
Gray, F. Gary **14, 49**
Greaves, William **38**
Grier, David Alan **28**
Grier, Pam **9, 31, 86**
Guillaume, Robert **3, 48**
Gunn, Moses **10**
Gurira, Danai **73**
Hairston, Jester **88**
Hall, Arsenio **58**
Hall, Juanita **62**
Hamilton, Lisa Gay **71**
Hamilton, Tanya **93**
Hampton, Henry **6**
Hardison, Kadeem **22**
Harewood, David **52**
Harper, Hill **32, 65**
Harris, Leslie **6**
Harris, Naomie **55**
Harris, Robin **7**
Hawkins, Screamin' Jay **30**
Hayes, Isaac **20, 58, 73**
Hayes, Teddy **40**
Hemsley, Sherman **19**
Henriques, Julian **37**
Henry, Lenny **9, 52**
Henson, Darrin **33**
Henson, Taraji P. **58, 77**
Hill, Lauryn **20, 53**
Hines, Gregory **1, 42**
Hooks, Robert **76**
Horne, Lena **5, 86**
Hounsou, Djimon **19, 45**
Houston, Whitney **7, 28, 83**
Howard, Sherri **36**
Howard, Terrence **59, 94**
Howell, Ayinde **91**
Hudlin, Reginald **9, 86**
Hudlin, Warrington **9**
Hudson, Ernie **72**
Hudson, Jennifer **63, 83**
Hughes, Albert **7**
Hughes, Allen **7**
Hughley, D. L. **23, 76**

Hurt, Byron 61
Ice Cube 8, 30, 60
Ice-T 6, 31
Ingram, Rex 5
Jackson, George 19
Jackson, Janet 6, 30, 68
Jackson, Rampage 83
Jackson, Samuel 8, 19, 63
Jean, Michaëlle; 70
Jean-Baptiste, Marianne 17, 46
Jean-Louis, Jimmy 76
Johnson, Beverly 2
Jones, James Earl 3, 49, 79
Jones, Orlando 30
Jones, Quincy 8, 30
Jorge, Seu 73
Julian, Hubert 90
Julien, Isaac 3
Kelley, Elijah 65
Keys, Alicia 32, 68
Khumalo, Leleti 51
King, Regina 22, 45
King, Woodie, Jr. 27
Kirby, George 14
Kitt, Eartha 16, 75
Kodjoe, Boris 34, 89
Kool Moe Dee 37
Kotto, Yaphet 7
Kunjufu, Jawanza 3, 50
Lane, Charles 3
Lathan, Sanaa 27
Lawrence, Martin 6, 27, 60
Lee, Joie 1
Lee, Malcolm D. 75
Lee, Spike 5, 19, 86
Lemmons, Kasi 20
LeNoire, Rosetta 37
Lester, Adrian 46
Lewis, Samella 25
Lil' Kim 28
Lincoln, Abbey 3, 88
Lindo, Delroy 18, 45
LisaRaye 27
LL Cool J 16, 49, 94
Long, Nia 17
Lover, Ed 10
Luke, Derek 61
Lumet, Jenny 80
Luna, Donyale 88
Lynch, Shola 61
Mac, Bernie 29, 61, 72
Malco, Romany 71
Mann, Tamela 92
Marsalis, Branford 34
Martin, Darnell 43, 78
Martin, Helen 31
Master P 21
Mbatha-Raw, Gugu 89
McBride, Chi 73
McDaniel, Hattie 5
McKee, Lonette 12
McKinney, Nina Mae 40
McQueen, Butterfly 6, 54
McQueen, Steve 84
Meadows, Tim 30
Mello, Breno 73
Merkerson, S. Epatha 47, 83
Micheaux, Oscar 7
Miller, Omar Benson 93
Miller, Wentworth 75
Mitchell, Kel 66
Mokae, Zakes 80
Mo'Nique 35, 84

Mooney, Paul 37
Moore, Chante 26
Moore, Juanita 83
Moore, Melba 21
Moore, Shemar 21
Morris, Garrett 31
Morrison, Vanessa 84
Morton, Joe 18
Mos Def 30
Moses, Gilbert 12
Moss, Carlton 17
Murphy, Eddie 4, 20, 61
Muse, Clarence Edouard 21
Nas 33
Nash, Johnny 40
Nash, Niecy 66
Neal, Elise 29
Nelson, Stanley 92
Newton, Thandie 26
Nicholas, Fayard 20, 57
Nicholas, Harold 20
Nichols, Nichelle 11
Norman, Maidie 20
Okonedo, Sophie 67
O'Neal, Ron 46
Onwurah, Ngozi 38
Oyelowo, David 82
Packer, Will 71
Palcy, Euzhan 94
Palmer, Keke 68
Parker, Nicole Ari 52
Parks, Gordon 1, 35, 58
Patton, Paula 62
Payne, Allen 13
Peck, Raoul 32
Perrineau, Harold, Jr. 51
Perry, Tyler 54
Phifer, Mekhi 25
Pierce, Wendell 90
Pinkett Smith, Jada 10, 41
Poitier, Sidney 11, 36
Poitier, Sydney Tamiia 65
Pounder, CCH 72
Pratt, Kyla 57
Preer, Evelyn 82
Prince 18, 65
Prince-Bythewood, Gina 31, 77
Pryor, Richard 3, 24, 56
Queen Latifah 1, 16, 58
Ralph, Sheryl Lee 18
Randle, Theresa 16
Reddick, Lance 52
Reuben, Gloria 15
Rhames, Ving 14, 50
Rhimes, Shonda Lynn 67
Rhymes, Busta 31
Richards, Beah 30
Richardson, LaTanya 71
Richardson, Salli 68
Ridley, John 69
Riggs, Marlon 5, 44
Roberts, Darryl 70
Roberts, Kimberly Rivers 72
Robinson, Matt 69
Robinson, Shaun 36
Rochon, Lela 16
Rock, Chris 3, 22, 66
Rock, The 29, 66
Rodrigues, Percy 68
Rolle, Esther 13, 21
Rollins, Howard E., Jr. 16
Rose, Anika Noni 70
Ross, Diana 8, 27

Roundtree, Richard 27
Rowell, Victoria 13, 68
St. Jacques, Raymond 8
St. John, Kristoff 25
Saldana, Zoe 72
Salter, Nikkole 73
Sands, Diana 87
Schultz, Michael A. 6
Scott, Hazel 66
Scott, Jill 29, 83
Sembène, Ousmane 13, 62
Shakur, Tupac 14
Shepherd, Sherri 55
Short, Columbus 79
Sidibe, Gabourey 84
Simpson, O. J. 15
Sinbad 1, 16
Sinclair, Madge 78
Singleton, John 2, 30
Sisqo 30
Smith, Anjela Lauren 44
Smith, Anna Deavere 6, 44
Smith, Jaden 82
Smith, Roger Guenveur 12
Smith, Tasha 73
Smith, Will 8, 18, 53
Smith, Willow 92
Snipes, Wesley 3, 24, 67
Souleymane, Mahamane 78
Sullivan, Maxine 37
Sykes, Wanda 48, 81
Tate, Larenz 15
Taylor, Meshach 4
Taylor, Regina 9, 46
Thigpen, Lynne 17, 41
Thomas, Sean Patrick 35
Thompson, Kenan 52
Thurman, Wallace 16
Tillman, George, Jr. 20
Torres, Gina 52
Torry, Guy 31
Toussaint, Lorraine 32
Townsend, Robert 4, 23
True, Rachel 82
Tucker, Chris 13, 23, 62
Tunie, Tamara 63
Turner, Tina 6, 27
Tyler, Aisha N. 36
Tyson, Cicely 7, 51
Uggams, Leslie 23
Underwood, Blair 7, 27, 76
Union, Gabrielle 31, 92
Usher 23, 56
Van Lierop, Robert 53
Van Peebles, Mario 2, 51
Van Peebles, Melvin 7
Vance, Courtney B. 15, 60
Vanity 67
Vereen, Ben 4
Walker, Eamonn 37
Wallace, William 75
Ward, Douglas Turner 42
Warfield, Marsha 2
Warner, Malcolm-Jamal 22, 36
Warren, Michael 27
Warwick, Dionne 18
Washington, Denzel 1, 16, 93
Washington, Fredi 10
Washington, Kerry 46
Waters, Ethel 7
Wayans, Damien 78
Wayans, Damon 8, 41
Wayans, Keenen Ivory 18

Wayans, Kim 80
Wayans, Marlon 29, 82
Wayans, Shawn 29
Weathers, Carl 10
Webb, Veronica 10
Wesley, Richard 73
Whitaker, Forest 2, 49, 67
White, Armond 80
White, Michael Jai 71
Whitfield, Lynn 18
Williams, Billy Dee 8
Williams, Clarence, III 26
Williams, Marco 53
Williams, Russell, II 70
Williams, Samm-Art 21
Williams, Saul 31
Williams, Vanessa A. 32, 66
Williams, Vanessa L. 4, 17
Williamson, Fred 67
Williamson, Mykelti 22
Wilson, Debra 38
Wilson, Dorien 55
Winfield, Paul 2, 45
Winfrey, Oprah 2, 15, 61
Witherspoon, John 38
Woodard, Alfre 9
Wright, Jeffrey 54
Yarbrough, Cedric 51
Yoba, Malik 11

**Government and politics--
international**
Abacha, Sani 11, 70
Abbott, Diane 9
Abiola, Moshood 70
Abubakar, Abdulsalami 66
Achebe, Chinua 6
Adebari, Rotimi 83
Ahidjo, Ahmadou 81
Akunyili, Dora Nkem 58
Ali Mahdi Mohamed 5
Amadi, Elechi 40
Amin, Idi 42
Amos, Valerie 41
Annan, Kofi Atta 15, 48
Aristide, Jean-Bertrand 6, 45
Arthur, Owen 33
Atta Mills, John 75
Augustine, Jean 53
Avant, Nicole A. 90
Awoonor, Kofi 37
Azikiwe, Nnamdi 13
Babangida, Ibrahim 4
Baker, Gwendolyn Calvert 9
Banda, Hastings Kamuzu 6, 54
Barnes, Melody 75
Barrow, Dean 69
Bartels, Peggielene 80
Bashir, Omar al- 77
Bedie, Henri Konan 21
Berry, Mary Frances 7
Biko, Steven 4
Bishop, Maurice 39
Biya, Chantal 89
Biya, Paul 28
Bizimungu, Pasteur 19
Boateng, Paul Yaw 56
Bongo, Ali Ben 80
Bongo, Omar 1, 79
Boye, Madior 30
Brown, Rosemary 62
Bunche, Ralph J. 5
Burnham, Forbes 66

Buthelezi, Mangosuthu Gatsha 9
Camara, Moussa Dadis 76
Césaire, Aimé 48, 69
Cham, Adongo Agada Akway 77
Charlemagne, Manno 11
Charles, Mary Eugenia 10, 55
Charles, Pierre 52
Chiluba, Frederick 56, 80
Chissano, Joaquim 7, 55, 67
Christie, Perry Gladstone 53
Christophe, Henri 9
Compaore, Blaise 87
Compton, John 65
Conneh, Sekou Damate, Jr. 51
Conté, Lansana 7, 76
Cools, Anne 64
Curling, Alvin 34
da Silva, Benedita 5
Dadié, Bernard 34
Dandala, Mvume 77
Davis, Ruth 37
Déby, Idriss 30
Diogo, Luisa Dias 63
Diop, Cheikh Anta 4
Diouf, Abdou 3
dos Santos, José Eduardo 43
Douglas, Denzil Llewellyn 53
Ekwensi, Cyprian 37
Eyadéma, Gnassingbé 7, 52
Fela 1, 42
Frazer, Jendayi 68
Gairy, Eric Matthew 83
Gbagbo, Laurent 43, 90
Gnassingbé, Faure 67
Golding, Bruce 78
Gordon, Pamela 17
Grant, Bernie 57
Guebuza, Armando 81
Habré, Hissène 6
Habyarimana, Juvenal 8
Haile Selassie 7
Haley, George Williford Boyce 21
Hani, Chris 6
Houphouët-Boigny, Félix 4, 64
Hussein, Lubna 80
Ifill, Gwen 28
Ingraham, Hubert A. 19
Isaac, Julius 34
Jagan, Cheddi 16
Jammeh, Yahya 23
Jawara, Dawda Kairaba 11
Jean, Michaëlle; 70
Jean, Wyclef 20, 86
Jonathan, Goodluck 83
Ka Dinizulu, Mcwayizeni 29
Kabbah, Ahmad Tejan 23
Kabila, Joseph 30
Kabila, Laurent 20
Kabunda, Kenneth 2
Kagame, Paul 54
Kariuki, J. M. 67
Kenyatta, Jomo 5
Kerekou, Ahmed (Mathieu) 1
Kibaki, Mwai 60
Kiir, Salva 85
Kikwete, Jakaya Mrisho 73
King, Oona 27
Koroma, Ernest Bai 84
Kufuor, John Agyekum 54, 82
Laraque, Paul 67
Lewis, Daurene 72
Liberia-Peters, Maria Philomena 12
Lumumba, Patrice 33

Luthuli, Albert 13
Maathai, Wangari 43
Mabuza, Lindiwe 18
Machel, Samora Moises 8
Magloire, Paul Eugène 68
Mandela, Nelson 1, 14, 77
Mandela, Winnie 2, 35
Manigat, Mirlande 90
Martelly, Michel 90
Masekela, Barbara 18
Masire, Quett 5
Mbeki, Govan A. 80
Mbeki, Thabo 14, 73
Mbuende, Kaire 12
Meles Zenawi 3
Mengistu, Haile Mariam 65
Mhlaba, Raymond 55
Mitchell, Keith 82
Mkapa, Benjamin W. 16, 77
Mobutu Sese Seko 1, 56
Mogae, Festus Gontebanye 19, 79
Moi, Daniel Arap 1, 35
Mongella, Gertrude 11
Motlanthe, Kgalema 74
Moyo, Dambisa 76
Moyo, Lovemore 76
Mswati III 56
Mugabe, Robert 10, 71
Mukoko, Jestina 75
Muluzi, Bakili 14, 76
Museveni, Yoweri 4
Mushikiwabo, Louise 88
Mutebi, Ronald 25
Muzorewa, Abel 85
Mwanawasa, Levy 72
Mwinyi, Ali Hassan 1, 77
Nascimento, Abdias do 93
Ndadaye, Melchior 7
Nelson, Sophia A. 93
Neto, António Agostinho 43
Ngilu, Charity 58
Ngubane, Ben 33
Nkoli, Simon 60
Nkomo, Joshua 4, 65
Nkrumah, Kwame 3
Nkurunziza, Pierre 78
Ntaryamira, Cyprien 8
Nujoma, Samuel 10
Nyanda, Siphiwe 21
Nyerere, Julius 5
Nzo, Alfred 15
Obasanjo, Olusegun 5, 22
Obasanjo, Stella 32, 56
Obote, Milton 63
Odinga, Raila 67
Okara, Gabriel 37
Ouattara, Alassane 90
Oyono, Ferdinand 38
Pascal-Trouillot, Ertha 3
Patterson, P. J. 6, 20
Pereira, Aristides 30
Perkins, Edward 5
Perry, Ruth 15
Pierre-Louis, Michèle 75
Pindling, Lynden 81
Pitt, David Thomas 10
Pitta, Celso 17
Préval, René 87
Ramaphosa, Cyril 3
Rawlings, Jerry 9
Rawlings, Nana Konadu Agyeman 13
Roberto, Holden 65

Robinson, Randall 7, 46
Sampson, Edith S. 4
Sanhá Malam Bacai 84
Sankara, Thomas 17
Sankoh, Foday 74
Savimbi, Jonas 2, 34
Sawyer, Amos 2
Senghor, Augustin Diamacoune 66
Senghor, Léopold Sédar 12, 66
Silva, Marina 80
Simpson-Miller, Portia 62
Sirleaf, Ellen Johnson 71
Sisulu, Walter 47
Skerrit, Roosevelt 72
Skinner, Kiron K. 65
Smith, Jennifer 21
Soglo, Nicephore 15
Spencer, Winston Baldwin 68
Tandja, Mamadou 33, 78
Taylor, Charles 20
Taylor, John (David Beckett) 16
Todman, Terence A. 55
Touré, Amadou Toumani 18
Touré, Sekou 6
Tsvangirai, Morgan 26, 72
Tutu, Desmond (Mpilo) 6, 44
Van Lierop, Robert 53
Vieira, João Bernardo 14, 84
Wade, Abdoulaye 66
Weah, George 58
Wharton, Clifton R., Jr. 7
Wharton, Clifton Reginald, Sr. 36
Williams, Eric Eustace 65
Wiwa, Ken 67
Yar'Adua, Umaru 69, 89
Yayi, Boni T. 84
Zuma, Jacob G. 33, 75
Zuma, Nkosazana Dlamini 34

Government and politics--U.S.
Adams, Floyd, Jr. 12
Adams, Grantley 82
Ahmed, Sharif 80
Alexander, Archie Alphonso 14
Alexander, Clifford 26
Allen, Claude 68
Allen, Ethel D. 13
Allen, Eugene 79
Archer, Dennis 7, 36
Arrington, Richard 24
Avant, Clarence 19, 86
Baker, Thurbert 22
Ballance, Frank W. 41
Baltimore, Richard Lewis, III 71
Barbee, Lloyd Augustus 71
Barrett, Andrew C. 12
Barrett, Jacqueline 28
Barry, Marion S. 7, 44
Bass, Karen 70
Bell, Michael 40
Bellamy, Terry 58
Belton, Sharon Sayles 9, 16
Berrien, Jacqueline A. 93
Berry, Edwin C. 81
Berry, Mary Frances 7
Berry, Theodore M. 31
Bethune, Mary McLeod 4
Bing, Dave 3, 59, 78
Blackwell, Kenneth, Sr. 61
Blackwell, Unita 17
Bobb, Robert C. 83
Bond, Julian 2, 35
Booker, Cory Anthony 68

Bosley, Freeman, Jr. 7
Bowman, Bertie 71
Boykin, Keith 14
Bradley, Jennette B. 40
Bradley, Thomas 2
Braun, Carol Moseley 4, 42
Brazile, Donna 25, 70
Brimmer, Andrew F. 2, 48
Brooke, Edward W. 8, 88
Brooks, Tyrone 59
Brown, Anthony G. 72
Brown, Byrd 49
Brown, Byron W. 72
Brown, Cora 33
Brown, Corrine 24, 90
Brown, Elaine 8
Brown, George Leslie 62
Brown, Jesse 6, 41
Brown, Kwame R. 91
Brown, Lee Patrick 24
Brown, Les 5
Brown, Ron 5
Brown, Willie 7, 85
Bruce, Blanche K. 33
Bryant, Wayne R. 6
Buckley, Victoria (Vicki) 24
Bunche, Ralph J. 5
Burke, Yvonne Brathwaite 42
Burris, Chuck 21
Burris, Roland W. 25, 75
Bush, Gordon 82
Butler, Jerry 26
Butts, Cassandra 78
Caesar, Shirley 19
Campbell, Bill 9, 76
Cardozo, Francis L. 33
Carson, André 69
Carson, Johnnie 85
Carson, Julia 23, 69
Carter, Pamela Lynn 67
Carter, Robert L. 51
Chavis, Benjamin 6
Chisholm, Shirley 2, 50
Christian-Green, Donna M. 17
Christie, Ron 83
Clarke, Yvette 92
Clay, William Lacy 8
Clayton, Eva M. 20
Cleaver, Eldridge 5
Cleaver, Emanuel 4, 45, 68
Clemente, Rosa 74
Clyburn, James E. 21, 71
Clyburn, Mignon 78
Cockrel, Kenneth V., Jr. 79
Cockrel, Kenneth Vern, Sr. 79
Coleman, Mary 46
Coleman, Michael B. 28, 79
Coleman, William T. 76
Collins, Barbara-Rose 7, 87
Collins, Cardiss 10, 80
Colter, Cyrus J. 36
Connerly, Ward 14
Conyers, John, Jr. 4, 45
Conyers, Monica 85
Cook, Mercer 40
Cose, Ellis 5, 50
Craig-Jones, Ellen Walker 44
Crockett, George W., Jr. 10, 64
Cummings, Elijah E. 24
Cunningham, Evelyn 23, 85
Currie, Betty 21
Currie, Ulysses 73
Davis, Angela 5

Davis, Artur 41
Davis, Benjamin O., Jr. 2, 43
Davis, Benjamin O., Sr. 4
Davis, Danny K. 24, 79
Davis, Gordon J. 76
Davis, James E. 50
Days, Drew S., III 10
De Priest, Oscar Stanton 80
DeJongh, John, Jr. 85
Delany, Martin R. 27
Delco, Wilhemina R. 33
Dellums, Ronald 2, 81
Diggs, Charles R. 21
Dinkins, David 4
Dixon, Julian C. 24
Dixon, Sharon Pratt 1
Dixon, Sheila 68
Dougherty, Mary Pearl 47
Douglas, Derek 88
Du Bois, W. E. B. 3
Dudley, Edward R. 58
Dukes, Hazel Nell 56
Dunbar-Nelson, Alice Ruth Moore 44
Dymally, Mervyn 42
Easley, Annie J. 61
Edmonds, Terry 17
Edwards, Donna 77
Elders, Joycelyn 6
Ellison, Keith 59
Ervin, Clark Kent 82
Espy, Mike 6
Evans, Melvin H. 88
Farmer, James 2, 64
Farrakhan, Louis 2
Farrell, Herman D., Jr. 81
Fattah, Chaka 11, 70
Fauntroy, Walter E. 11
Felix, Larry R. 64
Fenty, Adrian 60, 88
Ferguson, Roger W. 25
Fields, C. Virginia 25
Fields, Cleo 13
Fisher, Ada M. 76
Flake, Floyd H. 18
Fleming, Erik R. 75
Fletcher, Arthur A. 63
Flipper, Henry O. 3
Ford, Harold E(ugene) 42
Ford, Harold E(ugene), Jr. 16, 70
Ford, Jack 39
Ford, Johnny 70
Fortune, T. Thomas 6
Foster, Ezola 28
Foxx, Anthony 81
Franklin, Shirley 34, 80
Franks, Gary 2
Frazer, Jendayi 68
Frazier, Ryan 89
Fudge, Marcia L. 76
Fulani, Lenora 11
Fuller, Thomas O. 90
Gantt, Harvey 1
Garrett, Joyce Finley 59
Garvey, Marcus 1
Gaspard, Patrick 84
Gibson, Johnnie Mae 23
Gibson, Kenneth Allen 6
Gibson, William F. 6
Goode, W. Wilson 4
Gravely, Samuel L., Jr. 5, 49
Gray, Vincent C. 88
Gray, William H., III 3

Grimké, Archibald H. 9
Guinier, Lani 7, 30
Haley, George Williford Boyce 21
Hamer, Fannie Lou 6
Harmon, Clarence 26
Harris, Alice 7
Harris, Patricia Roberts 2
Harvard, Beverly 11
Hastie, William H. 8
Hastings, Alcee L. 16
Hatcher, Andrew T. 90
Hatcher, Richard G. 55
Hawkins, Augustus F. 68
Hayes, James C. 10
Henderson, Thelton E. 68
Henry, Aaron 19
Herenton, Willie W. 24, 81
Herman, Alexis M. 15
Hernandez, Aileen Clarke 13
Hill, Bonnie Guiton 20
Hilliard, Earl F. 24
Hobson, Julius W. 44
Holder, Eric H., Jr. 9, 76
Holmes, Amy 69
Holt Baker, Arlene 73
Horsford, Steven 88
Hughes, Dora 88
Ifill, Gwen 28
Irving, Larry, Jr. 12
Irvis, K. Leroy 67
Jackson, Alphonso R. 48
Jackson, Frank G. 76
Jackson, George 14
Jackson, Jesse 1, 27, 72
Jackson, Jesse, Jr. 14, 45, 81
Jackson, Lisa 77
Jackson, Mae 57
Jackson, Maynard 2, 41
Jackson, Shirley Ann 12
Jackson Lee, Sheila 20
Jacob, John E. 2
James, Sharpe 23, 69
Jarrett, Valerie 73
Jarvis, Charlene Drew 21
Jarvis, Kristen 85
Jefferson, William J. 25, 72
Johnson, Eddie Bernice 8, 90
Johnson, Hank, Jr. 80
Johnson, Harvey, Jr. 24, 82
Johnson, James Weldon 5
Johnson, Jeh C. 76
Johnson, Katherine (Coleman Goble) 61
Johnson, Kevin 70
Johnson, Leroy R. 89
Johnson, Norma L. Holloway 17
Johnson, Robert T. 17
Jones, Elaine R. 7, 45
Jones, Emil, Jr. 74
Jones, John 89
Jordan, Barbara 4, 78
Jordan, Vernon 3, 35
Kelley, Cliff 75
Kennard, William Earl 18
Keyes, Alan L. 11
Kidd, Mae Street 39
Kilpatrick, Carolyn Cheeks 16
Kilpatrick, Kwame 34, 71
Kincaid, Bernard 28
King, Martin Luther, III 20
Kirk, Ron 11, 75
Lafontant, Jewel Stradford 3, 51
Langford, Larry P. 74

Layton, William 87
Lee, Barbara 25
Leland, Mickey 2
Lewis, Delano 7
Lewis, John 2, 46, 83
Lewis, William Henry 89
Love, Reggie 77
Lowery, Myron 80
Majette, Denise 41
Mallett, Conrad, Jr. 16
Mallory, Mark 62
Marsh, Henry, III 32
Marshall, Bella 22
Marshall, Thurgood 1, 44
Martin, Louis E. 16
Martin, Ruby Grant 49
McCall, H. Carl 27
McGee, James D. 74
McGee, James Madison 46
McGlowan, Angela 64, 86
McHenry, Donald F. 83
McKinney, Cynthia 11, 52, 74
McKissick, Floyd B. 3
Meek, Carrie 6, 36
Meek, Kendrick 41, 89
Meeks, Gregory 25
Meeks, James T. 92
Melton, Frank 81
Menard, John Willis 90
Meredith, James H. 11
Metcalfe, Ralph 26
Mfume, Kweisi 6, 41
Millender-McDonald, Juanita 21, 61
Mitchell, Arthur Wergs 91
Mitchell, Parren J. 42, 66
Moore, Gwendolynne S. 55
Moore, Minyon 45
Morial, Ernest "Dutch" 26
Morial, Marc H. 20, 51
Morton, Azie Taylor 48
Morton, Ferdinand Q. 90
Moses, Robert Parris 11
Murrell, Sylvia Marilyn 49
Nagin, Ray 42, 57, 88
Nix, Robert N. C., Jr. 51
Norton, Eleanor Holmes 7, 93
Nutter, Michael 69
Obama, Barack 49, 74, 91
Obama, Michelle 61, 90
O'Leary, Hazel 6
Owens, Major 6
Page, Alan 7
Paige, Rod 29
Paterson, Basil A. 69
Paterson, David A. 59
Patrick, Deval 12, 61
Patterson, J. O., Jr. 80
Patterson, Louise 25
Payne, Donald M. 2, 57
Payne, William D. 60
Perez, Anna 1
Perkins, Edward 5
Perkins, James, Jr. 55
Perry, James 83
Perry, Lowell 30
Peterson, Karen Carter 90
Pinchback, P. B. S. 9
Pitts, Robb 84
Powell, Adam Clayton, Jr. 3
Powell, Colin 1, 28, 75
Powell, Debra A. 23
Powell, Michael 32
Pugh, Charles 81

Raines, Franklin Delano 14
Randolph, A. Philip 3
Rangel, Charles B. 3, 52, 85
Raoul, Kwame 55
Rapier, James T. 82
Rawlings-Blake, Stephanie 93
Redd, Dana 93
Reed, Kasim 82
Reeves, Gregory 49
Reeves, Martha 85
Reeves, Triette Lipsey 27
Rice, Condoleezza 3, 28, 72
Rice, Emmett J. 94
Rice, Norm 8
Rice, Susan E. 74
Richardson, Laura 81
Richardson, Rupert 67
Richmond, Cedric 93
Riles, Wilson C. 79
Roberts, Lillian 83
Robinson, Bishop L. 66
Robinson, Randall 7, 46
Rochon, Stephen W. 78
Rogers, Desirée 88
Rogers, Joe 27
Ross, Don 27
Rouse, Cecilia 93
Rush, Bobby 26, 76
Rustin, Bayard 4
Sampson, Edith S. 4
Sanders, Malika 48
Satcher, David 7, 57
Sawyer, Eugene 81
Sayles Belton, Sharon 9
Schmoke, Kurt 1, 48
Scott, David 41
Scott, Robert C. 23
Scott, Tim 87
Sewell, Terri 93
Shakur, Assata 6
Shavers, Cheryl 31
Shelton, Paula Young 86
Sherrod, Shirley 87
Simmons, E. Denise 79
Simmons, Jamal 72
Simpson, Carole 6, 30
Sisulu, Sheila Violet Makate 24
Slater, Rodney E. 15
Smith, Malcolm A. 75
Smith, Nate 49
Smith, Princella 86
Smyre, Calvin 90
Smythe Haith, Mabel 61
Spearman, Leonard H. O., Sr. 81
Spigner, Archie 81
Stanton, Robert 20
Staupers, Mabel K. 7
Steele, Michael 38, 73, 91
Stewart, Nzingha 89
Stokes, Carl 10, 73
Stokes, Louis 3
Stone, Chuck 9
Stoutt, H. Lavity 83
Strautmanis, Michael 87
Street, John F. 24
Sullivan, Louis 8
Sutphen, Mona 77
Sutton, Percy E. 42, 82
Terry, Clark 39
Thomas, Clarence 2, 39, 65
Thompson, Bennie G. 26
Thompson, Larry D. 39
Thompson, William C. 35

Tillman, Dorothy 76
Todman, Terence A. 55
Tolbert, Terence 74
Toote, Gloria E.A. 64
Towns, Edolphus 19, 75
Tribble, Israel, Jr. 8
Trotter, Donne E. 28
Tubbs Jones, Stephanie 24, 72
Tucker, C. Delores 12, 56
Turnbull, Charles Wesley 62
Turner, Henry McNeal 5
Usry, James L. 23
Vaughn, Gladys Gary 47
Von Lipsey, Roderick K. 11
Wallace, Phyllis A. 9
Washington, Harold 6
Washington, Val 12
Washington, Walter 45
Waters, Maxine 3, 67
Watkins, Joe 86
Watkins, Shirley R. 17
Watson, Diane 41
Watt, Melvin 26
Watts, J. C., Jr. 14, 38
Weaver, Robert C. 8, 46
Webb, Wellington 3, 81
West, Allen 89
Wharton, Clifton R., Jr. 7
Wharton, Clifton Reginald, Sr. 36
Wheat, Alan 14
White, Jesse 22, 75
White, Michael R. 5
Wilder, L. Douglas 3, 48
Williams, Anthony 21
Williams, Eddie N. 44
Williams, George Washington 18
Williams, Hosea Lorenzo 15, 31
Williams, Maggie 7, 71
Williams, Michael L. 86
Wilson, Frederica 92
Wilson, Margaret Bush 79
Wilson, Sunnie 7, 55
Woods, Abraham, Jr. 74
Wynn, Albert 25, 77
Young, Andrew 3, 48

Law
Alexander, Clifford 26
Alexander, Joyce London 18
Alexander, Sadie Tanner Mossell 22
Ali, Russlynn H. 92
Allen, Samuel W. 38
Amaker, Norman 63
Anderson, Reuben V. 81
Archer, Dennis 7, 36
Arnwine, Barbara 28
Bailey, Clyde 45
Baldwin, Cynthia A. 74
Banks, William 11
Barbee, Lloyd Augustus 71
Barrett, Andrew C. 12
Barrett, Jacqueline 28
Baugh, David 23
Bell, Derrick 6
Benham, Robert 78
Berrien, Jacqueline A. 93
Berry, Mary Frances 7
Berry, Theodore M. 31
Birch, Adolpho A., Jr. 85
Bishop, Sanford D., Jr. 24
Bolin, Jane 22, 59
Bolton, Terrell D. 25

Booker, Cory Anthony 68
Bosley, Freeman, Jr. 7
Boykin, Keith 14
Bradley, Thomas 2
Braun, Carol Moseley 4, 42
Brooke, Edward W. 8, 88
Brown, Byrd 49
Brown, Cora 33
Brown, Cupcake 63
Brown, Homer S. 47
Brown, Janice Rogers 43
Brown, Joe 29
Brown, Lee Patrick 1, 24
Brown, Ron 5
Bryant, Wayne R. 6
Bryant, William Benson 61
Bully-Cummings, Ella 48
Burke, Yvonne Brathwaite 42
Burris, Roland W. 25, 75
Butler, Louis 70
Butler, Paul D. 17
Bynoe, Peter C. B. 40
Campbell, Bill 9, 76
Carter, Pamela Lynn 67
Carter, Robert L. 51
Carter, Stephen L. 4
Cashin, Sheryll 63
Chambers, Julius 3
Chestnut, J. L., Jr. 73
Cleaver, Kathleen Neal 29
Clendenon, Donn 26, 56
Cochran, Johnnie 11, 39, 52
Coleman, James E., Jr. 79
Coleman, William T. 76
Colter, Cyrus J. 36
Conyers, John, Jr. 4, 45
Crenshaw, Kimberlé Williams 88
Darden, Christopher 13
Davis, Angela J. 88
Davis, Artur 41
Davis, Gordon J. 76
Days, Drew S., III 10
DeFrantz, Anita 37
Diggs-Taylor, Anna 20
Dillard, Godfrey J. 45
Dinkins, David 4
Dixon, Sharon Pratt 1
Edelman, Marian Wright 5, 42
Edley, Christopher 2, 48
Edley, Christopher F., Jr. 48
Ellington, E. David 11
Ephriam, Mablean 29
Ervin, Clark Kent 82
Espy, Mike 6
Evans, Warren C. 76
Farmer-Paellmann, Deadria 43
Feemster, Herbert 72
Fenty, Adrian 60, 88
Fields, Cleo 13
Finner-Williams, Paris Michele 62
Fisher, Ada Lois Sipuel 76
Ford, Wallace 58
Forman, James, Jr. 89
Foxx, Anthony 81
Frazier-Lyde, Jacqui 31
Freeman, Charles 19
Gaines, Lloyd 79
Gary, Willie E. 12
Gibson, Johnnie Mae 23
Glover, Nathaniel, Jr. 12
Gomez-Preston, Cheryl 9
Gordon-Reed, Annette 74
Gourdin, Edward O. 93

Graham, Lawrence Otis 12
Gray, Fred 37
Gray, Willie 46
Greenhouse, Bunnatine 57
Grimké, Archibald H. 9
Guinier, Lani 7, 30
Haley, George Williford Boyce 21
Hall, Elliott S. 24
Harris, Kamala D. 64
Harris, Maya Lakshmi 88
Harris, Patricia Roberts 2
Harvard, Beverly 11
Hassell, Leroy Rountree, Sr. 41
Hastie, William H. 8
Hastings, Alcee L. 16
Hatcher, Richard G. 55
Hatchett, Glenda 32
Hawkins, Augustus F. 68
Hawkins, Steven 14
Hayes, Dennis 54
Haywood, Margaret A. 24
Henderson, Thelton E. 68
Higginbotham, A. Leon, Jr. 13, 25
Hill, Anita 5, 65
Hillard, Terry 25
Hills, Oliver W. 24
Holder, Eric H., Jr. 9, 76
Hollowell, Donald L. 57
Holton, Hugh, Jr. 39
Hooks, Benjamin L. 2, 85
Houston, Charles Hamilton 4
Hubbard, Arnette Rhinehart 38
Hunter, Billy 22
Hurtt, Harold 46
Isaac, Julius 34
Jackson, Maynard 2, 41
Jackson Lee, Sheila 20
Johnson, Harry E. 57
Johnson, James Weldon 5
Johnson, Jeh C. 76
Johnson, Leroy R. 89
Johnson, Norma L. Holloway 17
Jones, Elaine R. 7, 45
Jones, Van 70
Jordan, Eddie 82
Jordan, Vernon E. 3, 35
Kearse, Amalya Lyle 12
Keith, Damon J. 16, 74
Kennard, William Earl 18
Kennedy, Florynce 12, 33
Kennedy, Randall 40
Kibaki, Mwai 60
Kirk, Ron 11, 75
Lafontant, Jewel Stradford 3, 51
Lewis, Delano 7
Lewis, Reginald F. 6
Lewis, William Henry 89
Lloyd, Reginald 64
Majette, Denise 41
Mallett, Conrad, Jr. 16
Mandela, Nelson 1, 14, 77
Marsh, Henry, III 32
Marshall, Thurgood 1, 44
Mathis, Greg 26
McAnulty, William E., Jr. 66
McCrary Anthony, Crystal 70
McDonald, Gabrielle Kirk 20
McDougall, Gay J. 11, 43
McKinnon, Isaiah 9
McKissick, Floyd B. 3
McPhail, Sharon 2
Meeks, Gregory 25
Melton, Harold D. 79

Mitchell, Arthur Wergs 91
Mitchell, Clarence M., Jr. 88
Moose, Charles 40
Morial, Ernest "Dutch" 26
Morton, Ferdinand Q. 90
Morton, Frederick A., Jr. 93
Motley, Constance Baker 10, 55
Muhammad, Ava 31
Murray, Pauli 38
Nance, Cynthia 71
Napoleon, Benny N. 23
Nash, Shannon King 84
Nelson, Sophia A. 93
Nix, Robert N. C., Jr. 51
Noble, Ronald 46
Nunn, Annetta 43
Obama, Michelle 61, 90
Ogletree, Charles, Jr. 12, 47
Ogunlesi, Adebayo O. 37
Oliver, Jerry 37
Page, Alan 7
Parker, Barrington D. 92
Parker, Kellis E. 30
Parks, Bernard C. 17
Parsons, James 14
Parsons, Richard Dean 11, 33
Pascal-Trouillot, Ertha 3
Paterson, Basil A. 69
Patrick, Deval 12
Payne, Ulice 42
Payton, John 48
Perry, Lowell 30
Philip, Marlene Nourbese 32
Pincham, R. Eugene, Sr. 69
Powell, Michael 32
Quince, Peggy A. 69
Ramsey, Charles H. 21, 69
Raoul, Kwame 55
Rawlinson, Johnnie B. 79
Ray, Charlotte E. 60
Redding, Louis L. 26
Reed, Kasim 82
Reynolds, Star Jones 10, 27, 61
Rice, Constance LaMay 60
Richie, Leroy C. 18
Robinson, Bishop L. 66
Robinson, Malcolm S. 44
Robinson, Randall 7, 46
Roundtree, Dovey 80
Russell-McCloud, Patricia 17
Sampson, Edith S. 4
Schmoke, Kurt 1, 48
Sears, Leah Ward 5, 79
Smith, DeMaurice 92
Solomon, Jimmie Lee 38
Sparks, Corinne Etta 53
Stokes, Louis 3
Stout, Juanita Kidd 24
Strautmanis, Michael 87
Sutton, Percy E. 42, 82
Taylor, John (David Beckett) 16
Thomas, Arthur Ray 52
Thomas, Clarence 2, 39, 65
Thomas, Franklin A. 5, 49
Thompson, Larry D. 39
Touré, Faya Ora Rose 56
Tubbs Jones, Stephanie 24, 72
Van Lierop, Robert 53
Vanzant, Iyanla 17, 47
Wagner, Annice 22
Wainwright, Joscelyn 46
Walker, Cora T. 68
Wallace, Perry E. 47

Ward, Benjamin 68
Washington, Harold 6
Watkins, Donald 35
Watt, Melvin 26
Wharton, Clifton Reginald, Sr. 36
Wilder, L. Douglas 3, 48
Wilkins, David 77
Williams, Ann Claire 82
Williams, Evelyn 10
Williams, Gregory 11
Williams, Patricia 11, 54
Williams, Willie L. 4
Wilson, Jimmy 45
Worthy, Kym 84
Wright, Bruce McMarion 3, 52
Wynn, Albert 25, 77

Military

Abacha, Sani 11, 70
Adams Early, Charity 13, 34
Adams-Ender, Clara 40
Alexander, Margaret Walker 22
Amin, Idi 42
Archer, Lee, Jr. 79
Babangida, Ibrahim 4
Baker, Vernon Joseph 65, 87
Bashir, Omar al- 77
Black, Barry C. 47
Bolden, Charles Frank, Jr. 7, 78
Brashear, Carl 29
Brown, Anthony G. 72
Brown, Erroll M. 23
Brown, Jesse 6, 41
Brown, Jesse Leroy 31
Brown, Willa 40
Bullard, Eugene 12
Cadoria, Sherian Grace 14
Chissano, Joaquim 7, 55, 67
Christophe, Henri 9
Clemmons, Reginal G. 41
Compaore, Blaise 87
Conté, Lansana 7, 76
Cooke, Marcia 60
Davis, Benjamin O., Jr. 2, 43
Davis, Benjamin O., Sr. 4
Drew, Alvin, Jr. 67
Duggins, George 64
Europe, James Reese 10
Eyadéma, Gnassingbé 7, 52
Fields, Evelyn J. 27
Flipper, Henry O. 3
Gravely, Samuel L., Jr. 5, 49
Gregory, Frederick 8, 51
Guéï, Robert 66
Habré, Hissène 6
Habyarimana, Juvenal 8
Harris, Marcelite Jordan 16
Healy, Michael 90
Honoré, Russel L. 64
Howard, Michelle 28
Jackson, Fred James 25
James, Daniel, Jr. 16
Johnson, Hazel 22
Johnson, Shoshana 47
Julian, Hubert 90
Kagame, Paul 54
Kerekou, Ahmed (Mathieu) 1
Kiir, Salva 85
King, Teresa 80
Laraque, Paul 67
Lawrence, Robert H., Jr. 16
Lyles, Lester 31
Maceo, Antonio 82

Magloire, Paul Eugène 68
Matthews, Mark 59
Miller, Dorie 29
Nkunda, Laurent 75
Nyanda, Siphiwe 21
Obasanjo, Olusegun 5, 22
Perry, Herman 89
Petersen, Frank E. 31
Powell, Colin 1, 28, 75
Pratt, Geronimo 18
Rawlings, Jerry 9
Reason, J. Paul 19
Rochon, Stephen W. 78
Rogers, Alan G. 72
Scantlebury, Janna 47
Smalls, Robert 82
Snow, Samuel 71
Stanford, John 20
Staupers, Mabel K. 7
Stokes, Louis 3
Touré, Amadou Toumani 18
Von Lipsey, Roderick K. 11
Watkins, Perry 12
West, Togo, D., Jr. 16
Wilson, Jimmy 45
Wright, Lewin 43
Young, Charles 77

Music

Aaliyah 30
Ace, Johnny 36
Adams, Johnny 39
Adams, Leslie 39
Adams, Oleta 18
Adams, Yolanda 17, 67
Adderley, Julian "Cannonball" 30
Adderley, Nat 29
Ade, King Sunny 41
Adebimpe, Tunde 75
Afro, Teddy 78
Akon 68
Albright, Gerald 23
Alert, Kool DJ 33
Ali, Rashied 79
Allen, Betty 83
Allen, Geri 92
Amerie 52
Anderson, Carl 48
Anderson, Fred 87
Anderson, Marian 2, 33
apl.de.ap 84
Ardoin, Alphonse 65
Armatrading, Joan 32
Armstrong, Louis 2
Armstrong, Vanessa Bell 24
Arroyo, Marina 30
Ashanti 37
Ashford, Nickolas 21
Ashong, Derrick 86
Astatke, Mulatu 81
Atkins, Juan 50
Austin, Lovie 40
Austin, Patti 24
Avant, Clarence 19, 86
Avant, Nicole A. 90
Ayers, Roy 16
Babyface 10, 31, 82
Baca, Susana 80
Badu, Erykah 22
Bailey, Buster 38
Bailey, DeFord 33
Bailey, Pearl 14
Bailey, Philip 63

Bailey Rae, Corinne 83
Baiocchi, Regina Harris 41
Baker, Anita 21, 48
Baker, Josephine 3
Baker, LaVern 26
Ballard, Hank 41
Bambaataa, Afrika 34
Banner, David 55
Banton, Buju 93
Barker, Danny 32
Barnes, Lloyd 77
Barnes, Roosevelt "Booba" 33
Barrino, Fantasia 53, 94
Basie, Count 23
Bassey, Shirley 25
Batiste, Alvin 66
Battle, Kathleen 70
Baylor, Helen 36
Bebey, Francis 45
Bechet, Sidney 18
Beenie Man 32
Belafonte, Harry 4, 65
Belgrave, Marcus 77
Belle, Regina 1, 51
Benét, Eric 28, 77
Benjamin, Andre 45
Bennett, Estelle 77
Bentley, Lamont 53
Berry, Chuck 29
Betts, Keter 85
Beverly, Frankie 25
Beyoncé 39, 70
Bibb, Eric 49
Big Daddy Kane 79
Bivins, Michael 72
Black Thought 63
Blackman, Toni 86
Blade, Brian 88
Blake, Eubie 29
Blakey, Art 37
Blanchard, Terence 43
Bland, Bobby "Blue" 36
Bleu, Corbin 65
Blige, Mary J. 20, 34, 60
Blondy, Alpha 30
Blow, Kurtis 31
B.o.B. 91
Bolden, Buddy 39
Bond, Beverly 53
Bonds, Margaret 39
Bonga, Kuenda 13
Boulogne, Joseph, Chevalier de
   Saint-Georges 94
Bow Wow 35
Boyz II Men 82
Bradley, J. Robert 65
Brae, C. Michael 61
Brandy 14, 34, 72
Braxton, Toni 15, 61, 91
Bridgetower, George 78
Bridgewater, Dee Dee 32, 92
Brooks, Avery 9
Brooks, Hadda 40
Broonzy, Big Bill 82
Brown, Angela M. 54
Brown, Anne 76
Brown, Bobby 58
Brown, Carlinhos 81
Brown, Charles 23
Brown, Chris 74
Brown, Chuck 78
Brown, Clarence Gatemouth 59
Brown, Clifford 86

Brown, Foxy 25
Brown, James 15, 60
Brown, Melanie 73
Brown, Nappy 73
Brown, Oscar, Jr. 53
Brown, Patrick "Sleepy" 50
Brown, Ruth 90
Brown, Uzee 42
Brownlee, Lawrence 88
Bumbry, Grace 5
Burke, Solomon 31, 86
Burleigh, Henry Thacker 56
Burning Spear 79
Burns, Eddie 44
Burnside, R. L. 56
Busby, Jheryl 3, 74
Butler, George, Jr. 70
Butler, Jerry 26
Butler, Jonathan 28
Caesar, Shirley 19
Cage, Byron 53
Calloway, Cab 1
Campbell-Martin, Tisha 8, 42
Cannon, Nick 47, 73
Carey, Mariah 32, 53, 69
Carr, Kurt 56
Carr, Leroy 49
Carroll, Diahann 9
Carter, Benny 46
Carter, Betty 19
Carter, Nell 39
Carter, Regina 23
Carter, Warrick L. 27
Cartiér, Xam Wilson 41
Caymmi, Dorival 72
Cee-Lo 70
Chamillionaire 82
Chanté, Keshia 50
Chapman, Tracy 26
Charlemagne, Manno 11
Charles, Ray 16, 48
Cheatham, Doc 17
Checker, Chubby 28
Chenault, John 40
Christie, Angella 36
Chuck D 9
Ciara 56
Clark, Mattie Moss 61
Clark-Cole, Dorinda 66
Clarke, Kenny 27
Clark-Sheard, Karen 22
Clemons, Clarence 41
Cleveland, James 19
Cliff, Jimmy 28, 92
Clinton, George 9, 93
Cole, Keyshia 63
Cole, Nat "King" 17
Cole, Natalie 17, 60, 84
Coleman, Ornette 39, 69
Coleridge-Taylor, Samuel 75
Collins, Albert 12
Collins, Bootsy 31
Collins, Lyn 53
Coltrane, Alice 70
Coltrane, John 19
Coltrane, Ravi 71
Combs, Sean 17, 43, 92
Common 31, 63
Conrad, Barbara Smith 90
Cook, Charles "Doc" 44
Cook, Will Marion 40
Cooke, Sam 17
Coppola, Imani Francesca 82

Cortez, Jayne 43
Count Basie 23
Cowboy Troy 54
Cox, Deborah 28
Cox, Ida 42
Craig, Carl 31, 71
Crawford, Hank 77
Crawford, Randy 19
Cray, Robert 30
Creagh, Milton 27
Crocker, Frankie 29
Crothers, Scatman 19
Crouch, Andraé 27
Crowder, Henry 16
Da Don, Polow 86
Daemyon, Jerald 64
D'Angelo 27
Danjah, Terror 91
Dara, Olu 35
Dash, Damon 31
Dash, Darien 29
David, Craig 31, 53
Davis, Anthony 11
Davis, Gary 41
Davis, Guy 36
Davis, Miles 4
Davis, Sammy, Jr. 18
Davis, Tyrone 54
Dawson, William Levi 39
Dawuni, Rocky 94
de Passe, Suzanne 25
DeBarge, El 89
Deezer D 53
Dennard, Brazeal 37
Derülo, Jason 93
DeVaughn, Raheem 91
Dickenson, Vic 38
Diddley, Bo 39, 72
Dixon, Bill 87
Dixon, Dean 68
Dixon, Willie 4
DJ Jazzy Jeff 32
DJ Lance Rock 94
DMX 28, 64
Dobbs, Mattiwilda 34
Domino, Fats 20
Donegan, Dorothy 19
Dorsey, Lee 65
Dorsey, Thomas 15
Downing, Will 19
Drake 86
Dre, Dr. 10, 14, 30
Dube, Lucky 77
Duke, George 21
Dumas, Henry 41
Duncan, Todd 76
Dunner, Leslie B. 45
Duplechan, Larry 55
Dupri, Jermaine 13, 46
Durham, Bobby 73
Dworkin, Aaron P. 52
Earthquake 55
Eckstine, Billy 28
Edmonds, Tracey 16, 64
Edwards, Esther Gordy 43
Eldridge, Roy 37
Ellington, Duke 5
Elliott, Missy 31, 90
Ellis, Alton 74
Escobar, Damien 56
Escobar, Tourie 56
Estelle 75
Estes, Simon 28

Estes, Sleepy John 33
Eubanks, Kevin 15
Europe, James Reese 10
Evans, Faith 22
Eve 29
Evora, Cesaria 12
Fabolous 93
Falana, Lola 42
Farmer, Art 38
Fat Boys 92
Feemster, Herbert 72
Fela 1, 42
Ferrell, Rachelle 29
Ferrer, Ibrahim 41
Fiasco, Lupe 64
50 Cent 46, 83
Fiona, Melanie 84
Fitzgerald, Ella 8, 18
Flack, Roberta 19
Flanagan, Tommy 69
Flavor Flav 67
Flo Rida 78
Ford, T-Model 91
Ford, Vincent 75
Forté, John 74
Fortune, James 92
Foster, George "Pops" 40
Foster, William P. 88
Foxx, Jamie 15, 48
Franklin, Aretha 11, 44
Franklin, Kirk 15, 49
Franti, Michael 93
Freelon, Nnenna 32
Freeman, Paul 39
Freeman, Yvette 27
Fresh, Doug E. 93
Fuller, Blind Boy 86
Fuqua, Antoine 35
Fuqua, Harvey 90
Gaines, Grady 38
Gamble, Kenny 85
Garner, Erroll 76
Garrett, Sean 57
Gaye, Marvin 2
Gaye, Nona 56
Gaynor, Gloria 36
George, Zelma Watson 42
Ghostface Killah 90
Gibson, Althea 8, 43
Gibson, Tyrese 27, 62
Gil, Gilberto 53
Gill, Johnny 51
Gillespie, Dizzy 1
Ginuwine 35
Glover, Corey 34
Goapele 55
Golson, Benny 37
Goodman, Al 87
Gordon, Dexter 25
Gordy, Berry, Jr. 1
Gotti, Irv 39
Grae, Jean 51
Grandmaster Flash 33, 60
Graves, Denyce Antoinette 19, 57
Gray, F. Gary 14, 49
Gray, Macy 29
Greaves, William 38
Greely, M. Gasby 27
Green, Al 13, 47, 74
Green, Grant 56
Greene, Jimmy 74
Griffey, Dick 89
Griffin, Johnny 71

Griffin, LaShell 51
Griffiths, Marcia 29
Grist, Reri 84
Güines, Tata 69
Guru 84
Guy, Buddy 31
Haddon, Dietrick 55
Hailey, JoJo 22
Hailey, K-Ci 22
Hairston, Jester 88
Hall, Aaron 57
Hall, Juanita 62
Hamilton, Anthony 61
Hammond, Fred 23
Hammond, Lenn 34
Hampton, Lionel 17, 41
Hancock, Herbie 20, 67
Handy, W. C. 8
Hardin Armstrong, Lil 39
Harper, Ben 34, 62
Harrell, Andre 9, 30
Harris, Barry 68
Harris, Corey 39, 73
Hart, Alvin Youngblood 61
Hathaway, Donny 18
Hathaway, Lalah 57, 88
Hawkins, Coleman 9
Hawkins, Erskine 14
Hawkins, Screamin' Jay 30
Hawkins, Tramaine 16
Hawkins, Walter 87
Hayes, Isaac 20, 58, 73
Hayes, Roland 4
Hayes, Teddy 40
Haynes, Roy 87
Heavy D 58
Hemphill, Jessie Mae 33, 59
Henderson, Fletcher 32
Hendricks, Barbara 3, 67
Hendrix, Jimi 10
Hendryx, Nona 56
Henry, Clarence "Frogman" 46
Higginbotham, J. C. 37
Higginsen, Vy 65
Hill, Andrew 66
Hill, Lauryn 20, 53
Hilson, Keri 84
Hinderas, Natalie 5
Hines, Earl "Fatha" 39
Hinton, Milt 30
Holiday, Billie 1
Holland-Dozier-Holland 36
Holloway, Brenda 65
Holmes, Clint 57
Holt, Nora 38
Hooker, John Lee 30
Hopkins, Lightnin' 83
Horn, Shirley 32, 56
Horne, Lena 5, 86
Horton, Gladys 92
Houghton, Israel 92
House, Son 8
Houston, Cissy 20, 83
Houston, Whitney 7, 28, 83
Howell, Ayinde 91
Howlin' Wolf 9
Hubbard, Freddie 75
Hudson, Jennifer 63, 83
Huff, Leon 86
Humphrey, Bobbi 20
Hunter, Alberta 42
Hurt, Mississippi John 84
Hutch, Willie 62

Hyman, Phyllis 19
Ice Cube 8, 30, 60
Ice-T 6, 31
India.Arie 34
Ingram, James 84
Isaacs, Gregory 89
Isley, Marvin 87
Isley, Ronald 25, 56
Ja Rule 35, 91
Jackson, Fred James 25
Jackson, George 19
Jackson, Hal 41
Jackson, Isaiah 3
Jackson, Janet 6, 30, 68
Jackson, Jermaine 79
Jackson, John 36
Jackson, Mahalia 5
Jackson, Michael 19, 53, 76
Jackson, Millie 25
Jackson, Milt 26
Jackson, Randy 40
Jackson, Tito 81
Jacquet, Illinois 49
Jaheim 58
Jamal, Ahmad 69
Jamelia 51
Jamerson, James 59
James, Etta 13, 52
James, Rick 17
James, Skip 38
Jarreau, Al 21, 65
Jay-Z 27, 69
Jean, Wyclef 20, 86
Jefferson, Blind Lemon 81
Jenkins, Ella 15
Jennings, Lyfe 56, 69
Jerkins, Rodney 31
Jeter, Claude 75
Jimmy Jam 13
Johnson, Beverly 2
Johnson, Buddy 36
Johnson, Hall 90
Johnson, J. J. 37
Johnson, James Weldon 5
Johnson, Johnnie 56
Johnson, Lonnie 85
Johnson, Robert 2
Johnson-George, Tamara 79
Jones, Bobby 20, 94
Jones, Booker T. 84
Jones, Donell 29
Jones, Elvin 14, 68
Jones, Etta 35
Jones, Hank 57, 86
Jones, Jonah 39
Jones, Quincy 8, 30
Jones, Robert G. 81
Jones, Sharon 86
Jones, Thad 68
Joplin, Scott 6
Jordan, Montell 23
Jordan, Ronny 26
Jorge, Seu 73
Joyner, Matilda Sissieretta 15
Kandi 83
Kay, Ulysses 37
Kee, John P. 43
Keita, Salif 83
Kelis 58
Kelley, Elijah 65
Kelly, R. 18, 44, 71
Kem 47
Kendricks, Eddie 22

Kenoly, Ron **45**
Kenyatta, Robin **54**
Keys, Alicia **32, 68**
Khan, Chaka **12, 50**
Kid Cudi **83**
Kidjo, Angelique **50**
Killings, Debra **57**
King, B. B. **7**
King, Freddie **92**
King Curtis **92**
Kingston, Sean **94**
Kitt, Eartha **16, 75**
Klugh, Earl **59**
K'naan **76**
Knight, Gladys **16, 66**
Knight, Marie **80**
Knight, Suge **11, 30**
Knowles, Tina **61**
Knuckles, Frankie **42**
Kolosoy, Wendo **73**
Kool Moe Dee **37**
Kravitz, Lenny **10, 34**
KRS-One **34**
K-Swift **73**
Kuti, Femi **47**
Kweli, Talib **93**
LaBelle, Patti **13, 30**
Larrieux, Amel **63**
Lateef, Yusef **91**
Lattimore, Kenny **35**
LaVette, Bettye **85**
Laws, Hubert **90**
Leadbelly **82**
Ledisi **73**
Lee, Consuela **84**
Lefel, Edith **41**
Legend, John **67**
León, Tania **13**
Lester, Julius **9**
Levert, Eddie **70**
Levert, Gerald **22, 59**
Lewis, Ananda **28**
Lewis, Butch **71**
Lewis, Henry **38**
Lewis, Leona **75**
Lewis, Ramsey **35, 70**
Lewis, Terry **13**
Lil' Kim **28**
Lil Wayne **66, 84**
Liles, Kevin **42**
Lincoln, Abbey **3, 88**
Lipscomb, Mance **49**
Lister, Marquita **65**
Little Milton **36, 54**
Little Richard **15**
Little Walter **36**
LL Cool J **16, 49, 94**
Locke, Eddie **44**
Long, Huey **79**
Lopes, Lisa "Left Eye" **36**
Loueke, Lionel **88**
Love, Darlene **23, 92**
Love, Ed **58**
Love, Laura **50**
Lover, Ed **10**
Lucie, Lawrence **80**
Lucien, Jon **66**
Luckett, Letoya **61**
Ludacris **37, 60**
Lymon, Frankie **22**
Maal, Baaba **66**
Madlib **88**
Mahal, Taj **39**

Mahlasela, Vusi **65**
Maitreya, Sananda **85**
Majors, Jeff **41**
Makeba, Miriam **2, 50, 74**
Mane, Gucci **91**
Mann, Tamela **92**
Mario **71**
Marley, Bob **5**
Marley, Rita **32, 70**
Marley, Ziggy **41**
Marrow, Queen Esther **24**
Marsalis, Branford **34**
Marsalis, Delfeayo **41**
Marsalis, Ellis **90**
Marsalis, Wynton **16, 90**
Martelly, Michel **90**
Martin, Roberta **58**
Martin, Sara **38**
Mary Mary **34, 92**
Mase **24**
Masekela, Hugh **1**
Massenburg, Kedar **23**
Master P **21**
Mathis, Johnny **20**
Matthews, Benjamin **93**
Maxwell **20, 81**
May, Derrick **41**
Mayfield, Curtis **2, 43**
Maynor, Dorothy **19**
MC Breed **75**
M.C. Hammer **20, 80**
MC Lyte **34**
McClendon, Lisa **61**
McClurkin, Donnie **25**
McCoo, Marilyn **53**
McDaniel, Hattie **5**
McFerrin, Bobby **68**
McFerrin, Robert, Sr. **94**
McGill, Anthony **76**
McGriff, Jimmy **72**
McKee, Lonette **12**
McKinney, Nina Mae **40**
McKnight, Brian **18, 34**
McLean, Jackie **78**
McPherson, David **32**
McRae, Carmen **77**
McTell, Blind Willie **89**
Memphis Minnie **33**
Method Man **81**
Miles, Buddy **69**
Miller, Marcus **84**
Mills, Stephanie **36**
Minaj, Nicki **86**
Mingus, Charles **15**
Minott, Sugar **86**
Mitchell, Leona **42**
Mitchell, Nicole **66**
Mo', Keb' **36**
Monáe, Janelle **86**
Monica **21**
Monk, Thelonious **1**
Montgomery, Wes **88**
Moody, James **83**
Moore, Chante **26**
Moore, Dorothy Rudd **46**
Moore, Johnny B. **38**
Moore, LeRoi **72**
Moore, Melba **21**
Moore, Undine Smith **28**
Moran, Jason **89**
Morton, Jelly Roll **29**
Mos Def **30**
Moses, Gilbert **12**

Moss, J **64**
Moten, Etta **18**
Moura, Paulo **87**
Mowatt, Judy **38**
Mullen, Nicole C. **45**
Mumba, Samantha **29**
Murphy, Eddie **4, 20, 61**
Murray, Tai **47**
Muse, Clarence Edouard **21**
Musiq **37, 84**
Mya **35**
Nas **33**
Nascimento, Milton **2, 64**
Nash, Johnny **40**
Nate Dogg **92**
Ndegeocello, Meshell **15, 83**
N'Dour, Youssou **1, 53, 79**
Neal, Raful **44**
Neale, Haydain **52**
Nelly **32, 90**
Neville, Aaron **21**
Newman, David **76**
Ne-Yo **65**
Nicholas, Fayard **20, 57**
Nicholas, Harold **20**
Noah, Yannick **4, 60**
Norman, Jessye **5**
Notorious B.I.G. **20**
Odetta **37, 74**
Okosuns, Sonny **71**
Ol' Dirty Bastard **52**
Olatunji, Babatunde **36**
Oliver, Joe "King" **42**
O'Neal, Shaquille **8, 30**
Ongala, Remmy **9, 91**
Osborne, Jeffrey **26**
Otis, Clyde **67**
OutKast **35**
Owens, Jack **38**
Palmer, Keke **68**
Palmer, Rissi **65**
Parker, Charlie **20**
Parker, Maceo **72**
Parker, Ray, Jr. **85**
Parks, Gordon **1, 35, 58**
Patton, Antwan **45**
Payne, Freda **58**
Pena, Paul **58**
Pendergrass, Teddy **22, 83**
Peoples, Dottie **22**
Perkins, Pinetop **70**
Perren, Freddie **60**
Perry, Ruth **19**
Peterson, James **38**
Peterson, Marvin "Hannibal" **27**
Peterson, Oscar **52**
Phillips, Helen L. **63**
Phipps, Wintley **59**
Pinkney, Fayette **80**
Pleasure P **84**
P.M. Dawn **54**
Portuondo, Omara **53**
Powell, Benny **87**
Powell, Bud **24**
Powell, Maxine **8**
Pratt, Awadagin **31**
Premice, Josephine **41**
Preston, Billy **39, 59**
Price, Florence **37**
Price, Kelly **23**
Price, Leontyne **1**
Pride, Charley **26**
Prince **18, 65**

Pritchard, Robert Starling **21**
Pryce, Trevor **89**
Pryor, Rain **65**
Purdie, Bernard **77**
Queen Latifah **1, 16, 58**
?uestlove **74**
Ragin, Derek Lee **84**
Rainey, Ma **33**
Ralph, Sheryl Lee **18**
Randall, Alice **38**
Ranglin, Ernest **78**
Rascal, Dizzee **82**
Ray J **86**
Razaf, Andy **19**
Reagon, Bernice Johnson **7**
Reagon, Toshi **76**
Record, Eugene **60**
Redman **81**
Redman, Joshua **30**
Reed, A. C. **36**
Reed, Jimmy **38**
Reese, Della **6, 20**
Reeves, Dianne **32**
Reeves, Martha **85**
Reid, Antonio "L.A." **28**
Reid, Vernon **34**
Rhoden, Wayne **70**
Rhone, Sylvia **2**
Rhymes, Busta **31**
Richard, Dawn **92**
Richie, Lionel **27, 65**
Rihanna **65**
Riley, Boots **89**
Riperton, Minnie **32**
Roach, Max **21, 63**
Roberts, Kimberly Rivers **72**
Roberts, Marcus **19**
Robeson, Paul **2**
Robinson, Fenton **38**
Robinson, Reginald R. **53**
Robinson, Smokey **3, 49**
Robinson, Sylvia **79**
Rodríguez, Arsenio **87**
Rogers, Jimmy **38**
Rollins, Sonny **37, 94**
Ross, Diana **8, 27**
Ross, Isaiah "Doc" **40**
Ross, Rick **79**
Roxanne Shante **33**
Rucker, Darius **34, 74**
Rudder, David **79**
Ruffins, Kermit **85**
Run **31, 73**
Run-DMC **31, 75**
RuPaul **17, 91**
Rush, Bobby **78**
Rush, Otis **38**
Rushen, Patrice **12**
Rushing, Jimmy **37**
Russell, Brenda **52**
RZA **80**
Sade **15, 92**
Sample, Joe **51**
Sanders, Angelia **86**
Sanders, Pharoah **64**
Sangare, Oumou **18**
Santamaria, Mongo **81**
Sapp, Marvin **74**
Scarlett, Millicent **49**
Schuyler, Philippa **50**
Scott, George **55**
Scott, Hazel **66**
Scott, Jill **29, 83**

Scott, "Little" Jimmy **48**
Scott-Heron, Gil **94**
Seal **14, 75**
Seals, Son **56**
Sermon, Erick **81**
Shaggy **31**
Shakur, Afeni **67**
Shakur, Tupac **14**
Sheard, Kierra "Kiki" **61**
Shider, Garry **87**
Shirley, George **33**
Short, Bobby **52**
Shorter, Wayne **75**
Shorty, Ras, I **47**
Siji **56**
Silver, Horace **26**
Simmons, Russell **1, 30**
Simone, Nina **15, 41**
Simpson, Valerie **21**
Simpson-Hoffman, N'kenge **52**
Sir Mix-A-Lot **82**
Sisqo **30**
Sissle, Noble **29**
Sister Souljah **11**
Slash **75**
Sledge, Percy **39**
Slick Rick **93**
Slim Thug **86**
Sly & Robbie **34**
Smith, Bessie **3**
Smith, Cladys "Jabbo" **32**
Smith, Dr. Lonnie **49**
Smith, Lonnie Liston **49**
Smith, Mamie **32**
Smith, Myrna **92**
Smith, Stuff **37**
Smith, Trixie **34**
Smith, Will **8, 18, 53**
Smith, Willow **92**
Snoop Dogg **35, 84**
Somi **85**
Songz, Trey **88**
Southern, Eileen **56**
Sowande, Fela **39**
Sparks, Jordin **66**
Spector, Ronnie **77**
Speech **82**
Spence, Joseph **49**
Stampley, Micah **54**
Stanford, Olivia Lee Dilworth **49**
Staples, Mavis **50, 88**
Staples, "Pops" **32**
Staton, Candi **27**
Staton, Dakota **62**
Steely **80**
Steinberg, Martha Jean "The
    Queen" **28**
Stew **69**
Sticky Fingaz **86**
Still, William Grant **37**
Stone, Angie **31**
Stone, Sly **85**
Stoute, Steve **38**
Strayhorn, Billy **31**
Streeter, Sarah **45**
Strong, Barrett **89**
Studdard, Ruben **46**
Sugarhill Gang, The **79**
Sullivan, Jazmine **81**
Sullivan, Maxine **37**
Summer, Donna **25**
Sun Ra **60**
Sundiata, Sekou **66**

Supremes, The **33**
Sweat, Keith **19**
Sykes, Roosevelt **20**
Tait, Michael **57**
Tamar-kali **63**
Tamia **24, 55**
Tampa Red **63**
Tatum, Art **28**
Taylor, Billy **23, 92**
Taylor, Cecil **70**
Taylor, Koko **40, 80**
Temptations, The **33**
Terrell, Tammi **32**
Terry, Clark **39**
Terry, Sonny **88**
Tharpe, Rosetta **65**
The-Dream **74**
Thomas, Irma **29**
Thomas, Rozonda **34, 78**
Thomas, Rufus **20**
Thornton, Big Mama **33**
Three Mo' Tenors **35**
Thurston, Stephen J. **49**
Tillis, Frederick **40**
Timbaland **32**
Tinsley, Boyd **50**
Tisdale, Wayman **50**
TLC **34**
Tonex **54**
Tosh, Peter **9**
Toussaint, Allen **60**
T-Pain **73**
Tresvant, Ralph **57**
Tribbett, Tye **81**
Turnbull, Walter **13, 60**
Turner, Big Joe **92**
Turner, Ike **68**
Turner, Tina **6, 27**
Tyner, McCoy **92**
Uggams, Leslie **23**
Ulmer, James **79**
Usher **23, 56**
Valdés, Bebo **75**
Valdés, Chucho **89**
Valentino, Bobby **62**
Vandross, Luther **13, 48, 59**
Vanity **67**
Vaughan, Sarah **13**
Vereen, Ben **4**
Verrett, Shirley **66, 91**
Wale **92**
Walker, Albertina **10, 58, 89**
Walker, Cedric **19**
Walker, George **37**
Walker, Hezekiah **34**
Wallace, Sippie **1**
Waller, Fats **29**
Warfield, William **94**
Warwick, Dionne **18**
Washington, Dinah **22**
Washington, Grover, Jr. **17, 44**
Waters, Benny **26**
Waters, Ethel **7**
Waters, Muddy **34**
Watley, Jody **54**
Watson, Johnny "Guitar" **18**
Watts, Andre **42**
Watts, Reggie **52**
Webster, Katie **29**
Wein, Joyce **62**
Welch, Elisabeth **52**
Wells, Mary **28**
West, Kanye **52, 93**

Whalum, Kirk **37, 64**
White, Barry **13, 41**
White, Josh **86**
White, Josh, Jr. **52**
White, Maurice **29**
White, Willard **53**
Whitfield, Norman **73**
Wilkins, Thomas Alphonso **71**
will.i.am **64**
Williams, Bert **18**
Williams, Clarence **33**
Williams, Claude **80**
Williams, Deniece **36**
Williams, Denise **40**
Williams, J. Mayo **83**
Williams, Joe **5, 25**
Williams, Mary Lou **15**
Williams, Michelle **73**
Williams, Nat D. **91**
Williams, Pharrell **47, 82**
Williams, Saul **31**
Williams, Tony **67**
Williams, Vanessa L. **4, 17**
Williamson, Sonny Boy **84**
Wilson, Brian Courtney **94**
Wilson, Cassandra **16**
Wilson, Charlie **31, 77**
Wilson, Gerald **49**
Wilson, Jackie **60**
Wilson, Mary **28**
Wilson, Nancy **10**
Wilson, Natalie **38**
Wilson, Sunnie **7, 55**
Winans, Angie **36**
Winans, BeBe **14**
Winans, CeCe **14, 43**
Winans, David **77**
Winans, Debbie **36**
Winans, Marvin L. **17**
Winans, Ronald **54**
Winans, Vickie **24**
Withers, Bill **61**
Withers-Mendes, Elisabeth **64**
Womack, Bobby **60, 92**
Wonder, Stevie **11, 53**
Woods, Georgie **57**
Woods, Scott **55**
Woodson, Ali Ollie **89**
Wright, Timothy **74**
Xzibit **78**
Yabby You **83**
Yarbrough, Camille **40**
Yoba, Malik **11**
York, Vincent **40**
Young, Lee **72**
Young, Lester **37**
Young Jeezy **63**

Religion
Abernathy, Ralph David **1**
Adams, Yolanda **17, 67**
Agyeman, Jaramogi Abebe **10, 63**
Akinola, Peter Jasper **65**
Akpan, Uwem **70**
Al-Amin, Jamil Abdullah **6**
Anthony, Wendell **25**
Arinze, Francis **19**
Aristide, Jean-Bertrand **6, 45**
Armstrong, Vanessa Bell **24**
Austin, Junius C. **44**
Banks, William **11**
Barrow, Willie T. **85**
Baylor, Helen **36**

Beauvoir, Max **74**
Bell, Ralph S. **5**
Ben-Israel, Ben Ami **11**
Berry, Moses **84**
Black, Barry C. **47**
Blake, Charles E. **82**
Blanks, Deborah K. **69**
Bloomer, George **86**
Borders, William Holmes **94**
Bowen, John W. E., Sr. **89**
Boyd, T. B., III **6**
Braxton, Brad **77**
Bryant, John R. **45**
Burgess, John **46**
Butts, Calvin O., III **9, 90**
Bynum, Juanita **31, 71**
Caesar, Shirley **19**
Cage, Byron **53**
Caldwell, Kirbyjon **55**
Cannon, Katie **10**
Cardozo, Francis L. **33**
Carr, Kurt **56**
Chavis, Benjamin **6**
Chineworth, Mary Alice **79**
Cleaver, Emanuel **4, 45, 68**
Clements, George **2**
Cleveland, James **19**
Colemon, Johnnie **11**
Collins, Janet **33, 64**
Coltrane, Alice **70**
Cone, James H. **3, 82**
Cook, Suzan D. Johnson **22**
Crouch, Andraé **27**
Dandala, Mvume **77**
DeLille, Henriette **30**
Divine, Father **7**
DuBois, Joshua **88**
Dyson, Michael Eric **11, 40**
Easton, Hosea **91**
Ellis, Charles H., III **79**
Elmore, Ronn **21**
Fabre, Shelton **71**
Farrakhan, Louis **2, 15**
Fauntroy, Walter E. **11**
Fisher, Miles Mark **91**
Flake, Floyd H. **18**
Forbes, James A., Jr. **71**
Franklin, C. L. **68**
Franklin, Kirk **15, 49**
Franklin, Robert M. **13**
Fuller, Thomas O. **90**
Funnye, Capers C., Jr. **73**
Gaither, Israel L. **65**
Gantin, Bernardin **70**
Gilmore, Marshall **46**
Gomes, Peter J. **15, 93**
Gray, Darius **69**
Gray, William H., III **3**
Green, Al **13, 47, 74**
Gregory, Wilton **37**
Grier, Roosevelt **13**
Haddon, Dietrick **55**
Haile Selassie **7**
Harding, Vincent **67**
Harris, Barbara **12**
Hawkins, Tramaine **16**
Hawkins, Walter **87**
Hayes, James C. **10**
Healy, James Augustine **30**
Holsey, Lucius Henry **92**
Hood, James Walker **91**
Hooks, Benjamin L. **2, 85**
Howard, M. William, Jr. **26**

Jackson, Jesse **1, 27, 72**
Jakes, Thomas "T. D." **17, 43**
Jasper, John J. **91**
Jean-Juste, Gérard **78**
Jemison, Major L. **48**
Johns, Vernon **38**
Jones, Absalom **52**
Jones, Alex **64**
Jones, E. Edward, Sr. **45**
Jones, Robert Elijah **90**
Jones, William A., Jr. **61**
Kalbani, Adil **77**
Karim, Benjamin **61**
Kelly, Leontine **33**
King, Barbara **22**
King, Bernice **4, 81**
King, Martin Luther, Jr. **1**
King, Martin Luther, Sr. **89**
Kobia, Samuel **43**
Lawson, James M., Jr. **90**
Lee, Eric P. **79**
Lester, Julius **9**
Lewis-Thornton, Rae **32**
Lincoln, C. Eric **38**
Little Richard **15**
Loguen, J. W. **91**
Long, Eddie L. **29, 89**
Lowery, Joseph **2**
Lowry, A. Leon **60**
Lyons, Henry **12**
Majors, Jeff **41**
Marino, Eugene Antonio **30**
Maxis, Theresa **62**
Mays, Benjamin E. **7**
McClellan, George Marion **91**
McClurkin, Donnie **25**
McGuire, George Alexander **80**
McKenzie, Vashti M. **29**
Meeks, James T. **92**
Michaux, Solomon Lightfoot **91**
Morgan, Gertrude **63**
Moss, J **64**
Moss, Otis, Jr. **72**
Moss, Otis, III **72**
Muhammad, Ava **31**
Muhammad, Elijah **4**
Muhammad, Jabir Herbert **72**
Muhammad, Khallid Abdul **10, 31**
Muhammad, W. Deen **27**
Murray, Cecil **12, 47**
Muzorewa, Abel **85**
Okaalet, Peter **58**
Otunga, Maurice Michael **55**
Patterson, Gilbert Earl **41**
Patterson, J. O., Jr. **80**
Peterson, Jesse Lee **81**
Phipps, Wintley **59**
Pierre, Andre **17**
Powell, Adam Clayton, Jr. **3**
Price, Frederick K. C. **21**
Redding, Ann Holmes **77**
Reems, Ernestine Cleveland **27**
Reese, Della **6, 20**
Reverend Ike **79**
Riley, Helen Caldwell Day **13**
Rivers, Eugene F., III **81**
Rogers, Alan G. **72**
Roundtree, Dovey **80**
Rugambwa, Laurean **20**
Sapp, Marvin **74**
Scott, George **55**
Senghor, Augustin Diamancoune **66**
Sentamu, John **58**

Shabazz, Betty **7, 26**
Sharpton, Al **21**
Shaw, William J. **30**
Shuttlesworth, Fred **47**
Slocumb, Jonathan **52**
Somé, Malidoma Patrice **10**
Stallings, George A., Jr. **6**
Stampley, Micah **54**
Stanton, Alysa **78**
Steinberg, Martha Jean "The Queen" **28**
Stith, Charles R. **73**
Sullivan, Leon H. **3, 30**
Taylor, Gardner C. **76**
Thurman, Howard **3**
Tillard, Conrad **47**
Tolton, Augustine **62**
Tonex **54**
Tribbett, Tye **81**
Turner, Henry McNeal **5**
Tutu, Desmond (Mpilo) **6, 44**
Ukpabio, Helen **86**
Vanity **67**
Vanzant, Iyanla **17, 47**
Waddles, Charleszetta "Mother" **10, 49**
Walker, Hezekiah **34**
Walker, John T. **50**
Walker, Lucius, Jr. **88**
Walker, Wyatt Tee **80**
Washington, James Melvin **50**
Waters, Ethel **7**
Watkins, Joe **86**
Weeks, Thomas, III **70**
Weems, Renita J. **44**
White, Reggie **6, 50**
White-Hammond, Gloria **61**
Williams, Frederick (B.) **63**
Williams, Hosea Lorenzo **15, 31**
Williams, Preston Warren, II **64**
Wilson, Natalie **38**
Winans, BeBe **14**
Winans, CeCe **14, 43**
Winans, Marvin L. **17**
Winans, Ronald **54**
Woods, Abraham, Jr. **74**
Wright, Jeremiah A., Jr. **45, 69**
Wright, Nathan, Jr. **56**
Wright, Timothy **74**
Wyatt, Addie L. **56**
X, Malcolm **1**
York, Dwight D. **71**
Youngblood, Johnny Ray **8**

Science and technology
Adams-Campbell, Lucille L. **60**
Adkins, Rod **41**
Adkins, Rutherford H. **21**
Alcorn, George Edward, Jr. **59**
Alexander, Archie Alphonso **14**
Allen, Ethel D. **13**
Allen, Will **74**
Anderson, Charles Edward **37**
Anderson, Michael P. **40**
Anderson, Norman B. **45**
Anderson, William G(ilchrist) **57**
Atim, Julian **66**
Auguste, Donna **29**
Auguste, Rose-Anne **13**
Austin, Wanda M. **94**
Bacon-Bercey, June **38**
Banda, Hastings Kamuzu **6, 54**
Banneker, Benjamin **93**

Bashir, Halima **73**
Bath, Patricia E. **37**
Benjamin, Regina **20, 75**
Benson, Angela **34**
Black, Keith Lanier **18, 84**
Blackwell, David **79**
Bluford, Guy **2, 35**
Bluitt, Juliann S. **14**
Bolden, Charles Frank, Jr. **7, 78**
Boykin, Otis **92**
Branson, Herman **87**
Brown, Vivian **27**
Brown, Willa **40**
Bullard, Eugene **12**
Callender, Clive O. **3**
Campbell, Donald J. **66**
Canady, Alexa **28**
Cargill, Victoria A. **43**
Carroll, L. Natalie **44**
Carruthers, George R. **40**
Carson, Benjamin **1, 35, 76**
Carter, Joye Maureen **41**
Carter, Majora **77**
Carver, George Washington **4**
CasSelle, Malcolm **11**
Chatard, Peter **44**
Chinn, May Edward **26**
Christian, Spencer **15**
Clack, Zoanne **73**
Clark, Mamie Phipps **79**
Cobb, W. Montague **39**
Cobbs, Price M. **9**
Cole, Rebecca **38**
Coleman, Bessie **9**
Coleman, Ken **57**
Comer, James P. **6**
Coney, PonJola **48**
Cooper, Edward S. **6**
Cooper, Lisa **73**
Cornwell, Edward E., III **70**
Counter, S. Allen **74**
Crosthwait, David **93**
Crumpler, Rebecca Lee **89**
Dabiri, John **93**
Dailey, Ulysses Grant **87**
Daly, Marie Maynard **37**
Davis, Allison **12**
Dean, Mark **35**
Deas, Gerald **85**
Deconge-Watson, Lovenia **55**
Delany, Bessie **12**
Delany, Martin R. **27**
Dennis, Gary C. **91**
Dickens, Helen Octavia **14, 64**
Diop, Cheikh Anta **4**
Drew, Alvin, Jr. **67**
Drew, Charles Richard **7**
Dunham, Katherine **4, 59**
Dunston, Georgia Mae **48**
Durham, James **90**
Edwards, Lena Frances **76**
Edwards, Willarda V. **59**
Elders, Joycelyn **6**
Ellington, E. David **11**
Ellis, Clarence A. **38**
Emeagwali, Dale **31**
Emeagwali, Philip **30**
Ericsson-Jackson, Aprille **28**
Fennoy, Ilene **72**
Fenton, Kevin **87**
Fields, Evelyn J. **27**
Fisher, Ada M. **76**
Fisher, Rudolph **17**

Flipper, Henry O. **3**
Flowers, Sylester **50**
Foster, Henry W., Jr. **26**
Freeman, Harold P. **23**
French, D. M. **94**
Fulani, Lenora **11**
Fuller, A. Oveta **43**
Fuller, Arthur **27**
Fuller, Solomon Carter, Jr. **15**
Gardere, Jeffrey **76**
Gaston, Marilyn Hughes **60**
Gates, Sylvester James, Jr. **15**
Gayle, Helene D. **3, 46**
Gibson, Kenneth Allen **6**
Gibson, William F. **6**
Giles, Roscoe C. **93**
Gilliard, Steve **69**
Goodlett, Carlton B. **91**
Gourdine, Meredith **33**
Grant, Augustus O. **71**
Granville, Evelyn Boyd **36**
Gray, Ida **41**
Gregory, Frederick **8, 51**
Grier, Eliza Ann **90**
Griffin, Anthony **71**
Griffin, Bessie Blout **43**
Griffith, Patrick A. **64**
Hall, Lloyd A. **8**
Hamburg, Margaret **78**
Hammonds, Evelynn **69**
Hannah, Marc **10**
Hansberry, Tony, II **93**
Harris, Bernard A. **90**
Harris, Gary L. **87**
Harris, Mary Styles **31**
Harris, Wesley L. **92**
Haynie, Sharon **94**
Haywood, Jimmy **58**
Henderson, Cornelius Langston **26**
Henderson, Henry Fairfax, Jr. **89**
Henson, Matthew **2**
Hill, Wyllstyne D. **94**
Hillary, Barbara **65**
Hinton, William Augustus **8**
Holmes, Hamilton E. **82**
Hopkins, Donald R. **89**
Hughes, Dora **88**
Howard, Ayanna **65**
Hutcherson, Hilda Yvonne **54**
Ibrahim, Mo **67**
Imes, Elmer Samuel **39**
Irving, Larry, Jr. **12**
Jackson, Deborah **94**
Jackson, Lisa **77**
Jackson, Shirley Ann **12**
Jarvis, Erich **67**
Jawara, Dawda Kairaba **11**
Jefferson, Mildred Fay **89**
Jemison, Mae C. **1, 35**
Jenifer, Franklyn G. **2**
Johnson, Anthony M. **92**
Johnson, Lonnie G. **32, 93**
Johnson, Sandra K. **94**
Jones, Edith Mae Irby **65**
Jones, Frederick McKinley **68**
Jones, Monty **66**
Jones, Randy **35**
Jones, Wayne **53**
Joseph, Kathie-Ann **56**
Julian, Hubert **90**
Julian, Percy Lavon **6**
Juma, Calestous **57**
Just, Ernest Everett **3**

Keith, Rachel Boone 63
Kenney, John A., Jr. 48
King, Reatha Clark 65
Kintaudi, Leon 62
Kittles, Rick 51
Knowling, Robert E., Jr. 38
Kong, B. Waine 50
Kountz, Samuel L. 10
Laroche, Joseph Philippe Lemercier 85
Laryea, Thomas Davies, III 67
Latimer, Lewis H. 4
Lavizzo-Mourey, Risa 48
Lawless, Theodore K. 8
Lawrence, Robert H., Jr. 16
Lee, Raphael C. 87
Leevy, Carrol M. 42
Leffall, Lasalle 3, 64
Lewis, Daurene 72
Lewis, Delano 7
Logan, Onnie Lee 14
Lushington, Augustus Nathaniel 56
Lyttle, Hulda Margaret 14
Madison, Romell 45
Malveaux, Floyd 54
Manley, Audrey Forbes 16
Massey, Walter E. 5, 45
Massie, Samuel P., Jr. 29
Maupin, John E., Jr. 92
Maxey, Randall 46
Mays, William G. 34
Mboup, Souleymane 10
McBay, Henry C. 91
McCoy, Elijah 8
McJunkin, George 93
McNair, Ronald 3, 58
Mensah, Thomas 48
Miller, Warren F., Jr. 53
Millines Dziko, Trish 28
Mills, Joseph C. 51
Morgan, Garrett 1
Mossell, Nathan Francis 91
Murray, Pauli 38
Nabrit, Samuel Milton 47
Naki, Hamilton 63
Neto, António Agostinho 43
Nour, Nawal M. 56
Ojikutu, Bisola 65
Olopade, Olufunmilayo Falusi 58
Osborne, Na'taki 54
Pace, Betty 59
Perry, Warren 56
Person, Waverly 9, 51
Peters, Lenrie 43
Pickett, Cecil 39
Pierre, Percy Anthony 46
Pinn, Vivian Winona 49
Pitt, David Thomas 10
Pitts, Derrick 77
Poindexter, Hildrus A. 87
Poussaint, Alvin F. 5, 67
Price, Richard 51
Prothrow-Stith, Deborah 10
Quarterman, Lloyd Albert 4
Rabb, Maurice F., Jr. 58
Randolph, Linda A. 52
Reece, E. Albert 63
Reese, Milous J., Jr. 51
Riley, Helen Caldwell Day 13
Rillieux, Norbert 92
Robeson, Eslanda Goode 13
Robinson, Rachel 16
Robinson-Berry, Joan 94

Roker, Al 12, 49
Ross-Lee, Barbara 67
Samara, Noah 15
Satcher, David 7, 57
Seacole, Mary 54
Shabazz, Betty 7, 26
Shavers, Cheryl 31
Sigur, Wanda 44
Sinkford, Jeanne C. 13
Slaughter, John Brooks 53
Smith, Ian 62
Smith, Richard 51
Spencer, Michael G. 87
Staples, Brent 8
Staupers, Mabel K. 7
Stewart, Ella 39
Sullivan, Louis 8
Sweet, Ossian 68
Taylor, Susan C. 62
Terrell, Dorothy A. 24
Thomas, Vivien 9
Thornton, Yvonne S. 69
Thurston, Baratunde 79
Tuckson, Reed V. 71
Tyson, Neil deGrasse 15, 65
Walker, Arthur, II 87
Wambugu, Florence 42
Washington, Patrice Clarke 12
Watkins, Levi, Jr. 9
Wein, Joyce 62
Welsing, Frances Cress 5
West, James E. 87
Westbrooks, Bobby 51
White-Hammond, Gloria 61
Wilkens, J. Ernest, Jr. 43
Williams, Daniel Hale 2
Williams, David Rudyard 50
Williams, O. S. 13
Wilson, Donald E. 88
Wilson, Stephanie 72
Wisdom, Kimberlydawn 57
Witt, Edwin T. 26
Woods, Granville T. 5
Wright, Louis Tompkins 4
Young, Roger Arliner 29

Social issues
Abbott, Diane 9
Abbott, Robert Sengstacke 27
Abernathy, Ralph David 1
Abu-Jamal, Mumia 15
Achebe, Chinua 6
Adams, Sheila J. 25
Agyeman, Jaramogi Abebe 10, 63
Ake, Claude 30
Al-Amin, Jamil Abdullah 6
Alexander, Clifford 26
Alexander, Sadie Tanner Mossell 22
Allen, Lucy 85
Allen, Will 74
Ali, Muhammad 2, 16, 52
Allen, Ethel D. 13
Amaker, Norman 63
Andrews, Benny 22, 59
Angelou, Maya 1, 15
Annan, Kofi Atta 15, 48
Anthony, Wendell 25
Appiah, Kwame Anthony 67
Arac de Nyeko, Monica 66
Archer, Dennis 7
Aristide, Jean-Bertrand 6, 45
Arnwine, Barbara 28

Asante, Molefi Kete 3
Ashe, Arthur 1, 18
Atyam, Angelina 55
Auguste, Rose-Anne 13
Autrey, Wesley 68
Avery, Byllye Y. 66
Azikiwe, Nnamdi 13
Ba, Mariama 30
Baisden, Michael 25, 66
Baker, Ella 5
Baker, Gwendolyn Calvert 9
Baker, Houston A., Jr. 6
Baker, Josephine 3
Baker, Thurbert 22
Baldwin, James 1
Banks, Paula A. 68
Barbee, Lloyd Augustus 71
Barlow, Roosevelt 49
Barnett, Etta Moten 56
Barrow, Willie T. 85
Bass, Charlotta Spears 40
Bates, Daisy 13
Bell, Derrick 6
Bell, Ralph S. 5
Berry, Bertice 8, 55
Berry, Edwin C. 81
Berry, Mary Frances 7
Berrysmith, Don Reginald 49
Bethune, Mary McLeod 4
Betsch, MaVynee 28
Betts, R. Dwayne 86
Bevel, James L. 75
Bibb, Henry and Mary 54
Biko, Steven 4
bin Wahad, Dhoruba 85
Birch, Glynn R. 61
Black, Albert 51
Blackwell, Unita 17
Blakely, Edward J. 88
Bobo, Lawrence 60
Bolin, Jane 22, 59
Bond, Julian 2, 35
Bonga, Kuenda 13
Booker, Cory Anthony 68
Bosley, Freeman, Jr. 7
Boyd, Gwendolyn 49
Boyd, John W., Jr. 20, 72
Boyd, T. B., III 6
Boykin, Keith 14
Bradley, David Henry, Jr. 39
Braun, Carol Moseley 4, 42
Bridges, Ruby 77
Broadbent, Hydeia 36
Brock, Roslyn McCallister 86
Brown, Byrd 49
Brown, Cora 33
Brown, Eddie C. 35
Brown, Elaine 8
Brown, Homer S. 47
Brown, Jesse 6, 41
Brown, Jim 11
Brown, Lee P. 1
Brown, Les 5
Brown, Lloyd Louis 10 42
Brown, Oliver Leon 94
Brown, Oscar, Jr. 53
Brown, Tony 3
Brown, Willa 40
Brown, Zora Kramer 12
Brutus, Dennis 38
Bryant, Wayne R. 6
Bullock, Steve 22
Bunch, Lonnie G., III 91

Bunche, Ralph J. 5
Burks, Mary Fair 40
Burroughs, Margaret Taylor 9
Butler, Paul D. 17
Butts, Calvin O., III 9, 90
Cameron, James 80
Campbell, Bebe Moore 6, 24, 59
Canada, Geoffrey 23
Carby, Hazel 27
Carmichael, Stokely 5, 26
Carr, Johnnie 69
Carr, Keela 74
Carter, Majora 77
Carter, Mandy 11
Carter, Robert L. 51
Carter, Rubin 26
Carter, Stephen L. 4
Cary, Lorene 3
Cary, Mary Ann Shadd 30
Catto, Octavius V. 83
Cayton, Horace 26
Chavis, Benjamin 6
Chestnut, J. L., Jr. 73
Chideya, Farai 14, 61
Childress, Alice 15
Chisholm, Daquan 93
Chissano, Joaquim 7, 55, 67
Christophe, Henri 9
Chuck D 9
Clark, Joe 1
Clark, Kenneth B. 5, 52
Clark, Septima 7
Clay, William Lacy 8
Clayton, Mayme Agnew 62
Claytor, Helen 14, 52
Cleaver, Eldridge 5
Cleaver, Kathleen Neal 29
Clements, George 2
Cobbs, Price M. 9
Cole, Johnnetta B. 5, 43
Cole, Lorraine 48
Coles, Alice 80
Collins, Patricia Hill 67
Colston, Hal 72
Comer, James P. 6
Compton-Rock, Malaak 86
Connerly, Ward 14
Conyers, John, Jr. 4, 45
Cook, Toni 23
Cooke, Marvel 31
Cooper, Anna Julia 20
Cooper, Edward S. 6
Cooper, Margaret J. 46
Correia, De'Jaun 93
Cosby, Bill 7, 26, 59
Cosby, Camille 14, 80
Cose, Ellis 5, 50
Cox, Donald Lee 93
Creagh, Milton 27
Crew, Spencer R. 55
Cruse, Harold 54
Cummings, Elijah E. 24
da Silva, Benedita 5
Davis, Angela 5
Davis, Artur 41
Davis, Danny K. 24
Dawson, Matel, Jr. 39
Dawson, Michael C. 63
DeBaptiste, George 32
Delany, Martin R. 27
Dellums, Ronald 2, 81
Dent, Thomas C. 50
Diallo, Amadou 27

Dickerson, Ernest 6
Dieudonné 67
Diop, Cheikh Anta 4
Dirie, Waris 56
Divine, Father 7
Dixon, Margaret 14
Dobbs, John Wesley 89
Dodson, Howard, Jr. 7, 52
Dortch, Thomas W., Jr. 45
Douglas, Derek 88
Douglass, Frederick 87
Drew, Charles Richard 7
Du Bois, W. E. B. 3
DuBois, Shirley Graham 21
Duggins, George 64
Dukes, Hazel Nell 56
Dumas, Henry 41
Dunham, Katherine 4, 59
Eagleson, William Lewis 90
Early, Gerald 15
Easton, Hosea 91
Edelin, Ramona Hoage 19
Edelman, Marian Wright 5, 42
Edley, Christopher 2, 48
Edwards, Harry 2
Edwards, Lena Frances 76
Elder, Larry 25
Elders, Joycelyn 6
Ellis-Lamkins, Phaedra 88
Ellison, Ralph 7
Esposito, Giancarlo 9
Espy, Mike 6
Eugene-Richard, Margie 63
Europe, James Reese 10
Evers, Medgar 3
Evers, Myrlie 8
Farmer, James 2, 64
Farrakhan, Louis 15
Farris, Isaac Newton, Jr. 63
Fauntroy, Walter E. 11
Fauset, Jessie 7
Fela 1, 42
Fields, C. Virginia 25
Finner-Williams, Paris Michele 62
Flavor Flav 67
Fletcher, Benjamin 90
Fletcher, Bill, Jr. 41
Forbes, James A., Jr. 71
Forman, James 7, 51
Fortune, T. Thomas 6
Foster, Marie 48
Franklin, C. L. 68
Franklin, Hardy R. 9
Franklin, John Hope 5, 77
Franklin, Robert M. 13
Frazier, E. Franklin 10
French, D. M. 94
Fulani, Lenora 11
Fuller, Arthur 27
Fuller, Charles 8
Gaines, Ernest J. 7
Gamble, Kenny 85
Gardner, Chris 65
Garvey, Marcus 1
Gates, Henry Louis, Jr. 3, 38, 67
Gayle, Helene D. 3
Gbowee, Leymah 76
George, Zelma Watson 42
Gibson, Kenneth Allen 6
Gibson, William F. 6
Gilbert, Christopher 50
Gist, Carole 1
Goldberg, Whoopi 4, 33, 69

Golden, Marita 19
Golston, Allan C. 55
Gomez, Jewelle 30
Gomez-Preston, Cheryl 9
Gomillion, Charles 90
Goss, Carol A. 55
Gossett, Louis, Jr. 7
Graham, Lawrence Otis 12
Granger, Lester B. 75
Gray, Fred 37
Greene, Petey 65
Gregory, Dick 1, 54
Gregory, Wilton 37
Grier, Roosevelt 13
Griffith, Mark Winston 8
Grimké, Archibald H. 9
Guinier, Lani 7, 30
Guy, Rosa 5
Hale, Lorraine 8
Haley, Alex 4
Hall, Elliott S. 24
Hall, Stuart 78
Hamblin, Ken 10
Hamer, Fannie Lou 6
Hampton, Fred 18
Hampton, Henry 6
Hani, Chris 6
Hansberry, Lorraine 6
Hansberry, William Leo 11
Harding, Vincent 67
Harper, Frances Ellen Watkins 11
Harrington, Oliver W. 9
Harris, Alice 7
Harris, Leslie 6
Harris, Marcelite Jordan 16
Harris, Patricia Roberts 2
Hastings, Alcee L. 16
Hawkins, Augustus F. 68
Hawkins, Steven 14
Hayes, Dennis 54
Haynes, George Edmund 8
Hedgeman, Anna Arnold 22
Height, Dorothy I. 2, 23, 78
Henderson, Thelton E. 68
Henderson, Wade J. 14
Henderson, Zelma 71
Henry, Aaron Edd 19
Henry, Lenny 9, 52
Henson, Josiah 90
Hernandez, Aileen Clarke 13
Herndon, Angelo 90
Hernton, Calvin C. 51
Hill, Anita 5, 65
Hill, Jesse, Jr. 13
Hill, Lauryn 20, 53
Hill, Oliver W. 24, 63
Hilliard, Asa Grant, III 66
Hilliard, David 7
Holland, Endesha Ida Mae 3, 57
Holt Baker, Arlene 73
Hood, James Walker 91
hooks, bell 5, 90
Hooks, Benjamin L. 2, 85
Hope, Lugenia Burns 89
Houston, Charles Hamilton 4
Howard, M. William, Jr. 26
Hoyte, Lenon 50
Hubbard, Arnette Rhinehart 38
Huggins, Nathan Irvin 52
Hughes, Albert 7
Hughes, Allen 7
Hughes, Langston 4
Hunt, Darnell 92

Hunter-Gault, Charlayne 6, 31
Hutchinson, Earl Ofari 24
Hutson, Jean Blackwell 16
Ibrahim, Mo 67
Iceberg Slim 11
Ice-T 6, 31
Ingram, Rex 5
Innis, Roy 5
Irvis, K. Leroy 67
Jackson, Edison O. 67
Jackson, Fred James 25
Jackson, George 14
Jackson, Janet 6, 30, 68
Jackson, Jesse 1, 27, 72
Jackson, Judith D. 57
Jackson, Mahalia 5
Jacob, John E. 2
Jagan, Cheddi 16
James, Daniel, Jr. 16
Jealous, Benjamin 70
Jean, Wyclef 20, 86
Jeffries, Leonard 8
Jenkins, Ray 77
Johnson, Charles S. 12
Johnson, Earvin "Magic" 3, 39
Johnson, James Weldon 5
Johnson, Kevin 70
Jolley, Willie 28
Jones, Cullen 73
Jones, Elaine R. 7, 45
Jones, Eugene Kinckle 79
Jones, John 89
Jones, Van 70
Jones, William A., Jr. 61
Jordan, June 7, 35
Jordan, Vernon E. 3, 35
Joseph, Kathie-Ann 56
Josey, E. J. 10
Joyner, Marjorie Stewart 26
Joyner, Tom 19, 90
Julian, Percy Lavon 6
Karim, Benjamin 61
Kaunda, Kenneth 2
Keita, Salif 83
Kelley, Cliff 75
Kennedy, Florynce 12, 33
Khanga, Yelena 6
Kidd, Mae Street 39
Kimbro, Warren 76
King, Bernice 4, 81
King, Coretta Scott 3, 57
King, Dexter 10
King, Martin Luther, III 20
King, Martin Luther, Jr. 1
King, Martin Luther, Sr. 89
King, Preston 28
King, Robert Hillary 84
King, Yolanda 6
Kitwana, Bakari 86
Kuzwayo, Ellen 68
Ladner, Joyce A. 42
LaGuma, Alex 30
Lampkin, Daisy 19
Lane, Charles 3
Lane, Vincent 5
Laraque, Paul 67
Lawson, James M., Jr. 90
Lee, Canada 8
Lee, Eric P. 79
Leland, Mickey 2
Lester, Julius 9
Lewis, Ananda 28
Lewis, Delano 7

Lewis, Thomas 19
Lewis-Thornton, Rae 32
Little, Robert L. 2
Logan, Rayford W. 40
Loguen, J. W. 91
Lorde, Audre 6
Louis, Errol T. 8
Loving, Mildred 69
Lowery, Joseph 2
Lowry, A. Leon 60
Lucas, John 7
Lucy, William 50
Lucy Foster, Autherine 35
Luper, Clara 94
Maathai, Wangari 43
Mabuza-Suttle, Felicia 43
Madison, Joseph E. 17
Makeba, Miriam 2, 50, 74
Malone Jones, Vivian 59
Malveaux, Julianne 32, 70
Mandela, Nelson 1, 14, 77
Mandela, Winnie 2, 35
Manley, Audrey Forbes 16
Marable, Manning 10
Marshall, Paule 7, 77
Marshall, Thurgood 1, 44
Martin, Louis E. 16
Masekela, Barbara 18
Masekela, Hugh 1
Mason, Biddy 89
Mason, Ronald 27
Mathabane, Mark 5
Maynard, Robert C. 7
Mays, Benjamin E. 7
Mbeki, Thabo 14, 73
McCabe, Jewell Jackson 10
McCarty, Osceola 16
McDougall, Gay J. 11, 43
McKay, Claude 6
McKenzie, Vashti M. 29
McKinney Hammond, Michelle 51
McKissick, Floyd B. 3
McMurray, Georgia L. 36
McQueen, Butterfly 6, 54
McWhorter, John 35
McWorter, Free Frank 91
Meredith, James H. 11
Mfume, Kweisi 6, 41
Mhlaba, Raymond 55
Micheaux, Oscar 7
Millender-McDonald, Juanita 21, 61
Miller-Travis, Vernice 64
Millines Dziko, Trish 28
Mitchell, Clarence M., Jr. 88
Mkapa, Benjamin W. 16, 77
Mongella, Gertrude 11
Moore, Gwendolynne S. 55
Moore, Harry T. 29
Morgan, Irene 65
Morial, Ernest "Dutch" 26
Moses, Robert Parris 11
Moss, Otis, Jr. 72
Mossell, Gertrude Bustill 40
Motley, Constance Baker 10, 55
Moton, Robert Russa 83
Moutoussamy-Ashe, Jeanne 7
Mowry, Jess 7
Muhammad, Elijah 4
Muhammad, Khallid Abdul 10, 31
Mukoko, Jestina 75
Murphy, Laura M. 43
Murray, Pauli 38
Nash, Diane 72

Ndadaye, Melchior 7
Nelson, Jill 6, 54
Newton, Huey 2
Niane, Katoucha 70
Nkoli, Simon 60
Nkrumah, Kwame 3
Noble, Gil 76
Norman, Pat 10
Nour, Nawal M. 56
Nzo, Alfred 15
Obasanjo, Olusegun 5
Oglesby, Zena 12
Ojikutu, Bisola 65
Orange, James 74
Ormes, Jackie 73
Osborne, Na'taki 54
Owens, Major 6
Page, Alan 7
Page, Clarence 4
Parker, Kellis E. 30
Parker, Pat 19
Parks, Rosa 1, 35, 56
Parr, Russ 51
Patterson, Frederick Douglass 12
Patterson, Louise 25
Patterson, Orlando 4
Patterson, P. J. 6, 20
Perkins, Edward 5
Perry, James 83
Peterson, Jesse Lee 81
Pitt, David Thomas 10
Pleasant, Mary Ellen 9
Plessy, Homer Adolph 31
Pough, Terrell 58
Poussaint, Alvin F. 5, 67
Powell, Adam Clayton, Jr. 3
Powell, Kevin 31, 74
Pratt, Geronimo 18
Pressley, Condace L. 41
Price, Hugh B. 9, 54
Primus, Pearl 6
Pritchard, Robert Starling 21
Prothrow-Stith, Deborah 10
Quarles, Benjamin Arthur 18
Quigless, Helen G. 49
Ramaphosa, Cyril 3
Ramphele, Mamphela 29
Ramsey, Charles H. 21, 69
Rand, A. Barry 6
Randolph, A. Philip 3
Randolph, Linda A. 52
Rawlings, Nana Konadu Agyeman 13
Reagon, Bernice Johnson 7
Reed, Ishmael 8
Rice, Louise Allen 54
Rice, Norm 8
Richards, Hilda 49
Richardson, Julieanna 81
Richardson, Rupert 67
Riggs, Marlon 5
Riley, Boots 89
Riley, Helen Caldwell Day 13
Rivers, Eugene F., III 81
Roberts, Lillian 83
Robeson, Eslanda Goode 13
Robeson, Paul 2
Robinson, Jackie 6
Robinson, Rachel 16
Robinson, Randall 7, 46
Robinson, Sharon 22
Robinson, Spottswood W., III 22
Roble, Abdi 71

Rodriguez, Cheryl 64
Rowan, Carl T. 1, 30
Rowell, Victoria 13, 68
Ruffin, Josephine St. Pierre 75
Rusesabagina, Paul 60
Rustin, Bayard 4
Sampson, Edith S. 4
Sanders, Malika 48
Sané, Pierre Gabriel 21
Sapphire 14
Saro-Wiwa, Kenule 39
Satcher, David 7, 57
Savimbi, Jonas 2, 34
Sawyer, Amos 2
Sayles Belton, Sharon 9, 16
Scantlebury-White, Velma 64
Seacole, Mary 54
Seale, Bobby 3
Sears, Stephanie 53
Seele, Pernessa 46
Senghor, Léopold Sédar 12
Shabazz, Attallah 6
Shabazz, Betty 7, 26
Shadd, Abraham D. 81
Shakur, Afeni 67
Shakur, Assata 6
Shakur, Yusef 85
Sherrod, Shirley 87
Shinhoster, Earl 32
Shuttlesworth, Fred 47
Sifford, Charlie 4, 49
Simms, Margaret 94
Simone, Nina 15, 41
Sisulu, Albertina 57
Sisulu, Sheila Violet Makate 24
Sleet, Moneta, Jr. 5
Smith, Anna Deavere 6
Smith, Barbara 28
Smith, Damu 54
Smith, Greg 28
Smith, Kemba 70
Smith, Marie F. 70
Smith, Nate 49
Snowden, Frank M., Jr. 67
Spriggs, William 67
Stallings, George A., Jr. 6
Staupers, Mabel K. 7
Steele, Claude Mason 13
Steele, Shelby 13, 82
Stewart, Alison 13
Stewart, Ella 39
Stewart, Maria W. Miller 19
Stone, Chuck 9
Sullivan, Leon H. 3, 30
Sweet, Ossian 68
Talbert, Mary B. 77
Tate, Eleanora E. 20, 55
Tatum, Wilbert 76
Taulbert, Clifton Lemoure 19
Taylor, Bo 72
Taylor, Mildred D. 26
Taylor, Recy 92
Terrell, Mary Church 9
Thomas, Arthur Ray 52
Thomas, Franklin A. 5, 49
Thomas, Jefferson 88
Thompson, Bennie G. 26
Thompson, Cynthia Bramlett 50
Thurman, Howard 3
Thurman, Wallace 16
Till, Emmett 7
Tobias, Channing H. 79
Toomer, Jean 6

Tosh, Peter 9
Touré, Askia (Muhammad Abu Bakr el) 47
Touré, Faya Ora Rose 56
Tribble, Israel, Jr. 8
Trotter, Donne E. 28
Trotter, Monroe 9
Tsvangirai, Morgan 26, 72
Tubman, Harriet 9
Tucker, C. Delores 12, 56
Tucker, Cynthia 15, 61
Tucker, Rosina 14
Tutu, Desmond 6
Tyree, Omar Rashad 21
Van Peebles, Melvin 7
Vanzant, Iyanla 17, 47
Vaughn, Viola 70
Vega, Marta Moreno 61
Velez-Rodriguez, Argelia 56
Vincent, Marjorie Judith 2
Waddles, Charleszetta "Mother" 10, 49
Walcott, Derek 5, 94
Walker, A'lelia 14
Walker, Alice 1, 43
Walker, Bernita Ruth 53
Walker, Lucius, Jr. 88
Wall, Orindatus S. B. 92
Wallace, Joaquin 49
Wallace, Michele Faith 13
Wallace, Phyllis A. 9
Wallace, William 75
Washington, Booker T. 4
Washington, Ebonya 79
Washington, Fredi 10
Washington, Harold 6
Washington, Pauletta Pearson 86
Waters, Maxine 3, 67
Wattleton, Faye 9
Wells, Henrietta Bell 69
Wells, James Lesesne 10
Wells-Barnett, Ida B. 8
Welsing, Frances Cress 5
West, Cornel 5, 33, 80
White, Michael R. 5
White, Reggie 6, 50
White, Walter F. 4
White, Willye 67
White-Hammond, Gloria 61
Wilkins, Roy 4
Williams, Armstrong 29
Williams, Evelyn 10
Williams, Fannie Barrier 27
Williams, George Washington 18
Williams, Hosea Lorenzo 15, 31
Williams, Maggie 7, 71
Williams, Montel 4, 57
Williams, Patricia 11, 54
Williams, Robert F. 11
Williams, Stanley "Tookie" 29, 57
Williams, Walter E. 4
Williams, Willie L. 4
Wilson, August 7, 33, 55
Wilson, Margaret Bush 79
Wilson, Phill 9
Wilson, Sunnie 7, 55
Wilson, William Julius 22
Withers, Ernest C. 68, 88
Wiwa, Ken 67
Wolfe, George C. 6, 43
Woodson, Robert L. 10
Worrill, Conrad 12
Wright, Charles H. 35

Wright, Louis Tompkins 4
Wright, Nathan, Jr. 56
Wright, Richard 5
Wyatt, Addie L. 56
X, Malcolm 1
Xuma, Madie Hall 59
Yancy, Dorothy Cowser 42
Yarbrough, Camille 40
Yeboah, Emmanuel Ofosu 53
Yoba, Malik 11
Young, Andrew 3, 48
Young, Jean Childs 14
Young, Whitney M., Jr. 4
Youngblood, Johnny Ray 8
Zulu, Princess Kasune 54

Sports
Aaron, Hank 5
Abdul-Jabbar, Kareem 8
Abdur-Rahim, Shareef 28
Adams, Paul 50
Adu, Freddy 67
Alexander, Shaun 58
Ali, Laila 27, 63
Ali, Muhammad 2, 16, 52
Allen, Dick 85
Allen, Marcus 20
Allen, Ray 82
Amaker, Tommy 62
Amos, John 8, 62
Anderson, Elmer 25
Anderson, Jamal 22
Anderson, Mike 63
Anderson, Viv 58
Anthony, Carmelo 46, 94
Archibald, Tiny 90
Arenas, Gilbert 84
Artest, Ron 52
Ashe, Arthur 1, 18
Ashford, Emmett 22
Ashford, Evelyn 63
Ashley, Maurice 15, 47
Baines, Harold 32
Baker, Dusty 8, 43, 72
Banks, Ernie 33
Barber, Ronde 41
Barber, Tiki 57
Barkley, Charles 5, 66
Barnes, Ernie 16, 78
Barnes, John 53
Barnes, Steven 54
Barney, Lem 26
Barnhill, David 30
Baugé, Grégory 86
Baylor, Don 6
Baylor, Elgin 93
Beamon, Bob 30
Beasley, Jamar 29
Bekele, Kenenisa 75
Bell, James "Cool Papa" 36
Belle, Albert 10
Bettis, Jerome 64
Bickerstaff, Bernie 21
Bing, Dave 3, 59, 78
Bivins, Michael 72
Black, Joe 75
Blair, Paul 36
Blake, James 43
Blanks, Billy 22
Blanton, Dain 29
Bogues, Tyrone "Muggsy" 56
Bol, Manute 1
Bolt, Usain 73

Bolton-Holifield, Ruthie **28**
Bonaly, Surya **7**
Bonds, Barry **6, 34, 63**
Bonds, Bobby **43**
Bonheur, Yannick **84**
Bosh, Chris **85**
Bowe, Riddick **6**
Bramlett, Joseph **91**
Brand, Elton **31**
Brandon, Terrell **16**
Branham, George, III **50**
Brashear, Donald **39**
Brathwaite, Fred **35**
Briscoe, Marlin **37**
Brock, Lou **18**
Brooks, Aaron **33**
Brooks, Derrick **43**
Brown, Antron **85**
Brown, James **22**
Brown, Jim **11**
Brown, Mike **77**
Brown, Sean **52**
Brown, Willard **36**
Bruce, Isaac **26**
Bryant, Cullen **81**
Bryant, Kobe **15, 31, 71**
Buchanan, Ray **32**
Bush, Reggie **59, 88**
Butler, Leroy, III **17**
Bynoe, Peter C. B. **40**
Caldwell, Jim **81**
Campanella, Roy **25**
Carew, Rod **20**
Carnegie, Herbert **25**
Carter, Anson **24**
Carter, Butch **27**
Carter, Cris **21**
Carter, Joe **30**
Carter, Kenneth **53**
Carter, Rubin **26**
Carter, Vince **26**
Cash, Swin **59**
Catchings, Tamika **43**
Chamberlain, Wilt **18, 47**
Chaney, John **67**
Charleston, Oscar **39**
Cheeks, Maurice **47**
Cherry, Deron **40**
Cheruiyot, Robert **69**
Christie, Linford **8**
Claiborne, Loretta **34**
Clay, Bryan **57, 74**
Clemons, Michael "Pinball" **64**
Clendenon, Donn **26, 56**
Clifton, Nathaniel "Sweetwater" **47**
Coachman, Alice **18**
Coleman, Leonard S., Jr. **12**
Cooper, Andy "Lefty" **63**
Cooper, Charles "Chuck" **47**
Cooper, Michael **31**
Cooper-Dyke, Cynthia **17, 89**
Copeland, Michael **47**
Corley, Tony **62**
Cottrell, Comer **11**
Cox, Bryan **83**
Crawford, Carl **90**
Crennel, Romeo **54**
Crooks, Garth **53**
Croom, Sylvester **50**
Culpepper, Daunte **32, 85**
Cunningham, Randall **23**
Curry, Michael **85**
Dandridge, Ray **36**

Dantley, Adrian **72**
Davis, Ernie **48**
Davis, Mike **41**
Davis, Milt **74**
Davis, Piper **19**
Davis, Shani **58, 84**
Davis, Terrell **20**
Dawes, Dominique **11**
Dawson, Andre **85**
Day, Leon **39**
DeFrantz, Anita **37**
DeGale, James **74**
Delaney, Joe **76**
Devers, Gail **7, 87**
Dibaba, Tirunesh **73**
Dickerson, Eric **27**
Dixon, George **52**
Doby, Lawrence Eugene, Sr. **16, 41**
Doig, Jason **45**
Dorrell, Karl **52**
dos Santos, Manuel Francisco **65**
Drew, Charles Richard **7**
Drexler, Clyde **4, 61**
Drogba, Didier **78**
Duerson, Dave **93**
Dumars, Joe **16, 65**
Duncan, Tim **20, 91**
Dungy, Tony **17, 42, 59**
Dunn, Jerry **27**
Dunn, Warrick **90**
Durant, Kevin **76**
Dye, Jermaine **58**
Edwards, Harry **2**
Edwards, Herman **51**
Edwards, Teresa **14**
Elder, Lee **6**
Ellerbe, Brian **22**
Elliott, Sean **26**
Ellis, Dock **78**
Ellis, Jimmy **44**
Ervin, Anthony **66**
Erving, Julius **18, 47**
Eto'o, Samuel **73**
Ewing, Patrick **17, 73**
Farr, Mel **24**
Faulk, Marshall **35**
Felix, Allyson **48**
Ferdinand, Rio **82**
Fielder, Cecil **2**
Fielder, Prince Semien **68**
Flood, Curt **10, 93**
Flowers, Vonetta **35**
Ford, Cheryl **45**
Foreman, George **1, 15**
Forrest, Vernon **40, 79**
Foster, Andrew **79**
Fowler, Reggie **51**
Fox, Rick **27**
Frazier, Joe **19**
Frazier, Walt **91**
Frazier-Lyde, Jacqui **31**
Freeman, Cathy **29**
Freeman, Marianna **23**
Fuhr, Grant **1, 49**
Fuller, Vivian **33**
Futch, Eddie **33**
Gaines, Clarence E., Sr. **55**
Gaither, Alonzo Smith (Jake) **14**
Gans, Joe **91**
Garnett, Kevin **14, 70**
Garrison, Zina **2**
Gaston, Cito **71**
Gebrselassie, Haile **70**

Gentry, Alvin **23**
George, Eddie **80**
Gervin, George **80**
Gibson, Althea **8, 43**
Gibson, Bob **33**
Gibson, Josh **22**
Gibson, Truman K., Jr. **60**
Gill, Turner **83**
Gilliam, Frank **23**
Gilliam, Joe **31**
Glanville, Douglas Metunwa **82**
Gooden, Dwight **20**
Gorden, W. C. **71**
Goss, Tom **23**
Gourdine, Meredith **33**
Gourdine, Simon **11**
Graham, Trevor **84**
Granderson, Curtis **66**
Grand-Pierre, Jean-Luc **46**
Gray, Yeshimbra "Shimmy" **55**
Green, A. C. **32**
Green, Darrell **39, 74**
Green, Dennis **5, 45**
Greene, Joe **10**
Greene, Maurice **27, 77**
Greer, Hal **92**
Gregg, Eric **16**
Gregory, Ann **63**
Grier, Mike **43**
Grier, Roosevelt **1**
Griffey, Ken, Jr. **12, 73**
Griffith, Yolanda **25**
Griffith-Joyner, Florence **28**
Gumbel, Greg **8**
Gwynn, Tony **18, 83**
Gyan, Asamoah **87**
Hairston, Sam **88**
Hamilton, Lewis **66**
Haney, Lee **77**
Hardaway, Anfernee (Penny) **13**
Hardaway, Tim **35**
Harris, James **79**
Harris, Sylvia **70**
Harrison, Alvin **28**
Harrison, Calvin **28**
Harris-Stewart, Lusia **90**
Haskins, Clem **23**
Hawkins, Connie **91**
Haye, David **82**
Hayes, Bob **77**
Hayes, Elvin **93**
Heard, Gar **25**
Hearns, Thomas **29**
Henderson, Rickey **28, 78**
Henry, Thierry **66**
Hickman, Fred **11**
Hill, Calvin **19**
Hill, Grant **13, 94**
Hillary, Barbara **65**
Hilliard, Wendy **53**
Hines, Garrett **35**
Holdsclaw, Chamique **24**
Holland, Kimberly N. **62**
Holmes, Kelly **47**
Holmes, Larry **20, 68**
Holmes, Santonio **87**
Holyfield, Evander **6**
Hopkins, Bernard **35, 69**
Horton, Andre **33**
Horton, Suki **33**
Howard, Desmond **16, 58**
Howard, Juwan **15**
Howard, Ryan **65**

Howard, Sherri **36**
Hunter, Billy **22**
Hunter, Torii **43**
Hyde, Cowan F. "Bubba" **47**
Iginla, Jarome **35**
Ince, Paul **83**
Irvin, Michael **64**
Irvin, Monte **31**
Isaacs, John **76**
Iverson, Allen **24, 46**
Ivey, Phil **72**
Jackson, Jamea **64**
Jackson, Mannie **14**
Jackson, Rampage **83**
Jackson, Reggie **15**
Jackson, Rickey **88**
Jackson, Tom **70**
Jacobs, Regina **38**
James, David **84**
James, G. Larry **74**
James, LeBron **46, 78**
James, Vanessa **84**
Jenkins, Fergie **46**
Jeter, Derek **27, 93**
Johnson, Avery **62**
Johnson, Ben **1**
Johnson, Chris **92**
Johnson, Clifford "Connie" **52**
Johnson, Dennis **89**
Johnson, Earvin "Magic" **3, 39**
Johnson, Gus **92**
Johnson, Jack **8**
Johnson, Joe **94**
Johnson, Kevin **70**
Johnson, Keyshawn **91**
Johnson, Larry **28**
Johnson, Levi **48**
Johnson, Mamie "Peanut" **40**
Johnson, Michael **13**
Johnson, Rafer **33**
Johnson, Rodney Van **28**
Jones, Cobi N'Gai **18**
Jones, Cullen **73**
Jones, Deacon **92**
Jones, Ed "Too Tall" **46**
Jones, K. C. **83**
Jones, Lou **64**
Jones, Marion **21, 66**
Jones, Merlakia **34**
Jones, Randy **35**
Jones, Roy, Jr. **22**
Jones, Sam **85**
Jordan, Eddie **83**
Jordan, Michael **6, 21**
Joyce, Dru **81**
Joyner-Kersee, Jackie **5**
Justice, David **18**
Kaiser, Cecil **42**
Kanouté, Fred **68**
Keflezighi, Meb **49**
Keith, Floyd A. **61**
Kellogg, Clark **64**
Kennedy-Overton, Jayne Harris **46**
Kerry, Leon G. **46**
Kidd, Jason **86**
Kimbro, Henry A. **25**
King, Don **14**
Lacy, Sam **30, 46**
Ladd, Ernie **64**
Lane, Dick **92**
Lanier, Bob **47**
Lanier, Willie **33**
Lankford, Ray **23**

Laraque, Georges **48**
Larkin, Barry **24**
Lashley, Bobby **63**
Lassiter, Roy **24**
Lee, Canada **8**
Lennox, Betty **31**
Leonard, Buck **67**
Leonard, Sugar Ray **15**
Leslie, Lisa **16, 73**
Lester, Bill **42, 85**
Lewis, Butch **71**
Lewis, Carl **4**
Lewis, Denise **33**
Lewis, Lennox **27**
Lewis, Marvin **51, 87**
Lewis, Oliver **56**
Lewis, Ray **33**
Liston, Sonny **33**
Little, Floyd **86**
Little, Larry **90**
Littlepage, Craig **35**
Lloyd, Earl **26**
Lloyd, John Henry "Pop" **30**
Lofton, James **42**
Lofton, Kenny **12**
Lopes, Davey **92**
Loroupe, Tegla **59**
Lott, Ronnie **9**
Louis, Joe **5**
Love, Nat **9**
Love, Reggie **77**
Lowe, Sidney **64**
Lucas, John **7**
Mackey, Biz **82**
Mahorn, Rick **60**
Malone, Karl **18, 51, 90**
Malone, Moses **79**
Manigault, Earl "The Goat" **15**
Manuel, Jerry **94**
Mariner, Jonathan **41**
Martinez, Pedro **81**
Master P **21**
Matson, Ollie **93**
Mayers, Jamal **39**
Mayhew, Martin R. **76**
Mays, Willie **3**
Mayweather, Floyd, Jr. **57**
McAdoo, Bob **75**
McBride, Bryant **18**
McCarthy, Sandy **64**
McCray, Nikki **18**
McDaniel, Randall Cornell **81**
McGrady, Tracy **80**
McGriff, Fred **24**
McKegney, Tony **3**
McLendon, John B., Jr. **89**
McNabb, Donovan **29**
McNair, Steve **22, 47, 79**
McNeil, Lori **1**
McRae, Hal **84**
Mello, Breno **73**
Mensah, John **87**
Metcalfe, Ralph **26**
Milla, Roger **2**
Miller, Cheryl **10, 74**
Miller, Larry G. **72**
Miller, Reggie **33**
Mills, Sam **33**
Milton, DeLisha **31**
Minor, DeWayne **32**
Minoso, Minnie **89**
Mitchell, Sam **82**
Mohammed, Nazr **64**

Monk, Art **38, 73**
Monroe, Earl **89**
Montgomery, Tim **41**
Moon, Warren **8, 66**
Moore, Maya **94**
Moorer, Michael **19**
Morgan, Joe Leonard **9**
Morris, Raheem **77**
Moses, Edwin **8**
Mosley, Shane **32**
Moss, Randy **23, 90**
Motley, Marion **26**
Mourning, Alonzo **17, 44**
Muhammad, Jabir Herbert **72**
Mundine, Anthony **56**
Murray, Eddie **12**
Murray, Lenda **10**
Mutola, Maria **12**
Mutombo, Dikembe **7**
Nakhid, David **25**
Newcombe, Don **24**
Newsome, Ozzie **26**
Noah, Yannick **4, 60**
Odom, Lamar **81**
Olajuwon, Hakeem **2, 72**
Oliver, Pam **54**
O'Neal, Shaquille **8, 30**
O'Neil, Buck **19, 59**
Onyewu, Oguchi **60**
O'Ree, Willie **5**
Ortiz, David **52, 82**
Owens, Jesse **2**
Owens, Terrell **53**
Pace, Orlando **21**
Page, Alan **7**
Page, Greg **78**
Paige, Satchel **7**
Palmer, Violet **59**
Parish, Robert **43**
Parker, Candace **74**
Parker, Jim **64**
Parker, Tony **75**
Patterson, Floyd **19, 58**
Paul, Chris **84**
Payne, Ulice **42**
Payton, Walter **11, 25**
Peck, Carolyn **23**
Peete, Calvin **11**
Peete, Rodney **60**
Pelé **7**
Perrot, Kim **23**
Perry, Lowell **30**
Peters, Margaret **43**
Peters, Matilda **43**
Phillips, Teresa L. **42**
Pickett, Bill **11**
Pierce, Paul **71**
Pippen, Scottie **15, 89**
Pollard, Fritz **53**
Porter, Terry **75**
Powell, Mike **7**
Powell, Renee **34**
Powell, William J. **82**
Pride, Charley **26**
Prince, Ron **64**
Prince, Tayshaun **68**
Pryce, Trevor **89**
Puckett, Kirby **4, 58**
Quirot, Ana **13**
Radcliffe, Ted **74**
Randle, John **87**
Randolph, Willie **53**
Rashad, Ahmad **18**

Ready, Stephanie **33**
Reagins, Tony **94**
Reed, Willis, Jr. **86**
Reese, Pokey **28**
Regis, Cyrille **51**
Reynolds, Harold **77**
Rhoden, William C. **67**
Rhodes, Ray **14**
Ribbs, Willy T. **2**
Rice, Jerry **5, 55, 89**
Rice, Jim **75**
Richard, J. R. **87**
Richards, Sanya **66**
Richardson, Donna **39**
Richardson, Nolan **9**
Richmond, Mitch **19**
Rivers, Doc **25, 81**
Robertson, Oscar **26**
Robinson, David **24, 90**
Robinson, Eddie G. **10, 61**
Robinson, Frank **9, 87**
Robinson, Jackie **6**
Robinson, Sugar Ray **18**
Robinson, Will **51, 69**
Rodman, Dennis **12, 44**
Rollins, Jimmy **70**
Ronaldinho **69**
Rose, Derrick **82**
Rose, Lionel **56**
Rubin, Chanda **37**
Rudolph, Wilma **4**
Russell, Bill **8**
Sabathia, CC **74**
St. Julien, Marlon **29**
Salvador, Bryce **51**
Sampson, Charles **13**
Sanders, Barry **1, 53**
Sanders, Bob **72**
Sanders, Deion **4, 31**
Sanders, Satch **77**
Sapp, Warren **38**
Sayers, Gale **28**
Scott, Stuart **34**
Scott, Wendell Oliver, Sr. **19**
Scurry, Briana **27**
Shannon, Randy **82**
Sharper, Darren **32**
Sheffield, Gary **16**
Shell, Art **1, 66**
Shippen, John **43**
Showers, Reggie **30**
Sifford, Charlie **4, 49**
Silas, Paul **24**
Simmons, Bob **29**
Simpson, O. J. **15**
Singletary, Mike **4, 76**
Slice, Kimbo **73**
Smith, Bruce **80**
Smith, Emmitt **7, 87**
Smith, Hilton **29**
Smith, Lovie **66**
Smith, Ozzie **77**
Smith, Randy **81**
Smith, Rick **72**
Smith, Stephen A. **69**
Smith, Tubby **18, 83**
Solomon, Jimmie Lee **38**
Sono, Jomo **86**
Sosa, Sammy **21, 44**
Spiller, Bill **64**
Sprewell, Latrell **23**
Stackhouse, Jerry **30**
Staley, Dawn **57**

Stargell, Willie **29**
Stearns, Norman "Turkey" **31**
Steward, Emanuel **18**
Stewart, James "Bubba," Jr. **60**
Stewart, Kordell **21**
Stingley, Darryl **69**
Stith, Tom **93**
Stone, Toni **15**
Stoudemire, Amaré **59**
Strahan, Michael **35, 81**
Strawberry, Darryl **22**
Stringer, C. Vivian **13, 66**
Stringer, Korey **35**
Swann, Lynn **28**
Swoopes, Sheryl **12, 56**
Tatum, Jack **87**
Taylor, Jason **70**
Taylor, Jermain **60**
Taylor, Lawrence **25**
Taylor, Marshall Walter "Major" **62**
Tergat, Paul **59**
Terrell-Kearney, Kim **83**
Thomas, Debi **26**
Thomas, Derrick **25**
Thomas, Emmitt **71**
Thomas, Frank **12, 51**
Thomas, Isiah **7, 26, 65**
Thomas, Thurman **75**
Thompson, Tina **25, 75**
Thrower, Willie **35**
Thugwane, Josia **21**
Thurmond, Nate **88**
Tirico, Mike **68**
Tisdale, Wayman **50**
Toler, Burl **80**
Tomlinson, LaDainian **65**
Toney, James **89**
Trouppe, Quincy Thomas, Sr. **84**
Tunnell, Emlen **54**
Tyson, Mike **28, 44, 93**
Unseld, Wes **23**
Upshaw, Gene **18, 47, 72**
Ussery, Terdema, II **29**
Vanessa James and Yannick Bonheur **84**
Vick, Michael **39, 65, 94**
Vincent, Troy **91**
Virgil, Ozzie **48**
Wade, Dwyane **61**
Walker, Herschel **1, 69**
Wallace, Ben **54**
Wallace, Perry E. **47**
Wallace, Rasheed **56**
Wanjiru, Sammy **94**
Ward, Andre **62**
Ward, Hines **84**
Ware, Andre **37**
Ware, DeMarcus **92**
Washington, Gene **63**
Washington, Kenny **50**
Washington, MaliVai **8**
Watson, Bob **25**
Watts, J. C., Jr. **14, 38**
Weah, George **58**
Weathers, Carl **10**
Webber, Chris **15, 30, 59**
Weekes, Kevin **67**
Wells, Vernon **91**
Westbrook, Peter **20**
Whitaker, Pernell **10, 89**
White, Bill **1, 48**
White, Jesse **22, 75**
White, Reggie **6, 50**

White, Willye 67
Whitfield, Fred 23
Whitfield, Mal 60
Wilbon, Michael 68
Wilkens, Lenny 11, 88
Wilkins, Dominique 74
Williams, Billy 86
Williams, Deron 92
Williams, Doug 22
Williams, J. Mayo 83
Williams, Ken 68
Williams, Lauryn 58
Williams, Natalie 31
Williams, Ricky 85
Williams, Serena 20, 41, 73
Williams, Stevie 71
Williams, Venus 17, 34, 62
Williamson, Fred 67
Willingham, Tyrone 43
Willis, Bill 68
Willis, Dontrelle 55
Wills, Harry 80
Wills, Maury 73
Wilson, Sunnie 7, 55
Winfield, Dave 5, 91
Winkfield, Jimmy 42
Winslow, Kellen 83
Wolfe, Ann 82
Woodard, Lynette 67
Woodruff, John 68
Woods, Tiger 14, 31, 81
Woodson, Mike 78
Woodson, Rod 79
Worthy, James 49
Wright, Rayfield 70
Yeboah, Emmanuel Ofosu 53
Young, Donald, Jr. 57
Young, Jimmy 54

Television

Akil, Mara Brock 60, 82
Akinnuoye-Agbaje, Adewale 56
Alexander, Khandi 43
Ali, Tatyana 73
Allen, Byron 3
Allen, Debbie 13, 42
Allen, Marcus 20
Alonso, Laz 87
Amos, John 8, 62
Anderson, Anthony 51, 77
Anderson, Eddie "Rochester" 30
Andrews, Tina 74
Arkadie, Kevin 17
Arnez J 53
Arnold, Tichina 63
Babatunde, Obba 35
Banks, Michelle 59
Banks, William 11
Barclay, Paris 37, 94
Bassett, Angela 6, 23, 62
Beach, Michael 26
Beaton, Norman 14
Beauvais, Garcelle 29
Bellamy, Bill 12
Bennett, Louise 69
Bentley, Lamont 53
Berry, Bertice 8, 55
Berry, Fred "Rerun" 48
Blackmon, Brenda 58
Blackwood, Maureen 37
Blacque, Taurean 58
Blake, Asha 26
Bleu, Corbin 65

Bonet, Lisa 58
Boston, Kelvin E. 25
Bowser, Yvette Lee 17
Bradley, Ed 2, 59
Brady, Wayne 32, 71
Brandy 14, 34, 72
Braugher, Andre 13, 58, 91
Bridges, Todd 37
Brooks, Avery 9
Brooks, Golden 62
Brooks, Hadda 40
Brooks, Mehcad 62
Brown, Chris 74
Brown, James 22
Brown, Joe 29
Brown, Les 5
Brown, Tony 3
Brown, Vivian 27
Brown, Warren 61
Browne, Roscoe Lee 66
Bruce, Bruce 56
Burnett, Charles 16, 68
Burton, LeVar 8
Byrd, Eugene 64
Byrd, Robert 11
Caldwell, Benjamin 46
Cameron, Earl 44
Campbell, Naomi 1, 31
Campbell-Martin, Tisha 8, 42
Cannon, Nick 47, 73
Cannon, Reuben 50
Cara, Irene 77
Carroll, Rocky 74
Carroll, Diahann 9
Carson, Lisa Nicole 21
Carter, Nell 39
Cash, Rosalind 28
Cedric the Entertainer 29, 60
Cenac, Wyatt 94
Chappelle, Dave 50
Cheadle, Don 19, 52
Chestnut, Morris 31
Chideya, Farai 14, 61
Christian, Spencer 15
Ciara, Barbara 69
Clack, Zoanne 73
Clash, Kevin 14, 93
Clayton, Xernona 3, 45
CoCo Brother 93
Cole, Nat "King" 17
Coleman, Gary 35, 86
Corbi, Lana 42
Cornelius, Don 4
Cosby, Bill 7, 26, 59
Crothers, Scatman 19
Curry, Mark 17
Curtis-Hall, Vondie 17
Davidson, Tommy 21
Davis, Eisa 68
Davis, Mia Amber 94
Davis, Ossie 5, 50
Davis, Viola 34, 76
de Passe, Suzanne 25
De Shields, André 72
Dee, Ruby 8, 50, 68
Deezer D 53
Devine, Loretta 24
Dickerson, Eric 27
Dickerson, Ernest 6
Diggs, Taye 25, 63
Dixon, Ivan 69
DJ Lance Rock 94
Dourdan, Gary 37

Drake 86
Dre, Dr. 10
Duke, Bill 3
Dungey, Merrin 62
Dutton, Charles S. 4, 22
Earthquake 55
Ejiofor, Chiwetel 67
Elba, Idris 49, 89
Elder, Larry 25
Elise, Kimberly 32
Emmanuel, Alphonsia 38
Ephriam, Mablean 29
Epperson, Sharon 54
Erving, Julius 18, 47
Esposito, Giancarlo 9
Eubanks, Kevin 15
Evans, Harry 25
Faison, Donald 50
Faison, Frankie 55
Falana, Lola 42
Fales-Hill, Susan 88
Fargas, Antonio 50
Fields, Kim 36
Fishburne, Laurence 4, 22, 70
Fisher, Gail 85
Flavor Flav 67
Fox, Rick 27
Foxx, Jamie 15, 48
Foxx, Redd 2
Frazier, Kevin 58
Freeman, Aaron 52
Freeman, Al, Jr. 11
Freeman, Morgan 2, 20, 62
Freeman, Yvette 27
Gaines, Ernest J. 7
Gardere, Jeffrey 76
Garvin, Gerry 78
Gibbs, Marla 86
Gibson, Tyrese 27, 62
Givens, Adele 62
Givens, Robin 4, 25, 58
Glover, Danny 3, 24
Glover, Donald 85
Glover, Savion 14
Goldberg, Whoopi 4, 33, 69
Goode, Mal 13
Gooding, Cuba, Jr. 16, 62
Gordon, Carl 87
Gordon, Ed 10, 53
Gossett, Louis, Jr. 7
Gray, Darius 69
Greely, M. Gasby 27
Greene, Petey 65
Grier, David Alan 28
Grier, Pam 9, 31, 86
Griffin, Angela 80
Guillaume, Robert 3, 48
Gumbel, Bryant 14, 80
Gumbel, Greg 8
Gunn, Moses 10
Gurira, Danai 73
Guy, Jasmine 2
Hairston, Jester 88
Haley, Alex 4
Hall, Arsenio 58
Hamilton, Lisa Gay 71
Hampton, Henry 6
Hardison, Kadeem 22
Harewood, David 52
Harper, Hill 32, 65
Harrell, Andre 9, 30
Harris, Naomie 55
Harris, Robin 7

Harvey, Steve 18, 58
Hatchett, Glenda 32
Hayes, Isaac 20, 58, 73
Haynes, Trudy 44
Haysbert, Dennis 42
Hemsley, Sherman 19
Henderson, Jeff 72
Henriques, Julian 37
Henry, Lenny 9, 52
Henson, Darrin 33
Henson, Taraji P. 58, 77
Hickman, Fred 11
Hill, Dulé 29
Hill, Lauryn 20, 53
Hill, Marc Lamont 80
Hinderas, Natalie 5
Hines, Gregory 1, 42
Holmes, Amy 69
Holt, Lester 66
Hooks, Robert 76
Hounsou, Djimon 19, 45
Howard, Sherri 36
Howard, Terrence 59, 94
Hudson, Ernie 72
Huggins, Edie 71
Hughley, D. L. 23, 76
Hunter-Gault, Charlayne 6, 31
Hyman, Earle 25, 79
Ice-T 6, 31
Ifill, Gwen 28
Ingram, Rex 5
Jackson, George 19
Jackson, Janet 6, 30, 68
Jackson, Randy 40
Jackson, Tom 70
Jarrett, Vernon D. 42
Joe, Yolanda 21
Johnson, Beverly 2
Johnson, Linton Kwesi 37
Johnson, Robert L. 3, 39
Johnson, Rodney Van 28
Jones, James Earl 3, 49, 79
Jones, Orlando 30
Jones, Quincy 8, 30
Kandi 83
Kaufman, Monica 66
Kelley, Malcolm David 59
Kennedy-Overton, Jayne Harris 46
Keys, Alicia 32, 68
Kid Cudi 83
King, Gayle 19
King, Regina 22, 45
King, Woodie, Jr. 27
Kirby, George 14
Kitt, Eartha 16, 75
Knight, Gladys 16, 66
Kodjoe, Boris 34, 89
Kotto, Yaphet 7
Kwei-Armah, Kwame 84
La Salle, Eriq 12
LaBelle, Patti 13, 30
Langhart Cohen, Janet 19, 60
Lathan, Sanaa 27
Lawrence, Martin 6, 27, 60
Lawson, Jennifer 1, 50
Lee, Leslie 85
Lemmons, Kasi 20
Lemon, Don 94
Lesure, James 64
Lewis, Ananda 28
Lewis, Byron E. 13
Lewis, Emmanuel 36
Lil' Kim 28

Lindo, Delroy **18, 45**
LisaRaye **27**
LL Cool J **16, 49, 94**
Lofton, James **42**
Long, Loretta **58**
Long, Nia **17**
Lover, Ed **10**
Luke, Derek **61**
Lumbly, Carl **47**
Mabrey, Vicki **26**
Mabuza-Suttle, Felicia **43**
Mac, Bernie **29, 61, 72**
Madison, Paula **37**
Malco, Romany **71**
Malveaux, Suzanne **88**
Manigault-Stallworth, Omarosa **69**
Mann, Tamela **92**
Martin, Helen **31**
Martin, Jesse L. **31**
Mathis, Greg **26**
Mayo, Whitman **32**
Mbatha-Raw, Gugu **89**
McBride, Chi **73**
McCrary Anthony, Crystal **70**
McDaniel, Hattie **5**
McDaniels, Ralph **79**
McEwen, Mark **5**
McFarland, Roland **49**
McGlowan, Angela **64, 86**
McKee, Lonette **12**
McKenzie, Vashti M. **29**
McKinney, Nina Mae **40**
McQueen, Butterfly **6, 54**
Meadows, Tim **30**
Mello, Breno **73**
Melton, Frank **81**
Mercado-Valdes, Frank **43**
Merkerson, S. Epatha **47, 83**
Michele, Michael **31**
Mickelbury, Penny **28**
Miller, Omar Benson **93**
Miller, Wentworth **75**
Mitchell, Brian Stokes **21**
Mitchell, Kel **66**
Mitchell, Russ **21, 73**
Mokae, Zakes **80**
Mo'Nique **35, 84**
Mooney, Paul **37**
Moore, Chante **26**
Moore, Melba **21**
Moore, Shemar **21**
Morgan, Joe Leonard **9**
Morgan, Tracy **61**
Morris, Garrett **31**
Morris, Greg **28**
Morton, Frederick A., Jr. **93**
Morton, Joe **18**
Mos Def **30**
Moses, Gilbert **12**
Moss, Carlton **17**
Mowry, Tamera **79**
Mowry, Tia **78**
Murphy, Eddie **4, 20, 61**
Muse, Clarence Edouard **21**
Myles, Kim **69**
Nash, Johnny **40**
Nash, Niecy **66**
Neal, Elise **29**
Nicholas, Denise **82**
Nichols, Nichelle **11**
Nissel, Angela **42**
Neville, Arthel **53**
Noble, Gil **76**

Norman, Christina **47**
Norman, Maidie **20**
O'Brien, Soledad **88**
Odetta **37, 74**
Okonedo, Sophie **67**
Oliver, Pam **54**
Onwurah, Ngozi **38**
Orman, Roscoe **55**
Palcy, Euzhan **94**
Palmer, Keke **68**
Parker, Nicole Ari **52**
Parr, Russ **51**
Payne, Allen **13**
Peete, Holly Robinson **20**
Peete, Rodney **60**
Perkins, Tony **24**
Perrineau, Harold, Jr. **51**
Perry, Lowell **30**
Perry, Tyler **40**
Phifer, Mekhi **25**
Phillips, Joseph C. **73**
Pickens, James, Jr. **59**
Pierce, Wendell **90**
Pinckney, Sandra **56**
Pinkett Smith, Jada **10, 41**
Pinkston, W. Randall **24**
Pitts, Byron **71**
Poitier, Sydney Tamiia **65**
Pounder, CCH **72**
Poussaint, Renee **78**
Price, Frederick K. C. **21**
Price, Hugh B. **9, 54**
Prince-Bythewood, Gina **31, 77**
Pugh, Charles **81**
Quarles, Norma **25**
Queen Latifah **1, 16, 58**
Quivers, Robin **61**
Ralph, Sheryl Lee **18**
Randle, Theresa **16**
Rashad, Ahmad **18**
Rashad, Phylicia **21**
Raven **44**
Ray, Gene Anthony **47**
Ray J **86**
Reddick, Lance **52**
Reed Hall, Alaina **83**
Reese, Della **6, 20**
Reid, Tim **56**
Reuben, Gloria **15**
Reynolds, Star Jones **10, 27, 61**
Rhimes, Shonda Lynn **67**
Ribeiro, Alfonso **17**
Richards, Beah **30**
Richardson, Donna **39**
Richardson, LaTanya **71**
Richardson, Salli **68**
Ridley, John **69**
Roberts, Deborah **35**
Roberts, Robin **16, 54**
Robinson, Matt **69**
Robinson, Max **3**
Robinson, Shaun **36**
Rochon, Lela **16**
Rock, Chris **3, 22, 66**
Rodgers, Johnathan **6, 51**
Rodrigues, Percy **68**
Roker, Al **12, 49**
Roker, Roxie **68**
Rolle, Esther **13, 21**
Rollins, Howard E., Jr. **16**
Ross, Diana **8, 27**
Ross, Tracee Ellis **35**
Roundtree, Richard **27**

Rowan, Carl T. **1, 30**
Rowell, Victoria **13, 68**
Rudolph, Maya **46**
Run **31, 73**
RuPaul **17, 91**
Russell, Bill **8**
Russell, Nipsey **66**
Rust, Art, Jr. **83**
St. Jacques, Raymond **8**
St. John, Kristoff **25**
St. Patrick, Mathew **48**
Saldana, Zoe **72**
Salters, Lisa **71**
Sands, Diana **87**
Sanford, Isabel **53**
Santiago-Hudson, Ruben **85**
Schultz, Michael A. **6**
Scott, Hazel **66**
Scott, Jill **29, 83**
Scott, Stuart **34**
Shaw, Bernard **2, 28**
Shepherd, Sherri **55**
Simmons, Henry **55**
Simmons, Jamal **72**
Simmons, Kimora Lee **51, 83**
Simpson, Carole **6, 30**
Simpson, O. J. **15**
Sinbad **1, 16**
Sinclair, Madge **78**
Smiley, Tavis **20, 68**
Smith, Anjela Lauren **44**
Smith, B(arbara) **11**
Smith, Ian **62**
Smith, Roger Guenveur **12**
Smith, Tasha **73**
Smith, Will **8, 18, 53**
Stewart, Alison **13**
Stewart, Nzingha **89**
Stokes, Carl **10, 73**
Stone, Chuck **9**
Strahan, Michael **35, 81**
Stuart, Moira **82**
Sykes, Wanda **48, 81**
Syler, Rene **53**
Swann, Lynn **28**
Tate, Larenz **15**
Taylor, Jason **70**
Taylor, Karin **34**
Taylor, Meshach **4**
Taylor, Regina **9, 46**
Thigpen, Lynne **17, 41**
Thomas-Graham, Pamela **29**
Thomason, Marsha **47**
Thompson, Kenan **52**
Thoms, Tracie **61**
Tirico, Mike **68**
Torres, Gina **52**
Torry, Guy **31**
Toussaint, Lorraine **32**
Townsend, Robert **4, 23**
True, Rachel **82**
Tucker, Chris **13, 23, 62**
Tunie, Tamara **63**
Tyler, Aisha N. **36**
Tyson, Cicely **7, 51**
Uggams, Leslie **23**
Underwood, Blair **7, 27, 76**
Union, Gabrielle **31, 92**
Usher **23, 56**
Van Peebles, Mario **2, 51**
Van Peebles, Melvin **7**
Vaughn, Countess **53**
Vereen, Ben **4**

Walker, Eamonn **37**
Ware, Andre **37**
Warfield, Marsha **2**
Warner, Malcolm-Jamal **22, 36**
Warren, Michael **27**
Warwick, Dionne **18**
Washington, Denzel **1, 16, 93**
Washington, Hayma **86**
Washington, Isaiah **62**
Watson, Carlos **50**
Wattleton, Faye **9**
Watts, Rolonda **9**
Wayans, Damien **78**
Wayans, Damon **8, 41**
Wayans, Kim **80**
Wayans, Keenen Ivory **18**
Wayans, Marlon **29, 82**
Wayans, Shawn **29**
Weathers, Carl **10**
Wesley, Richard **73**
Whack, Rita Coburn **36**
Whitfield, Lynn **1, 18**
Wilbon, Michael **68**
Williams, Armstrong **29**
Williams, Billy Dee **8**
Williams, Clarence, III **26**
Williams, Juan **35, 80**
Williams, Malinda **57**
Williams, Montel **4, 57**
Williams, Russell, II **70**
Williams, Samm-Art **21**
Williams, Vanessa A. **32, 66**
Williams, Vanessa L. **4, 17**
Williams, Wendy **62**
Williamson, Mykelti **22**
Wills, Maury **53**
Wilson, Chandra **57**
Wilson, Debra **38**
Wilson, Dorien **55**
Wilson, Flip **21**
Winfield, Paul **2, 45**
Winfrey, Oprah **2, 15, 61**
Witherspoon, John **38**
Wright, Jeffrey **54**
Yarbrough, Cedric **51**
Yoba, Malik **11**

Theater
Adams, Osceola Macarthy **31**
Ailey, Alvin **8**
Alexander, Khandi **43**
Allen, Debbie **13, 42**
Amos, John **8, 62**
Anderson, Carl **48**
Andrews, Bert **13**
Angelou, Maya **1, 15**
Anthony, Trey **63**
Arkadie, Kevin **17**
Armstrong, Vanessa Bell **24**
Arnez J **53**
Babatunde, Obba **35**
Bandele, Biyi **68**
Baraka, Amiri **1, 38**
Barclay, Paris **37, 94**
Barnett, Etta Moten **56**
Barrett, Lindsay **43**
Bassett, Angela **6, 23, 62**
Beach, Michael **26**
Beaton, Norman **14**
Belafonte, Harry **4, 65**
Belgrave, Cynthia **75**
Bennett, Louise **69**
Borders, James **9**

Branch, William Blackwell 39
Braugher, Andre 13, 58, 91
Brooks, Avery 9
Brown, Oscar, Jr. 53
Brown, Ruth 90
Browne, Roscoe Lee 66
Bruce, Bruce 56
Caldwell, Benjamin 46
Calloway, Cab 14
Cameron, Earl 44
Campbell, Naomi 1
Cara, Irene 77
Carroll, Diahann 9
Carroll, Rocky 74
Carroll, Vinnette 29
Carter, Nell 39
Cash, Rosalind 28
Cheadle, Don 19, 52
Chenault, John 40
Childress, Alice 15
Clarke, Hope 14
Cleage, Pearl 17, 64
Cook, Will Marion 40
Cooper, Chuck 75
Corthron, Kia 43
Curtis-Hall, Vondie 17
Dadié, Bernard 34
David, Keith 27
Davis, Altovise 76
Davis, Eisa 68
Davis, Ossie 5, 50
Davis, Sammy, Jr. 18
Davis, Viola 34, 76
Dawn, Marpessa 75
De Shields, André 72
Dee, Ruby 8, 50, 68
Devine, Loretta 24
Dieudonné 67
Diggs, Taye 25, 63
Dixon, Ivan 69
Dodson, Owen Vincent 38
Domingo, Colman 94
Duke, Bill 3
Dunham, Katherine 4, 59
Dutton, Charles S. 4, 22
Ejiofor, Chiwetel 67
Elba, Idris 49, 89
Elder, Lonne, III 38
Emmanuel, Alphonsia 38
Epps, Mike 60
Esposito, Giancarlo 9
Europe, James Reese 10
Faison, Frankie 55
Falana, Lola 42
Fargas, Antonio 50
Fields, Felicia P. 60
Fishburne, Laurence 4, 22, 70
Francis, Thais 93
Franklin, J. E. 44
Freeman, Aaron 52
Freeman, Al, Jr. 11
Freeman, Morgan 2, 20, 62
Freeman, Yvette 27
Fuller, Charles 8
Gibson, John Trusty 87
Gilpin, Charles Sidney 81
Givens, Adele 62
Glover, Danny 1, 24
Glover, Keith 79
Glover, Savion 14
Goldberg, Whoopi 4, 33, 69
Gordone, Charles 15
Gossett, Louis, Jr. 7

Graves, Denyce Antoinette 19, 57
Greaves, William 38
Grier, Pam 9, 31, 86
Guillaume, Robert 3, 48
Gunn, Moses 10
Gurira, Danai 73
Hall, Juanita 62
Hamilton, Lisa Gay 71
Hamlin, Larry Leon 49, 62
Hansberry, Lorraine 6
Harewood, David 52
Harris, Bill 72
Harris, Robin 7
Hayes, Teddy 40
Hemsley, Sherman 19
Henry, Joshua 94
Higginsen, Vy 65
Hill, Dulé 29
Hill, Errol 40
Hill, Hugh Morgan 83
Hines, Gregory 1, 42
Holder, Geoffrey 78
Holder, Laurence 34
Holland, Endesha Ida Mae 3, 57
Hooks, Robert 76
Hyman, Earle 25, 79
Hyman, Phyllis 19
Ingram, Rex 5
Jackson, Millie 25
Jackson, Samuel 8, 19, 63
James, Nikki M. 94
Jamison, Judith 7, 67
Jean-Baptiste, Marianne 17, 46
Johnson, Je'Caryous 63
Jones, James Earl 3, 49, 79
Jones, Sarah 39
Joyner, Matilda Sissieretta 15
Kente, Gibson 52
Khumalo, Leleti 51
King, Woodie, Jr. 27
King, Yolanda 6
Kitt, Eartha 16, 75
Kotto, Yaphet 7
Kwei-Armah, Kwame 84
La Salle, Eriq 12
LaChanze 93
Lampley, Oni Faida 43, 71
Lathan, Sanaa 27
Lee, Canada 8
Lee, Leslie 85
Leggs, Kingsley 62
Lemmons, Kasi 20
LeNoire, Rosetta 37
Lenox, Adriane 59
Leon, Kenny 10
Lester, Adrian 46
Letson, Al 39
Lindo, Delroy 18, 45
Lister, Marquita 65
Mann, Tamela 92
Marrow, Queen Esther 24
Martin, Helen 31
Martin, Jesse L. 31
Mbatha-Raw, Gugu 89
McClendon, Forrest 94
McClinton, Marion Isaac 77
McDaniel, Hattie 5
McDonald, Audra 20, 62
McFarlan, Tyron 60
McKee, Lonette 12
McQueen, Butterfly 6, 54
Merkerson, S. Epatha 47, 83
Mickelbury, Penny 28

Miller, Patina 94
Mills, Florence 22
Milner, Ron 39
Mitchell, Brian Stokes 21
Mokae, Zakes 80
Mollel, Tololwa 38
Moore, Melba 21
Morgan, Tracy 61
Moses, Gilbert 12
Moss, Carlton 17
Moss, Preacher 63
Moten, Etta 18
Muse, Clarence Edouard 21
Nascimento, Abdias do 93
Ngaujah, Sahr 86
Nicholas, Fayard 20, 57
Nicholas, Harold 20
Norman, Maidie 20
Nottage, Lynn 66
Ntshona, Winston 52
Okonedo, Sophie 67
Orlandersmith, Dael 42
Oyelowo, David 82
Payne, Allen 13
Perrineau, Harold, Jr. 51
Perry, Tyler 54
Pierce, Wendell 90
Pounder, CCH 72
Powell, Maxine 8
Power, Will 83
Preer, Evelyn 82
Premice, Josephine 41
Primus, Pearl 6
Pryor, Rain 65
Ralph, Sheryl Lee 18
Randle, Theresa 16
Rashad, Phylicia 21
Raven 44
Redwood, John Henry 78
Reese, Della 6, 20
Reid, Tim 56
Rhames, Ving 14, 50
Richards, Beah 30
Richards, Lloyd 2
Richardson, Desmond 39
Richardson, LaTanya 71
Robeson, Paul 2
Rolle, Esther 13, 21
Rollins, Howard E., Jr. 16
Rose, Anika Noni 70
Rotimi, Ola 1
St. Jacques, Raymond 8
Salter, Nikkole 73
Sands, Diana 87
Sanford, Isabel 53
Santiago-Hudson, Ruben 85
Schultz, Michael A. 6
Scott, Harold Russell, Jr. 61
Shabazz, Attallah 6
Slocumb, Jonathan 52
Smiley, Rickey 59
Smith, Anjela Lauren 44
Smith, Anna Deavere 6, 44
Smith, Roger Guenveur 12
Snipes, Wesley 3, 24, 67
Sommore 61
Soyinka, Wole 4, 93
Stew 69
Stewart, Tonea Harris 78
Sundiata, Sekou 66
Talbert, David E. 34, 93
Taylor, Meshach 4
Taylor, Regina 9, 46

Taylor, Ron 35
Teer, Barbara Ann 81
Thigpen, Lynne 17, 41
Thompson, John Douglas 81
Thompson, Tazewell 13
Thurman, Wallace 16
Torres, Gina 52
Toussaint, Lorraine 32
Townsend, Robert 4, 23
Tyson, Cicely 7, 51
Uggams, Leslie 23
Underwood, Blair 7, 27, 76
Van Peebles, Melvin 7
Vance, Courtney B. 15, 60
Vereen, Ben 4
Walcott, Derek 5, 94
Walker, Eamonn 37
Ward, Douglas Turner 42
Warfield, William 94
Washington, Fredi 10
Waters, Ethel 7
Watts, Reggie 52
Whitaker, Forest 2, 49, 67
White, Terri 82
White, Willard 53
Whitfield, Lynn 18
Williams, Bert 18
Williams, Billy Dee 8
Williams, Clarence, III 26
Williams, Michelle 73
Williams, Samm-Art 21
Williamson, Mykelti 22
Wilson, August 7, 33, 55
Wilson, Dorien 55
Wilson, Tracey Scott 777
Winfield, Paul 2, 45
Withers-Mendes, Elisabeth 64
Wolfe, George C. 6, 43
Woodard, Alfre 9
Wright, Jeffrey 54
Yarbrough, Cedric 51

Writing
Abani, Chris 77
Abrahams, Peter 39
Abu-Jamal, Mumia 15
Achebe, Chinua 6
Adams, Jenoyne 60
Adams-Ender, Clara 40
Adichie, Chimamanda Ngozi 64
Aidoo, Ama Ata 38
Ake, Claude 30
Akpan, Uwem 70
Al-Amin, Jamil Abdullah 6
Alexander, Elizabeth 75
Alexander, Margaret Walker 22
Ali, Ayaan Hirsi 58, 92
Ali, Hana Yasmeen 52
Ali, Mohammed Naseehu 60
Allen, Robert L. 38
Allen, Samuel W. 38
Amadi, Elechi 40
Ames, Wilmer 27
Anderson, Ho Che 54
Andrews, Raymond 4
Andrews, Tina 74
Angelou, Maya 1, 15
Ansa, Tina McElroy 14
Anthony, Michael 29
Appiah, Kwame Anthony 67
Arac de Nyeko, Monica 66
Aristide, Jean-Bertrand 6, 45
Arkadie, Kevin 17

Armah, Ayi Kwei 49
Armah, Esther 87
Asante, Molefi Kete 3
Ashley-Ward, Amelia 23
Asim, Jabari 71
Atkins, Cholly 40
Atkins, Russell 45
Aubert, Alvin 41
Auguste, Arnold A. 47
Awoonor, Kofi 37
Azikiwe, Nnamdi 13
Ba, Mariama 30
Bahati, Wambui 60
Bailey, Chauncey 68
Baiocchi, Regina Harris 41
Baisden, Michael 25, 66
Baker, Augusta 38
Baker, Houston A., Jr. 6
Baldwin, James 1
Ballard, Allen Butler, Jr. 40
Bambara, Toni Cade 10
Bandele, Asha 36
Bandele, Biyi 68
Baquet, Dean 63
Baraka, Amiri 1, 38
Barnes, Steven 54
Barnett, Amy Du Bois 46
Barrax, Gerald William 45
Barrett, Lindsay 43
Bashir, Halima 73
Bass, Charlotta Spears 40
Baszile, Jennifer 79
Bates, Karen Grigsby 40
Beah, Ishmael 69
Beals, Melba Pattillo 15, 94
Bebey, Francis 45
Beckham, Barry 41
Bell, Derrick 6
Bell, James Madison 40
Benberry, Cuesta 65
Bennett, George Harold 45
Bennett, Gwendolyn B. 59
Bennett, Lerone, Jr. 5, 84
Bennett, Louise 69
Benson, Angela 34
Berry, James 41
Berry, Mary Frances 7
Best, Carrie 80
Beti, Mongo 36
Betts, R. Dwayne 86
Bishop, Maurice 39
Blackman, Toni 86
Blair, Jayson 50
Bland, Eleanor Taylor 39
Blassingame, John Wesley 40
Blockson, Charles L. 42
Blow, Charles M. 73
Bluitt, Juliann S. 14
Bolden, Tonya 32
Bontemps, Arna 8
Booker, Simeon 23
Borders, James 9
Boston, Lloyd 24
Boyd, Gerald M. 32, 59
Boyd, Melba Joyce 86
Boyd, Suzanne 52
Bradley, David Henry, Jr. 39
Bradley, Ed 2, 59
Braithwaite, William Stanley 52
Branch, William Blackwell 39
Brand, Dionne 32
Brathwaite, Kamau 36
Brawley, Benjamin 44

Breeze, Jean "Binta" 37
Bridges, Sheila 36
Brimmer, Andrew F. 2, 48
Briscoe, Connie 15
Britt, Donna 28
Brooks, Gwendolyn 1, 28
Brower, William 49
Brown, Cecil M. 46
Brown, Claude 38
Brown, Elaine 8
Brown, Les 5
Brown, Lloyd Louis 10, 42
Brown, Marie Dutton 12
Brown, Sterling Allen 10, 64
Brown, Tony 3
Brown, Wesley 23
Broyard, Anatole 68
Broyard, Bliss 68
Brutus, Dennis 38
Bryan, Ashley F. 41
Buckley, Gail Lumet 39
Bullins, Ed 25
Bunche, Ralph J. 5
Bunkley, Anita Richmond 39
Burgess, Marjorie L. 55
Burroughs, Margaret Taylor 9
Burwell, Bryan 83
Butler, Octavia 8, 43, 58
Bynum, Juanita 31, 71
Caldwell, Earl 60
Calhoun, Lillian Scott 87
Campbell, Bebe Moore 6, 24, 59
Carby, Hazel 27
Carmichael, Stokely 5, 26
Carroll, Vinnette 29
Carter, Joye Maureen 41
Carter, Martin 49
Carter, Stephen L. 4
Cartey, Wilfred 47
Cartiér, Xam Wilson 41
Cary, Lorene 3
Cary, Mary Ann Shadd 30
Cayton, Horace 26
Cenac, Wyatt 94
Césaire, Aimé 48, 69
Chadiha, Jeffri 57
Channer, Colin 36
Chase-Riboud, Barbara 20, 46
Chenault, John 40
Cheney-Coker, Syl 43
Chesnutt, Charles 29
Chideya, Farai 14, 61
Childress, Alice 15
Christian, Barbara T. 44
Churchwell, Robert, Sr. 76
Clack, Zoanne 73
Clark, Kenneth B. 5, 52
Clark, Septima 7
Clark-Bekederemo, J. P. 44
Clarke, Austin C. 32
Clarke, Cheryl 32
Clarke, George 32
Cleage, Pearl 17, 64
Cleaver, Eldridge 5
Cliff, Michelle 42
Clifton, Lucille 14, 64, 91
Coates, Ta-Nehisi 76
Cobb, William Jelani 59
Cobbs, Price M. 9
Cohen, Anthony 15
Cole, Johnnetta B. 5, 43
Coleman, Wanda 48
Collins, Patricia Hill 67

Colter, Cyrus J. 36
Comer, James P. 6
Common 31, 63
Contee, Cheryl 88
Cook, Suzan D. Johnson 22
Cooke, Marvel 31
Coombs, Orde M. 44
Cooper, Afua 53
Cooper, Andrew W. 36
Cooper, Anna Julia 20
Cooper, Helene 74
Cooper, J. California 12, 85
Cornish, Sam 50
Cortez, Jayne 43
Cosby, Bill 7, 26, 59
Cose, Ellis 5, 50
Cotter, Joseph Seamon, Sr. 40
Couto, Mia 45
Cox, Joseph Mason Andrew 51
Creagh, Milton 27
Croal, N'Gai 76
Crouch, Stanley 11, 87
Cruse, Harold 54
Crutchfield, James N. 55
Cullen, Countee 8
Cuney, William Waring 44
Cunningham, Evelyn 23, 85
Curry, George E. 23
Curtis, Christopher Paul 26
Curtis-Hall, Vondie 17
Dabydeen, David 48
Dadié, Bernard 34
D'Aguiar, Fred 50
Damas, Léon-Gontran 46
Dandridge, Raymond Garfield 45
Danner, Margaret Esse 49
Danquah, Meri Nana Ama 93
Danticat, Edwidge 15, 68
Dash, Leon 47
Datcher, Michael 60
Dathorne, O. R. 52
Davis, Allison 12
Davis, Angela 5
Davis, Charles T. 48
Davis, Eisa 68
Davis, Frank Marshall 47
Davis, George 36
Davis, Nolan 45
Davis, Ossie 5, 50
Davis, Thulani 61
Dawkins, Wayne 20
de Passe, Suzanne 25
De Veaux, Alexis 44
Deggans, Eric 71
Delany, Martin R. 27
Delany, Samuel R., Jr. 9
DeLoach, Nora 30
Demby, William 51
Dent, Thomas C. 50
Dickerson, Debra J. 60
Dickey, Eric Jerome 21, 56
Diop, Birago 53
Diop, Cheikh Anta 4
Dodson, Howard, Jr. 7, 52
Dodson, Owen Vincent 38
Douglass, Frederick 87
Dove, Rita 6, 78
Draper, Sharon Mills 16, 43
Driskell, David C. 7
Driver, David E. 11
Drummond, William J. 40
Du Bois, David Graham 45
Du Bois, W. E. B. 3

DuBois, Shirley Graham 21
Due, Tananarive 30
Dumas, Henry 41
Dunbar, Paul Laurence 8
Dunbar-Nelson, Alice Ruth Moore 44
Dungy, Camille 86
Dunham, Katherine 4, 59
Dunnigan, Alice Allison 41
Duplechan, Larry 55
Dyson, Michael Eric 11, 40
Eagleson, William Lewis 90
Edmonds, Terry 17
Ekwensi, Cyprian 37
Elder, Lonne, III 38
Elliot, Lorris 37
Ellison, Ralph 7
Elmore, Ronn 21
Emanuel, James A. 46
Emecheta, Buchi 30
Equiano, Olaudah 78
Estes, Rufus 29
Evans, Diana 72
Evans, Mari 26
Everett, Percival 93
Fabio, Sarah Webster 48
Fair, Ronald L. 47
Fales-Hill, Susan 88
Fanon, Frantz 44
Farah, Nuruddin 27
Farley, Christopher John 54
Farrakhan, Louis 15
Fauset, Jessie 7
Feelings, Muriel 44
Feelings, Tom 11, 47
Fields, Julia 45
Figueroa, John J. 40
Files, Lolita 35
Finner-Williams, Paris Michele 62
Fisher, Antwone 40
Fisher, Rudolph 17
Fleming, Raymond 48
Fletcher, Bill, Jr. 41
Fletcher, Geoffrey 85
Forbes, Calvin 46
Ford, Clyde W. 40
Ford, Nick Aaron 44
Ford, Wallace 58
Forman, James 7, 51
Forrest, Leon 44
Fortune, T. Thomas 6
Foster, Cecil 32
Foster, Jylla Moore 45
Franklin, John Hope 5, 77
Franklin, Robert M. 13
Frazier, E. Franklin 10
Frazier, Oscar 58
French, Albert 18
Fuller, Charles 8
Fuller, Hoyt 44
Gabre-Medhin, Tsegaye 64
Gaines, Ernest J. 7
Gaiter, Dorothy J. 80
Gardner, Chris 65
Gaston, Marilyn Hughes 60
Gates, Henry Louis, Jr. 3, 38, 67
Gayle, Addison, Jr. 41
George, Nelson 12
Gibson, Donald Bernard 40
Giddings, Paula 11
Gilbert, Christopher 50
Gilliard, Steve 69
Giovanni, Nikki 9, 39, 85

Givhan, Robin Deneen 72
Gladwell, Malcolm 62
Gloster, Hugh Morris, Sr. 90
Glover, Donald 85
Goines, Donald 19
Golden, Marita 19
Gomez, Jewelle 30
Goodison, Lorna 71
Goodlett, Carlton B. 91
Gordon-Reed, Annette 74
Graham, Lawrence Otis 12
Graham, Lorenz 48
Grant, Gwendolyn Goldsby 28
Gray, Darius 69
Greaves, William 38
Greenfield, Eloise 9
Greenlee, Sam 48
Greenwood, Monique 38
Griffith, Mark Winston 8
Grimké, Archibald H. 9
Guinier, Lani 7, 30
Guy, Rosa 5
Guy-Sheftall, Beverly 13, 92
Haley, Alex 4
Halliburton, Warren J. 49
Hamblin, Ken 10
Hamilton, Virginia 10
Hansberry, Lorraine 6
Harding, Vincent 67
Hare, Nathan 44
Harkless, Necia Desiree 19
Harper, Frances Ellen Watkins 11
Harper, Michael S. 34
Harper, Rachel M. 92
Harrington, Oliver W. 9
Harris, Bill 72
Harris, Claire 34
Harris, Eddy L. 18
Harris, Jay 19
Harris, Jessica B. 91
Harris, Leslie 6
Harris, Monica 18
Harrison, Alvin 28
Harrison, Calvin 28
Haskins, James 36, 54
Hayden, Robert 12
Hayes, Teddy 40
Haygood, Wil 83
Haywood, Gar Anthony 43
Head, Bessie 28
Heard, Nathan C. 45
Hearne, John Edgar Caulwell 45
Hemphill, Essex 10
Henderson, David 53
Henderson, Stephen E. 45
Henries, A. Doris Banks 44
Henriques, Julian 37
Henry, Lenny 9, 52
Henson, Josiah 90
Henson, Matthew 2
Herbert, Bob 63
Hercules, Frank 44
Herndon, Angelo 90
Hernton, Calvin C. 51
Hill, Donna 32
Hill, Errol 40
Hill, Leslie Pinckney 44
Hilliard, David 7
Hoagland, Everett H. 45
Hobson, Julius W. 44
Holland, Endesha Ida Mae 3, 57
Holmes, Shannon 70
Holt, Nora 38

Holton, Hugh, Jr. 39
hooks, bell 5, 90
Horne, Frank 44
Hrabowski, Freeman A., III 22
Hudlin, Reginald 9, 86
Hudson, Cheryl 15
Hudson, Wade 15
Hughes, Langston 4
Hull, Akasha Gloria 45
Hunter-Gault, Charlayne 6, 31
Hurston, Zora Neale 3
Iceberg Slim 11
Ifill, Gwen 28
Ilibagiza, Immaculée 66
Jackson, Brenda 87
Jackson, Fred James 25
Jackson, George 14
Jackson, James A. 90
Jackson, Sheneska 18
James, Marlon 85
Jarrett, Vernon D. 42
Jasper, Kenji 39
Jenkins, Beverly 14
Joachim, Paulin 34
Joe, Yolanda 21
Johnson, Angela 52
Johnson, Charles 1, 82
Johnson, Charles S. 12
Johnson, Fenton 91
Johnson, Georgia Douglas 41
Johnson, James Weldon 5
Johnson, John H. 3, 54
Johnson, Linton Kwesi 37
Johnson, Mat 31
Johnson, R. M. 36
Johnson, Sandra K. 94
Johnson, William 91
Jolley, Willie 28
Jones, Edward P. 43, 67
Jones, Gayl 37
Jones, Orlando 30
Jones, Sarah 39
Jordan, June 7, 35
Josey, E. J. 10
July, William 27
Just, Ernest Everett 3
Kamau, Kwadwo Agymah 28
Karenga, Maulana 10, 71
Kariuki, J. M. 67
Kay, Jackie 37
Kayira, Legson 40
Kearney, Janis 54
Keckley, Elizabeth 90
Keene, John 73
Kendrick, Erika 57
Kennedy, Adrienne 11
Kennedy, Florynce 12, 33
Kennedy, Randall 40
Khanga, Yelena 6
Killens, John O. 54
Kimbro, Dennis 10
Kincaid, Jamaica 4
King, Colbert I. 69
King, Coretta Scott 3, 57
King, Preston 28
King, Woodie, Jr. 27
King, Yolanda 6
Kitt, Sandra 23
Kitwana, Bakari 86
Knight, Etheridge 37
Kobia, Samuel 43
Komunyakaa, Yusef 9
Kunjufu, Jawanza 3, 50

Lacy, Sam 30, 46
Ladner, Joyce A. 42
Laferriere, Dany 33
LaGuma, Alex 30
Lamming, George 35
Lampley, Oni Faida 43, 71
Lane, Lunsford 93
Larsen, Nella 10
Lateef, Yusef 91
Lattany, Kristin Hunter 88
Lawrence, Martin 6, 27, 60
Lawrence-Lightfoot, Sara 10
Lemmons, Kasi 20
Lemon, Don 94
Lester, Julius 9
Letson, Al 39
Lewis, David Levering 9
Lewis, Samella 25
Lincoln, C. Eric 38
Little, Benilde 21
Locke, Alain 10
Locke, Attica 85
Lomax, Louis E. 90
Lorde, Audre 6
Louis, Errol T. 8
Loury, Glenn 36
Lowe, Herbert 57
Mabry, Marcus 70
Mabuza-Suttle, Felicia 43
Machado de Assis 74
Mackey, Nathaniel 75
Madhubuti, Haki 7, 85
Madison, Paula 37
Major, Clarence 9
Makeba, Miriam 2, 50, 74
Malveaux, Julianne 32, 70
Manley, Ruth 34
Marechera, Dambudzo 39
Markham, E. A. 37
Marshall, Paule 7, 77
Martin, Roland S. 49, 84
Mason, Felicia 31
Mason, Herman, Jr. 83
Massaquoi, Hans J. 30
Matejka, Adrian 87
Mathabane, Mark 5
Maynard, Nancy Hicks 73
Maynard, Robert C. 7
Mays, Benjamin E. 7
Mbaye, Mariétou 31
McBride, James 35, 87
McCall, Nathan 8
McCauley, Gina 76
McClellan, George Marion 91
McCrary Anthony, Crystal 70
McDuffie, Dwayne 62
McFadden, Bernice L. 39
McGruder, Robert 22, 35
McKay, Claude 6
McKinney Hammond, Michelle 51
McKinney-Whetstone, Diane 27
McMillan, Rosalynn A. 36
McMillan, Terry 4, 17, 53
McMillan, Tracy 93
McPherson, James Alan 70
Memmi, Albert 37
Menard, John Willis 90
Mengestu, Dinaw 66
Meredith, James H. 11
Mfume, Kweisi 6, 41
Micheaux, Oscar 7
Mickelbury, Penny 28
Millner, Denene 76

Milner, Ron 39
Mitchell, Elvis 67
Mitchell, Loften 31
Mitchell, Russ 21, 73
Mitchell, Sharon 36
Mofolo, Thomas Mokopu 37
Mollel, Tololwa 38
Monroe, Bryan 71
Monroe, Mary 35
Moore, Jessica Care 30
Moore, Wes 86
Morrison, Toni 2, 15, 86
Mosley, Walter 5, 25, 68
Moss, Carlton 17
Mossell, Gertrude Bustill 40
Moutoussamy-Ashe, Jeanne 7
Mowry, Jess 7
Mphalele, Es'kia (Ezekiel) 40
Mudimbe, V.Y. 61
Mugo, Micere Githae 32
Mullen, Harryette 34
Murphy, John H. 42
Murray, Albert L. 33
Murray, Pauli 38
Mwangi, Meja 40
Myers, Walter Dean 8, 70
Nash, Shannon King 84
Naylor, Gloria 10, 42
Neal, Larry 38
Neal, Mark Anthony 74
Nelson, Jill 6, 54
Neto, António Agostinho 43
Newkirk, Pamela 69
Newton, Huey 2
Ngugi wa Thiong'o 29, 61
Nissel, Angela 42
Njawe, Pius 87
Nkosi, Lewis 46
Norris, Michele 83
Norton, Meredith 72
Nugent, Richard Bruce 39
Nunez, Elizabeth 62
Ojikutu, Bayo 66
Okara, Gabriel 37
Oliver, John J., Jr. 48
Onwueme, Tess Osonye 23
Orlandersmith, Dael 42
Oyono, Ferdinand 38
Packer, Z. Z. 64
Page, Clarence 4
Painter, Nell Irvin 24, 88
Palmer, Everard 37
Parker, Pat 19
Parker, Star 70
Parks, Suzan-Lori 34, 85
Patterson, Orlando 4
Payne, Ethel L. 28
Payne, Les 89
Peters, Lenrie 43
Petry, Ann 19
Philip, Marlene Nourbese 32
Phillips, Joseph C. 73
Piper, Adrian 71
Pitts, Leonard, Jr. 54, 85
Plaatje, Sol. T. 80
Polite, Carlene Hatcher 82
Poussaint, Alvin F. 5, 67
Poussaint, Renee 78
Powell, Adam Clayton, Jr. 3
Powell, Kevin 31, 74
Power, Will 83
Pressley, Condace L. 41
Prince, Richard E. 71

Pryce, Trevor 89
Pryor, Rain 65
Pryor, Richard 3, 24, 56
Quarles, Benjamin Arthur 18
Rahman, Aishah 37
Randall, Alice 38
Randall, Dudley 8, 55
Rapier, James T. 82
Raspberry, William 2
Reagon, Bernice Johnson 7
Reddick, Lawrence Dunbar 20
Redding, J. Saunders 26
Redmond, Eugene 23
Reed, Ishmael 8
Rhimes, Shonda Lynn 67
Rhoden, William C. 67
Rhodes, Jewell Parker 84
Rhone, Trevor 80
Richards, Beah 30
Ridley, John 69
Riggs, Marlon 5
Riley, Rochelle 50
Ringgold, Faith 4, 81
Robertson, Gil L., IV 85
Robeson, Eslanda Goode 13
Robinson, Aminah 50
Robinson, Eugene 77
Robinson, Matt 69
Roby, Kimberla Lawson 86
Rogers, Joel Augustus 30
Rollins, Charlamae Hill 27
Rotimi, Ola 1
Rowan, Carl T. 1, 30
Ruffin, Josephine St. Pierre 75
Run 31, 73
Rust, Art, Jr. 83
Sadlier, Rosemary 62
Saint James, Synthia 12
St. John, Kristoff 25
Salih, Al-Tayyib 37
Sanchez, Sonia 17, 51
Sanders, Dori 8
Sapphire 14
Saro-Wiwa, Kenule 39
Shelton, Paula Young 86
Schomburg, Arthur Alfonso 9
Schuyler, George Samuel 40
Scott-Heron, Gil 94
Seale, Bobby 3
Sembène, Ousmane 13, 62

Senghor, Léopold Sédar 12, 66
Sengstacke, John 18
Senior, Olive 37
Senna, Danzy 93
Shabazz, Attallah 6
Shabazz, Ilyasah 36
Shakur, Assata 6
Shakur, Yusef 85
Shange, Ntozake 8, 89
Shaw, Bernard 2, 28
Shipp, E. R. 15
Shockley, Ann Allen 84
Simone, Nina 15, 41
Simpson, Carole 6, 30
Singletary, Mike 4, 76
Singleton, John 2, 30
Sister Souljah 11
Skinner, Kiron K. 65
Smiley, Tavis 20, 68
Smith, Anna Deavere 6
Smith, B(arbara) 11
Smith, Barbara 28
Smith, Bruce W. 53
Smith, Danyel 40
Smith, Jessie Carney 35
Smith, Mary Carter 26
Smith, Stephen A. 69
Smith, Zadie 51
Snowden, Frank M., Jr. 67
Somé, Malidoma Patrice 10
Southgate, Martha 58
Sowell, Thomas 2
Soyinka, Wole 4, 93
Spencer, Anne 27
Spriggs, William 67
Staples, Brent 8
Stewart, Alison 13
Stone, Chuck 9
Stringer, Vickie 58
Sundiata, Sekou 66
Tademy, Lalita 36
Talbert, David E. 34, 93
Talley, André Leon 56
Tate, Eleanora E. 20, 55
Tatum, Beverly Daniel 42, 84
Tatum, Elinor R. 78
Tatum, Wilbert 76
Taulbert, Clifton Lemoure 19
Taylor, Kristin Clark 8
Taylor, Mildred D. 26

Taylor, Susan C. 62
Taylor, Susan L. 10, 86
Teasley, Lisa 92
Thomas, Michael 69
Thomas, Trisha R. 65
Thomas-Graham, Pamela 29
Thornton, Yvonne S. 69
Thurman, Howard 3
Thurston, Baratunde 79
Tillis, Frederick 40
Tolson, Melvin 37
Toomer, Jean 6
Touré, Askia (Muhammad Abu Bakr
   el) 47
Townsend, Robert 4
Trotter, Monroe 9
Troupe, Quincy 83
Tucker, Cynthia 15, 61
Turner, Henry McNeal 5
Tutuola, Amos 30
Tyree, Omar Rashad 21
Tyson, Asha 39
Tyson, Neil deGrasse 15, 65
Van Peebles, Melvin 7
van Sertima, Ivan 25
Vega, Marta Moreno 61
Vera, Yvonne 32
Verdelle, A. J. 26
Wade-Gayles, Gloria Jean 41
Walcott, Derek 5, 94
Walker, Alice 1, 43
Walker, Margaret 29
Walker, Rebecca 50
Wallace, Michele Faith 13
Wallace, Phyllis A. 9
Walters, Ronald 83
Ward, Douglas Turner 42
Washington, Booker T. 4
Washington, Elsie B. 78
Washington, Harriet A. 69
Washington, James, Jr. 38
Washington, Laura S. 18
Wattleton, Faye 9
Wayans, Damon 8, 41
Weaver, Afaa Michael 37
Webb, Veronica 10
Weems, Renita J. 44
Wells-Barnett, Ida B. 8
Wesley, Dorothy Porter 19
Wesley, Richard 73

Wesley, Valerie Wilson 18
West, Cornel 5, 33, 80
West, Dorothy 12, 54
Whack, Rita Coburn 36
Wharton, Clifton R., Jr. 7
Whitaker, Mark 21, 47
White, Armond 80
White, Walter F. 4
Whitehead, Colson 77
Whitfield, LeRoy 84
Whitfield, Van 34
Whitlock, Jason 78
Wideman, John Edgar 5, 87
Wilbekin, Emil 63
Wiley, Ralph 8, 78
Wilkerson, Isabel 71
Wilkins, Roger 2, 84
Wilkins, Roy 4
Williams, Armstrong 29
Williams, George Washington 18
Williams, John A. 27
Williams, Juan 35, 80
Williams, Patricia 11, 54
Williams, Robert F. 11
Williams, Roy 89
Williams, Samm-Art 21
Williams, Saul 31
Williams, Sherley Anne 25
Williams, Stanley "Tookie" 29, 57
Williams, Wendy 62
Wilson, August 7, 33, 55
Wilson, Mary 28
Wilson, William Julius 22
Winans, Marvin L. 17
Wiwa, Ken 67
Wolfe, George C. 6, 43
Woods, Mattiebelle 63
Woods, Scott 55
Woods, Teri 69
Woodson, Carter G. 2
Worrill, Conrad 12
Wright, Bruce McMarion 3, 52
Wright, Richard 5
X, Marvin 45
Yarbrough, Camille 40
Yette, Samuel F. 63
Young, Al 82
Young, Whitney M., Jr. 4
Youngblood, Shay 32
Zane 71
Zook, Kristal Brent 62

Cumulative Subject Index

Volume numbers appear in **bold**

A cappella
Cooke, Sam **17**
Reagon, Bernice Johnson **7**

AA
See Alcoholics Anonymous

AAAS
See American Association for the Advancement of Science

AARP
Dixon, Margaret **14**
Smith, Marie F. **70**

ABC
See American Broadcasting Company

Abstract expressionism
Lewis, Norman **39**

Academy awards
Austin, Patti **24**
Cara, Irene **77**
Fletcher, Geoffrey **85**
Freeman, Morgan **2, 20, 62**
Goldberg, Whoopi **4, 33, 69**
Gooding, Cuba, Jr. **16, 62**
Gossett, Louis, Jr. **7**
Jean-Baptiste, Marianne **17, 46**
McDaniel, Hattie **5**
Mo'Nique **35, 84**
Poitier, Sidney **11, 36**
Prince **18, 65**
Richie, Lionel **27, 65**
Washington, Denzel **1, 16, 93**
Whitaker, Forest **2, 49, 67**
Williams, Russell, II **70**
Wonder, Stevie **11, 53**

ACLU
See American Civil Liberties Union

Acquired immune deficiency syndrome (AIDS)
Ashe, Arthur **1, 18**
Atim, Julian **66**
Broadbent, Hydeia **36**
Cargill, Victoria A. **43**
Fenton, Kevin **87**
Gayle, Helene D. **3, 46**
Hale, Lorraine **8**
Johnson, Earvin "Magic" **3, 39**
Lewis-Thornton, Rae **32**
Mboup, Souleymane **10**

Moutoussamy-Ashe, Jeanne **7**
Norman, Pat **10**
Ojikutu, Bisola **65**
Okaalet, Peter **58**
Pickett, Cecil **39**
Riggs, Marlon **5, 44**
Satcher, David **7, 57**
Seele, Pernessa **46**
Whitfield, LeRoy **84**
Wilson, Phill **9**
Zulu, Princess Kasune **54**

ACT UP
See AIDS Coalition to Unleash Power

Acting
Aaliyah **30**
Aaron, Quinton **82**
Adams, Osceola Macarthy **31**
Adebimpe, Tunde **75**
Akinnuoye-Agbaje, Adewale **56**
Alexander, Khandi **43**
Ali, Tatyana **73**
Allen, Debbie **13, 42**
Alonso, Laz **87**
Amos, John **8, 62**
Anderson, Anthony **51, 77**
Anderson, Carl **48**
Anderson, Eddie "Rochester" **30**
Andrews, Tina **74**
Angelou, Maya **1, 15**
Armstrong, Vanessa Bell **24**
Ashanti **37**
Babatunde, Obba **35**
Bahati, Wambui **60**
Bailey, Pearl **14**
Baker, Josephine **3**
Banks, Michelle **59**
Banks, Tyra **11, 50**
Barnett, Etta Moten **56**
Bassett, Angela **6, 23, 62**
Beach, Michael **26**
Beals, Jennifer **12**
Beaton, Norman **14**
Beauvais, Garcelle **29**
Belgrave, Cynthia **75**
Bennett, Louise **69**
Bentley, Lamont **53**
Berry, Fred "Rerun" **48**
Berry, Halle **4, 19, 57, 91**
Beyoncé **39, 70**
Bivins, Michael **72**
Blacque, Taurean **58**

Blanks, Billy **22**
Blige, Mary J. **20, 34, 60**
Bonet, Lisa **58**
Borders, James **9**
Bow Wow **35**
Brady, Wayne **32, 71**
Branch, William Blackwell **39**
Braugher, Andre **13, 58, 91**
Bridges, Todd **37**
Brooks, Avery **9**
Brooks, Golden **62**
Brooks, Mehcad **62**
Brown, Chris **74**
Brown, Jim **11**
Browne, Roscoe Lee **66**
Byrd, Eugene **64**
Caesar, Shirley **19**
Calloway, Cab **14**
Cameron, Earl **44**
Campbell, Naomi **1, 31**
Campbell-Martin, Tisha **8, 42**
Cannon, Nick **47, 73**
Cara, Irene **77**
Carroll, Diahann **9**
Carroll, Rocky **74**
Carson, Lisa Nicole **21**
Carey, Mariah **32, 53, 69**
Cash, Rosalind **28**
Cedric the Entertainer **29, 60**
Cheadle, Don **19, 52**
Chestnut, Morris **31**
Childress, Alice **15**
Chong, Rae Dawn **62**
Chweneyagae, Presley **63**
Clarke, Hope **14**
Cole, Nat "King" **17**
Coleman, Gary **35, 86**
Combs, Sean **17, 43, 92**
Cooper, Chuck **75**
Cosby, Bill **7, 26, 59**
Crothers, Scatman **19**
Curry, Mark **17**
Curtis-Hall, Vondie **17**
Dandridge, Dorothy **3**
David, Keith **27**
Davidson, Jaye **5**
Davis, Altovise **76**
Davis, Eisa **68**
Davis, Guy **36**
Davis, Ossie **5, 50**
Davis, Sammy, Jr. **18**
Davis, Viola **34, 76**
Dawn, Marpessa **75**
Dawson, Rosario **72**

De Bankolé, Isaach **78**
De Shields, André **72**
Dee, Ruby **8, 50, 68**
Devine, Loretta **24**
Diesel, Vin **29**
Diggs, Taye **25, 63**
Dixon, Ivan **69**
DMX **28, 64**
Domingo, Colman **94**
Dourdan, Gary **37**
Duke, Bill **3**
Duncan, Michael Clarke **26**
Dungey, Merrin **62**
Dutton, Charles S. **4, 22**
Ejiofor, Chiwetel **67**
Elba, Idris **49, 89**
Elise, Kimberly **32**
Emmanuel, Alphonsia **38**
Epps, Mike **60**
Epps, Omar **23, 59**
Esposito, Giancarlo **9**
Everett, Francine **23**
Faison, Donald **50**
Faison, Frankie **55**
Falana, Lola **42**
Fargas, Antonio **50**
Fetchit, Stepin **32**
Fields, Felicia P. **60**
Fields, Kim **36**
Fishburne, Laurence **4, 22, 70**
Fisher, Gail **85**
Fox, Rick **27**
Fox, Vivica A. **15, 53**
Foxx, Jamie **15, 48**
Foxx, Redd **2**
Francis, Thais **93**
Freeman, Al, Jr. **11**
Freeman, Morgan **2, 20, 62**
Freeman, Yvette **27**
Gaye, Nona **56**
Gibbs, Marla **86**
Gibson, Tyrese **27, 62**
Gilpin, Charles Sidney **81**
Ginuwine **35**
Givens, Adele **62**
Givens, Robin **4, 25, 58**
Glover, Danny **1, 24**
Glover, Donald **85**
Goldberg, Whoopi **4, 33, 69**
Gooding, Cuba, Jr. **16, 62**
Gordon, Dexter **25**
Gossett, Louis, Jr. **7**
Greaves, William **38**
Grier, David Alan **28**

Grier, Pam 9, 31, 86
Griffin, Angela 80
Guillaume, Robert 3, 48
Gunn, Moses 10
Gurira, Danai 73
Guy, Jasmine 2
Hairston, Jester 88
Hall, Arsenio 58
Hamilton, Lisa Gay 71
Hamlin, Larry Leon 49, 62
Hammond, Fred 23
Hardison, Kadeem 22
Harewood, David 52
Harper, Hill 32, 65
Harris, Naomie 55
Harris, Robin 7
Harvey, Steve 18, 58
Hawkins, Screamin' Jay 30
Hayes, Isaac 20, 58, 73
Haysbert, Dennis 42
Hemsley, Sherman 19
Henry, Joshua 94
Henry, Lenny 9, 52
Henson, Taraji P. 58, 77
Hill, Dulé 29
Hill, Lauryn 20, 53
Hines, Gregory 1, 42
Holder, Geoffrey 78
Hooks, Robert 76
Horne, Lena 5, 86
Hounsou, Djimon 19, 45
Houston, Whitney 7, 28, 83
Howard, Sherri 36
Howard, Terrence 59, 94
Howell, Ayinde 91
Hudson, Ernie 72
Hudson, Jennifer 63, 83
Hughley, D. L. 23, 76
Hyman, Earle 25, 79
Ice Cube 8, 30, 60
Ingram, Rex 5
Jackson, Millie 25
Jackson, Samuel 8, 19, 63
James, Nikki M. 94
Jean-Baptiste, Marianne 17, 46
Jean-Louis, Jimmy 76
Johnson, Rafer 33
Johnson, Rodney Van 28
Jones, James Earl 3, 49, 79
Jones, Orlando 30
Jorge, Seu 73
Kelley, Elijah 65
Kelley, Malcolm David 59
Kennedy-Overton, Jayne Harris 46
Khumalo, Leleti 51
Kid Cudi 83
King, Regina 22, 45
King, Woodie, Jr. 27
Kirby, George 14
Kitt, Eartha 16, 75
Knight, Gladys 16, 66
Kodjoe, Boris 34, 89
Kotto, Yaphet 7
La Salle, Eriq 12
LaBelle, Patti 13, 30
LaChanze 93
Lampley, Oni Faida 43, 71
Lane, Charles 3
Lassiter, Roy 24
Lathan, Sanaa 27
Lawrence, Martin 6, 27, 60
Lee, Canada 8
Lee, Joie 1

Leggs, Kingsley 62
Lemmons, Kasi 20
LeNoire, Rosetta 37
Lenox, Adriane 59
Lester, Adrian 46
Lesure, James 64
Lewis, Emmanuel 36
Lil' Kim 28
Lincoln, Abbey 3, 88
Lindo, Delroy 18, 45
LisaRaye 27
LL Cool J 16, 49, 94
Luke, Derek 61
Lumbly, Carl 47
Mabley, Jackie "Moms" 15
Mac, Bernie 29, 61, 72
Malco, Romany 71
Mann, Tamela 92
Mario 71
Marrow, Queen Esther 24
Martin, Helen 31
Martin, Jesse L. 31
Master P 21
Mayo, Whitman 32
Mbatha-Raw, Gugu 89
M.C. Hammer 20, 80
McBride, Chi 73
McClendon, Forrest 94
McClinton, Marion Isaac 77
McDaniel, Hattie 5
McDonald, Audra 20, 62
McKee, Lonette 12
McKinney, Nina Mae 40
McQueen, Butterfly 6, 54
Meadows, Tim 30
Mello, Breno 73
Merkerson, S. Epatha 47, 83
Michele, Michael 31
Miller, Omar Benson 93
Miller, Patina 94
Miller, Wentworth 75
Mitchell, Brian Stokes 21
Mitchell, Kel 66
Mokae, Zakes 80
Mo'Nique 35, 84
Moore, Chante 26
Moore, Juanita 83
Moore, Shemar 21
Morris, Garrett 31
Morris, Greg 28
Morton, Joe 18
Mos Def 30
Moten, Etta 18
Mowry, Tamera 79
Mowry, Tia 78
Murphy, Eddie 4, 20, 61
Muse, Clarence Edouard 21
Nash, Johnny 40
Nash, Niecy 66
Neal, Elise 29
Newton, Thandie 26
Ngaujah, Sahr 86
Nicholas, Fayard 20, 57
Nicholas, Harold 20
Nichols, Nichelle 11
Norman, Maidie 20
Notorious B.I.G. 20
Ntshona, Winston 52
Okonedo, Sophie 67
O'Neal, Ron 46
Orlandersmith, Dael 42
Orman, Roscoe 55
Oyelowo, David 82

Parker, Nicole Ari 52
Patton, Paula 62
Payne, Allen 13
Payne, Freda 58
Peete, Holly Robinson 20
Perrineau, Harold, Jr. 51
Perry, Tyler 40, 54
Phifer, Mekhi 25
Phillips, Joseph C. 73
Pickens, James, Jr. 59
Pierce, Wendell 90
Pinkett Smith, Jada 10, 41
Poitier, Sidney 11, 36
Poitier, Sydney Tamiia 65
Pounder, CCH 72
Pratt, Kyla 57
Preer, Evelyn 82
Premice, Josephine 41
Prince 18, 65
Pryor, Rain 65
Pryor, Richard 3, 24, 56
Queen Latifah 1, 16, 58
Randle, Theresa 16
Rashad, Phylicia 21
Raven 44
Ray, Gene Anthony 47
Reddick, Lance 52
Reed Hall, Alaina 83
Reese, Della 6, 20
Reid, Tim 56
Reuben, Gloria 15
Rhames, Ving 14, 50
Rhymes, Busta 31
Ribeiro, Alfonso 17
Richards, Beah 30
Richards, Lloyd 2
Richardson, LaTanya 71
Richardson, Salli 68
Robeson, Paul 2
Robinson, Shaun 36
Rock, Chris 3, 22, 66
Rock, The 29 66
Rodgers, Rod 36
Rodrigues, Percy 68
Roker, Roxie 68
Rolle, Esther 13, 21
Rose, Anika Noni 70
Ross, Diana 8, 27
Ross, Tracee Ellis 35
Roundtree, Richard 27
Rowell, Victoria 13, 68
Rudolph, Maya 46
Russell, Nipsey 66
St. Jacques, Raymond 8
St. John, Kristoff 25
St. Patrick, Mathew 48
Saldana, Zoe 72
Salter, Nikkole 73
Sands, Diana 87
Santiago-Hudson, Ruben 85
Scott, Hazel 66
Scott, Jill 29, 83
Shakur, Tupac 14
Short, Columbus 79
Sidibe, Gabourey 84
Simmons, Henry 55
Sinbad 1, 16
Sinclair, Madge 78
Sisqo 30
Smith, Anjela Lauren 44
Smith, Anna Deavere 6, 44
Smith, B(arbara) 11
Smith, Jaden 82

Smith, Roger Guenveur 12
Smith, Tasha 73
Smith, Will 8, 18, 53
Smith, Willow 92
Snipes, Wesley 3, 24, 67
Snoop Dogg 35, 84
Sommore 61
Stewart, Tonea Harris 78
Sticky Fingaz 86
Tamia 24, 55
Tate, Larenz 15
Taylor, Meshach 4
Taylor, Regina 9, 46
Taylor, Ron 35
Thomas, Sean Patrick 35
Thomason, Marsha 47
Thompson, John Douglas 81
Thompson, Kenan 52
Thompson, Tazewell 13
Thoms, Tracie 61
Torres, Gina 52
Torry, Guy 31
Toussaint, Lorraine 32
Townsend, Robert 4, 23
True, Rachel 82
Tucker, Chris 13, 23, 62
Tunie, Tamara 63
Turner, Tina 6, 27
Tyler, Aisha N. 36
Tyson, Cicely 7, 51
Uggams, Leslie 23
Underwood, Blair 7, 27, 76
Union, Gabrielle 31, 92
Usher 23, 56
Van Peebles, Mario 2, 51
Van Peebles, Melvin 7
Vance, Courtney B. 15, 60
Vanity 67
Vereen, Ben 4
Walker, Eamonn 37
Ward, Douglas Turner 42
Warfield, Marsha 2
Warfield, William 94
Warner, Malcolm-Jamal 22, 36
Warren, Michael 27
Washington, Denzel 1, 16, 93
Washington, Fredi 10
Washington, Isaiah 62
Washington, Kerry 46
Waters, Ethel 7
Wayans, Damon 8, 41
Wayans, Keenen Ivory 18
Wayans, Kim 80
Wayans, Marlon 29, 82
Wayans, Shawn 29
Weathers, Carl 10
Webb, Veronica 10
Whitaker, Forest 2, 49, 67
White, Michael Jai 71
White, Terri 82
Whitfield, Lynn 18
Williams, Bert 18
Williams, Billy Dee 8
Williams, Clarence, III 26
Wilson, Chandra 57
Wilson, Dorien 55
Williams, Joe 5, 25
Williams, Malinda 57
Williams, Samm-Art 21
Williams, Saul 31
Williams, Vanessa A. 32, 66
Williams, Vanessa L. 4, 17
Williamson, Fred 67

Williamson, Mykelti 22
Wilson, Debra 38
Wilson, Flip 21
Winfield, Paul 2, 45
Winfrey, Oprah 2, 15, 61
Withers-Mendes, Elisabeth 64
Witherspoon, John 38
Woodard, Alfre 9
Woodson, Ali Ollie 89
Wright, Jeffrey 54
Yarbrough, Cedric 51
Yoba, Malik 11

Adoption and foster care
Clements, George 2
Hale, Clara 16
Hale, Lorraine 8
Oglesby, Zena 12
Rowell, Victoria 13, 68

Advertising
Barboza, Anthony 10
Boyd, Edward 70
Burrell, Tom 21, 51
Campbell, E. Simms 13
Chisholm, Samuel J. 32
Coleman, Donald 24, 62
Cullers, Vincent T. 49
Gaskins, Rudy 74
Johnson, Beverly 2
Jones, Caroline R. 29
Jordan, Montell 23
Kemp, Herb 94
Lewis, Byron E. 13
McKinney Hammond, Michelle 51
Mingo, Frank 32
Olden, Georg(e) 44
Pinderhughes, John 47
Roche, Joyce M. 17

Affirmative action
Arnwine, Barbara 28
Berry, Mary Frances 7
Coleman, William T. 76
Edley, Christopher F., Jr. 48
Higginbotham, A. Leon, Jr. 13, 25
Maynard, Robert C. 7
Rand, A. Barry 6
Thompson, Bennie G. 26
Waters, Maxine 3, 67

AFL-CIO
See American Federation of Labor and Congress of Industrial Organizations

African American art
Jones, Paul R. 76

African American Dance Ensemble
Davis, Chuck 33

African American folklore
Bailey, Xenobia 11
Brown, Sterling Allen 10, 64
Driskell, David C. 7
Ellison, Ralph 7
Gaines, Ernest J. 7
Hamilton, Virginia 10
Hughes, Langston 4
Hurston, Zora Neale 3
Lester, Julius 9
Primus, Pearl 6
Tillman, George, Jr. 20

Williams, Bert 18
Yarbrough, Camille 40

African American history
Appiah, Kwame Anthony 67
Benberry, Cuesta 65
Bennett, Lerone, Jr. 5, 84
Berry, Mary Frances 7
Blackshear, Leonard 52
Blockson, Charles L. 42
Burroughs, Margaret Taylor 9
Camp, Kimberly 19
Chase-Riboud, Barbara 20, 46
Cheadle, Don 19, 52
Clarke, John Henrik 20
Clayton, Mayme Agnew 62
Cobb, William Jelani 59
Coombs, Orde M. 44
Cooper, Anna Julia 20
Dodson, Howard, Jr. 7, 52
Douglas, Aaron 7
Du Bois, W. E. B. 3
DuBois, Shirley Graham 21
Dyson, Michael Eric 11, 40
Feelings, Tom 11, 47
Franklin, John Hope 5, 77
Gaines, Ernest J. 7
Gates, Henry Louis, Jr. 3, 38, 67
Gill, Gerald 69
Gordon-Reed, Annette 74
Haley, Alex 4
Halliburton, Warren J. 49
Harkless, Necia Desiree 19
Harris, Richard E. 61
Hine, Darlene Clark 24
Hughes, Langston 4
Johnson, James Weldon 5
Jones, Edward P. 43, 67
Lewis, David Levering 9
Marable, Manning 10
Mason, Herman, Jr. 83
Painter, Nell Irvin 24, 88
Pritchard, Robert Starling 21
Putney, Martha S. 75
Quarles, Benjamin Arthur 18
Reagon, Bernice Johnson 7
Richardson, Julieanna 81
Schomburg, Arthur Alfonso 9
Shadd, Abraham D. 81
Southern, Eileen 56
Tancil, Gladys Quander 59
Wilson, August 7, 33, 55
Woodson, Carter G. 2
Yarbrough, Camille 40

African American literature
Andrews, Raymond 4
Angelou, Maya 1, 15
Appiah, Kwame Anthony 67
Baisden, Michael 25, 66
Baker, Houston A., Jr. 6
Baldwin, James 1
Bambara, Toni Cade 1
Baraka, Amiri 1, 38
Bennett, George Harold "Hal" 45
Bontemps, Arna 8
Briscoe, Connie 15
Brooks, Gwendolyn 1, 28
Brown, Claude 38
Brown, Wesley 23
Burroughs, Margaret Taylor 9
Campbell, Bebe Moore 6, 24, 59
Cary, Lorene 3

Childress, Alice 15
Cleage, Pearl 17, 64
Cullen, Countee 8
Curtis, Christopher Paul 26
Davis, Arthur P. 41
Davis, Nolan 45
Dickey, Eric Jerome 21, 56
Dove, Rita 6, 78
Du Bois, W. E. B. 3
Dunbar, Paul Laurence 8
Ellison, Ralph 7
Evans, Mari 26
Fair, Ronald L. 47
Fauset, Jessie 7
Feelings, Tom 11, 47
Fisher, Rudolph 17
Ford, Nick Aaron 44
Fuller, Charles 8
Gaines, Ernest J. 7
Gates, Henry Louis, Jr. 3, 38, 67
Gayle, Addison, Jr. 41
Gibson, Donald Bernard 40
Giddings, Paula 11
Giovanni, Nikki 9, 39, 85
Goines, Donald 19
Golden, Marita 19
Guy, Rosa 5
Haley, Alex 4
Hansberry, Lorraine 6
Harper, Frances Ellen Watkins 11
Heard, Nathan C. 45
Himes, Chester 8
Holland, Endesha Ida Mae 3, 57
Holmes, Shannon 70
Hughes, Langston 4
Hull, Akasha Gloria 45
Hurston, Zora Neale 3
Iceberg Slim 11
Joe, Yolanda 21
Johnson, Charles 1, 82
Johnson, James Weldon 5
Jones, Gayl 37
Jordan, June 7, 35
July, William 27
Kitt, Sandra 23
Larsen, Nella 10
Lester, Julius 9
Little, Benilde 21
Lorde, Audre 6
Madhubuti, Haki 7, 85
Major, Clarence 9
Marshall, Paule 7, 77
McKay, Claude 6
McKay, Nellie Yvonne 17, 57
McKinney-Whetstone, Diane 27
McMillan, Terry 4, 17, 53
McPherson, James Alan 70
Morrison, Toni 2, 15, 86
Mowry, Jess 7
Myers, Walter Dean 8, 20
Naylor, Gloria 10, 42
Petry, Ann 19
Pinkney, Jerry 15
Rahman, Aishah 37
Randall, Dudley 8, 55
Redding, J. Saunders 26
Redmond, Eugene 23
Reed, Ishmael 8
Ringgold, Faith 4, 81
Sanchez, Sonia 17, 51
Schomburg, Arthur Alfonso 9
Schuyler, George Samuel 40
Shange, Ntozake 8, 89

Smith, Mary Carter 26
Taylor, Mildred D. 26
Thomas, Trisha R. 65
Thurman, Wallace 16
Toomer, Jean 6
Tyree, Omar Rashad 21
Van Peebles, Melvin 7
Verdelle, A. J. 26
Villarosa, Clara 85
Walker, Alice 1, 43
Wesley, Valerie Wilson 18
Wideman, John Edgar 5, 87
Williams, John A. 27
Williams, Sherley Anne 25
Wilson, August 7, 33, 55
Wolfe, George C. 6, 43
Wright, Richard 5
Yarbrough, Camille 40

African American studies
Alexander, Elizabeth 75
Baszile, Jennifer 79
Brawley, Benjamin 44
Carby, Hazel 27
Christian, Barbara T. 44
De Veaux, Alexis 44
Ford, Nick Aaron 44
Hare, Nathan 44
Harris-Lacewell, Melissa 81
Henderson, Stephen E. 45
Huggins, Nathan Irvin 52
Long, Richard Alexander 65
Neal, Mark Anthony 74
Peterson, James 81
West, Cornel 5, 33, 80

African Burial Ground Project
Perry, Warren 56

African Canadian literature
Elliott, Lorris 37
Foster, Cecil 32
Senior, Olive 37

African dance
Acogny, Germaine 55
Adams, Jenoyne 60
Ailey, Alvin 8
Davis, Chuck 33
Fagan, Garth 18
Primus, Pearl 6

African history
Appiah, Kwame Anthony 67
Chase-Riboud, Barbara 20, 46
Clarke, John Henrik 20
Counter, S. Allen 74
Diop, Cheikh Anta 4
Dodson, Howard, Jr. 7, 52
DuBois, Shirley Graham 21
Feelings, Muriel 44
Halliburton, Warren J. 49
Hansberry, William Leo 11
Harkless, Necia Desiree 19
Henries, A. Doris Banks 44
Hilliard, Asa Grant, III 66
Jawara, Dawda Kairaba 11
Marshall, Paule 7, 77
van Sertima, Ivan 25

African literature
Aidoo, Ama Ata 38
Akpan, Uwem 70
Appiah, Kwame Anthony 67
Arac de Nyeko, Monica 66

Armah, Ayi Kwei 49
Awoonor, Kofi 37
Bandele, Biyi 68
Cartey, Wilfred 47
Cheney-Coker, Syl 43
Couto, Mia 45
Dadié, Bernard 34
Dathorne, O. R. 52
Ekwensi, Cyprian 37
Farah, Nuruddin 27
Gabre-Medhin, Tsegaye 64
Head, Bessie 28
Kayira, Legson 40
Memmi, Albert 37
Mphalele, Es'kia 40
Mwangi, Meja 40
Oyono, Ferdinand 38
Peters, Lenrie 43
Salih, Al-Tayyib 37

African Methodist Episcopal Church (AME)
Blanks, Deborah K. 69
Bryant, John R. 45
Flake, Floyd H. 18
Loguen, J. W. 91
McKenzie, Vashti M. 29
Mudimbe, V. Y. 61
Murray, Cecil 12, 47
Roundtree, Dovey 80
Shuttlesworth, Fred 47
Turner, Henry McNeal 5
Youngblood, Johnny Ray 8

African music
Ade, King Sunny 41
Afro, Teddy 78
Ashong, Derrick 86
Fela 1, 42
Keita, Salif 83
Kidjo, Angelique 50
Kolosoy, Wendo 73
Kuti, Femi 47
Maal, Baaba 66
Mahlasela, Vusi 65
Makeba, Miriam 2, 50, 74
Nascimento, Milton 2 64
Somi 85

African National Congress (ANC)
Baker, Ella 5
Hani, Chris 6
Ka Dinizulu, Mcwayizeni 29
Kaunda, Kenneth 2
Kuzwayo, Ellen 68
Luthuli, Albert 13
Mandela, Nelson 1, 14, 77
Mandela, Winnie 2, 35
Masekela, Barbara 18
Mbeki, Govan A. 80
Mbeki, Thabo 14, 73
Mhlaba, Raymond 55
Motlanthe, Kgalema 74
Nkomo, Joshua 4, 65
Nyanda, Siphiwe 21
Nzo, Alfred 15
Ramaphosa, Cyril 3
Sisulu, Albertina 57
Sisulu, Walter 47
Tutu, Desmond Mpilo 6, 44
Weems, Renita J. 44
Xuma, Madie Hall 59
Zuma, Jacob 33, 75

Zuma, Nkosazana Dlamini 34

Afro-Beat music
Fela 1, 42

Afro-Brazilian music
Brown, Carlinhos 81
Caymmi, Dorival 72
Gil, Gilberto 53
Jorge, Seu 73
Moura, Paulo 87

Afrocentricity
Asante, Molefi Kete 3
Biggers, John 20, 33
Diop, Cheikh Anta 4
Hansberry, Lorraine 6
Hansberry, William Leo 11
Sanchez, Sonia 17, 51
Turner, Henry McNeal 5

Afro-Cuban music
Lefel, Edith 41
Rodríguez, Arsenio 87
Santamaria, Mongo 81

Afro-Peruvian music
Baca, Susana 80

Agency for International Development (AID)
Gayle, Helene D. 3, 46
Perkins, Edward 5

Agriculture
Allen, Will 74
Boyd, John W., Jr. 20, 72
Carver, George Washington 4
Hall, Lloyd A. 8
Jones, Monty 66
Masire, Quett 5
Sanders, Dori 8
Wambugu, Florence 42

AHA
See American Heart Association

AID
See Agency for International Development

AIDS
See Acquired immune deficiency syndrome

AIDS Coalition to Unleash Power (ACT UP)
Norman, Pat 10

Akron Beacon Journal
Crutchfield, James N. 55

ALA
See American Library Association

Alabama state government
Davis, Artur 41
Ford, Johnny 70
Gray, Fred 37
Rapier, James T. 82

Alcoholics Anonymous (AA)
Hilliard, David 7
Lucas, John 7

All Afrikan People's Revolutionary Party
Carmichael, Stokely 5, 26
Moses, Robert Parris 11

Allied Arts Academy
Bonds, Margaret 39

Alpha & Omega Ministry
White, Reggie 6, 50

Alpha Kappa Alpha Sorority
White, Linda M. 45

Alvin Ailey American Dance Theater
Ailey, Alvin 8
Clarke, Hope 14
Dove, Ulysses 5
Faison, George 16
Jamison, Judith 7, 67
Jefferson, Denise 87
Primus, Pearl 6
Rhoden, Dwight 40
Richardson, Desmond 39
Spears, Warren 52
Tyson, Andre 40
Williams, Dudley 60

Alvin Ailey Repertory Ensemble
Ailey, Alvin 8
Miller, Bebe 3

Ambassadors
Avant, Nicole A. 90
Braun, Carol Moseley 4, 42
Carson, Johnnie 85
Cook, Mercer 40
Davis, Ruth 37
Dudley, Edward R. 58
Dymally, Mervyn 42
Frazer, Jendayi 68
Mbuende, Kaire 12
Poitier, Sidney 11, 36
Smythe Haith, Mabel 61
Spearman, Leonard H. O., Sr. 81
Stith, Charles R. 73
Todman, Terence A. 55
Watson, Diane 41
Wharton, Clifton Reginald, Sr. 36
Whitfield, Mal 60

AME
See African Methodist Episcopal Church

American Academy of Arts and Sciences
Loury, Glenn 36

American Art Award
Simpson, Lorna 4, 36

American Association for the Advancement of Science (AAAS)
Cobb, W. Montague 39
Massey, Walter E. 5, 45
Pickett, Cecil 39

American Association of University Women
Granville, Evelyn Boyd 36

American Ballet Theatre
Dove, Ulysses 5
Richardson, Desmond 39

American Bar Association
Archer, Dennis 7, 36
Pincham, R. Eugene, Sr. 69

Thompson, Larry D. 39
Walker, Cora T. 68

American Beach
Betsch, MaVynee 28

American Book Award
Baraka, Amiri 1, 38
Bates, Daisy 13
Bradley, David Henry, Jr. 39
Clark, Septima 7
Gates, Henry Louis, Jr. 3, 38, 67
Lorde, Audre 6
Loury, Glenn 36
Marshall, Paule 7, 77
Sanchez, Sonia 17, 51
Troupe, Quincy 83
Walker, Alice 1, 43

American Broadcasting Company (ABC)
Christian, Spencer 15
Goode, Mal 13
Mickebury, Penny 28
Reynolds, Star Jones 10, 27, 61
Roberts, Robin 16, 54
Robinson, Max 3
Simpson, Carole 6, 30

American Cancer Society
Ashe, Arthur 1, 18
Leffall, Lasalle 3, 64
Riperton, Minnie 32
Thomas, Arthur Ray 52

American Choral Directors Association
Adams, Leslie 39

American Civil Liberties Union (ACLU)
Baugh, David 23
Harris, Maya Lakshmi 88
Murphy, Laura M. 43
Murray, Pauli 38
Pincham, R. Eugene, Sr. 69

American Community Housing Associates, Inc.
Lane, Vincent 5

American Composers Alliance
Tillis, Frederick 40

American Counseling Association
Mitchell, Sharon 36

American Economic Association
Loury Glenn 36

American Enterprise Institute
Woodson, Robert L. 10

American Express Company
Adams, Eula L. 39
Chapman, Susan E. 94
Chenault, Kenneth I. 4, 36
Goodman, Kim C. 94

American Federation of Labor and Congress of Industrial Organizations (AFL-CIO)
Fletcher, Bill, Jr. 41
Holt Baker, Arlene 73

Randolph, A. Philip **3**

American Guild of Organists
Adams, Leslie **39**

American Heart Association (AHA)
Cooper, Edward S. **6**
Grant, Augustus O. **71**
Richardson, Donna **39**

American Idol
Barrino, Fantasia **53, 94**
Hudson, Jennifer **63, 83**
Jackson, Randy **40**

American Institute for the Prevention of Blindness
Bath, Patricia E. **37**

American Library Association (ALA)
Franklin, Hardy R. **9, 87**
Hayden, Carla D. **47**
Jones, Clara Stanton **51**
Josey, E. J. **10**
McFadden, Bernice L. **39**
Rollins, Charlamae Hill **27**
Wedgeworth, Robert W. **42**

American Negro Academy
Grimké, Archibald H. **9**
Schomburg, Arthur Alfonso **9**

American Negro Theater
Martin, Helen **31**

American Nuclear Society
Wilkens, J. Ernest, Jr. **43**

American Nurses Association (ANA)
Kennedy, Adrienne **11**
Staupers, Mabel K. **7**

American Postal Workers Union
Burrus, William Henry "Bill" **45**

American Psychological Association (APA)
Anderson, Norman B. **45**
Mitchell, Sharon **36**

American Red Cross
Bullock, Steve **22**
Drew, Charles Richard **7**

American Society of Magazine Editors
Curry, George E. **23**

American Tennis Association
Gibson, Althea **8, 43**
Peters, Margaret and Matilda **43**

American Writers Association
Schuyler, George Samuel **40**

Amsterdam News
Cooper, Andrew W. **36**
Holt, Nora **38**
Tatum, Elinor R. **78**
Tatum, Wilbert **76**

ANA
See American Nurses Association

ANC
See African National Congress

Anglican Church hierarchy
Akinola, Peter Jasper **65**
Tutu, Desmond Mpilo **6, 44**

Angolan government
dos Santos, José Eduardo **43**
Neto, António Agostinho **43**

Anheuser-Busch distribution
Cherry, Deron **40**

Anthropology
Asante, Molefi Kete **3**
Bunche, Ralph J. **5**
Cole, Johnnetta B. **5, 43**
Davis, Allison **12**
Diop, Cheikh Anta **4**
Dunham, Katherine **4, 59**
Hansberry, William Leo **11**
Primus, Pearl **6**
Robeson, Eslanda Goode **13**
Rodriguez, Cheryl **64**

Antoinette Perry awards
See Tony awards

APA
See American Psychological Association

Apartheid
Abrahams, Peter **39**
Ashe, Arthur **18**
Berry, Mary Frances **7**
Biko, Steven **4**
Brutus, Dennis **38**
Butler, Jonathan **28**
Howard, M. William, Jr. **26**
Ka Dinizulu, Mcwayizeni **29**
Kuzwayo, Ellen **68**
LaGuma, Alex **30**
Luthuli, Albert **13**
Mahlasela, Vusi **65**
Makeba, Miriam **2, 50, 74**
Mandela, Nelson **1, 14, 77**
Mandela, Winnie **2, 35**
Masekela, Hugh **1**
Mathabane, Mark **5**
Mbeki, Thabo **14, 73**
Mbuende, Kaire **12**
McDougall, Gay J. **11, 43**
Mhlaba, Raymond **55**
Mphalele, Es'kia **40**
Nkoli, Simon **60**
Ntshona, Winston **52**
Nyanda, Siphiwe **21**
Nzo, Alfred **15**
Plaatje, Sol. T. **80**
Ramaphosa, Cyril **3**
Ramphele, Maphela **29**
Robinson, Randall **7, 46**
Sisulu, Albertina **57**
Sisulu, Walter **47**
Sullivan, Leon H. **13, 30**
Tutu, Desmond Mpilo **6, 44**

Apollo
Williams, O. S. **13**

Apollo Theater
Sims, Howard **48**
Sutton, Percy E. **42, 82**

APWU
See American Postal Workers Union

Archaeology
Gilbert, John Wesley **91**
McJunkin, George **93**

Architecture
Abele, Julian **55**
Adjaye, David **38, 78**
Bond, J. Max, Jr. **76**
Gantt, Harvey **1**
Johnson, Jeh Vincent **44**
King, Robert Arthur **58**
McKissack, Leatrice **80**
Sklarek, Norma Merrick **25**
Taylor, Robert Robinson **80**
Williams, Paul R. **9**

Argonne National Laboratory
Massey, Walter E. **5, 45**
Quarterman, Lloyd Albert **4**

Ariel Capital Management
Hobson, Mellody **40**
Rogers, John W., Jr. **5, 52**

Arista Records
Lattimore, Kenny **35**
Reid, Antonio "L.A." **28**

Arkansas government
Elders, Joycelyn **6**

Art history
Amaki, Amalia **76**
Benjamin, Tritobia Hayes **53**
Campbell, Mary Schmidt **43**

Arthur Andersen
Scott, Milton **51**

Astronauts
Anderson, Michael P. **40**
Bluford, Guy **2, 35**
Bolden, Charles Frank, Jr. **7, 78**
Gregory, Frederick **8, 51**
Harris, Bernard A. **90**
Jemison, Mae C. **1, 35**
Lawrence, Robert H., Jr. **16**
McNair, Ronald **3, 58**
Wilson, Stephanie **72**

Astronomy
Banneker, Benjamin **93**
Pitts, Derrick **77**

Astrophysics
Alcorn, George Edward, Jr. **59**
Carruthers, George R. **40**
Walker, Arthur, II **87**

Athletic administration
Goss, Tom **23**
Littlepage, Craig **35**

Atlanta Baptist College
See Morehouse College

Atlanta Board of Education
Mays, Benjamin E. **7**

Atlanta Braves baseball team
Aaron, Hank **5**
Baker, Dusty **8, 43, 72**
Justice, David **18**

McGriff, Fred **24**
Sanders, Deion **4, 31**

Atlanta city government
Campbell, Bill **9, 76**
Franklin, Shirley **34, 80**
Jackson, Maynard **2, 41**
Pitts, Robb **84**
Reed, Kasim **82**
Williams, Hosea Lorenzo **15, 31**
Young, Andrew **3, 48**

Atlanta Falcons football team
Anderson, Jamal **22**
Buchanan, Ray **32**
Sanders, Deion **4, 31**
Vick, Michael **39, 65, 94**

Atlanta Police Department
Brown, Lee Patrick **1, 24**
Harvard, Beverly **11**

Audelco awards
Holder, Laurence **34**
Rodgers, Rod **36**
Wesley, Richard **73**

Aurelian Honor Society Award
Lewis, William M., Jr. **40**

Authors Guild
Davis, George **36**
Gayle, Addison, Jr. **41**
Schuyler, George Samuel **40**

Authors League of America
Abrahams, Peter **39**
Cotter, Joseph Seamon, Sr. **40**
Davis, George **36**
Gayle, Addison, Jr. **41**

Automobile dealership
Farr, Mel **24**
Gidron, Richard D. **68**
Parker, Jim **64**

Aviation
Brown, Jesse Leroy **31**
Brown, Willa **40**
Bullard, Eugene **12**
Coleman, Bessie **9**
Julian, Hubert **90**
McLeod, Gus **27**
Petersen, Frank E. **31**
Roy, Kenny **51**

"Back to Africa" movement
Turner, Henry McNeal **5**

Bahamian government
Christie, Perry Gladstone **53**
Pindling, Lynden **81**

Ballet
Ailey, Alvin **8**
Allen, Debbie **13, 42**
Anderson, Lauren **72**
Collins, Janet **33, 64**
Dove, Ulysses **5**
Faison, George **16**
Jamison, Judith **7, 67**
Johnson, Virginia **9**
Jones, Doris W. **62**
Mitchell, Arthur **2, 47**
Nichols, Nichelle **11**
Parks, Gordon **1, 35, 58**

Rhoden, Dwight **40**
Richardson, Desmond **39**
Rowell, Victoria **13, 68**
Tyson, Andre **40**

Balm in Gilead, The
Seele, Pernessa **46**

Baltimore Black Sox baseball team
Day, Leon **39**

Baltimore city government
Dixon, Sheila **68**
Rawlings-Blake, Stephanie **93**
Robinson, Bishop L. **66**
Schmoke, Kurt **1, 48**

Baltimore Colts football team
Davis, Milt **74**
Parker, Jim **64**

Baltimore Elite Giants baseball team
Campanella, Roy **25**
Day, Leon **39**
Kimbro, Henry A. **25**

Baltimore Orioles baseball team
Baylor, Don **6**
Blair, Paul **36**
Carter, Joe **30**
Jackson, Reggie **15**
Robinson, Frank **9, 87**

Banking
Blaylock, Ronald **86**
Boyd, T. B., III **6**
Bradley, Jennette B. **40**
Bridgforth, Glinda **36**
Brimmer, Andrew F. **2, 48**
Bryant, John **26**
Chapman, Nathan A., Jr. **21**
Chappell, Emma **18**
Ferguson, Roger W. **25**
Forte, Linda Diane **54**
Funderburg, I. Owen **38**
Greene, Richard Thaddeus, Sr. **67**
Griffith, Mark Winston **8**
Harris, Carla A. **67**
Lawless, Theodore K. **8**
Louis, Errol T. **8**
March, William Carrington **56**
McGuire, Raymond J. **57**
Morgan, Rose **11**
Parsons, Richard Dean **11**
Utendahl, John **23**
Walker, Maggie Lena **17**
Watkins, Donald **35**
Watkins, Walter C. **24**
Willie, Louis, Jr. **68**
Wright, Deborah C. **25**

Baptist
Austin, Junius C. **44**
Borders, William Holmes **94**
Bradley, J. Robert **65**
Braxton, Brad **77**
Butts, Calvin O., III **9, 90**
Davis, Gary **41**
Forbes, James A., Jr. **71**
Franklin, C. L. **68**
Fuller, Thomas O. **90**
Gomes, Peter J. **15, 93**

Hooks, Benjamin L. **2, 85**
Jasper, John J. **91**
Jemison, Major L. **48**
Jones, E. Edward, Sr. **45**
King, Martin Luther, Sr. **89**
Long, Eddie L. **29, 89**
Meeks, James T. **92**
Moss, Otis, Jr. **72**
Rogers, Alan G. **72**
Taylor, Gardner C. **76**
Thurston, Stephen J. **49**
Walker, Lucius, Jr. **88**
Walker, Wyatt Tee **80**

Baseball
Aaron, Hank **5**
Allen, Dick **85**
Anderson, Elmer **25**
Ashford, Emmett **22**
Baines, Harold **32**
Baker, Dusty **8, 43, 72**
Banks, Ernie **33**
Barnhill, David **30**
Baylor, Don **6**
Bell, James "Cool Papa" **36**
Belle, Albert **10**
Black, Joe **75**
Blair, Paul **36**
Bonds, Barry **6, 34, 63**
Bonds, Bobby **43**
Brock, Lou **18**
Brown, Willard **36**
Campanella, Roy **25**
Carew, Rod **20**
Carter, Joe **30**
Charleston, Oscar **39**
Clendenon, Donn **26, 56**
Coleman, Leonard S., Jr. **12**
Cooper, Andy "Lefty" **63**
Cottrell, Comer **11**
Crawford, Carl **90**
Dandridge, Ray **36**
Davis, Piper **19**
Dawson, Andre **85**
Day, Leon **39**
Doby, Lawrence Eugene, Sr. **16**
Dye, Jermaine **58**
Ellis, Dock **78**
Fielder, Cecil **2**
Fielder, Prince Semien **68**
Flood, Curt **10, 93**
Foster, Andrew **79**
Gaston, Cito **71**
Gibson, Bob **33**
Gibson, Josh **22**
Glanville, Douglas Metunwa **82**
Gooden, Dwight **20**
Granderson, Curtis **66**
Gregg, Eric **16**
Griffey, Ken, Jr. **12, 73**
Gwynn, Tony **18, 83**
Henderson, Rickey **28, 78**
Howard, Ryan **65**
Hunter, Torii **43**
Hyde, Cowan F. "Bubba" **47**
Irvin, Monte **31**
Jackson, Reggie **15**
Jenkins, Fergie **46**
Jeter, Derek **27, 93**
Johnson, Clifford "Connie" **52**
Johnson, Mamie "Peanut" **40**
Justice, David **18**
Kaiser, Cecil **42**

Kimbro, Henry A. **25**
Lacy, Sam **30, 46**
Lankford, Ray **23**
Larkin, Barry **24**
Lloyd, John Henry "Pop" **30**
Lofton, Kenny **12**
Lopes, Davey **92**
Mackey, Biz **82**
Manuel, Jerry **94**
Mariner, Jonathan **41**
Martinez, Pedro **81**
Mays, Willie **3**
McGriff, Fred **24**
McRae, Hal **84**
Minoso, Minnie **89**
Morgan, Joe **9**
Murray, Eddie **12**
Newcombe, Don **24**
O'Neil, Buck **19, 59**
Ortiz, David **52, 82**
Paige, Satchel **7**
Payne, Ulice **42**
Pride, Charley **26**
Puckett, Kirby **4, 58**
Radcliffe, Ted **74**
Randolph, Willie **53**
Reagins, Tony **94**
Reese, Pokey **28**
Reynolds, Harold **77**
Rice, Jim **75**
Richard, J. R. **87**
Robinson, Frank **9, 87**
Robinson, Jackie **6**
Robinson, Sharon **22**
Rollins, Jimmy **70**
Sabathia, CC **74**
Sanders, Deion **4, 31**
Sheffield, Gary **16**
Smith, Hilton **29**
Smith, Ozzie **77**
Sosa, Sammy **21, 44**
Stargell, Willie **29**
Stearnes, Norman "Turkey" **31**
Stone, Toni **15**
Strawberry, Darryl **22**
Thomas, Frank **12, 51**
Trouppe, Quincy Thomas, Sr. **84**
Vaughn, Mo **16**
Virgil, Ozzie **48**
Watson, Bob **25**
Wells, Vernon **91**
White, Bill **1, 48**
Williams, Billy **86**
Williams, Ken **68**
Willis, Dontrelle **55**
Wills, Maury **73**
Winfield, Dave **5, 91**

Baseball Hall of Fame
Banks, Ernie **33**
Bell, James "Cool Papa" **36**
Brown, Willard **36**
Campanella, Roy **25**
Charleston, Oscar **39**
Dandridge, Ray **36**
Dawson, Andre **85**
Day, Leon **39**
Doby, Lawrence Eugene, Sr. **16, 41**
Gibson, Josh **22**
Gwynn, Tony **18, 83**
Henderson, Rickey **28, 78**
Irvin, Monte **31**
Leonard, Buck **67**

Lloyd, John Henry "Pop" **30**
Morgan, Joe **9**
Paige, Satchel **7**
Rice, Jim **75**
Robinson, Frank **9, 87**
Robinson, Jackie **6**
Smith, Hilton **29**
Smith, Ozzie **77**
Stearnes, Norman "Turkey" **31**
Williams, Billy **86**
Winfield, Dave **5, 91**

Barbadian government
Adams, Grantley **82**
Arthur, Owen **33**

Basket making
Jackson, Mary **73**

Basketball
Abdul-Jabbar, Kareem **8**
Abdur-Rahim, Shareef **28**
Allen, Ray **82**
Amaker, Tommy **62**
Anderson, Mike **63**
Anthony, Carmelo **46, 94**
Archibald, Tiny **90**
Arenas, Gilbert **84**
Artest, Ron **52**
Barkley, Charles **5, 66**
Baylor, Elgin **93**
Bing, Dave **3, 59, 78**
Bogues, Tyrone "Muggsy" **56**
Bol, Manute **1**
Bolton-Holifield, Ruthie **28**
Bosh, Chris **85**
Brand, Elton **31**
Brandon, Terrell **16**
Brown, Mike **77**
Bryant, Kobe **15, 31, 71**
Bynoe, Peter C. B. **40**
Carter, Butch **27**
Carter, Kenneth **53**
Carter, Vince **26**
Catchings, Tamika **43**
Chamberlain, Wilt **18, 47**
Chaney, John **67**
Cheeks, Maurice **47**
Clifton, Nathaniel "Sweetwater" **47**
Cooper, Charles "Chuck" **47**
Cooper, Michael **31**
Cooper-Dyke, Cynthia **17, 89**
Curry, Michael **85**
Dantley, Adrian **72**
Davis, Mike **41**
Drexler, Clyde **4, 61**
Dumars, Joe **16, 65**
Duncan, Tim **20, 91**
Dunn, Jerry **27**
Durant, Kevin **76**
Edwards, Teresa **14**
Ellerbe, Brian **22**
Elliott, Sean **26**
Erving, Julius **18, 47**
Ewing, Patrick **17, 73**
Fox, Rick **27**
Frazier, Walt **91**
Freeman, Marianna **23**
Gaines, Clarence E., Sr. **55**
Garnett, Kevin **14, 70**
Gentry, Alvin **23**
Gourdine, Simon **11**
Gray, Yeshimbra "Shimmy" **55**
Green, A. C. **32**

Greer, Hal **92**
Griffith, Yolanda **25**
Hardaway, Anfernee (Penny) **13**
Hardaway, Tim **35**
Harris-Stewart, Lusia **90**
Haskins, Clem **23**
Hawkins, Connie **91**
Hayes, Elvin **93**
Haynes, Marques **22**
Heard, Gar **25**
Hill, Grant **13, 94**
Holdsclaw, Chamique **24**
Howard, Juwan **15**
Hunter, Billy **22**
Isaacs, John **76**
Iverson, Allen **24, 46**
James, LeBron **46, 78**
Johnson, Avery **62**
Johnson, Dennis **89**
Johnson, Earvin "Magic" **3, 39**
Johnson, Gus **92**
Johnson, Joe **94**
Johnson, Kevin **70**
Johnson, Larry **28**
Jones, K. C. **83**
Jones, Merlakia **34**
Jones, Roy, Jr. **22**
Jones, Sam **85**
Jordan, Eddie **83**
Jordan, Michael **6, 21**
Joyce, Dru **81**
Justice, David **18**
Kellogg, Clark **64**
Kidd, Jason **86**
Lanier, Bob **47**
Lennox, Betty **31**
Leslie, Lisa **16, 73**
Lloyd, Earl **26**
Lofton, Kenny **12**
Lowe, Sidney **64**
Lucas, John **7**
Mahorn, Rick **60**
Malone, Karl **18, 51, 90**
Malone, Moses **79**
Manigault, Earl "The Goat" **15**
Master P **21**
McAdoo, Bob **75**
McGrady, Tracy **80**
McLendon, John B., Jr. **89**
Miller, Cheryl **10, 74**
Milton, DeLisha **31**
Mitchell, Sam **82**
Mohammed, Nazr **64**
Monroe, Earl **89**
Mourning, Alonzo **17, 44**
Mutombo, Dikembe **7**
Odom, Lamar **81**
Olajuwon, Hakeem **2, 72**
O'Neal, Shaquille **8, 30**
Palmer, Violet **59**
Parish, Robert **43**
Parker, Candace **74**
Parker, Tony **75**
Paul, Chris **84**
Peck, Carolyn **23**
Phillips, Teresa L. **42**
Pierce, Paul **71**
Pippen, Scottie **15, 89**
Porter, Terry **75**
Prince, Tayshaun **68**
Reed, Willis, Jr. **86**
Richardson, Nolan **9**
Richmond, Mitch **19**

Rivers, Doc **25, 81**
Robertson, Oscar **26**
Robinson, David **24, 90**
Robinson, Will **51, 69**
Rodman, Dennis **12, 44**
Rose, Derrick **82**
Russell, Bill **8**
Sanders, Satch **77**
Silas, Paul **24**
Smith, Randy **81**
Smith, Stephen A. **69**
Smith, Tubby **18, 83**
Sprewell, Latrell **23**
Stackhouse, Jerry **30**
Staley, Dawn **57**
Stith, Tom **93**
Stoudemire, Amaré **59**
Stringer, C. Vivian **13, 66**
Swoopes, Sheryl **12, 56**
Ussery, Terdema, II **29**
Thomas, Isiah **7, 26, 65**
Thompson, Tina **25, 75**
Thurmond, Nate **88**
Tisdale, Wayman **50**
Unseld, Wes **23**
Wade, Dwyane **61**
Wallace, Ben **54**
Wallace, Perry E. **47**
Wallace, Rasheed **56**
Webber, Chris **15, 30, 59**
Wilkens, Lenny **11, 88**
Williams, Deron **92**
Williams, Natalie **31**
Woodard, Lynette **67**
Woodson, Mike **78**
Worthy, James **49**

Basketball Hall of Fame
Abdul-Jabbar, Kareem **8**
Archibald, Tiny **90**
Barkley, Charles **5, 66**
Baylor, Elgin **93**
Bing, Dave **3, 59, 78**
Chamberlain, Wilt **18, 47**
Chaney, John **67**
Cooper-Dyke, Cynthia **17, 89**
Dantley, Adrian **72**
Drexler, Clyde **4, 61**
Dumars, Joe **16, 65**
Ewing, Patrick **17, 73**
Frazier, Walt **91**
Gaines, Clarence E., Sr. **55**
Gervin, George **80**
Greer, Hal **92**
Harris-Stewart, Lusia **90**
Hawkins, Connie **91**
Hayes, Elvin **93**
Haynes, Marques **22**
Johnson, Dennis **89**
Johnson, Earvin "Magic"
Johnson, Gus **92**
Jones, K. C. **83**
Jones, Sam **85**
Lanier, Bob **47**
Lloyd, Earl **26**
Malone, Karl **18, 51, 90**
Malone, Moses **79**
McAdoo, Bob **75**
McLendon, John B., Jr. **89**
Miller, Cheryl **10, 74**
Monroe, Earl **89**
Olajuwon, Hakeem **2, 72**
Parish, Robert **43**

Pippen, Scottie **15, 89**
Reed, Willis, Jr. **86**
Robertson, Oscar **26**
Robinson, David **24, 90**
Russell, Bill **8**
Sanders, Satch **77**
Thomas, Isiah **7, 26, 65**
Thurmond, Nate **88**
Unseld, Wes **23**
Wilkens, Lenny **11, 88**
Wilkins, Dominique **74**
Woodard, Lynette **67**
Worthy, James **49**

Bass
Foster, George "Pops" **40**
Isley, Marvin **87**
Jamerson, James **59**

BBC
See British Broadcasting Company

Beale Streeters
Ace, Johnny **36**
Bland, Bobby "Blue" **36**
King, B. B. **7**

Beatrice International
See TLC Beatrice International
   Holdings, Inc.

Beauty salons and products
Fine, Sam **60**
Gibson, Ted **66**
Stanford, Olivia Lee Dilworth **49**

Bebop
Carter, Betty **19**
Clarke, Kenny **27**
Coltrane, John **19**
Davis, Miles **4**
Eckstine, Billy **28**
Fitzgerald, Ella **8, 18**
Gillespie, Dizzy **1**
Gordon, Dexter **25**
Hancock, Herbie **20, 67**
Harris, Barry **68**
Hawkins, Coleman **9**
Jackson, Milt **26**
Parker, Charlie **20**
Powell, Bud **24**
Roach, Max **21, 63**
Vaughan, Sarah **13**

**Ben & Jerry's Homemade Ice
Cream, Inc.**
Holland, Robert, Jr. **11**

Bennett College
Cole, Johnnetta B. **5, 43**
Player, Willa B. **43**

Benin government
Kerekou, Ahmed **1**
Soglo, Nicéphore **15**
Yayi, Boni T. **84**

Bessie award
Richardson, Desmond **39**

BET
See Black Entertainment Television

Bethune-Cookman College
Bethune, Mary McLeod **4**
Joyner, Marjorie Stewart **26**

A Better Chance
Lewis, William M., Jr. **40**

Big Easy Award
Adams, Johnny **39**

Bill and Melinda Gates Foundation
Golston, Allan C. **55**

Billy Graham Evangelistic Association
Bell, Ralph S. **5**
Waters, Ethel **7**

Bing Group, The
Bing, Dave **3, 59, 78**
Lloyd, Earl **26**

Biology
Cobb, Jewel Plummer **42**
Emeagwali, Dale **31**
Jarvis, Erich **67**
Just, Ernest Everett **3**
Malveaux, Floyd **54**
Pickett, Cecil **39**

Biotechnology
Dabiri, John **93**
Haynie, Sharon **94**
Juma, Calestous **57**
Wambugu, Florence **42**

Birmingham (AL) city government
Kincaid, Bernard **28**
Langford, Larry P. **74**
Nunn, Annetta **43**

Birmingham (AL) Police Department
Nunn, Annetta **43**
Woods, Abraham, Jr. **74**

Birth control
Elders, Joycelyn **6**
Williams, Maggie **7, 71**

Bishop College
Cottrell, Comer **11**

Black Academy of Arts & Letters
White, Charles **39**

Black Alliance for Educational Options
Fuller, Howard L. **37**

Black American West Museum
Stewart, Paul Wilbur **12**

Black Americans for Family Values
Foster, Ezola **28**

Black arts movement
Barrett, Lindsay **43**
Caldwell, Benjamin **46**
Cornish, Sam **50**
Cortez, Jayne **43**
Cruse, Harold **54**
Dent, Thomas C. **50**
Donaldson, Jeff **46**
Dumas, Henry **41**
Gayle, Addison, Jr. **41**
Giovanni, Nikki **9, 39, 85**

Henderson, David 53
Hoagland, Everett H. 45
Neal, Larry 38
Pomare, Eleo 72
Smith, Vincent D. 48
Touré, Askia (Muhammad Abu Bakr el) 47
X, Marvin 45

Black Cabinet
Hastie, William H. 8

Black Coaches Association (BCA)
Freeman, Marianna 23
Keith, Floyd A. 61

Black Consciousness movement
Biko, Steven 4
Fanon, Frantz 44
Fuller, Hoyt 44
Muhammad, Elijah 4
Ramaphosa, Cyril 3
Ramphele, Maphela 29
Tutu, Desmond Mpilo 6, 44

Black Economic Union (BEU)
Brown, Jim 11

Black Enterprise magazine
Brimmer, Andrew F. 2, 48
Graves, Butch 77
Graves, Earl G. 1, 35
Wallace, Phyllis A. 9

Black Entertainment Television (BET)
Ames, Wilmer 27
Gordon, Ed 10, 53
Greely, M. Gasby 27
Johnson, Robert L. 3, 39
Johnson, Sheila Crump 48
Jones, Bobby 20, 94
Lee, Debra L. 62
McCrary Anthony, Crystal 70
Smiley, Tavis 20, 68

Black Filmmakers Hall of Fame
Browne, Roscoe Lee 66
Dee, Ruby 8, 50, 68
Dixon, Ivan 69
McKinney, Nina Mae 40

Black History Month
Woodson, Carter G. 2

Black Horizons on the Hill
Wilson, August 7, 33, 55

Black Manifesto
Forman, James 7, 51

Black Music Center
Moore, Undine Smith 28

Black Muslims
Abdul-Jabbar, Kareem 8
Ali, Muhammad 2, 16, 52
Farrakhan, Louis 2
Muhammad, Elijah 4
Muhammed, W. Deen 27
Redding, Ann Holmes 77

X, Malcolm 1

Black nationalism
Baker, Houston A., Jr. 6
Baraka, Amiri 1, 38
Caldwell, Benjamin 46
Carmichael, Stokely 5, 26
Donaldson, Jeff 46
Farrakhan, Louis 2
Forman, James 7, 51
Garvey, Marcus 1
Heard, Nathan C. 45
Innis, Roy 5
Muhammad, Elijah 4
Obadele, Imari 84
Turner, Henry McNeal 5
X, Malcolm 1
York, Dwight D. 71

Black Panther Party (BPP)
Abu-Jamal, Mumia 15
Al-Amin, Jamil Abdullah 6
bin Wahad, Dhoruba 85
Brown, Elaine 8
Carmichael, Stokely 5
Cleaver, Eldridge 5
Cleaver, Kathleen Neal 29
Coates, Ta-Nehisi 76
Cox, Donald Lee 93
Davis, Angela 5
Douglas, Emory 89
Forman, James 7, 51
Hampton, Fred 18
Hilliard, David 7
Jackson, George Lester 14
Kimbro, Warren 76
Neal, Larry 38
Newton, Huey 2
Pratt, Geronimo 18
Rush, Bobby 26, 76
Seale, Bobby 3
Shakur, Afeni 67
Shakur, Assata 6

Black Power movement
Al-Amin, Jamil Abdullah 6
Baker, Houston A., Jr. 6
Brown, Elaine 8
Carmichael, Stokely 5, 26
Dodson, Howard, Jr. 7, 52
Donaldson, Jeff 46
Dumas, Henry 41
Hare, Nathan 44
McKissick, Floyd B. 3
Stone, Chuck 9

Black Think Tank
Hare, Nathan 44

Blackvoices.com
Cooper, Barry 33

Blackwell Consulting Services
Blackwell, Robert D., Sr. 52

Black World magazine
See Negro Digest magazine

Black Writers Conference
McMillan, Rosalynn A. 36

Blind Boys of Alabama
Scott, George 55

Blogging
Contee, Cheryl 88

Blues
Ace, Johnny 36
Austin, Lovie 40
Barnes, Roosevelt "Booba" 33
Bibb, Eric 49
Bland, Bobby "Blue" 36
Broonzy, Big Bill 82
Brown, Charles 23
Brown, Nappy 73
Burns, Eddie 44
Burnside, R. L. 56
Carr, Leroy 49
Clarke, Kenny 27
Collins, Albert 12
Cox, Ida 42
Cray, Robert 30
Davis, Gary 41
Davis, Guy 36
Davis, Tyrone 54
Dixon, Willie 4
Dorsey, Thomas 15
Estes, Sleepy John 33
Evora, Cesaria 12
Ford, T-Model 91
Freeman, Yvette 27
Fuller, Blind Boy 86
Gaines, Grady 38
Guy, Buddy 31
Handy, W. C. 8
Harris, Corey 39, 73
Hemphill, Jessie Mae 33, 59
Holiday, Billie 1
Hooker, John Lee 30
Hopkins, Lightnin' 83
House, Son 8
Howlin' Wolf 9
Hunter, Alberta 42
Hurt, Mississippi John 84
Jackson, John 36
James, Skip 38
Jefferson, Blind Lemon 81
Johnson, Buddy 36
Johnson, Lonnie 85
King, B. B. 7
King, Freddie 92
LaVette, Bettye 85
Leadbelly 82
Lipscomb, Mance 49
Little Milton 36
Little Walter 36
Mahal, Taj 39
Martin, Sara 38
McGriff, Jimmy 72
McTell, Blind Willie 89
Mo', Keb' 36
Moore, Johnny B. 38
Muse, Clarence Edouard 21
Neal, Raful 44
Odetta 37, 74
Owens, Jack 38
Parker, Charlie 20
Pena, Paul 58
Perkins, Pinetop 70
Peterson, James 38
Rawls, Lou 17, 57
Reed, A. C. 36
Reed, Jimmy 38
Reese, Della 6, 20
Robinson, Fenton 38
Rogers, Jimmy 38
Ross, Isaiah "Doc" 40
Rush, Bobby 78
Rush, Otis 38

Seals, Son 56
Smith, Bessie 3
Smith, Mamie 32
Smith, Trixie 34
Streeter, Sarah 45
Sykes, Roosevelt 20
Tampa Red 63
Taylor, Koko 40, 80
Terry, Sonny 88
Turner, Big Joe 92
Turner, Ike 68
Wallace, Sippie 1
Washington, Dinah 22
Waters, Ethel 7
Waters, Muddy 34
Watson, Johnny "Guitar" 18
Webster, Katie 29
White, Josh, Jr. 52
Williams, Joe 5, 25
Williamson, Sonny Boy 84
Wilson, August 7, 33, 55

Blues Hall of Fame
Broonzy, Big Bill 82
Hopkins, Lightnin' 83
Hunter, Alberta 42
Hurt, Mississippi John 84
Little Milton 36
Williamson, Sonny Boy 84

Blues vernacular
Baker, Houston A., Jr. 6

Bobsledding
Flowers, Vonetta 35
Hines, Garrett 35
Jones, Randy 35
Moses, Edwin 8

Bodybuilding
Haney, Lee 77
Murray, Lenda 10

Boeing Company, The
Bell, James A. 50
Grooms, Henry R(andall) 50
Mills, Joseph C. 51
Robinson-Berry, Joan 94

Bola Press
Cortez, Jayne 43

Bolero music
Ferrer, Ibrahim 41

Boogie music
Brooks, Hadda 40

The Boondocks
McGruder, Aaron 28, 56

Boston Bruins hockey team
O'Ree, Willie 5

Boston Celtics basketball team
Allen, Ray 82
Cooper, Charles "Chuck" 47
Fox, Rick 27
Garnett, Kevin 14, 70
Parish, Robert 43
Pierce, Paul 71
Rivers, Doc 25, 81
Russell, Bill 8
Sanders, Satch 77

Silas, Paul 24

Boston Red Sox baseball team
Baylor, Don 6
Ortiz, David 52, 82
Rice, Jim 75
Vaughn, Mo 16

Boston University
Loury, Glenn 36
Mitchell, Sharon 36

Botswanan government
Masire, Quett 5
Mogae, Festus Gontebanye 19, 79

Bowling
Branham, George, III 50
Terrell-Kearney, Kim 83

Boxing
Ali, Laila 27, 63
Ali, Muhammad 2, 16, 52
Bowe, Riddick 6
Carter, Rubin 26
DeGale, James 74
Dixon, George 52
Ellis, Jimmy 44
Foreman, George 1, 15
Forrest, Vernon 40, 79
Frazier, Joe 19
Frazier-Lyde, Jacqui 31
Futch, Eddie 33
Gans, Joe 91
Gibson, Truman K., Jr. 60
Haye, David 82
Hearns, Thomas 29
Holmes, Larry 20, 68
Holyfield, Evander 6
Hopkins, Bernard 35, 69
Johnson, Jack 8
Jones, Roy, Jr. 22
King, Don 14
Lee, Canada 8
Leonard, Sugar Ray 15
Lewis, Butch 71
Lewis, Lennox 27
Louis, Joe 5
Mayweather, Floyd, Jr. 57
Moorer, Michael 19
Mosley, Shane 32
Muhammad, Jabir Herbert 72
Mundine, Anthony 56
Page, Greg 78
Patterson, Floyd 19, 58
Robinson, Sugar Ray 18
Rose, Lionel 56
Steward, Emanuel 18
Taylor, Jermain 60
Toney, James 89
Tyson, Mike 28, 44, 93
Ward, Andre 62
Whitaker, Pernell 10, 89
Wills, Harry 80
Wolfe, Ann 82
Young, Jimmy 54

Boys and Girls Clubs
Brooks, Derrick 43
Gaines, Brenda 41

Boys Choir of Harlem
Turnbull, Walter 13, 60

BPP
See Black Panther Party

Brazilian government
da Silva, Benedita 5
Nascimento, Abdias do 93
Silva, Marina 80

Breast cancer awareness
Brown, Zora Kramer 12
Norton, Meredith 72
Riperton, Minnie 32

Bristol-Myers Squibb Inc.
Potter, Myrtle 40

British Broadcasting Company (BBC)
Armah, Esther 87
Figueroa, John J. 40
Stuart, Moira 82

British Film Institute
Akomfrah, John 37

British government
Abbott, Diane 9
Amos, Valerie 41
Boateng, Paul Yaw 56
Grant, Bernie 57
King, Oona 27
Pitt, David Thomas 10

British Virgin Islands government
Stoutt, H. Lavity 83

Broadcasting
Allen, Byron 3, 24
Ashley, Maurice 15, 47
Banks, William 11
Bettis, Jerome 64
Blackmon, Brenda 58
Bradley, Ed 2, 59
Branch, William Blackwell 39
Brown, Les 5
Brown, Tony 3
Brown, Vivian 27
Brunson, Dorothy 1, 87
Clayton, Xernona 3, 45
Cornelius, Don 4
Dee, Merri 55
Elder, Larry 25
Evans, Harry 25
Figueroa, John J. 40
Freeman, Aaron 52
Goode, Mal 13
Gumbel, Bryant 14, 80
Gumbel, Greg 8
Hamblin, Ken 10
Hickman, Fred 11
Holt, Lester 66
Hunter-Gault, Charlayne 6, 31
Jackson, Hal 41
Johnson, Rafer 33
Johnson, Robert L. 3, 39
Joyner, Tom 19, 90
Kellogg, Clark 64
Kennedy-Overton, Jayne Harris 46
Langhart Cohen, Janet 19, 60
Lawson, Jennifer 1, 50
Lemon, Don 94
Lewis, Delano 7
Lofton, James 42
Lomax, Louis E. 90

Mabrey, Vicki 26
Madison, Joseph E. 17
Madison, Paula 37
McEwen, Mark 5
McFarland, Roland 49
Melton, Frank 81
Mickelbury, Penny 28
Miller, Cheryl 10, 74
Mitchell, Russ 21, 73
Morgan, Joe 9
Morton, Frederick A., Jr. 93
Neville, Arthel 53
Peete, Rodney 60
Pinckney, Sandra 56
Pinkston, W. Randall 24
Quarles, Norma 25
Reynolds, Star Jones 10, 27, 61
Roberts, Deborah 35
Roberts, Robin 16, 54
Rodgers, Johnathan 6, 51
Russell, Bill 8
Shaw, Bernard 2, 28
Simmons, Jamal 72
Simpson, Carole 6, 30
Simpson, O. J. 15
Smiley, Tavis 20, 68
Stewart, Alison 13
Swann, Lynn 28
Syler, Rene 53
Tirico, Mike 68
Watts, Rolonda 9
White, Bill 1, 48
Williams, Armstrong 29
Williams, Juan 35, 80
Williams, Montel 4, 57
Winfrey, Oprah 2, 15, 61

Broadside Press
Hoagland, Everett H. 45
Randall, Dudley 8, 55

Brookings Institute
Ladner, Joyce A. 42

Brooklyn Academy of Music
Miller, Bebe 3

Brooklyn Dodgers baseball team
Black, Joe 75
Campanella, Roy 25
Newcombe, Don 24
Robinson, Jackie 6

Brooklyn Eagles baseball team
Day, Leon 39

Brotherhood of Sleeping Car Porters
Randolph, A. Philip 3
Tucker, Rosina 14

Brown University
Beckham, Barry 41
Gibson, Donald Bernard 40
Simmons, Ruth 13, 38

Brown v. Board of Education of Topeka
Bell, Derrick 6
Brown, Oliver Leon 94
Carter, Robert L. 51
Clark, Kenneth B. 5, 52
Franklin, John Hope 5, 77

Henderson, Zelma 71
Hill, Oliver W. 24, 63
Houston, Charles Hamilton 4
Malone Jones, Vivian 59
Marshall, Thurgood 1, 44
Motley, Constance Baker 10, 55
Redding, Louis L. 26
Robinson, Spottswood W., III 22

Buena Vista Social Club
Ferrer, Ibrahim 41

Buffalo Bills football team
Lofton, James 42
Simpson, O. J. 15
Smith, Bruce 80
Thomas, Thurman 75

Bull-riding
Sampson, Charles 13

Burundian government
Ndadaye, Melchior 7
Nkurunziza, Pierre 78
Ntaryamira, Cyprien 8

Busing (anti-busing legislation)
Bosley, Freeman, Jr. 7

Cabinet
See U.S. Cabinet

Cable News Network (CNN)
Chideya, Farai 14, 61
Hickman, Fred 11
Malveaux, Suzanne 88
O'Brien, Soledad 88
Quarles, Norma 25
Shaw, Bernard 2, 28
Watson, Carlos 50

Calabash International Literary Festival
Channer, Colin 36

Calgary Flames hockey team
Iginla, Jarome 35

California Angels baseball team
See Los Angeles Angels baseball team

***California Eagle* newspaper**
Bass, Charlotta Spears 40
Jackson, Vera 40

California state government
Bass, Karen 70
Brown, Janice Rogers 43
Brown, Willie 7, 85
Dixon, Julian C. 24
Dymally, Mervyn 42
Hawkins, Augustus F. 68
Lee, Barbara 25
Millender-McDonald, Juanita 21, 61
Richardson, Laura 81
Riles, Wilson C. 79
Waters, Maxine 3, 67
Watson, Diane 41

California State University
Cobb, Jewel Plummer 42
Granville, Evelyn Boyd 36

Karenga, Maulana 10, 71

California Supreme Court
Brown, Janice Rogers 43

Calypso
Belafonte, Harry 4, 65
Premice, Josephine 41
Rhoden, Wayne 70
Rudder, David 79

Cameroonian government
Ahidjo, Ahmadou 81
Biya, Paul 28
Oyono, Ferdinand 38

Canadian Football League (CFL)
Clemons, Michael "Pinball" 64
Gilliam, Frank 23
Moon, Warren 8, 66
Thrower, Willie 35
Weathers, Carl 10

Canadian government
Augustine, Jean 53
Brown, Rosemary 62
Cools, Anne 64
Jean, Michaëlle; 70
Lewis, Daurene 72
Sparks, Corinne Etta 53

Cancer research
Adams-Campbell, Lucille L. 60
Chinn, May Edward 26
Clark, Celeste 15
Daly, Marie Maynard 37
Dunston, Georgia Mae 48
Freeman, Harold P. 23
Leffall, Lasalle 3, 64
Olopade, Olufunmilayo Falusi 58

Capital punishment
Correia, De'Jaun 93
Hawkins, Steven 14

Cardiac research
Watkins, Levi, Jr. 9

CARE
Gossett, Louis, Jr. 7
Stone, Chuck 9

Caribbean Artists' Movement
Brathwaite, Kamau 36

Caribbean dance
Ailey, Alvin 8
Dunham, Katherine 4, 59
Fagan, Garth 18
Nichols, Nichelle 11
Primus, Pearl 6

Caribbean literature
Breeze, Jean "Binta" 37
Carter, Martin 49
Cartey, Wilfred 47
Dabydeen, David 48
Hearne, John Edgar Caulwell 45

Caribbean music
Ellis, Alton 74
Lefel, Edith 41
Ranglin, Ernest 78

Casting
Cannon, Reuben 50

Cartoonists
Armstrong, Robb 15
Bell, Darrin 77
Brandon, Barbara 3
Brown, Robert 65
Campbell, E. Simms 13
Fax, Elton 48
Harrington, Oliver W. 9
McDuffie, Dwayne 62
McGruder, Aaron 28, 56
Ormes, Jackie 73
Smith, Bruce W. 53

Catering
See Restaurants/Catering/Cooking

Catholicism
See Roman Catholic Church

CBC
See Congressional Black Caucus

CBS
See Columbia Broadcasting System

CDC
See Centers for Disease Control and Prevention

CDF
See Children's Defense Fund

Celebrities for a Drug-Free America
Vereen, Ben 4

Censorship
Butts, Calvin O., III 9, 90
Ice-T 6, 31

Centers for Disease Control and Prevention (CDC)
Fenton, Kevin 87
Gayle, Helene D. 3
Satcher, David 7, 57
Wisdom, Kimberlydawn 57

Central Intercollegiate Athletic Association (CIAA)
Kerry, Leon G. 46
Yancy, Dorothy Cowser 42

Certified public accountant
Jones, Thomas W. 41
Washington, Mary T. 57

CFL
See Canadian Football League

Chadian government
Déby, Idriss 30
Habré, Hissène 6

Challenged Athletes Foundation
Yeboah, Emmanuel Ofosu 53

Challenger
McNair, Ronald 3, 58

Challenger Air Pilot's Association
Brown, Willa 40

Chama Cha Mapinduzi (Tanzania; Revolutionary Party)
Kikwete, Jakaya Mrisho 73
Mkapa, Benjamin W. 16, 77

Mongella, Gertrude 11
Mwinyi, Ali Hassan 1, 77
Nyerere, Julius 5

Charles H. Wright Museum of African American History
Wright, Charles H. 35

Charles R. Drew University
Bath, Patricia E. 37

Charlotte Hornets basketball team
Bryant, Kobe 15, 31, 71
Parish, Robert 43

Charter Schools USA
Mariner, Jonathan 41

Chemistry
Daly, Marie Maynard 37
Donald, Arnold Wayne 36
Hall, Lloyd A. 8
Haynie, Sharon 94
Humphries, Frederick 20
Julian, Percy Lavon 6
King, Reatha Clark 65
Massie, Samuel Proctor, Jr. 29
Mays, William G. 34
McBay, Henry C. 91
Mensah, Thomas 48
Quarterman, Lloyd Albert 4

Chess
Ashley, Maurice 15, 47

Chicago American Giants baseball team
Bell, James "Cool Papa" 36
Charleston, Oscar 39

Chicago Art League
Wilson, Ellis 39

Chicago Bears football team
Page, Alan 7
Payton, Walter 11, 25
Sayers, Gale 28
Singletary, Mike 4, 76
Thrower, Willie 35

Chicago Black Arts Movement
Cortor, Eldzier 42
Sebree, Charles 40

Chicago Bulls basketball team
Brand, Elton 31
Jordan, Michael 6, 21
Parish, Robert 43

Chicago city government
Berry, Edwin C. 81
De Priest, Oscar Stanton 80
Jones, Emil, Jr. 74
Jones, John 89
Kelley, Cliff 75
Lane, Vincent 5
Metcalfe, Ralph 26
Sawyer, Eugene 81
Tillman, Dorothy 76
Washington, Harold 6

Chicago Cubs baseball team
Baker, Dusty 8, 43, 72
Banks, Ernie 33
Bonds, Bobby 43
Carter, Joe 30

Sosa, Sammy 21, 44
Williams, Billy 86

Chicago Defender
Abbott, Robert Sengstacke 27
Holt, Nora 38
Martin, Roland S. 49, 84
Ormes, Jackie 73
Payne, Ethel L. 28

Chicago Defender Charities
Joyner, Marjorie Stewart 26

Chicago Eight
Seale, Bobby 3

Chicago Library Board
Williams, Fannie Barrier 27

Chicago Negro Chamber of Commerce
Fuller, S. B. 13

Chicago Police Department
Hillard, Terry 25
Holton, Hugh, Jr. 39

Chicago Reporter
Calhoun, Lillian Scott 87
Washington, Laura S. 18

Chicago Tribune
Page, Clarence 4

Chicago White Sox baseball team
Baines, Harold 32
Bonds, Bobby 43
Doby, Lawrence Eugene, Sr. 16, 41
Johnson, Clifford "Connie" 52
Thomas, Frank 12, 51
Williams, Ken 68

Chicago Women's Club
Williams, Fannie Barrier 27

Children's Defense Fund (CDF)
Edelman, Marian Wright 5, 42
Williams, Maggie 7, 71

Children's literature
Asim, Jabari 71
Berry, James 41
Bryan, Ashley F. 41
Common 31, 63
De Veaux, Alexis 44
Feelings, Muriel 44
Graham, Lorenz 48
Greenfield, Eloise 9
Johnson, Angela 52
Mollel, Tololwa 38
Myers, Walter Dean 8, 20
Okara, Gabriel 37
Palmer, Everard 37
Shelton, Paula Young 86
Yarbrough, Camille 40

Chi-Lites
Record, Eugene 60

Chiropractics
Ford, Clyde W. 40
Reese, Milous J., Jr. 51

Westbrooks, Bobby 51

Chisholm-Mingo Group, Inc.
Chisholm, Samuel J. 32
Mingo, Frank 32

Choreography
Acogny, Germaine 55
Ailey, Alvin 8
Alexander, Khandi 43
Allen, Debbie 13, 42
Atkins, Cholly 40
Babatunde, Obba 35
Beatty, Talley 35
Brooks, Avery 9
Brown, Ronald K. 91
Byrd, Donald 10
Campbell-Martin, Tisha 8, 42
Collins, Janet 33, 64
Davis, Chuck 33
de Lavallade, Carmen 78
de Passe, Suzanne 25
De Shields, André 72
Dove, Ulysses 5
Dunham, Katherine 4, 59
Ellington, Mercedes 34
Fagan, Garth 18
Faison, George 16
Glover, Savion 14
Hall, Arthur 39
Henson, Darrin 33
Jamison, Judith 7, 67
Johnson, Virginia 9
Jones, Bill T. 1, 46, 80
King, Alonzo 38
LeTang, Henry 66
Manning, Frankie 78
Miller, Bebe 3
Mitchell, Arthur 2, 47
Nicholas, Fayard 20, 57
Nicholas, Harold 20
Pomare, Eleo 72
Primus, Pearl 6
Rhoden, Dwight 40
Richardson, Desmond 39
Robinson, Cleo Parker 38
Robinson, Fatima 34
Rodgers, Rod 36
Spears, Warren 52
Tyson, Andre 40
Zollar, Jawole 28

Christian Financial Ministries, Inc.
Ross, Charles 27

Christian Science Monitor
Khanga, Yelena 6

Chrysler Corporation
Colbert, Virgis William 17
Farmer, Forest 1
Gilles, Ralph 61
Richie, Leroy C. 18

Church of God in Christ
Blake, Charles E. 82
Franklin, Robert M. 13
Hayes, James C. 10
Patterson, Gilbert Earl 41

CIAA
See Central Intercollegiate Athletic Association

Cincinnati city government
Berry, Theodore M. 31
Mallory, Mark 62

Cincinnati Reds baseball team
Baker, Dusty 8, 43, 72
Blair, Paul 36
Larkin, Barry 24
Morgan, Joe 9
Reese, Pokey 28
Robinson, Frank 9, 87
Sanders, Deion 4, 31

Cinematography
Dickerson, Ernest 6, 17

Circus
McFarlan, Tyron 60
Walker, Cedric "Ricky" 19

Citadel Press
Achebe, Chinua 6

Citigroup
Gaines, Brenda 41
Jones, Thomas W. 41
McGuire, Raymond J. 57

City government--U.S.
Bell, Michael 40
Bellamy, Terry 58
Bobb, Robert C. 83
Bradley, Jennette B. 40
Brown, Lee P. 1, 24
Brown, Willie 7, 85
Burris, Chuck 21
Bush, Gordon 82
Caesar, Shirley 19
Clayton, Constance 1
Cleaver, Emanuel 4, 45, 68
Coleman, Michael 28, 79
Craig-Jones, Ellen Walker 44
Dellums, Ronald 2, 81
Ford, Jack 39
Ford, Johnny 70
Foxx, Anthony 81
Hatcher, Richard G. 55
Hayes, James C. 10
Herenton, Willie W. 24, 81
Johnson, Harvey, Jr. 24, 82
Lowery, Myron 80
Mallett, Conrad, Jr. 16
Marsh, Henry 32
McPhail, Sharon 2
Melton, Frank 81
Millender-McDonald, Juanita 21, 61
Morial, Ernest "Dutch" 26
Morial, Marc H. 20, 51
Murrell, Sylvia Marilyn 49
Patterson, J. O., Jr. 80
Perkins, James, Jr. 55
Powell, Adam Clayton, Jr. 3
Powell, Debra A. 23
Redd, Dana 93
Usry, James L. 23

City Sun newspaper
Cooper, Andrew W. 36

City University of New York
Ballard, Allen Butler, Jr. 40
Davis, George 36
Gayle, Addison, Jr. 41

Shabazz, Ilyasah 36

Civil rights
Abbott, Diane 9
Abernathy, Ralph 1
Agyeman, Jaramogi Abebe 10, 63
Al-Amin, Jamil Abdullah 6
Alexander, Clifford 26
Ali, Muhammad 2, 16, 52
Amaker, Norman 63
Angelou, Maya 1, 15
Anthony, Wendell 25
Aristide, Jean-Bertrand 6, 45
Arnwine, Barbara 28
Baker, Ella 5
Baker, Houston A., Jr. 6
Baker, Josephine 3
Ballance, Frank W. 41
Barbee, Lloyd Augustus 71
Barrow, Willie T. 85
Bashir, Halima 73
Bass, Charlotta Spears 40
Bates, Daisy 13
Baugh, David 23
Beals, Melba Pattillo 15, 94
Belafonte, Harry 4, 65
Bell, Derrick 6
Bell, James Madison 40
Berry, Mary Frances 7
Berry, Theodore M. 31
Bevel, James L. 75
Biko, Steven 4
Bishop, Sanford D., Jr. 24
Bond, Julian 2, 35
Booker, Simeon 23
Borders, William Holmes 94
Boyd, John W., Jr. 20, 72
Bradle, David Henry, Jr. 39
Bridges, Ruby 77
Brock, Roslyn McCallister 86
Brooks, Tyrone 59
Brown, Byrd 49
Brown, Elaine 8
Brown, Homer S. 47
Brown, Tony 3
Brown, Wesley 23
Brown, Willa 40
Burks, Mary Fair 40
Caldwell, Earl 60
Cameron, James 80
Campbell, Bebe Moore 6, 24, 59
Carmichael, Stokely 5, 26
Carr, Johnnie 69
Carter, Mandy 11
Carter, Rubin 26
Cary, Mary Ann Shadd 30
Catto, Octavius V. 83
Cayton, Horace 26
Chambers, Julius 3
Chavis, Benjamin 6
Chestnut, J. L., Jr. 73
Clark, Septima 7
Clay, William Lacy 8
Cleaver, Eldridge 5
Cleaver, Kathleen Neal 29
Clyburn, James E. 21, 71
Cobb, W. Montague 39
Cobbs, Price M. 9
Cockrel, Kenneth Vern, Sr. 79
Coleman, James E., Jr. 79
Cooper, Anna Julia 20
Cosby, Bill 7, 26, 59
Crockett, George W., Jr. 10, 64

Cunningham, Evelyn 23, 85
Davis, Angela 5
Davis, Artur 41
Davis, James E. 50
Days, Drew S., III 10
Dee, Ruby 8, 50, 68
Dent, Thomas C. 50
Diallo, Amadou 27
Diggs, Charles C. 21
Diggs-Taylor, Anna 20
Divine, Father 7
Dobbs, John Wesley 89
Dodson, Howard, Jr. 7, 52
Douglass, Frederick 87
Du Bois, W. E. B. 3
Dudley, Edward R. 58
Dukes, Hazel Nell 56
Dumas, Henry 41
Eagleson, William Lewis 90
Edelman, Marian Wright 5, 42
Ellison, Ralph 7
Evers, Medgar 3
Evers, Myrlie 8
Farmer, James 2, 64
Farmer-Paellmann, Deadria 43
Fauntroy, Walter E. 11
Fisher, Ada Lois Sipuel 76
Fletcher, Bill, Jr. 41
Forman, James 7, 51
Fortune, T. Thomas 6
Foster, Marie 48
Franklin, C. L. 68
Franklin, John Hope 5, 77
Gaines, Ernest J. 7
Gaines, Lloyd 79
George, Zelma Watson 42
Gibson, William F. 6
Gomillion, Charles 90
Granger, Lester B. 75
Gray, Fred 37
Gregory, Dick 1, 54
Grimké, Archibald H. 9
Guinier, Lani 7, 30
Haley, Alex 4
Haley, George Williford Boyce 21
Hall, Elliott S. 24
Hamer, Fannie Lou 6
Hampton, Fred 18
Hampton, Henry 6
Hansberry, Lorraine 6
Harding, Vincent 67
Harper, Frances Ellen Watkins 11
Harris, Patricia Roberts 2
Hastie, William H. 8
Hatcher, Richard G. 55
Hawkins, Augustus F. 68
Hawkins, Steven 14
Hayes, Dennis 54
Hedgeman, Anna Arnold 22
Height, Dorothy I. 2, 23, 78
Henderson, Thelton E. 68
Henderson, Wade J. 14
Henry, Aaron 19
Higginbotham, A. Leon, Jr. 13, 25
Hill, Jesse, Jr. 13
Hill, Oliver W. 24, 63
Hilliard, David 7
Hobson, Julius W. 44
Holland, Endesha Ida Mae 3, 57
Hollowell, Donald L. 57
Hooks, Benjamin L. 2, 85
Hope, Lugenia Burns 89

Houston, Charles Hamilton **4**
Howard, M. William, Jr. **26**
Innis, Roy **5**
Irvis, K. Leroy **67**
Jackson, Alexine Clement **22**
Jackson, Jesse **1, 27, 72**
James, Daniel, Jr. **16**
Jarrett, Vernon D. **42**
Jenkins, Ray **77**
Johns, Vernon **38**
Johnson, Georgia Douglas **41**
Johnson, James Weldon **5**
Johnson, Norma L. Holloway **17**
Jones, Elaine R. **7, 45**
Jones, John **89**
Jones, William A., Jr. **61**
Jordan, Barbara **4, 78**
Jordan, June **7, 35**
Jordan, Vernon E. **3, 35**
Julian, Percy Lavon **6**
Karim, Benjamin **61**
Kennedy, Florynce **12, 33**
Kenyatta, Jomo **5**
Kidd, Mae Street **39**
King, Bernice **4, 81**
King, Coretta Scott **3, 57**
King, Martin Luther, III **20**
King, Martin Luther, Jr. **1**
King, Martin Luther, Sr. **89**
King, Preston **28**
King, Robert Hillary **84**
King, Yolanda **6**
Ladner, Joyce A. **42**
Lampkin, Daisy **19**
Lawson, James M., Jr. **90**
Lester, Julius **9**
Lewis, John **2, 46, 83**
Lewis, William Henry **89**
Logan, Rayford W. **40**
Lorde, Audre **6**
Loving, Mildred **69**
Lowery, Joseph **2**
Lowry, A. Leon **60**
Lucy Foster, Autherine **35**
Luper, Clara **94**
Makeba, Miriam **2, 50, 74**
Malone Jones, Vivian **59**
Mandela, Nelson **1, 14, 77**
Mandela, Winnie **2, 35**
Martin, Louis E. **16**
Martin, Ruby Grant **49**
Mays, Benjamin E. **7**
Mbeki, Thabo **14, 73**
McDonald, Gabrielle Kirk **20**
McDougall, Gay J. **11, 43**
McKissick, Floyd B. **3**
Meredith, James H. **11**
Metcalfe, Ralph **26**
Mitchell, Clarence M., Jr. **88**
Morgan, Irene **65**
Moore, Barbara C. **49**
Moore, Harry T. **29**
Morial, Ernest "Dutch" **26**
Moses, Robert Parris **11**
Moss, Otis, Jr. **72**
Motley, Constance Baker **10, 55**
Mowry, Jess **7**
Mukoko, Jestina **75**
Murphy, Laura M. **43**
Murray, Pauli **38**
Nash, Diane **72**
Ndadaye, Melchior **7**
Nelson, Jill **6, 54**

Newton, Huey **2**
Nkoli, Simon **60**
Nkomo, Joshua **4, 65**
Noble, Gil **76**
Norman, Pat **10**
Nunn, Annetta **43**
Nzo, Alfred **15**
Orange, James **74**
Parker, Kellis E. **30**
Parks, Rosa **1, 35, 56**
Patrick, Deval **12, 61**
Patterson, Louise **25**
Patterson, Orlando **4**
Perkins, Edward **5**
Pincham, R. Eugene, Sr. **69**
Pinchback, P. B. S. **9**
Player, Willa B. **43**
Pleasant, Mary Ellen **9**
Plessy, Homer Adolph **31**
Poitier, Sidney **11, 36**
Powell, Adam Clayton, Jr. **3**
Price, Hugh B. **9, 54**
Ramaphosa, Cyril **3**
Randolph, A. Philip **3**
Reagon, Bernice Johnson **7**
Redding, Louis L. **26**
Riggs, Marlon **5, 44**
Rivers, Eugene F., III **81**
Robeson, Paul **2**
Robinson, Jackie **6**
Robinson, Rachel **16**
Robinson, Randall **7, 46**
Robinson, Sharon **22**
Robinson, Spottswood W., III **22**
Roundtree, Dovey **80**
Rowan, Carl T. **1, 30**
Rush, Bobby **26, 76**
Rustin, Bayard **4**
Sadlier, Rosemary **62**
Sanders, Malika **48**
Sané, Pierre Gabriel **21**
Saro-Wiwa, Kenule **39**
Seale, Bobby **3**
Shabazz, Attallah **6**
Shabazz, Betty **7, 26**
Shakur, Assata **6**
Shelton, Paula Young **86**
Shinhoster, Earl **32**
Shuttlesworth, Fred **47**
Simone, Nina **15, 41**
Sisulu, Albertina **57**
Sisulu, Sheila Violet Makate **24**
Sleet, Moneta, Jr. **5**
Smith, Barbara **28**
Staupers, Mabel K. **7**
Sullivan, Leon H. **3, 30**
Sutton, Percy E. **42, 82**
Sweet, Ossian **68**
Taylor, Recy **92**
Thompson, Bennie G. **26**
Thurman, Howard **3**
Till, Emmett **7**
Tillman, Dorothy **76**
Tolson, Melvin B. **37**
Touré, Faya Ora Rose **56**
Trotter, Monroe **9**
Tsvangirai, Morgan **26, 72**
Turner, Henry McNeal **5**
Tutu, Desmond Mpilo **6, 44**
Underwood, Blair **7, 27, 76**
Walker, Rebecca **50**
Washington, Booker T. **4**
Washington, Fredi **10**

Watt, Melvin **26**
Weaver, Robert C. **8, 46**
Wells, James Lesesne **10**
Wells-Barnett, Ida B. **8**
White, Walter F. **4**
Wilkins, Roy **4**
Williams, Evelyn **10**
Williams, Fannie Barrier **27**
Williams, Hosea Lorenzo **15, 31**
Williams, Robert F. **11**
Williams, Walter E. **4**
Wilson, August **7, 33, 55**
Wilson, Sunnie **7, 55**
Wilson, William Julius **22**
Woods, Abraham, Jr. **74**
Woodson, Robert L. **10**
Wright, Nathan, Jr. **56**
X, Malcolm **1**
Yoba, Malik **11**
Young, Andrew **3, 48**
Young, Jean Childs **14**
Young, Whitney M., Jr. **4**

Civilian Pilots Training Program
Brown, Willa **40**

Clarinet
Bechet, Sidney **18**
McGill, Anthony **76**

Classical music
Adams, Leslie **39**
Baiocchi, Regina Harris **41**
Bonds, Margaret **39**
Brown, Uzee **42**
Burleigh, Henry Thacker **56**
Coleridge-Taylor, Samuel **75**
Cook, Will Marion **40**
Dawson, William Levi **39**
DePreist, James **37**
Dixon, Dean **68**
Dunner, Leslie B. **45**
Freeman, Paul **39**
Kay, Ulysses **37**
Lewis, Henry **38**
McFerrin, Bobby **68**
McGill, Anthony **76**
Moore, Dorothy Rudd **46**
Murray, Tai **47**
Pratt, Awadagin **31**
Price, Florence **37**
Schuyler, Philippa **50**
Sowande, Fela **39**
Still, William Grant **37**
Tillis, Frederick **40**
Walker, George **37**
Wilkins, Thomas Alphonso **71**
Williams, Denise **40**

Classical singers
Anderson, Marian **2, 33**
Battle, Kathleen **70**
Bumbry, Grace **5**
Burleigh, Henry Thacker **56**
Hayes, Roland **4**
Hendricks, Barbara **3, 67**
Lister, Marquita **65**
Norman, Jessye **5**
Price, Leontyne **1**
Three Mo' Tenors **35**

Williams, Denise **40**

Clearview Golf Club
Powell, Renee **34**

Cleo Parker Robinson Dance Ensemble
Robinson, Cleo Parker **38**

Clergy
Agyeman, Jaramogi Abebe **10, 63**
Anthony, Wendell **25**
Austin, Junius C. **44**
Berry, Moses **84**
Black, Barry C. **47**
Bloomer, George **86**
Bowen, John W. E., Sr. **89**
Burgess, John **46**
Bynum, Juanita **31, 71**
Caesar, Shirley **19**
Caldwell, Kirbyjon **55**
Cleveland, James **19**
Cook, Suzan D. Johnson **22**
Dyson, Michael Eric **11, 40**
Easton, Hosea **91**
Ellis, Charles H., III **79**
Falana, Lola **42**
Gilmore, Marshall **46**
Gregory, Wilton **37**
Henson, Josiah **90**
Holsey, Lucius Henry **92**
Hood, James Walker **91**
Howard, M. William, Jr. **26**
Jakes, Thomas "T. D." **17, 43**
James, Skip **38**
Jemison, Major L. **48**
Johns, Vernon **38**
Jones, Absalom **52**
Jones, Alex **64**
Jones, Robert Elijah **90**
Jones, William A., Jr. **61**
Karim, Benjamin **61**
Kee, John P. **43**
Kelly, Leontine **33**
King, Barbara **22**
King, Bernice **4, 81**
Kobia, Samuel **43**
Lee, Eric P. **79**
Lincoln, C. Eric **38**
Maxis, Theresa **62**
McClurkin, Donnie **25**
McGuire, George Alexander **80**
McKenzie, Vashti M. **29**
Michaux, Solomon Lightfoot **91**
Morgan, Gertrude **63**
Okaalet, Peter **58**
Otunga, Maurice Michael **55**
Peterson, Jesse Lee **81**
Phipps, Wintley **59**
Reems, Ernestine Cleveland **27**
Reese, Della **6, 20**
Reverend Ike **79**
Sentamu, John **58**
Taylor, Gardner C. **76**
Thurman, Howard **3**
Thurston, Stephen J. **49**
Tillard, Conrad **47**
Tolton, Augustine **62**
Ukpabio, Helen **86**
Walker, John T. **50**
Washington, James Melvin **50**
Watkins, Joe **86**
Weeks, Thomas, III **70**
Weems, Renita J. **44**

White-Hammond, Gloria **61**
Williams, David Rudyard **50**
Williams, Frederick (B.) **63**
Williams, Preston Warren, II **64**
Winans, Marvin L. **17**
Wright, Nathan, Jr. **56**

Cleveland Browns football team
Brown, Jim **11**
Crennel, Romeo **54**
Hill, Calvin **19**
Motley, Marion **26**
Newsome, Ozzie **26**
Willis, Bill **68**

Cleveland city government
Jackson, Frank G. **76**
Stokes, Carl **10, 73**
White, Michael R. **5**

Cleveland Foundation
Adams, Leslie **39**

Cleveland Indians baseball team
Belle, Albert **10**
Bonds, Bobby **43**
Carter, Joe **30**
Doby, Lawrence Eugene, Sr. **16, 41**
Justice, David **18**
Lofton, Kenny **12**
Murray, Eddie **12**
Paige, Satchel **7**
Robinson, Frank **9, 87**
Sabathia, CC **74**

CLIO Awards
Lewis, Emmanuel **36**

Clothing design
Aberra, Amsale **67**
Bailey, Xenobia **11**
Burrows, Stephen **31**
Gaskins, Eric **64**
Henderson, Gordon **5**
John, Daymond **23**
Jones, Carl **7**
Kani, Karl **10**
Kelly, Patrick **3**
Lars, Byron **32**
Malone, Maurice **32**
Pinkett Smith, Jada **10, 41**
Robinson, Patrick **19, 71**
Smith, Willi **8**
Walker, T. J. **7**
Williams, Serena **20, 41, 73**

CNBC
Epperson, Sharon **54**
Thomas-Graham, Pamela **29**

CNN
See Cable News Network

Coaching
Amaker, Tommy **62**
Anderson, Mike **63**
Ashley, Maurice **15, 47**
Baker, Dusty **8, 43, 72**
Baylor, Don **6**
Bickerstaff, Bernie **21**
Bonds, Bobby **43**
Brown, Mike **77**
Caldwell, Jim **81**
Campanella, Roy **25**
Carew, Rod **20**
Carter, Butch **27**
Carter, Kenneth **53**
Chaney, John **67**
Cheeks, Maurice **47**
Cooper, Michael **31**
Cox, Bryan **83**
Crennel, Romeo **54**
Curry, Michael **85**
Davis, Mike **41**
Dorrell, Karl **52**
Dungy, Tony **17, 42, 59**
Dunn, Jerry **27**
Edwards, Herman **51**
Ellerbe, Brian **22**
Freeman, Marianna **23**
Gaines, Clarence E., Sr. **55**
Gaither, Alonzo Smith (Jake) **14**
Gaston, Cito **71**
Gentry, Alvin **23**
Gibson, Althea **8, 43**
Gibson, Bob **33**
Gill, Turner **83**
Gorden, W. C. **71**
Graham, Trevor **84**
Gray, Yeshimbra "Shimmy" **55**
Green, Dennis **5, 45**
Greene, Joe **10**
Haskins, Clem **23**
Heard, Gar **25**
Johnson, Avery **62**
Jordan, Eddie **83**
Joyce, Dru **81**
Keith, Floyd A. **61**
Lewis, Marvin **51, 87**
Lofton, James **42**
Manuel, Jerry **94**
Miller, Cheryl **10, 74**
Mitchell, Sam **82**
Morris, Raheem **77**
O'Neil, Buck **19, 59**
Parish, Robert **43**
Phillips, Teresa L. **42**
Rhodes, Ray **14**
Richardson, Nolan **9**
Rivers, Doc **25, 81**
Robinson, Eddie G. **10, 61**
Robinson, Frank **9, 87**
Robinson, Will **51, 69**
Russell, Bill **8**
Sanders, Satch **77**
Shannon, Randy **82**
Shell, Art **1, 66**
Silas, Paul **24**
Simmons, Bob **29**
Singletary, Mike **4, 76**
Smith, Lovie **66**
Smith, Tubby **18, 83**
Stringer, C. Vivian **13, 66**
Thomas, Emmitt **71**
Tunnell, Emlen **54**
White, Jesse **22, 75**
Williams, Doug **22**
Willingham, Tyrone **43**
Wills, Maury **73**

Coalition of Black Trade Unionists
Lucy, William **50**
Wyatt, Addie L. **56**

Coca-Cola Company
Llewellyn, J. Bruce **13, 85**
Ware, Carl T. **30**

Coca-Cola Foundation
Jones, Ingrid Saunders **18**

Collage
Andrews, Benny **22, 59**
Bearden, Romare **2, 50**
Bradford, Mark **89**
Driskell, David C. **7**
Pindell, Howardena **55**
Pinder, Jefferson **77**
Robinson, Aminah **50**
Saar, Betye **80**
Thomas, Mickalene **61**
Verna, Gelsy **70**

College and university administration
Ammons, James H. **81**
Archie-Hudson, Marguerite **44**
Barnett, Marguerite **46**
Bromery, Randolph Wilson **85**
Burnim, Mickey L. **48**
Christian, Barbara T. **44**
Cross, Dolores E. **23**
Davis, Erroll B., Jr. **57**
Dogan, Matthew Winifred **91**
Ford, Nick Aaron **44**
Gilbert, John Wesley **91**
Hill, Leslie Pinckney **44**
Hogan, Beverly Wade **50**
Horne, Frank **44**
Jackson, Edison O. **67**
King, Reatha Clark **65**
Lee, Joe A. **45**
Lewis, Shirley A. R. **14**
Mason, Ronald **27**
Massey, Walter E. **5, 45**
Maupin, John E., Jr. **92**
Mell, Patricia **49**
Moody-Adams, Michele **76**
Morón, Alonzo G. **91**
Nance, Cynthia **71**
Newman, Lester C. **51**
Page, Inman **82**
Pollard, William L. **91**
Ribeau, Sidney **70**
Trueheart, William E. **49**

Colorado Rockies baseball team
Baylor, Don **6**

Colorado state government
Brown, George Leslie **62**
Rogers, Joe **27**

Columbia Broadcasting System (CBS)
Bradley, Ed **2, 59**
Kellogg, Clark **64**
Mabrey, Vicki **26**
McEwen, Mark **5**
Mitchell, Russ **21, 73**
Olden, Georg(e) **44**
Pinkston, W. Randall **24**
Pitts, Byron **71**
Rodgers, Johnathan **6, 51**
Ware, Andre **37**

Columbia Records
Jackson, Randy **40**
Knowles, Tina **61**

Coca-Cola Company
Olatunji, Babatunde **36**
Williams, Deniece **36**

Columbia University
Huggins, Nathan Irvin **52**
Marable, Manning **10**
Moody-Adams, Michele **76**

Comedy
Allen, Byron **3, 24**
Amos, John **8, 62**
Anderson, Anthony **51, 77**
Anderson, Eddie "Rochester" **30**
Anthony, Trey **63**
Arnez J **53**
Beaton, Norman **14**
Bellamy, Bill **12**
Berry, Bertice **8, 55**
Brady, Wayne **32, 71**
Bruce, Bruce **56**
Cannon, Nick **47, 73**
Cedric the Entertainer **29, 60**
Cenac, Wyatt **94**
Chappelle, Dave **50**
Cosby, Bill **7, 26, 59**
Curry, Mark **17**
Davidson, Tommy **21**
Davis, Sammy, Jr. **18**
Dieudonné **67**
Earthquake **55**
Epps, Mike **60**
Foxx, Jamie **15, 48**
Foxx, Redd **2**
Freeman, Aaron **52**
Givens, Adele **62**
Glover, Donald **85**
Goldberg, Whoopi **4, 33, 69**
Harris, Robin **7**
Harvey, Steve **18, 58**
Henry, Lenny **9, 52**
Hughley, D. L. **23, 76**
Kirby, George **14**
Lawrence, Martin **6, 27, 60**
Mabley, Jackie "Moms" **15**
Mac, Bernie **29, 61, 72**
Mayo, Whitman **32**
McEwen, Mark **5**
Meadows, Tim **30**
Mooney, Paul **37**
Morgan, Tracy **61**
Morris, Garrett **31**
Moss, Preacher **63**
Murphy, Eddie **4, 20, 61**
Nash, Niecy **66**
Perry, Tyler **40, 54**
Pryor, Richard **3, 24, 56**
Rock, Chris **3, 22, 66**
Russell, Nipsey **66**
Schultz, Michael A. **6**
Slocumb, Jonathan **52**
Smiley, Rickey **59**
Sommore **61**
Sykes, Wanda **48, 81**
Thompson, Kenan **52**
Thurston, Baratunde **79**
Torry, Guy **31**
Townsend, Robert **4, 23**
Tucker, Chris **13, 23, 62**
Tyler, Aisha N. **36**
Wayans, Damon **8, 41**
Wayans, Keenen Ivory **18**
Wayans, Kim **80**
Wayans, Marlon **29, 82**

Wayans, Shawn 29
Wilson, Debra 38
Wilson, Flip 21
Witherspoon, John 38
Yarbrough, Cedric 51

Comerica Bank
Forte, Linda Diane 54

Commercial art
Freeman, Leonard 27

Communist Party
Brown, Lloyd Louis 42
Davis, Angela 5
Du Bois, W. E. B. 3
Herndon, Angelo 90
Jagan, Cheddi 16
Patterson, Louise 25
Wright, Richard 5

Community activism
Kimbro, Warren 76
Shakur, Yusef 85

Complete Energy Partners
Scott, Milton 51

Complexions dance troupe
Rhoden, Dwight 40
Richardson, Desmond 39
Tyson, Andre 40

Computer graphics
Coleman, Ken 57
Hannah, Marc 10

Computer science
Adkins, Rod 41
Auguste, Donna 29
Dean, Mark 35
Easley, Annie J. 61
Ellis, Clarence 38
Emeagwali, Philip 30
Hannah, Marc 10
Irvin, Vernon 65
Laryea, Thomas Davies, III 67
Mensah, Thomas 48
Millines Dziko, Trish 28
Zollar, Alfred 40

Conceptual art
Allen, Tina 22, 75
Bailey, Xenobia 11
Harris, Lyle Ashton 83
O'Grady, Lorraine 73
Piper, Adrian 71
Pope.L, William 72
Robinson, Aminah 50
Shonibare, Yinka 58
Simpson, Lorna 4, 36

Conductors
Calloway, Cab 14
Cook, Will Marion 40
Dawson, William Levi 39
DePreist, James 37
Dixon, Dean 68
Dunner, Leslie B. 45
Foster, William P. 88
Freeman, Paul 39
Hairston, Jester 88
Jackson, Isaiah 3
León, Tania 13

Lewis, Henry 38

Congress of Racial Equality (CORE)
Dee, Ruby 8, 50, 68
Farmer, James 2, 64
Hobson, Julius W. 44
Innis, Roy 5
Jackson, Jesse 1, 27, 72
McKissick, Floyd B. 3
Rustin, Bayard 4

Congressional Black Caucus (CBC)
Christian-Green, Donna M. 17
Clay, William Lacy 8
Clyburn, James E. 21, 71
Collins, Cardiss 10, 80
Conyers, John, Jr. 4, 45
Dellums, Ronald 2, 81
Diggs, Charles C. 21
Fauntroy, Walter E. 11
Gray, William H., III 3
Hastings, Alcee L. 16
Hawkins, Augustus F. 68
Johnson, Eddie Bernice 8, 90
Mfume, Kweisi 6, 41
Mitchell, Parren J. 42, 66
Owens, Major 6
Payton, John 48
Rangel, Charles B. 3, 52, 85
Scott, Robert C. 23
Stokes, Louis 3
Thompson, Bennie G. 26
Towns, Edolphus 19, 75

Contemporary Christian music
Griffin, LaShell 51
Tait, Michael 57

Continental Basketball Association (CBA)
Davis, Mike 41
Thomas, Isiah 7, 26, 65
Ussery, Terdema, II 29

Cooking
See Restaurants/Catering/Cooking

Coppin State College
Blair, Paul 36

CORE
See Congress of Racial Equality

Coretta Scott King Awards
Clifton, Lucille 14, 64, 91
Curtis, Christopher Paul 26
Draper, Sharon Mills 16, 43
Fax, Elton 48
Greenfield, Eloise 9
Hamilton, Virginia 10
Haskins, James 36, 54
Johnson, Angela 52
Lester, Julius 9
Morrison, Toni 2, 15, 86
Rollins, Charlemae Hill 27
Taylor, Mildred D. 26

Coronet
Oliver, Joe "King" 42

Corporate executive
Adams, Eula L. 39
Cottrell, Comer 11

Hill, Wyllstyne D. 94
Jackson, Mannie 14
Johnson, George E. 29
Siméus, Dumas M. 25
Smith, Joshua 10

Corporation for Public Broadcasting (CPB)
Brown, Tony 3

Cosmetology
Cottrell, Comer 11
Fuller, S. B. 13
McGrath, Pat 72
Morgan, Rose 11
Powell, Maxine 8
Roche, Joyce M. 17
Walker, A'lelia 14
Walker, Madame C. J. 7

Cotton Club Revue
Johnson, Buddy 36

Council on Legal Education Opportunities (CLEO)
Henderson, Wade J. 14
Henry, Aaron 19

Count Basie Orchestra
Eldridge, Roy 37
Johnson, J. J. 37
Powell, Benny 87
Rushing, Jimmy 37
Williams, Joe 5, 25
Young, Lester 37

Country music
Bailey, DeFord 33
Cowboy Troy 54
Palmer, Rissi 65
Pride, Charley 26
Randall, Alice 38
Rucker, Darius 34, 74

Covad Communications
Knowling, Robert 38

Cowboys
Love, Nat 9
Pickett, Bill 11

CPB
See Corporation for Public Broadcasting

Craftwork
Hill, Peter 92

Creative Artists Agency
Nelson Meigs, Andrea 48

Credit Suisse First Boston, Inc.
Ogunlesi, Adebayo 37

Creole music
Ardoin, Alphonse 65

Cricket
Adams, Paul 50

Critics' Choice Award
Channer, Colin 36

Critical race theory
Crenshaw, Kimberlé Williams 88
Williams, Patricia 11, 54

Cross Colours
Jones, Carl 7
Kani, Karl 10

Walker, T. J. 7

Crown Media
Corbi, Lana 42

Crusader
Williams, Robert F. 11

Cuban League
Charleston, Oscar 39
Day, Leon 39

Cuban military
Maceo, Antonio 82

Cuban music
Ferrer, Ibrahim 41
Portuondo, Omara 53
Valdés, Bebo 75
Valdés, Chucho 89

Cubism
Bearden, Romare 2, 50
Green, Jonathan 54

Culinary arts
Allen, Eugene 79
Brown, Warren 61
Calabrese, Karyn 89
Chase, Leah 57
Clark, Patrick 14
Estes, Rufus 29
Evans, Darryl 22
Garvin, Gerry 78
Henderson, Jeff 72
Ouattara, Morou 74
Samuelsson, Marcus 53

Cultural Hangups
Ham, Cynthia Parker 58

Cultural pluralism
Locke, Alain 10

Curator/exhibition designer
Amaki, Amalia 76
Camp, Kimberly 19
Campbell, Mary Schmidt 43
Golden, Thelma 10, 55
Hoyte, Lenon 50
Hutson, Jean Blackwell 16
Pindell, Howardena 55
Sanders, Joseph R., Jr. 11
Sims, Lowery Stokes 27
Stewart, Paul Wilbur 12

Cy Young Award
Gibson, Bob 33
Gooden, Dwight 20
Jenkins, Fergie 46
Martinez, Pedro 81
Newcombe, Don 24
Sabathia, CC 74

Cycling
Baugé, Grégory 86
Taylor, Marshall Walter "Major" 62
Yeboah, Emmanuel Ofosu 53

Cytogenetics
Satcher, David 7, 57

Dallas city government
Kirk, Ron 11, 75

Dallas Cowboys football team
Hayes, Bob 77
Hill, Calvin 19

Irvin, Michael **64**
Jones, Ed "Too Tall" **46**
Sanders, Deion **4, 31**
Smith, Emmitt **7, 87**
Wright, Rayfield **70**

Dallas Police Department
Bolton, Terrell D. **25**

DanceAfrica
Davis, Chuck **33**

Dance Theatre of Harlem
Johnson, Virginia **9**
King, Alonzo **38**
Mitchell, Arthur **2, 47**
Nicholas, Fayard **20, 57**
Nicholas, Harold **20**
Tyson, Cicely **7, 51**

DAV
See Disabled American Veterans

Daytona Institute
See Bethune-Cookman College

D.C. sniper
Moose, Charles **40**

Death Row Records
Dre, Dr. **10, 14, 30**
Knight, Suge **11, 30**
Shakur, Tupac **14**

Decca Records
Hardin Armstrong, Lil **39**

Def Jam Records
Jay-Z **27, 69**
Liles, Kevin **42**
LL Cool J **16, 49, 94**
Simmons, Russell **1, 30**

Defense Communications Agency
Gravely, Samuel L., Jr. **5, 49**

Delta Sigma Theta Sorority
Rice, Louise Allen **54**

Democratic National Committee (DNC)
Brown, Ron **5**
Dixon, Sharon Pratt **1**
Fattah, Chaka **11, 70**
Hamer, Fannie Lou **6**
Horsford, Steven **88**
Jackson, Maynard **2, 41**
Jordan, Barbara **4, 78**
Joyner, Marjorie Stewart **26**
Mallett, Conrad, Jr. **16**
Martin, Louis E. **16**
Moore, Minyon **45**
Waters, Maxine **3, 67**
Williams, Maggie **7, 71**

Dentistry
Bluitt, Juliann S. **14**
Delany, Bessie **12**
Gray, Ida **41**
Madison, Romell **45**
Maupin, John E., Jr. **92**
Sinkford, Jeanne C. **13**

Denver Broncos football team
Barnes, Ernie **16, 78**
Briscoe, Marlin **37**

Davis, Terrell **20**
Jackson, Tom **70**
Little, Floyd **86**

Denver city government
Webb, Wellington **3, 81**

Denver Nuggets basketball team
Bickerstaff, Bernie **21**
Bynoe, Peter C. B. **40**
Hardaway, Tim **35**
Lee, Bertram M., Sr. **46**
Mutombo, Dikembe **7**

DePaul University
Braun, Carol Moseley **4, 42**
Sizemore, Barbara A. **26**

Depression/The Great Depression
Hampton, Henry **6**

Dermatology
Taylor, Susan C. **62**

Desert Shield/Desert Storm
See Operation Desert Shield/Operation Desert Storm

Destiny's Child
Beyoncé **39, 70**
Knowles, Tina **61**
Luckett, Letoya **61**
Williams, Michelle **73**

Detective fiction
See Mystery/Detective fiction

Detroit city government
Archer, Dennis **7, 36**
Bing, Dave **3, 59, 78**
Cockrel, Kenneth V., Jr. **79**
Cockrel, Kenneth Vern, Sr. **79**
Collins, Barbara-Rose **7, 87**
Conyers, Monica **85**
Crockett, George W., Jr. **10, 64**
Evans, Warren C. **76**
Garrett, Joyce Finley **59**
Kilpatrick, Kwame **34, 71**
Marshall, Bella **22**
Pugh, Charles **81**
Reeves, Martha **85**
Young, Coleman **1, 20**

Detroit Golden Gloves
Wilson, Sunnie **7, 55**

Detroit Lions football team
Barney, Lem **26**
Farr, Mel **24**
Johnson, Levi **48**
Mayhew, Martin R. **76**
Sanders, Barry **1, 53**
Ware, Andre **37**

Detroit Pistons basketball team
Bing, Dave **3, 59, 78**
Dumars, Joe **16, 65**
Gentry, Alvin **23**
Hill, Grant **13, 94**
Lanier, Bob **47**
Lloyd, Earl **26**
Lowe, Sidney **64**
Mahorn, Rick **60**
Mohammed, Nazr **64**

Prince, Tayshaun **68**
Robinson, Will **51, 69**
Stackhouse, Jerry **30**
Thomas, Isiah **7, 26, 65**
Wallace, Ben **54**
Webber, Chris **15, 30, 59**

Detroit Police Department
Bully-Cummings, Ella **48**
Gomez-Preston, Cheryl **9**
McKinnon, Isaiah **9**
Napoleon, Benny N. **23**

Detroit Public Schools
Coleman, William F., III **61**

Detroit Tigers baseball team
Fielder, Cecil **2**
Granderson, Curtis **66**
Virgil, Ozzie **48**

Diabetes
Fennoy, Ilene **72**
Wisdom, Kimberlydawn **57**

Diamond mining
Masire, Quett **5**

Dictators
Abacha, Sani **11, 70**
Ahidjo, Ahmadou **81**
Amin, Idi **42**
Biya, Paul **28**
Compaore, Blaise **87**
Eyadéma, Gnassingbé **7, 52**
Gbagbo, Laurent **43, 90**
Habré, Hissène **6**
Kabila, Laurent **20**
Meles Zenawi **3**
Mengistu, Haile Mariam **65**
Moi, Daniel Arap **1, 35**
Mswati III **56**
Mugabe, Robert **10, 71**
Touré, Sekou **6**

Dillard University
Cook, Samuel DuBois **14**
Lomax, Michael L. **58**

Dime Savings Bank
Parsons, Richard Dean **11**

Diner's Club
Gaines, Brenda **41**

Diplomatic Corps
See U.S. Department of State

Disabled American Veterans (DAV)
Brown, Jesse **6, 41**

Disco
Gaynor, Gloria **36**
Payne, Freda **58**
Perren, Freddie **60**
Staton, Candi **27**
Summer, Donna **25**

Distance running
Cheruiyot, Robert **69**
Loroupe, Tegla **59**
Tergat, Paul **59**
Wanjiru, Sammy **94**

Diving
Brashear, Carl **29**

DJ
Alert, Kool DJ Red **32**
Atkins, Juan **50**
Bond, Beverly **53**
DJ Jazzy Jeff **32**
DJ Lance Rock **94**
Grandmaster Flash **33, 60**
Knuckles, Frankie **42**
Love, Ed **58**

DNC
See Democratic National Committee

Documentary film
Billops, Camille **82**
Blackwood, Maureen **37**
Branch, William Blackwell **39**
Byrd, Robert **11**
Dash, Julie **4**
Davis, Ossie **5, 50**
Gray, Darius **69**
Greaves, William **38**
Hampton, Henry **6**
Henry, Lenny **9, 52**
Hudlin, Reginald **9, 86**
Hudlin, Warrington **9**
Hurt, Byron **61**
Jean, Michaëlle; **70**
Julien, Isaac **3**
Lynch, Shola **61**
Nelson, Stanley **92**
Peck, Raoul **32**
Riggs, Marlon **5, 44**
Roberts, Kimberly Rivers **72**
Whack, Rita Coburn **36**
Williams, Marco **53**

Dollmaking
El Wilson, Barbara **35**

Dominica government
Charles, Mary Eugenia **10, 55**
Charles, Pierre **52**
Skerrit, Roosevelt **72**

Dove Award
Baylor, Helen **36**
Winans, CeCe **14, 43**

***Down Beat* Jazz Hall of Fame**
Terry, Clark **39**

Drama Desk Awards
Carter, Nell **39**
Taylor, Ron **35**
Wesley, Richard **73**

Dreamland Orchestra
Cook, Charles "Doc" **44**

Drug abuse prevention
Clements, George **2**
Creagh, Milton **27**
Hale, Lorraine **8**
Harris, Alice **7**
Lucas, John **7**

Drug synthesis
Julian, Percy Lavon **6**
Pickett, Cecil **39**

Drums
Ali, Rashied **79**
Blade, Brian **88**
Blakey, Art **37**

Brown, Carlinhos 81
Durham, Bobby 73
Güines, Tata 69
Haynes, Roy 87
Jones, Elvin 14, 68
Locke, Eddie 44
Miles, Buddy 69
Purdie, Bernard 77
Rodríguez, Arsenio 87
Williams, Tony 67
Young, Lee 72

Duke Ellington School of Arts
Cooper Cafritz, Peggy 43

Duke Records
Bland, Bobby "Blue" 36

Dunham Dance Company
Dunham, Katherine 4, 59

**DuSable Museum of African
American History**
Burroughs, Margaret Taylor 9
Wright, Antoinette 60

Dynegy
Scott, Milton 51

E Street Band
Clemons, Clarence 41

**East Harlem School at Exo-
dus House**
Hageman, Hans 36
Hageman, Ivan 36

Ebonics
Cook, Toni 23

***Ebony* magazine**
Bennett, Lerone, Jr. 5, 84
Branch, William Blackwell 39
Cullers, Vincent T. 49
Fuller, Hoyt 44
Johnson, Eunice W. 83
Johnson, John H. 3, 54
Massaquoi, Hans J. 30
Rice, Linda Johnson 9, 41
Sleet, Moneta, Jr. 5

**Ebony Museum of African
American History**
See DuSable Museum of African
   American History

Economics
Ake, Claude 30
Arthur, Owen 33
Boyd, T. B., III 6
Brimmer, Andrew F. 2, 48
Brown, Tony 3
Conrad, Cecilia A. 94
Fryer, Roland G. 56
Gibson, William F. 6
Hamer, Fannie Lou 6
Hampton, Henry 6
Juma, Calestous 57
Machel, Graca Simbine 16
Malveaux, Julianne 32, 70
Masire, Quett 5
Moyo, Dambisa 76
Pitta, Celso 17
Raines, Franklin Delano 14
Robinson, Randall 7, 46
Simms, Margaret 94

Sowell, Thomas 2
Spriggs, William 67
Sullivan, Leon H. 3, 30
Van Peebles, Melvin 7
Wallace, Phyllis A. 9
Washington, Ebonya 79
Wharton, Clifton R., Jr. 7
White, Michael R. 5
Williams, Walter E. 4
Woodson, Robert L. 10

Editing
Abani, Chris 77
Aubert, Alvin 41
Bass, Charlotta Spears 40
Brown, Lloyd Louis 42
Curry, George E. 23
Delany, Martin R. 27
Dumas, Henry 41
Murphy, John H. 42
Schuyler, George Samuel 40

Edmonton Oilers hockey team
Fuhr, Grant 1, 49
Grier, Mike 43
Laraque, Georges 48

Educational Testing Service
Stone, Chuck 9

EEC
See European Economic Community

EEOC
See Equal Employment Opportunity
   Commission

Egyptology
Diop, Cheikh Anta 4

Elder Foundation
Elder, Lee 6

Electronic music
Craig, Carl 31, 71

Elektra Records
McPherson, David 32

***Emerge (Savoy)* magazine**
Ames, Wilmer 27
Curry, George E. 23

Emmy awards
Allen, Debbie 13, 42
Amos, John 8, 62
Ashe, Arthur 1, 18
Barclay, Paris 37, 94
Belafonte, Harry 4, 65
Bradley, Ed 2, 59
Branch, William Blackwell 39
Brown, James 22
Brown, Les 5
Browne, Roscoe Lee 66
Carter, Nell 39
Clayton, Xernona 3, 45
Cosby, Bill 7, 26, 59
Curtis-Hall, Vondie 17
De Shields, André 72
Dee, Ruby 8, 50, 68
Fisher, Gail 85
Foxx, Redd 2
Freeman, Al, Jr. 11
Goldberg, Whoopi 4, 33, 69
Gossett, Louis, Jr. 7

Guillaume, Robert 3, 48
Gumbel, Greg 8
Hunter-Gault, Charlayne 6, 31
Jones, James Earl 3, 49, 79
Kitt, Eartha 16, 75
La Salle, Eriq 12
Mabrey, Vicki 26
McQueen, Butterfly 6, 54
Moore, Shemar 21
Parks, Gordon 1, 35, 58
Pinkston, W. Randall 24
Quarles, Norma 25
Richards, Beah 30
Robinson, Max 3
Rock, Chris 3, 22, 66
Rolle, Esther 13, 21
St. John, Kristoff 25
Taylor, Billy 23, 92
Thigpen, Lynne 17, 41
Tyson, Cicely 7, 51
Uggams, Leslie 23
Washington, Hayma 86
Wayans, Damon 8, 41
Whack, Rita Coburn 36
Whitfield, Lynn 18
Williams, Montel 4, 57
Williams, Russell, II 70
Williams, Sherley Anne 25
Winfrey, Oprah 2, 15, 61
Woodard, Alfre 9

Emory University
Cole, Johnnetta B. 5, 43

Endocrinology
Elders, Joycelyn 6
Fennoy, Ilene 72

Energy
Cose, Ellis 5, 50
Lawal, Kase L. 45
O'Leary, Hazel 6

Engineering
Alexander, Archie Alphonso 14
Anderson, Charles Edward 37
Auguste, Donna 29
Austin, Wanda M. 94
Benson, Angela 34
Boyd, Gwendolyn 49
Boykin, Otis 92
Burns, Ursula 60
Crosthwait, David 93
Dabiri, John 93
Emeagwali, Philip 30
Ericsson-Jackson, Aprille 28
Gibson, Kenneth Allen 6
Gourdine, Meredith 33
Grooms, Henry R(andall) 50
Hannah, Marc 10
Harris, Gary L. 87
Harris, Wesley L. 92
Henderson, Cornelius Langston 26
Henderson, Henry Fairfax, Jr. 89
Howard, Ayanna 65
Johnson, Anthony M. 92
Johnson, Sandra K. 94
Jones, Wayne 53
Laroche, Joseph Philippe Lemercier
   85
Laryea, Thomas Davies, III 67
McCoy, Elijah 8
Miller, Warren F., Jr. 53
Mills, Joseph C. 51

O'Neal, Rodney 88
Pierre, Percy Anthony 46
Price, Richard 51
Rillieux, Norbert 92
Robinson-Berry, Joan 94
Sigur, Wanda 44
Slaughter, John Brooks 53
Spencer, Michael G. 87
Trotter, Lloyd G. 56
West, James E. 87
Wilkens, J. Ernest, Jr. 43
Williams, O. S. 13

Entertainment promotion
Bowen, Ruth 83
Lewis, Butch 71

Entrepreneur
Barden, Donald H. 9, 20, 89
Chenault, Kenneth I. 5, 36
Downing, George T. 91
Fletcher, Alphonse, Jr. 16
Fudge, Ann (Marie) 11, 55
Gardner, Edward G. 45
Gaston, Arthur George 3, 38, 59
Gordy, Berry, Jr. 1
Graves, Earl G. 1, 35
Henderson, Henry Fairfax, Jr. 89
Herndon, Alonzo Franklin 89
Johnson, John H. 3, 54
Lewis, Reginald F. 6
McCann, Renetta 44
Otis, Clarence, Jr. 55
Parks, Henry Green, Jr. 89
Payton, Philip A., Jr. 88
Perry, Tyler 40, 54
Spaulding, Charles Clinton 9
Steward, David L. 36
Walker, Madame C. J. 7
Walker, Maggie Lena 17
Winfrey, Oprah 2, 15, 61
Woods, Granville T. 5

Environmental issues
Carter, Majora 77
Ellis-Lamkins, Phaedra 88
Eugene-Richard, Margie 63
Hill, Bonnie Guiton 20
Jackson, Lisa 77
Jones, Van 70
Miller-Travis, Vernice 64
Osborne, Na'taki 54
Saro-Wiwa, Kenule 39

Epic Records
McPherson, David 32
Mo', Keb' 36

Epidemiology
Fenton, Kevin 87
Gayle, Helene D. 3
Poindexter, Hildrus A. 87

Episcopalian
Burgess, John 46
Harris, Barbara 12
Jones, Absalom 52
Redding, Ann Holmes 77
Walker, John T. 50
Williams, Frederick (B.) 63

**Equal Employment Opportu-
nity Commission (EEOC)**
Alexander, Clifford 26
Berrien, Jacqueline A. 93

Hill, Anita 5, 65
Lewis, Delano 7
Norton, Eleanor Holmes 7, 93
Thomas, Clarence 2, 39, 65
Wallace, Phyllis A. 9

Esalen Institute
Olatunji, Babatunde 36

ESPN
Jackson, Tom 70
Roberts, Robin 16, 54
Salters, Lisa 71
Scott, Stuart 34
Smith, Stephen A. 69
Tirico, Mike 68
Wilbon, Michael 68

Essence magazine
Bandele, Asha 36
Burt-Murray, Angela 59
Channer, Colin 36
De Veaux, Alexis 44
Ebanks, Michelle 60
Grant, Gwendolyn Goldsby 28
Greenwood, Monique 38
Lewis, Edward T. 21
Parks, Gordon 1, 35, 58
Smith, Clarence O. 21
Taylor, Susan L. 10, 86
Wesley, Valerie Wilson 18

Essence Award
Broadbent, Hydeia 36
McMurray, Georgia L. 36

Ethiopian government
Haile Selassie 7
Meles Zenawi 3
Mengistu, Haile Mariam 65

Etiquette
Bates, Karen Grigsby 40

European Economic Community (EEC)
Diouf, Abdou 3

Event planning
Bailey, Preston 64
Williams, Lindsey 75

Executive Leadership Council
Jackson, Mannie 14

Exiled heads of state
Amin, Idi 42
Aristide, Jean-Bertrand 6, 45
Mengistu, Haile Mariam 65
Mobutu Sese Seko 1, 56

Exploration
Henson, Matthew 2

Famine relief
See World hunger

FAN
See Forces Armées du Nord (Chad)

Fannie Mae
Jackson, Maynard 2, 41
Raines, Franklin Delano 14

Fashion
Aberra, Amsale 67
Biya, Chantal 89

Boateng, Ozwald 35
Boyd, Suzanne 52
Chanticleer, Raven 91
Darego, Agbani 52
Delice, Ronald 48
Delice, Rony 48
Evans, Etu 55
Fine, Sam 60
Gaskins, Eric 64
Givhan, Robin Deneen 72
Hall, Kevan 61
Hendy, Francis 47
Keckley, Elizabeth 90
Knowles, Tina 61
Lars, Byron 32
Luna, Donyale 88
Malone, Maurice 32
McGrath, Pat 72
Reese, Tracy 54
Simmons, Kimora Lee 51, 83
Smaltz, Audrey 12
Steele, Lawrence 28
Stoney, Michael 50
Sy, Oumou 65
Talley, André Leon 56
White, Jessica 83

Fashion Institute of Technology (FIT)
Brown, Joyce F. 25

FCC
See Federal Communications Commission

Federal Bureau of Investigation (FBI)
Gibson, Johnnie Mae 23
Harvard, Beverly 11

Federal Communications Commission (FCC)
Barrett, Andrew C. 12
Clyburn, Mignon 78
Hughes, Cathy 27
Kennard, William Earl 18
Powell, Michael 32
Russell-McCloud, Patricia A. 17

Federal Court of Canada
Isaac, Julius 34

Federal Reserve Bank
Brimmer, Andrew F. 2, 48
Ferguson, Roger W. 25
Layton, William 87
Rice, Emmett J. 94

Federation of Nigeria
Sowande, Fela 39

Feed the Hungry program
Williams, Hosea Lorenzo 15, 31

Fellowship of Reconciliation (FOR)
Farmer, James 2, 64
Rustin, Bayard 4

Fencing
Boulogne, Joseph, Chevalier de Saint-Georges 94
Westbrook, Peter 20

Fiction
Adams, Jenoyne 60
Adichie, Chimamanda Ngozi 64

Alexander, Margaret Walker 22
Ali, Mohammed Naseehu 60
Amadi, Elechi 40
Anthony, Michael 29
Ansa, Tina McElroy 14
Armah, Ayi Kwei 49
Ba, Mariama 30
Baiocchi, Regina Harris 41
Baisden, Michael 25, 66
Ballard, Allen Butler, Jr. 40
Bandele, Biyi 68
Barrett, Lindsay 43
Bates, Karen Grigsby 40
Beckham, Barry 41
Benson, Angela 34
Berry, James 41
Bland, Eleanor Taylor 39
Bolden, Tonya 32
Bradley, David Henry, Jr. 39
Brand, Dionne 32
Briscoe, Connie 15
Brown, Cecil M. 46
Brown, Lloyd Louis 42
Bunkley, Anita Richmond 39
Butler, Octavia 8, 43, 58
Campbell, Bebe Moore 6, 24, 59
Cartiér, Xam Wilson 41
Chase-Riboud, Barbara 20, 46
Cheney-Coker, Syl 43
Chesnutt, Charles 29
Clarke, Austin 32
Cleage, Pearl 17, 64
Cliff, Michelle 42
Cooper, J. California 12, 85
Creagh, Milton 27
Curtis, Christopher Paul 26
Danticat, Edwidge 15, 68
Dathorne, O. R. 52
Demby, William 51
Diop, Birago 53
Draper, Sharon Mills 16, 43
Due, Tananarive 30
Dumas, Henry 41
Dunbar-Nelson, Alice Ruth Moore 44
Duplechan, Larry 55
Emecheta, Buchi 30
Evans, Diana 72
Everett, Percival 93
Fair, Ronald L. 47
Fales-Hill, Susan 88
Farah, Nuruddin 27
Farley, Christopher John 54
Files, Lolita 35
Ford, Nick Aaron 44
Ford, Wallace 58
Forrest, Leon 44
Gomez, Jewelle 30
Gray, Darius 69
Greenlee, Sam 48
Harper, Rachel M. 92
Harris, E. Lynn 12, 33
Haywood, Gar Anthony 43
Hercules, Frank 44
Hill, Donna 32
Holton, Hugh, Jr. 39
Horne, Frank 44
Jackson, Sheneska 18
Jakes, Thomas "T. D." 17, 43
James, Marlon 85
Jasper, Kenji 39
Jenkins, Beverly 14
Johnson, Georgia Douglas 41

Johnson, Mat 31
Jones, Edward P. 43, 67
Jones, Gayl 37
Kamau, Kwadwo Agymah 28
Kay, Jackie 37
Kayira, Legson 40
Keene, John 73
Kendrick, Erika 57
Killens, John O. 54
Laferriere, Dany 33
LaGuma, Alex 30
Lamming, George 35
Lattany, Kristin Hunter 88
Locke, Attica 85
Machado de Assis 74
Marechera, Dambudzo 39
Markham, E. A. 37
Mason, Felicia 31
Mbaye, Mariétou 31
McCrary Anthony, Crystal 70
McFadden, Bernice L. 39
McKinney-Whetstone, Diane 27
McMillan, Terry 4, 17, 53
Memmi, Albert 37
Mengestu, Dinaw 66
Monroe, Mary 35
Mosley, Walter 5, 25, 68
Mossell, Gertrude Bustill 40
Mphalele, Es'kia 40
Mwangi, Meja 40
Naylor, Gloria 10, 42
Ngugi wa Thiong'o 29, 61
Nkosi, Lewis 46
Nugent, Richard Bruce 39
Nunez, Elizabeth 62
Okara, Gabriel 37
Ojikutu, Bayo 66
Packer, Z. Z. 64
Peters, Lenrie 43
Philip, Marlene Nourbese 32
Polite, Carlene Hatcher 82
Randall, Alice 38
Ridley, John 69
Roby, Kimberla Lawson 86
Schuyler, George Samuel 40
Senior, Olive 37
Senna, Danzy 93
Smith, Danyel 40
Smith, Zadie 51
Southgate, Martha 58
Tate, Eleanora E. 20, 55
Taylor, Mildred D. 26
Teasley, Lisa 92
Thomas, Michael 69
Thomas-Graham, Pamela 29
Tutuola, Amos 30
Vera, Yvonne 32
Verdelle, A. J. 26
Walker, Margaret 29
Weaver, Afaa Michael 37
Whitehead, Colson 77
Whitfield, Van 34
Williams, Sherley Anne 25
Williams, Stanley "Tookie" 29, 57
Woods, Teri 69
Yarbrough, Camille 40
Young, Al 82
Youngblood, Shay 32
Zane 71

Figure skating
Bonaly, Surya 7
Bonheur, Yannick 84

James, Vanessa **84**
Thomas, Debi **26**
Vanessa James and Yannick Bonheur **84**

Film criticism
Mitchell, Elvis **67**

Film direction/video direction
Akomfrah, John **37**
Allain, Stephanie **49**
Barclay, Paris **37, 94**
Blackwood, Maureen **37**
Burnett, Charles **16, 68**
Byrd, Robert **11**
Cortez, Jayne **43**
Curtis-Hall, Vondie **17**
Daniels, Lee **36, 76**
Dash, Julie **4**
Davis, Ossie **5, 50**
Dickerson, Ernest **6, 17**
Duke, Bill **3**
Franklin, Carl **11**
Freeman, Al, Jr. **11**
Fuqua, Antoine **35**
Gerima, Haile **38, 80**
Gray, Darius **69**
Gray, F. Gary **14, 49**
Greaves, William **38**
Hamilton, Tanya **93**
Harris, Leslie **6**
Hayes, Teddy **40**
Henriques, Julian **37**
Hudlin, Reginald **9, 86**
Hudlin, Warrington **9**
Hughes, Albert **7**
Hughes, Allen **7**
Hurt, Byron **61**
Jackson, George **19**
Julien, Isaac **3**
Lane, Charles **3**
Lee, Malcolm D. **75**
Lee, Spike **5, 19, 86**
Lemmons, Kasi **20**
Lewis, Samella **25**
Martin, Darnell **43, 78**
McQueen, Steve **84**
Micheaux, Oscar **7**
Morton, Joe **18**
Moses, Gilbert **12**
Moss, Carlton **17**
Mwangi, Meja **40**
Onwurah, Ngozi **38**
Palcy, Euzhan **94**
Peck, Raoul **32**
Perry, Tyler **40, 54**
Pinkett Smith, Jada **10, 41**
Poitier, Sidney **11, 36**
Prince-Bythewood, Gina **31, 77**
Riggs, Marlon **5, 44**
Roberts, Darryl **70**
St. Jacques, Raymond **8**
Schultz, Michael A. **6**
Sembène, Ousmane **13, 62**
Singleton, John **2, 30**
Smith, Roger Guenveur **12**
Souleymane, Mahamane **78**
Tillman, George, Jr. **20**
Townsend, Robert **4, 23**
Tyler, Aisha N. **36**
Underwood, Blair **7, 27, 76**
Van Peebles, Mario **2, 51**
Van Peebles, Melvin **7**

Wallace, William **75**
Ward, Douglas Turner **42**
Wayans, Damon **8, 41**
Wayans, Keenen Ivory **18**
Whitaker, Forest **2, 49, 67**

Film production
Allain, Stephanie **49**
Chase, Debra Martin **49**
Daniels, Lee **36, 76**
Gerima, Haile **38, 80**
Greaves, William **38**
Julian, Hubert **90**
Morrison, Vanessa **84**
Onwurah, Ngozi **38**
Packer, Will **71**
Patton, Paula **62**
Randall, Alice **38**
Robinson, Matt **69**
Stewart, Nzingha **89**
Tyler, Aisha N. **36**
Van Lierop, Robert **53**
Ward, Douglas Turner **42**
Wayans, Damien **78**
Whitaker, Forest **2, 49, 67**
Williams, Marco **53**
Williams, Russell, II **70**
Williamson, Fred **67**

Film scores
Blanchard, Terence **43**
Crouch, Andraé **27**
Hancock, Herbie **20, 67**
Jones, Quincy **8, 30**
Prince **18, 65**
RZA **80**

Finance
Adams, Eula L. **39**
Banks, Jeffrey **17**
Bell, James A. **50**
Boston, Kelvin E. **25**
Brown, Eddie C. **35**
Bryant, John **26**
Chapman, Nathan A., Jr. **21**
Chapman, Susan E. **94**
Doley, Harold, Jr. **26**
Epperson, Sharon **54**
Ferguson, Roger W. **25**
Fletcher, Alphonse, Jr. **16**
Funderburg, I. Owen **38**
Gaines, Brenda **41**
Griffith, Mark Winston **8**
Hall, Alvin D. **86**
Harris, Carla A. **67**
Hobson, Mellody **40**
Jones, Thomas W. **41**
Lawless, Theodore K. **8**
Lewis, William M., Jr. **40**
Louis, Errol T. **8**
Marshall, Bella **22**
Moyo, Dambisa **76**
Nash, Shannon King **84**
O'Neal, Stanley **38, 67**
Rogers, John W., Jr. **5, 52**
Ross, Charles **27**
Shank, Suzanne F. **77**
Taylor, Ephren W., II **61**
Thompson, William C. **35**
Travis, Tracey T. **94**

Firefighters
Barlow, Roosevelt **49**
Bell, Michael **40**

Fisk University
Harvey, William R. **42**
Imes, Elmer Samuel **39**
Johnson, Charles S. **12**
Phillips, Teresa L. **42**
Smith, John L. **22**

Fitness
Richardson, Donna **39**
Smith, Ian **62**

Florida A & M University
Ammons, James H. **81**
Foster, William P. **88**
Gaither, Alonzo Smith (Jake) **14**
Humphries, Frederick **20**

Florida Marlins baseball team
Mariner, Jonathan **41**

Florida state government
Brown, Corrine **24, 90**
Meek, Carrie **6, 36**
Meek, Kendrick **41, 89**
Menard, John Willis **90**
Tribble, Israel, Jr. **8**
Wilson, Frederica **92**

Florida State Supreme Court
Quince, Peggy A. **69**

Flute
Laws, Hubert **90**

Folk music
Bailey, DeFord **33**
Broonzy, Big Bill **82**
Chapman, Tracy **26**
Charlemagne, Manno **11**
Cuney, William Waring **44**
Davis, Gary **41**
Dawson, William Levi **39**
Handy, W. C. **8**
Harper, Ben **34, 62**
House, Son **8**
Jenkins, Ella **15**
Johnson, James Weldon **5**
Lester, Julius **9**
Love, Laura **50**
Odetta **37, 74**
Reagon, Toshi **76**
Southern, Eileen **56**
Spence, Joseph **49**
White, Josh **86**
Williams, Denise **40**

Food products
Amos, Wally **9**
Briggs, Curtis **84**
Parks, Henry Green, Jr. **89**
Siméus, Dumas M. **25**

Football
Buchanan, Ray **32**
Carter, Cris **21**
Clemons, Michael "Pinball" **64**
Davis, Ernie **48**
Dorrell, Karl **52**
Dungy, Tony **17, 42, 59**
Gaither, Alonzo Smith (Jake) **14**
Gill, Turner **83**
Gorden, W. C. **71**
Grier, Roosevelt **13**
Jones, Ed "Too Tall" **46**
Keith, Floyd A. **61**

Lanier, Willie **33**
Lewis, Marvin **51, 87**
Lewis, William Henry **89**
McNabb, Donovan **29**
Parker, Jim **64**
Perry, Lowell **30**
Pollard, Fritz **53**
Prince, Ron **64**
Robinson, Eddie G. **10, 61**
Shannon, Randy **82**
Simmons, Bob **29**
Smith, Lovie **66**
Watts, J. C., Jr. **14, 38**
Weathers, Carl **10**
Willingham, Tyrone **43**
Willis, Bill **68**
Woodson, Rod **79**

Football Hall of Fame, professional
Allen, Marcus **20**
Barney, Lem **26**
Briscoe, Marlin **37**
Brown, Jim **11**
Dickerson, Eric **27**
Faulk, Marshall **35**
Green, Darrell **39, 74**
Greene, Joe **10**
Hayes, Bob **77**
Irvin, Michael **64**
Jackson, Rickey **88**
Jones, Deacon **92**
Lane, Dick **92**
Lanier, Willie **33**
Little, Floyd **86**
Little, Larry **90**
Lofton, James **42**
Lott, Ronnie **9**
Matson, Ollie **93**
McDaniel, Randall Cornell **81**
Monk, Art **38, 73**
Moon, Warren **8, 66**
Motley, Marion **26**
Newsome, Ozzie **26**
Page, Alan (Cedric) **7**
Parker, Jim **64**
Payton, Walter (Jerry) **11, 25**
Pollard, Fritz **53**
Randle, John **87**
Rice, Jerry **5, 55, 89**
Sanders, Barry **1, 53**
Sanders, Deion **4, 31**
Sayers, Gale **28**
Shell, Art **1, 66**
Simpson, O. J. **15**
Singletary, Mike **4, 76**
Smith, Bruce **80**
Smith, Emmitt **7, 87**
Swann, Lynn **28**
Taylor, Lawrence **25**
Thomas, Derrick **25**
Thomas, Emmitt **71**
Thomas, Thurman **75**
Tunnell, Emlen **54**
Upshaw, Gene **18, 47, 72**
White, Reggie **6, 50**
Willis, Bill **68**
Winslow, Kellen **83**
Woodson, Rod **79**
Wright, Rayfield **70**

FOR
See Fellowship of Reconciliation

Forces Armées du Nord (Chad; FAN)
Déby, Idriss 30
Habré, Hissène 6

Ford Foundation
Franklin, Robert M. 13
Thomas, Franklin A. 5, 49

Ford Motor Company
Cherry, Deron 40
Dawson, Matel, Jr. 39
Goldsberry, Ronald 18
Hazel, Darryl B. 50
McMillan, Rosalynn A. 36

Fordham University
Blair, Paul 36
McMurray, Georgia L. 36

Foreign investment
Amoudi, Mohammed al- 88

Foreign policy
Bunche, Ralph J. 5
Frazer, Jendayi 68
Rice, Condoleezza 3, 28, 72
Robinson, Randall 7, 46

Forensic science
Griffin, Bessie Blout 43

Forest Club
Wilson, Sunnie 7, 55

Foster care
Hale, Clara 16
Hale, Lorraine 8

Fox Broadcasting Company
Corbi, Lana 42
McFarland, Roland 49
Oliver, Pam 54
Strahan, Michael 35, 81

Franklin H. Williams Caribbean Cultural Center African Diaspora Institute
Vega, Marta Moreno 61

Freddie Mac
Baker, Maxine 28

Frederick Douglass Caring Award
Broadbent, Hydeia 36

French West Africa
Camara, Moussa Dadis 76
Diouf, Abdou 3
Ndiaye, Iba 74

Funeral homes
March, William Carrington 56

Funk music
Ayers, Roy 16
Brown, James 15, 60
Clinton, George 9, 93
Collins, Bootsy 31
Collins, Lyn 53
Love, Laura 50
Monáe, Janelle 86
Parker, Maceo 72
Parker, Ray, Jr. 85
Purdie, Bernard 77
Richie, Lionel 27, 65

Shider, Garry 87
Stone, Sly 85
Watson, Johnny "Guitar" 18

Fusion
Davis, Miles 4
Jones, Quincy 8, 30
Williams, Tony 67

Gabonese government
Bongo, Ali Ben 80
Bongo, Omar 1, 79

Gambling
Ivey, Phil 72

Gangs
Taylor, Bo 72
Shakur, Yusef 85
Williams, Stanley "Tookie" 29, 57

Gary Post-Tribune
Ross, Don 27

Gassaway, Crosson, Turner & Parsons
Parsons, James 14

Gay and lesbian activism
De Veaux, Alexis 44

Gay Men of Color Consortium
Wilson, Phill 9

Genealogy
Allen, Lucy 85
Blockson, Charles L. 42
Dash, Julie 4
Haley, Alex 4

General Hospital TV series
Cash, Rosalind 28

General Motors Corporation
O'Neal, Stanley 38, 67
Roberts, Roy S. 14
Welburn, Edward T. 50

Genetech
Potter, Myrtle 40

Genetics
Dunston, Georgia Mae 48
Harris, Mary Styles 31
Kittles, Rick 51
Olopade, Olufunmilayo Falusi 58

Geometric symbolism
Douglas, Aaron 7

Geophysics
Person, Waverly 9, 51

George Foster Peabody Broadcasting Award
Bradley, Ed 2, 59
Hunter-Gault, Charlayne 6, 31
Mac, Bernie 29, 61, 72
Shaw, Bernard 2

George Mason University
Dunn, Jerry 27
Wilkins, Roger 2, 84

George Washington University
Carter, Joye Maureen 41

Georgia state government
Baker, Thurbert 22
Bishop, Sanford D., Jr. 24

Bond, Julian 2, 35
Brooks, Tyrone 59
Johnson, Hank, Jr. 80
Johnson, Leroy R. 89
Majette, Denise 41
McKinney, Cynthia 11, 52, 74
Reed, Kasim 82
Scott, David 41
Smyre, Calvin 90
Williams, Hosea Lorenzo 15, 31

Georgia State Supreme Court
Benham, Robert 78
Melton, Harold D. 79
Sears, Leah Ward 5, 79

Ghanaian government
Atta Mills, John 75
Awoonor, Kofi 37
Bartels, Peggielene 80
Kufuor, John Agyekum 54, 82
Nkrumah, Kwame 3
Rawlings, Jerry 9

Girl Scouts of the USA
Thompson, Cynthia Bramlett 50

Goddard Space Flight Center
Ericsson-Jackson, Aprille 28

Golden Globe awards
Allen, Debbie 13, 42
Bassett, Angela 6, 23, 62
Cara, Irene 77
Carroll, Diahann 9
Fisher, Gail 85
Freeman, Morgan 2, 20, 62
Ross, Diana 8, 27
Taylor, Regina 9, 46

Golden Pen award
McFadden, Bernice L. 39

Golden State Warriors basketball team
Parish, Robert 43
Sprewell, Latrell 23

Golf
Bramlett, Joseph 91
Elder, Lee 6
Gibson, Althea 8, 43
Gregory, Ann 63
Jackson, Fred James 25
Peete, Calvin 11
Powell, William J. 82
Richmond, Mitch 19
Shippen, John 43
Sifford, Charlie 4, 49
Spiller, Bill 64
Woods, Tiger 14, 31, 81

Goodwill ambassador
Terry, Clark 39

Gospel music
Adams, Oleta 18
Adams, Yolanda 17, 67
Armstrong, Vanessa Bell 24
Baylor Helen 36
Bonds, Margaret 39
Bradley, J. Robert 65
Caesar, Shirley 19
Cage, Byron 53
Clark, Mattie Moss 61
Clark-Cole, Dorinda 66

Clark-Sheard, Karen 22
Cleveland, James 19
Christie, Angella 36
Cooke, Sam 17
Crouch, Andraé 27
Davis, Gary 41
Dorsey, Thomas 15
Fortune, James 92
Franklin, Aretha 11, 44
Franklin, Kirk 15, 49
Gaynor, Gloria 36
Green, Al 13, 47, 74
Haddon, Dietrick 55
Hammond, Fred 23
Hawkins, Tramaine 16
Hawkins, Walter 87
Higginsen, Vy 65
Houghton, Israel 92
Houston, Cissy 20, 83
Jackson, Mahalia 5
Jakes, Thomas "T. D." 17, 43
Jeter, Claude 75
Jones, Bobby 20, 94
Kee, John P. 43
Kenoly, Ron 45
Killings, Debra 57
Knight, Gladys 16, 66
Knight, Marie 80
Lassiter, Roy 24
Little Richard 15
Majors, Jeff 41
Mann, Tamela 92
Marrow, Queen Esther 24
Martin, Roberta 58
Mary Mary 34, 92
Mayfield, Curtis 2, 43
McClendon, Lisa 61
McClurkin, Donnie 25
Mills, Stephanie 36
Monica 21
Moss, J 64
Mullen, Nicole C. 45
Peoples, Dottie 22
Phipps, Wintley 59
Preston, Billy 39, 59
Reagon, Bernice Johnson 7
Reese, Della 6, 20
Sapp, Marvin 74
Scott, George 55
Sheard, Kierra "Kiki" 61
Stampley, Micah 54
Staples, Mavis 50, 88
Staples, "Pops" 32
Staton, Candi 27
Steinberg, Martha Jean "The Queen" 28
Tharpe, Rosetta 65
Tonex 54
Tribbett, Tye 81
Walker, Albertina 10, 58, 89
Walker, Hezekiah 34
Wilson, Brian Courtney 94
Washington, Dinah 22
Whalum, Kirk 37, 64
Williams, Deniece 36
Williams, Michelle 73
Wilson, Natalie 38
Winans, Angie 36
Winans, BeBe 14
Winans, CeCe 14, 43
Winans, David 77
Winans, Debbie 36
Winans, Marvin L. 17

Winans, Ronald 54
Winans, Vickie 24
Wright, Timothy 74

Graffiti art
White, Dondi 34

Grambling State University
Favors, Steve 23

Grammy awards
Adams, Oleta 18
Adderley, Nat 29
Babyface 10, 31, 82
Badu, Erykah 22
Battle, Kathleen 70
Belafonte, Harry 4, 65
Beyoncé 39, 70
Blade, Brian 88
Blige, Mary J. 20, 34, 60
Brandy 14, 34, 72
Caesar, Shirley 19
Cara, Irene 77
Chapman, Tracy 26
Cleveland, James 19
Cole, Natalie 17, 60, 84
Combs, Sean 17, 43, 92
Cosby, Bill 7, 26, 59
Cray, Robert 30
Crouch, Andraé 27
Davis, Miles 4
Dee, Ruby 8, 50, 68
Ellington, Duke 5
Estelle 75
Ferrer, Ibrahim 41
Fitzgerald, Ella 8
Forté, John 74
Franklin, Aretha 11, 44
Gamble, Kenny 85
Gaye, Marvin 2
Gaynor, Gloria 36
Gibson, Tyrese 27, 62
Glover, Corey 34
Goldberg, Whoopi 4, 33, 69
Gray, Macy 29
Guy, Buddy 31
Hathaway, Donny 18
Hawkins, Tramaine 16
Hawkins, Walter 87
Hayes, Isaac 20, 58, 73
Hill, Lauryn 20, 53
Holland-Dozier-Holland 36
Hooker, John Lee 30
Houston, Cissy 20, 83
Houston, Whitney 7, 28, 83
Hubbard, Freddie 75
Isley, Ronald 25, 56
Jackson, Janet 6, 30, 68
Jackson, Michael 19, 53, 76
James, Etta 13, 52
Jay-Z 27, 69
Jean, Wyclef 20, 86
Jimmy Jam 13
Jones, Bobby 20, 94
Jones, Quincy 8, 30
Kee, John P. 43
Kelly, R. 18, 44, 71
Keys, Alicia 32, 68
Knight, Gladys 16, 66
Knuckles, Frankie 42
LaBelle, Patti 13, 30
Legend, John 67
Lewis, Terry 13
Lopes, Lisa "Left Eye" 36

Mahal, Taj 39
Maitreya, Sananda 85
Makeba, Miriam 2, 50, 74
Marley, Ziggy 41
Marsalis, Branford 34
M.C. Hammer 20, 80
Method Man 81
Mills, Stephanie 36
Mo', Keb' 36
Moore, LeRoi 72
Murphy, Eddie 4, 20, 61
Norman, Jessye 5
Olatunji, Babatunde 36
Perkins, Pinetop 70
Poitier, Sidney 11, 36
Price, Leontyne 1
Pride, Charley 26
Prince 18, 65
Queen Latifah 1, 16, 58
?uestlove 74
Reagon, Bernice Johnson 7
Redding, Otis 16
Reid, Vernon 34
Richie, Lionel 27, 65
Robinson, Smokey 3, 49
Rollins, Sonny 37, 94
Ross, Isaiah "Doc" 40
Rucker, Darius 34, 74
Sade 15, 92
Scott, Jill 29, 83
Seal 14, 75
Shaggy 31
Shorter, Wayne 75
Slash 75
Smith, Will 8, 18
Summer, Donna 25
Turner, Tina 6, 27
Walker, Hezekiah 34
Warwick, Dionne 18
West, Kanye 52, 93
White, Barry 13, 41
White, Maurice 29
Whitfield, Norman 73
Williams, Deniece 36
Williams, Joe 5, 25
Williams, Michelle 73
Wilson, Nancy 10
Winans, CeCe 14, 43
Winans, Marvin L. 17
Wonder, Stevie 11, 53

Grand Ole Opry
Bailey, DeFord 33

Graphic novels
Anderson, Ho Che 54
McDuffie, Dwayne 62
Tooks, Lance 62

Green Bay Packers football team
Brooks, Aaron 33
Butler, Leroy, III 17
Howard, Desmond 16, 58
Lofton, James 42
Sharper, Darren 32
White, Reggie 6, 50

Green Belt Movement
Maathai, Wangari 43

Green Party
Clemente, Rosa 74
McKinney, Cynthia 11, 52, 74

Grenadian government
Bishop, Maurice 39
Gairy, Eric Matthew 83
Mitchell, Keith 82

Groupe de Recherche Choréographique de
Dove, Ulysses 5

Guardian
Trotter, Monroe 9

Guggenheim fellowship
Pope.L, William 72
Rollins, Sonny 37, 94
Taylor, Cecil 70
Wilson, Ellis 39

Guinea government
Camara, Moussa Dadis 76
Conté, Lansana 7, 76
Touré, Sekou 6

Guinea-Bissau government
Sanhá Malam Bacai 84
Vieira, João 14, 84

Guitar
Ade, King Sunny 41
Barker, Danny 32
Barnes, Roosevelt "Booba" 33
Bibb, Eric 49
Brown, Clarence Gatemouth 59
Butler, Jonathan 28
Burns, Eddie 44
Burnside, R. L. 56
Caymmi, Dorival 72
Collins, Bootsy 31
Cray, Robert 30
Davis, Gary 41
Diddley, Bo 39, 72
Estes, Sleepy John 33
Fuller, Blind Boy 86
Green, Grant 56
Guy, Buddy 31
Harris, Corey 39, 73
Hemphill, Jessie Mae 33, 59
Hendrix, Jimi 10
House, Son 8
Hooker, John Lee 30
Hopkins, Lightnin' 83
Howlin' Wolf 9
Johnson, Robert 2
Jordan, Ronny 26
Killings, Debra 57
King, B. B. 7
King, Freddie 92
Klugh, Earl 59
Kolosoy, Wendo 73
Kravitz, Lenny 10, 34
Leadbelly 82
Lipscomb, Mance 49
Long, Huey 79
Loueke, Lionel 88
Marley, Bob 5
Mayfield, Curtis 2, 43
McTell, Blind Willie 89
Montgomery, Wes 88
Ndegeocello, Meshell 15, 83
Ongala, Remmy 9, 91
Parker, Ray, Jr. 85
Pena, Paul 58
Ranglin, Ernest 78
Rodríguez, Arsenio 87

Rush, Bobby 78
Seals, Son 56
Shider, Garry 87
Slash 75
Spence, Joseph 49
Ulmer, James 79
Watson, Johnny "Guitar" 18
White, Josh 86

Gulf War
Powell, Colin 1, 28, 75
Shaw, Bernard 2
Von Lipsey, Roderick K. 11

Gurdjieff Institute
Toomer, Jean 6

Guyanese government
Burnham, Forbes 66

Gymnastics
Dawes, Dominique 11
Hilliard, Wendy 53
White, Jesse 22, 75

Hair care
Cottrell, Comer 11
Fuller, S. B. 13
Gardner, Edward G. 45
Gibson, Ted 66
Johnson, George E. 29
Johnson, William 91
Joyner, Marjorie Stewart 26
Malone, Annie 13
Roche, Joyce M. 17
Walker, Madame C. J. 7

Haitian government
Aristide, Jean-Bertrand 6, 45
Manigat, Mirlande 90
Martelly, Michel 90
Pascal-Trouillot, Ertha 3
Pierre-Louis, Michèle 75
Préval, René 87

Hale House
Hale, Clara 16
Hale, Lorraine 8

Hallmark Channel
Corbi, Lana 42

Hampton University
Harvey, William R. 42

Handy Award
Hunter, Alberta 42

Harlem Artist Guild
Nugent, Richard Bruce 39
Wilson, Ellis 39

Harlem Globetrotters
Chamberlain, Wilt 18, 47
Haynes, Marques 22
Jackson, Mannie 14
Woodard, Lynette 67

Harlem Renaissance
Alexander, Margaret Walker 22
Bennett, Gwendolyn B. 59
Christian, Barbara T. 44
Crichlow, Ernest 75
Cullen, Countee 8
Cuney, William Waring 44
Dandridge, Raymond Garfield 45
Davis, Arthur P. 41

Delaney, Beauford **19**
Ellington, Duke **5**
Fauset, Jessie **7**
Fisher, Rudolph **17**
Frazier, E. Franklin **10**
Horne, Frank **44**
Hughes, Langston **4**
Hurston, Zora Neale **3**
Imes, Elmer Samuel **39**
Johnson, Georgia Douglas **41**
Johnson, James Weldon **5**
Johnson, William Henry **3**
Larsen, Nella **10**
Locke, Alain **10**
McKay, Claude **6**
Mills, Florence **22**
Morton, Ferdinand Q. **90**
Nail, John E. **92**
Nugent, Richard Bruce **39**
Payton, Philip A., Jr. **88**
Petry, Ann **19**
Thurman, Wallace **16**
Toomer, Jean **6**
VanDerZee, James **6**
West, Dorothy **12, 54**
Wilson, Ellis **39**

Harlem Writers Guild
Guy, Rosa **5**
Killens, John O. **54**
Wesley, Valerie Wilson **18**

Harlem Youth Opportunities Unlimited (HARYOU)
Clark, Kenneth B. **5, 52**

Harmonica
Bailey, DeFord **33**
Barnes, Roosevelt "Booba" **33**
Burns, Eddie **44**
Howlin' Wolf **9**
Neal, Raful **44**
Ross, Isaiah "Doc" **40**
Terry, Sonny **88**

Harness racing
Minor, DeWayne **32**

Harp
Coltrane, Alice **70**
Majors, Jeff **41**

Harvard Law School
Bell, Derrick **6**
Dickerson, Debra J. **60**
Ogletree, Charles, Jr. **12, 47**
Wilkins, David **77**

Harvard University
Amaker, Tommy **62**
Epps, Archie C., III **45**
Ferguson, Ronald F. **75**
Gomes, Peter J. **15, 93**
Hammonds, Evelynn **69**
Huggins, Nathan Irvin **52**
Loury, Glenn **36**
Poindexter, Hildrus A. **87**

HARYOU
See Harlem Youth Opportunities Unlimited

Hazelitt Award for Excellence in Arts
Bradley, David Henry, Jr. **39**

Head Start
Edelman, Marian Wright **5, 42**
Taylor, Helen **30**

Health care reform
Adams-Campbell, Lucille L. **60**
Berrysmith, Don Reginald **49**
Brown, Jesse **6, 41**
Carroll, L. Natalie **44**
Cole, Lorraine **48**
Cooper, Edward S. **6**
Dirie, Waris **56**
Gibson, Kenneth A. **6**
Hughes, Dora **88**
Hughes, Ebony **57**
Kintaudi, Leon **62**
Lavizzo-Mourey, Risa **48**
Norman, Pat **10**
Potter, Myrtle **40**
Richardson, Rupert **67**
Satcher, David **7, 57**
Tuckson, Reed V. **71**
Vaughn, Viola **70**
Williams, Daniel Hale **2**
Williams, David Rudyard **50**

Heart disease
Cooper, Edward S. **6**
Grant, Augustus O. **71**

Heidelberg Project
Guyton, Tyree **9, 94**

Heisman Trophy
Allen, Marcus **20**
Bush, Reggie **59, 88**
Davis, Ernie **48**
George, Eddie **80**
Howard, Desmond **16, 58**
Sanders, Barry **1, 53**
Simpson, O. J. **15**
Walker, Herschel **1, 69**
Ware, Andre **37**
Williams, Ricky **85**

Heritage Network, The
Mercado-Valdes, Frank **43**

Heroism
Autrey, Wesley **68**
Delaney, Joe **76**

HEW
See U.S. Department of Health, Education, and Welfare

HHS
See U.S. Department of Health and Human Services

Hip-hop music
Akon **68**
apl.de.ap **84**
Ashanti **37**
Benjamin, Andre **45**
Blackman, Toni **86**
B.o.B. **91**
Combs, Sean **17, 43, 92**
Elliott, Missy **31, 90**
Estelle **75**
Fabolous **93**
Fat Boys **92**
Fiasco, Lupe **64**
Forté, John **74**
Franti, Michael **93**
Fresh, Doug E. **93**

Garrett, Sean **57**
Ghostface Killah **90**
Guru **84**
Jean, Wyclef **20, 86**
Jennings, Lyfe **56, 69**
Kid Cudi **83**
Kitwana, Bakari **86**
K-Swift **73**
Kweli, Talib **93**
Lil Wayne **66, 84**
Madlib **88**
Mane, Gucci **91**
Method Man **81**
Minaj, Nicki **86**
Nelly **32, 90**
Nate Dogg **92**
Patton, Antwan **45**
Peterson, James **81**
?uestlove **74**
Rascal, Dizzee **82**
Redman **81**
Run **31, 73**
Sermon, Erick **81**
Slick Rick **93**
Smith, Danyel **40**
Wale **92**
West, Kanye **52, 93**
will.i.am **64**
Williams, Pharrell **47, 82**

Hip-hop theater
Power, Will **83**

Historians
Ballard, Allen Butler, Jr. **40**
Berry, Mary Frances **7**
Blassingame, John Wesley **40**
Blockson, Charles L. **42**
Bogle, Donald **34**
Chase-Riboud, Barbara **20, 46**
Cooper, Afua **53**
Cooper, Anna Julia **20**
Cruse, Harold **54**
Diop, Cheikh Anta **4**
Dodson, Howard, Jr. **7, 52**
Du Bois, W. E. B. **3**
Fisher, Miles Mark **91**
Franklin, John Hope **5, 77**
Gates, Henry Louis, Jr. **3, 38, 67**
Giddings, Paula **11**
Gill, Gerald **69**
Gordon-Reed, Annette **74**
Hammonds, Evelynn **69**
Hansberry, William Leo **11**
Harkless, Necia Desiree **19**
Harris, Jessica B. **91**
Hine, Darlene Clark **24**
Horton, James Oliver **58**
Huggins, Nathan Irvin **52**
Logan, Rayford W. **40**
Marable, Manning **10**
Moore, Wes **86**
Painter, Nell Irvin **24, 88**
Patterson, Orlando **4**
Quarles, Benjamin Arthur **18**
Querino, Manuel Raimundo **84**
Reagon, Bernice Johnson **7**
Reddick, Lawrence Dunbar **20**
Rogers, Joel Augustus **30**
Sadlier, Rosemary **62**
Schomburg, Arthur Alfonso **9**
Skinner, Kiron K. **65**

Snowden, Frank M., Jr. **67**
van Sertima, Ivan **25**
Washington, James Melvin **50**
Williams, George Washington **18**
Williams, Rhonda Y. **86**
Woodson, Carter G. **2**

Hitman Records
Brae, C. Michael **61**

Hockey
Carnegie, Herbert **25**
Doig, Jason **45**
Grand-Pierre, Jean-Luc **46**

Homosexuality
Carter, Mandy **11**
Clarke, Cheryl **32**
Delany, Samuel R., Jr. **9**
Harris, E. Lynn **12, 33**
Hemphill, Essex **10**
Julien, Isaac **3**
Norman, Pat **10**
Nugent, Richard Bruce **39**
Parker, Pat **19**
Riggs, Marlon S. **44**
RuPaul **17, 91**
Wilson, Phill **9**

Horse racing
Harris, Sylvia **70**
St. Julien, Marlon **29**
Winkfield, Jimmy **42**

House of Representatives
See U.S. House of Representatives

Houston Astros baseball team
Morgan, Joe **9**
Richard, J. R. **87**
Watson, Bob **25**

Houston Oilers football team
McNair, Steve **22, 47, 79**
Moon, Warren **8, 66**

Houston Rockets basketball team
Lucas, John **7**
Olajuwon, Hakeem **2, 72**

Howard University
Adams-Campbell, Lucille L. **60**
Benjamin, Tritobia Hayes **53**
Branson, Herman **87**
Cardozo, Francis L. **33**
Carter, Joye Maureen **41**
Cobb, W. Montague **39**
Davis, Arthur P. **41**
Dodson, Owen **38**
Gerima, Haile **38, 80**
Harris, Gary L. **87**
Jenifer, Franklyn G. **2**
Johnson, Mordecai Wyatt **79**
Ladner, Joyce A. **42**
Locke, Alain **10**
Logan, Rayford W. **40**
Malveaux, Floyd **54**
Mays, Benjamin E. **7**
Neal, Larry **38**
Payton, Benjamin F. **23**
Porter, James A. **11**
Reid, Irvin D. **20**
Ribeau, Sidney **70**
Robinson, Spottswood W., III **22**

Snowden, Frank M., Jr. 67
Sowande, Fela 39
Spriggs, William 67
Swygert, H. Patrick 22
Wells, James Lesesne 10
Wesley, Dorothy Porter 19
White, Charles 39
Young, Roger Arliner 29

HUD
See U.S. Department of Housing and Urban Development

Hugo awards
Butler, Octavia 8, 43, 58
Delany, Samuel R., Jr. 9

Human resources
Howroyd, Janice Bryant 42

Human rights
Atyam, Angelina 55
Bond, Julian 2, 35
Carter, Mandy 11
McDougall, Gay J. 11, 43
Williams, Robert F. 11

Hunter College
DeCarava, Roy 42, 81
Mayhew, Richard 39
Thomas, Michael 69

IBM
Adkins, Rod 41
Blackwell, Robert D., Sr. 52
Chenault, Kenneth I. 5, 36
Dean, Mark 35
Foster, Jylla Moore 45
Thompson, John W. 26
Zollar, Alfred 40

Ice Hockey in Harlem
Mayers, Jamal 39

Ice skating
See Figure skating

Igbo people/traditions
Achebe, Chinua 6

Illinois state government
Braun, Carol Moseley 4, 42
Burris, Roland W. 25, 75
Colter, Cyrus J. 36
Jones, Emil, Jr. 74
Meeks, James T. 92
Obama, Barack 49, 74, 91
Raoul, Kwame 55
Trotter, Donne E. 28
Washington, Harold 6
White, Jesse 22, 75

Illustrations
Anderson, Ho Che 54
Baker, Matt 76
Biggers, John 20, 33
Bryan, Ashley F. 41
Campbell, E. Simms 13
Crichlow, Ernest 75
Fax, Elton 48
Honeywood, Varnette P. 54, 88
Hudson, Cheryl 15
Kitt, Sandra 23
Pinkney, Jerry 15
Ransome, James E. 88
Saint James, Synthia 12

Simmons, Gary 58

IMF
See International Monetary Fund

Indiana state government
Carson, Julia 23, 69
Carter, Pamela Lynn 67

Indianapolis Colts football team
Caldwell, Jim 81
Dickerson, Eric 27
Dungy, Tony 17, 42, 59
Sanders, Bob 72

Indianapolis 500
Ribbs, Willy T. 2

Industrial design
Harrison, Charles 72

Information technology
Blackwell, Robert D., Sr. 52
Coleman, Ken 57
Council, LaVerne 94
Gooden, Linda 94
Hill, Wyllstyne D. 94
Mayberry-Stewart, Melodie 94
Pinkett, Randal 61
Smith, Joshua 10
Steward, David L. 36
Woods, Jacqueline 52
Zollar, Alfred 40

Insurance
Gaston, Arthur George 3, 38, 59
Herndon, Alonzo Franklin 89
Hill, Jesse, Jr. 13
Holstein, Casper 89
James, Donna A. 51
Kidd, Mae Street 39
Killingsworth, Cleve, Jr. 54
Procope, Ernesta 23
Procope, John Levy 56
Scott, Tim 87
Spaulding, Charles Clinton 9
Vaughns, Cleopatra 46
Williams, Ronald A. 57
Willie, Louis, Jr. 68

Interior design
Ashford, Calvin, Jr. 74
Bridges, Sheila 36
De' Alexander, Quinton 57
Ham, Cynthia Parker 58
Hayes, Cecil N. 46
King, Robert Arthur 58
Myles, Kim 69
Steave-Dickerson, Kia 57
Taylor, Karin 34

Internal Revenue Service
Colter, Cyrus J. 36

International Association of Fire Chiefs
Bell, Michael 40
Day, Leon 39

International Federation of Library Associations and Institutions
Wedgeworth, Robert W. 42

International Free and Accepted Masons and Eastern Star
Banks, William 11

International Ladies' Auxiliary
Tucker, Rosina 14

International law
Payne, Ulice 42

International Monetary Fund (IMF)
Babangida, Ibrahim 4
Chissano, Joaquim 7, 55, 67
Diouf, Abdou 3
Patterson, P. J. 6, 20

International Workers Organization (IWO)
Patterson, Louise 25

Internet
CasSelle, Malcolm 11
Cooper, Barry 33
Ellington, E. David 11
Gilliard, Steve 69
Knowling, Robert 38
Mitchell, Shireen 89
Thomas-Graham, Pamela 29
Thompson, John W. 26

Interpol
Noble, Ronald 46

Interscope Geffen A & M Records
Stoute, Steve 38

In the Black television show
Jones, Caroline R. 29

Inventions
Chisholm, Daquan 93
Johnson, Lonnie G. 32, 93
Jones, Frederick McKinley 68
Julian, Percy Lavon 6
Latimer, Lewis H. 4
Matzeliger, Jan 93
McCoy, Elijah 8
Morgan, Garrett 1
West, James E. 87
Woods, Granville T. 5

Investment management
Beal, Bernard B. 46
Bryant, John 26
Ford, Wallace 58
Gardner, Chris 65
Goings, Russell 59
Green, Isaac H. 79
Harris, Carla A. 67
Procope, Ernesta 23
Rogers, John W., Jr. 5, 52
Utendahl, John 23

Islam
Ali, Ayaan Hirsi 58, 92
Kalbani, Adil 77
Muhammed, W. Deen 27

Ivory Coast government
Gbagbo, Laurent 43, 90
Guéï, Robert 66

Ouattara, Alassane 90

Jackie Robinson Foundation
Robinson, Rachel 16

Jackson State University
Mason, Ronald 27

Jamaican government
Golding, Bruce 78
Simpson-Miller, Portia 62

Jazz
Adderley, Julian "Cannonball" 30
Adderley, Nat 29
Albright, Gerald 23
Ali, Rashied 79
Allen, Geri 92
Anderson, Carl 48
Anderson, Fred 87
Armstrong, Louis 2
Astatke, Mulatu 81
Austin, Lovie 40
Austin, Patti 24
Ayers, Roy 16
Bailey, Buster 38
Bailey, Philip 63
Barker, Danny 32
Basie, Count 23
Batiste, Alvin 66
Bechet, Sidney 18
Belgrave, Marcus 77
Belle, Regina 1, 51
Betts, Keter 85
Blade, Brian 88
Blakey, Art 37
Blanchard, Terence 43
Bolden, Buddy 39
Bridgewater, Dee Dee 32, 92
Brooks, Avery 9
Brown, Clifford 86
Butler, Jonathan 28
Calloway, Cab 14
Carter, Benny 46
Carter, Betty 19
Carter, Regina 23
Carter, Warrick L. 27
Cartiér, Xam Wilson 41
Charles, Ray 16, 48
Cheatham, Doc 17
Clarke, Kenny 27
Cole, Nat "King" 17
Cole, Natalie 17, 60, 84
Coleman, Ornette 39, 69
Coltrane, Alice 70
Coltrane, John 19
Coltrane, Ravi 71
Cook, Charles "Doc" 44
Count Basie 23
Crawford, Hank 77
Crawford, Randy 19
Crothers, Scatman 19
Crouch, Stanley 11, 87
Crowder, Henry 16
Daemyon, Jerald 64
Dara, Olu 35
Davis, Anthony 11
Davis, Frank Marshall 47
Davis, Miles 4
Dickenson, Vic 38
Dixon, Bill 87
Donegan, Dorothy 19
Downing, Will 19
Duke, George 21

Dumas, Henry 41
Durham, Bobby 73
Eckstine, Billy 28
Eldridge, Roy 37
Ellington, Duke 5
Ellison, Ralph 7
Eubanks, Kevin 15
Farmer, Art 38
Ferrell, Rachelle 29
Fitzgerald, Ella 8, 18
Flanagan, Tommy 69
Foster, George "Pops" 40
Freelon, Nnenna 32
Freeman, Yvette 27
Fuller, Arthur 27
Garner, Erroll 76
Gillespie, Dizzy 1
Golson, Benny 37
Gordon, Dexter 25
Green, Grant 56
Greene, Jimmy 74
Griffin, Johnny 71
Güines, Tata 69
Hampton, Lionel 17, 41
Hancock, Herbie 20, 67
Hardin Armstrong, Lil 39
Harris, Barry 68
Hawkins, Coleman 9
Haynes, Roy 87
Henderson, Fletcher 32
Higginbotham, J. C. 37
Hill, Andrew 66
Hines, Earl "Fatha" 39
Hinton, Milt 30
Holiday, Billie 1
Horn, Shirley 32, 56
Hubbard, Freddie 75
Hyman, Phyllis 19
Jackson, Milt 26
Jacquet, Illinois 49
Jamal, Ahmad 69
James, Etta 13, 52
Jarreau, Al 21, 65
Johnson, Buddy 36
Johnson, J. J. 37
Johnson, Lonnie 85
Jones, Elvin 14, 68
Jones, Etta 35
Jones, Hank 57, 86
Jones, Jonah 39
Jones, Quincy 8, 30
Jones, Thad 68
Jordan, Ronny 26
Kenyatta, Robin 54
Klugh, Earl 59
Lateef, Yusef 91
Laws, Hubert 90
Ledisi 73
Lee, Consuela 84
Lewis, Ramsey 35, 70
Lincoln, Abbey 3, 88
Locke, Eddie 44
Long, Huey 79
Loueke, Lionel 88
Lucie, Lawrence 80
Lucien, Jon 66
Marsalis, Branford 34
Marsalis, Delfeayo 41
Marsalis, Ellis 90
Marsalis, Wynton 16, 90
McBride, James 35, 87
McGriff, Jimmy 72
McLean, Jackie 78

McRae, Carmen 77
Miller, Marcus 84
Mills, Florence 22
Mingus, Charles 15
Mitchell, Nicole 66
Monk, Thelonious 1
Montgomery, Wes 88
Moody, James 83
Moore, Melba 21
Moran, Jason 89
Morton, Jelly Roll 29
Muse, Clarence Edouard 21
Nascimento, Milton 2, 64
Newman, David 76
Oliver, Joe "King" 42
Parker, Charlie 20
Parker, Maceo 72
Payne, Freda 58
Peterson, Marvin "Hannibal" 27
Peterson, Oscar 52
Powell, Benny 87
Powell, Bud 24
Purdie, Bernard 77
Redman, Joshua 30
Reese, Della 6, 20
Reeves, Dianne 32
Roach, Max 21, 63
Roberts, Marcus 19
Rollins, Sonny 37, 94
Ruffins, Kermit 85
Rushing, Jimmy 37
Sample, Joe 51
Santamaria, Mongo 81
Scarlett, Millicent 49
Scott, Hazel 66
Scott, "Little" Jimmy 48
Shorter, Wayne 75
Silver, Horace 26
Simpson-Hoffman, N'kenge 52
Sissle, Noble 29
Smith, Bessie 3
Smith, Cladys "Jabbo" 32
Smith, Dr. Lonnie 49
Smith, Lonnie Liston 49
Smith, Stuff 37
Somi 85
Staton, Dakota 62
Strayhorn, Billy 31
Sullivan, Maxine 37
Sun Ra 60
Swann, Lynn 28
Tampa Red 63
Taylor, Billy 23, 92
Taylor, Cecil 70
Terry, Clark 39
Tisdale, Wayman 50
Tyner, McCoy 92
Ulmer, James 79
Valdés, Bebo 75
Valdés, Chucho 89
Vaughan, Sarah 13
Waller, Fats 29
Washington, Dinah 22
Washington, Grover, Jr. 17, 44
Waters, Benny 26
Watson, Johnny "Guitar" 18
Watts, Reggie 52
Webster, Katie 29
Wein, Joyce 62
Whalum, Kirk 37, 64
White, Maurice 29
Williams, Claude 80
Williams, Joe 5, 25

Williams, Mary Lou 15
Williams, Tony 67
Wilson, Cassandra 16
Wilson, Gerald 49
Wilson, Nancy 10
York, Vincent 40
Young, Lee 72
Young, Lester 37

Jet magazine
Johnson, John H. 3, 54
Massaquoi, Hans J. 30
Sleet, Moneta, Jr. 5

Jive Records
McPherson, David 32

Jockeys
Harris, Sylvia 70
Lewis, Oliver 56
Winkfield, Jimmy 42

Johnson C. Smith University
Yancy, Dorothy Cowser 42

Johnson Products
Johnson, George E. 29

Johnson Publishing Company, Inc.
Booker, Simeon 23
Johnson, Eunice W. 83
Johnson, John H. 3, 54
Monroe, Bryan 71
Rice, Linda Johnson 9, 41
Rogers, Desirée 88
Sleet, Moneta, Jr. 5

Joint Center for Political Studies
Williams, Eddie N. 44

Joint Chiefs of Staff
See U.S. Joint Chiefs of Staff

Jones Haywood School of Ballet
Jones, Doris W. 62

Journalism
Abbott, Robert Sengstacke 27
Abrahams, Peter 39
Abu-Jamal, Mumia 15
Ansa, Tina McElroy 14
Ashley-Ward, Amelia 23
Asim, Jabari 71
Auguste, Arnold A. 47
Azikiwe, Nnamdi 13
Bailey, Chauncey 68
Baquet, Dean 63
Barnett, Amy Du Bois 46
Barrett, Lindsay 43
Bass, Charlotta Spears 40
Bates, Karen Grigsby 40
Bennett, Gwendolyn B. 59
Bennett, Lerone, Jr. 5, 84
Best, Carrie 80
Blair, Jayson 50
Blake, Asha 26
Blow, Charles M. 73
Bolden, Frank E. 44
Booker, Simeon 23
Borders, James 9
Boyd, Gerald M. 32, 59
Boyd, Suzanne 52
Bradley, Ed 2, 59

Britt, Donna 28
Brower, William 49
Brown, George Leslie 62
Brown, Lloyd Louis 42
Brown, Tony 3
Buckley, Gail Lumet 39
Burt-Murray, Angela 59
Burwell, Bryan 83
Caldwell, Earl 60
Campbell, Bebe Moore 6, 24, 59
Cary, Mary Ann Shadd 30
Cayton, Horace 26
Chadiha, Jeffri 57
Chideya, Farai 14, 61
Churchwell, Robert, Sr. 76
Ciara, Barbara 69
Cooke, Marvel 31
Cooper, Barry 33
Cooper, Helene 74
Cose, Ellis 5, 50
Croal, N'Gai 76
Crouch, Stanley 11, 87
Crutchfield, James N. 55
Cullen, Countee 8
Cunningham, Evelyn 23, 85
Dash, Leon 47
Datcher, Michael 60
Davis, Belva 61
Davis, Frank Marshall 47
Davis, Thulani 61
Dawkins, Wayne 20
Deggans, Eric 71
Douglass, Frederick 87
Drummond, William J. 40
Due, Tananarive 30
Dunbar, Paul Laurence 8
Dunnigan, Alice Allison 41
Eagleson, William Lewis 90
Edmonds, Terry 17
Epperson, Sharon 54
Farley, Christopher John 54
Forman, James 7, 51
Fortune, T. Thomas 6
Fuller, Hoyt 44
Gaiter, Dorothy J. 80
Giddings, Paula 11
Gilliard, Steve 69
Givhan, Robin Deneen 72
Goode, Mal 13
Gordon, Ed 10, 53
Grimké, Archibald H. 9
Gumbel, Bryant 14, 80
Gumbel, Greg 8
Hansberry, Lorraine 6
Hare, Nathan 44
Harrington, Oliver W. 9
Harris, Claire 34
Harris, Jay 19
Harris, Richard E. 61
Hatcher, Andrew T. 90
Haygood, Wil 83
Haynes, Trudy 44
Henriques, Julian 37
Herbert, Bob 63
Hickman, Fred 11
Holt, Lester 66
Huggins, Edie 71
Hunter-Gault, Charlayne 6, 31
Ifill, Gwen 28
Jackson, James A. 90
Jarrett, Vernon D. 42
Jasper, Kenji 39
Jealous, Benjamin 70

Joachim, Paulin 34
Johnson, Georgia Douglas 41
Johnson, James Weldon 5
Kaufman, Monica 66
Kearney, Janis 54
Khanga, Yelena 6
Killens, John O. 54
King, Colbert I. 69
Kitwana, Bakari 86
Knight, Etheridge 37
LaGuma, Alex 30
Lacy, Sam 30, 46
Lampkin, Daisy 19
Leavell, Dorothy R. 17
Lemon, Don 94
Lewis, Edward T. 21
Lomax, Louis E. 90
Lowe, Herbert 57
Mabrey, Vicki 26
Mabry, Marcus 70
Mabuza-Suttle, Felicia 43
Madison, Paula 37
Malveaux, Suzanne 88
Martin, Louis E. 16
Mason, Felicia 31
Maynard, Nancy Hicks 73
Maynard, Robert C. 7
Mbeki, Govan A. 80
McBride, James 35, 87
McCall, Nathan 8
McGruder, Robert 22, 35
McKay, Claude 6
Mickelbury, Penny 28
Mitchell, Elvis 67
Mitchell, Russ 21, 73
Mkapa, Benjamin W. 16, 77
Monroe, Bryan 71
Mossell, Gertrude Bustill 40
Mukoko, Jestina 75
Murphy, John H. 42
Murray, Pauli 38
Nelson, Jill 6, 54
Neville, Arthel 53
Newkirk, Pamela 69
Njawe, Pius 87
Nkosi, Lewis 46
Noble, Gil 76
Norris, Michele 83
O'Brien, Soledad 88
Oliver, Pam 54
Olojede, Dele 59
Page, Clarence 4
Palmer, Everard 37
Parham, Marjorie B. 71
Parker, Star 70
Parks, Gordon 1, 35, 58
Payne, Ethel L. 28
Payne, Les 89
Perez, Anna 1
Perkins, Tony 24
Phillips, Joseph C. 73
Pinkston, W. Randall 24
Pitts, Byron 78
Pitts, Leonard, Jr. 54, 85
Plaatje, Sol. T. 80
Poussaint, Renee 78
Pressley, Condace L. 41
Price, Hugh B. 9, 54
Prince, Richard E. 71
Pugh, Charles 81
Quarles, Norma 25
Rapier, James T. 82
Raspberry, William 2

Reed, Ishmael 8
Reeves, Rachel J. 23
Rhoden, William C. 67
Riley, Rochelle 50
Roberts, Robin 16, 54
Robertson, Gil L., IV 85
Robinson, Eugene 77
Robinson, Max 3
Rodgers, Johnathan 6, 51
Rowan, Carl T. 1, 30
Rust, Art, Jr. 83
Salih, Al-Tayyib 37
Salters, Lisa 71
Sanders, Pharoah 64
Schuyler, George Samuel 40
Schuyler, Philippa 50
Senior, Olive 37
Shaw, Bernard 2, 28
Shipp, E. R. 15
Simpson, Carole 6, 30
Smith, Clarence O. 21
Smith, Danyel 40
Smith, Stephen A. 69
Sowell, Thomas 2
Staples, Brent 8
Stewart, Alison 13
Stokes, Carl 10, 73
Stone, Chuck 9
Syler, Rene 53
Tate, Eleanora E. 20, 55
Tatum, Elinor R. 78
Tatum, Wilbert 76
Taylor, Kristin Clark 8
Thurman, Wallace 16
Tolson, Melvin B. 37
Trotter, Monroe 9
Tucker, Cynthia 15, 61
Wallace, Michele Faith 13
Washington, Elsie B. 78
Washington, Harriet A. 69
Watson, Carlos 50
Watts, Rolonda 9
Webb, Veronica 10
Wells-Barnett, Ida B. 8
Wesley, Valerie Wilson 18
Whitaker, Mark 21, 47
White, Armond 80
Whitfield, LeRoy 84
Whitlock, Jason 78
Wilbekin, Emil 63
Wilbon, Michael 68
Wiley, Ralph 8, 78
Wilkerson, Isabel 71
Wilkins, Roger 2, 84
Williams, Armstrong 29
Williams, Clarence 70
Williams, Juan 35, 80
Wiwa, Ken 67
Woods, Mattiebelle 63
Yette, Samuel F. 63
Zook, Kristal Brent 62

Judaism
Funnye, Capers C., Jr. 73
Stanton, Alysa 78

Judiciary
Hatchett, Glenda 32
Hubbard, Arnette 38
Sampson, Edith S. 4

Just Us Books
Hudson, Cheryl 15
Hudson, Wade 15

Kansas City Chiefs football team
Allen, Marcus 20
Cherry, Deron 40
Delaney, Joe 76
Dungy, Tony 17, 42, 59
Thomas, Derrick 25
Thomas, Emmitt 71

Kansas City (MO) government
Cleaver, Emanuel 4, 45, 68

Kansas City Monarchs baseball team
Bell, James "Cool Papa" 36
Brown, Willard 36

Kansas State University
Prince, Ron 64

KANU
See Kenya African National Union

Kappa Alpha Psi
Hamilton, Samuel C. 47

Kentucky Derby
Winkfield, Jimmy 42

Kentucky Negro Educational Association
Cotter, Joseph Seamon, Sr. 40

Kentucky state government
Kidd, Mae Street 39

Kenya African National Union (KANU)
Kariuki, J. M. 67
Kenyatta, Jomo 5
Kibaki, Mwai 60
Moi, Daniel Arap 1, 35
Ngilu, Charity 58
Odinga, Raila 67

Kenya National Council of Churches (NCCK)
Kobia, Samuel 43

Kenyan government
Kariuki, J. M. 67
Kibaki, Mwai 60
Maathai, Wangari 43
Moi, Daniel Arap 1, 35
Ngilu, Charity 58
Odinga, Raila 67

King Center
See Martin Luther King Jr. Center for Nonviolent Social Change

King Oliver's Creole Band
Armstrong, Louis 2
Hardin Armstrong, Lil 39
Oliver, Joe "King" 42

King's Troop of the Royal Horse Artillery
Scantlebury, Janna 47

Kraft General Foods
Fudge, Ann (Marie) 11, 55
Sneed, Paula A. 18

Kunta Kinte–Alex Haley Foundation
Blackshear, Leonard 52

Kwanzaa
Karenga, Maulana 10, 71

Kwazulu Territorial Authority
Buthelezi, Mangosuthu Gatsha 9

Labour Party
Amos, Valerie 41

Ladies Professional Golfers' Association (LPGA)
Gibson, Althea 8, 43
Powell, Renee 34

LaFace Records
Babyface 10, 31, 82
Benjamin, Andre 45
OutKast 35
Patton, Antwan 45
Reid, Antonio "L.A." 28

LAPD
See Los Angeles Police Department

Latin American folk music
Nascimento, Milton 2, 64

Latin baseball leagues
Kaiser, Cecil 42

Law education
Bell, Derrick 6
Carter, Stephen L. 4
Forman, James, Jr. 89
Guinier, Lani 7, 30
Williams, Patricia 11, 54

Law enforcement
Alexander, Joyce London 18
Barrett, Jacquelyn 28
Bolton, Terrell D. 25
Bradley, Thomas 2, 20
Brown, Lee P. 1, 24
Bully-Cummings, Ella 48
Evans, Warren C. 76
Feemster, Herbert 72
Freeman, Charles 19
Gibson, Johnnie Mae 23
Glover, Nathaniel, Jr. 12
Gomez-Preston, Cheryl 9
Harvard, Beverly 11
Hillard, Terry 25
Holton, Hugh, Jr. 39
Hurtt, Harold 46
Johnson, Norma L. Holloway 17
Johnson, Robert T. 17
Jordan, Eddie 82
McKinnon, Isaiah 9
Moose, Charles 40
Napoleon, Benny N. 23
Noble, Ronald 46
Oliver, Jerry 37
Parks, Bernard C. 17
Ramsey, Charles H. 21, 69
Robinson, Bishop L. 66
Schmoke, Kurt 1, 48
Smith, Richard 51
Thomas, Franklin A. 5, 49
Wainwright, Joscelyn 46
Ward, Benjamin 68
Williams, Willie L. 4
Wilson, Jimmy 45

LDF
See NAACP Legal Defense and
Educational Fund

League of Nations
Haile Selassie 7

Legal Defense Fund
See NAACP Legal Defense and
Educational Fund

Lexicography
Major, Clarence 9

Liberian government
Henries, A. Doris Banks 44
Sawyer, Amos 2
Sirleaf, Ellen Johnson 71
Weah, George 58

**Liberians United for Recon-
ciliation and Democracy
(LURD)**
Conneh, Sekou Damate, Jr. 51

Library science
Bontemps, Arna 8
Franklin, Hardy R. 9, 87
Harsh, Vivian Gordon 14
Hutson, Jean Blackwell 16
Jones, Clara Stanton 51
Josey, E. J. 10
Kitt, Sandra 23
Larsen, Nella 10
Morrison, Sam 50
Owens, Major 6
Rollins, Charlemae Hill 27
Schomburg, Arthur Alfonso 9
Shockley, Ann Allen 84
Smith, Jessie Carney 35
Spencer, Anne 27
Wedgeworth, Robert W. 42
Wesley, Dorothy Porter 19

Librettos
Chenault, John 40

Lincoln University (MO)
Page, Inman 82
Randall, Dudley 8, 55

Lincoln University (PA)
Cuney, William Waring 44
Sudarkasa, Niara 4

**Literacy Volunteers of
America**
Amos, Wally 9

Literary criticism
Baker, Houston A., Jr. 6
Braithwaite, William Stanley 52
Brown, Sterling Allen 10, 64
Broyard, Anatole 68
Cartey, Wilfred 47
Christian, Barbara T. 44
Cook, Mercer 40
De Veaux, Alexis 44
Emanuel, James A. 46
Fleming, Raymond 48
Ford, Nick Aaron 44
Joachim, Paulin 34
Mackey, Nathaniel 75
Mugo, Micere Githae 32
Ngugi wa Thiong'o 29, 61
Redding, J. Saunders 26

Reed, Ishmael 8
Smith, Barbara 28
Wesley, Valerie Wilson 18
West, Cornel 5, 33, 80

**Literary Hall of Fame for Writ-
ers of African Descent**
Colter, Cyrus J. 36

Lithography
White, Charles 39

Litigation
Allen, Lucy 85
Baldwin, Cynthia A. 74
Cochran, Johnnie 11, 39, 52
Gary, Willie E. 12
Worthy, Kym 84

"Little Rock Nine"
Bates, Daisy 13
Thomas, Jefferson 88

Liver research
Leevy, Carrol M. 42

Lobbying
Boyd, John W., Jr. 20, 72
Brown, Elaine 8
Brown, Jesse 6, 41
Brown, Ron 5
Christie, Ron 83
Edelman, Marian Wright 5, 42
Lee, Canada 8
Mallett, Conrad, Jr. 16
Reeves, Gregory 49
Robinson, Randall 7, 46
Wynn, Albert R. 25, 77

**Los Angeles Angels baseball
team**
Baylor, Don 6
Bonds, Bobby 43
Reagins, Tony 94

Los Angeles city government
Bradley, Thomas 2, 20
Evers, Myrlie 8

**Los Angeles Clippers basket-
ball team**
Baylor, Elgin 93
Brand, Elton 31

**Los Angeles Dodgers base-
ball team**
Baker, Dusty 8, 43, 72
Newcombe, Don 24
Strawberry, Darryl 22
Wills, Maury 73

**Los Angeles Lakers basket-
ball team**
Abdul-Jabbar, Kareem 8
Baylor, Elgin 93
Bryant, Kobe 15, 31, 71
Chamberlain, Wilt 18, 47
Fox, Rick 27
Green, A. C. 32
Johnson, Earvin "Magic" 3, 39
Odom, Lamar 81
O'Neal, Shaquille 8, 30
Worthy, James 49

Los Angeles Philharmonic
Lewis, Henry 38

**Los Angeles Police Depart-
ment (LAPD)**
Parks, Bernard C. 17
Smith, Richard 51
Williams, Willie L. 4

**Los Angeles Raiders football
team**
Allen, Marcus 20
Lofton, James 42
Lott, Ronnie 9
Shell, Art 1, 66

**Los Angeles Rams football
team**
Bryant, Cullen 81
Dickerson, Eric 27
Washington, Kenny 50

Los Angeles Times newspaper
Baquet, Dean 63
Drummond, William J. 40

Lost-Found Nation of Islam
Ali, Muhammad 2, 16, 52
Ellison, Keith 59
Farrakhan, Louis 2, 15
Heard, Nathan C. 45
Karim, Benjamin 61
Muhammad, Ava 31
Muhammad, Elijah 4
Muhammad, Jabir Herbert 72
Muhammad, Khallid Abdul 10, 31
Muhammed, W. Deen 27
Sutton, Percy E. 42, 82
Tillard, Conrad 47
X, Malcolm 1
X, Marvin 45

Louisiana state government
Fields, Cleo 13
Francis, Norman (C.) 60
Jefferson, William J. 25, 72
Morial, Ernest "Dutch" 26
Peterson, Karen Carter 90
Pinchback, P. B. S. 9
Richardson, Rupert 67
Richmond, Cedric 93

LPGA
See Ladies Professional Golfers'
Association

**Lunar surface ultraviolet cam-
era**
See Ultraviolet
camera/spectrograph

**Lynching (anti-lynching legis-
lation)**
Johnson, James Weldon 5
Moore, Harry T. 29
Till, Emmett 7

Lyrics
Crouch, Andraé 27
D'Angelo 27
Dunbar, Paul Laurence 8
Fitzgerald, Ella 8
Jefferson, Blind Lemon 81
Johnson, James Weldon 5
KRS-One 34
Lil' Kim 28
MC Lyte 34
Randall, Alice 38

Run-DMC 31, 75

**MacArthur Foundation Fellow-
ship**
Allen, Will 74
Benjamin, Regina 20, 75
Butler, Octavia 8, 43, 58
Carter, Majora 77
Carter, Regina 23
Cooper, Lisa 73
Dabiri, John 93
Gordon-Reed, Annette 74
Hammons, David 69
Harris, Corey 39, 73
Jackson, Mary 73
Johnson, Angela 52
Johnson, Charles 1, 82
Jones, Edward P. 43, 67
Lee, Raphael C. 87
Lindsey, Tommie 51
Lovell, Whitfield 74
Mehretu, Julie 85
Moran, Jason 89
Nelson, Stanley 92
Olopade, Olufunmilayo Falusi 58
Parks, Suzan-Lori 34, 85
Robinson, Aminah 50
Taylor, Cecil 70
Walcott, Derek 5, 94
Whitehead, Colson 77
Williams, Patricia 11, 54

MacNeil/Lehrer NewsHour
Hunter-Gault, Charlayne 6, 31

Mad TV
Jones, Orlando 30
Wilson, Debra 38

**Madame C. J. Walker Manu-
facturing Company**
Joyner, Marjorie Stewart 26
Walker, A'lelia 14
Walker, Madame C. J. 7

**Major League Baseball admin-
istration**
Solomon, Jimmie Lee 38

Malaco Records
Bland, Bobby "Blue" 36

Malawi Congress Party (MCP)
Banda, Hastings Kamuzu 6, 54

Malawian government
Muluzi, Bakili 14, 76

Manhattan Project
Quarterman, Lloyd Albert 4
Wilkens, J. Ernest, Jr. 43

MARC Corp.
See Metropolitan Applied Research
Center

**March on
Washington/Freedom March**
Baker, Josephine 3
Belafonte, Harry 4, 65
Bunche, Ralph J. 5
Davis, Ossie 5, 50
Fauntroy, Walter E. 11
Forman, James 7, 51
Franklin, John Hope 5, 77
Hedgeman, Anna Arnold 22

Jackson, Mahalia 5
King, Coretta Scott 3, 57
King, Martin Luther, Jr. 1
Lewis, John 2, 46, 83
Meredith, James H. 11
Randolph, A. Philip 3
Rustin, Bayard 4
Sleet, Moneta, Jr. 5
Wilkins, Roy 4
Woods, Abraham, Jr. 74
Young, Whitney M., Jr. 4

Marketing
DeVard, Jerri 61
Edwards, Trevor 54
Fils-Aimé, Reggie 74
Gaskins, Rudy 74
Jackson, James A. 90
Kaigler, Denise 63
Kendrick, Erika 57
Moyo, Karega Kofi 36
Moyo, Yvette Jackson 36

Martial arts
Barnes, Steven 54
Copeland, Michael 47
Slice, Kimbo 73

Martin Luther King Jr. Center for Nonviolent Social Change
Dodson, Howard, Jr. 7, 52
Farris, Isaac Newton, Jr. 63
King, Bernice 4, 81
King, Coretta Scott 3, 57
King, Dexter 10
King, Martin Luther, Jr. 1
King, Yolanda 6

Martin Luther King Jr. Drum Major Award
Broadbent, Hydeia 36
Mfume, Kweisi 6, 41

Martin Luther King Jr. National Memorial Project
Johnson, Harry E. 57

Marxism
Baraka, Amiri 1, 38
Bishop, Maurice 39
Jagan, Cheddi 16
Machel, Samora Moises 8
Nkrumah, Kwame 3
Sankara, Thomas 17

Maryland state government
Brown, Anthony G. 72
Currie, Ulysses 73
Steele, Michael 38, 73, 91

Massachusetts state government
Brooke, Edward W. 8, 88
Gourdin, Edward O. 93
Lewis, William Henry 89
Patrick, Deval 12, 61

Masters Golf Tournament
Elder, Lee 6
Woods, Tiger 14, 31, 81

Mathematics
Alcorn, George Edward, Jr. 59
Banneker, Benjamin 93
Blackwell, David 79
Deconge-Watson, Lovenia 55

Emeagwali, Philip 30
Falconer, Etta Zuber 59
Gates, Sylvester James, Jr. 15
Johnson, Katherine (Coleman Goble) 61
Price, Richard 51
Wilkens, J. Ernest, Jr. 43

Maxwell House Coffee Company
Fudge, Ann (Marie) 11, 55

McDonald's Corporation
Thompson, Don 56

McGill University (Canada)
Elliott, Lorris 37

MCP
See Malawi Congress Party

Medical examiners
Carter, Joye Maureen 41

Medicine
Adams-Campbell, Lucille L. 60
Anderson, William G(ilchrist) 57
Atim, Julian 66
Banda, Hastings Kamuzu 6, 54
Bashir, Halima 73
Benjamin, Regina 20, 75
Black, Keith Lanier 18, 84
Callender, Clive O. 3
Canady, Alexa 28
Carroll, L. Natalie 44
Carson, Benjamin 1, 35, 76
Carter, Joye Maureen 41
Chatard, Peter 44
Chinn, May Edward 26
Christian-Green, Donna M. 17
Cobb, W. Montague 39
Cole, Rebecca 38
Comer, James P. 6
Coney, PonJola 48
Cooper, Edward S. 6
Cooper, Lisa 73
Cornwell, Edward E., III 70
Counter, S. Allen 74
Crumpler, Rebecca Lee 89
Dailey, Ulysses Grant 87
Deas, Gerald 85
Dickens, Helen Octavia 14, 64
Drew, Charles Richard 7
Durham, James 90
Edwards, Lena Frances 76
Edwards, Willarda V. 59
Elders, Joycelyn 6
Fennoy, Ilene 72
Fisher, Ada M. 76
Fisher, Rudolph 17
Flowers, Sylester 50
Foster, Henry W., Jr. 26
Freeman, Harold P. 23
French, D. M. 94
Fuller, Solomon Carter, Jr. 15
Gayle, Helene D. 3
Gibson, William F. 6
Giles, Roscoe C. 93
Goodlett, Carlton B. 91
Grant, Augustus O. 71
Grier, Eliza Ann 90
Griffin, Anthony 71
Griffith, Patrick A. 64
Hamburg, Margaret 78
Hansberry, Tony, II 93

Harris, Bernard A. 90
Hinton, William Augustus 8
Holmes, Hamilton E. 82
Hopkins, Donald R. 89
Hutcherson, Hilda Yvonne 54
Jefferson, Mildred Fay 89
Jemison, Mae C. 1, 35
Johnson, R. M. 36
Jones, Edith Mae Irby 65
Joseph, Kathie-Ann 56
Keith, Rachel Boone 63
Kenney, John A., Jr. 48
Kintaudi, Leon 62
Kong, B. Waine 50
Kountz, Samuel L. 10
Lavizzo-Mourey, Risa 48
Lawless, Theodore K. 8
Lee, Raphael C. 87
Leffall, Lasalle 3, 64
Logan, Onnie Lee 14
Malveaux, Floyd 54
Maxey, Randall 46
Mossell, Nathan Francis 91
Naki, Hamilton 63
Nour, Nawal M. 56
Okaalet, Peter 58
Olopade, Olufunmilayo Falusi 58
Pace, Betty 59
Pinn, Vivian Winona 49
Pitt, David Thomas 10
Poussaint, Alvin F. 5, 67
Rabb, Maurice F., Jr. 58
Randolph, Linda A. 52
Reece, E. Albert 63
Ross-Lee, Barbara 67
Satcher, David 7, 57
Scantlebury-White, Velma 64
Smith, Ian 62
Stewart, Ella 39
Sullivan, Louis 8
Sweet, Ossian 68
Taylor, Susan C. 62
Thomas, Claudia Lynn 64
Thomas, Vivien 9
Thornton, Yvonne S. 69
Tuckson, Reed V. 71
Washington, Harriet A. 69
Watkins, Levi, Jr. 9
Welsing, Frances Cress 5
White-Hammond, Gloria 61
Williams, Daniel Hale 2
Wilson, Donald E. 88
Witt, Edwin T. 26
Wright, Charles H. 35
Wright, Louis Tompkins 4

Meharry Medical College
Coney, PonJola 48
Foster, Henry W., Jr. 26
Griffith, Patrick A. 64
Lyttle, Hulda Margaret 14

Melody Makers
Marley, Ziggy 41

Men's movement
Somé, Malidoma Patrice 10

Merce Cunningham Dance Company
Dove, Ulysses 5

Merrill Lynch & Co., Inc.
Ford, Harold E(ugene), Jr. 16, 70
Matthews Shatteen, Westina 51

O'Neal, Stanley 38, 67

Meteorology
Anderson, Charles Edward 37
Bacon-Bercey, June 38

Metropolitan Applied Research Center (MARC Corp.)
Clark, Kenneth B. 5, 52

Mexican baseball league
Bell, James "Cool Papa" 36
Dandridge, Ray 36

Miami Dolphins football team
Cox, Bryan 83
Greene, Joe 10
Little, Larry 90
Williams, Ricky 85

Michigan state government
Brown, Cora 33
Collins, Barbara-Rose 7, 87
Kilpatrick, Carolyn Cheeks 16
Kilpatrick, Kwame 34, 71
Reeves, Triette Lipsey 27
Wisdom, Kimberlydawn 57

Michigan State Supreme Court
Archer, Dennis 7, 36
Mallett, Conrad, Jr. 16

Michigan State University
Wharton, Clifton R., Jr. 7
Willingham, Tyrone 43

Microsoft Corporation
Millines Dziko, Trish 28

Midwest Stamping
Thompson, Cynthia Bramlett 50

Midwifery
Logan, Onnie Lee 14
Mason, Biddy 89
Robinson, Sharon 22

Military police
Cadoria, Sherian Grace 14

Militia
Nkunda, Laurent 75

Millennium Digital Media
Westbrook, Kelvin 50

Miller Brewing Company
Colbert, Virgis William 17
Shropshire, Thomas B. 49

Millinery
Bailey, Xenobia 11

Million Man March
Farrakhan, Louis 2, 15
Hawkins, La-Van 17, 54
Worrill, Conrad 12

Milwaukee Brewers baseball team
Aaron, Hank 5
Baylor, Don 6
Fielder, Prince Semien 68
Payne, Ulice 42

Sheffield, Gary 16

Milwaukee Bucks basketball team
Abdul-Jabbar, Kareem 8
Robertson, Oscar 26

Mingo-Jones Advertising
Chisholm, Samuel J. 32
Jones, Caroline R. 29
Mingo, Frank 32

Minneapolis city government
Sayles Belton, Sharon 9, 16

Minnesota State Supreme Court
Page, Alan 7

Minnesota Timberwolves basketball team
Garnett, Kevin 14, 70

Minnesota Twins baseball team
Baylor, Don 6
Carew, Rod 20
Hunter, Torii 43
Puckett, Kirby 4, 58

Minnesota Vikings football team
Carter, Cris 21
Culpepper, Daunte 32, 85
Cunningham, Randall 23
Dungy, Tony 17, 42, 59
Fowler, Reggie 51
Gilliam, Frank 23
Green, Dennis 5, 45
McDaniel, Randall Cornell 81
Moon, Warren 8, 66
Moss, Randy 23, 90
Page, Alan 7
Randle, John 87
Rashad, Ahmad 18
Stringer, Korey 35

Minority Business Enterprise Legal Defense and Education Fund
Mitchell, Parren J. 42, 66

Minstrel shows
Lane, William Henry 90
McDaniel, Hattie 5

Miracle Network Telethon
Warner, Malcolm-Jamal 22, 36

Miss America
Dunlap, Ericka 55
Harold, Erika 54
Vincent, Marjorie Judith 2
Williams, Vanessa L. 4, 17

Miss USA
Gist, Carole 1

Miss World
Darego, Agbani 52

Mississippi state government
Anderson, Reuben V. 81
Fleming, Erik R. 75

Hamer, Fannie Lou 6

Missouri state government
Wilson, Margaret Bush 79

Mixed martial arts
Jackson, Rampage 83

MLA
See Modern Language Association of America

Model Inner City Community Organization (MICCO)
Fauntroy, Walter E. 11

Modeling
Allen-Buillard, Melba 55
Banks, Tyra 11, 50
Beckford, Tyson 11, 68
Berry, Halle 4, 19, 57, 91
Campbell, Naomi 1, 31
Darego, Agbani 52
Davis, Mia Amber 94
Dirie, Waris 56
Ebanks, Selita 67
Gibson, Tyrese 27, 62
Hardison, Bethann 12
Hounsou, Djimon 19, 45
Iman 4, 33, 87
Iman, Chanel 66
Johnson, Beverly 2
Kebede, Liya 59
Kodjoe, Boris 34, 89
Langhart Cohen, Janet 19, 60
Leslie, Lisa 16, 73
LisaRaye 27
McKenzie, Jaunel 73
Michele, Michael 31
Niane, Katoucha 70
Onwurah, Ngozi 38
Powell, Maxine 8
Rochon, Lela 16
RuPaul 17, 91
Simmons, Kimora Lee 51, 83
Sims, Naomi 29, 79
Smith, B(arbara) 11
Tamia 24, 55
Taylor, Karin 34
Tyson, Cicely 7, 51
Watley, Jody 54
Webb, Veronica 10
Wek, Alek 18, 63

Modern dance
Ailey, Alvin 8
Allen, Debbie 13, 42
Brown, Ronald K. 91
Byrd, Donald 10
Collins, Janet 33, 64
Davis, Chuck 33
Diggs, Taye 25, 63
Dove, Ulysses 5
Fagan, Garth 18
Faison, George 16
Henson, Darrin 33
Jamison, Judith 7, 67
Jones, Bill T. 1, 46, 80
King, Alonzo 38
Kitt, Eartha 16, 75
Miller, Bebe 3
Pomare, Eleo 72
Primus, Pearl 6
Spears, Warren 52
Vereen, Ben 4

Williams, Dudley 60

Modern Language Association of America (MLA)
Baker, Houston A., Jr. 6

Modern Records
Brooks, Hadda 40

Montgomery bus boycott
Abernathy, Ralph David 1
Baker, Ella 5
Burks, Mary Fair 40
Carr, Johnnie 69
Jackson, Mahalia 5
Killens, John O. 54
King, Martin Luther, Jr. 1
Parks, Rosa 1, 35, 56
Rustin, Bayard 4

Montgomery County (MD) Police Department
Moose, Charles 40

Montreal Canadiens hockey team
Brashear, Donald 39

Montreal Expos baseball team
Dawson, Andre 85
Doby, Lawrence Eugene, Sr. 16, 41

Morehouse College
Brown, Uzee 42
Gloster, Hugh Morris, Sr. 90
Hope, John 8
Mays, Benjamin E. 7

Morgan Stanley
Lewis, William M., Jr. 40

Moscow World News
Khanga, Yelena 6
Sullivan, Louis 8

Motivational speaking
Bahati, Wambui 60
Baisden, Michael 66
Brown, Les 5
Bunkley, Anita Richmond 39
Creagh, Milton 27
Gardner, Chris 65
Grant, Gwendolyn Goldsby 28
Gray, Farrah 59
Jolley, Willie 28
July, William 27
Kimbro, Dennis 10
Russell-McCloud, Patricia 17
Tyson, Asha 39

Motorcycle racing
Brown, Antron 85
Showers, Reggie 30
Stewart, James "Bubba," Jr. 60

Motown Records
Atkins, Cholly 40
Avant, Clarence 19, 86
Bizimungu, Pasteur 19
Busby, Jheryl 3, 74
de Passe, Suzanne 25
Edwards, Esther Gordy 43
Gaye, Marvin 2
Gordy, Berry, Jr. 1
Harrell, Andre 9, 30
Holland-Dozier-Holland 36

Holloway, Brenda 65
Hutch, Willie 62
Jackson, George 19
Jamerson, James 59
Jones, Robert G. 81
Kendricks, Eddie 22
Knight, Gladys 16, 66
Massenburg, Kedar 23
Powell, Maxine 8
Richie, Lionel 27, 65
Robinson, Smokey 3, 49
Ross, Diana 8, 27
Sanders, Angelia 86
Terrell, Tammi 32
Wells, Mary 28
Whitfield, Norman 73
Wilson, Mary 28
Wonder, Stevie 11, 53

Mount Holyoke College
Tatum, Beverly Daniel 42, 84

Movement for Democratic Change (MDC)
Moyo, Lovemore 76
Tsvangirai, Morgan 26, 72

Movimento Popular de Libertação de Angola (MPLA)
dos Santos, José Eduardo 43
Neto, António Agostinho 43

Mozambican government
Chissano, Joaquim 7, 55, 67
Diogo, Luisa Dias 63
Guebuza, Armando 81
Machel, Samora Moises 8

MPLA
See Movimento Popular de Libertação de Angola

Multimedia art
Amaki, Amalia 76
Bailey, Xenobia 11
Lovell, Whitfield 74
Pinder, Jefferson 77
Robinson, Aminah 50
Simpson, Lorna 4, 36

Muppets, The
Clash, Kevin 14, 93

Murals
Alston, Charles 33
Biggers, John 20, 33
Douglas, Aaron 7
Lee-Smith, Hughie 5
Walker, Kara 16, 80

Museum of Modern Art
Pindell, Howardena 55

Music Critics Circle
Holt, Nora 38

Music One, Inc.
Majors, Jeff 41

Music publishing
Avant, Nicole A. 90
Edmonds, Tracey 16, 64
Griffey, Dick 89
Handy, W. C. 8
Holland-Dozier-Holland 36
Humphrey, Bobbi 20
Jackson, George 19

James, Rick 17
Knight, Suge 11, 30
Master P 21
Mayfield, Curtis 2, 43
Otis, Clyde 67
Pryce, Trevor 89
Redding, Otis 16
Riley, Boots 89
Shakur, Afeni 67
Shorty, Ras, I 47
Strong, Barrett 89

Music Television (MTV)
Bellamy, Bill 12
Chideya, Farai 14, 61
Morton, Frederick A., Jr. 93
Norman, Christina 47
Powell, Kevin 31, 74
Run 31, 73

Musical composition
Armatrading, Joan 32
Ashford, Nickolas 21
Baiocchi, Regina Harris 41
Ballard, Hank 41
Bebey, Francis 45
Blanchard, Terence 43
Blige, Mary J. 20, 34, 60
Bonds, Margaret 39
Bonga, Kuenda 13
Boulogne, Joseph, Chevalier de Saint-Georges 94
Bridgetower, George 78
Brown, Patrick "Sleepy" 50
Brown, Uzee 42
Burke, Solomon 31, 86
Burleigh, Henry Thacker 56
Caesar, Shirley 19
Carter, Warrick L. 27
Chapman, Tracy 26
Charlemagne, Manno 11
Charles, Ray 16, 48
Cleveland, James 19
Cole, Natalie 17, 60, 84
Coleman, Ornette 39, 69
Collins, Bootsy 31
Cook, Will Marion 40
Davis, Anthony 11
Davis, Miles 4
Davis, Sammy, Jr. 18
Dawson, William Levi 39
Diddley, Bo 39, 72
Domino, Fats 20
Ellington, Duke 5
Europe, James Reese 10
Evans, Faith 22
Freeman, Paul 39
Fuller, Arthur 27
Gamble, Kenny 85
Garrett, Sean 57
Gaynor, Gloria 36
George, Nelson 12
Gillespie, Dizzy 1
Golson, Benny 37
Green, Al 13, 47, 74
Hailey, JoJo 22
Hailey, K-Ci 22
Handy, W. C. 8
Harris, Corey 39, 73
Hathaway, Donny 18
Hayes, Isaac 20, 58, 73
Hayes, Teddy 40
Hill, Lauryn 20, 53

Holland-Dozier-Holland 36
Holmes, Clint 57
Holt, Nora 38
Humphrey, Bobbi 20
Hutch, Willie 62
Isley, Ronald 25, 56
Jackson, Fred James 25
Jackson, Michael 19, 53, 76
Jackson, Randy 40
James, Rick 17
Jerkins, Rodney 31
Johnson, Buddy 36
Johnson, Georgia Douglas 41
Jones, Jonah 39
Jones, Quincy 8, 30
Jones, Thad 68
Joplin, Scott 6
Jordan, Montell 23
Jordan, Ronny 26
Kay, Ulysses 37
Kee, John P. 43
Kelly, R. 18, 44, 71
Keys, Alicia 32, 68
Kidjo, Angelique 50
Killings, Debra 57
King, B. B. 7
León, Tania 13
Little Milton 36, 54
Little Walter 36
Lopes, Lisa "Left Eye" 36
Mahlasela, Vusi 65
Majors, Jeff 41
Marsalis, Delfeayo 41
Martin, Roberta 58
Master P 21
Maxwell 20, 81
Mayfield, Curtis 2, 43
M.C. Hammer 20, 80
McClurkin, Donnie 25
McFerrin, Bobby 68
Mills, Stephanie 36
Mitchell, Brian Stokes 21
Mo', Keb' 36
Monica 21
Moore, Chante 26
Moore, Dorothy Rudd 46
Moore, Undine Smith 28
Muse, Clarence Edouard 21
Nash, Johnny 40
Ndegeocello, Meshell 15, 83
Osborne, Jeffrey 26
Otis, Clyde 67
Parker, Ray, Jr. 85
Pratt, Awadagin 31
Price, Florence 37
Prince 18, 65
Pritchard, Robert Starling 21
Reagon, Bernice Johnson 7
Redding, Otis 16
Reed, A. C. 36
Reid, Antonio "L.A." 28
Roach, Max 21, 63
Robinson, Reginald R. 53
Run-DMC 31, 75
Rushen, Patrice 12
Russell, Brenda 52
Sangare, Oumou 18
Scott-Heron, Gil 94
Seal 14, 75
Shorty, Ras, I 47
Silver, Horace 26
Simone, Nina 15, 41
Simpson, Valerie 21

Somi 85
Sowande, Fela 39
Still, William Grant 37
Strayhorn, Billy 31
Sundiata, Sekou 66
Sweat, Keith 19
Tillis, Frederick 40
Usher 23, 56
Van Peebles, Melvin 7
Walker, George 37
Warwick, Dionne 18
Washington, Grover, Jr. 17, 44
Williams, Deniece 36
Williams, Tony 67
Winans, Angie 36
Winans, Debbie 36
Withers, Bill 61

Musicology
George, Zelma Watson 42

Mysteries
Bland, Eleanor Taylor 39
Creagh, Milton 27
DeLoach, Nora 30
Himes, Chester 8
Holton, Hugh, Jr. 39
Mickelbury, Penny 28
Mosley, Walter 5, 25, 68
Thomas-Graham 29
Wesley, Valerie Wilson 18

Mystery/Detective fiction
Bates, Karen Grigsby 40
Bland, Eleanor Taylor 39
DeLoach, Nora 30
Hayes, Teddy 40
Haywood, Gar Anthony 43
Himes, Chester 8
Holton, Hugh, Jr. 39
Mosley, Walter 5, 25, 68
Wesley, Valerie Wilson 18

Mystic Seaport Museum
Pinckney, Bill 42

NAACP
See National Association for the Advancement of Colored People

NAACP Image Awards
Brandy 14, 34, 72
Fields, Kim 36
Lawrence, Martin 6, 27, 60
Mac, Bernie 29, 61, 72
McRae, Carmen 77
Okonedo, Sophie 67
Prince-Bythewood, Gina 31, 77
Rhimes, Shonda Lynn 67
Warner, Malcolm-Jamal 22, 36
Wesley, Richard 73

NAACP Legal Defense and Educational Fund (LDF)
Bell, Derrick 6
Berrien, Jacqueline A. 93
Carter, Robert L. 51
Chambers, Julius 3
Coleman, James E., Jr. 79
Coleman, William T. 76
Edelman, Marian Wright 5, 42
Fisher, Ada Lois Sipuel 76
Guinier, Lani 7, 30
Jones, Elaine R. 7, 45
Julian, Percy Lavon 6

Marshall, Thurgood 1, 44
Motley, Constance Baker 10, 55
Rice, Constance LaMay 60
Smith, Kemba 70
Smythe Haith, Mabel 61

NABJ
See National Association of Black Journalists

NAC
See Nyasaland African Congress

NACW
See National Association of Colored Women

Namibian government
Mbuende, Kaire 12
Nujoma, Samuel 10

NASA
See National Aeronautics and Space Administration

NASCAR
See National Association of Stock Car Auto Racing

Nation of Islam
See Lost-Found Nation of Islam

National Academy of Design
White, Charles 39

National Action Council for Minorities in Engineering
Pierre, Percy Anthony 46
Slaughter, John Brooks 53

National Action Network
Sharpton, Al 21

National Aeronautics and Space Administration (NASA)
Anderson, Michael P. 40
Bluford, Guy 2, 35
Bolden, Charles Frank, Jr. 7, 78
Campbell, Donald J. 66
Carruthers, George R. 40
Drew, Alvin, Jr. 67
Easley, Annie J. 61
Gregory, Frederick 8, 51
Harris, Bernard A. 90
Jemison, Mae C. 1, 35
Johnson, Katherine (Coleman Goble) 61
Johnson, Lonnie G. 32, 93
McNair, Ronald 3, 58
Mills, Joseph C. 51
Nichols, Nichelle 11
Sigur, Wanda 44
Wilson, Stephanie 72

National Afro-American Council
Fortune, T. Thomas 6
Mossell, Gertrude Bustill 40

National Airmen's Association of America
Brown, Willa 40

National Alliance of Postal and Federal Employees
McGee, James Madison 46

National Association for the Advancement of Colored People (NAACP)
Anderson, Reuben V. 81
Anderson, William G(ilchrist) 57
Anthony, Wendell 25
Austin, Junius C. 44
Baker, Ella 5
Ballance, Frank W. 41
Bates, Daisy 13
Bell, Derrick 6
Bond, Julian 2, 35
Bontemps, Arna 8
Brock, Roslyn McCallister 86
Brooks, Gwendolyn 1
Brown, Homer S. 47
Bunche, Ralph J. 5
Chambers, Julius 3
Chavis, Benjamin 6
Clark, Kenneth B. 5, 52
Clark, Septima 7
Cobb, W. Montague 39
Colter, Cyrus, J. 36
Cotter, Joseph Seamon, Sr. 40
Creagh, Milton 27
Days, Drew S., III 10
Dee, Ruby 8, 50, 68
Du Bois, W. E. B. 3
DuBois, Shirley Graham 21
Dukes, Hazel Nell 56
Edelman, Marian Wright 5, 42
Evers, Medgar 3
Evers, Myrlie 8
Farmer, James 2, 64
Ford, Clyde W. 40
Fuller, S. B. 13
Grimké, Archibald H. 9
Hampton, Fred 18
Harrington, Oliver W. 9
Hayes, Dennis 54
Henderson, Wade 14
Hobson, Julius W. 44
Hollowell, Donald L. 57
Hooks, Benjamin L. 2, 85
Houston, Charles Hamilton 4
Jackson, Vera 40
Jealous, Benjamin 70
Johnson, James Weldon 5
Jordan, Vernon E. 3, 35
Kidd, Mae Street 39
Lampkin, Daisy 19
Madison, Joseph E. 17
Marshall, Thurgood 1, 44
McKissick, Floyd B. 3
McPhail, Sharon 2
Meredith, James H. 11
Mfume, Kweisi 6, 41
Mitchell, Clarence M., Jr. 88
Mitchell, Sharon 36
Moore, Harry T. 29
Morgan, Irene 65
Moses, Robert Parris 11
Motley, Constance Baker 10, 55
Moyo, Yvette Jackson 36
Owens, Major 6
Payton, John 48
Richardson, Rupert 67
Rustin, Bayard 4
Sutton, Percy E. 42, 82
Talbert, Mary B. 77
Terrell, Mary Church 9
Tobias, Channing H. 79
Tucker, C. Delores 12, 56

Van Lierop, Robert 53
White, Walter F. 4
Wilkins, Roy 4
Williams, Hosea Lorenzo 15, 31
Williams, Robert F. 11
Wilson, Margaret Bush 79
Wright, Louis Tompkins 4

National Association of Black Journalists (NABJ)
Curry, George E. 23
Dawkins, Wayne 20
Harris, Jay T. 19
Jarrett, Vernon D. 42
Lowe, Herbert 57
Madison, Paula 37
Payne, Les 89
Pressley, Condace L. 41
Rice, Linda Johnson 9, 41
Shipp, E. R. 15
Stone, Chuck 9
Washington, Laura S. 18

National Association of Colored Women (NACW)
Bethune, Mary McLeod 4
Cooper, Margaret J. 46
Harper, Frances Ellen Watkins 11
Lampkin, Daisy 19
Ruffin, Josephine St. Pierre 75
Stewart, Ella 39
Talbert, Mary B. 77
Terrell, Mary Church 9

National Association of Negro Business and Professional Women's Clubs
Vaughns, Cleopatra 46

National Association of Negro Musicians
Bonds, Margaret 39
Brown, Uzee 42

National Association of Regulatory Utility Commissioners
Colter, Cyrus, J. 36

National Association of Social Workers
Jackson, Judith D. 57
McMurray, Georgia L. 36

National Association for Stock Car Auto Racing
Lester, Bill 42, 85

National Baptist Convention USA
Bradley, J. Robert 65
Jones, E. Edward, Sr. 45
Lyons, Henry 12
Shaw, William J. 30
Thurston, Stephen J. 49

National Bar Association
Alexander, Joyce London 18
Alexander, Sadie Tanner Mossell 22
Archer, Dennis 7, 36
Bailey, Clyde 45
Hubbard, Arnette 38
McPhail, Sharon 2
Pincham, R. Eugene, Sr. 69
Quince, Peggy A. 69
Ray, Charlotte E. 60

Robinson, Malcolm S. 44
Thompson, Larry D. 39
Walker, Cora T. 68

National Basketball Players Association
Erving, Julius 18, 47
Ewing, Patrick 17, 73
Gourdine, Simon 11
Hunter, Billy 22

National Black Arts Festival (NBAF)
Borders, James 9
Brooks, Avery 9

National Black College Hall of Fame
Dortch, Thomas W., Jr. 45

National Black Farmers Association (NBFA)
Boyd, John W., Jr. 20, 72

National Black Fine Art Show
Wainwright, Joscelyn 46

National Black Gay and Lesbian Conference
Wilson, Phill 9

National Black Gay and Lesbian Leadership Forum (NB-GLLF)
Boykin, Keith 14
Carter, Mandy 11
Wilson, Phill 9

National Black Women's Health Project
Avery, Byllye Y. 66

National Book Award
Ellison, Ralph 7
Haley, Alex 4
Johnson, Charles 1, 82
Mackey, Nathaniel 75
Patterson, Orlando 4

National Broadcasting Company (NBC)
Allen, Byron 3, 24
Gumbel, Bryant 14, 80
Hinderas, Natalie 5
Holt, Lester 66
Ifill, Gwen 28
Johnson, Rodney Van 28
Madison, Paula 37
Reynolds, Star Jones 10, 27, 61
Roker, Al 12, 49
Simpson, Carole 6, 30
Thomas-Graham, Pamela 29
Williams, Montel 4, 57

National Brotherhood of Skiers (NBS)
Horton, Andre 33
Horton, Suki 33

National Center for Neighborhood Enterprise (NCNE)
Woodson, Robert L. 10

National Coalition of 100 Black Women (NCBW)
Mays, Leslie A. 41
McCabe, Jewell Jackson 10

National Coalition to Abolish the Dealth Penalty (NCADP)
Hawkins, Steven 14

National Council of Churches
Howard, M. William, Jr. 26

National Council of Negro Women (NCNW)
Bethune, Mary McLeod 4
Blackwell, Unita 17
Cole, Johnnetta B. 5, 43
Hamer, Fannie Lou 6
Height, Dorothy I. 2, 23, 78
Lampkin, Daisy 19
Sampson, Edith S. 4
Smith, Jane E. 24
Staupers, Mabel K. 7

National Council of Nigeria and the Cameroons (NCNC)
Azikiwe, Nnamdi 13

National Council of Teachers of Mathematics
Granville, Evelyn Boyd 36

National Council on the Arts
Robinson, Cleo Parker 38

National Cowboys of Color Museum and Hall of Fame
Austin, Gloria 63
Austin, Jim 63
Pickett, Bill 11
Pride, Charley 26
Sampson, Charles 13

National Dental Association
Madison, Romell 45

National Earthquake Information Center
Person, Waverly 9, 51

National Education Association (NEA)
Futrell, Mary Hatwood 33

National Endowment for the Arts (NEA)
Barthé, Earl 78
Bradley, David Henry, Jr. 39
Brown, Chuck 78
Hall, Arthur 39
Hemphill, Essex 10
Pope.L, William 72
Serrano, Andres 3
Williams, John A. 27
Williams, William T. 11

National Endowment for the Arts Jazz Hall of Fame
Terry, Clark 39

National Endowment for the Humanities
Gibson, Donald Bernard 40

National Equal Rights League
Trotter, Monroe 9

National Football League (NFL)
Alexander, Shaun 58
Allen, Marcus 20
Anderson, Jamal 22

Barber, Ronde 41
Barber, Tiki 57
Barney, Lem 26
Bettis, Jerome 64
Briscoe, Marlin 37
Brooks, Aaron 33
Brooks, Derrick 43
Brown, Jim 11
Bruce, Isaac 26
Bryant, Cullen 81
Bush, Reggie 59, 88
Butler, Leroy, III 17
Caldwell, Jim 81
Cherry, Deron 40
Cox, Bryan 83
Crennel, Romeo 54
Croom, Sylvester 50
Culpepper, Daunte 32, 85
Cunningham, Randall 23
Davis, Milt 74
Davis, Terrell 20
Delaney, Joe 76
Dickerson, Eric 27
Duerson, Dave 93
Dunn, Warrick 90
Edwards, Herman 51
Farr, Mel 24
Faulk, Marshall 35
Fowler, Reggie 51
George, Eddie 80
Gilliam, Frank 23
Gilliam, Joe 31
Green, Darrell 39, 74
Green, Dennis 5, 45
Greene, Joe 10
Harris, James 79
Hill, Calvin 19
Holmes, Santonio 87
Howard, Desmond 16, 58
Irvin, Michael 64
Jackson, Rickey 88
Jackson, Tom 70
Johnson, Chris 92
Johnson, Keyshawn 91
Johnson, Levi 48
Jones, Deacon 92
Ladd, Ernie 64
Lane, Dick 92
Little, Floyd 86
Little, Larry 90
Lofton, James 42
Lott, Ronnie 9
Matson, Ollie 93
Mayhew, Martin R. 76
McDaniel, Randall Cornell 81
McNair, Steve 22, 47, 79
Monk, Art 38, 73
Moon, Warren 8, 66
Moss, Randy 23, 90
Motley, Marion 26
Newsome, Ozzie 26
Oliver, Pam 54
Owens, Terrell 53
Pace, Orlando 21
Page, Alan 7
Payton, Walter 11, 25
Peete, Rodney 60
Pryce, Trevor 89
Randle, John 87
Rashad, Ahmad 18
Rhodes, Ray 14
Rice, Jerry 5, 55, 89
Sanders, Barry 1, 53

Sanders, Bob 72
Sanders, Deion 4, 31
Sapp, Warren 38
Sayers, Gale 28
Sharper, Darren 32
Shell, Art 1, 66
Simpson, O.J. 15
Singletary, Mike 4, 76
Smith, Bruce 80
Smith, DeMaurice 92
Smith, Emmitt 7, 87
Smith, Rick 72
Stewart, Kordell 21
Stingley, Darryl 69
Strahan, Michael 35, 81
Stringer, Korey 35
Swann, Lynn 28
Tatum, Jack 87
Taylor, Jason 70
Taylor, Lawrence 25
Thomas, Derrick 25
Thomas, Emmitt 71
Thomas, Thurman 75
Thrower, Willie 35
Toler, Burl 80
Tomlinson, LaDainian 65
Tunnell, Emlen 54
Upshaw, Gene 18, 47, 72
Vick, Michael 39, 65, 94
Vincent, Troy 91
Walker, Herschel 1, 69
Ward, Hines 84
Ware, Andre 37
Ware, DeMarcus 92
Washington, Kenny 50
White, Reggie 6, 50
Williams, Doug 22
Williams, J. Mayo 83
Williams, Ricky 85
Williamson, Fred 67
Winslow, Kellen 83
Wright, Rayfield 70

National Heritage "Living Treasure" Fellowship
Jackson, John 36

National Hockey League (NHL)
Brashear, Donald 39
Brathwaite, Fred 35
Brown, Sean 52
Doig, Jason 45
Fuhr, Grant 1, 49
Grand-Pierre, Jean-Luc 46
Grier, Mike 43
Iginla, Jarome 35
Laraque, Georges 48
Mayers, Jamal 39
McBride, Bryant 18
McCarthy, Sandy 64
McKegney, Tony 3
O'Ree, Willie 5
Salvador, Bryce 51
Weekes, Kevin 67

National Institute of Arts & Letters
Lewis, Norman 39
White, Charles 39

National Institute of Education
Baker, Gwendolyn Calvert 9

National Institutes of Health (NIH)
Anderson, Norman B. 45
Cargill, Victoria A. 43
Dunston, Georgia Mae 48
Pinn, Vivian Winona 49

National Inventors Hall of Fame
Carruthers, George R. 40

National Lawn & Garden Distributor Association
Donald, Arnold Wayne 36

National Medical Association
Cole, Lorraine 48
Giles, Roscoe C. 93
Maxey, Randall 46
Ojikutu, Bisola 65

National Minority Business Council
Leary, Kathryn D. 10

National Museum of American History
Crew, Spencer R. 55
Reagon, Bernice Johnson 7

National Negro Congress
Bunche, Ralph J. 5

National Negro Suffrage League
Trotter, Monroe 9

National Newspaper Publishers Association
Cooper, Andrew W. 36
Jealous, Benjamin 70
Oliver, John J., Jr. 48

National Oceanic and Atmospheric Administration
Bacon-Bercey, June 38
Fields, Evelyn J. 27

National Organization for Women (NOW)
Hernandez, Aileen Clarke 13
Kennedy, Florynce 12, 33
Murray, Pauli 38

National Political Congress of Black Women
Chisholm, Shirley 2, 50
Tucker, C. Delores 12, 56
Waters, Maxine 3, 67

National Public Radio (NPR)
Abu-Jamal, Mumia 15
Bates, Karen Grigsby 40
Drummond, William J. 40
Early, Gerald 15
Lewis, Delano 7
Mitchell, Elvis 67
Norris, Michele 83
Smiley, Tavis 20, 68
Williams, Juan 35, 80
Zook, Kristal Brent 62

National Resistance Army (Uganda; NRA)
Museveni, Yoweri 4

National Resistance Movement
Museveni, Yoweri 4

National Revolutionary Movement for Development
See Mouvement Revolutionnaire National pour le Developpement

National Rifle Association (NRA)
Williams, Robert F. 11

National Science Foundation (NSF)
Jackson, Deborah 94
Massey, Walter E. 5, 45

National Security Council
Frazer, Jendayi 68
Powell, Colin 1, 28, 75
Rice, Condoleezza 3, 28, 72
Rice, Susan E. 74
Sutphen, Mona 77

National Society of Black Engineers
Donald, Arnold Wayne 36
Price, Richard 51

National Union for the Total Independence of Angola (UNITA)
Roberto, Holden 65
Savimbi, Jonas 2, 34

National Union of Mineworkers (South Africa)
Motlanthe, Kgalema 74
Ramaphosa, Cyril 3

National Urban Coalition (NUC)
Edelin, Ramona Hoage 19

National Urban League
Barrow, Willie T. 85
Berry, Edwin C. 81
Brown, Ron 5
Gordon, Bruce S. 41, 53, 82
Granger, Lester B. 75
Greely, M. Gasby 27
Haynes, George Edmund 8
Jacob, John E. 2
Jones, Eugene Kinckle 79
Jordan, Vernon E. 3, 35
Price, Hugh B. 9, 54
Spriggs, William 67
Young, Whitney M., Jr. 4

National War College
Clemmons, Reginal G. 41

National Wildlife Federation
Osborne, Na'taki 54

National Women's Hall of Fame
Cary, Mary Ann Shadd 30
Kelly, Leontine 33
Talbert, Mary B. 77

National Youth Administration (NYA)
Bethune, Mary McLeod 4
Primus, Pearl 6

Nationwide
James, Donna A. **51**

Naval Research Laboratory (NRL)
Carruthers, George R. **40**

NBAF
See National Black Arts Festival

NBC
See National Broadcasting Company

NBGLLF
See National Black Gay and Lesbian Leadership Forum

NCBL
See National Conference on Black Lawyers

NCBW
See National Coalition of 100 Black Women

NCCK
See Kenya National Council of Churches

NCNE
See National Center for Neighborhood Enterprise

NCNW
See National Council of Negro Women

NEA
See National Education Association; National Endowment for the Arts

Nebula awards
Butler, Octavia **8, 43, 58**
Delany, Samuel R., Jr. **9**

Négritude
Césaire, Aimé **48, 69**
Damas, Léon-Gontran **46**
Ndiaye, Iba **74**

Negro American Political League
Trotter, Monroe **9**

Negro Ensemble Company
Cash, Rosalind **28**
Gordon, Carl **87**
Hooks, Robert **76**
Rolle, Esther **13, 21**
Schultz, Michael A. **6**
Ward, Douglas Turner **42**

Negro Leagues
Banks, Ernie **33**
Barnhill, David **30**
Bell, James "Cool Papa" **36**
Black, Joe **75**
Brown, Willard **36**
Campanella, Roy **25**
Charleston, Oscar **39**
Dandridge, Ray **36**
Davis, Piper **19**
Day, Leon **39**
Foster, Andrew **79**
Gibson, Josh **22**
Hairston, Sam **88**

Hyde, Cowan F. "Bubba" **47**
Irvin, Monte **31**
Johnson, Clifford "Connie" **52**
Johnson, Mamie "Peanut" **40**
Kaiser, Cecil **42**
Kimbro, Henry A. **25**
Leonard, Buck **67**
Lloyd, John Henry "Pop" **30**
Mackey, Biz **82**
Morton, Ferdinand Q. **90**
O'Neil, Buck **19, 59**
Paige, Satchel **7**
Pride, Charley **26**
Radcliffe, Ted **74**
Smith, Hilton **29**
Stearnes, Norman "Turkey" **31**
Stone, Toni **15**

Netherlands Antilles government
Liberia-Peters, Maria Philomena **12**

Neurosurgery
Black, Keith Lanier **18, 84**
Canady, Alexa **28**
Carson, Benjamin **1, 35, 76**
Dennis, Gary C. **91**

Neustadt International Prize for Literature
Brathwaite, Kamau **36**

Nevada state government
Horsford, Steven **88**

New Jersey state government
Bryant, Wayne R. **6**
Payne, William D. **60**

New Life Community Choir
Kee, John P. **43**

New Negro movement
See Harlem Renaissance

New Orleans city government
Henry, Troy **85**
Mason, Ronald **27**
Nagin, Ray **42, 57, 88**
Perry, James **83**

New Orleans Saints football team
Brooks, Aaron **33**
Mills, Sam **33**

New York City government
Campbell, Mary Schmidt **43**
Crew, Rudolph F. **16**
Davis, Gordon J. **76**
Dinkins, David **4**
Farrell, Herman D., Jr. **81**
Fields, C. Virginia **25**
Ford, Wallace **58**
Hageman, Hans **36**
Paterson, Basil A. **69**
Spigner, Archie **81**
Sutton, Percy E. **42**
Thompson, William **35**
Tolbert, Terence **74**

New York Coalition of 100 Black Woman
Wein, Joyce **62**

New York Daily News
Cose, Ellis **5, 50**

New York Drama Critics Circle Award
Hansberry, Lorraine **6**

New York Giants baseball team
Dandridge, Ray **36**
Mays, Willie **3**
Tunnell, Emlen **54**

New York Giants football team
Barber, Tiki **57**
Strahan, Michael **35, 81**
Taylor, Lawrence **25**

New York Jets football team
Lott, Ronnie **9**

New York Knicks basketball team
Ewing, Patrick **17, 73**
Johnson, Larry **28**
Reed, Willis, Jr. **86**
Sprewell, Latrell **23**
Stith, Tom **93**

New York Mets baseball team
Clendenon, Donn **26, 56**
Manuel, Jerry **94**

New York Philharmonic
DePreist, James **37**

New York Public Library
Baker, Augusta **38**
Dodson, Howard, Jr. **7, 52**
Schomburg, Arthur Alfonso **9**

New York Shakespeare Festival
Browne, Roscoe Lee **66**
Gunn, Moses **10**
Wolfe, George C. **6, 43**

New York state government
Brown, Byron W. **72**
Farrell, Herman D., Jr. **81**
McCall, H. Carl **27**
Meeks, Gregory **25**
Motley, Constance Baker **10, 55**
Owens, Major **6**
Paterson, Basil A. **69**
Paterson, David A. **59**
Smith, Malcolm A. **75**

New York State Supreme Court
Dudley, Edward R. **58**
Wright, Bruce McMarion **3, 52**

New York Stock Exchange
Doley, Harold, Jr. **26**

New York Times
Blair, Jayson **50**
Blow, Charles M. **73**
Boyd, Gerald M. **32, 59**
Broyard, Anatole **68**
Caldwell, Earl **60**
Cooper, Helene **74**
Davis, George **36**
Hunter-Gault, Charlayne **6, 31**
Ifill, Gwen **28**
Mabry, Marcus **70**

Price, Hugh B. **9, 54**
Rhoden, William C. **67**
Wilkins, Roger **2, 84**

New York University
Brathwaite, Kamau **36**
Campbell, Mary Schmidt **43**
Newkirk, Pamela **69**

New York Yankees baseball team
Baylor, Don **6**
Bonds, Bobby **43**
Jackson, Reggie **15**
Jeter, Derek **27, 93**
Sabathia, CC **74**
Strawberry, Darryl **22**
Watson, Bob **25**
Winfield, Dave **5, 91**

Newark (NJ) city government
Booker, Cory Anthony **68**
Gibson, Kenneth Allen **6**
James, Sharpe **23, 69**

Newark Housing Authority
Gibson, Kenneth Allen **6**

The News Hour with Jim Lehrer TV series
Ifill, Gwen **28**

Newsday
Olojede, Dele **59**

Newsweek
Mabry, Marcus **70**

NFL
See National Football League

NHL
See National Hockey League

Niagara movement
Du Bois, W. E. B. **3**
Hope, John **8**
Talbert, Mary B. **77**
Trotter, Monroe **9**

Nickelodeon
DJ Lance Rock **94**
Thompson, Kenan **52**

Nigerian Armed Forces
Abacha, Sani **11, 70**
Abiola, Moshood **70**
Babangida, Ibrahim **4**
Obasanjo, Olusegun **5, 22**

Nigerian Association of Patriotic Writers and Artists
Barrett, Lindsay **43**

Nigerian government
Abiola, Moshood **70**
Abubakar, Abdulsalami **66**
Akunyili, Dora Nkem **58**
Jonathan, Goodluck **83**
Obasanjo, Olusegun **5**
Yar'Adua, Umaru **69, 89**

Nigerian literature
Achebe, Chinua **6**
Akpan, Uwem **70**
Amadi, Elechi **40**
Bandele, Biyi **68**

Barrett, Lindsay 43
Ekwensi, Cyprian 37
Onwueme, Tess Osonye 23
Rotimi, Ola 1
Saro-Wiwa, Kenule 39
Soyinka, Wole 4, 93

Nigerien government
Tandja, Mamadou 33, 78

NIH
See National Institutes of Health

Nike, Inc.
Edwards, Trevor 54
Miller, Larry G. 72

Nobel Peace Prize
Annan, Kofi Atta 15, 48
Bunche, Ralph J. 5
King, Martin Luther, Jr. 1
Luthuli, Albert 13
Tutu, Desmond Mpilo 6, 44

Nobel Prize for Literature
Morrison, Toni 2, 15, 86
Soyinka, Wole 4, 93
Walcott, Derek 5, 94

Noma Award for Publishing in African
Ba, Mariama 30

Nonfiction
Abrahams, Peter 39
Adams-Ender, Clara 40
Ali, Hana Yasmeen 52
Allen, Debbie 13, 42
Allen, Robert L. 38
Andrews, Tina 74
Atkins, Cholly 40
Baisden, Michael 66
Ballard, Allen Butler, Jr. 40
Bashir, Halima 73
Beah, Ishmael 69
Blassingame, John Wesley 40
Blockson, Charles L. 42
Bogle, Donald 34
Brown, Cecil M. 46
Brown, Lloyd Louis 42
Broyard, Bliss 68
Buckley, Gail Lumet 39
Carby, Hazel 27
Carter, Joye Maureen 41
Carter, Stephen L. 4
Cashin, Sheryll 63
Cobb, William Jelani 59
Cole, Johnnetta B. 5, 43
Cook, Mercer 40
Cox, Joseph Mason Andrew 51
Crew, Spencer R. 55
Cruse, Harold 54
Danquah, Meri Nana Ama 93
Datcher, Michael 60
Davis, Angela J. 88
Davis, Arthur P. 41
Davis, Thulani 61
Dickerson, Debra J. 60
Dunnigan, Alice Allison 41
Edelman, Marian Wright 5, 42
Elliott, Lorris 37
Fax, Elton 48
Fine, Sam 60
Finner-Williams, Paris Michele 62
Fisher, Antwone 40

Fletcher, Bill, Jr. 41
Ford, Clyde W. 40
Foster, Cecil 32
Gayle, Addison, Jr. 41
Gibson, Donald Bernard 40
Gladwell, Malcolm 62
Greenwood, Monique 38
Harrison, Alvin 28
Harrison, Calvin 28
Henderson, David 53
Henries, A. Doris Banks 44
Henriques, Julian 37
Hercules, Frank 44
Hernton, Calvin C. 51
Hill, Errol 40
Hobson, Julius W. 44
Horne, Frank 44
Ilibagiza, Immaculée 66
Jakes, Thomas "T. D." 17, 43
Johnson, Sandra K. 94
Johnson, William 91
Jolley, Willie 28
Jordan, Vernon E. 7, 35
Kayira, Legson 40
Kearney, Janis 54
Kennedy, Randall 40
Knight, Etheridge 37
Kobia, Samuel 43
Ladner, Joyce A. 42
Lampley, Oni Faida 43, 71
Lane, Lunsford 93
Lincoln, C. Eric 38
Mabuza-Suttle, Felicia 43
Malveaux, Julianne 32, 70
Manley, Ruth 34
Matthews Shatteen, Westina 51
McKenzie, Vashti M. 29
McKinney Hammond, Michelle 51
McWhorter, John 35
Mossell, Gertrude Bustill 40
Murray, Pauli 38
Myers, Walter Dean 8, 20
Naylor, Gloria 10, 42
Neal, Mark Anthony 74
Newkirk, Pamela 69
Nissel, Angela 42
Norton, Meredith 72
Parks, Rosa 1, 35, 56
Pitts, Leonard, Jr. 54, 85
Run 31, 73
Rusesabagina, Paul 60
Sadlier, Rosemary 62
Shakur, Yusef 85
Smith, Jessie Carney 35
Steele, Shelby 13, 82
Thornton, Yvonne S. 69
Tillis, Frederick 40
Wade-Gayles, Gloria Jean 41
Walker, Rebecca 50
Wambugu, Florence 42
Wilkens, J. Ernest, Jr. 43
Williams, Terrie 35
Williams, Wendy 62
Wiwa, Ken 67
Wright, Nathan, Jr. 56
Zook, Kristal Brent 62

North Carolina state government
Ballance, Frank W. 41
Fuller, Thomas O. 90

North Carolina State University
Lowe, Sidney 64

North Pole
Counter, S. Allen 74
Delany, Martin R. 27
Henson, Matthew 2
Hillary, Barbara 65
McLeod, Gus 27

NOW
See National Organization for Women

NPR
See National Public Radio

NRA
See National Resistance Army (Uganda); National Rifle Association

NRL
See Naval Research Laboratory

NSF
See National Science Foundation

Nuclear energy
O'Leary, Hazel 6
Packer, Daniel 56
Quarterman, Lloyd Albert 4

Nuclear Regulatory Commission
Jackson, Shirley Ann 12

Nucleus
King, Yolanda 6
Shabazz, Attallah 6

Nursing
Adams-Ender, Clara 40
Auguste, Rose-Anne 13
Hillary, Barbara 65
Hughes, Ebony 57
Hunter, Alberta 42
Johnson, Hazel 22
Johnson, Mamie "Peanut" 40
Larsen, Nella 10
Lewis, Daurene 72
Lyttle, Hulda Margaret 14
Richards, Hilda 49
Riley, Helen Caldwell Day 13
Robinson, Rachel 16
Robinson, Sharon 22
Seacole, Mary 54
Shabazz, Betty 7, 26
Staupers, Mabel K. 7
Taylor, Susie King 13

Nutrition
Clark, Celeste 15
Gregory, Dick 1, 54
Smith, Ian 62
Watkins, Shirley R. 17

Nuwaubianism
York, Dwight D. 71

NYA
See National Youth Administration

Nyasaland African Congress (NAC)
Banda, Hastings Kamuzu 6, 54

Oakland Athletics baseball team
Baylor, Don 6
Henderson, Rickey 28, 78
Jackson, Reggie 15

Oakland Raiders football team
Howard, Desmond 16, 58
Tatum, Jack 87
Upshaw, Gene 18, 47, 72

Oakland Tribune
Bailey, Chauncey 68
Maynard, Nancy Hicks 73
Maynard, Robert C. 7

OAU
See Organization of African Unity

Obie awards
Browne, Roscoe Lee 66
Carter, Nell 39
De Shields, André 72
Freeman, Yvette 27
Orlandersmith, Dael 42
Sands, Diana 87
Thigpen, Lynne 17, 41

Office of Civil Rights
See U.S. Department of Education

Office of Management and Budget
Raines, Franklin Delano 14

Ohio state government
Brown, Les 5
Ford, Jack 39
Stokes, Carl 10, 73
White, Michael R. 5
Williams, George Washington 18

Ohio Women's Hall of Fame
Craig-Jones, Ellen Walker 44
Stewart, Ella 39

OKeh record label
Brooks, Hadda 40
Mo', Keb' 36

Oklahoma Eagle
Ross, Don 27

Oklahoma Hall of Fame
Mitchell, Leona 42

Oklahoma state government
Ross, Don 27

Olatunji Center for African Culture
Olatunji, Babatunde 36

Olympics
Ali, Muhammad 2, 16, 52
Beamon, Bob 30
Bekele, Kenenisa 75
Bolt, Usain 73
Bonaly, Surya 7
Bonheur, Yannick 84
Bowe, Riddick 6
Christie, Linford 8
Clay, Bryan 57, 74
Coachman, Alice 18
Davis, Shani 58, 84
Dawes, Dominique 11
DeFrantz, Anita 37

DeGale, James **74**
Devers, Gail **7, 87**
Dibaba, Tirunesh **73**
Edwards, Teresa **14**
Ervin, Anthony **66**
Eto'o, Samuel **73**
Felix, Allyson **48**
Flowers, Vonetta **35**
Freeman, Cathy **29**
Garrison, Zina **2**
Gebrselassie, Haile **70**
Gourdin, Edward O. **93**
Gourdine, Meredith **33**
Greene, Maurice **27, 77**
Griffith, Yolanda **25**
Griffith-Joyner, Florence **28**
Harrison, Alvin **28**
Harrison, Calvin **28**
Harris-Stewart, Lusia **90**
Hayes, Bob **77**
Hines, Garrett **35**
Holmes, Kelly **47**
Holyfield, Evander **6**
Howard, Sherri **36**
Iginla, Jarome **35**
James, G. Larry **74**
James, Vanessa **84**
Johnson, Ben **1**
Johnson, Michael **13**
Johnson, Rafer **33**
Jones, Cullen **73**
Jones, Lou **64**
Jones, Randy **35**
Joyner-Kersee, Jackie **5**
Keflezighi, Meb **49**
Kidd, Jason **86**
Lewis, Carl **4**
Malone, Karl **18, 51, 90**
Matson, Ollie **93**
Metcalfe, Ralph **26**
Miller, Cheryl **10, 74**
Montgomery, Tim **41**
Moses, Edwin **8**
Mutola, Maria **12**
Owens, Jesse **2**
Powell, Mike **7**
Quirot, Ana **13**
Richards, Sanya **66**
Rudolph, Wilma **4**
Scurry, Briana **27**
Thomas, Debi **26**
Thugwane, Josia **21**
Vanessa James and Yannick Bonheur **84**
Wanjiru, Sammy **94**
Ward, Andre **62**
Ward, Lloyd **21, 46**
Westbrook, Peter **20**
Whitaker, Pernell **10, 89**
White, Willye **67**
Whitfield, Mal **60**
Williams, Lauryn **58**
Woodruff, John **68**

***On a Roll* Radio**
Smith, Greg **28**

Oncology
Leffall, Lasalle **3, 64**

100 Black Men of America
Dortch, Thomas W., Jr. **45**
Llewellyn, J. Bruce **13, 85**

Ontario Legislature
Curling, Alvin **34**

Opera
Adams, Leslie **39**
Allen, Betty **83**
Anderson, Marian **2, 33**
Arroyo, Martina **30**
Battle, Kathleen **70**
Brooks, Avery **9**
Brown, Angela M. **54**
Brown, Anne **76**
Brown, Uzee **42**
Brownlee, Lawrence **88**
Bumbry, Grace **5**
Collins, Janet **33, 64**
Conrad, Barbara Smith **90**
Davis, Anthony **11**
Dobbs, Mattiwilda **34**
Duncan, Todd **76**
Estes, Simon **28**
Freeman, Paul **39**
Graves, Denyce Antoinette **19, 57**
Greely, M. Gasby **27**
Grist, Reri **84**
Hendricks, Barbara **3, 67**
Joplin, Scott **6**
Joyner, Matilda Sissieretta **15**
Lister, Marquita **65**
Matthews, Benjamin **93**
Maynor, Dorothy **19**
McDonald, Audra **20, 62**
McFerrin, Robert, Sr. **94**
Mitchell, Leona **42**
Norman, Jessye **5**
Phillips, Helen L. **63**
Price, Leontyne **1**
Ragin, Derek Lee **84**
Simpson-Hoffman, N'kenge **52**
Still, William Grant **37**
Three Mo' Tenors **35**
Verrett, Shirley **66, 91**
Warfield, William **94**
White, Willard **53**

Operation Desert Shield/Operation Desert Storm
Powell, Colin **1, 28, 75**

Operation HOPE
Bryant, John **26**

Ophthalmology
Bath, Patricia E. **37**

Oracle Corporation
Phillips, Charles E., Jr. **57**
Woods, Jacqueline **52**

Organ
McGriff, Jimmy **72**

Organization of African States
Museveni, Yoweri **4**

Organization of African Unity (OAU)
Diouf, Abdou **3**
Haile Selassie **7**
Kaunda, Kenneth **2**
Kenyatta, Jomo **5**
Nkrumah, Kwame **3**
Nujoma, Samuel **10**
Nyerere, Julius **5**

Touré, Sekou **6**

Organization of Women Writers of African Descent
Cortez, Jayne **43**

Organization Us
Karenga, Maulana **10, 71**

Orlando Magic basketball team
Erving, Julius **18, 47**
O'Neal, Shaquille **8, 30**

Osteopathy
Allen, Ethel D. **13**
Anderson, William G(ilchrist) **57**
Ross-Lee, Barbara **67**

Overbrook Entertainment
Pinkett Smith, Jada **10, 41**

Painting
Alston, Charles **33**
Amos, Emma **63**
Andrews, Benny **22, 59**
Bailey, Radcliffe **19**
Bannister, Edward Mitchell **88**
Barnes, Ernie **16, 78**
Barthe, Richmond **15**
Basquiat, Jean-Michel **5**
Bearden, Romare **2, 50**
Beasley, Phoebe **34**
Biggers, John **20, 33**
Bradford, Mark **89**
Campbell, E. Simms **13**
Colescott, Robert **69**
Collins, Paul **61**
Cortor, Eldzier **42**
Cowans, Adger W. **20**
Crichlow, Ernest **75**
Crite, Alan Rohan **29**
Davis, Bing **84**
Delaney, Beauford **19**
Delaney, Joseph **30**
Delsarte, Louis **34**
Douglas, Aaron **7**
Driskell, David C. **7**
Ferguson, Amos **81**
Freeman, Leonard **27**
Gilliam, Sam **16**
Goodnight, Paul **32**
Green, Jonathan **54**
Guyton, Tyree **9, 94**
Harkless, Necia Desiree **19**
Hayden, Palmer **13**
Holder, Geoffrey **78**
Honeywood, Varnette P. **54, 88**
Hunter, Clementine **45**
Jackson, Earl **31**
Johnson, William Henry **3**
Jones, Lois Mailou **13**
Knight, Gwendolyn **63**
Knox, Simmie **49**
Lawrence, Jacob **4, 28**
Lee, Annie Frances **22**
Lee-Smith, Hughie **5, 22**
Lewis, Norman **39**
Lewis, Samella **25**
Ligon, Glenn **82**
Loving, Alvin, Jr. **35, 53**
Major, Clarence **9**
Marshall, Kerry James **59**
Mayhew, Richard **39**
McGee, Charles **10**

Mehretu, Julie **85**
Mitchell, Corinne **8**
Motley, Archibald, Jr. **30**
Mutu, Wangechi **44**
Nascimento, Abdias do **93**
Ndiaye, Iba **74**
Neals, Otto **73**
Nugent, Richard Bruce **39**
Ouattara **43**
Pierre, Andre **17**
Pindell, Howardena **55**
Pippin, Horace **9**
Porter, James A. **11**
Ransome, James E. **88**
Reid, Senghor **55**
Ringgold, Faith **4, 81**
Ruley, Ellis **38**
Sallee, Charles **38**
Sebree, Charles **40**
Smith, Vincent D. **48**
Sudduth, Jimmy Lee **65**
Tanksley, Ann **37**
Tanner, Henry Ossawa **1**
Thomas, Alma **14**
Thomas, Mickalene **61**
Tolliver, Mose **60**
Tolliver, William **9**
Verna, Gelsy **70**
Wagner, Albert **78**
Washington, James, Jr. **38**
Wells, James Lesesne **10**
White, Charles **39**
Wiley, Kehinde **62**
Williams, Billy Dee **8**
Williams, William T. **11**
Wilson, Ellis **39**
Woodruff, Hale **9**

Pan African Orthodox Christian Church
Agyeman, Jaramogi Abebe **10, 63**

Pan-Africanism
Carmichael, Stokely **5, 26**
Clarke, John Henrik **20**
Du Bois, David Graham **45**
Du Bois, W. E. B. **3**
Garvey, Marcus **1**
Haile Selassie **7**
Kenyatta, Jomo **5**
Logan, Rayford W. **40**
Madhubuti, Haki **7, 85**
Marshall, Paule **7, 77**
Nkrumah, Kwame **3**
Nyerere, Julius **5**
Touré, Sekou **6**
Turner, Henry McNeal **5**

Papal Medal
Hampton, Lionel **17, 41**

Parti Démocratique de la Côte d'Ivoire (Democratic Party of the Ivory Coast; PDCI)
Bedie, Henri Konan **21**
Houphouët-Boigny, Félix **4, 64**

PATC
See Performing Arts Training Center

Pathology
Fuller, Solomon Carter, Jr. **15**

PBS
See Public Broadcasting Service

PDCI
See Parti Démocratique de la Côte d'Ivoire (Democratic Party of the Ivory Coast)

PDP
See People's Democratic Party

Peace Corps
See U.S. Peace Corps

Peck School of the Fine Arts
Tyson, Andre **40**

Pediatrics
Carson, Benjamin **1, 35, 76**
Elders, Joycelyn **6**
Fennoy, Ilene **72**
Witt, Edwin T. **26**
Zuma, Nkosazana Dlamini **34**

PEN/Faulkner award
Bradley, David Henry, Jr. **39**
Mayhew, Richard **39**
Wideman, John Edgar **5, 87**

Pennsylvania state government
Allen, Ethel D. **13**
Brown, Homer S. **47**
Fattah, Chaka **11, 70**
Irvis, K. Leroy **67**
Nix, Robert N. C., Jr. **51**

Pennsylvania State University
Dunn, Jerry **27**

Pennsylvania Supreme Court
Baldwin, Cynthia A. **74**

Pentecostal church
DuBois, Joshua **88**
Patterson, Gilbert Earl **41**
Patterson, J. O., Jr. **80**
Rivers, Eugene F., III **81**
Sapp, Marvin **74**
Wright, Timothy **74**

People United to Serve Humanity (PUSH)
Barrow, Willie T. **85**
Jackson, Jesse **1, 27, 72**
Jackson, Jesse, Jr. **14, 45, 81**

People's Democratic Party (Nigeria; PDP)
Jonathan, Goodluck **83**
Obasanjo, Stella **32**
Yar'Adua, Umaru **69, 89**

People's National Party (Jamaica; PNP)
Patterson, P. J. **6, 20**

People's Progressive Party (Gambia; PPP)
Jagan, Cheddi **16**
Jawara, Dawda Kairaba **11**

PepsiCo Inc.
Banks, Paula A. **68**
Boyd, Edward **70**

Harvey, William R. **42**

Performing Arts Training Center (PATC)
Dunham, Katherine **4, 59**

Perkins Prize
Jones, Thomas W. **41**

PGA
See Professional Golfers' Association

Pharmaceutical research
Pickett, Cecil **39**

Pharmaceuticals
Flowers, Sylester **50**
Potter, Myrtle **40**

Pharmacist
Akunyili, Dora Nkem **58**
Flowers, Sylester **50**
Pickett, Cecil **39**
Stewart, Ella **39**

Phelps Stokes Fund
Patterson, Frederick Douglass **12**

Phi Beta Sigma Fraternity
Thomas, Arthur Ray **52**

Philadelphia city government
Allen, Ethel D. **13**
Goode, W. Wilson **4**
Nutter, Michael **69**
Street, John F. **24**

Philadelphia Eagles football team
Cunningham, Randall **23**
McNabb, Donovan **29**
Rhodes, Ray **14**
Vick, Michael **39, 65, 94**
White, Reggie **6, 50**

Philadelphia Flyers hockey team
Brashear, Donald **39**
Charleston, Oscar **39**

Philadelphia Phillies baseball team
Howard, Ryan **65**
Rollins, Jimmy **70**

Philadelphia public schools
Clayton, Constance **1**

Philadelphia 76ers basketball team
Barkley, Charles **5, 66**
Bol, Manute **1**
Chamberlain, Wilt **18, 47**
Erving, Julius **18, 47**
Iverson, Allen **24, 46**
Stackhouse, Jerry **30**

Philadelphia Warriors
Chamberlain, Wilt **18, 47**

Philanthropy
Banks, Paula A. **68**
Brown, Eddie C. **35**
Cooper, Evern **40**
Cosby, Bill **7, 26, 59**
Cosby, Camille **14, 80**
Dawson, Matel, Jr. **39**

Edley, Christopher **2, 48**
Gardner, Chris **65**
Golden, Marita **19**
Gray, Willie **46**
Johnson, Kevin **70**
Johnson, Sheila Crump **48**
Jones, Paul R. **76**
Lavizzo-Mourey, Risa **48**
Malone, Annie **13**
McCarty, Osceola **16**
Millines Dziko, Trish **28**
Pleasant, Mary Ellen **9**
Reeves, Rachel J. **23**
Thomas, Franklin A. **5, 49**
Waddles, Charleszetta "Mother" **10, 49**
Walker, Madame C. J. **7**
Washington, Pauletta Pearson **86**
Wein, Joyce **62**
White, Reggie **6, 50**
Williams, Fannie Barrier **27**
Wonder, Stevie **11, 53**

Philosophy
Appiah, Kwame Anthony **67**
Baker, Houston A., Jr. **6**
Hall, Stuart **78**
Piper, Adrian **71**
Toomer, Jean **6**
West, Cornel **5, 33, 80**

Phoenix Suns basketball team
Barkley, Charles **5, 66**
Heard, Gar **25**
Hill, Grant **13, 94**
Johnson, Kevin **70**

Photography
Andrews, Bert **13**
Barboza, Anthony **10**
Cowans, Adger W. **20**
Cox, Renée **67**
DeCarava, Roy **42, 81**
Hansen, Austin **88**
Harris, Lyle Ashton **83**
Hinton, Milt **30**
Jackson, Vera **40**
Lester, Julius **9**
Moutoussamy-Ashe, Jeanne **7**
Parks, Gordon **1, 35, 58**
Pinderhughes, John **47**
Robeson, Eslanda Goode **13**
Roble, Abdi **71**
Serrano, Andres **3**
Simpson, Lorna **4, 36**
Sleet, Moneta, Jr. **5**
Smith, Marvin **46**
Smith, Morgan **46**
Tanner, Henry Ossawa **1**
Thomas, Mickalene **61**
VanDerZee, James **6**
Weems, Carrie Mae **63**
White, John H. **27**
Williams, Clarence **70**
Willis, Deborah **85**

Photojournalism
Ashley-Ward, Amelia **23**
du Cille, Michel **74**
Jackson, Vera **40**
Moutoussamy-Ashe, Jeanne **7**
Parks, Gordon **1, 35, 58**
Sleet, Moneta, Jr. **5**
Van Lierop, Robert **53**

Wallace, William **75**
White, John H. **27**
Williams, Clarence **70**
Withers, Ernest C. **68, 88**
Yette, Samuel F. **63**

Physical therapy
Elders, Joycelyn **6**
Griffin, Bessie Blout **43**

Physics
Adkins, Rutherford H. **21**
Branson, Herman **87**
Carruthers, George R. **40**
Gates, Sylvester James, Jr. **15**
Gourdine, Meredith **33**
Imes, Elmer Samuel **39**
Jackson, Deborah **94**
Jackson, Shirley Ann **12**
Johnson, Anthony M. **92**
Massey, Walter E. **5, 45**
Tyson, Neil deGrasse **15, 65**

Piano
Adams, Leslie **39**
Allen, Geri **92**
Austin, Lovie **40**
Basie, Count **23**
Bonds, Margaret **39**
Brooks, Hadda **40**
Cartiér, Xam Wilson **41**
Cole, Nat "King" **17**
Coltrane, Alice **70**
Cook, Charles "Doc" **44**
Domino, Fats **20**
Donegan, Dorothy **19**
Duke, George **21**
Ellington, Duke **5**
Flanagan, Tommy **69**
Garner, Erroll **76**
Hancock, Herbie **20, 67**
Hardin Armstrong, Lil **39**
Harris, Barry **68**
Hayes, Isaac **20, 58, 73**
Hinderas, Natalie **5**
Hines, Earl "Fatha" **39**
Horn, Shirley **32, 56**
Jamal, Ahmad **69**
Johnson, Johnnie **56**
Jones, Hank **57, 86**
Joplin, Scott **6**
Keys, Alicia **32, 68**
Lee, Consuela **84**
Marsalis, Ellis **90**
McRae, Carmen **77**
Monk, Thelonious **1**
Moran, Jason **89**
Perkins, Pinetop **70**
Peterson, Oscar **52**
Powell, Bud **24**
Pratt, Awadagin **31**
Preston, Billy **39, 59**
Price, Florence **37**
Pritchard, Robert Starling **21**
Roberts, Marcus **19**
Robinson, Reginald R. **53**
Sample, Joe **51**
Schuyler, Philippa **50**
Scott, Hazel **66**
Silver, Horace **26**
Simone, Nina **15, 41**
Sun Ra **60**
Swann, Lynn **28**
Southern, Eileen **56**

Sykes, Roosevelt 20
Taylor, Billy 23, 92
Taylor, Cecil 70
Turner, Ike 68
Tyner, McCoy 92
Valdés, Bebo 75
Valdés, Chucho 89
Vaughan, Sarah 13
Walker, George 37
Waller, Fats 29
Watts, Andre 42
Webster, Katie 29
Williams, Mary Lou 15

Pittsburgh Pirates baseball team
Bonds, Barry 6, 34, 63
Clendenon, Donn 26, 56
Ellis, Dock 78
Stargell, Willie 29

Pittsburgh Steelers football team
Dungy, Tony 17, 42, 59
Gilliam, Joe 31
Greene, Joe 10
Perry, Lowell 30
Stargell, Willie 29
Stewart, Kordell 21
Swann, Lynn 28
Ward, Hines 84
Woodson, Rod 79

Planned Parenthood Federation of America Inc.
Wattleton, Faye 9

Playboy
Brown, Robert 65
Taylor, Karin 34

Playwright
Anthony, Trey 63
Arkadie, Kevin 17
Armah, Esther 87
Baldwin, James 1
Bandele, Biyi 68
Barrett, Lindsay 43
Beckham, Barry 41
Branch, William Blackwell 39
Brown, Cecil M. 46
Brown, Oscar, Jr. 53
Bullins, Ed 25
Caldwell, Benjamin 46
Carroll, Vinnette 29
Césaire, Aimé 48, 69
Chenault, John 40
Childress, Alice 15
Clark-Bekedermo, J. P. 44
Clarke, George 32
Cleage, Pearl 17, 64
Corthron, Kia 43
Cotter, Joseph Seamon, Sr. 40
Cox, Joseph Mason Andrew 51
Dadié, Bernard 34
Davis, Eisa 68
De Veaux, Alexis 44
Dent, Thomas C. 50
Dodson, Owen 38
Domingo, Colman 94
Elder, Larry, III 38
Evans, Mari 26
Farah, Nuruddin 27
Franklin, J. E. 44

Glover, Keith 79
Gordone, Charles 15
Gurira, Danai 73
Hansberry, Lorraine 6
Harris, Bill 72
Hayes, Teddy 40
Hill, Errol 40
Hill, Leslie Pinckney 44
Holder, Laurence 34
Hughes, Langston 4
Johnson, Georgia Douglas 41
Johnson, Je'Caryous 63
Jones, Sarah 39
Kennedy, Adrienne 11
Kente, Gibson 52
King, Woodie, Jr. 27
Kwei-Armah, Kwame 84
Lampley, Oni Faida 43, 71
Lee, Leslie 85
Long, Richard Alexander 65
Marechera, Dambudzo 39
McClinton, Marion Isaac 77
Milner, Ron 39
Mitchell, Loften 31
Moss, Carlton 17
Mugo, Micere Githae 32
Nottage, Lynn 66
Onwueme, Tess Osonye 23
Orlandersmith, Dael 42
Parks, Suzan-Lori 34, 85
Perry, Tyler 40, 54
Rahman, Aishah 37
Redwood, John Henry 78
Rhone, Trevor 80
Salter, Nikkole 73
Sanchez, Sonia 17, 51
Santiago-Hudson, Ruben 85
Schuyler, George Samuel 40
Sebree, Charles 40
Smith, Anna Deavere 6, 44
Talbert, David E. 34, 93
Taylor, Regina 9, 46
Teer, Barbara Ann 81
Thurman, Wallace 17
Tolson, Melvin B. 37
Walcott, Derek 5, 94
Ward, Douglas Turner 42
Wesley, Richard 73
Williams, Roy 89
Williams, Samm-Art 21
Wilson, August 7, 33, 55
Wilson, Tracey Scott 777
Wolfe, George C. 6, 43
Youngblood, Shay 32

PNP
See People's National Party (Jamaica)

Poet laureate (U.S.)
Dove, Rita 6, 78

Poetry
Abani, Chris 77
Adams, Jenoyne 60
Alexander, Elizabeth 75
Alexander, Margaret Walker 22
Allen, Samuel L. 38
Angelou, Maya 1, 15
Atkins, Russell 45
Aubert, Alvin 41
Baiocchi, Regina Harris 41
Bandele, Asha 36
Barrax, Gerald William 45

Barrett, Lindsay 43
Bell, James Madison 40
Bennett, Gwendolyn B. 59
Bennett, Louise 69
Berry, James 41
Bontemps, Arna 8
Boyd, Melba Joyce 86
Braithwaite, William Stanley 52
Brand, Dionne 32
Breeze, Jean "Binta" 37
Brooks, Gwendolyn 1, 28
Brown, Cecil M. 46
Brutus, Dennis 38
Burgess, Marjorie L. 55
Carter, Martin 49
Cartey, Wilfred 47
Césaire, Aimé 48, 69
Chenault, John 40
Cheney-Coker, Syl 43
Clark-Bekedermo, J. P. 44
Clarke, Cheryl 32
Clarke, George 32
Cleage, Pearl 17, 64
Cliff, Michelle 42
Clifton, Lucille 14, 64, 91
Coleman, Wanda 48
Cooper, Afua 53
Cornish, Sam 50
Cortez, Jayne 43
Cotter, Joseph Seamon, Sr. 40
Cox, Joseph Mason Andrew 51
Cuney, William Waring 44
Dabydeen, David 48
Dadié, Bernard 34
D'Aguiar, Fred 50
Damas, Léon-Gontran 46
Dandridge, Raymond Garfield 45
Danner, Margaret Esse 49
Datcher, Michael 60
Davis, Charles T. 48
Davis, Frank Marshall 47
De Veaux, Alexis 44
Dent, Thomas C. 50
Dodson, Owen 38
Dove, Rita 6, 78
Draper, Sharon Mills 16, 43
Dumas, Henry 41
Dunbar-Nelson, Alice Ruth Moore 44
Dungy, Camille 86
Emanuel, James A. 46
Evans, Mari 26
Fabio, Sarah Webster 48
Fair, Ronald L. 47
Figueroa, John J. 40
Fisher, Antwone 40
Fleming, Raymond 48
Forbes, Calvin 46
Ford, Nick Aaron 44
Frazier, Oscar 58
Gabre-Medhin, Tsegaye 64
Gilbert, Christopher 50
Goings, Russell 59
Goodison, Lorna 71
Harkless, Necia Desiree 19
Harper, Frances Ellen Watkins 11
Harper, Michael S. 34
Harris, Bill 72
Harris, Claire 34
Hayden, Robert 12
Henderson, David 53
Hernton, Calvin C. 51
Hill, Leslie Pinckney 44

Hoagland, Everett H. 45
Horne, Frank 44
Hughes, Langston 7
Jackson, Fred James 25
Joachim, Paulin 34
Johnson, Fenton 91
Johnson, Georgia Douglas 41
Johnson, Linton Kwesi 37
Jones, Sarah 39
Kay, Jackie 37
Keene, John 73
Knight, Etheridge 37
Laraque, Paul 67
Letson, Al 39
Lorde, Audre 6
Mackey, Nathaniel 75
Manley, Ruth 34
Marechera, Dambudzo 39
Matejka, Adrian 87
McClellan, George Marion 91
Moore, Jessica Care 30
Mugo, Micere Githae 32
Mullen, Harryette 34
Naylor, Gloria 10, 42
Neto, António Agostinho 43
Nugent, Richard Bruce 39
Okara, Gabriel 37
Parker, Pat 19
Peters, Lenrie 43
Philip, Marlene Nourbese 32
Powell, Kevin 31, 74
Quigless, Helen G. 49
Randall, Dudley 8, 55
Redmond, Eugene 23
Richards, Beah 30
Sanchez, Sonia 17, 51
Sapphire 14
Scott-Heron, Gil 94
Senghor, Léopold Sédar 12
Senior, Olive 37
Smith, Mary Carter 26
Spencer, Anne 27
Sundiata, Sekou 66
Tillis, Frederick 40
Tolson, Melvin B. 37
Touré, Askia (Muhammad Abu Bakr el) 47
Troupe, Quincy 83
van Sertima, Ivan 25
Walker, Margaret 29
Washington, James, Jr. 38
Weaver, Afaa Michael 37
Williams, Saul 31
Williams, Sherley Anne 25
Woods, Scott 55
Young, Al 82

Poetry Slam, Inc.
Woods, Scott 55

Political science
Ake, Claude 30
Cohen, Cathy J. 88
Dawson, Michael C. 63
Harris-Lacewell, Melissa 81
Skinner, Kiron K. 65
Walters, Ronald 83
Watson, Carlos 50

Politics
Adebari, Rotimi 83
Alexander, Archie Alphonso 14
Ali, Ayaan Hirsi 58, 92
Allen, Claude 68

Arthur, Owen 33
Austin, Junius C. 44
Avant, Clarence 19, 86
Baker, Thurbert 22
Ballance, Frank W. 41
Barnes, Melody 75
Barrow, Dean 69
Bass, Charlotta Spears 40
Belton, Sharon Sayles 9, 16
Bishop, Sanford D., Jr. 24
Blackwell, Unita 17
Boateng, Paul Yaw 56
Booker, Cory Anthony 68
Boye, Madior 30
Brazile, Donna 25, 70
Brown, Oscar, Jr. 53
Buckley, Victoria (Vikki) 24
Burris, Chuck 21
Burris, Roland W. 25, 75
Butler, Jerry 26
Cain, Herman 15, 92
Césaire, Aimé 48, 69
Chideya, Farai 14, 61
Christian-Green, Donna M. 17
Clayton, Eva M. 20
Coleman, Mary 46
Compton, John 65
Connerly, Ward 14
Cummings, Elijah E. 24
Curling, Alvin 34
Currie, Betty 21
Davis, Artur 41
Davis, James E. 50
Dixon, Julian C. 24
Dixon, Sheila 68
dos Santos, José Eduardo 43
Dymally, Mervyn 42
Edmonds, Terry 17
Ellison, Keith 59
Fields, C. Virginia 25
Fields, Julia 45
Fleming, Erik R. 75
Ford, Jack 39
Frazier, Ryan 89
Gordon, Pamela 17
Greenlee, Sam 48
Hatcher, Andrew T. 90
Hatcher, Richard G. 55
Henry, Aaron 19
Hilliard, Earl F. 24
Hobson, Julius W. 44
Holmes, Amy 69
Ingraham, Hubert A. 19
Isaac, Julius 34
Jackson, Mae 57
Jackson Lee, Sheila 20
James, Sharpe 23, 69
Jammeh, Yahya 23
Jarrett, Valerie 73
Jarvis, Charlene Drew 21
Jefferson, William J. 25, 72
Kabbah, Ahmad Tejan 23
Kabila, Joseph 30
Kariuki, J. M. 67
Kelley, Cliff 75
Lee, Barbara 25
Lumumba, Patrice 33
Maathai, Wangari 43
Magloire, Paul Eugène 68
Majette, Denise 41
McGlowan, Angela 64, 86
Metcalfe, Ralph 26
Millender-McDonald, Juanita 21, 61

Moore, Gwendolynne S. 55
Moore, Harry T. 29
Morial, Ernest "Dutch" 26
Morial, Marc H. 20, 51
Morton, Ferdinand Q. 90
Nelson, Sophia A. 93
Pereira, Aristides 30
Perry, Ruth 15
Pitta, Celso 17
Powell, Debra A. 23
Sankoh, Foday 74
Scott, David 41
Scott, Robert C. 23
Simmons, E. Denise 79
Simmons, Jamal 72
Sisulu, Sheila Violet Makate 24
Smith, Jennifer 21
Smith, Princella 86
Spencer, Winston Baldwin 68
Thompson, Bennie G. 26
Thurston, Baratunde 79
Touré, Amadou Toumani 18
Watkins, Joe 86
Watt, Melvin 26
Watts, J. C., Jr. 14, 38
Wheat, Alan 14
Williams, Anthony 21
Williams, Eddie N. 44
Williams, Eric Eustace 65
Williams, George Washington 18
Yar'Adua, Umaru 69, 89

Pop music
Ashanti 37
Ashford, Nickolas 21
Babyface 10, 31, 82
Bailey, Pearl 14
Bailey Rae, Corinne 83
Bassey, Shirley 25
Bleu, Corbin 65
Blige, Mary J. 20, 34, 60
Brown, Bobby 58
Brown, Melanie 73
Butler, Jonathan 28
Cannon, Nick 47, 73
Carey, Mariah 32, 53, 69
Cee-Lo 70
Chanté, Keshia 50
Checker, Chubby 28
Cole, Nat "King" 17
Coppola, Imani Francesca 82
Cox, Deborah 28
David, Craig 31, 53
Derülo, Jason 93
Duke, George 21
Ferrell, Rachelle 29
Franklin, Aretha 11, 44
Franklin, Kirk 15, 49
Gray, Macy 29
Hailey, JoJo 22
Hailey, K-Ci 22
Hawkins, Screamin' Jay 30
Hayes, Isaac 20, 58, 73
Hill, Lauryn 20, 53
Holmes, Clint 57
Horton, Gladys 92
Houston, Whitney 7, 28, 83
Hudson, Jennifer 63, 83
Humphrey, Bobbi 20
Isley, Ronald 25, 56
Jackson, Janet 6, 30, 68
Jackson, Jermaine 79
Jackson, Michael 19, 53, 76

James, Rick 17
Jarreau, Al 21, 65
Jones, Booker T. 84
Jones, Quincy 8, 30
Jordan, Montell 23
Kelis 58
Kendricks, Eddie 22
Keys, Alicia 32, 68
Khan, Chaka 12, 50
Kingston, Sean 94
LaBelle, Patti 13, 30
Lewis, Leona 75
Luckett, Letoya 61
Martelly, Michel 90
Massenburg, Kedar 23
Mathis, Johnny 20
McFerrin, Bobby 68
Monica 21
Moore, Chante 26
Mumba, Samantha 29
Mya 35
Neville, Aaron 21
Ne-Yo 65
Noah, Yannick 4, 60
Osborne, Jeffrey 26
Otis, Clyde 67
Palmer, Keke 68
P.M. Dawn 54
Preston, Billy 39, 59
Prince 18, 65
Reid, Antonio "L.A." 28
Reid, Vernon 34
Richie, Lionel 27, 65
Rihanna 65
Robinson, Smokey 3, 49
Rucker, Darius 34, 74
Seal 14, 75
Senghor, Léopold Sédar 12
Short, Bobby 52
Simpson, Valerie 21
Sisqo 30
Smith, Myrna 92
Smith, Willow 92
Staton, Candi 27
Summer, Donna 25
Supremes, The 33
Sweat, Keith 19
Temptations, The 33
The-Dream 74
Thomas, Irma 29
TLC 34
Turner, Tina 6, 27
Usher 23, 56
Vanity 67
Washington, Dinah 22
Washington, Grover, Jr. 17, 44
Washington, Val 12
Welch, Elisabeth 52
White, Barry 13, 41
White, Josh, Jr. 52
White, Maurice 29
will.i.am 64
Williams, Vanessa L. 4, 17
Wilson, Jackie 60
Wilson, Mary 28
Wilson, Nancy 10
Withers-Mendes, Elisabeth 64
Wonder, Stevie 11, 53

Portland (OR) Police Department
Moose, Charles 40

Portland Trail Blazers basketball team
Drexler, Clyde 4, 61
Miller, Larry G. 72
Porter, Terry 75

PPP
See People's Progressive Party
(Gambia)

Pratt Institute
Mayhew, Richard 39

Presbyterianism
Cannon, Katie 10

Pride Economic Enterprises
Barry, Marion S. 7, 44

Princeton University
Blanks, Deborah K. 69
Harris-Lacewell, Melissa 81
Rouse, Cecilia 93
Simmons, Ruth 13, 38

Printmaking
Blackburn, Robert 28
Crichlow, Ernest 75
Neals, Otto 73
Tanksley, Ann 37
Thrash, Dox 35
Wells, James Lesesne 10

Prison ministry
Bell, Ralph S. 5

Prison reform
Betts, R. Dwayne 86

Procter & Gamble
Clement-Holmes, Linda 94

Professional Golfers' Association (PGA)
Bramlett, Joseph 91
Elder, Lee 6
Powell, Renee 34
Sifford, Charlie 4, 49
Woods, Tiger 14, 31, 81

Professional Women's Club of Chicago
Gray, Ida 41

Progressive Labour Party
Smith, Jennifer 21

Progressive Party
Bass, Charlotta Spears 40

Proposition 209
Connerly, Ward 14

Prosecution
Darden, Christopher 13
Worthy, Kym 84

Provincial Freeman
Cary, Mary Ann Shadd 30

Psychiatry
Cobbs, Price M. 9
Comer, James P. 6
Fanon, Frantz 44
Fuller, Solomon Carter, Jr. 15
Hamburg, Beatrix 84
Poussaint, Alvin F. 5, 67

Welsing, Frances Cress 5

Psychic health
Ford, Clyde W. 40

Psychology
Anderson, Norman B. 45
Archie-Hudson, Marguerite 44
Brown, Joyce F. 25
Clark, Mamie Phipps 79
Edwards, Harry 2
Finner-Williams, Paris Michele 62
Fulani, Lenora 11
Gardere, Jeffrey 76
Gilbert, Christopher 50
Hale, Lorraine 8
Hare, Nathan 44
Hilliard, Asa Grant, III 66
Staples, Brent 8
Steele, Claude Mason 13
Tatum, Beverly Daniel 42, 84

Psychotheraphy
Berrysmith, Don Reginald 49
Ford, Clyde W. 40

Public Broadcasting Service (PBS)
Brown, Les 5
Brown, Tony 3
Creagh, Milton 27
Davis, Ossie 5, 50
Duke, Bill 3
Hampton, Henry 6
Hunter-Gault, Charlayne 6, 31
Ifill, Gwen 28
Lawson, Jennifer 1, 50
Long, Loretta 58
Lynch, Shola 61
Riggs, Marlon 5, 44
Roker, Al 12, 49

Public housing
Hamer, Fannie Lou 6
Lane, Vincent 5
Perry, James 83
Reems, Ernestine Cleveland 27

Public policy
Douglas, Derek 88

Public relations
Barrett, Andrew C. 12
Calhoun, Lillian Scott 87
Compton-Rock, Malaak 86
Edmonds, Terry 17
Graham, Stedman 13
Hedgeman, Anna Arnold 22
Jones, Robert G. 81
McCabe, Jewell Jackson 10
Perez, Anna 1
Pritchard, Robert Starling 21
Rowan, Carl T. 1, 30
Taylor, Kristin Clark 8
Tobin, Patricia 75
Williams, Maggie 7, 71

Public speaking
Bell, James Madison 40
Douglass, Frederick 87
Kennedy, Randall 40

Publishing
Abbott, Robert Sengstacke 27
Achebe, Chinua 6

Ames, Wilmer 27
Ashley-Ward, Amelia 23
Aubert, Alvin 41
Auguste, Arnold A. 47
Baisden, Michael 25, 66
Bass, Charlotta Spears 40
Bates, Daisy 13
Boston, Lloyd 24
Boyd, T. B., III 6
Brown, Jamie Foster 91
Brown, Marie Dutton 12
Cary, Mary Ann Shadd 30
Coombs, Orde M. 44
Cox, William E. 68
Dawkins, Wayne 20
Driver, David E. 11
Ducksworth, Marilyn 12
Dumas, Henry 41
Fuller, Hoyt 44
Giddings, Paula 11
Goodlett, Carlton B. 91
Graves, Butch 77
Graves, Earl G. 1, 35
Harris, Jay 19
Harris, Monica 18
Hill, Bonnie Guiton 20
Hudson, Cheryl 15
Hudson, Wade 15
James, Juanita 13
Jones, Quincy 8, 30
Kunjufu, Jawanza 3, 50
Lawson, Jennifer 1, 50
Leavell, Dorothy R. 17
Lewis, Edward T. 21
Lorde, Audre 6
Madhubuti, Haki 7, 85
Maynard, Nancy Hicks 73
Maynard, Robert C. 7
McDonald, Erroll 1
Moore, Jessica Care 30
Morgan, Garrett 1
Murphy, John H. 42
Myers, Walter Dean 8, 20
Parks, Gordon 1, 35, 58
Perez, Anna 1
Randall, Dudley 8, 55
Scott, C. A. 29
Sengstacke, John 18
Smith, Clarence O. 21
Stinson, Denise L. 59
Stringer, Vickie 58
Tyree, Omar Rashad 21
Vanzant, Iyanla 17, 47
Walker, Alice 1, 43
Washington, Alonzo 29
Washington, Laura S. 18
Wells-Barnett, Ida B. 8
Williams, Armstrong 29
Woods, Teri 69

Pulitzer Prize
Brooks, Gwendolyn 1, 28
Dove, Rita 6, 78
Fuller, Charles 8
Givhan, Robin Deneen 72
Gordone, Charles 15
Haley, Alex 4
Komunyakaa, Yusef 9
Lewis, David Levering 9
McPherson, James Alan 70
Morrison, Toni 2, 15, 86
Newkirk, Pamela 69
Page, Clarence 4

Parks, Suzan-Lori 34, 85
Payne, Les 89
Pitts, Leonard, Jr. 54, 85
Robinson, Eugene 77
Shipp, E. R. 15
Sleet, Moneta, Jr. 5
Walker, Alice 1, 43
Walker, George 37
White, John H. 27
Wilkins, Roger 2, 84
Wilson, August 7, 33, 55

Puppetry
Clash, Kevin 14, 93

PUSH
See People United to Serve Humanity

Quiltmaking
Benberry, Cuesta 65
Ringgold, Faith 4, 81

Qwest Records
Jones, Quincy 8, 30

Race car driving
Brown, Antron 85
Hamilton, Lewis 66
Lester, Bill 42, 85
Ribbs, Willy T. 2
Scott, Wendell Oliver, Sr. 19

Race relations
Abbott, Diane 9
Achebe, Chinua 6
Alexander, Clifford 26
Anthony, Wendell 25
Asante, Molefi Kete 3
Baker, Ella 5
Baker, Houston A., Jr. 6
Baldwin, James 1
Bell, Derrick 6
Bethune, Mary McLeod 4
Bobo, Lawrence 60
Booker, Simeon 23
Bosley, Freeman, Jr. 7
Boyd, T. B., III 6
Bradley, David Henry, Jr. 39
Branch, William Blackwell 39
Brown, Elaine 8
Bunche, Ralph J. 5
Butler, Paul D. 17
Cary, Lorene 3
Cashin, Sheryll 63
Cayton, Horace 26
Chavis, Benjamin 6
Clark, Kenneth B. 5, 52
Clark, Septima 7
Cobbs, Price M. 9
Cochran, Johnnie 11, 39, 52
Cole, Johnnetta B. 5, 43
Comer, James P. 6
Cone, James H. 3, 82
Conyers, John, Jr. 4, 45
Cook, Suzan D. Johnson 22
Cook, Toni 23
Cosby, Bill 7, 26, 59
Davis, Angela 5
Davis, Benjamin O., Jr. 2, 43
Davis, Benjamin O., Sr. 4
Dee, Ruby 8, 50, 68
Delany, Martin R. 27
Diallo, Amadou 27
Dickerson, Debra J. 60

Divine, Father 7
DuBois, Shirley Graham 21
Dunbar, Paul Laurence 8
Dunbar-Nelson, Alice Ruth Moore 44
Dyson, Michael Eric 11, 40
Edelman, Marian Wright 5, 42
Elder, Lee 6
Ellison, Ralph 7
Farmer, James 2, 64
Farmer-Paellmann, Deadria 43
Farrakhan, Louis 2
Fauset, Jessie 7
Franklin, John Hope 5, 77
Fuller, Charles 8
Gaines, Ernest J. 7
Gibson, William F. 6
Goode, W. Wilson 4
Graham, Lawrence Otis 12
Gregory, Dick 1, 54
Grimké, Archibald H. 9
Guy, Rosa 5
Haley, Alex 4
Hall, Elliott S. 24
Hampton, Henry 6
Hansberry, Lorraine 6
Harris, Alice 7
Hastie, William H. 8
Haynes, George Edmund 8
Hedgeman, Anna Arnold 22
Henry, Aaron 19
Henry, Lenny 9, 52
Hill, Oliver W. 24, 63
Hope, John 8
Howard, M. William, Jr. 26
Hunt, Darnell 92
Ingram, Rex 5
Innis, Roy 5
Jeffries, Leonard 8
Johnson, James Weldon 5
Jones, Elaine R. 7, 45
Jordan, Vernon E. 3, 35
Khanga, Yelena 6
King, Bernice 4, 81
King, Coretta Scott 3, 57
King, Martin Luther, Jr. 1
King, Yolanda 6
Lane, Charles 3
Lee-Smith, Hughie 5, 22
Lorde, Audre 6
Mabuza-Suttle, Felicia 43
Mandela, Nelson 1, 14, 77
Martin, Louis E. 16
Mathabane, Mark 5
Maynard, Robert C. 7
Mays, Benjamin E. 7
McDougall, Gay J. 11, 43
McKay, Claude 6
Meredith, James H. 11
Micheaux, Oscar 7
Moore, Harry T. 29
Mosley, Walter 5, 25, 68
Muhammad, Khallid Abdul 10, 31
Page, Clarence 4
Perkins, Edward 5
Pitt, David Thomas 10
Poussaint, Alvin F. 5, 67
Price, Frederick K. C. 21
Price, Hugh B. 9, 54
Robeson, Paul 2
Robinson, Spottswood W., III 22
Sampson, Edith S. 4
Shabazz, Attallah 6

Sifford, Charlie **4**, **49**
Simpson, Carole **6**, **30**
Sister Souljah **11**
Sisulu, Sheila Violet Makate **24**
Smith, Anna Deavere **6**, **44**
Sowell, Thomas **2**
Spaulding, Charles Clinton **9**
Staples, Brent **8**
Steele, Claude Mason **13**
Steele, Shelby **13**, **82**
Taulbert, Clifton Lemoure **19**
Till, Emmett **7**
Tutu, Desmond Mpilo **6**, **44**
Tutu, Nontombi Naomi **57**
Tyree, Omar Rashad **21**
Walcott, Derek **5**, **94**
Walker, Maggie **17**
Washington, Booker T. **4**
Washington, Harold **6**
Wells-Barnett, Ida B. **8**
Welsing, Frances Cress **5**
Wiley, Ralph **8**, **78**
Wilkins, Roy **4**
Williams, Fannie Barrier **27**
Williams, Gregory **11**
Williams, Hosea Lorenzo **15**, **31**
Williams, Walter E. **4**
Wilson, Sunnie **7**, **55**
Wright, Richard **5**
Young, Whitney M., Jr. **4**

Radio
Abrahams, Peter **39**
Abu-Jamal, Mumia **15**
Alert, Kool DJ Red **33**
Anderson, Eddie "Rochester" **30**
Ashong, Derrick **86**
Banks, William **11**
Bates, Karen Grigsby **40**
Beasley, Phoebe **34**
Blayton, Jesse B., Sr. **55**
Booker, Simeon **23**
Branch, William Blackwell **39**
CoCo Brother **93**
Crocker, Frankie **29**
Dee, Ruby **8**, **50**, **68**
Dre, Dr. **10**, **14**, **30**
Elder, Larry **25**
Fuller, Charles **8**
Gibson, Truman K., Jr. **60**
Goode, Mal **13**
Greene, Petey **65**
Gumbel, Greg **8**
Hamblin, Ken **10**
Haynes, Trudy **44**
Holt, Nora **38**
Hughes, Cathy **27**
Jackson, Hal **41**
Jarrett, Vernon D. **42**
Joe, Yolanda **21**
Joyner, Tom **19**, **90**
Kelley, Cliff **75**
Keyes, Alan L. **11**
Lewis, Delano **7**
Lewis, Ramsey **35**, **70**
Ligging, Alfred, III **43**
Love, Ed **58**
Lover, Ed **10**
Ludacris **37**, **60**
Luper, Clara **94**
Madison, Joseph E. **17**
Majors, Jeff **41**
Michaux, Solomon Lightfoot **91**

Mickelbury, Penny **28**
Moss, Carlton **17**
Parr, Russ **51**
Pressley, Condace L. **41**
Pugh, Charles **81**
Quivers, Robin **61**
Samara, Noah **15**
Smiley, Rickey **59**
Smiley, Tavis **20**, **68**
Smith, Greg **28**
Steinberg, Martha Jean "The
    Queen" **28**
Stuart, Moira **82**
Tirico, Mike **68**
Whack, Rita Coburn **36**
Williams, Armstrong **29**
Williams, Nat D. **91**
Williams, Ted **91**
Williams, Wendy **62**
Woods, Georgie **57**
Yarbrough, Camille **40**

Ragtime
Blake, Eubie **29**
Europe, James Reese **10**
Joplin, Scott **6**
Robinson, Reginald R. **53**
Sissle, Noble **29**

Rainbow Coalition
Chappell, Emma **18**
Jackson, Jesse **1**, **27**, **72**
Jackson, Jesse, Jr. **14**, **45**, **81**
Moore, Minyon **45**

Rap music
Alert, Kool DJ Red **33**
Baker, Houston A., Jr. **6**
Bambaataa, Afrika **34**
Banner, David **55**
Benjamin, Andre **45**
Big Daddy Kane **79**
Black Thought **63**
Blackman, Toni **86**
Blow, Kurtis **31**
B.o.B. **91**
Bow Wow **35**
Brown, Foxy **25**
Cee-Lo **70**
Chamillionaire **82**
Chuck D. **9**
Combs, Sean **17**, **43**, **92**
Common **31**, **63**
Da Don, Polow **86**
Deezer D **53**
DJ Jazzy Jeff **32**
DMX **28**, **64**
Drake **86**
Dre, Dr. **10**, **14**, **30**
Dupri, Jermaine **13**, **46**
Dyson, Michael Eric **11**, **40**
Elliott, Missy **31**, **90**
Eve **29**
Fabolous **93**
Fat Boys **92**
50 Cent **46**, **83**
Flavor Flav **67**
Flo Rida **78**
Ghostface Killah **90**
Gotti, Irv **39**
Grae, Jean **51**
Grandmaster Flash **33**, **60**
Gray, F. Gary **14**, **49**
Harrell, Andre **9**, **30**

Heavy D **58**
Hill, Lauryn **20**, **53**
Ice Cube **8**, **30**, **60**
Ice-T **6**, **31**
Ja Rule **35**, **91**
Jay-Z **27**, **69**
Jones, Quincy **8**, **30**
Kid Cudi **83**
K'naan **76**
Knight, Suge **11**, **30**
KRS-One **34**
Kweli, Talib **93**
Lil' Kim **28**
Lil Wayne **66**, **84**
Liles, Kevin **42**
LL Cool J **16**, **49**, **94**
Lopes, Lisa "Left Eye" **36**
Lover, Ed **10**
Ludacris **37**, **60**
Madlib **88**
Mane, Gucci **91**
Mase **24**
Master P **21**
MC Breed **75**
M.C. Hammer **20**, **80**
MC Lyte **34**
McDaniels, Ralph **79**
Method Man **81**
Mos Def **30**
Nate Dogg **92**
Nelly **32**, **90**
Notorious B.I.G. **20**
Ol' Dirty Bastard **52**
OutKast **35**
Peterson, James **81**
Queen Latifah **1**, **16**, **58**
?uestlove **74**
Ray J **86**
Redman **81**
Rhymes, Busta **31**
Riley, Boots **89**
Roberts, Kimberly Rivers **72**
Ross, Rick **79**
Run-DMC **31**, **75**
RZA **80**
Sermon, Erick **81**
Shakur, Afeni **67**
Shakur, Tupac **14**
Simmons, Russell **1**, **30**
Sir Mix-A-Lot **82**
Sister Souljah **11**
Slick Rick **93**
Slim Thug **86**
Smith, Will **8**, **18**, **53**
Snoop Dogg **35**, **84**
Speech **82**
Sticky Fingaz **86**
Sugarhill Gang, The **79**
Timbaland **32**
T-Pain **73**
Wale **92**
Xzibit **78**
Yarbrough, Camille **40**
Young Jeezy **63**

**Rassemblement Démocra-
tique Africain (African Democratic Rally; RDA)**
Houphouët-Boigny, Félix **4**, **64**
Touré, Sekou **6**

Rastafarianism
Burning Spear **79**
Dube, Lucky **77**

Heavy D **58**
Marley, Bob **5**
Marley, Rita **32**, **70**
Tosh, Peter **9**

RDA
See Rassemblement Démocratique
    Africain (African Democratic
    Rally)

Reader's Choice Award
Holton, Hugh, Jr. **39**

Reading Is Fundamental
Trueheart, William E. **49**

Real estate development
Amoudi, Mohammed al- **88**
Chapman, Susan E. **94**
Lane, Vincent **5**
Marshall, Bella **22**
Nail, John E. **92**
Payton, Philip A., Jr. **88**
Russell, Herman Jerome **17**
Toote, Gloria E. A. **64**

Record producer
Albright, Gerald **23**
Ayers, Roy **16**
Babyface **10**, **31**, **82**
Bambaataa, Afrika **34**
Barnes, Lloyd **77**
Bivins, Michael **72**
Butler, George, Jr. **70**
Coleman, Ornette **39**, **69**
Da Don, Polow **86**
Danjah, Terror **91**
de Passe, Suzanne **25**
DJ Jazzy Jeff **32**
Dre, Dr. **10**, **14**, **30**
Duke, George **21**
Dupri, Jermaine **13**, **46**
Elliott, Missy **31**, **90**
Fuqua, Harvey **90**
Gotti, Irv **39**
Hailey, JoJo **22**
Hailey, K-Ci **22**
Hammond, Fred **23**
Hawkins, Walter **87**
Hill, Lauryn **20**, **53**
Huff, Leon **86**
Ice Cube **8**, **30**, **60**
Ja Rule **35**, **91**
Jackson, George **19**
Jackson, Joe **78**
Jackson, Michael **19**, **53**, **76**
Jackson, Randy **40**
Jean, Wyclef **20**, **86**
Jerkins, Rodney **31**
Jimmy Jam **13**
Jones, Quincy **8**, **30**
Kelly, R. **18**, **44**, **71**
Lewis, Terry **13**
Liles, Kevin **42**
Marley, Rita **32**, **70**
Master P **21**
Mayfield, Curtis **2**, **43**
Minott, Sugar **86**
Osborne, Jeffrey **26**
Prince **18**, **65**
Queen Latifah **1**, **16**, **58**
Reid, Antonio "L.A." **28**
Robinson, Sylvia **79**
Sermon, Erick **81**

Sweat, Keith 19
Timbaland 32
Turner, Ike 68
Vandross, Luther 13, 48, 59
White, Barry 13, 41
Whitfield, Norman 73
Williams, J. Mayo 83
Williams, Pharrell 47, 82
Yabby You 83
Young, Lee 72

Recording executives
Busby, Jheryl 3, 74
Butler, George, Jr. 70
de Passe, Suzanne 25
Dupri, Jermaine 13, 46
Gordy, Berry, Jr. 1
Gotti, Irv 39
Harrell, Andre 9, 30
Jackson, George 19
Jackson, Randy 40
Jimmy Jam 13
Jones, Quincy 8, 30
Knight, Suge 11, 30
Lewis, Terry 13
Liles, Kevin 42
Massenburg, Kedar 23
Master P 21
Mayfield, Curtis 2, 43
Reid, Antonio "L.A." 28
Rhone, Sylvia 2
Sanders, Angelia 86
Simmons, Russell 1, 30
Williams, J. Mayo 83

Reform Party
Foster, Ezola 28

Reggae
Afro, Teddy 78
Banton, Buju 93
Barnes, Lloyd 77
Beenie Man 32
Blondy, Alpha 30
Burning Spear 79
Cliff, Jimmy 28, 92
Dawuni, Rocky 94
Dube, Lucky 77
Ellis, Alton 74
Ford, Vincent 75
Griffiths, Marcia 29
Hammond, Lenn 34
Isaacs, Gregory 89
Johnson, Linton Kwesi 37
Marley, Bob 5
Marley, Rita 32, 70
Marley, Ziggy 41
Minott, Sugar 86
Mowatt, Judy 38
Perry, Ruth 19
Rhoden, Wayne 70
Shaggy 31
Sly & Robbie 34
Steely 80
Tosh, Peter 9
Yabby You 83

Republic of New Afrika (RNA)
Williams, Robert F. 11

Republican Party
Allen, Ethel D. 13
Fisher, Ada M. 76
Scott, Tim 87

Steele, Michael 38, 73, 91
Toote, Gloria E. A. 64

Restaurants/Catering/Cooking
Armstrong, Govind 81
Cain, Herman 15, 92
Calabrese, Karyn 89
Daniels-Carter, Valerie 23
Dorsey, Thomas J. 90
Downing, George T. 91
Ford, Barney 90
Garvin, Gerry 78
Hawkins, La-Van 17, 54
Howell, Ayinde 91
James, Charles H., III 62
Lewis, Aylwin B. 51, 88
Otis, Clarence, Jr. 55
Ouattara, Morou 74
Pierce, Harold 75
Rodriguez, Jimmy 47
Samuelsson, Marcus 53
Sbraga, Kevin 88
Smith, B(arbara) 11
Thompson, Don 56
Washington, Regynald G. 44
Williams, Lindsey 75

Rhode Island School of Design
Bannister, Edward Mitchell 88
Prophet, Nancy Elizabeth 42

Rhodes scholar
Braxton, Brad 77
Kennedy, Randall 40
Locke, Alain 10
Rice, Susan E. 74

Rhythm and blues/soul music
Aaliyah 30
Ace, Johnny 36
Adams, Johnny 39
Adams, Oleta 18
Akon 68
Amerie 52
Ashanti 37
Ashford, Nickolas 21
Austin, Patti 24
Ayers, Roy 16
Babyface 10, 31, 82
Badu, Erykah 22
Bailey, Philip 63
Baker, Anita 21, 48
Baker, LaVern 26
Ballard, Hank 41
Barrino, Fantasia 53, 94
Baylor, Helen 36
Belgrave, Marcus 77
Belle, Regina 1, 51
Benét, Eric 28, 77
Berry, Chuck 29
Beverly, Frankie 25
Beyoncé 39, 70
Bivins, Michael 72
Blige, Mary J. 20, 34, 60
Boyz II Men 82
Brandy 14, 34, 72
Braxton, Toni 15, 61, 91
Brooks, Hadda 40
Brown, Bobby 58
Brown, Charles 23
Brown, Chris 74
Brown, Chuck 78
Brown, Clarence Gatemouth 59

Brown, James 15, 60
Brown, Nappy 73
Brown, Oscar, Jr. 53
Brown, Ruth 90
Burke, Solomon 31, 86
Busby, Jheryl 3, 74
Butler, Jerry 26
Carey, Mariah 32, 53, 69
Charles, Ray 16, 48
Ciara 56
Clinton, George 9, 93
Cole, Keyshia 63
Cole, Natalie 17, 60, 84
Cooke, Sam 17
Cox, Deborah 28
Crawford, Hank 77
D'Angelo 27
David, Craig 31, 53
Davis, Tyrone 54
DeBarge, El 89
Derülo, Jason 93
DeVaughn, Raheem 91
Diddley, Bo 39, 72
Domino, Fats 20
Dorsey, Lee 65
Downing, Will 19
Dre, Dr. 14, 30
Dupri, Jermaine 13, 46
Escobar, Damien 56
Escobar, Tourie 56
Evans, Faith 22
Feemster, Herbert 72
Fiona, Melanie 84
Franklin, Aretha 11, 44
Fuqua, Harvey 90
Gamble, Kenny 85
Garrett, Sean 57
Gaye, Marvin 2
Gaynor, Gloria 36
Gibson, Tyrese 27, 62
Gill, Johnny 51
Ginuwine 35
Goapele 55
Goodman, Al 87
Gotti, Irv 39
Gray, Macy 29
Green, Al 13, 47, 74
Hailey, JoJo 22
Hailey, K-Ci 22
Hall, Aaron 57
Hamilton, Anthony 61
Harris, Corey 39, 73
Hart, Alvin Youngblood 61
Hathaway, Donny 18
Hathaway, Lalah 57, 88
Hayes, Isaac 20, 58, 73
Hendryx, Nona 56
Henry, Clarence "Frogman" 46
Hill, Lauryn 20, 53
Hilson, Keri 84
Holloway, Brenda 65
Houston, Cissy 20, 83
Houston, Whitney 7, 28, 83
Huff, Leon 86
Hyman, Phyllis 19
India.Arie 34
Ingram, James 84
Isley, Marvin 87
Isley, Ronald 25, 56
Jackson, Janet 6, 30, 68
Jackson, Michael 19, 53, 76
Jackson, Millie 25
Jackson, Tito 81

Jaheim 58
Jamelia 51
James, Etta 13, 52
James, Rick 17
Jarreau, Al 21, 65
Jennings, Lyfe 56, 69
Johnson, Robert 2
Johnson-George, Tamara 79
Jones, Booker T. 84
Jones, Donell 29
Jones, Quincy 8, 30
Jones, Sharon 86
Jordan, Montell 23
Kandi 83
Kelly, R. 18, 44, 71
Kem 47
Kendricks, Eddie 22
Keys, Alicia 32, 68
King Curtis 92
Knight, Gladys 16, 66
Knight, Marie 80
LaBelle, Patti 13, 30
Larrieux, Amel 63
Lattimore, Kenny 35
LaVette, Bettye 85
Ledisi 73
Legend, John 67
Levert, Eddie 70
Levert, Gerald 22, 59
Little Richard 15
Lopes, Lisa "Left Eye" 36
Love, Darlene 23, 92
Luckett, Letoya 61
Maitreya, Sananda 85
Mario 71
Massenburg, Kedar 23
Master P 21
Maxwell 20, 81
Mayfield, Curtis 2, 43
McCoo, Marilyn 53
McKnight, Brian 18, 34
Miles, Buddy 69
Monáe, Janelle 86
Monica 21
Moore, Chante 26
Moore, Melba 21
Musiq 37, 84
Mya 35
Nash, Johnny 40
Ndegeocello, Meshell 15, 83
Neale, Haydain 52
Neville, Aaron 21
Ne-Yo 65
Notorious B.I.G. 20
Otis, Clyde 67
Parker, Maceo 72
Parker, Ray, Jr. 85
Pendergrass, Teddy 22, 83
Pinkney, Fayette 80
Pleasure P 84
Preston, Billy 39, 59
Price, Kelly 23
Prince 18, 65
Reagon, Toshi 76
Record, Eugene 60
Redding, Otis 16
Reed, A. C. 36
Reeves, Martha 85
Richard, Dawn 92
Richie, Lionel 27, 65
Rihanna 65
Riperton, Minnie 32
Robinson, Smokey 3, 49

Ross, Diana **8, 27**
Russell, Brenda **52**
Sade **15, 92**
Sample, Joe **51**
Scott, Jill **29, 83**
Scott, "Little" Jimmy **48**
Scott-Heron, Gil **94**
Siji **56**
Simpson, Valerie **21**
Sisqo **30**
Sledge, Percy **39**
Songz, Trey **88**
Sparks, Jordin **66**
Staton, Candi **27**
Steinberg, Martha Jean "The Queen" **28**
Stone, Angie **31**
Strong, Barrett **89**
Studdard, Ruben **46**
Sullivan, Jazmine **81**
Supremes, The **33**
Sweat, Keith **19**
Tamia **24, 55**
Temptations, The **33**
Terrell, Tammi **32**
The-Dream **74**
Thomas, Irma **29**
Thomas, Rozonda **34, 78**
Thomas, Rufus **20**
TLC **34**
Tresvant, Ralph **57**
Turner, Ike **68**
Turner, Tina **6, 27**
Ulmer, James **79**
Usher **23, 56**
Valentino, Bobby **62**
Vandross, Luther **13, 48, 59**
Watley, Jody **54**
Watts, Reggie **52**
Wells, Mary **28**
West, Kanye **52, 93**
White, Barry **13, 41**
Williams, Michelle **73**
Williams, Vanessa L. **4, 17**
Wilson, Cassandra **16**
Wilson, Charlie **31, 77**
Wilson, Mary **28**
Wilson, Nancy **10**
Withers, Bill **61**
Womack, Bobby **60, 92**
Wonder, Stevie **11, 53**
Woodson, Ali Ollie **89**

RNA
See Republic of New Afrika

Robert C. Maynard Institute for Journalism Education
Harris, Jay T. **19**
Maynard, Nancy Hicks **73**
Maynard, Robert C. **7**

Roberts Companies, The
Roberts, Mike **57**

Roc-A-Fella
Dash, Damon **31**
Jay-Z **27, 69**

Rock and Roll Hall of Fame
Ballard, Hank **41**
Bennett, Estelle **77**
Berry, Chuck **29**
Bland, Bobby "Blue" **36**

Brown, Charles **23**
Burke, Solomon **31, 86**
Clinton, George **9, 93**
Cole, Nat "King" **17**
Davis, Miles **4**
Diddley, Bo **39, 72**
Franklin, Aretha **11, 44**
Gamble, Kenny **85**
Grandmaster Flash **33, 60**
Green, Al **13, 47, 74**
Guy, Buddy **31**
Hayes, Isaac **20, 58, 73**
Holiday, Billie **1**
Holland-Dozier-Holland **36**
Hooker, John Lee **30**
Isley, Marvin **87**
Isley, Ronald **25, 56**
Jackson, Mahalia **5**
Jackson, Michael **19, 53, 76**
Jackson, Tito **81**
Jamerson, James **59**
James, Etta **13, 52**
Johnson, Johnnie **56**
Jones, Booker T. **84**
Knight, Gladys **16, 66**
Mayfield, Curtis **2, 43**
Morton, Jelly Roll **29**
Prince **18, 65**
Reeves, Martha **85**
Run-DMC **31, 75**
Shider, Garry **87**
Sledge, Percy **39**
Spector, Ronnie **77**
Steinberg, Martha Jean "The Queen" **28**
Stone, Sly **85**
Toussaint, Allen **60**
Turner, Big Joe **92**
Turner, Ike **68**
Turner, Tina **6, 27**
Wilson, Jackie **60**
Wilson, Mary **28**
Wonder, Stevie **11, 53**

Rock music
Adebimpe, Tunde **75**
Ballard, Hank **41**
Bennett, Estelle **77**
Berry, Chuck **29**
Clemons, Clarence **41**
Diddley, Bo **39, 72**
Domino, Fats **20**
Edwards, Esther Gordy **43**
Glover, Corey **34**
Hendrix, Jimi **10**
Ice-T **6, 31**
Johnson, Johnnie **56**
King Curtis **92**
Kravitz, Lenny **10, 34**
Little Richard **15**
Lymon, Frankie **22**
Mayfield, Curtis **2, 43**
Miles, Buddy **69**
Moore, LeRoi **72**
Preston, Billy **39, 59**
Prince **18, 65**
Reagon, Toshi **76**
Reid, Vernon **34**
Run-DMC **31, 75**
Slash **75**
Spector, Ronnie **77**
Stew **69**
Stone, Sly **85**

Tait, Michael **57**
Tamar-kali **63**
Tinsley, Boyd **50**
Toussaint, Allen **60**
Turner, Ike **68**
Turner, Big Joe **92**
Turner, Tina **6, 27**
will.i.am **64**
Wilson, Jackie **60**

Rockefeller Foundation
Price, Hugh B. **9, 54**

Rockets
Williams, O. S. **13**

Rodeo
Nash, Johnny **40**
Pickett, Bill **11**
Sampson, Charles **13**
Whitfield, Fred **23**

Roman Catholic Church
Akpan, Uwem **70**
Arinze, Francis **19**
Aristide, Jean-Bertrand **6, 45**
Chineworth, Mary Alice **79**
Clements, George **2**
DeLille, Henriette **30**
Fabre, Shelton **71**
Gantin, Bernardin **70**
Gregory, Wilton D. **37**
Guy, Rosa **5**
Healy, James Augustine **30**
Jean-Juste, Gérard **78**
Jones, Alex **64**
Marino, Eugene Antonio **30**
Otunga, Maurice Michael **55**
Rugambwa, Laurean **20**
Senghor, Augustin Diamacoune **66**
Stallings, George A., Jr. **6**

Romance fiction
Bunkley, Anita Richmond **39**
Hill, Donna **32**
Jackson, Brenda **87**
Washington, Elsie B. **78**

Royalty
Christophe, Henri **9**
Ka Dinizulu, Mcwayizeni **29**
Mswati III **56**
Mutebi, Ronald **25**

Rugby
Mundine, Anthony **56**

Rutgers University
Davis, George **36**
Gibson, Donald Bernard **40**

Rwandan government
Habyarimana, Juvenal **8**
Kagame, Paul **54**
Mushikiwabo, Louise **88**

SAA
See Syndicat Agricole Africain

Sacramento Kings basketball team
Russell, Bill **8**
Webber, Chris **15, 30, 59**

SADCC
See Southern African Development Coordination Conference

Sailing
Pinckney, Bill **42**

St. Kitts and Nevis government
Douglas, Denzil Llewellyn **53**

St. Louis Blues hockey team
Brathwaite, Fred **35**
Mayers, Jamal **39**

St. Louis Browns baseball team
Brown, Willard **36**
Paige, Satchel **7**

St. Louis Cardinals baseball team
Baylor, Don **6**
Bonds, Bobby **43**
Brock, Lou **18**
Flood, Curt **10, 93**
Gibson, Bob **33**
Lankford, Ray **23**
Smith, Ozzie **77**

St. Louis city government
Bosley, Freeman, Jr. **7**
Harmon, Clarence **26**

St. Louis Rams football team
Bruce, Isaac **26**
Faulk, Marshall **35**
Pace, Orlando **21**

Sainte Beuve Prize
Beti, Mongo **36**

Salvation Army
Gaither, Israel L. **65**

Sammy Davis Jr. National Liver Institute University Hospital
Leevy, Carrol M. **42**

San Antonio Spurs basketball team
Duncan, Tim **20, 91**
Elliott, Sean **26**
Gervin, George **80**
Mohammed, Nazr **64**
Parker, Tony **75**
Robinson, David **24, 90**

San Diego Chargers football team
Barnes, Ernie **16, 78**
Lofton, James **42**
Tomlinson, LaDainian **65**
Winslow, Kellen **83**

San Diego Conquistadors
Chamberlain, Wilt **18, 47**

San Diego Padres baseball team
Carter, Joe **30**
Gwynn, Tony **18, 83**
McGriff, Fred **24**
Smith, Ozzie **77**
Winfield, Dave **5, 91**

San Francisco 49ers football team
Green, Dennis **5, 45**
Hayes, Bob **77**

Lott, Ronnie 9
Rice, Jerry 5, 55, 89
Simpson, O. J. 15
Singletary, Mike 4, 76
Washington, Gene 63

San Francisco Giants baseball team
Baker, Dusty 8, 43, 72
Bonds, Barry 6, 34, 63
Bonds, Bobby 43
Carter, Joe 30
Mays, Willie 3
Morgan, Joe 9
Strawberry, Darryl 22

San Francisco public schools
Coleman, William F., III 61

Saturday Night Live
Meadows, Tim 30
Morgan, Tracy 61
Morris, Garrett 31
Murphy, Eddie 4, 20, 61
Rock, Chris 3, 22, 66
Rudolph, Maya 46
Thompson, Kenan 52

Savoy Ballroom
Johnson, Buddy 36

Saxophone
Adderley, Julian "Cannonball" 30
Albright, Gerald 23
Anderson, Fred 87
Bechet, Sidney 18
Clemons, Clarence 41
Coltrane, John 19
Coltrane, Ravi 71
Crawford, Hank 77
Golson, Benny 37
Gordon, Dexter 25
Greene, Jimmy 74
Griffin, Johnny 71
Hawkins, Coleman 9
Jacquet, Illinois 49
Kay, Ulyssess 37
Kenyatta, Robin 54
King Curtis 92
McLean, Jackie 78
Moody, James 83
Moore, LeRoi 72
Moura, Paulo 87
Newman, David 76
Parker, Charlie 20
Parker, Maceo 72
Redman, Joshua 30
Rollins, Sonny 37, 94
Sanders, Pharoah 64
Shider, Garry 87
Shorter, Wayne 75
Washington, Grover, Jr. 17, 44
Waters, Benny 26
Whalum, Kirk 37, 64
York, Vincent 40
Young, Lester 37

Schomburg Center for Research in Black Culture
Andrews, Bert 13
Dodson, Howard, Jr. 7, 52
Hutson, Jean Blackwell 16
Morrison, Sam 50
Reddick, Lawrence Dunbar 20

Schomburg, Arthur Alfonso 9

School desegregation
Bridges, Ruby 77
Brown, Oliver Leon 94
Chestnut, J. L., Jr. 73
Fortune, T. Thomas 6
Hamer, Fannie Lou 6
Hobson, Julius W. 44
Holmes, Hamilton E. 82

Science fiction
Barnes, Steven 54
Butler, Octavia 8, 43, 58
Delany, Samuel R., Jr. 9

SCLC
See Southern Christian Leadership
Conference

Scotland Yard
Griffin, Bessie Blout 43

Screenplay writing
Akil, Mara Brock 60, 82
Brown, Cecil M. 46
Clack, Zoanne 73
Davis, Thulani 61
Elder, Lonne, III 38
Fisher, Antwone 40
Fletcher, Geoffrey 85
Greaves, William 38
Jones, Orlando 30
Lumet, Jenny 80
McMillan, Tracy 93
Nissel, Angela 42
Prince-Bythewood, Gina 31, 77
Pryce, Trevor 89
Rhimes, Shonda Lynn 67
Rhone, Trevor 80
Ridley, John 69
Robinson, Matt 69
Singleton, John 2, 30
Talbert, David E. 34, 93
Wesley, Richard 73

Sculpture
Allen, Tina 22, 75
Amos, Emma 63
Bailey, Radcliffe 19
Barthe, Richmond 15
Biggers, John 20, 33
Biggers, Sanford 62
Billops, Camille 82
Brown, Donald 19
Burke, Selma 16
Catlett, Elizabeth 2
Chanticleer, Raven 91
Chase-Riboud, Barbara 20, 46
Cortor, Eldzier 42
Dwight, Edward 65
Edwards, Melvin 22
Fuller, Meta Vaux Warrick 27
Guyton, Tyree 9, 94
Hammons, David 69
Hathaway, Isaac Scott 33
Hunt, Richard 6
Lewis, Edmonia 10
Lewis, Samella 25
Manley, Edna 26
Marshall, Kerry James 59
McCullough, Geraldine 58, 79
McGee, Charles 10
Moody, Ronald 30
Neals, Otto 73

Perkins, Marion 38
Pierce, Elijah 84
Prophet, Nancy Elizabeth 42
Puryear, Martin 42
Ringgold, Faith 4, 81
Saar, Alison 16
Saar, Betye 80
Savage, Augusta 12
Scott, John T. 65
Shabazz, Attallah 6
Simmons, Gary 58
Stout, Renee 63
Washington, James, Jr. 38

Seattle city government
Rice, Norm 8

Seattle Mariners baseball team
Griffey, Ken, Jr. 12, 73
Reynolds, Harold 77

Seattle Supersonics basketball team
Bickerstaff, Bernie 21
Durant, Kevin 76
Silas, Paul 24

Security and defense services
Garrett, James F. 78

Seismology
Person, Waverly 9, 51

Senegalese government
Diouf, Abdou 3
Senghor, Léopold Sédar 66
Wade, Abdoulaye 66

Sesame Street
Byrd, Eugene 64
Clash, Kevin 14, 93
Glover, Savion 14
Long, Loretta 58
Orman, Roscoe 55
Reed Hall, Alaina 83
Robinson, Matt 69

Sexual harassment
Gomez-Preston, Cheryl 9
Hill, Anita 5, 65
McCauley, Gina 76
Thomas, Clarence 2, 39, 65

Share
Auguste, Arnold A. 47

Sheila Bridges Design Inc.
Bridges, Sheila 36

Shell Oil Company
Mays, Leslie A. 41

Shrine of the Black Madonna
Agyeman, Jaramogi Abebe 10, 63

Sickle cell anemia
Edwards, Willarda V. 59
Pace, Betty 59
Satcher, David 7, 57

Sierra Leone government
Kabbah, Ahmad Tejan 23
Koroma, Ernest Bai 84

Silicon Graphics Incorporated
Coleman, Ken 57
Hannah, Marc 10

Skateboarding
Williams, Stevie 71

Sketches
Crite, Alan Rohan 29
Sallee, Charles 38

Skiing
Horton, Andre 33
Horton, Suki 33

Skillman Foundation
Goss, Carol A. 55

Slavery
Asante, Molefi Kete 3
Bibb, Henry and Mary 54
Blackshear, Leonard 52
Blassingame, John Wesley 40
Chase-Riboud, Barbara 20, 46
Cooper, Anna Julia 20
Douglas, Aaron 7
Du Bois, W. E. B. 3
Dunbar, Paul Laurence 8
Durham, James 90
Easton, Hosea 91
Equiano, Olaudah 78
Farmer-Paellmann, Deadria 43
Gaines, Ernest J. 7
Gordon-Reed, Annette 74
Haley, Alex 4
Harper, Frances Ellen Watkins 11
Henson, Josiah 90
Huggins, Nathan Irvin 52
Johnson, Charles 1, 82
Jones, Edward P. 43, 67
Keckley, Elizabeth 90
Lane, Lunsford 93
Mason, Biddy 89
McWorter, Free Frank 91
Montgomery, Isaiah T. 91
Muhammad, Elijah 4
Patterson, Orlando 4
Pleasant, Mary Ellen 9
Stephens, Charlotte Andrews 14
Stewart, Maria W. Miller 19
Tancil, Gladys Quander 59
Taylor, Susie King 13
Tubman, Harriet 9
Wall, Orindatus S. B. 92

Smithsonian Institution
Bunch, Lonnie G., III 91

Smith College
Mayhew, Richard 39
Simmons, Ruth 13, 38

SNCC
See Student Nonviolent Coordinating Committee

Soccer
Adu, Freddy 67
Anderson, Viv 58
Barnes, John 53
Beasley, Jamar 29
Crooks, Garth 53
dos Santos, Manuel Francisco 65
Drogba, Didier 78
Eto'o, Samuel 73

Ferdinand, Rio 82
Gyan, Asamoah 87
Henry, Thierry 66
Ince, Paul 83
James, David 84
Jones, Cobi N'Gai 18
Kanouté, Fred 68
Mello, Breno 73
Mensah, John 87
Milla, Roger 2
Nakhid, David 25
Onyewu, Oguchi 60
Pelé 7
Regis, Cyrille 51
Ronaldinho 69
Scurry, Briana 27
Sono, Jomo 86
Weah, George 58

Social science/social criticism
Berry, Mary Frances 7
Black, Albert 51
Bobo, Lawrence 60
Bunche, Ralph J. 5
Cayton, Horace 26
Clark, Kenneth B. 5, 52
Cobbs, Price M. 9
Collins, Patricia Hill 67
Edwards, Harry 2
Frazier, E. Franklin 10
George, Zelma Watson 42
Hall, Stuart 78
Hare, Nathan 44
Harris, Eddy L. 18
Haynes, George Edmund 8
hooks, bell 5, 90
Hunt, Darnell 92
Ladner, Joyce A. 42
Lawrence-Lightfoot, Sara 10
Marable, Manning 10
Steele, Claude Mason 13
Williams, David Rudyard 50
Woodson, Robert L. 10

Social work
Auguste, Rose-Anne 13
Berry, Bertice 8, 55
Berrysmith, Don Reginald 49
Brown, Cora 33
Canada, Geoffrey 23
Coles, Alice 80
Colston, Hal 72
Compton-Rock, Malaak 86
Dunham, Katherine 4, 59
Fields, C. Virginia 25
Finner-Williams, Paris Michele 62
Gbowee, Leymah 76
Granger, Lester B. 75
Hale, Clara 16
Hale, Lorraine 8
Harris, Alice 7
Haynes, George Edmund 8
Jackson, Judith D. 57
Jackson, Mae 57
King, Barbara 22
Lewis, Thomas 19
Little, Robert L. 2
Robinson, Rachel 16
Sears, Stephanie 53
Smith, Damu 54
Vaughn, Viola 70
Waddles, Charleszetta "Mother" 10, 49

Walker, Bernita Ruth 53
Wallace, Joaquin 49
Wells, Henrietta Bell 69
White-Hammond, Gloria 61
Williams, Fannie Barrier 27
Thrower, Willie 35
Young, Whitney M., Jr. 4

Soledad Brothers
Jackson, George Lester 14

Somalian government
Ahmed, Sharif 80

Soul City, NC
McKissick, Floyd B. 3

Soul food
Williams, Lindsey 75
Woods, Sylvia 34

Soul Train
Baylor, Helen 36
Cornelius, Don 4
D'Angelo 27
Lil' Kim 28
Winans, CeCe 14, 43

South African Communist Party
Hani, Chris 6
Mhlaba, Raymond 55

South African government
Dandala, Mvume 77
Mhlaba, Raymond 55
Motlanthe, Kgalema 74
Sisulu, Walter 47
Zuma, Jacob 33, 75
Zuma, Nkosazana Dlamini 34

South African literature
Abrahams, Peter 39
Brutus, Dennis 38
Head, Bessie 28
Mathabane, Mark 5
Mofolo, Thomas 37
Mphalele, Es'kia 40

South Carolina state government
Cardozo, Francis L. 33
Scott, Tim 87

Southeastern University
Jarvis, Charlene Drew 21

Southern African Development Coordination Conference (SADCC)
Masire, Quett 5
Nujoma, Samuel 10

Southern Christian Leadership Conference (SCLC)
Abernathy, Ralph 1
Angelou, Maya 1, 15
Baker, Ella 5
Barrow, Willie T. 85
Brooks, Tyrone 59
Chavis, Benjamin 6
Dee, Ruby 8, 50, 68
Fauntroy, Walter E. 11
Hooks, Benjamin L. 2, 85
Jackson, Jesse 1, 27, 72
Jones, William A., Jr. 61

King, Bernice 4, 81
King, Martin Luther, Jr. 1
King, Martin Luther, III 20
Lawson, James M., Jr. 90
Lee, Eric P. 79
Lowery, Joseph 2
Moses, Robert Parris 11
Moss, Otis, Jr. 72
Nash, Diane 72
Orange, James 74
Rustin, Bayard 4
Shuttlesworth, Fred 47
Walker, Wyatt Tee 80
Williams, Hosea Lorenzo 15, 31
Young, Andrew 3, 48

Southern Syncopated Orchestra
Cook, Will Marion 40

Space shuttle
Gregory, Frederick 8, 51
Jemison, Mae C. 1, 35
McNair, Ronald 3, 58
Wilson, Stephanie 72

Special Olympics
Clairborne, Loretta 34

Speedskating
Davis, Shani 58, 84

Spelman College
Cobb, William Jelani 59
Cole, Johnnetta B. 5, 43
Falconer, Etta Zuber 59
Price, Glenda 22
Simmons, Ruth 13, 38
Tatum, Beverly Daniel 42, 84
Wade-Gayles, Gloria Jean 41

Sphinx Organization
Dworkin, Aaron P. 52

Spingarn medal
Aaron, Hank 5
Ailey, Alvin 8
Anderson, Marian 2, 33
Angelou, Maya 1, 15
Bates, Daisy 13
Bethune, Mary McLeod 4
Bradley, Thomas 2, 20
Brooke, Edward W. 8, 88
Bunche, Ralph J. 5
Carver, George Washington 4
Chesnutt, Charles 29
Clark, Kenneth B. 5, 52
Cosby, Bill 7, 26, 59
Davis, Sammy, Jr. 18
Drew, Charles Richard 7
Du Bois, W. E. B. 3
Ellington, Duke 5
Evers, Medgar 3
Franklin, John Hope 5, 77
Grimké, Archibald H. 9
Haley, Alex 4
Hastie, William H. 8
Hayes, Roland 4
Height, Dorothy I. 2, 23, 78
Higginbotham, A. Leon, Jr. 13, 25
Hinton, William Augustus 8
Hooks, Benjamin L. 2, 85
Horne, Lena 5, 86
Houston, Charles Hamilton 4
Hughes, Langston 4

Jackson, Jesse 1, 27, 72
Johnson, James Weldon 5
Jordan, Barbara 4, 78
Julian, Percy Lavon 6
Just, Ernest Everett 3
Keith, Damon J. 16, 74
King, Martin Luther, Jr. 1
Lawless, Theodore K. 8
Lawrence, Jacob 4
Logan, Rayford 40
Marshall, Thurgood 1, 44
Mays, Benjamin E. 7
Moore, Harry T. 29
Parks, Gordon 1, 35, 58
Parks, Rosa 1, 35, 56
Powell, Colin 1, 28, 75
Price, Leontyne 1
Randolph, A. Philip 3
Robeson, Paul 2
Robinson, Jackie 6
Staupers, Mabel K. 7
Sullivan, Leon H. 3, 30
Tobias, Channing H. 79
Weaver, Robert C. 8, 46
White, Walter F. 4
Wilder, L. Douglas 3, 48
Wilkins, Roy 4
Williams, Paul R. 9
Woodson, Carter G. 2
Wright, Louis Tompkins 4
Wright, Richard 5
Young, Andrew 3, 48
Young, Coleman 1, 20

Spirituals
Anderson, Marian 2, 33
Carr, Kurt 56
Fisher, Miles Mark 91
Hairston, Jester 88
Hayes, Roland 4
Jackson, Mahalia 5
Johnson, Hall 90
Joyner, Matilda Sissieretta 15
Norman, Jessye 5
Reese, Della 6, 20
Williams, Denise 40

Sports administration
Fuller, Vivian 33
Kerry, Leon G. 46
Lee, Bertram M., Sr. 46
Mills, Steve 47
Phillips, Teresa L. 42
Randolph, Willie 53
Ussery, Terdema, II 29

Sports agent
Holland, Kimberly N. 62

Stanford University
Bobo, Lawrence 60
Rice, Condoleezza 3, 28, 72
Walker, Arthur, II 87
Washington, Gene 63
Willingham, Tyrone 43

State University of New York
Ballard, Allen Butler, Jr. 40
Baraka, Amiri 1, 38
Butts, Calvin O., III 9, 90
Clemente, Rosa 74

Wharton, Clifton R., Jr. 7

Stellar Awards
Baylor, Helen 36
Hawkins, Walter 87
Sapp, Marvin 74
Tribbett, Tye 81
Walker, Hezekiah 34

Stonewall 25
Norman, Pat 10

Stop the Violence Movement
KRS-One 34
MC Lyte 34

Storytelling
Baker, Augusta 38
Bennett, Louise 69
Hill, Hugh Morgan 83

Student Nonviolent Coordinating Committee (SNCC)
Al-Amin, Jamil Abdullah 6
Anderson, William G(ilchrist) 57
Baker, Ella 5
Barry, Marion S. 7, 44
Blackwell, Unita 17
Bond, Julian 2, 35
Carmichael, Stokely 5, 26
Clark, Septima 7
Davis, Angela 5
Forman, James 7, 51
Hamer, Fannie Lou 6
Holland, Endesha Ida Mae 3, 57
Lester, Julius 9
Lewis, John 2, 46, 83
Moses, Robert Parris 11
Nash, Diane 72
Poussaint, Alvin F. 5, 67
Reagon, Bernice Johnson 7
Touré, Askia (Muhammad Abu Bakr el) 47

Sudan government
Bashir, Omar al- 77
Cham, Adongo Agada Akway 77
Kiir, Salva 85

Sun Microsystems
Tademy, Lalita 36

Sundance Film Festival
Harris, Leslie 6
Nelson, Stanley 92

Sunny Alade Records
Ade, King Sunny 41

Supreme Court
See U.S. Supreme Court

Surfing
Corley, Tony 62

Surrealism
Ellison, Ralph 7
Lee-Smith, Hughie 5, 22

Swaziland government
Mswati III 56

Sweet Honey in the Rock
Reagon, Bernice Johnson 7

Swimming
Jones, Cullen 73

Sylvia's Restaurant
Washington, Regynald G. 44
Woods, Sylvia 34

Syndicat Agricole Africain (SAA)
Houphouët-Boigny, Félix 4, 64

Talk Soup
Tyler, Aisha N. 36

Talladega College
Archie-Hudson, Marguerite 44

Tampa Bay Buccaneers football team
Barber, Ronde 41
Brooks, Derrick 43
Dungy, Tony 17, 42, 59
McDaniel, Randall Cornell 81
Morris, Raheem 77
Sapp, Warren 38
Williams, Doug 22

Tanganyikan African National Union (TANU)
Kikwete, Jakaya Mrisho 73
Nyerere, Julius 5

TANU
See Tanganyikan African National Union

Tanzanian African National Union (TANU)
See Tanganyikan African National Union

Tap dancing
Atkins, Cholly 40
Bates, Peg Leg 14
Brown, Ernest 80
Glover, Savion 14
Hines, Gregory 1, 42
Lane, William Henry 90
Robinson, LaVaughn 69
Sims, Howard "Sandman" 48
Slyde, Jimmy 70
Walker, Dianne 57

TBS
See Turner Broadcasting System

Teacher of the Year Award
Draper, Sharon Mills 16, 43
Oliver, Kimberly 60

Teachers Insurance and Annuity Association and the College Retirement Equities Fund (TIAA-CREF)
Wharton, Clifton R., Jr. 7

Teaching
Abani, Chris 77
Adams-Ender, Clara 40
Alexander, Margaret Walker 22
Amadi, Elechi 40
Archie-Hudson, Marguerite 44
Aubert, Alvin 41
Baiocchi, Regina Harris 41
Ballard, Allen Butler, Jr. 40
Beals, Melba Pattillo 15, 94
Belgrave, Marcus 77
Bibb, Henry and Mary 54
Blassingame, John Wesley 40
Branch, William Blackwell 39

Brawley, Benjamin 44
Brown, Uzee 42
Brown, Willa 40
Bryan, Ashley F. 41
Campbell, Mary Schmidt 43
Cardozo, Francis L. 33
Carruthers, George R. 40
Carter, Joye Maureen 41
Chenault, John 40
Cheney-Coker, Syl 43
Clarke, John Henrik 20
Clemmons, Reginal G. 41
Cobb, Jewel Plummer 42
Cobb, W. Montague 39
Cole, Johnnetta B. 5, 43
Colescott, Robert 69
Collins, Patricia Hill 67
Cook, Mercer 40
Cooper Cafritz, Peggy 43
Cortez, Jayne 43
Cortor, Eldzier 42
Cotter, Joseph Seamon, Sr. 40
Dailey, Ulysses Grant 87
Davis, Arthur P. 41
Davis, Gary 41
Davis, Milt 74
De Veaux, Alexis 44
Dennard, Brazeal 37
Draper, Sharon Mills 16, 43
Drummond, William J. 40
Dumas, Henry 41
Dunnigan, Alice Allison 41
Dymally, Mervyn 42
Early, Gerald 15
Everett, Percival 93
Falconer, Etta Zuber 59
Feelings, Muriel 44
Ferguson, Ronald F. 75
Figueroa, John J. 40
Fletcher, Bill, Jr. 41
Ford, Nick Aaron 44
Forrest, Leon 44
Fuller, A. Oveta 43
Fuller, Arthur 27
Fuller, Howard L. 37
Gates, Sylvester James, Jr. 15
Gayle, Addison, Jr. 41
George, Zelma Watson 42
Gibson, Donald Bernard 40
Gill, Gerald 69
Hall, Arthur 39
Hamburg, Beatrix 84
Hammonds, Evelynn 69
Harding, Vincent 67
Hare, Nathan 44
Harris, Barry 68
Harvey, William R. 42
Henries, A. Doris Banks 44
Hill, Errol 40
Hill, Leslie Pinckney 44
Horne, Frank 44
Humphries, Frederick 20
Imes, Elmer Samuel 39
Jackson, Fred James 25
Jarrett, Vernon D. 42
Jarvis, Erich 67
Kennedy, Randall 40
Ladner, Joyce A. 42
Leevy, Carrol M. 42
Lewis, Norman 39
Lindsey, Tommie 51
Luper, Clara 94
Logan, Rayford W. 40

Maathai, Wangari 43
McCullough, Geraldine 58, 79
Mitchell, Parren J. 42, 66
Moore, Harry T. 29
Mphalele, Es'kia 40
Naylor, Gloria 10, 42
Norman, Maidie 20
Oliver, Kimberly 60
Owens, Helen 48
Palmer, Everard 37
Patterson, Mary Jane 54
Peters, Margaret and Matilda 43
Player, Willa B. 43
Prophet, Nancy Elizabeth 42
Puryear, Martin 42
Putney, Martha S. 75
Querino, Manuel Raimundo 84
Ray, Charlotte E. 60
Redmond, Eugene 23
Reid, Senghor 55
Rhodes, Jewell Parker 84
Ross-Lee, Barbara 67
Shockley, Ann Allen 84
Simpson-Hoffman, N'kenge 52
Smith, Anna Deavere 6, 44
Smith, John L. 22
Tillis, Frederick 40
Toler, Burl 80
Tutu, Nontombi Naomi 57
Tyson, Andre 40
Wambugu, Florence 42
Watson, Diane 41
Wells, Henrietta Bell 69
Wesley, Richard 73
Wilkens, J. Ernest, Jr. 43
Yancy, Dorothy Cowser 42
Yarbrough, Camille 40
York, Vincent 40

Teatro Experimental do Negro
Nascimento, Abdias do 93

Techno music
Atkins, Juan 50
Craig, Carl 31, 71
May, Derrick 41

TEF
See Theological Education Fund

Telecommunications
Clyburn, Mignon 78
Gordon, Bruce S. 41, 53, 82
Ibrahim, Mo 67
Irvin, Vernon 65
Wilkins, Ray 47

Television
Akil, Mara Brock 60, 82
Anderson, Eddie "Rochester" 30
Andrews, Tina 74
Arkadie, Kevin 17
Arnold, Tichina 63
Banks, Tyra 11, 50
Beach, Michael 26
Bentley, Lamont 53
Blacque, Taurean 58
Blake, Asha 26
Bonet, Lisa 58
Bowser, Yvette Lee 17
Brady, Wayne 32, 71
Branch, William Blackwell 39
Bridges, Todd 37
Brooks, Golden 62

Brooks, Hadda 40
Brooks, Mehcad 62
Brown, Bobby 58
Brown, James 22
Brown, Joe 29
Brown, Vivian 27
Burnett, Charles 16, 68
Carson, Lisa Nicole 21
Carter, Nell 39
Cash, Rosalind 28
Cedric the Entertainer 29, 60
Cheadle, Don 19, 52
Clack, Zoanne 73
CoCo Brother 93
Coleman, Gary 35, 86
Corbi, Lana 42
Cosby, Bill 7, 26, 59
Creagh, Milton 27
Curtis-Hall, Vondie 17
Davis, Viola 34, 76
de Passe, Suzanne 25
Deezer D 53
Diggs, Taye 25, 63
Dourdan, Gary 37
Dungey, Merrin 62
Earthquake 55
Elba, Idris 49, 89
Elder, Larry 25
Ephriam, Mablean 29
Eubanks, Kevin 15
Evans, Harry 25
Faison, Donald 50
Falana, Lola 42
Fales-Hill, Susan 88
Fields, Kim 36
Flavor Flav 67
Fox, Rick 27
Frazier, Kevin 58
Freeman, Yvette 27
Gardere, Jeffrey 76
Gibbs, Marla 86
Givens, Robin 4, 25, 58
Gray, Willie 46
Greely, M. Gasby 27
Greene, Petey 65
Grier, David Alan 28
Griffin, Angela 80
Hall, Arsenio 58
Hardison, Kadeem 22
Harewood, David 52
Hatchett, Glenda 32
Haynes, Trudy 44
Haysbert, Dennis 42
Hemsley, Sherman 19
Henriques, Julian 37
Hill, Lauryn 20, 53
Hill, Marc Lamont 80
Hughley, D. L. 23, 76
Hyman, Earle 25, 79
Jackson, George 19
Jackson, Randy 40
Jackson, Tom 70
Jarrett, Vernon D. 42
Jean-Louis, Jimmy 76
Joe, Yolanda 21
Johnson, Rodney Van 28
Kandi 83
Kodjoe, Boris 34, 89
Lathan, Sanaa 27
Lesure, James 64
Lewis, Emmanuel 36
Long, Loretta 58
Lomax, Louis E. 90

Lumbly, Carl 47
Mabuza-Suttle, Felicia 43
Mac, Bernie 29, 61, 72
Mahorn, Rick 60
Manigault-Stallworth, Omarosa 69
Mann, Tamela 92
Marsalis, Branford 34
Martin, Helen 31
Martin, Jesse L. 31
Mathis, Greg 26
McCrary Anthony, Crystal 70
McFarland, Roland 49
McGlowan, Angela 64, 86
McKenzie, Vashti M. 29
McKinney, Nina Mae 40
Meadows, Tim 30
Mercado-Valdes, Frank 43
Michele, Michael 31
Miller, Wentworth 75
Mitchell, Brian Stokes 21
Mitchell, Russ 21, 73
Moss, Carlton 16
Nash, Johnny 40
Nash, Niecy 66
Neal, Elise 29
Neville, Arthel 53
Nicholas, Denise 82
Nissel, Angela 42
Norman, Christina 47
Orman, Roscoe 55
Palmer, Keke 68
Parker, Nicole Ari 52
Perry, Tyler 40, 54
Phifer, Mekhi 25
Pickens, James, Jr. 59
Pitts, Byron 71
Poussaint, Renee 78
Pratt, Kyla 57
Premice, Josephine 41
Price, Frederick K. C. 21
Prince-Bythewood, Gina 31, 77
Quarles, Norma 25
Ray, Gene Anthony 47
Reddick, Lance 52
Reynolds, Star Jones 10, 27, 61
Rhimes, Shonda Lynn 67
Richards, Beah 30
Richardson, Salli 68
Ridley, John 69
Roberts, Deborah 35
Robinson, Shaun 36
Rock, Chris 3, 22, 66
Rodrigues, Percy 68
Roker, Al 12, 49
Roker, Roxie 68
Rollins, Howard E., Jr. 17
Russell, Nipsey 66
St. Patrick, Mathew 48
Salters, Lisa 71
Sanford, Isabel 53
Shepherd, Sherri 55
Simmons, Henry 55
Simmons, Kimora Lee 51, 83
Smiley, Tavis 20, 68
Snipes, Wesley 3, 24, 67
Stewart, Nzingha 89
Stuart, Moira 82
Sykes, Wanda 48, 81
Taylor, Jason 70
Taylor, Karin 34
Taylor, Regina 9, 46
Thigpen, Lynne 17, 41
Thompson, Kenan 52

Torres, Gina 52
Tyler, Aisha N. 36
Union, Gabrielle 31, 92
Usher 23, 56
Vaughn, Countess 53
Wainwright, Joscelyn 46
Warner, Malcolm-Jamal 22, 36
Warren, Michael 27
Washington, Hayma 86
Watson, Carlos 50
Wayans, Damien 78
Wayans, Damon 8, 41
Wayans, Marlon 29, 82
Wayans, Shawn 29
Whitaker, Forest 2, 49, 67
Williams, Armstrong 29
Williams, Clarence, III 26
Williams, Serena 20, 41, 73
Williams, Vanessa A. 32, 66
Williams, Wendy 62
Williamson, Mykelti 22
Wilson, Chandra 57
Wilson, Dorien 55

Television direction
Barclay, Paris 37, 94
Warner, Malcolm-Jamal 22, 36
Whack, Rita Coburn 36

Tennessee state government
Ford, Harold E(ugene) 42

Tennessee State University
Phillips, Teresa L. 42

Tennessee Supreme Court
Birch, Adolpho A., Jr. 85

Tennessee Titans football team
George, Eddie 80
McNair, Steve 22, 47, 79

Tennis
Ashe, Arthur 1, 18
Blake, James 43
Garrison, Zina 2
Gibson, Althea 8, 43
Jackson, Jamea 64
McNeil, Lori 1
Noah, Yannick 4, 60
Peters, Margaret and Matilda 43
Rubin, Chanda 37
Washington, MaliVai 8
Williams, Samm-Art 21
Williams, Serena 20, 41, 73
Williams, Venus 17, 34, 62
Young, Donald, Jr. 57

Texas Rangers baseball team
Bonds, Bobby 43
Cottrell, Comer 11

Texas state government
Delco, Wilhemina 33
Johnson, Eddie Bernice 8, 90
Jordan, Barbara 4, 78

Theater administration/ownership
Austin, Lovie 40
Banks, Michelle 59
Borders, James 9
Cortez, Jayne 43
Cox, Ida 42

Gibson, John Trusty 87
Hamlin, Larry Leon 49, 62
Leggs, Kingsley 62
LeNoire, Rosetta 37
Leon, Kenny 10
Marsalis, Delfeayo 41
Spears, Warren 52

Theatrical direction/production
Belgrave, Cynthia 75
Glover, Keith 79
Hall, Juanita 62
Hayes, Teddy 40
McClinton, Marion Isaac 77
Milner, Ron 39
Perry, Tyler 40, 54
Scott, Harold Russell, Jr. 61
Teer, Barbara Ann 81
Thompson, Tazewell 13
Wolfe, George C. 6, 43

Thelonius Monk Institute of Jazz Performance
Blanchard, Terence 43

Theological Education Fund (TEF)
Gordon, Pamela 17
Tutu, Desmond Mpilo 6, 44

Theology
Cone, James H. 3, 82
Franklin, Robert M. 13
Harding, Vincent 67
Wright, Jeremiah A., Jr. 45, 69

Threads 4 Life
Jones, Carl 7
Kani, Karl 10
Walker, T. J. 7

Three Fifths Productions
Marsalis, Delfeayo 41

TIAA-CREF
See Teachers Insurance and Annuity Association and the College Retirement Equities Fund

Time Warner Inc.
Ames, Wilmer 27
Parsons, Richard Dean 11, 33

TLC Beatrice International Holdings, Inc.
Lewis, Reginald F. 6

Togolese government
Eyadéma, Gnassingbé 7, 52
Gnassingbé, Faure 67

The Tonight Show
Eubanks, Kevin 15

Tony awards
Allen, Debbie 13, 42
Bailey, Pearl 14
Belafonte, Harry 4, 65
Carroll, Diahann 9
Carter, Nell 39
Clarke, Hope 14
Cooper, Chuck 75
Davis, Viola 34, 76
Faison, George 16
Falana, Lola 42
Fishburne, Laurence 4, 22, 70

Glover, Savion **14**
Goldberg, Whoopi **4, 33, 69**
Hall, Juanita **62**
Hines, Gregory **1, 42**
Horne, Lena **5, 86**
Hyman, Phyllis **19**
James, Nikki M. **94**
Jones, Bill T. **1, 46, 80**
Jones, James Earl **3, 49, 79**
Jones, Sarah **39**
LaChanze **93**
Lenox, Adriane **59**
McDonald, Audra **20, 62**
Mitchell, Brian Stokes **21**
Mokae, Zakes **80**
Moore, Melba **21**
Premice, Josephine **41**
Rashad, Phylicia **21**
Richards, Lloyd **2**
Rose, Anika Noni **70**
Santiago-Hudson, Ruben **85**
Thigpen, Lynne **17, 41**
Uggams, Leslie **23**
Vereen, Ben **4**
Washington, Denzel **1, 16, 93**
Wilson, August **7, 33, 55**
Wolfe, George C. **6, 43**
Wright, Jeffrey **54**

Toronto Blue Jays baseball team
Carter, Joe **30**
Gaston, Cito **71**
McGriff, Fred **24**

Toronto Raptors basketball team
Carter, Butch **27**
Carter, Vince **26**
Olajuwon, Hakeem **2, 72**
Thomas, Isiah **7, 26, 65**

Tourism
Edmunds, Gladys **48**

Track and field
Ashford, Evelyn **63**
Beamon, Bob **30**
Bekele, Kenenisa **75**
Bolt, Usain **73**
Christie, Linford **8**
Clay, Bryan **57, 74**
Devers, Gail **7, 87**
Dibaba, Tirunesh **73**
Felix, Allyson **48**
Freeman, Cathy **29**
Gebrselassie, Haile **70**
Graham, Trevor **84**
Greene, Maurice **27, 77**
Griffith-Joyner, Florence **28**
Harrison, Alvin **28**
Harrison, Calvin **28**
Hayes, Bob **77**
Holmes, Kelly **47**
Jacobs, Regina **38**
James, G. Larry **74**
Johnson, Michael **13**
Johnson, Rodney Van **28**
Jones, Lou **64**
Jones, Marion **21, 66**
Joyner-Kersee, Jackie **5**
Keflezighi, Meb **49**
Lewis, Carl **4**
Matson, Ollie **93**

Metcalfe, Ralph **26**
Montgomery, Tim **41**
Moses, Edwin **8**
Mutola, Maria **12**
Owens, Jesse **2**
Pollard, Fritz **53**
Powell, Mike **7**
Quirot, Ana **13**
Richards, Sanya **66**
Rudolph, Wilma **4**
Thugwane, Josia **21**
White, Willye **67**
Whitfield, Mal **60**
Williams, Lauryn **58**
Woodruff, John **68**

TransAfrica Forum, Inc.
Fletcher, Bill, Jr. **41**
Robinson, Randall **7, 46**

Transplant surgery
Callender, Clive O. **3**
Kountz, Samuel L. **10**

Transport and General Workers' Union
Morris, William "Bill" **51**

"Trial of the Century"
Cochran, Johnnie **11, 39, 52**
Darden, Christopher **13**
Simpson, O. J. **15**

Trombone
Marsalis, Delfeayo **41**
Powell, Benny **87**

Trumpet
Adderley, Nat **29**
Armstrong, Louis **2**
Belgrave, Marcus **77**
Blanchard, Terence **43**
Brown, Clifford **86**
Dara, Olu **35**
Davis, Miles **4**
Dixon, Bill **87**
Eldridge, Roy **37**
Ellison, Ralph **7**
Farmer, Art **38**
Gillespie, Dizzy **1**
Hubbard, Freddie **75**
Jones, Jonah **39**
Jones, Thad **68**
Marsalis, Wynton **16, 90**
Smith, Cladys "Jabbo" **32**
Terry, Clark **39**
Wilson, Gerald **49**

Turner Broadcasting System (TBS)
Clayton, Xernona **3, 45**

Tuskegee Airmen
Archer, Lee, Jr. **79**
Bromery, Randolph Wilson **85**
Brown, Willa **40**
Davis, Benjamin O., Jr. **2, 43**
Haysbert, Raymond V., Sr. **87**
James, Daniel, Jr. **16**
Patterson, Frederick Douglass **12**

Tuskegee University
Carver, George Washington **4**
Dawson, William Levi **39**
Gomillion, Charles **90**

Harvey, William R. **42**
Moton, Robert Russa **83**
Payton, Benjamin F. **23**
Taylor, Robert Robinson **80**

TV One
Ligging, Alfred, III **43**

UAW
See United Auto Workers

UCC
See United Church of Christ

UFBL
See Universal Foundation for Better Living

UGA
See United Golf Association

Ugandan government
Amin, Idi **42**
Museveni, Yoweri **4**
Obote, Milton **63**

Ultraviolet camera/spectrograph (UVC)
Carruthers, George R. **40**

Umkhonto we Sizwe
Hani, Chris **6**
Mandela, Nelson **1, 14, 77**
Motlanthe, Kgalema **74**
Zuma, Jacob **33, 75**

UN
See United Nations

UNCF
See United Negro College Fund

Underground Railroad
Blockson, Charles L. **42**
Cohen, Anthony **15**
Crew, Spencer R. **55**
DeBaptiste, George **32**
Shadd, Abraham D. **81**

Unemployment and Poverty Action Committee
Forman, James **7, 51**

UNESCO
See United Nations Educational, Scientific, and Cultural Organization

UNESCO Medals
Dadié, Bernard **34**

UNIA
See Universal Negro Improvement Association

UNICEF
See United Nations Children's Fund

Unions
Brown, Lloyd Louis **42**
Clay, William Lacy **8**
Crockett, George W., Jr. **10, 64**
Ellis-Lamkins, Phaedra **88**
Europe, James Reese **10**
Farmer, James **2, 64**
Fletcher, Benjamin **90**
Fletcher, Bill, Jr. **41**
Hilliard, David **7**

Holt Baker, Arlene **73**
Lucy, William **50**
Morris, William "Bill" **51**
Ramaphosa, Cyril **3**
Randolph, A. Philip **3**
Roberts, Lillian **83**
Smith, Nate **49**
Touré, Sekou **6**
Wyatt, Addie L. **56**

UNIP
See United National Independence Party

UNITA
See National Union for the Total Independence of Angola

United Auto Workers (UAW)
Fletcher, Bill, Jr. **41**

United Church of Christ (UCC)
Chavis, Benjamin **6**
Forbes, James A., Jr. **71**
Moss, Otis, III **72**

United Democratic Front (UDF; Malawi)
Muluzi, Bakili **14, 76**

United Golf Association (UGA)
Elder, Lee **6**
Sifford, Charlie **4, 49**

United Methodist Church
Caldwell, Kirbyjon **55**
Lawson, James M., Jr. **90**
Lewis, Shirley A. R. **14**
Muzorewa, Abel **85**
Stith, Charles R. **73**

United Nations (UN)
Annan, Kofi Atta **15, 48**
Bunche, Ralph J. **5**
Cleaver, Emanuel **4, 45, 68**
Diouf, Abdou **3**
Juma, Calestous **57**
Lafontant, Jewel Stradford **3, 51**
McDonald, Gabrielle Kirk **20**
McHenry, Donald F. **83**
Mongella, Gertrude **11**
Perkins, Edward **5**
Sampson, Edith S. **4**
Young, Andrew **3, 48**

United Nations Children's Fund (UNICEF)
Baker, Gwendolyn Calvert **9**
Belafonte, Harry **4, 65**
Machel, Graca Simbine **16**
Weah, George **58**

United Nations Educational, Scientific, and Cultural Organization (UNESCO)
Diop, Cheikh Anta **4**
Frazier, E. Franklin **10**
Machel, Graca Simbine **16**
Smythe Haith, Mabel **61**

United Negro College Fund (UNCF)
Boyd, T. B., III **6**
Bunkley, Anita Richmond **39**
Creagh, Milton **27**
Dawson, Matel, Jr. **39**

Edley, Christopher **2, 48**
Gray, William H., III **3**
Jordan, Vernon E. **3, 35**
Lomax, Michael L. **58**
Mays, Benjamin E. **7**
Patterson, Frederick Douglass **12**
Tillis, Frederick **40**

United Parcel Service
Cooper, Evern **40**
Darden, Calvin **38**
Washington, Patrice Clarke **12**

United Parcel Service Foundation
Cooper, Evern **40**

United Somali Congress
Ali Mahdi Mohamed **5**

United States Delegations
Shabazz, Ilyasah **36**

United States Football League (USFL)
White, Reggie **6, 50**
Williams, Doug **22**

United Way
Donald, Arnold Wayne **36**

United Workers Union of South Africa (UWUSA)
Buthelezi, Mangosuthu Gatsha **9**

Universal Foundation for Better Living (UFBL)
Colemon, Johnnie **11**
Reese, Della **6, 20**

Universal Negro Improvement Association (UNIA)
Austin, Junius C. **44**
Garvey, Marcus **1**
McGuire, George Alexander **80**

University administration
See College and university administration

University of Alabama
Davis, Mike **41**
Lucy Foster, Autherine **35**

University of California–Berkeley
Blackwell, David **79**
Drummond, William J. **40**
Edley, Christopher F., Jr. **48**

University of Cape Town
Ramphele, Maphela **29**

University of Chicago Hospitals
Lee, Raphael C. **87**

University of Colorado
Berry, Mary Frances **7**

University of Delaware
Mitchell, Sharon **36**

University of Florida
Haskins, James **36, 54**

University of Michigan
Amaker, Tommy **62**
Dillard, Godfrey J. **45**

Fuller, A. Oveta **43**
Goss, Tom **23**
Gray, Ida **41**
Imes, Elmer Samuel **39**

University of Missouri
Anderson, Mike **63**
Floyd, Elson S. **41**

University of North Carolina
Floyd, Elson S. **41**

University of Notre Dame
Willingham, Tyrone **43**

University of Texas
Granville, Evelyn Boyd **36**

University of the West Indies
Brathwaite, Kamau **36**
Hill, Errol **40**

University of Virginia
Littlepage, Craig **35**

Upscale magazine
Bronner, Nathaniel H., Sr. **32**

Urban League (regional)
Adams, Sheila J. **25**
Clayton, Xernona **3, 45**
Jacob, John E. **2**
Layton, William **87**
Mays, Benjamin E. **7**
Young, Whitney M., Jr. **4**

Urban planning/renewal
Allen, Will **74**
Archer, Dennis **7, 36**
Blakely, Edward J. **88**
Bosley, Freeman, Jr. **7**
Carter, Majora **77**
Harris, Alice **7**
Lane, Vincent **5**
Waters, Maxine **3, 67**

U.S. Air Force
Anderson, Michael P. **40**
Carter, Joye Maureen **41**
Davis, Benjamin O., Jr. **2, 43**
Drew, Alvin, Jr. **67**
Dwight, Edward **65**
Gregory, Frederick **8, 51**
Harris, Marcelite Jordan **16**
James, Daniel, Jr. **16**
Johnson, Lonnie G. **32, 93**
Jones, Wayne **53**
Lyles, Lester **31**

U.S. Army
Adams-Ender, Clara **40**
Baker, Vernon Joseph **65, 87**
Brown, Anthony G. **72**
Cadoria, Sherian Grace **14**
Clemmons, Reginal G. **41**
Davis, Benjamin O., Sr. **4**
Delany, Martin R. **27**
Flipper, Henry O. **3**
Greenhouse, Bunnatine "Bunny" **57**
Honoré, Russel L. **64**
Jackson, Fred James **25**
Johnson, Hazel **22**
Johnson, Shoshana **47**
King, Teresa **80**
Matthews, Mark **59**
Perry, Herman **89**

Poindexter, Hildrus A. **87**
Powell, Colin **1, 28, 75**
Rogers, Alan G. **72**
Snow, Samuel **71**
Stanford, John **20**
Watkins, Perry **12**
West, Allen **89**
West, Togo D., Jr. **16**
Young, Charles **77**

U.S. Army Air Corps
Anderson, Charles Edward **37**

U.S. Atomic Energy Commission
Nabrit, Samuel Milton **47**

U.S. Attorney's Office
Jordan, Eddie **82**
Lafontant, Jewel Stradford **3, 51**

U.S. Bureau of Engraving and Printing
Felix, Larry R. **64**

U.S. Cabinet
Brown, Ron **5**
Elders, Joycelyn **6**
Espy, Mike **6**
Harris, Patricia Roberts **2**
Herman, Alexis M. **15**
Kirk, Ron **11, 75**
O'Leary, Hazel **6**
Powell, Colin **1, 28, 75**
Rice, Condoleezza **3, 28, 72**
Slater, Rodney E. **15**
Sullivan, Louis **8**
Weaver, Robert C. **8, 46**

U.S. Coast Guard
Brown, Erroll M. **23**
Healy, Michael **90**
Rochon, Stephen W. **78**

U.S. Commission on Civil Rights
Berry, Mary Frances **7**
Edley, Christopher **2, 48**
Fletcher, Arthur A. **63**

U.S. Conference of Catholic Bishops
Gregory, Wilton D. **37**

U.S. Court of Appeals
Hastie, William H. **8**
Higginbotham, A. Leon, Jr. **13, 25**
Kearse, Amalya Lyle **12**
Keith, Damon J. **16, 74**
Rawlinson, Johnnie B. **79**
Williams, Ann Claire **82**

U.S. Department of Agriculture (USDA)
Espy, Mike **6**
Layton, William **87**
Sherrod, Shirley **87**
Vaughn, Gladys Gary **47**
Watkins, Shirley R. **17**
Williams, Hosea Lorenzo **15, 31**

U.S. Department of Commerce
Brown, Ron **5**
Irving, Larry, Jr. **12**
Person, Waverly **9, 51**

Shavers, Cheryl **31**

U.S. Department of Defense
Greenhouse, Bunnatine "Bunny" **57**
Johnson, Jeh C. **76**
Tribble, Israel, Jr. **8**

U.S. Department of Education
Ali, Russlynn H. **92**
Hill, Anita **5, 65**
Hill, Bonnie Guiton **20**
Paige, Rod **29**
Purnell, Silas **59**
Thomas, Clarence **2, 39, 65**
Tribble, Israel, Jr. **8**
Velez-Rodriguez, Argelia **56**

U.S. Department of Energy
O'Leary, Hazel **6**

U.S. Department of Health and Human Services (HHS)
See also U.S. Department of Health, Education, and Welfare
Gaston, Marilyn Hughes **60**
Hamburg, Margaret **78**
Hughes, Dora **88**

U.S. Department of Health, Education, and Welfare (HEW)
Bell, Derrick **6**
Berry, Mary Frances **7**
Harris, Patricia Roberts **2**
Randolph, Linda A. **52**
Spearman, Leonard H. O., Sr. **81**
Sullivan, Louis **8**

U.S. Department of Housing and Urban Development (HUD)
Blackwell, J. Kenneth, Sr. **61**
Gaines, Brenda **41**
Harris, Patricia Roberts **2**
Jackson, Alphonso R. **48**
Weaver, Robert C. **8, 46**

U.S. Department of Justice
Bell, Derrick **6**
Campbell, Bill **9, 76**
Days, Drew S., III **10**
Guinier, Lani **7, 30**
Harris, Maya Lakshmi **88**
Holder, Eric H., Jr. **9, 76**
Lafontant, Jewel Stradford **3, 51**
Lewis, Delano **7**
Patrick, Deval **12, 61**
Payton, John **48**
Thompson, Larry D. **39**
Williams, Michael L. **86**

U.S. Department of Labor
Crockett, George W., Jr. **10, 64**
Fletcher, Arthur A. **63**
Herman, Alexis M. **15**

U.S. Department of State
Baltimore, Richard Lewis, III **71**
Bethune, Mary McLeod **4**
Bunche, Ralph J. **5**
Davis, Ruth **37**
Dougherty, Mary Pearl **47**
Frazer, Jendayi **68**
Ervin, Clark Kent **82**
Garrett, Joyce Finley **59**
Grimké, Archibald H. **9**
Haley, George Williford Boyce **21**

Harris, Patricia Roberts **2**
Keyes, Alan L. **11**
Lafontant, Jewel Stradford **3, 51**
McGee, James D. **74**
Perkins, Edward **5**
Powell, Colin **1, 28, 75**
Rice, Condoleezza **3, 28, 72**
Rice, Susan E. **74**
Stokes, Carl **10, 73**
Sutphen, Mona **77**
Van Lierop, Robert **53**
Wharton, Clifton R., Jr. **7**
Wharton, Clifton Reginald, Sr. **36**

U.S. Department of the Interior
Person, Waverly **9, 51**

U.S. Department of the Treasury
Morton, Azie Taylor **48**

U.S. Department of Transportation
Coleman, William T. **76**
Davis, Benjamin O., Jr. **2, 43**

U.S. Department of Veterans Affairs
Brown, Jesse **6, 41**

U.S. Diplomatic Corps
See U.S. Department of State

U.S. District Attorney
Harris, Kamala D. **64**
Lloyd, Reginald **64**

U.S. District Court judge
Bryant, William Benson **61**
Carter, Robert L. **51**
Cooke, Marcia **60**
Diggs-Taylor, Anna **20**
Henderson, Thelton E. **68**
Keith, Damon J. **16, 74**
Parker, Barrington D. **92**
Parsons, James **14**
Williams, Ann Claire **82**

U.S. Dream Academy
Phipps, Wintley **59**

U.S. Environmental Protection Agency
Jackson, Lisa **77**

U.S. Foreign Service
See U.S. Department of State

U.S. Geological Survey
Bromery, Randolph Wilson **85**
Person, Waverly **9, 51**

U.S. House of Representatives
Archie-Hudson, Marguerite **44**
Ballance, Frank W. **41**
Bishop, Sanford D., Jr. **24**
Brown, Corrine **24, 90**
Burke, Yvonne Brathwaite **42**
Carson, André **69**
Carson, Julia **23, 69**
Chisholm, Shirley **2, 50**
Clarke, Yvette **92**
Clay, William Lacy **8**
Clayton, Eva M. **20**

Cleaver, Emanuel **4, 45, 68**
Clyburn, James E. **21, 71**
Collins, Barbara-Rose **7, 87**
Collins, Cardiss **10, 80**
Conyers, John, Jr. **4, 45**
Crockett, George W., Jr. **10, 64**
Cummings, Elijah E. **24**
Davis, Artur **41**
Davis, Danny K. **24, 79**
De Priest, Oscar Stanton **80**
Dellums, Ronald **2, 81**
Diggs, Charles C. **21**
Dixon, Julian C. **24**
Dymally, Mervyn **42**
Edwards, Donna **77**
Ellison, Keith **59**
Espy, Mike **6**
Fattah, Chaka **11, 70**
Fauntroy, Walter E. **11**
Fields, Cleo **13**
Flake, Floyd H. **18**
Ford, Harold E(ugene) **42**
Ford, Harold E(ugene), Jr. **16, 70**
Franks, Gary **2**
Fudge, Marcia L. **76**
Gray, William H., III **3**
Hastings, Alcee L. **16**
Hawkins, Augustus F. **68**
Hilliard, Earl F. **24**
Jackson, Jesse, Jr. **14, 45, 81**
Jackson Lee, Sheila **20**
Jefferson, William J. **25, 72**
Johnson, Eddie Bernice **8, 90**
Johnson, Hank, Jr. **80**
Jordan, Barbara **4, 78**
Kilpatrick, Carolyn Cheeks **16**
Lee, Barbara **25**
Leland, Mickey **2**
Lewis, John **2, 46, 83**
Majette, Denise **41**
McKinney, Cynthia **11, 52, 74**
Meek, Carrie **6, 36**
Meek, Kendrick **41, 89**
Meeks, Gregory **25**
Menard, John Willis **90**
Metcalfe, Ralph **26**
Mfume, Kweisi **6, 41**
Millender-McDonald, Juanita **21, 61**
Mitchell, Arthur Wergs **91**
Mitchell, Parren J. **42, 66**
Moore, Gwendolynne S. **55**
Norton, Eleanor Holmes **7, 93**
Owens, Major **6**
Payne, Donald M. **2, 57**
Pinchback, P. B. S. **9**
Powell, Adam Clayton, Jr. **3**
Rangel, Charles B. **3, 52, 85**
Rapier, James T. **82**
Richardson, Laura **81**
Richmond, Cedric **93**
Rush, Bobby **26, 76**
Scott, David **41**
Scott, Robert C. **23**
Sewell, Terri **93**
Smalls, Robert **82**
Stokes, Louis **3**
Towns, Edolphus **19, 75**
Tubbs Jones, Stephanie **24, 72**
Washington, Harold **6**
Waters, Maxine **3, 67**
Watson, Diane **41**
Watt, Melvin **26**
Watts, J. C., Jr. **14, 38**

West, Allen **89**
Wheat, Alan **14**
Wilson, Frederica **92**
Wynn, Albert R. **25, 77**
Young, Andrew **3, 48**

U.S. Information Agency
Allen, Samuel **38**

U.S. Joint Chiefs of Staff
Howard, Michelle **28**
Powell, Colin **1, 28, 75**
Rice, Condoleezza **3, 28, 72**

U.S. Marines
Bolden, Charles Frank, Jr. **7, 78**
Brown, Jesse **6, 41**
Petersen, Franke E. **31**
Von Lipsey, Roderick K. **11**

U.S. Navy
Black, Barry C. **47**
Brashear, Carl **29**
Brown, Jesse Leroy **31**
Doby, Lawrence Eugene, Sr. **16, 41**
Fields, Evelyn J. **27**
Gravely, Samuel L., Jr. **5, 49**
Howard, Michelle **28**
Miller, Dorie **29**
Pinckney, Bill **42**
Reason, J. Paul **19**
Wright, Lewin **43**

U.S. Open tennis tournament
Williams, Venus **17, 34, 62**

U.S. Peace Corps
Days, Drew S., III **10**
Johnson, Rafer **33**
Lewis, Delano **7**

U.S. presidency
Obama, Barack **49, 74, 91**

U.S. Register of the Treasury
Bruce, Blanche Kelso **33**

U.S. Senate
Black, Barry C. **47**
Bowman, Bertie **71**
Braun, Carol Moseley **4, 42**
Brooke, Edward W. **8, 88**
Bruce, Blanche Kelso **33**
Burris, Roland W. **25, 75**
Obama, Barack **49, 74, 91**
Pinchback, P. B. S. **9**

U.S. State Department
See U.S. Department of State

U.S. Supreme Court
Marshall, Thurgood **1, 44**
Thomas, Clarence **2, 39, 65**

U.S. Surgeon General
Elders, Joycelyn **6**
Satcher, David **7, 57**

U.S. Virgin Islands government
DeJongh, John, Jr. **85**
Evans, Melvin H. **88**
Hastie, William H. **8**
Turnbull, Charles Wesley **62**

USDA
See U.S. Department of Agriculture

USFL
See United States Football League

U.S.S. *Constitution*
Wright, Lewin **43**

UVC
See Ultraviolet
   camera/spectrograph

UWUSA
See United Workers Union of South
   Africa

Vancouver Canucks hockey team
Brashear, Donald **39**

Vancouver Grizzlies basketball team
Abdur-Rahim, Shareef **28**

Vaudeville
Anderson, Eddie "Rochester" **30**
Austin, Lovie **40**
Bates, Peg Leg **14**
Cox, Ida **42**
Davis, Sammy, Jr. **18**
Gilpin, Charles Sidney **81**
Johnson, Jack **8**
Martin, Sara **38**
McDaniel, Hattie **5**
Mills, Florence **22**
Robinson, Bill "Bojangles" **11**
Waters, Ethel **7**

Veterans's issues
Carr, Keela **74**

Veterinary science
Jawara, Dawda Kairaba **11**
Lushington, Augustus Nathaniel **56**
Maathai, Wangari **43**
Patterson, Frederick Douglass **12**
Thomas, Vivien **9**

Vibe
Jones, Quincy **8, 30**
Smith, Danyel **40**
Wilbekin, Emil **63**

Vibraphone
Hampton, Lionel **17, 41**

Victim's Bill of Rights
Dee, Merri **55**

Video gaming
Croal, N'Gai **76**
Fils-Aimé, Reggie **74**

Vietnam Veterans of America
Duggins, George **64**

Village Voice
Cooper, Andrew W. **36**
Crouch, Stanley **11**

Violin
Boulogne, Joseph, Chevalier de
   Saint-Georges **94**
Bridgetower, George **78**
Daemyon, Jerald **64**
Dworkin, Aaron P. **52**
Escobar, Damien **56**
Escobar, Tourie **56**
Murray, Tai **47**
Smith, Stuff **37**

Tinsley, Boyd 50
Williams, Claude 80

VIP Memphis magazine
McMillan, Rosalynn A. 36

Virgin Records
Brooks, Hadda 40
Sledge, Percy 39

Virginia state government
Marsh, Henry 32
Martin, Ruby Grant 49
Wilder, L. Douglas 3, 48

Virginia State Supreme Court
Hassell, Leroy Rountree, Sr. 41

Virology
Fuller, A. Oveta 43

Vogue magazine
Talley, André Leon 56

Volleyball
Blanton, Dain 29

Voodoo
Beauvoir, Max 74
Dunham, Katherine 4, 59
Guy, Rosa 5
Hurston, Zora Neale 3
Pierre, Andre 17

Voting rights
Cary, Mary Ann Shadd 30
Chestnut, J. L., Jr. 73
Clark, Septima 7
Forman, James 7, 51
Hamer, Fannie Lou 6
Harper, Frances Ellen Watkins 11
Hill, Jesse, Jr. 13
Lampkin, Daisy 19
Mandela, Nelson 1, 14, 77
Moore, Harry T. 29
Moses, Robert Parris 11
Terrell, Mary Church 9
Touré, Faya Ora Rose 56
Trotter, Monroe 9
Tubman, Harriet 9
Wells-Barnett, Ida B. 8
Williams, Fannie Barrier 27
Williams, Hosea Lorenzo 15, 31
Woodard, Alfre 9

WAAC (Women's Auxiliary Army Corps)
See Women's Army Corps

WAC
See Women's Army Corps

Wall Street
Lewis, William M., Jr. 40
McGuire, Raymond J. 57
Phillips, Charles E., Jr. 57

War criminals
Sankoh, Foday 74

Washington, D.C., city government
Barry, Marion S. 7, 44
Brown, Kwame R. 91
Cooper Cafritz, Peggy 43
Dixon, Sharon Pratt 1
Fauntroy, Walter E. 11

Fenty, Adrian 60, 88
Gray, Vincent C. 88
Hobson, Julius W. 44
Jarvis, Charlene Drew 21
Norton, Eleanor Holmes 7, 93
Washington, Walter 45
Williams, Anthony 21

Washington, D.C., Commission on the Arts and Humanities
Neal, Larry 38

Washington Post
Britt, Donna 28
Davis, George 36
Givhan, Robin Deneen 72
Haygood, Wil 83
Ifill, Gwen 28
King, Colbert I. 69
Maynard, Robert C. 7
McCall, Nathan 8
Nelson, Jill 6, 54
Raspberry, William 2

Washington Redskins football team
Green, Darrell 39, 74
Monk, Art 38, 73
Sanders, Deion 4, 31

Washington State Higher Education Coordinating Board
Floyd, Elson S. 41

Washington Week in Review
TV series
Ifill, Gwen 28

Washington Wizards basketball team
Bickerstaff, Bernie 21
Heard, Gar 25
Howard, Juwan 15
Unseld, Wes 23
Webber, Chris 15, 30, 59

WCC
See World Council of Churches

Weather
Brown, Vivian 27
Christian, Spencer 15
McEwen, Mark 5
Roker, Al 12, 49

Welfare reform
Bryant, Wayne R. 6
Carson, Julia 23, 69
Parker, Star 70
Wallace, Joaquin 49
Williams, Walter E. 4

West Indian folk songs
Belafonte, Harry 4, 65
Rhoden, Wayne 70

West Indian literature
Coombs, Orde M. 44
Guy, Rosa 5
Kincaid, Jamaica 4
Markham, E. A. 37
Marshall, Paule 7, 77
McKay, Claude 6

Walcott, Derek 5, 94

West Point
Davis, Benjamin O., Jr. 2, 43
Flipper, Henry O. 3
Young, Charles 77

West Side Preparatory School
Collins, Marva 3, 71

Western Michigan University
Floyd, Elson S. 41

White House
Allen, Eugene 79
Butts, Cassandra 78
Christie, Ron 83
Gaspard, Patrick 84
Hatcher, Andrew T. 90
Jarvis, Kristen 85
Keckley, Elizabeth 90
Love, Reggie 77
Obama, Michelle 61, 90
Rochon, Stephen W. 78
Rogers, Desirée 88
Rouse, Cecilia 93
Strautmanis, Michael 87

Whitney Museum of American Art
Golden, Thelma 10, 55
Simpson, Lorna 4, 36

Wimbledon
Williams, Venus 17, 34, 62

Wine and winemaking
Allen-Buillard, Melba 55
Rideau, Iris 46

Wisconsin State Supreme Court
Butler, Louis 70

Women Helping Offenders
Holland, Endesha Ida Mae 3, 57

Women's Army Corps (WAC)
Adams Earley, Charity 13, 34
Cadoria, Sherian Grace 14

Women's Auxiliary Army Corps
See Women's Army Corps

Women's issues
Allen, Ethel D. 13
Angelou, Maya 1, 15
Avery, Byllye Y. 66
Ba, Mariama 30
Baker, Ella 5
Bashir, Halima 73
Berry, Mary Frances 7
Brown, Elaine 8
Campbell, Bebe Moore 6, 24, 59
Cannon, Katie 10
Carby, Hazel 27
Cary, Mary Ann Shadd 30
Charles, Mary Eugenia 10, 55
Chinn, May Edward 26
Christian, Barbara T. 44
Christian-Green, Donna M. 17
Clark, Septima 7
Cole, Johnnetta B. 5, 43
Cooper, Anna Julia 20
Davis, Angela 5

De Veaux, Alexis 44
Edelman, Marian Wright 5, 42
Edwards, Lena Frances 76
Elders, Joycelyn 6
Evans, Diana 72
Fauset, Jessie 7
Giddings, Paula 11
Gomez, Jewelle 30
Grimké, Archibald H. 9
Guy-Sheftall, Beverly 13, 92
Hale, Clara 16
Hale, Lorraine 8
Hamer, Fannie Lou 6
Harper, Frances Ellen Watkins 11
Harris, Leslie 6
Harris, Patricia Roberts 2
Height, Dorothy I. 2, 23, 78
Hernandez, Aileen Clarke 13
Hill, Anita 5, 65
Hine, Darlene Clark 24
Holland, Endesha Ida Mae 3, 57
hooks, bell 5, 90
Hughes, Ebony 57
Hull, Akasha Gloria 45
Hussein, Lubna 80
Jackson, Alexine Clement 22
Joe, Yolanda 21
Jordan, June 7, 35
Lampkin, Daisy 19
Larsen, Nella 10
Lorde, Audre 6
Maathai, Wangari 43
Marshall, Paule 7, 77
Mbaye, Mariétou 31
McCabe, Jewell Jackson 10
McCauley, Gina 76
McKenzie, Vashti M. 29
McMillan, Terry 4, 17, 53
Millender-McDonald, Juanita 21, 61
Millner, Denene 76
Mongella, Gertrude 11
Mossell, Gertrude Bustill 40
Naylor, Gloria 10, 42
Nelson, Jill 6, 54
Niane, Katoucha 70
Nichols, Nichelle 11
Norman, Pat 10
Ormes, Jackie 73
Parker, Pat 19
Rawlings, Nana Konadu Agyeman 13
Ruffin, Josephine St. Pierre 75
Shange, Ntozake 8, 89
Sherrod, Shirley 87
Simpson, Carole 6, 30
Smith, Barbara 28
Smith, Jane E. 24
Talbert, Mary B. 77
Terrell, Mary Church 9
Tubman, Harriet 9
Vanzant, Iyanla 17, 47
Walker, Alice 1, 43
Walker, Rebecca 50
Wallace, Michele Faith 13
Waters, Maxine 3, 67
Wattleton, Faye 9
Williams, Fannie Barrier 27
Xuma, Madie Hall 59

Women's Leadership Forum
Shabazz, Ilyasah 36

Women's National Basketball Association (WNBA)
Bolton-Holifield, Ruthie 28
Cash, Swin 59
Catchings, Tamika 43
Cooper, Cynthia 17
Edwards, Teresa 14
Ford, Cheryl 45
Griffith, Yolanda 25
Holdsclaw, Chamique 24
Jones, Merlakia 34
Lennox, Betty 31
Leslie, Lisa 16, 73
McCray, Nikki 18
Miller, Cheryl 10, 74
Milton, DeLisha 31
Moore, Maya 94
Palmer, Violet 59
Parker, Candace 74
Peck, Carolyn 23
Perrot, Kim 23
Staley, Dawn 57
Swoopes, Sheryl 12, 56
Thompson, Tina 25, 75
Williams, Natalie 31
Woodard, Lynette 67

Workplace equity
Clark, Septima 7
Hill, Anita 5, 65
Nelson, Jill 6, 54
Simpson, Carole 6, 30

Works Progress (Projects) Administration (WPA)
Alexander, Margaret Walker 22
Baker, Ella 5
Blackburn, Robert 28
DeCarava, Roy 42, 81
Douglas, Aaron 7
Dunham, Katherine 4, 59
Hall, Juanita 62
Lawrence, Jacob 4, 28
Lee-Smith, Hughie 5, 22
Murray, Pauli 38
Sallee, Charles 38
Sebree, Charles 40

Winkfield, Jimmy 42
Wright, Richard 5

World African Hebrew Israelite Community
Ben-Israel, Ben Ami 11

World Bank
Soglo, Nicéphore 15

World beat
Belafonte, Harry 4, 65
Fela 1, 42
Maal, Baaba 66
N'Dour, Youssou 1, 53, 79
Okosuns, Sonny 71
Ongala, Remmy 9, 91

World Council of Churches (WCC)
Kobia, Samuel 43
Mays, Benjamin E. 7
Tutu, Desmond Mpilo 6, 44

World Cup
dos Santos, Manuel Francisco 65
Gyan, Asamoah 87
Mensah, John 87
Milla, Roger 2
Pelé 7
Scurry, Briana 27

World hunger
Belafonte, Harry 4, 65
Iman 4, 33, 87
Jones, Quincy 8, 30
Leland, Mickey 2
Masire, Quett 5

World Wrestling Entertainment (WWE) Hall of Fame
Ladd, Ernie 64

World Wrestling Federation (WWF)
Ladd, Ernie 64
Lashley, Bobby 63

Rock, The 29, 66

WPA
See Works Progress (Projects) Administration

Wrestling
Ladd, Ernie 64
Lashley, Bobby 63
Rock, The 29, 66

WWF
See World Wrestling Federation

Xavier University of Louisiana
Francis, Norman (C.) 60

Xerox Corp.
Burns, Ursula 60
Rand, A. Barry 6

Yale Repertory Theater
Dutton, Charles S. 4, 22
Richards, Lloyd 2
Wilson, August 7, 33, 55

Yale University
Blassingame, John Wesley 40
Carby, Hazel 27
Davis, Charles T. 48
Hill, Errol 40
Neal, Larry 38

YMCA
See Young Men's Christian Association

Yoruban folklore
Soyinka, Wole 4, 93
Vanzant, Iyanla 17, 47

Young adult literature
Anderson, Ho Che 54
Bolden, Tonya 32
Ekwensi, Cyprian 37
Johnson, Angela 52
Millner, Denene 76

Young Men's Christian Association (YMCA)
Goode, Mal 13
Hope, John 8

Mays, Benjamin E. 7
Tobias, Channing H. 79

Young Women's Christian Association (YWCA)
Baker, Ella 5
Baker, Gwendolyn Calvert 9
Clark, Septima 7
Claytor, Helen 14, 52
Hedgeman, Anna Arnold 22
Height, Dorothy I. 2, 23, 78
Jackson, Alexine Clement 22
Jenkins, Ella 15
Sampson, Edith S. 4
Stewart, Ella 39
Xuma, Madie Hall 59

YWCA
See Young Women's Christian Association

Zairian government
Mobutu Sese Seko 1, 56

Zambian government
Chiluba, Frederick 56, 80
Mwanawasa, Levy 72

ZCTU
See Zimbabwe Congress of Trade Unions

Zimbabwe Congress of Trade Unions (ZCTU)
Tsvangirai, Morgan 26, 72
Young, Roger Arliner 29

Zimbabwean government
Moyo, Lovemore 76
Mugabe, Robert 10, 71
Mukoko, Jestina 75
Muzorewa, Abel 85
Nkomo, Joshua 4, 65

ZTA
See Zululand Territorial Authority

Zululand Territorial Authority (ZTA)
Buthelezi, Mangosuthu Gatsha 9

Cumulative Name Index

Volume numbers appear in **bold**

Aaliyah 1979–2001 **30**

Aaron, Hank 1934— **5**

Aaron, Henry Louis *See Aaron, Hank*

Aaron, Quinton 1984— **82**

Abacha, Sani 1943–1998 **11, 70**

Abani, Chris 1966— **77**

Abbott, Diane (Julie) 1953— **9**

Abbott, Robert Sengstacke 1868–1940 **27**

Abdul-Jabbar, Kareem 1947— **8**

Abdullah, Imaam Isa *See York, Dwight D.*

Abdulmajid, Iman Mohamed *See Iman*

Abdur-Rahim, Shareef 1976— **28**

Abele, Julian 1881–1950 **55**

Abernathy, Ralph David 1926–1990 **1**

Aberra, Amsale 1954— **67**

Abiola, Moshood 1937–1998 **70**

Abrahams, Peter 1919— **39**

Abubakar, Abdulsalami 1942— **66**

Abu-Jamal, Mumia 1954— **15**

Ace, Johnny 1929–1954 **36**

Achebe, (Albert) Chinua(lumogu) 1930— **6**

Acogny, Germaine 1944— **55**

Adams, Eula L. 1950— **39**

Adams, Floyd, Jr. 1945— **12**

Adams, Grantley 1898–1971 **82**

Adams, H. Leslie *See Adams, Leslie*

Adams, Jenoyne (?)— **60**

Adams, Johnny 1932–1998 **39**

Adams, Leslie 1932— **39**

Adams, Oleta 19(?)(?)— **18**

Adams, Osceola Macarthy 1890–1983 **31**

Adams, Paul 1977— **50**

Adams, Sheila J. 1943— **25**

Adams, Yolanda 1961— **17, 67**

Adams-Campbell, Lucille L. 1953— **60**

Adams Earley, Charity (Edna) 1918— **13, 34**

Adams-Ender, Clara 1939— **40**

Adderley, Julian "Cannonball" 1928–1975 **30**

Adderley, Nat 1931–2000 **29**

Adderley, Nathaniel *See Adderley, Nat*

Ade, Sunny King 1946— **41**

Adebari, Rotimi 1963(?)— **83**

Adebimpe, Tunde 1975— **75**

Adeniyi, Sunday *See Ade, Sunny King*

Adichie, Chimamanda Ngozi 1977— **64**

Adjaye, David 1966— **38, 78**

Adkins, Rod 1958— **41**

Adkins, Rutherford H. 1924–1998 **21**

Adu, Freddy 1989— **67**

Adu, Fredua Koranteng *See Adu, Freddy*

Adu, Helen Folasade *See Sade*

Afro, Teddy 1976— **78**

Agyeman, Jaramogi Abebe 1911–2000 **10, 63**

Agyeman Rawlings, Nana Konadu 1948— **13**

Ahidjo, Ahmadou 1924–1989 **81**

Ahmed, Sharif 1964— **80**

Aidoo, Ama Ata 1942— **38**

Aiken, Loretta Mary *See Mabley, Jackie "Moms"*

Ailey, Alvin 1931–1989 **8**

Ake, Claude 1939–1996 **30**

Akil, Mara Brock 1970— **60, 82**

Akinnuoye-Agbaje, Adewale 1967— **56**

Akinola, Peter Jasper 1944— **65**

Akintimehin, Olubowale Victor *See Wale*

Akomfrah, John 1957— **37**

Akon 1973(?)— **68**

Akpan, Uwem 1971— **70**

Akunyili, Dora Nkem 1954— **58**

Al-Amin, Jamil Abdullah 1943— **6**

Albright, Gerald 1947— **23**

Alcindor, Ferdinand Lewis *See Abdul-Jabbar, Kareem*

Alcorn, George Edward, Jr. 1940— **59**

Alert, Kool DJ Red 19(?)(?)— **33**

Alexander, Archie Alphonso 1888–1958 **14**

Alexander, Clifford 1933— **26**

Alexander, Elizabeth 1962— **75**

Alexander, John Marshall *See Ace, Johnny*

Alexander, Joyce London 1949— **18**

Alexander, Khandi 1957— **43**

Alexander, Margaret Walker 1915–1998 **22**

Alexander, Sadie Tanner Mossell 1898–1989 **22**

Alexander, Shaun 1977— **58**

Ali, Ayaan Hirsi 1969— **58, 92**

Ali, Hana Yasmeen 1976— **52**

Ali, Laila 1977— **27, 63**

Ali, Mohammed Naseehu 1971— **60**

Ali, Muhammad 1942— **2, 16, 52**

Ali, Rashied 1935–2009 **79**

Ali, Russlynn H. 1971(?)— **92**

Ali, Tatyana 1979— **73**

Ali Mahdi Mohamed 1940— **5**

Allain, Stephanie 1959— **49**

Allen, Betty 1927–2009 **83**

Allen, Byron 1961— **3, 24**

Allen, Claude 1960— **68**

Allen, Debbie 1950— **13, 42**

Allen, Dick 1942— **85**

Allen, Ethel D. 1929–1981 **13**

Allen, Eugene 1919— **79**

Allen, Fulton *See Fuller, Blind Boy*

Allen, Geri 1957— **92**

Allen, Lucy 1932— **85**

Allen, Marcus 1960— **20**

Allen, Ray 1975— **82**

Allen, Richard 1760–1831 **14**

Allen, Robert L. 1942— **38**

Allen, Samuel W. 1917— **38**

Allen, Tina 1949–2008 **22, 75**

Allen, Will 1949— **74**

Allen-Buillard, Melba 1960— **55**

Alonso, Laz 1974— **87**

Alston, Charles Henry 1907–1997 **33**

Amadi, Elechi 1934— **40**

Amaker, Harold Tommy, Jr. *See Amaker, Tommy*

Amaker, Norman 1935–2000 **63**

Amaker, Tommy 1965— **62**

Amaki, Amalia 1949— **76**

Amerie 1980— **52**

Ames, Wilmer 1950–1993 **27**

Amin, Idi 1925–2003 **42**

Ammons, James H. 1952(?)— **81**

Amos, Emma 1938— **63**

Amos, John 1941— **8, 62**

Amos, Valerie 1954— **41**

Amos, Wally 1937— **9**

Amoudi, Mohammed al- 1946— **88**

Anderson, Anthony 1970— **51, 77**

Anderson, Carl 1945–2004 **48**

Anderson, Charles Edward 1919–1994 **37**

Anderson, Eddie "Rochester" 1905–1977 **30**

Anderson, Elmer 1941— **25**

Anderson, Fred 1929–2010 **87**

Anderson, Ho Che 1969— **54**

Anderson, Jamal 1972— **22**

Anderson, Kisean *See Kingston, Sean*

Anderson, Lauren 1965— **72**

Anderson, Marian 1902— **2, 33**

Anderson, Michael P. 1959–2003 **40**

Anderson, Mike 1959— **63**

Anderson, Norman B. 1955— **45**

Anderson, Reuben V. 1942— **81**

Anderson, Viv 1956— **58**

Anderson, William G(ilchrist) 1927— **57**

Andre 3000 *See Benjamin, Andre*

Andrews, Benny 1930–2006 **22, 59**

Andrews, Bert 1929–1993 **13**

Andrews, Mark *See Sisqo*

Andrews, Raymond 1934–1991 **4**

Andrews, Tina 1951— **74**

Angelou, Maya 1928— **1, 15**

Anna Marie *See Lincoln, Abbey*

Annan, Kofi Atta 1938— **15, 48**

Ansa, Tina McElroy 1949— **14**

Anthony, Carmelo 1984— **46, 94**

Anthony, Crystal *See McCrary Anthony, Crystal*

Anthony, Michael 1930(?)— **29**

Anthony, Trey 1974— **63**

Anthony, Wendell 1950— **25**

apl.de.ap 1974— **84**

Appiah, Kwame Anthony 1954— **67**

Arac de Nyeko, Monica 1979— **66**

Arach, Monica *See Arac de Nyeko, Monica*

Archer, Dennis (Wayne) 1942— **7, 36**

Archer, Lee, Jr. 1919— **79**

Archer, Michael D'Angelo *See D'Angelo*

Archer, Osceola *See Adams, Osceola Macarthy*

Archibald, Nathaniel *See Archibald, Tiny*

Archibald, Tiny 1948— **90**

Archie-Hudson, Marguerite 1937— **44**

Ardoin, Alphonse 1915–2007 **65**

Arenas, Gilbert 1982— **84**

Arinze, Francis 1932— **19**

Aristide, Jean-Bertrand 1953— **6, 45**

Arkadie, Kevin 1957— **17**

Armah, Ayi Kwei 1939— 49
Armah, Esther 1963— 87
Armatrading, Joan 1950— 32
Armstrong, Govind 1968— 81
Armstrong, (Daniel) Louis 1900–1971 2
Armstrong, Robb 1962— 15
Armstrong, Vanessa Bell 1953— 24
Arnez J, 1966(?)— 53
Arnold, Monica See Monica
Arnold, Tichina 1971— 63
Arnwine, Barbara 1951(?)— 28
Arrington, Richard 1934— 24
Arroyo, Martina 1936— 30
Artest, Ron 1979— 52
Arthur, Owen 1949— 33
Asante, Molefi Kete 1942— 3
Ashanti 1980— 37
Ashe, Arthur Robert, Jr. 1943–1993 1, 18
Ashford, Calvin, Jr. 1935(?)–2008 74
Ashford, Emmett 1914–1980 22
Ashford, Evelyn 1957— 63
Ashford, Nickolas 1942— 21
Ashley, Maurice 1966— 15, 47
Ashley-Ward, Amelia 1957— 23
Ashong, Derrick 1975— 86
Asim, Jabari 1962— 71
Astatke, Mulatu 1942(?)— 81
Atim, Julian 1980(?)— 66
Atkins, Cholly 1930–2003 40
Atkins, David See Sinbad
Atkins, Erica 1972— See Mary Mary
Atkins, Jeffrey See Ja Rule
Atkins, Juan 1962— 50
Atkins, Russell 1926— 45
Atkins, Tina 1974— See Mary Mary
Atta Mills, John 1944— 75
Atyam, Angelina 1946— 55
Aubert, Alvin 1930— 41
Auguste, Arnold A. 1946— 47
Auguste, Donna 1958— 29
Auguste, (Marie Carmele) Rose-Anne 1963— 13
Augustine, Jean 1937— 53
Austin, Gloria 1956— 63
Austin, Jim 1951— 63
Austin, Junius C. 1887–1968 44
Austin, Lovie 1887–1972 40
Austin, Patti 1948— 24
Austin, Wanda M. 1953(?)— 94
Autrey, Wesley 1956— 68
Avant, Clarence 1931— 19, 86
Avant, Nicole A. 1968— 90
Avery, Byllye Y. 1937— 66
Awoonor, Kofi 1935— 37
Awoonor-Williams, George See Awoonor, Kofi
Awoyinka, Adesiji See Siji
Ayers, Roy 1940— 16
Azikiwe, Nnamdi 1904–1996 13
Ba, Mariama 1929–1981 30
Babangida, Ibrahim (Badamasi) 1941— 4
Babatunde, Obba 19(?)(?)— 35
Babyface 1959— 10, 31, 82
Baca, Susana 1954— 80
Bacon-Bercey, June 1942— 38
Badu, Erykah 1971(?)— 22
Bahati, Wambui 1950(?)— 60
Bailey, Buster 1902–1967 38

Bailey, Chauncey 1949–2007 68
Bailey, Clyde 1946— 45
Bailey, DeFord 1899–1982 33
Bailey, Pearl Mae 1918–1990 14
Bailey, Philip 1951— 63
Bailey, Preston 1948(?)— 64
Bailey, Radcliffe 1968— 19
Bailey, William C. See Bailey, Buster
Bailey, Xenobia 1955(?)— 11
Bailey Rae, Corinne 1979— 83
Baines, Harold 1959— 32
Baiocchi, Regina Harris 1956— 41
Baisden, Michael 1963— 25, 66
Baker, Anita 1957— 21, 48
Baker, Arlene Holt See Holt Baker, Arlene
Baker, Augusta 1911–1998 38
Baker, Constance See Motley, Constance Baker
Baker, Dusty 1949— 8, 43, 72
Baker, Ella 1903–1986 5
Baker, George See Divine, Father
Baker, Gwendolyn Calvert 1931— 9
Baker, Houston A(lfred), Jr. 1943— 6
Baker, Johnnie B., Jr. See Baker, Dusty
Baker, Josephine 1906–1975 3
Baker, LaVern 1929–1997 26
Baker, Matt 1921–1959 76
Baker, Maxine 1952— 28
Baker, Thurbert 1952— 22
Baker, Vernon Joseph 1919–2010 65, 87
Balance, Frank W. 1942— 41
Baldwin, Cynthia A. 1945— 74
Baldwin, James 1924–1987 1
Ballard, Allen B(utler), Jr. 1930— 40
Ballard, Hank 1927–2003 41
Baltimore, Richard Lewis, III 1946— 71
Bambaataa, Afrika 1958— 34
Bambara, Toni Cade 1939— 10
Banda, Hastings Kamuzu 1898(?)–1997 6, 54
Bandele, Asha 1970(?)— 36
Bandele, Biyi 1967— 68
Bandele-Thomas, Biyi See Bandele, Biyi
Banks, A. Doris See Henries, A. Doris Banks
Banks, Ernie 1931— 33
Banks, Jeffrey 1953— 17
Banks, Michelle 1968(?)— 59
Banks, Paula A. 1950— 68
Banks, Tyra 1973— 11, 50
Banks, William (Venoid) 1903–1985 11
Banneker, Benjamin 1731–1806 93
Banner, David 1975(?)— 55
Bannister, Edward Mitchell 1828–1901 88
Banton, Buju 1973— 93
Baquet, Dean 1956— 63
Baraka, Amiri 1934— 1, 38
Barbee, Lloyd Augustus 1925–2002 71
Barber, Atiim Kiambu See Barber, Tiki
Barber, Ronde 1975— 41
Barber, Tiki 1975— 57
Barboza, Anthony 1944— 10

Barclay, Paris 1956— 37, 94
Barden, Donald H. 1943— 9, 20, 89
Barker, Danny 1909–1994 32
Barkley, Charles 1963— 5, 66
Barlow, Roosevelt 1917–2003 49
Barnes, Ernie 1938–2009 16, 78
Barnes, John 1963— 53
Barnes, Lloyd 1944— 77
Barnes, Melody 1964— 75
Barnes, Roosevelt "Booba" 1936–1996 33
Barnes, Steven 1952— 54
Barnett, Amy Du Bois 1969— 46
Barnett, Etta Moten 1901–2004 18, 56
Barnett, Marguerite 1942–1992 46
Barney, Lem 1945— 26
Barnhill, David 1914–1983 30
Barrax, Gerald William 1933— 45
Barrett, Andrew C. 1942(?)— 12
Barrett, Jacqueline 1950— 28
Barrett, Lindsay 1941— 43
Barrett, Mario Dewar See Mario
Barrino, Fantasia 1984— 53, 94
Barrow, Dean 1951— 69
Barrow, Joseph Louis See Louis, Joe
Barrow, Willie T. 1924— 85
Barry, Marion S(hepilov, Jr.) 1936— 7, 44
Bartels, Peggielene 1953(?)— 80
Barthé, Earl 19(?)(?)— 78
Barthe, Richmond 1901–1989 15
Bashir, Halima 1979— 73
Bashir, Omar al- 1944— 77
Basie, William James See Count Basie
Basquiat, Jean-Michel 1960–1988 5
Bass, Charlotta Amanda Spears 1874–1969 40
Bass, Karen 1953— 70
Bassett, Angela 1958— 6, 23, 62
Bassey, Shirley 1937— 25
Baszile, Jennifer 1969(?)— 79
Bates, Clayton See Bates, Peg Leg
Bates, Daisy (Lee Gatson) 1914(?)— 13
Bates, Elias See Diddley, Bo
Bates, Karen Grigsby 19(?)(?)— 40
Bates, Peg Leg 1907— 14
Bath, Patricia E. 1942— 37
Batiste, Alvin 1932–2007 66
Battle, Kathleen 1948— 70
Baugé, Grégory 1985— 86
Baugh, David 1947— 23
Baylor, Don(ald Edward) 1949— 6
Baylor, Elgin 1934— 93
Baylor, Helen 1953— 36
Beach, Michael 1963— 26
Beah, Ishmael 1980— 69
Beal, Bernard B. 1954(?)— 46
Beals, Jennifer 1963— 12
Beals, Melba Pattillo 1941— 15, 94
Beamon, Bob 1946— 30
Bearden, Romare 1912–1988 2, 50
Beasley, Jamar 1979— 29
Beasley, Myrlie See Evers, Myrlie
Beasley, Phoebe 1943— 34
Beaton, Norman Lugard 1934–1994 14
Beatty, Talley 1923(?)–1995 35
Beauvais, Garcelle 1966— 29

Beauvoir, Max 1936(?)— 74
Bebey, Francis 1929–2001 45
Bechet, Sidney 1897–1959 18
Beck, Robert See Iceberg Slim
Beckford, Tyson 1970— 11, 68
Beckham, Barry 1944— 41
Bedie, Henri Konan 1934— 21
Beenie Man 1973— 32
Bekele, Kenenisa 1982— 75
Belafonte, Harold George, Jr. See Belafonte, Harry
Belafonte, Harry 1927— 4, 65
Belgrave, Cynthia 1920–1997 75
Belgrave, Marcus 1936— 77
Bell, Cool Papa See Bell, James "Cool Papa"
Bell, Darrin 1975— 77
Bell, Derrick (Albert, Jr.) 1930— 6
Bell, James "Cool Papa" 1901–1991 36
Bell, James A. 1948— 50
Bell, James Madison 1826–1902 40
Bell, Michael 1955— 40
Bell, Ralph S. 1934— 5
Bell, Robert Mack 1943— 22
Bellamy, Bill 1967— 12
Bellamy, Terry 1972— 58
Belle, Albert (Jojuan) 1966— 10
Belle, Regina 1963— 1, 51
Belton, Sharon Sayles 1951— 9, 16
Benberry, Cuesta 1923–2007 65
Benét, Eric 1966— 28, 77
Benham, Robert 1946— 78
Ben-Israel, Ben Ami 1940(?)— 11
Benjamin, Andre 1975— 45
Benjamin, Andre (3000) 1975(?)— See OutKast
Benjamin, Regina 1956— 20, 75
Benjamin, Tritobia Hayes 1944— 53
Bennett, Estelle 1941–2009 77
Bennett, George Harold "Hal" 1930— 45
Bennett, Gwendolyn B. 1902–1981 59
Bennett, Lerone, Jr. 1928— 5, 84
Bennett, Louise 1919–2006 69
Benson, Angela 19(?)(?)— 34
Bentley, Lamont 1973–2005 53
Berrien, Jacqueline A. 1961— 93
Berry, Bertice 1960— 8, 55
Berry, Bill See Berry, Edwin C.
Berry, Charles Edward Anderson See Berry, Chuck
Berry, Chuck 1926— 29
Berry, Edwin C. 1910–1987 81
Berry, Fred "Rerun" 1951–2003 48
Berry, Halle 1966— 4, 19, 57, 91
Berry, James 1925— 41
Berry, Mary Frances 1938— 7
Berry, Moses 1950(?)— 84
Berry, Theodore M. 1905–2000 31
Berrysmith, Don Reginald 1936— 49
Best, Carrie 1903–2001 80
Betha, Mason Durrell 1977(?)— 24
Bethune, Mary (Jane) McLeod 1875–1955 4
Beti, Mongo 1932–2001 36
Betsch, MaVynee 1935— 28
Bettis, Jerome 1972— 64
Betts, Keter 1928–2005 85

Betts, R. Dwayne 1979(?)— **86**
Bevel, James L. 1936–2008 **75**
Beverly, Frankie 1946— **25**
Beyoncé 1981— **39, 70**
Beze, Dante Terrell *See Mos Def*
Bibb, Eric 1951— **49**
Bibb, Henry 1815–1854 **54**
Bibb, Mary 1820–1877 **54**
Bickerstaff, Bernard Tyrone 1944— **21**
Big Bank Hank *See Sugarhill Gang, The*
Big Boi *See Patton, Antwan*
Big Daddy Kane 1968— **79**
Biggers, John 1924–2001 **20, 33**
Biggers, Sanford 1970— **62**
Biko, Stephen *See Biko, Steven (Bantu)*
Biko, Steven (Bantu) 1946–1977 **4**
Billops, Camille 1933— **82**
bin Wahad, Dhoruba 1943— **85**
Bing, Dave 1943— **3, 59, 78**
Birch, Adolpho A., Jr. 1932— **85**
Birch, Glynn R. 195(?)— **61**
Bishop, Eric *See Foxx, Jamie*
Bishop, Maurice 1944–1983 **39**
Bishop, Sanford D. Jr. 1947— **24**
Bivins, Michael 1968— **72**
Biya, Chantal 1970— **89**
Biya, Paul 1933— **28**
Biyidi-Awala, Alexandre *See Beti, Mongo*
Bizimungu, Pasteur 1951— **19**
Black, Albert 1940— **51**
Black, Barry C. 1948— **47**
Black, Joe 1924–2002 **75**
Black, Keith Lanier 1957— **18, 84**
Black Kold Madina *See Roberts, Kimberly Rivers*
Black Thought 1972— **63**
Blackburn, Robert 1920— **28**
Blackman, Toni 1968— **86**
Blackmon, Brenda 1952— **58**
Blackshear, Leonard 1943— **52**
Blackwell, David 1919— **79**
Blackwell, Kenneth, Sr. 1948— **61**
Blackwell, Robert D., Sr. 1937— **52**
Blackwell, Unita 1933— **17**
Blackwood, Maureen 1960— **37**
Blacque, Taurean 1941— **58**
Blade, Brian 1970— **88**
Blair, Jayson 1976— **50**
Blair, Maxine *See Powell, Maxine*
Blair, Paul 1944— **36**
Blake, Asha 1961(?)— **26**
Blake, Charles E. 1940— **82**
Blake, Eubie 1883–1983 **29**
Blake, James 1979— **43**
Blake, James Hubert *See Blake, Eubie*
Blakely, Edward J. 1938— **88**
Blakey, Art(hur) 1919–1990 **37**
Blanchard, Terence 1962— **43**
Bland, Bobby "Blue" 1930— **36**
Bland, Eleanor Taylor 1944— **39**
Bland, Robert Calvin *See Bland, Bobby "Blue"*
Blanks, Billy 1955(?)— **22**
Blanks, Deborah K. 1958— **69**
Blanton, Dain 1971— **29**
Blassingame, John Wesley 1940–2000 **40**
Blaylock, Ronald 1960(?)— **86**

Blayton, Jesse B., Sr. 1897–1977 **55**
Bleu, Corbin 1989— **65**
Blige, Mary J. 1971— **20, 34, 60**
Blockson, Charles L. 1933— **42**
Blondy, Alpha 1953— **30**
Bloomer, George 1963— **86**
Blow, Charles M. 1968(?)— **73**
Blow, Kurtis 1959— **31**
Bluford, Guion Stewart, Jr. *See Bluford, Guy*
Bluford, Guy 1942— **2, 35**
Bluitt, Juliann Stephanie 1938— **14**
Boateng, Ozwald 1968— **35**
Boateng, Paul Yaw 1951— **56**
B.o.B. 1988— **91**
Bobb, Robert C. 1945— **83**
Bobo, Lawrence 1958— **60**
Bogle, Donald 19(?)(?)— **34**
Bogues, Tyrone "Muggsy" 1965— **56**
Bol, Manute 1963— **1**
Bolden, Buddy 1877–1931 **39**
Bolden, Charles Frank, Jr. 1946— **7, 78**
Bolden, Charles Joseph *See Bolden, Buddy*
Bolden, Frank E. 1913–2003 **44**
Bolden, Tonya 1959— **32**
Bolin, Jane 1908–2007 **22, 59**
Bolt, Usain 1986— **73**
Bolton, Terrell D. 1959(?)— **25**
Bolton-Holifield, Ruthie 1967— **28**
Bonaly, Surya 1973— **7**
Bond, Beverly 1970— **53**
Bond, J. Max, Jr. 1935— **76**
Bond, (Horace) Julian 1940— **2, 35**
Bonds, Barry 1964— **6, 34, 63**
Bonds, Bobby 1946— **43**
Bonds, Margaret 1913–1972 **39**
Bonet, Lisa 1967— **58**
Boney, Lisa Michelle *See Bonet, Lisa*
Bonga, Kuenda 1942— **13**
Bongo, Albert-Bernard *See Bongo, Omar*
Bongo, Ali Ben 1959— **80**
Bongo, Omar 1935–2009 **1, 79**
Bonheur, Yannick 1982— **84**
Bontemps, Arna(ud Wendell) 1902–1973 **8**
Booker, Cory Anthony 1969— **68**
Booker, Simeon 1918— **23**
Borders, James (Buchanan, IV) 1949— **9**
Borders, William Holmes 1905–1993 **94**
Bosh, Chris 1984— **85**
Bosley, Freeman (Robertson), Jr. 1954— **7**
Boston, Kelvin E. 1955(?)— **25**
Boston, Lloyd 1970(?)— **24**
Boulogne, Joseph, Chevalier de Saint-Georges 1745(?)–1799 **94**
Bow Wow 1987— **35**
Bowe, Riddick (Lamont) 1967— **6**
Bowen, John W. E., Sr. 1855–1933 **89**
Bowen, Ruth 1924–2009 **83**
Bowman, Bertie 1931— **71**
Bowman, Herbert *See Bowman, Bertie*
Bowser, Yvette Lee 1965(?)— **17**
Boyd, Edward 1914–2007 **70**

Boyd, Gerald M. 1950–2006 **32, 59**
Boyd, Gwendolyn 1955— **49**
Boyd, John W., Jr. 1965— **20, 72**
Boyd, Melba Joyce 1950— **86**
Boyd, Suzanne 1963— **52**
Boyd, T(heophilus) B(artholomew), III 1947— **6**
Boye, Madior 1940— **30**
Boykin, Keith 1965— **14**
Boykin, Otis 1920–1982 **92**
Boyz II Men **82**
Bradford, Mark 1961— **89**
Bradley, David Henry, Jr. 1950— **39**
Bradley, Ed 1941–2006 **2, 59**
Bradley, J. Robert 1919–2007 **65**
Bradley, Jennette B. 1952— **40**
Bradley, Thomas 1917— **2, 20**
Brady, Wayne 1972— **32, 71**
Brae, C. Michael 1963(?)— **61**
Braithwaite, William Stanley 1878–1962 **52**
Bramlett, Joseph 1988— **91**
Branch, William Blackwell 1927— **39**
Brand, Dionne 1953— **32**
Brand, Elton 1979— **31**
Brandon, Barbara 1960(?)— **3**
Brandon, Thomas Terrell 1970— **16**
Brandy 1979— **14, 34, 72**
Branham, George, III 1962— **50**
Branson, Herman 1914–1995 **87**
Brashear, Carl Maxie 1931— **29**
Brashear, Donald 1972— **39**
Brathwaite, Fred 1972— **35**
Brathwaite, Kamau 1930— **36**
Brathwaite, Lawson Edward *See Kamau Brathwaite*
Braugher, Andre 1962— **13, 58, 91**
Braun, Carol Moseley 1947— **4, 42**
Brawley, Benjamin 1882–1939 **44**
Braxton, Brad 1969(?)— **77**
Braxton, Gene *See Herndon, Angelo*
Braxton, Toni 1967— **15, 61, 91**
Brazile, Donna 1959— **25, 70**
Breed, Eric T. *See MC Breed*
Breed, MC *See MC Breed*
Breedlove, Sarah *See Walker, Madame C. J.*
Breeze, Jean "Binta" 1956— **37**
Bridges, Christopher *See Ludacris*
Bridges, Ruby 1954— **77**
Bridges, Sheila 1964— **36**
Bridges, Todd 1965— **37**
Bridgetower, George 1780(?)–1860 **78**
Bridgewater, Dee Dee 1950— **32, 92**
Bridgforth, Glinda 1952— **36**
Briggs, Curtis 1952(?)— **84**
Brimmer, Andrew F. 1926— **2, 48**
Briscoe, Connie 1952— **15**
Briscoe, Marlin 1946(?)— **37**
Britt, Donna 1954(?)— **28**
Broadbent, Hydeia 1984— **36**
Brock, Lou 1939— **18**
Brock, Roslyn McCallister 1965— **86**
Bromery, Randolph Wilson 1926— **85**
Bronner, Nathaniel H., Sr. 1914–1993 **32**
Brooke, Edward W. 1919— **8, 88**

Brooks, Aaron 1976— **33**
Brooks, Avery 1949— **9**
Brooks, Derrick 1973— **43**
Brooks, Golden 1970— **62**
Brooks, Gwendolyn 1917–2000 **1, 28**
Brooks, Hadda 1916–2002 **40**
Brooks, Mehcad 1980— **62**
Brooks, Tyrone 1945— **59**
Broonzy, Big Bill 1893–1958 **82**
Brother Blue *See Hill, Hugh Morgan*
Brower, William 1916–2004 **49**
Brown, Andre *See Dre, Dr.*
Brown, Angela M. 1964(?)— **54**
Brown, Anne 1912–2009 **76**
Brown, Anthony G. 1961— **72**
Brown, Antron 1976— **85**
Brown, Bobby 1969— **58**
Brown, Buck *See Brown, Robert*
Brown, Byrd 1930–2001 **49**
Brown, Byron W. 1958— **72**
Brown, Carlinhos 1962— **81**
Brown, Cecil M. 1943— **46**
Brown, Charles 1922–1999 **23**
Brown, Chris 1989— **74**
Brown, Chuck 1939— **78**
Brown, Clarence Gatemouth 1924–2005 **59**
Brown, Claude 1937–2002 **38**
Brown, Clifford 1930–1956 **86**
Brown, Cora 1914–1972 **33**
Brown, Corrine 1946— **24, 90**
Brown, Cupcake 1964— **63**
Brown, Donald 1963— **19**
Brown, Eddie C. 1940— **35**
Brown, Elaine 1943— **8**
Brown, Ernest 1916–2009 **80**
Brown, Erroll M. 1950(?)— **23**
Brown, Foxy 1979— **25**
Brown, George Leslie 1926–2006 **62**
Brown, H. Rap *See Al-Amin, Jamil Abdullah*
Brown, Homer S. 1896–1977 **47**
Brown, Hubert Gerold *See Al-Amin, Jamil Abdullah*
Brown, James 1933–2006 **15, 60**
Brown, James 1951— **22**
Brown, James Nathaniel *See Brown, Jim*
Brown, James Willie, Jr. *See Komunyakaa, Yusef*
Brown, Jamie Foster 19(?)(?)— **91**
Brown, Janice Rogers 1949— **43**
Brown, Jesse 1944–2003 **6, 41**
Brown, Jesse Leroy 1926–1950 **31**
Brown, Jim 1936— **11**
Brown, Joe 19(?)(?)— **29**
Brown, Joyce F. 1946— **25**
Brown, Kwame R. 1970— **91**
Brown, Lee P(atrick) 1937— **1, 24**
Brown, Les(lie Calvin) 1945— **5**
Brown, Lloyd Louis 1913–2003 **42**
Brown, Melanie 1975— **73**
Brown, Mike 1970— **77**
Brown, Nappy 1929–2008 **73**
Brown, Oliver Leon 1918–1961 **94**
Brown, Oscar, Jr. 1926–2005 **53**
Brown, Patrick "Sleepy" 1970— **50**
Brown, Robert 1936–2007 **65**
Brown, Ron(ald Harmon) 1941–1996 **5**

Brown, Ronald K. 1966— **91**
Brown, Rosemary 1930–2003 **62**
Brown, Ruth 1928–2006 **90**
Brown, Sean 1976— **52**
Brown, Sterling Allen 1901–1989 **10, 64**
Brown, Tony 1933— **3**
Brown, Uzee 1950— **42**
Brown, Vivian 1964— **27**
Brown, Warren 1971(?)— **61**
Brown, Wesley 1945— **23**
Brown, Willa Beatrice 1906–1992 **40**
Brown, Willard 1911(?)–1996 **36**
Brown, William Anthony *See Brown, Tony*
Brown, Willie 1934— **7, 85**
Brown, Zora Kramer 1949— **12**
Brown Bomber, The *See Louis, Joe*
Browne, Roscoe Lee 1925–2007 **66**
Brownlee, Lawrence 1972(?)— **88**
Broyard, Anatole 1920–1990 **68**
Broyard, Bliss 1966— **68**
Bruce, Blanche Kelso 1849–1898 **33**
Bruce, Bruce 19(?)(?)— **56**
Bruce, Isaac 1972— **26**
Brunson, Dorothy 1938— **1, 87**
Brutus, Dennis 1924— **38**
Bryan, Ashley F. 1923— **41**
Bryant, Cullen 1951–2009 **81**
Bryant, John 1966— **26**
Bryant, John R. 1943— **45**
Bryant, Kobe 1978— **15, 31, 71**
Bryant, Wayne R(ichard) 1947— **6**
Bryant, William Benson 1911–2005 **61**
Bryant, William Cullen *See Bryant, Cullen*
Buchanan, Ray 1971— **32**
Buckley, Gail Lumet 1937— **39**
Buckley, Victoria (Vikki) 1947–1999 **24**
Buff Love *See Fat Boys*
Bullard, Eugene Jacques 1894–1961 **12**
Bullins, Ed 1935— **25**
Bullock, Anna Mae *See Turner, Tina*
Bullock, Steve 1936— **22**
Bully-Cummings, Ella 1957(?)— **48**
Bumbry, Grace (Ann) 1937— **5**
Bunch, Lonnie G., III 1952— **91**
Bunche, Ralph J(ohnson) 1904–1971 **5**
Bunkley, Anita Richmond 19(?)(?)— **39**
Burgess, John 1909–2003 **46**
Burgess, Marjorie L. 1929— **55**
Burke, Selma Hortense 1900–1995 **16**
Burke, Solomon 1940— **31, 86**
Burke, Yvonne Brathwaite 1932— **42**
Burks, Mary Fair 1920–1991 **40**
Burleigh, Henry Thacker 1866–1949 **56**
Burley, Mary Lou *See Williams, Mary Lou*
Burnett, Charles 1944— **16, 68**
Burnett, Chester Arthur *See Howlin' Wolf*
Burnett, Dorothy 1905–1995 **19**

Burnham, Forbes 1923–1985 **66**
Burnim, Mickey L. 1949— **48**
Burning Spear 194(?)— **79**
Burns, Eddie 1928— **44**
Burns, Jesse Louis *See Jackson, Jesse*
Burns, Ursula 1958— **60**
Burnside, R. L. 1926–2005 **56**
Burrell, Orville Richard *See Shaggy*
Burrell, Stanley Kirk *See M.C. Hammer*
Burrell, Tom 1939— **21, 51**
Burris, Chuck 1951— **21**
Burris, Roland W. 1937— **25, 75**
Burroughs, Margaret Taylor 1917— **9**
Burrows, Stephen 1943— **31**
Burrus, William Henry "Bill" 1936— **45**
Burruss, Kandi *See Kandi*
Burt-Murray, Angela 1970— **59**
Burton, LeVar 1957— **8**
Burwell, Bryan 1955— **83**
Busby, Jheryl 1949–2008 **3, 74**
Bush, Gordon 1942— **82**
Bush, Reggie 1985— **59, 88**
Buthelezi, Mangosuthu Gatsha 1928— **9**
Butler, George, Jr. 1931–2008 **70**
Butler, Jerry 1939— **26**
Butler, Jonathan 1961— **28**
Butler, Leroy, III 1968— **17**
Butler, Louis 1952— **70**
Butler, Octavia 1947–2006 **8, 43, 58**
Butler, Paul D. 1961— **17**
Butts, Calvin O, III 1949— **9, 90**
Butts, Cassandra 1965— **78**
Bynoe, Peter C. B. 1951— **40**
Bynum, Juanita 1959— **31, 71**
Byrd, Donald 1949— **10**
Byrd, Eugene 1975— **64**
Byrd, Michelle 1965— **19**
Byrd, Robert (Oliver Daniel, III) 1952— **11**
Byron, JoAnne Deborah *See Shakur, Assata*
Cade, Toni *See Bambara, Toni Cade*
Cadoria, Sherian Grace 1940— **14**
Caesar, Shirley 1938— **19**
Cage, Byron 1965(?)— **53**
Cain, Herman 1945— **15, 92**
Calabrese, Karyn 1947— **89**
Caldwell, Benjamin 1937— **46**
Caldwell, Earl 1941(?)— **60**
Caldwell, Jim 1955— **81**
Caldwell, Kirbyjon 1953(?)— **55**
Calhoun, Cora *See Austin, Lovie*
Calhoun, Lillian Scott 1923–2006 **87**
Callaway, Thomas DeCarlo *See Cee-Lo*
Callender, Clive O(rville) 1936— **3**
Calloway, Cab 1907–1994 **14**
Camara, Moussa Dadis 1964— **76**
Cameron, Earl 1917— **44**
Cameron, James 1914–2006 **80**
Camp, Georgia Blanche Douglas *See Johnson, Georgia Douglas*
Camp, Kimberly 1956— **19**
Campanella, Roy 1921–1993 **25**

Campbell, Bebe Moore 1950–2006 **6, 24, 59**
Campbell, Bill 1954— **9, 76**
Campbell, Charleszetta Lena *See Waddles, Charleszetta (Mother)*
Campbell, Donald J. 1935— **66**
Campbell, E(lmer) Simms 1906–1971 **13**
Campbell, Mary Schmidt 1947— **43**
Campbell, Milton *See Little Milton*
Campbell, Naomi 1970— **1, 31**
Campbell, Tisha *See Campbell-Martin, Tisha*
Campbell-Martin, Tisha 1969— **8, 42**
Canada, Geoffrey 1954— **23**
Canady, Alexa 1950— **28**
Canegata, Leonard Lionel Cornelius *See Lee, Canada*
Cannon, Katie 1950— **10**
Cannon, Nick 1980— **47, 73**
Cannon, Reuben 1946— **50**
Cara, Irene 1959— **77**
Carby, Hazel 1948— **27**
Cardozo, Francis L. 1837–1903 **33**
Carew, Rod 1945— **20**
Carey, Mariah 1970— **32, 53, 69**
Cargill, Victoria A. 19(?)(?)— **43**
Carmichael, Stokely 1941–1998 **5, 26**
Carnegie, Herbert 1919— **25**
Carr, Johnnie 1911–2008 **69**
Carr, Keela 1973— **74**
Carr, Kurt 196(?)— **56**
Carr, Leroy 1905–1935 **49**
Carroll, Diahann 1935— **9**
Carroll, L. Natalie 1950— **44**
Carroll, Rocky 1963— **74**
Carroll, Vinnette 1922— **29**
Carruthers, George R. 1939— **40**
Carson, André 1974— **69**
Carson, Benjamin 1951— **1, 35, 76**
Carson, Johnnie 1943— **85**
Carson, Josephine *See Baker, Josephine*
Carson, Julia 1938–2007 **23, 69**
Carson, Lisa Nicole 1969— **21**
Carter, Anson 1974— **24**
Carter, Ben *See Ben-Israel, Ben Ami*
Carter, Benny 1907–2003 **46**
Carter, Betty 1930— **19**
Carter, Butch 1958— **27**
Carter, Cris 1965— **21**
Carter, Dwayne Michael, Jr. *See Lil Wayne*
Carter, Joe 1960— **30**
Carter, Joye Maureen 1957— **41**
Carter, Kenneth 1959(?)— **53**
Carter, Majora 1966— **77**
Carter, Mandy 1946— **11**
Carter, Martin 1927–1997 **49**
Carter, Nell 1948–2003 **39**
Carter, Pamela Lynn 1949— **67**
Carter, Regina 1966(?)— **23**
Carter, Robert L. 1917— **51**
Carter, Rubin 1937— **26**
Carter, Shawn *See Jay-Z*
Carter, Stephen L(isle) 1954— **4**
Carter, Vince 1977— **26**
Carter, Warrick L. 1942— **27**
Cartey, Wilfred 1931–1992 **47**
Cartiér, Xam Wilson 1949— **41**

Carver, George Washington 1861(?)–1943 **4**
Cary, Lorene 1956— **3**
Cary, Mary Ann Shadd 1823–1893 **30**
Cash, Rosalind 1938–1995 **28**
Cash, Swin 1979— **59**
Cashin, Sheryll 1962— **63**
CasSelle, Malcolm 1970— **11**
Catchings, Tamika 1979— **43**
Catlett, Elizabeth 1919— **2**
Catto, Octavius V. 1839–1871 **83**
Caymmi, Dorival 1914–2008 **72**
Cayton, Horace 1903–1970 **26**
Cedric the Entertainer 1964— **29, 60**
Cee-Lo 1974— **70**
Cenac, Wyatt 1976— **94**
Césaire, Aimé 1913–2008 **48, 69**
Chadiha, Jeffri 1970— **57**
Cham, Adongo Agada Akway 1954(?)— **77**
Chamberlain, Wilt 1936–1999 **18, 47**
Chambers, James *See Cliff, Jimmy*
Chambers, Julius (LeVonne) 1936— **3**
Chamillionaire 1979— **82**
Chaney, John 1932— **67**
Channer, Colin 1963— **36**
Chanté, Keshia 1988— **50**
Chanticleer, Raven 1928–2002 **91**
Chapman, Nathan A., Jr. 1957— **21**
Chapman, Susan E. 1968— **94**
Chapman, Tracy 1964— **26**
Chappell, Emma C. 1941— **18**
Chappelle, Dave 1973— **50**
Charlemagne, Emmanuel *See Charlemagne, Manno*
Charlemagne, Manno 1948— **11**
Charles, Mary Eugenia 1919–2005 **10, 55**
Charles, Pierre 1954–2004 **52**
Charles, Ray 1930–2004 **16, 48**
Charleston, Oscar 1896–1954 **39**
Chase, Debra Martin 1956(?)— **49**
Chase, Leah 1923— **57**
Chase-Riboud, Barbara 1939— **20, 46**
Chatard, Peter 1936— **44**
Chavis, Benjamin (Franklin, Jr.) 1948— **6**
Cheadle, Don 1964— **19, 52**
Cheatham, Doc 1905–1997 **17**
Checker, Chubby 1941— **28**
Cheeks, Maurice 1956— **47**
Chenault, John 1952— **40**
Chenault, Kenneth I. 1952— **4, 36**
Cheney-Coker, Syl 1945— **43**
Cheruiyot, Robert 1978— **69**
Cherry, Deron 1959— **40**
Chesimard, JoAnne (Deborah) *See Shakur, Assata*
Chesnutt, Charles 1858–1932 **29**
Chestnut, J. L., Jr. 1930–2008 **73**
Chestnut, Morris 1969— **31**
Chideya, Farai 1969— **14, 61**
Chief Black Thunderbird Eagle *See York, Dwight D.*
Childress, Alice 1920–1994 **15**
Chiluba, Frederick 1943— **56, 80**
Chineworth, Mary Alice 1917— **79**
Chinn, May Edward 1896–1980 **26**
Chisholm, Daquan 1993— **93**

Chisholm, Samuel J. 1942— **32**
Chisholm, Shirley 1924–2005 **2, 50**
Chissano, Joaquim 1939— **7, 55, 67**
Chong, Rae Dawn 1961— **62**
Christian, Barbara T. 1946–2000 **44**
Christian, Spencer 1947— **15**
Christian-Green, Donna M. 1945— **17**
Christie, Angella **36**
Christie, Linford 1960— **8**
Christie, Perry Gladstone 1944— **53**
Christie, Ron 1969(?)— **83**
Christophe, Henri 1767–1820 **9**
Chuck D 1960— **9**
Church, Bruce *See Bruce, Bruce*
Churchwell, Robert, Sr. 1917–2009 **76**
Chweneyagae, Presley 1984— **63**
Ciara 1985— **56**
Ciara, Barbara 195(?)— **69**
Cissé, Souleymane *See Souleymane, Mahamane*
Clack, Zoanne 1968(?)— **73**
Claiborne, Loretta 1953— **34**
Clark, Celeste (Clesteen) Abraham 1953— **15**
Clark, Joe 1939— **1**
Clark, John Pepper *See Clark-Bekedermo, J. P.*
Clark, Kenneth B. 1914–2005 **5, 52**
Clark, Kristin *See Taylor, Kristin Clark*
Clark, Mamie Phipps 1917–1983 **79**
Clark, Mattie Moss 1925–1994 **61**
Clark, Patrick 1955— **14**
Clark, Septima (Poinsette) 1898–1987 **7**
Clark-Bekedermo, J. P. 1935— **44**
Clark-Cole, Dorinda 1957— **66**
Clarke, Austin C. 1934— **32**
Clarke, Cheryl 1947— **32**
Clarke, George Elliott 1960— **32**
Clarke, Hope 1943(?)— **14**
Clarke, John Henrik 1915–1998 **20**
Clarke, Kenny 1914–1985 **27**
Clarke, Patrice Francise *See Washington, Patrice Clarke*
Clarke, Yvette 1964— **92**
Clark-Sheard, Karen 19(?)(?)— **22**
Clash, Kevin 1960— **14, 93**
Clay, Bryan 1980— **57, 74**
Clay, Cassius Marcellus, Jr. *See Ali, Muhammad*
Clay, William Lacy 1931— **8**
Clayton, Constance 1937— **1**
Clayton, Eva M. 1934— **20**
Clayton, Mayme Agnew 1923–2006 **62**
Clayton, Xernona 1930— **3, 45**
Claytor, Helen 1907–2005 **14, 52**
Cleage, Albert B., Jr. *See Agyeman, Jaramogi Abebe*
Cleage, Pearl 1948— **17, 64**
Cleaver, (Leroy) Eldridge 1935— **5, 45**
Cleaver, Emanuel (II) 1944— **4, 68**
Cleaver, Kathleen Neal 1945— **29**
Clemente, Rosa 1972— **74**
Clement-Holmes, Linda 1962— **94**
Clements, George (Harold) 1932— **2**

Clemmons, Reginal G. 19(?)(?)— **41**
Clemons, Clarence 1942— **41**
Clemons, Michael "Pinball" 1965— **64**
Clendenon, Donn 1935–2005 **26, 56**
Cleveland, James 1932(?)–1991 **19**
Cliff, Jimmy 1948— **28, 92**
Cliff, Michelle 1946— **42**
Clifton, Lucille 1936–2010 **14, 64, 91**
Clifton, Nathaniel "Sweetwater" 1922(?)–1990 **47**
Clinton, George 1941— **9, 93**
Clyburn, James E. 1940— **21, 71**
Clyburn, Mignon 1962— **78**
Coachman, Alice 1923— **18**
Coates, Ta-Nehisi 1975— **76**
Cobb, Jewel Plummer 1924— **42**
Cobb, Monty *See Cobb, W. Montague*
Cobb, W. Montague 1904–1990 **39**
Cobb, William Jelani 1969— **59**
Cobbs, Price M(ashaw) 1928— **9**
Cochran, Johnnie 1937–2005 **11, 39, 52**
Cockrel, Kenneth V., Jr. 1965— **79**
Cockrel, Kenneth Vern, Sr. 1938–1989 **79**
CoCo Brother 19(?)(?)— **93**
Cohen, Anthony 1963— **15**
Cohen, Cathy J. 1962— **88**
Colbert, Virgis William 1939— **17**
Cole, Johnnetta B(etsch) 1936— **5, 43**
Cole, Keyshia 1983— **63**
Cole, Lorraine 195(?)— **48**
Cole, Nat "King" 1919–1965 **17**
Cole, Natalie 1950— **17, 60, 84**
Cole, Rebecca 1846–1922 **38**
Coleman, Bessie 1892–1926 **9**
Coleman, Donald 1952— **24, 62**
Coleman, Gary 1968–2010 **35, 86**
Coleman, James E., Jr. 1948(?)— **79**
Coleman, Ken 1942— **57**
Coleman, Leonard S., Jr. 1949— **12**
Coleman, Mary 1946— **46**
Coleman, Michael B. 1954— **28, 79**
Coleman, Ornette 1930— **39, 69**
Coleman, Troy *See Cowboy Troy*
Coleman, Wanda 1946— **48**
Coleman, William F., III 1955(?)— **61**
Coleman, William T. 1920— **76**
Colemon, Johnnie 1921(?)— **11**
Coleridge-Taylor, Samuel 1875–1912 **75**
Coles, Alice 1951(?)— **80**
Coles, Dennis *See Ghostface Killah*
Colescott, Robert 1925— **69**
Collins, Albert 1932–1993 **12**
Collins, Barbara-Rose 1939— **7, 87**
Collins, Bootsy 1951— **31**
Collins, Cardiss 1931— **10, 80**
Collins, Janet 1917–2003 **33, 64**
Collins, Lyn 1948–2005 **53**
Collins, Marva 1936— **3, 71**
Collins, Patricia Hill 1948— **67**
Collins, Paul 1936— **61**
Collins, William *See Collins, Bootsy*
Colston, Hal 1953(?)— **72**

Colter, Cyrus J. 1910–2002 **36**
Coltrane, Alice 1937–2007 **70**
Coltrane, John William 1926–1967 **19**
Coltrane, Ravi 1965— **71**
Combs, Sean 1969— **17, 43, 92**
Comer, James P(ierpont) 1934— **6**
Common 1972— **31, 63**
Compaore, Blaise 1951— **87**
Compton, John 1925–2007 **65**
Compton-Rock, Malaak 1969— **86**
Condrey, Cory *See CoCo Brother*
Cone, James H. 1938— **3, 82**
Coney, PonJola 1951— **48**
Conneh, Sekou Damate, Jr. 1960— **51**
Connerly, Ward 1939— **14**
Conrad, Barbara Smith 1940(?)— **90**
Conrad, Cecilia A. 1955— **94**
Conté, Lansana 1934(?)–2008 **7, 76**
Contee, Cheryl 1971— **88**
Conyers, John, Jr. 1929— **4, 45**
Conyers, Monica 1964— **85**
Conyers, Nathan G. 1932— **24**
Cook, Charles "Doc" 1891–1958 **44**
Cook, (Will) Mercer 1903–1987 **40**
Cook, Sam 1931–1964 **17**
Cook, Samuel DuBois 1928— **14**
Cook, Suzan D. Johnson 1957— **22**
Cook, Toni 1944— **23**
Cook, Victor Trent 19(?)(?)— *See Three Mo' Tenors*
Cook, Wesley *See Abu-Jamal, Mumia*
Cook, Will Marion 1869–1944 **40**
Cooke, Charles L. *See Cook, Charles "Doc"*
Cooke, Marcia 1954— **60**
Cooke, Marvel 1901(?)–2000 **31**
Cooks, Patricia 1944–1989 **19**
Cools, Anne 1943— **64**
Coombs, Orde M. 1939–1984 **44**
Cooper, Afua 1957— **53**
Cooper, Andrew Lewis *See Cooper, Andy "Lefty"*
Cooper, Andrew W. 1928–2002 **36**
Cooper, Andy "Lefty" 1898–1941 **63**
Cooper, Anna Julia 1858–1964 **20**
Cooper, Barry 1956— **33**
Cooper, Charles "Chuck" 1926–1984 **47**
Cooper, Chuck 1954— **75**
Cooper, Cynthia *See Cooper-Dyke, Cynthia*
Cooper, Edward S(awyer) 1926— **6**
Cooper, Evern 19(?)(?)— **40**
Cooper, Helene 1966— **74**
Cooper, J. California 1932(?)— **12, 85**
Cooper, Lisa 1963— **73**
Cooper, Marcus *See Pleasure P*
Cooper, Margaret J. 194(?)— **46**
Cooper, Michael 1956— **31**
Cooper Cafritz, Peggy 1947— **43**
Cooper-Dyke, Cynthia 1963— **17, 89**
Copeland, Michael 1954— **47**
Coppola, Imani Francesca 1978— **82**
Corbi, Lana 1955— **42**
Corley, Tony 1949— **62**

Cornelius, Don 1936— **4**
Cornish, Sam 1935— **50**
Cornwell, Edward E., III 1956— **70**
Correia, Antoné De'Jaun *See Correia, De'Jaun*
Correia, De'Jaun 1994— **93**
Cortez, Jayne 1936— **43**
Corthron, Kia 1961— **43**
Cortor, Eldzier 1916— **42**
Cosby, Bill 1937— **7, 26, 59**
Cosby, Camille 1945— **14, 80**
Cosby, William Henry, Jr. *See Cosby, Bill*
Cose, Ellis 1951— **5, 50**
Cotter, Joseph Seamon, Sr. 1861–1949 **40**
Cottrell, Comer 1931— **11**
Council, LaVerne 1961(?)— **94**
Count Basie 1904–1984 **23**
Counter, S. Allen 1944— **74**
Couto, Mia 1955— **45**
Coverley, Louise Bennett *See Bennett, Louise*
Cowans, Adger W. 1936— **20**
Cowboy Troy, 1970— **54**
Cox, Bryan 1968— **83**
Cox, Deborah 1974(?)— **28**
Cox, Donald Lee 1936–2011 **93**
Cox, Ida 1896–1967 **42**
Cox, Joseph Mason Andrew 1930— **51**
Cox, Renée 1960— **67**
Cox, William E. 1942— **68**
Craig, Carl 1969— **31, 71**
Craig-Jones, Ellen Walker 1906–2000 **44**
Crawford, Carl 1981— **90**
Crawford, Hank 1934–2009 **77**
Crawford, Randy 1952— **19**
Crawford, Veronica *See Crawford, Randy*
Cray, Robert 1953— **30**
Creagh, Milton 1957— **27**
Crennel, Romeo 1947— **54**
Crenshaw, Kimberlé Williams 1959— **88**
Crew, Rudolph F. 1950(?)— **16**
Crew, Spencer R. 1949— **55**
Crichlow, Ernest 1914–2005 **75**
Crite, Alan Rohan 1910— **29**
Croal, N'Gai 1972— **76**
Crocker, Frankie 1937–2000 **29**
Crockett, George W., Jr. 1909–1997 **10, 64**
Crooks, Garth 1958— **53**
Croom, Sylvester 1954— **50**
Cross, Dolores E. 1938— **23**
Crosthwait, David 1892–1976 **93**
Crothers, Benjamin Sherman *See Crothers, Scatman*
Crothers, Scatman 1910–1986 **19**
Crouch, Andraé 1942— **27**
Crouch, Stanley 1945— **11, 87**
Crowder, Henry 1895–1954(?) **16**
Crump, Lavell *See Banner, David*
Crumpler, Rebecca Lee 1831–1895 **89**
Cruse, Harold 1916–2005 **54**
Crutchfield, James N. 1947— **55**
Cullen, Countee 1903–1946 **8**
Cullers, Vincent T. 1924(?)–2003 **49**
Culp, Napoleon Brown Goodson *See Brown, Nappy*

Culpepper, Daunte 1977— **32, 85**
Cummings, Elijah E. 1951— **24**
Cuney, William Waring 1906–1976 **44**
Cunningham, Evelyn 1916–2010 **23, 85**
Cunningham, Randall 1963— **23**
Curling, Alvin 1939— **34**
Currie, Betty 1939(?)— **21**
Currie, Ulysses 1937— **73**
Curry, George E. 1947— **23**
Curry, Mark 1964— **17**
Curry, Michael 1968— **85**
Curtis, Christopher Paul 1954(?)— **26**
Curtis-Hall, Vondie 1956— **17**
Da Don, Polow 1978— **86**
da Silva, Benedita 1942— **5**
da Silva, Jorge Mário *See Jorge, Seu*
Dabiri, John 1980(?)— **93**
Dabydeen, David 1956— **48**
Dadié, Bernard 1916— **34**
Daemyon, Jerald 1970(?)— **64**
D'Aguiar, Fred 1960— **50**
Dailey, Ulysses Grant 1885–1961 **87**
Daly, Marie Maynard 1921— **37**
Damas, Léon-Gontran 1912–1978 **46**
Dance, Kelvin *See Kitwana, Bakari*
Dandala, Mvume 1951— **77**
Dandridge, Dorothy 1922–1965 **3**
Dandridge, Ray 1913–1994 **36**
Dandridge, Raymond Garfield 1882–1930 **45**
D'Angelo 1974— **27**
Daniels, Gertrude *See Haynes, Trudy*
Daniels, Lee 1959— **36, 76**
Daniels-Carter, Valerie 19(?)(?)— **23**
Danjah, Terror 1977— **91**
Danner, Margaret Esse 1915–1986 **49**
Danquah, Meri Nana Ama 1967— **93**
Danticat, Edwidge 1969— **15, 68**
Dantley, Adrian 1956— **72**
Dara, Olu 1941— **335**
D'Arby, Terence Trent *See Maitreya, Sananda*
Darden, Calvin 1950— **38**
Darden, Christopher 1957— **13**
Darego, Agbani 1982— **52**
Dash, Damon 19(?)(?)— **31**
Dash, Darien 1972(?)— **29**
Dash, Julie 1952— **4**
Dash, Leon 1944— **47**
Datcher, Michael 1967— **60**
Dathorne, O. R. 1934— **52**
Davenport, Arthur *See Fattah, Chaka*
David, Craig 1981— **31, 53**
David, Keith 1954— **27**
Davidson, Jaye 1967(?)— **5**
Davidson, Tommy 1963(?)— **21**
Davis, Allison 1902–1983 **12**
Davis, Altovise 1943–2009 **76**
Davis, Angela (Yvonne) 1944— **5**
Davis, Angela J. 1956— **88**
Davis, Anthony 1951— **11**
Davis, Anthony Moses *See Beenie Man*

Davis, Arthur P. 1904–1996 **41**
Davis, Artur 1967— **41**
Davis, Belva 1932— **61**
Davis, Benjamin O(liver), Jr. 1912–2002 **2, 43**
Davis, Benjamin O(liver), Sr. 1877–1970 **4**
Davis, Bing 1937— **84**
Davis, Charles T. 1918–1981 **48**
Davis, Chuck 1937— **33**
Davis, Danny K. 1941— **24, 79**
Davis, Douglas E. *See Fresh, Doug E.*
Davis, Ed 1911–1999 **24**
Davis, Eisa 1971— **68**
Davis, Ernie 1939–1963 **48**
Davis, Erroll B., Jr. 1944— **57**
Davis, Frank Marshall 1905–1987 **47**
Davis, Gary 1896–1972 **41**
Davis, George 1939— **36**
Davis, Gordon D. 1941— **76**
Davis, Guy 1952— **36**
Davis, Jamelia Niela *See Jamelia*
Davis, James E. 1962–2003 **50**
Davis, Lorenzo "Piper" 1917–1997 **19**
Davis, Mia Amber 1974–2011 **94**
Davis, Mike 1960— **41**
Davis, Miles (Dewey, III) 1926–1991 **4**
Davis, Milt 1929–2008 **74**
Davis, Nolan 1942— **45**
Davis, Ossie 1917–2005 **5, 50**
Davis, Ruth 1943— **37**
Davis, Sammy, Jr. 1925–1990 **18**
Davis, Shani 1982— **58, 84**
Davis, Terrell 1972— **20**
Davis, Thulani 1948— **61**
Davis, Tyrone 1938–2005 **54**
Davis, Viola 1965— **34, 76**
Dawes, Dominique (Margaux) 1976— **11**
Dawkins, Wayne 1955— **20**
Dawn, Marpessa 1934–2008 **75**
Dawson, Andre 1954— **85**
Dawson, Matel "Mat," Jr. 1921–2002 **39**
Dawson, Michael C. 1951— **63**
Dawson, Rosario 1979— **72**
Dawson, William Levi 1899–1900 **39**
Dawuni, Rocky 1969— **94**
Day, Leon 1916–1995 **39**
Days, Drew S(aunders, III) 1941— **10**
De' Alexander, Quinton 19??— **57**
de Assís Moreira, Ronaldo *See Ronaldinho*
De Bankolé, Isaach 1957— **78**
de Carvalho, Barcelo *See Bonga, Kuenda*
de Lavallade, Carmen 1931— **78**
de Passe, Suzanne 1948(?)— **25**
De Priest, Oscar Stanton 1871–1951 **80**
De Shields, André 1946— **72**
De Veaux, Alexis 1948— **44**
"Deadwood Dick" *See Love, Nat*
Dean, Mark E. 1957— **35**
Deas, Gerald 1931— **85**
DeBaptiste, George 1814(?)–1875 **32**
DeBarge, El 1961— **89**

Déby, Idriss 1952— **30**
DeCarava, Roy 1919–2009 **42, 81**
Deconge-Watson, Lovenia 1933— **55**
Dee, Merri 1936— **55**
Dee, Ruby 1924— **8, 50, 68**
Deezer D 1965— **53**
DeFrantz, Anita 1952— **37**
DeGale, James 1986— **74**
Deggans, Eric 1965— **71**
DeJongh, John, Jr. 1957— **85**
Delaney, Beauford 1901–1979 **19**
Delaney, Joe 1958–1983 **76**
Delaney, Joseph 1904–1991 **30**
Delany, Annie Elizabeth 1891–1995 **12**
Delany, Martin R. 1812–1885 **27**
Delany, Samuel R(ay), Jr. 1942— **9**
Delany, Sarah (Sadie) 1889— **12**
Delco, Wilhemina R. 1929— **33**
Delice, Ronald 1966— **48**
Delice, Rony 1966— **48**
DeLille, Henriette 1813–1862 **30**
Dellums, Ronald 1935— **2, 81**
DeLoach, Nora 1940–2001 **30**
Delsarte, Louis 1944— **34**
Demby, William 1922— **51**
Dennard, Brazeal 1929— **37**
Dennis, Gary C. 1950— **91**
Dent, Thomas C. 1932–1998 **50**
Dent, Tom *See Dent, Thomas C.*
DePreist, James 1936— **37**
Derham, James *See Durham, James*
Derûlo, Jason 1989— **93**
Desrouleaux, Jason *See Derûlo, Jason*
DeVard, Jerri 1957(?)— **61**
DeVaughn, Raheem 1975— **91**
Devers, Gail 1966— **7, 87**
Devine, Loretta 1953— **24**
Devine, Major J. *See Divine, Father*
DeWese, Mohandas *See Kool Moe Dee*
Diallo, Amadou 1976–1999 **27**
Dibaba, Tirunesh 1985— **73**
Dickens, Helen Octavia 1909–2001 **14, 64**
Dickenson, Vic 1906–1984 **38**
Dickerson, Debra J. 1959— **60**
Dickerson, Eric 1960— **27**
Dickerson, Ernest 1952(?)— **6, 17**
Dickey, Eric Jerome 1961— **21, 56**
Diddley, Bo 1928–2008 **39, 72**
Diesel, Vin 1967(?)— **29**
Dieudonné 1966— **67**
Diggs, Charles C. 1922–1998 **21**
Diggs, Robert Fitzgerald *See RZA*
Diggs, Scott *See Diggs, Taye*
Diggs, Taye 1972— **25, 63**
Diggs-Taylor, Anna 1932— **20**
Dillard, Godfrey J. 1948— **45**
Dillard, Tramar *See Flo Rida*
Dinkins, David (Norman) 1927— **4**
Diogo, Luisa Dias 1958— **63**
Diop, Birago 1906–1989 **53**
Diop, Cheikh Anta 1923–1986 **4**
Diouf, Abdou 1935— **3**
Dirie, Waris 1965(?)— **56**
Divine, Father 1877(?)–1965 **7**
Dixon, Bill 1925–2010 **87**
Dixon, Dean 1915–1976 **68**
Dixon, George 1870–1909 **52**

Dixon, Ivan 1931–2008 **69**
Dixon, Julian C. 1934— **24**
Dixon, Margaret 192(?)— **14**
Dixon, Rodrick 19(?)(?)— *See Three Mo' Tenors*
Dixon, Sharon Pratt 1944— **1**
Dixon, Sheila 1953— **68**
Dixon, Willie (James) 1915–1992 **4**
DJ Jazzy Jeff 1965— **32**
DJ Lance Rock 1965— **94**
DJ Red Alert *See Alert, Kool DJ Red*
DMC *See Run-DMC*
DMX 1970— **28, 64**
do Nascimento, Edson Arantes *See Pelé*
Dobbs, John Wesley 1882–1961 **89**
Dobbs, Mattiwilda 1925— **34**
Doby, Larry *See Doby, Lawrence Eugene, Sr.*
Doby, Lawrence Eugene, Sr. 1924–2003 **16, 41**
Dodson, Howard, Jr. 1939— **7, 52**
Dodson, Owen 1914–1983 **38**
Dogan, Matthew Winifred 1863–1947 **91**
Doig, Jason 1977— **45**
Doley, Harold, Jr. 1947— **26**
Domingo, Colman 1969— **94**
Domini, Rey *See Lorde, Audre (Geraldine)*
Domino, Fats 1928— **20**
Donald, Arnold Wayne 1954— **36**
Donaldson, Jeff 1932–2004 **46**
Donegan, Dorothy 1922–1998 **19**
Donovan, Kevin *See Bambaataa, Afrika*
Dorrell, Karl 1963— **52**
Dorsey, Lee 1926–1986 **65**
Dorsey, Thomas Andrew 1899–1993 **15**
Dorsey, Thomas J. 1812(?)–1875 **90**
Dortch, Thomas W., Jr. 1950— **45**
dos Santos, José Eduardo 1942— **43**
dos Santos, Manuel Francisco 1933 **65**
Dougherty, Mary Pearl 1915–2003 **47**
Douglas, Aaron 1899–1979 **7**
Douglas, Ashanti *See Ashanti*
Douglas, Denzil Llewellyn 1953— **53**
Douglas, Derek 1971— **88**
Douglas, Emory 1943— **89**
Douglas, Lizzie *See Memphis Minnie*
Douglass, Frederick 1817(?)–1895 **87**
Dourdan, Gary 1966— **37**
Dove, Rita 1952— **6, 78**
Dove, Ulysses 1947— **5**
Downing, George T. 1819–1903 **91**
Downing, Will 19(?)(?)— **19**
Dozier, Lamont *See Holland-Dozier-Holland*
Dr. J *See Erving, Julius*
Drake 1986— **86**
Draper, Sharon Mills 1952— **16, 43**
Drayton, William Jonathan, Jr. *See Flavor Flav*
Dre, Dr. 1965(?)— **10, 14, 30**
Dream, The *See The-Dream*

Drew, Alvin, Jr. 1962— **67**
Drew, Charles Richard 1904–1950 **7**
Drexler, Clyde 1962— **4, 61**
Driskell, David C(lyde) 1931— **7**
Driver, David E. 1955— **11**
Drogba, Didier 1978— **78**
Drummond, William J. 1944— **40**
Du Bois, David Graham 1925— **45**
Du Bois, W(illiam) E(dward) B(urghardt) 1868–1963 **3**
du Cille, Michel 1955(?)— **74**
Dube, Lucky 1964–2007 **77**
DuBois, Joshua 1982— **88**
DuBois, Shirley Graham 1907–1977 **21**
Duchemin, Alamaine See Maxis, Theresa
Duchemin, Marie See Maxis, Theresa
Duchemin, Theresa Maxis See Maxis, Theresa
Ducksworth, Marilyn 1957— **12**
Dudley, Edward R. 1911–2005 **58**
Due, Tananarive 1966— **30**
Duerson, Dave 1960–2011 **93**
Duggins, George 1943–2005 **64**
Duke, Bill 1943— **3**
Duke, George 1946— **21**
Dukes, Hazel Nell 1932— **56**
Dumars, Joe 1963— **16, 65**
Dumas, Henry 1934–1968 **41**
Dunbar, Alice See Dunbar-Nelson, Alice Ruth Moore
Dunbar, Paul Laurence 1872–1906 **8**
Dunbar, Sly 1952— See Sly & Robbie
Dunbar-Nelson, Alice Ruth Moore 1875–1935 **44**
Duncan, Michael Clarke 1957— **26**
Duncan, Tim 1976— **20, 91**
Duncan, Todd 1903–1998 **76**
Dungey, Merrin 1971— **62**
Dungy, Camille 1972— **86**
Dungy, Tony 1955— **17, 42, 59**
Dunham, Katherine 1910–2006 **4, 59**
Dunlap, Ericka 1982(?)— **55**
Dunn, Jerry 1953— **27**
Dunn, Warrick 1975— **90**
Dunner, Leslie B. 1956— **45**
Dunnigan, Alice Allison 1906–1983 **41**
Dunston, Georgia Mae 1944— **48**
Duplechan, Larry 1956— **55**
Dupri, Jermaine 1972— **13, 46**
Durant, Kevin 1988— **76**
Durham, Bobby 1937–2008 **73**
Durham, James 1762–1834(?) **90**
Durham, Robert Joseph See Durham, Bobby
Dutton, Charles S. 1951— **4, 22**
Dutton, Marie Elizabeth 1940— **12**
Dwight, Edward 1933— **65**
Dworkin, Aaron P. 1970— **52**
Dye, Jermaine 1974— **58**
Dymally, Mervyn 1926— **42**
Dyson, Michael Eric 1958— **11, 40**
Eagleson, William Lewis 1835–1899 **90**
Early, Deloreese Patricia See Reese, Della
Early, Gerald (Lyn) 1952— **15**

Earthquake, 1963— **55**
Easley, Annie J. 1933— **61**
Easton, Hosea 1798–1837 **91**
Ebanks, Michelle 1962— **60**
Ebanks, Selita 1983— **67**
Eckstein, William Clarence See Eckstine, Billy
Eckstine, Billy 1914–1993 **28**
Edelin, Ramona Hoage 1945— **19**
Edelman, Marian Wright 1939— **5, 42**
Edgerton, Khia Danielle See K-Swift
Edley, Christopher 1928–2003 **2, 48**
Edley, Christopher F., Jr. 1953— **48**
Edmonds, Kenneth See Babyface
Edmonds, Terry 1950(?)— **17**
Edmonds, Tracey 1967— **16, 64**
Edmunds, Gladys 1951(?)— **48**
Edwards, Donna 1958— **77**
Edwards, Eli See McKay, Claude
Edwards, Esther Gordy 1920(?)— **43**
Edwards, Harry 1942— **2**
Edwards, Herman 1954— **51**
Edwards, Lena Frances 1900–1986 **76**
Edwards, Melvin 1937— **22**
Edwards, Teresa 1964— **14**
Edwards, Trevor 1962— **54**
Edwards, Willarda V. 1951— **59**
Eikerenkoetter, Frederick J., II See Reverend Ike
Ejiofor, Chiwetal 1977(?)— **67**
Ekwensi, Cyprian 1921— **37**
El Wilson, Barbara 1959— **35**
Elam, Keith See Guru
Elba, Idris 1972— **49, 89**
Elder, Larry 1952— **25**
Elder, (Robert) Lee 1934— **6**
Elder, Lonne, III 1931–1996 **38**
Elders, Joycelyn (Minnie) 1933— **6**
Eldridge, Roy 1911–1989 **37**
El-Hajj Malik El-Shabazz See X, Malcolm
Elise, Kimberly 1967— **32**
Ellerbe, Brian 1963— **22**
Ellington, Duke 1899–1974 **5**
Ellington, E. David 1960— **11**
Ellington, Edward Kennedy See Ellington, Duke
Ellington, Mercedes 1939— **34**
Elliott, Lorris 1931–1999 **37**
Elliott, Missy 1971— **31, 90**
Elliott, Sean 1968— **26**
Ellis, Alton 1938–2008 **74**
Ellis, Charles H., III 1958(?)— **79**
Ellis, Clarence A. 1943— **38**
Ellis, Dock 1945–2008 **78**
Ellis, Jimmy 1940— **44**
Ellis-Lamkins, Phaedra 1976— **88**
Ellison, Keith 1963— **59**
Ellison, Ralph (Waldo) 1914–1994 **7**
Elmore, Ronn 1957— **21**
El-Shabazz, El-Hajj Malik See X, Malcolm
Emanuel, James A. 1921— **46**
Emeagwali, Dale 1954— **31**
Emeagwali, Philip 1954— **30**
Emecheta, Buchi 1944— **30**
Emmanuel, Alphonsia 1956— **38**

Ensley, Carol Denis See Nash, Niecy
Ephriam, Mablean 1949(?)— **29**
Epperson, Sharon 1969(?)— **54**
Epps, Archie C., III 1937–2003 **45**
Epps, Mike 1970— **60**
Epps, Omar 1973— **23, 59**
Equiano, Olaudah 1745(?)–1797 **78**
Ericsson-Jackson, Aprille 19(?)(?)— **28**
Ervin, Anthony 1981— **66**
Ervin, Clark Kent 1959— **82**
Erving, Julius 1950— **18, 47**
Escobar, Damien 1987— **56**
Escobar, Tourie 1985— **56**
Esposito, Giancarlo (Giuseppi Alessandro) 1958— **9**
Espy, Alphonso Michael See Espy, Mike
Espy, Mike 1953— **6**
Estelle 1980— **75**
Esters, Monica Ann See Conyers, Monica
Estes, Rufus 1857–19(?)(?) **29**
Estes, Simon 1938— **28**
Estes, Sleepy John 1899–1977 **33**
Eto'o, Samuel 1981— **73**
Eubanks, Kevin 1957— **15**
Eugene-Richard, Margie 1941— **63**
Europe, (William) James Reese 1880–1919 **10**
Evans, Darryl 1961— **22**
Evans, Diana 1972(?)— **72**
Evans, Ernest See Checker, Chubby
Evans, Etu 1969— **55**
Evans, Faith 1973(?)— **22**
Evans, Harry 1956(?)— **25**
Evans, Mari 1923— **26**
Evans, Melvin H. 1917–1984 **88**
Evans, Warren C. 1948— **76**
Eve 1979— **29**
Everett, Francine 1917–1999 **23**
Everett, Percival 1956— **93**
Everett, Ronald McKinley See Karenga, Maulana
Evers, Medgar (Riley) 1925–1963 **3**
Evers, Myrlie 1933— **8**
Evora, Cesaria 1941— **12**
Ewing, Patrick 1962— **17, 73**
Eyadéma, Gnassingbé 1937–2005 **7, 52**
Fabio, Sarah Webster 1928–1979 **48**
Fabolous 1977— **93**
Fabre, Shelton 1963— **71**
Fagan, Garth 1940— **18**
Fair, Ronald L. 1932— **47**
Faison, Donald 1974— **50**
Faison, Frankie 1949— **55**
Faison, George William 1946— **16**
Falana, Lola 1942— **42**
Falconer, Etta Zuber 1933–2002 **59**
Fales-Hill, Susan 1962— **88**
Fanon, Frantz 1925–1961 **44**
Fantasia See Barrino, Fantasia
Farah, Nuruddin 1945— **27**
Fargas, Antonio 1946(?)— **50**
Farley, Christopher John 1966— **54**
Farmer, Art(hur Stewart) 1928–1999 **38**
Farmer, Forest J(ackson) 1941— **1**
Farmer, James 1920–1999 **2, 64**

Farmer-Paellmann, Deadria 1966— **43**
Farr, Mel 1944— **24**
Farrakhan, Louis 1933— **2, 15**
Farrell, Herman D., Jr. 1932— **81**
Farris, Isaac Newton, Jr. 1962— **63**
Fat Boys **92**
Father Goose See Rhoden, Wayne
Fattah, Chaka 1956— **11, 70**
Faulk, Marshall 1973— **35**
Fauntroy, Walter E(dward) 1933— **11**
Fauset, Jessie (Redmon) 1882–1961 **7**
Favors, Steve 1948— **23**
Fax, Elton 1909–1993 **48**
Feaster, Robert Franklin See Sundiata, Sekou
Feelings, Muriel 1938— **44**
Feelings, Tom 1933–2003 **11, 47**
Feemster, Herbert 1942— **72**
Fela 1938–1997 **1, 42**
Felix, Allyson 1985— **48**
Felix, Larry R. (?)— **64**
Fennoy, Ilene 1947— **72**
Fenton, Kevin 1966(?)— **87**
Fentry, Robyn See Rihanna
Fenty, Adrian 1970— **60, 88**
Ferdinand, Rio 1978— **82**
Ferguson, Amos 1920–2009 **81**
Ferguson, Kevin See Slice, Kimbo
Ferguson, Roger W. 1951— **25**
Ferguson, Ronald F. 1950(?)— **75**
Ferrell, Rachelle 1961— **29**
Ferrer, Ibrahim 1927— **41**
Fetchit, Stepin 1892–1985 **32**
Fiasco, Lupe 1982— **64**
Fielder, Cecil (Grant) 1963— **2**
Fielder, Prince Semien 1984— **68**
Fields, C. Virginia 1946— **25**
Fields, Cleo 1962— **13**
Fields, Evelyn J. 1949— **27**
Fields, Felicia P. (?)— **60**
Fields, Julia 1938— **45**
Fields, Kim 1969— **36**
50 Cent 1976— **46, 83**
Figueroa, John J. 1920–1999 **40**
Files, Lolita 1964(?)— **35**
Fils-Aimé, Reggie 1961— **74**
Fine, Sam 1969— **60**
Finner-Williams, Paris Michele 1951— **62**
Fiona, Melanie 1983— **84**
Fishburne, Larry See Fishburne, Laurence
Fishburne, Laurence 1961— **4, 22, 70**
Fisher, Ada Lois Sipuel 1924–1995 **76**
Fisher, Ada M. 1947— **76**
Fisher, Antwone Quenton 1959— **40**
Fisher, Gail 1935–2000 **85**
Fisher, Miles Mark 1899–1970 **91**
Fisher, Rudolph John Chauncey 1897–1934 **17**
Fitzgerald, Ella 1918–1996 **8, 18**
Flack, Roberta 1940— **19**
Flake, Floyd H. 1945— **18**
Flanagan, Tommy 1930–2001 **69**
Flash, Grandmaster See Grandmaster Flash
Flavor Flav 1959— **67**

Fleming, Erik R. 1965— **75**
Fleming, Raymond 1945— **48**
Fletcher, Alphonse, Jr. 1965— **16**
Fletcher, Arthur A. 1924–2005 **63**
Fletcher, Benjamin 1890–1949 **90**
Fletcher, Bill, Jr. 1954— **41**
Fletcher, Geoffrey 1970— **85**
Flipper, Henry O(ssian) 1856–1940 **3**
Flo Rida 1979— **78**
Flood, Curt 1938–1997 **10, 93**
Flowers, Sylester 1935— **50**
Flowers, Vonetta 1973— **35**
Floyd, Elson S. 1956— **41**
Folks, Byron See Allen, Byron
Forbes, Audrey Manley 1934— **16**
Forbes, Calvin 1945— **46**
Forbes, James A., Jr. 1935— **71**
Ford, Barney 1822–1902 **90**
Ford, Cheryl 1981— **45**
Ford, Clyde W. 1951— **40**
Ford, Harold E(ugene) 1945— **42**
Ford, Harold E(ugene), Jr. 1970— **16, 70**
Ford, Jack 1947— **39**
Ford, James Lewis Carter See Ford, T-Model
Ford, Johnny 1942— **70**
Ford, Nick Aaron 1904–1982 **44**
Ford, T-Model 1920(?)— **91**
Ford, Vincent 1940(?)–2008 **75**
Ford, Wallace 1950— **58**
Foreman, George 1948— **1, 15**
Forman, James 1928–2005 **7, 51**
Forman, James, Jr. 1967— **89**
Forrest, Leon 1937–1997 **44**
Forrest, Vernon 1971–2009 **40, 79**
Forté, John 1975— **74**
Forte, Linda Diane 1952— **54**
Fortune, James 1977(?)— **92**
Fortune, T(imothy) Thomas 1856–1928 **6**
Foster, Andrew 1879–1930 **79**
Foster, Cecil (A.) 1954— **32**
Foster, Ezola 1938— **28**
Foster, George "Pops" 1892–1969 **40**
Foster, Henry W., Jr. 1933— **26**
Foster, Jylla Moore 1954— **45**
Foster, Marie 1917–2003 **48**
Foster, Rube See Foster, Andrew
Foster, William P. 1919–2010 **88**
Fowler, Reggie 1959— **51**
Fowles, Gloria See Gaynor, Gloria
Fox, Rick 1969— **27**
Fox, Ulrich Alexander See Fox, Rick
Fox, Vivica A. **15, 53**
Foxx, Anthony 1971— **81**
Foxx, Jamie 1967— **15, 48**
Foxx, Redd 1922–1991 **2**
Francis, Norman (C.) 1931— **60**
Francis, Thais 1980— **93**
Franklin, Aretha 1942— **11, 44**
Franklin, C. L. 1915–1984 **68**
Franklin, Carl 1949— **11**
Franklin, Hardy R. 1929–2004 **9, 87**
Franklin, J. E. 1937— **44**
Franklin, John Hope 1915–2009 **5, 77**
Franklin, Kirk 1970(?)— **15, 49**
Franklin, Robert M(ichael) 1954— **13**

Franklin, Shirley 1945— **34, 80**
Franks, Gary 1954(?)— **2**
Franti, Michael 1966— **93**
Frazer, Jendayi 196(?)— **68**
Frazier, Edward Franklin 1894–1962 **10**
Frazier, Joe 1944— **19**
Frazier, Kevin 1964— **58**
Frazier, Oscar 1956–2005 **58**
Frazier, Ryan 1977— **89**
Frazier, Walt 1945— **91**
Frazier-Lyde, Jacqui 1961— **31**
Fredericks, Henry Saint Claire See Mahal, Taj
Freelon, Nnenna 1954— **32**
Freeman, Aaron 1956— **52**
Freeman, Al(bert Cornelius), Jr. 1934— **11**
Freeman, Cathy 1973— **29**
Freeman, Charles Eldridge 1933— **19**
Freeman, Harold P. 1933— **23**
Freeman, Leonard 1950— **27**
Freeman, Marianna 1957— **23**
Freeman, Morgan 1937— **2, 20, 62**
Freeman, Paul 1936— **39**
Freeman, Yvette **27**
French, Albert 1943— **18**
French, D. M. 1924–2011 **94**
Fresh, Doug E. 1966— **93**
Fresh Prince, The See Smith, Will
Friday, Jeff 1964(?)— **24**
Fryer, Roland G. 1977— **56**
Fudge, Ann (Marie) 1951— **11, 55**
Fudge, Marcia L. 1952— **76**
Fuhr, Grant 1962— **1, 49**
Fulani, Lenora (Branch) 1950— **11**
Fuller, A. Oveta 1955— **43**
Fuller, Arthur 1972— **27**
Fuller, Blind Boy 1907(?)–1941 **86**
Fuller, Charles (Henry) 1939— **8**
Fuller, Howard L. 1941— **37**
Fuller, Hoyt 1923–1981 **44**
Fuller, Meta Vaux Warrick 1877–1968 **27**
Fuller, S. B. 1895–1988 **13**
Fuller, Solomon Carter, Jr. 1872–1953 **15**
Fuller, Thomas O. 1867–1942 **90**
Fuller, Vivian 1954— **33**
Funderburg, I. Owen 1924–2002 **38**
Funnye, Capers C., Jr. 1952(?)— **73**
Fuqua, Antoine 1966— **35**
Fuqua, Harvey 1927–2010 **90**
Futch, Eddie 1911–2001 **33**
Gabre-Medhin, Tsegaye 1936–2006 **64**
Gaines, Brenda 19(?)(?)— **41**
Gaines, Clarence E., Sr. 1923–2005 **55**
Gaines, Ernest J(ames) 1933— **7**
Gaines, Grady 1934— **38**
Gaines, Lloyd 1911–19(?)(?) **79**
Gairy, Eric Matthew 1922–1997 **83**
Gaiter, Dorothy J. 1950(?)— **80**
Gaither, Israel L. 1944— **65**
Gaither, Jake 1903–1994 **14**
Gamble, Kenny 1943— **85**
Gans, Joe 1874–1910 **91**
Gantin, Bernardin 1922–2008 **70**
Gantt, Harvey (Bernard) 1943— **1**
Gardere, Jeffrey 1956— **76**

Gardner, Chris 1954— **65**
Gardner, Edward G. 1925— **45**
Garner, Erroll 1921–1977 **76**
Garnett, Kevin (Maurice) 1976— **14, 70**
Garrett, James F. 1942— **78**
Garrett, Joyce Finley 1931–1997 **59**
Garrett, Sean 1979— **57**
Garrincha See dos Santos, Manuel Francisco
Garrison, Zina 1963— **2**
Garvey, Marcus 1887–1940 **1**
Garvin, Gerry 1967(?)— **78**
Gary, Willie Edward 1947— **12**
Gaskins, Eric 1958— **64**
Gaskins, Rudy 1960(?)— **74**
Gaspard, Patrick 1967— **84**
Gaston, Arthur George 1892–1996 **3, 38, 59**
Gaston, Cito 1944— **71**
Gaston, Clarence Edwin See Gaston, Cito
Gaston, Marilyn Hughes 1939— **60**
Gates, Henry Louis, Jr. 1950— **3, 38, 67**
Gates, Sylvester James, Jr. 1950— **15**
Gay, Marvin Pentz, Jr. See Gaye, Marvin
Gaye, Marvin 1939–1984 **2**
Gaye, Nona 1974— **56**
Gayle, Addison, Jr. 1932–1991 **41**
Gayle, Helene D. 1955— **3, 46**
Gaynor, Gloria 1947— **36**
Gbagbo, Laurent 1945— **43, 90**
Gbowee, Leymah 1971(?)— **76**
Gebrselassie, Haile 1973— **70**
Gentry, Alvin 1954— **23**
George, Eddie 1973— **80**
George, Nelson 1957— **12**
George, Zelma Watson 1903–1994 **42**
Gerima, Haile 1946— **38, 80**
Gervin, George 1952— **80**
Ghostface Killah 1970— **90**
Gibbs, Marla 1931— **86**
Gibson, Althea 1927–2003 **8, 43**
Gibson, Bob 1935— **33**
Gibson, Donald Bernard 1933— **40**
Gibson, John Trusty 1878–1937 **87**
Gibson, Johnnie Mae 1949— **23**
Gibson, Josh 1911–1947 **22**
Gibson, Kenneth Allen 1932— **6**
Gibson, Ted 1965— **66**
Gibson, Truman K., Jr. 1912–2005 **60**
Gibson, Tyrese 1978— **27, 62**
Gibson, William F(rank) 1933— **6**
Giddings, Paula (Jane) 1947— **11**
Gidron, Richard D. 1939–2007 **68**
Gil, Gilberto 1942— **53**
Gilbert, Christopher 1949— **50**
Gilbert, John Wesley 1864–1923 **91**
Giles, Roscoe C. 1890–1970 **93**
Gill, Gerald 1948–2007 **69**
Gill, Johnny 1966— **51**
Gill, Turner 1962— **83**
Gilles, Ralph 1970— **61**
Gillespie, Dizzy 1917–1993 **1**
Gillespie, John Birks See Gillespie, Dizzy
Gilliam, Frank 1934(?)— **23**
Gilliam, Joe, Jr. 1950–2000 **31**

Gilliam, Sam 1933— **16**
Gilliard, Steve 1964–2007 **69**
Gilmore, Marshall 1931— **46**
Gilpin, Charles Sidney 1878–1930 **81**
Ginuwine 1975(?)— **35**
Giovanni, Nikki 1943— **9, 39, 85**
Gist, Carole 1970(?)— **1**
Givens, Adele 19(?)(?)— **62**
Givens, Robin 1964— **4, 25, 58**
Givhan, Robin Deneen 1964— **72**
Gladwell, Malcolm 1963— **62**
Glanville, Douglas Metunwa 1970— **82**
Gloster, Hugh Morris, Sr. 1911–2002 **90**
Glover, Corey 1964— **34**
Glover, Danny 1948— **1, 24**
Glover, Donald 1983— **85**
Glover, Keith 1966— **79**
Glover, Nathaniel, Jr. 1943— **12**
Glover, Savion 1974— **14**
Gnassingbé, Faure 1966— **67**
Goapele 1977— **55**
"The Goat" See Manigault, Earl "The Goat"
Godbolt, James Titus See Slyde, Jimmy
Goines, Donald 1937(?)–1974 **19**
Goings, Russell 1932(?)— **59**
Goldberg, Whoopi 1955— **4, 33, 69**
Golden, Marita 1950— **19**
Golden, Thelma 1965— **10, 55**
Golding, Bruce 1947— **78**
Goldsberry, Ronald 1942— **18**
Golson, Benny 1929— **37**
Golston, Allan C. 1967(?)— **55**
Gomes, Peter J. 1942–2011 **15, 93**
Gomez, Jewelle 1948— **30**
Gomez-Preston, Cheryl 1954— **9**
Gomillion, Charles 1900–1995 **90**
Goode, Mal(vin Russell) 1908–1995 **13**
Goode, W(oodrow) Wilson 1938— **4**
Gooden, Dwight 1964— **20**
Gooden, Linda 1953(?)— **94**
Gooden, Lolita See Roxanne Shante
Gooding, Cuba, Jr. 1968— **16, 62**
Goodison, Lorna 1947— **71**
Goodlett, Carlton B. 1914–1997 **91**
Goodman, Al 1943–2010 **87**
Goodman, Kim C. 1966— **94**
Goodnight, Paul 1946— **32**
Gorden, W. C. 1930— **71**
Gorden, William C. See Gorden, W. C.
Gordon, Bruce S. 1946— **41, 53, 82**
Gordon, Carl 1932–2010 **87**
Gordon, Dexter 1923–1990 **25**
Gordon, Ed 1960— **10, 53**
Gordon, Pamela 1955— **17**
Gordone, Charles 1925–1995 **15**
Gordon-Reed, Annette 1958— **74**
Gordy, Berry, Jr. 1929— **1**
Goreed, Joseph See Williams, Joe
Goss, Carol A. 1947— **55**
Goss, Tom 1946— **23**
Gossett, Louis, Jr. 1936— **7**
Gotti, Irv 1971— **39**
Gourdin, Edward O. 1897–1966 **93**

Gourdine, Meredith 1929–1998 **33**
Gourdine, Simon (Peter) 1940— **11**
Grace, George H. 1948— **48**
Grae, Jean 1976— **51**
Graham, Aubrey Drake *See Drake*
Graham, Lawrence Otis 1962— **12**
Graham, Lorenz 1902–1989 **48**
Graham, Stedman 1951(?)— **13**
Graham, Trevor 1962(?)— **84**
Granderson, Curtis 1981— **66**
Grandmaster Flash 1958— **33, 60**
Grand-Pierre, Jean-Luc 1977— **46**
Granger, Lester B. 1896–1976 **75**
Grant, Augustus O. 1946(?)— **71**
Grant, Bernie 1944–2000 **57**
Grant, Gwendolyn Goldsby
19(?)(?)— **28**
Granville, Evelyn Boyd 1924— **36**
Gravely, Samuel L., Jr. 1922–2004
5, 49
Graves, Butch 1962— **77**
Graves, Denyce Antoinette 1964—
19, 57
Graves, Earl G(ilbert) 1935— **1, 35**
Graves, Earl Gilbert, Jr. *See
Graves, Butch*
Gray, Darius 1945— **69**
Gray, F. Gary 1969— **14, 49**
Gray, Farrah 1984— **59**
Gray, Fred Sr. 1930— **37**
Gray, Frizzell *See Mfume, Kweisi*
Gray (Nelson Rollins), Ida
1867–1953 **41**
Gray, Macy 1970— **29**
Gray, Vincent C. 1942— **88**
Gray, William H., III 1941— **3**
Gray, Willie 1947— **46**
Gray, Yeshimbra "Shimmy" 1972—
55
Greaves, William 1926— **38**
Greely, M. Gasby 1946— **27**
Greely, Margaret Gasby *See
Greely, M. Gasby*
Green, A. C. 1963— **32**
Green, Al 1946— **13, 47, 74**
Green, Cee-Lo *See Cee-Lo*
Green, Darrell 1960— **39, 74**
Green, Dennis 1949— **5, 45**
Green, Grant 1935–1979 **56**
Green, Isaac H. 1959— **79**
Green, Jonathan 1955— **54**
Greene, Jimmy 1975— **74**
Greene, Joe 1946— **10**
Greene, Maurice 1974— **27, 77**
Greene, Petey 1931–1984 **65**
Greene, Ralph Waldo *See Greene,
Petey*
Greene, Richard Thaddeus, Sr.
1913–2006 **67**
Greene, Talib Kweli *See Kweli,
Talib*
Greenfield, Eloise 1929— **9**
Greenfield, Ronnie Spector *See
Spector, Ronnie*
Greenhouse, Bunnatine "Bunny"
1944— **57**
Greenlee, Sam 1930— **48**
Greenwood, Monique 1959— **38**
Greer, Hal 1936— **92**
Gregg, Eric 1951— **16**
Gregory, Ann 1912–1990 **63**
Gregory, Dick 1932— **1, 54**
Gregory, Frederick 1941— **8, 51**

Gregory, Wilton 1947— **37**
Grier, David Alan 1955— **28**
Grier, Eliza Ann 1863(?)–1902 **90**
Grier, Mike 1975— **43**
Grier, Pam 1949— **9, 31, 86**
Grier, Roosevelt (Rosey) 1932— **13**
Griffey, Dick 1938–2010 **89**
Griffey, Ken, Jr. 1969— **12, 73**
Griffin, Angela 1976— **80**
Griffin, Anthony 1960— **71**
Griffin, Bessie Blout 1914— **43**
Griffin, John Arnold, III *See Griffin,
Johnny*
Griffin, Johnny 1928–2008 **71**
Griffin, LaShell 1967— **51**
Griffith, Mark Winston 1963— **8**
Griffith, Patrick A. 1944— **64**
Griffith, Yolanda 1970— **25**
Griffith-Joyner, Florence 1959–1998
28
Griffiths, Marcia 1948(?)— **29**
Grimké, Archibald H(enry)
1849–1930 **9**
Grist, Reri 1932— **84**
Grooms, Henry R(andall) 1944—
50
Guarionex *See Schomburg, Arthur
Alfonso*
Guebuza, Armando 1943— **81**
Guéï, Robert 1941–2002 **66**
Guillaume, Robert 1927— **3, 48**
Güines, Tata 1930–2008 **69**
Guinier, (Carol) Lani 1950— **7, 30**
Gumbel, Bryant 1948— **14, 80**
Gumbel, Greg 1946— **8**
Gunn, Moses 1929–1993 **10**
Gurira, Danai 1978(?)— **73**
Guru 1961–2010 **84**
Guy, (George) Buddy 1936— **31**
Guy, Jasmine 1964(?)— **2**
Guy, Rosa 1925(?)— **5**
Guy-Sheftall, Beverly 1946— **13,
92**
Guyton, Tyree 1955— **9, 94**
Gwynn, Tony 1960— **18, 83**
Gyan, Asamoah 1985— **87**
Habré, Hissène 1942— **6**
Habyarimana, Juvenal 1937–1994
8
Haddon, Dietrick 1973(?)— **55**
Hageman, Hans 19(?)(?)— **36**
Hageman, Ivan 19(?)(?)— **36**
Haile Selassie 1892–1975 **7**
Hailey, JoJo 1971— **22**
Hailey, K-Ci 1969— **22**
Hairston, Jester 1901–2000 **88**
Hairston, Sam 1920–1997 **88**
Hale, Clara 1902–1992 **16**
Hale, Lorraine 1926(?)— **8**
Hale, Nathaniel Dawayne *See Nate
Dogg*
Haley, Alex (Palmer) 1921–1992 **4**
Haley, George Williford Boyce
1925— **21**
Hall, Aaron 1963— **57**
Hall, Alvin D. 1952— **86**
Hall, Arsenio 1955— **58**
Hall, Arthur 1943–2000 **39**
Hall, Elliott S. 1938(?)— **24**
Hall, Juanita 1901–1968 **62**
Hall, Kevan 19(?)(?)— **61**
Hall, Lloyd A(ugustus) 1894–1971 **8**
Hall, Syren *See Fiona, Melanie*

Hall, Stuart 1932— **78**
Halliburton, Warren J. 1924— **49**
Hallim, Melanie Fiona *See Fiona,
Melanie*
Ham, Cynthia Parker 1970(?)— **58**
Hamblin, Ken 1940— **10**
Hamburg, Beatrix 1923— **84**
Hamburg, Margaret 1955— **78**
Hamer, Fannie Lou (Townsend)
1917–1977 **6**
Hamilton, Anthony 1971— **61**
Hamilton, Lewis 1985— **66**
Hamilton, Lisa Gay 1964— **71**
Hamilton, Samuel C. 19(?)(?)— **47**
Hamilton, Tanya 1968— **93**
Hamilton, Virginia 1936— **10**
Hamlin, Larry Leon 1948–2007 **49,
62**
Hammer, M. C. *See M.C. Hammer*
Hammond, Fred 1960— **23**
Hammond, Lenn 1970(?)— **34**
Hammonds, Evelynn 1953— **69**
Hammons, David 1943— **69**
Hampton, Fred 1948–1969 **18**
Hampton, Henry (Eugene, Jr.)
1940— **6**
Hampton, Lionel 1908(?)–2002 **17,
41**
Hancock, Herbie 1940— **20, 67**
Handy, W(illiam) C(hristopher)
1873–1937 **8**
Haney, Lee 1959— **77**
Hani, Chris 1942–1993 **6**
Hani, Martin Thembisile *See Hani,
Chris*
Hannah, Marc (Regis) 1956— **10**
Hansberry, Lorraine (Vivian)
1930–1965 **6**
Hansberry, Tony, II 1994— **93**
Hansberry, William Leo 1894–1965
11
Hansen, Austin 1910–1996 **88**
Hardaway, Anfernee (Penny)
1971— **13**
Hardaway, Penny *See Hardaway,
Anfernee (Penny)*
Hardaway, Tim 1966— **35**
Hardin Armstrong, Lil 1898–1971
39
Hardin, Lillian Beatrice *See Hardin
Armstrong, Lil*
Harding, Vincent 1931— **67**
Hardison, Bethann 19(?)(?)— **12**
Hardison, Kadeem 1966— **22**
Hardy, Antonio *See Big Daddy
Kane*
Hardy, Nell *See Carter, Nell*
Hare, Nathan 1934— **44**
Harewood, David 1965— **52**
Harkless, Necia Desiree 1920— **19**
Harmon, Clarence 1940(?)— **26**
Harold, Erika 1980(?)— **54**
Harper, Ben 1969— **34, 62**
Harper, Frances E(llen) W(atkins)
1825–1911 **11**
Harper, Frank *See Harper, Hill*
Harper, Hill 1966— **32, 65**
Harper, Michael S. 1938— **34**
Harper, Rachel M. 1972— **92**
Harrell, Andre (O'Neal) 1962(?)—
9, 30
Harrington, Oliver W(endell) 1912—
9
Harris, Alice 1934— **7**

Harris, Barbara 1930— **12**
Harris, Barry 1929— **68**
Harris, Bernard A. 1956— **90**
Harris, Bill 1941— **72**
Harris, Carla A. 1962— **67**
Harris, Ciara Princess *See Ciara*
Harris, Claire 1937— **34**
Harris, Corey 1969— **39, 73**
Harris, E. Lynn 1957— **12, 33**
Harris, Eddy L. 1956— **18**
Harris, Gary L. 1953— **87**
Harris, James 1947— **79**
Harris, James, III *See Jimmy Jam*
Harris, Jay **19**
Harris, Jessica B. 1948— **91**
Harris, Kamala D. 1964— **64**
Harris, Leslie 1961— **6**
Harris, Lyle Ashton 1965— **83**
Harris, Marcelite Jordon 1943— **16**
Harris, Mary Styles 1949— **31**
Harris, Maya Lakshmi 1966— **88**
Harris, Monica 1968— **18**
Harris, Naomie 1976— **55**
Harris, Patricia Roberts 1924–1985
2
Harris, Richard E. 1912(?)— **61**
Harris, Robin 1953–1990 **7**
Harris, Shack *See Harris, James*
Harris, "Sweet" Alice *See Harris,
Alice*
Harris, Sylvia 1967(?)— **70**
Harris, Wesley L. 1941— **92**
Harris, William Anthony *See Harris,
Bill*
Harris-Lacewell, Melissa 1973— **81**
Harrison, Alvin 1974— **28**
Harrison, Calvin 1974— **28**
Harrison, Charles 1931— **72**
Harrison, Mya *See Mya*
Harris-Stewart, Lusia 1955— **90**
Harsh, Vivian Gordon 1890–1960
14
Hart, Alvin Youngblood 1963— **61**
Hart, Gregory Edward *See Hart,
Alvin Youngblood*
Harvard, Beverly (Joyce Bailey)
1950— **11**
Harvey, Steve 1956— **18, 58**
Harvey, William R. 1941— **42**
Haskins, Clem 1943— **23**
Haskins, James 1941–2005 **36, 54**
Hassell, Leroy Rountree, Sr.
1955— **41**
Hastie, William H(enry) 1904–1976
8
Hastings, Alcee Lamar 1936— **16**
Hatcher, Andrew T. 1923–1990 **90**
Hatcher, Richard G. 1933— **55**
Hatchett, Glenda 1951(?)— **32**
Hathaway, Donny 1945–1979 **18**
Hathaway, Isaac Scott 1874–1967
33
Hathaway, Lalah 1968— **57, 88**
Haughton, Aaliyah *See Aaliyah*
Hawkins, Adrienne Lita *See
Kennedy, Adrienne*
Hawkins, Augustus F. 1907–2007
68
Hawkins, Coleman 1904–1969 **9**
Hawkins, Connie 1942— **91**
Hawkins, Erskine Ramsey
1914–1993 **14**

Hawkins, Jamesetta *See James, Etta*
Hawkins, La-Van 1960— **17, 54**
Hawkins, "Screamin'" Jay 1929–2000 **30**
Hawkins, Steven Wayne 1962— **14**
Hawkins, Tramaine Aunzola 1951— **16**
Hawkins, Walter 1949–2010 **87**
Hayden, Carla D. 1952— **47**
Hayden, Palmer 1890–1973 **13**
Hayden, Robert Earl 1913–1980 **12**
Haye, David 1980— **82**
Hayes, Bob 1942–2002 **77**
Hayes, Cecil N. 1945— **46**
Hayes, Dennis 1951— **54**
Hayes, Elvin 1945— **93**
Hayes, Isaac 1942–2008 **20, 58, 73**
Hayes, James C. 1946— **10**
Hayes, Robert Lee *See Hayes, Bob*
Hayes, Roland 1887–1977 **4**
Hayes, Teddy 1951— **40**
Haygood, Wil 1954— **83**
Haynes, Cornell, Jr. *See Nelly*
Haynes, George Edmund 1880–1960 **8**
Haynes, Marques 1926— **22**
Haynes, Roy 1925— **87**
Haynes, Trudy 1926— **44**
Haynie, Sharon 1955— **94**
Haysbert, Dennis 1955— **42**
Haysbert, Raymond V., Sr. 1920–2010 **87**
Haywood, Gar Anthony 1954— **43**
Haywood, Jimmy 1993(?)— **58**
Haywood, Margaret A. 1912— **24**
Hazel, Darryl B. 1949— **50**
Head, Bessie 1937–1986 **28**
Healy, James Augustine 1830–1900 **30**
Healy, Michael 1839–1904 **90**
Heard, Gar 1948— **25**
Heard, Nathan C. 1936–2004 **45**
Hearne, John Edgar Caulwell 1926–1994 **45**
Hearns, Thomas 1958— **29**
Heavy D 1967— **58**
Hedgeman, Anna Arnold 1899–1990 **22**
Hedgeman, Peyton Cole *See Hayden, Palmer*
Height, Dorothy I. 1912— **2, 23, 78**
Hemphill, Essex 1957— **10**
Hemphill, Jessie Mae 1923–2006 **33, 59**
Hemsley, Sherman 1938— **19**
Henderson, Cornelius Langston 1888(?)–1976 **26**
Henderson, David 1942— **53**
Henderson, Fletcher 1897–1952 **32**
Henderson, Gordon 1957— **5**
Henderson, Henry Fairfax, Jr. 1928— **89**
Henderson, Jeff 1964— **72**
Henderson, Natalie Leota *See Hinderas, Natalie*
Henderson, Rickey 1958— **28, 78**
Henderson, Stephen E. 1925–1997 **45**
Henderson, Thelton E. 1933— **68**
Henderson, Wade 1944(?)— **14**
Henderson, Zelma 1920–2008 **71**
Hendricks, Barbara 1948— **3, 67**

Hendrix, James Marshall *See Hendrix, Jimi*
Hendrix, Jimi 1942–1970 **10**
Hendrix, Johnny Allen *See Hendrix, Jimi*
Hendryx, Nona 1944— **56**
Hendy, Francis 195(?)— **47**
Henries, A. Doris Banks 1913–1981 **44**
Henriques, Julian 1955(?)— **37**
Henry, Aaron Edd 1922–1997 **19**
Henry, Clarence "Frogman" 1937— **46**
Henry, Joshua 1994— **94**
Henry, Lenny 1958— **9, 52**
Henry, Richard Bullock *See Obadele, Imari*
Henry, Thierry 1977— **66**
Henry, Troy 1960(?)— **85**
Henson, Darrin 1970(?)— **33**
Henson, Josiah 1789–1883 **90**
Henson, Matthew (Alexander) 1866–1955 **2**
Henson, Taraji P. 1970— **58, 77**
Herbert, Bob 1945— **63**
Hercules, Frank 1911–1996 **44**
Herenton, Willie W. 1940— **24, 81**
Herman, Alexis Margaret 1947— **15**
Hernandez, Aileen Clarke 1926— **13**
Herndon, Alonzo Franklin 1858–1927 **89**
Herndon, Angelo 1913–1997 **90**
Hernton, Calvin C. 1932–2001 **51**
Hickman, Fred(erick Douglass) 1951— **11**
Hicks Maynard, Nancy *See Maynard, Nancy Hicks*
Higginbotham, A(loysius) Leon, Jr. 1928–1998 **13, 25**
Higginbotham, Jack *See Higginbotham, Jay C.*
Higginbotham, Jay C. 1906–1973 **37**
Higginsen, Vy 1945(?)— **65**
Hightower, Dennis F(owler) 1941— **13**
Hill, Andrew 1931–2007 **66**
Hill, Anita 1956— **5, 65**
Hill, Beatrice *See Moore, Melba*
Hill, Bonnie Guiton 1941— **20**
Hill, Calvin 1947— **19**
Hill, Donna 1955— **32**
Hill, Dulé 1975(?)— **29**
Hill, Errol 1921— **40**
Hill, Grant 1972— **13, 94**
Hill, Hugh Morgan 1921–2009 **83**
Hill, Janet 1947— **19**
Hill, Jesse, Jr. 1927— **13**
Hill, Lauryn 1975— **20, 53**
Hill, Leslie Pinckney 1880–1960 **44**
Hill, Marc Lamont 1978— **80**
Hill, Oliver W. 1907–2007 **24, 63**
Hill, Peter 1767–1829 **92**
Hill, Tamia *See Tamia*
Hill, Wyllstyne D. 1949(?)— **94**
Hillard, Terry 1954— **25**
Hillary, Barbara 1923(?)— **65**
Hilliard, Asa Grant, III 1933–2007 **66**
Hilliard, David 1942— **7**
Hilliard, Earl F. 1942— **24**
Hilliard, Wendy 196(?)— **53**
Hilson, Keri 1982— **84**

Himes, Chester 1909–1984 **8**
Hinderas, Natalie 1927–1987 **5**
Hine, Darlene Clark 1947— **24**
Hines, Earl "Fatha" 1905–1983 **39**
Hines, Garrett 1969— **35**
Hines, Gregory (Oliver) 1946–2003 **1, 42**
Hinton, Milt 1910–2000 **30**
Hinton, William Augustus 1883–1959 **8**
Hoagland, Everett H. 1942— **45**
Hoagland, Jaheim *See Jaheim*
Hobson, Julius W. 1919–1977 **44**
Hobson, Mellody 1969— **40**
Hogan, Beverly Wade 1951— **50**
Holder, Eric H., Jr. 1951— **9, 76**
Holder, Geoffrey 1930— **78**
Holder, Laurence 1939— **34**
Holdsclaw, Chamique 1977— **24**
Holiday, Billie 1915–1959 **1**
Holland, Brian *See Holland-Dozier-Holland*
Holland, Eddie *See Holland-Dozier-Holland*
Holland, Endesha Ida Mae 1944–2006 **3, 57**
Holland, Kimberly N. 19(?)(?)— **62**
Holland, Robert, Jr. 1940— **11**
Holland-Dozier-Holland **36**
Holloway, Brenda 1946— **65**
Hollowell, Donald L. 1917–2004 **57**
Holmes, Amy 1973— **69**
Holmes, Clint 1946— **57**
Holmes, Hamilton E. 1941–1995 **82**
Holmes, Kelly 1970— **47**
Holmes, Larry 1949— **20, 68**
Holmes, Santonio 1984— **87**
Holmes, Shannon 1973(?)— **70**
Holsey, Lucius Henry 1842–1920 **92**
Holstein, Casper 1876–1944 **89**
Holt, Lester 1959— **66**
Holt, Nora 1885(?)–1974 **38**
Holt Baker, Arlene 1951— **73**
Holte, Patricia Louise *See LaBelle, Patti*
Holton, Hugh, Jr. 1947–2001 **39**
Holyfield, Evander 1962— **6**
Holyfield, Varnette P. 1950–2010 **54, 88**
Honoré, Russel L. 1947— **64**
Hood, James Walker 1831–1918 **91**
Hooker, John Lee 1917–2000 **30**
hooks, bell 1952— **5, 90**
Hooks, Benjamin L. 1925–2010 **2, 85**
Hooks, Robert 1937— **76**
Hope, John 1868–1936 **8**
Hope, Lugenia Burns 1871–1947 **89**
Hopgood, Hadda *See Brooks, Hadda*
Hopkins, Bernard 1965— **35, 69**
Hopkins, Donald R. 1941— **89**
Hopkins, Lightnin' 1912–1982 **83**
Hopkins, Sam *See Hopkins, Lightnin'*
Horn, Shirley 1934–2005 **32, 56**
Horne, Frank 1899–1974 **44**
Horne, Lena 1917–2010 **5, 86**
Horsford, Steven 1973— **88**
Horton, Andre 1979— **33**
Horton, Gladys 1945–2011 **92**
Horton, James Oliver 1943— **58**

Horton, (Andreana) "Suki" 1982— **33**
Houghton, Israel 1971— **92**
Hounsou, Djimon 1964— **19, 45**
Houphouët, Dia *See Houphouët-Boigny, Félix*
Houphouët-Boigny, Félix 1905–1993 **4, 64**
House, Eddie James, Jr. *See House, Son*
House, Eugene *See House, Son*
House, Son 1902–1988 **8**
Houston, Charles Hamilton 1895–1950 **4**
Houston, Cissy 1933— **20, 83**
Houston, Whitney 1963— **7, 28, 83**
Howard, Ayanna 1972— **65**
Howard, Corinne *See Mitchell, Corinne*
Howard, Desmond 1970— **16, 58**
Howard, Juwan Antonio 1973— **15**
Howard, M. William, Jr. 1946— **26**
Howard, Michelle 1960— **28**
Howard, Ryan 1979— **65**
Howard, Sherri 1962— **36**
Howard, Terrence 1969— **59, 94**
Howell, Ayinde 1978— **91**
Howlin' Wolf 1910–1976 **9**
Howroyd, Janice Bryant 1953— **42**
Hoyte, Lenon 1905–1999 **50**
Hrabowski, Freeman A., III 1950— **22**
Hubbard, Arnette 19(?)(?)— **38**
Hubbard, Freddie 1948–2008 **75**
Hubbard, Frederick DeWayne *See Hubbard, Freddie*
Huddleston, William Emanuel *See Lateef, Yusef*
Hudlin, Reginald 1961— **9, 86**
Hudlin, Warrington, Jr. 1953(?)— **9**
Hudson, Cheryl 19(?)(?)— **15**
Hudson, Ernie 1945— **72**
Hudson, Jennifer 1981— **63, 83**
Hudson, Saul *See Slash*
Hudson, Wade 1946— **15**
Huff, Leon 1942— **86**
Huggins, Edie 1935–2008 **71**
Huggins, Larry 1950— **21**
Huggins, Nathan Irvin 1927–1989 **52**
Hughes, Albert 1972— **7**
Hughes, Allen 1972— **7**
Hughes, Cathy 1947(?)— **27**
Hughes, Dora 1970(?)— **88**
Hughes, Ebony 1948— **57**
Hughes, (James Mercer) Langston 1902–1967 **4**
Hughley, D. L. 1963— **23, 76**
Hughley, Darryl Lynn *See Hughley, D. L.*
Hull, Akasha Gloria 1944— **45**
Humphrey, Bobbi 1950— **20**
Humphries, Frederick 1935— **20**
Hunt, Darnell 1962— **92**
Hunt, Richard (Howard) 1935— **6**
Hunter, Alberta 1895–1984 **42**
Hunter, Billy 1943— **22**
Hunter, Charlayne *See Hunter-Gault, Charlayne*
Hunter, Clementine 1887–1988 **45**
Hunter, George William *See Hunter, Billy*
Hunter, Torii 1975— **43**

Hunter-Gault, Charlayne 1942— **6, 31**
Hurston, Zora Neale 1891–1960 **3**
Hurt, Byron 1970— **61**
Hurt, Mississippi John 1892(?)—1966 **84**
Hurtt, Harold 1947(?)— **46**
Hussein, Lubna 1970(?)— **80**
Hutch, Willie 1944–2005 **62**
Hutcherson, Hilda Yvonne 1955— **54**
Hutchinson, Earl Ofari 1945— **24**
Hutson, Jean Blackwell 1914— **16**
Hyde, Cowan F. "Bubba" 1908–2003 **47**
Hyman, Earle 1926— **25, 79**
Hyman, Phyllis 1949(?)–1995 **19**
Ibrahim, Mo 1946— **67**
Ice Cube 1969— **8, 30, 60**
Iceberg Slim 1918–1992 **11**
Ice-T 1958(?)— **6, 31**
Ifill, Gwen 1955— **28**
Iginla, Jarome 1977— **35**
Ilibagiza, Immaculée 1972(?)— **66**
Iman 1955— **4, 33, 87**
Iman, Chanel 1989— **66**
Imes, Elmer Samuel 1883–1941 **39**
Ince, Paul 1967— **83**
India.Arie 1975— **34**
Ingraham, Hubert A. 1947— **19**
Ingram, James 1952— **84**
Ingram, Rex 1895–1969 **5**
Innis, Roy (Emile Alfredo) 1934— **5**
Irvin, Michael 1966— **64**
Irvin, (Monford Merrill) Monte 1919— **31**
Irvin, Vernon 1961— **65**
Irving, Clarence (Larry) 1955— **12**
Irvis, K. Leroy 1917(?)–2006 **67**
Isaac, Julius 1928— **34**
Isaacs, Gregory 1951–2010 **89**
Isaacs, John 1915–2009 **76**
Isley, Marvin 1953–2010 **87**
Isley, Ronald 1941— **25, 56**
Iverson, Allen 1975— **24, 46**
Ivey, Phil 1976— **72**
Ja Rule 1976— **35, 91**
Jackson, Alexine Clement 1936— **22**
Jackson, Alphonso R. 1946— **48**
Jackson, Brenda 1953— **87**
Jackson, Deborah 1952— **94**
Jackson, Earl 1948— **31**
Jackson, Edison O. 1943(?)— **67**
Jackson, Frank G. 1946— **76**
Jackson, Fred James 1950— **25**
Jackson, George 1960(?)— **19**
Jackson, George Lester 1941–1971 **14**
Jackson, Hal 1915— **41**
Jackson, Isaiah (Allen) 1945— **3**
Jackson, Jamea 1986— **64**
Jackson, James A. 1878–1960 **90**
Jackson, James Curtis, III See 50 Cent
Jackson, Janet 1966— **6, 30, 68**
Jackson, Jermaine 1954— **79**
Jackson, Jesse 1941— **1, 27, 72**
Jackson, Jesse, Jr. 1965— **14, 45, 81**
Jackson, Joe 1929— **78**
Jackson, John 1924–2002 **36**
Jackson, John David See Fabolous

Jackson, Judith D. 1950— **57**
Jackson, Lisa 1962— **77**
Jackson, Mae 1941–2005 **57**
Jackson, Mahalia 1911–1972 **5**
Jackson, Mannie 1939— **14**
Jackson, Mary 1945— **73**
Jackson, Maynard (Holbrook, Jr.) 1938–2003 **2, 41**
Jackson, Michael 1958–2009 **19, 53, 76**
Jackson, Millie 1944— **25**
Jackson, Milt 1923–1999 **26**
Jackson, O'Shea See Ice Cube
Jackson, Otis, Jr. See Madlib
Jackson, Quinton See Jackson, Rampage
Jackson, Rampage 1978— **83**
Jackson, Randy 1956— **40**
Jackson, Reginald Martinez 1946— **15**
Jackson, Rickey 1958— **88**
Jackson, Samuel 1948— **8, 19, 63**
Jackson, Sheneska 1970(?)— **18**
Jackson, Shirley Ann 1946— **12**
Jackson, Tito 1953— **81**
Jackson, Tom 1951— **70**
Jackson, Vera 1912— **40**
Jackson, Vivian See Yabby You
Jackson, Zelda Mavin See Ormes, Jackie
Jackson Lee, Sheila 1950— **20**
Jaco, Wasalu Muhammad See Fiasco, Lupe
Jacob, John E(dward) 1934— **2**
Jacobs, Marion Walter See Little Walter
Jacobs, Regina 1963— **38**
Jacquet, Illinois 1922(?)–2004 **49**
Jagan, Cheddi 1918–1997 **16**
Jaheim 1978— **58**
Jakes, Thomas "T.D." 1957— **17, 43**
Jam, Jimmy See Jimmy Jam
Jam Master Jay See Run-DMC
Jamal, Ahmad 1930— **69**
Jamelia 1981— **51**
Jamerson, James 1936–1983 **59**
James, Charles H., III 1959(?)— **62**
James, Daniel "Chappie," Jr. 1920–1978 **16**
James, David 1970— **84**
James, Donna A. 1957— **51**
James, Etta 1938— **13, 52**
James, G. Larry 1947–2008 **74**
James, Juanita (Therese) 1952— **13**
James, LeBron 1984— **46, 78**
James, Marlon 1970— **85**
James, Nikki M. 1981— **94**
James, Sharpe 1936— **23, 69**
James, Skip 1902–1969 **38**
James, Vanessa 1987— **84**
Jamison, Judith 1943— **7, 67**
Jammeh, Yahya 1965— **23**
Jarreau, Al 1940— **21, 65**
Jarrett, Valerie 1956— **73**
Jarrett, Vernon D. 1921— **42**
Jarvis, Charlene Drew 1941— **21**
Jarvis, Erich 1965— **67**
Jarvis, Kristen 1981(?)— **85**
Jasper, John J. 1812–1901 **91**
Jasper, Kenji 1976(?)— **39**
Jawara, Dawda Kairaba 1924— **11**

Jay-Z 1970— **27, 69**
Jealous, Benjamin 1973— **70**
Jean, Michaëlle 1957— **70**
Jean, Wyclef 1970— **20, 86**
Jean-Baptiste, Marianne 1967— **17, 46**
Jean-Juste, Gérard 1946–2009 **78**
Jean-Louis, Jimmy 1968— **76**
Jeffers, Eve Jihan See Eve
Jefferson, Blind Lemon 1893(?)–1929 **81**
Jefferson, Denise 1944–2010 **87**
Jefferson, Mildred Fay 1927–2010 **89**
Jefferson, William J. 1947— **25, 72**
Jeffries, Leonard 1937— **8**
Jemison, Mae C. 1957— **1, 35**
Jemison, Major L. 1955(?)— **48**
Jenifer, Franklyn G(reen) 1939— **2**
Jenkins, Beverly 1951— **14**
Jenkins, Ella (Louise) 1924— **15**
Jenkins, Fergie 1943— **46**
Jenkins, Jay See Young Jeezy
Jenkins, Ray 1920–2009 **77**
Jennings, Chester See Jennings, Lyfe
Jennings, Lyfe 1973— **56, 69**
Jerkins, Rodney 1978(?)— **31**
Jeter, Claude 1914–2009 **75**
Jeter, Derek 1974— **27, 93**
Jimmy Jam 1959— **13**
Joachim, Paulin 1931— **34**
Joe, Yolanda 19(?)(?)— **21**
John, Daymond 1969(?)— **23**
Johns, Vernon 1892–1965 **38**
Johnson, Angela 1961— **52**
Johnson, Anthony M. 1954— **92**
Johnson, Arnez See Arnez J
Johnson, Avery 1965— **62**
Johnson, Ben 1961— **1**
Johnson, Beverly 1952— **2**
Johnson, Buddy 1915–1977 **36**
Johnson, Carol Diann See Carroll, Diahann
Johnson, Caryn E. See Goldberg, Whoopi
Johnson, Charles 1948— **1, 82**
Johnson, Charles Arthur See St. Jacques, Raymond
Johnson, Charles Spurgeon 1893–1956 **12**
Johnson, Chris 1985— **92**
Johnson, Clifford "Connie" 1922–2004 **52**
Johnson, Dennis 1954–2007 **89**
Johnson, Dwayne See Rock, The
Johnson, Earvin "Magic" 1959— **3, 39**
Johnson, Eddie Bernice 1935— **8, 90**
Johnson, Eunice W. 1916–2010 **83**
Johnson, Fenton 1888–1958 **91**
Johnson, George E. 1927— **29**
Johnson, Georgia Douglas 1880–1966 **41**
Johnson, Gus 1938–1987 **92**
Johnson, Hall 1888–1970 **90**
Johnson, Hank, Jr. 1954— **80**
Johnson, Harry E. 1954— **57**
Johnson, Harvey, Jr. 1947(?)— **24, 82**
Johnson, Hazel 1927— **22**
Johnson, J. J. 1924–2001 **37**
Johnson, Jack 1878–1946 **8**

Johnson, James Louis See Johnson, J. J.
Johnson, James Weldon 1871–1938 **5**
Johnson, James William See Johnson, James Weldon
Johnson, Je'Caryous 1977— **63**
Johnson, Jeh C. 1957— **76**
Johnson, Jeh Vincent 1931— **44**
Johnson, Joe 1981— **94**
Johnson, John Arthur See Johnson, Jack
Johnson, John H. 1918–2005 **3, 54**
Johnson, Johnnie 1924–2005 **56**
Johnson, Katherine (Coleman Goble) 1918— **61**
Johnson, Kevin 1966— **70**
Johnson, Keyshawn 1972— **91**
Johnson, Larry 1969— **28**
Johnson, Leroy R. 1928— **89**
Johnson, Levi 1950— **48**
Johnson, Linton Kwesi 1952— **37**
Johnson, Lonnie 1899(?)–1970 **85**
Johnson, Lonnie G. 1949— **32, 93**
Johnson, "Magic" See Johnson, Earvin "Magic"
Johnson, Mamie "Peanut" 1932— **40**
Johnson, Marguerite See Angelou, Maya
Johnson, Mat 1971(?)— **31**
Johnson, Michael (Duane) 1967— **13**
Johnson, Michelle See Ndegeocello, Meshell
Johnson, Mordecai Wyatt 1890–1976 **79**
Johnson, Norma L. Holloway 1932— **17**
Johnson, R. M. 1968— **36**
Johnson, Rafer 1934— **33**
Johnson, Robert 1911–1938 **2**
Johnson, Robert L. 1946(?)— **3, 39**
Johnson, Robert T. 1948— **17**
Johnson, Rodney Van 19(?)(?)— **28**
Johnson, Sandra K. 1960(?)— **94**
Johnson, Sheila Crump 1949(?)— **48**
Johnson, Shoshana 1973— **47**
Johnson, Taalib See Musiq
Johnson, Virginia (Alma Fairfax) 1950— **9**
Johnson, William 1809–1851 **91**
Johnson, William Henry 1901–1970 **3**
Johnson, Woodrow Wilson See Johnson, Buddy
Johnson, Wycliffe See Steely
Johnson-Brown, Hazel W. See Johnson, Hazel
Johnson-George, Tamara 1971— **79**
Joiner, Alvin Nathaniel See Xzibit
Jolley, Willie 1956— **28**
Jonathan, Goodluck 1957— **83**
Jones, Absalom 1746–1818 **52**
Jones, Alex 1941— **64**
Jones, Anthony See Jones, Van
Jones, Bill T. 1952— **1, 46, 80**
Jones, Bob See Jones, Robert G.
Jones, Bobby 1938— **20, 94**
Jones, Booker T. 1944— **84**
Jones, Carl 1955(?)— **7**

Jones, Caroline R. 1942— **29**
Jones, Clara Stanton 1913— **51**
Jones, Cobi N'Gai 1970— **18**
Jones, Cullen 1984— **73**
Jones, Deacon 1938— **92**
Jones, Donell 1973— **29**
Jones, Doris W. 1914(?)–2006 **62**
Jones, E. Edward, Sr. 1931— **45**
Jones, Ed "Too Tall" 1951— **46**
Jones, Edith Mae Irby 1927— **65**
Jones, Edward P. 1950— **43, 67**
Jones, Elaine R. 1944— **7, 45**
Jones, Elvin 1927–2004 **14, 68**
Jones, Emil, Jr. 1935— **74**
Jones, Etta 1928–2001 **35**
Jones, Eugene Kinckle 1885–1954 **79**
Jones, Frederick McKinley 1893–1961 **68**
Jones, Frederick Russell See Jamal, Ahmad
Jones, Gayl 1949— **37**
Jones, Hank 1918–2010 **57, 86**
Jones, Ingrid Saunders 1945— **18**
Jones, James Earl 1931— **3, 49, 79**
Jones, John 1816–1879 **89**
Jones, Jonah 1909–2000 **39**
Jones, K. C. 1932— **83**
Jones, Kelis See Kelis
Jones, Kimberly Denise See Lil' Kim
Jones, Kirk See Sticky Fingaz
Jones, Le Roi See Baraka, Amiri
Jones, Lillie Mae See Carter, Betty
Jones, Lois Mailou 1905— **13**
Jones, Lou 1932–2006 **64**
Jones, Marion 1975— **21, 66**
Jones, Merlakia 1973— **34**
Jones, Monty 1951(?)— **66**
Jones, Nasir See Nas
Jones, Orlando 1968— **30**
Jones, Paul R. 1928— **76**
Jones, Quincy (Delight) 1933— **8, 30**
Jones, Randy 1969— **35**
Jones, Robert Elijah 1872–1960 **90**
Jones, Robert Elliott See Jones, Jonah
Jones, Robert G. 1936–2008 **81**
Jones, Roy Jr. 1969— **22**
Jones, Russell See Ol' Dirty Bastard
Jones, Ruth Lee See Washington, Dinah
Jones, Sam 1933— **85**
Jones, Sarah 1974— **39**
Jones, Sharon 1955(?)— **86**
Jones, Sissieretta See Joyner, Matilda Sissieretta
Jones, Star See Reynolds, Star Jones
Jones, Thad 1923–1986 **68**
Jones, Thomas W. 1949— **41**
Jones, Van 1968— **70**
Jones, Wayne 1952— **53**
Jones, William A., Jr. 1934–2006 **61**
Joplin, Scott 1868–1917 **6**
Jordan, Barbara 1936–1996 **4, 78**
Jordan, Eddie 1952— **82**
Jordan, Eddie 1955— **83**
Jordan, Eric Benét See Benét, Eric

Jordan, June 1936— **7, 35**
Jordan, Michael (Jeffrey) 1963— **6, 21**
Jordan, Montell 1968(?)— **23**
Jordan, Ronny 1962— **26**
Jordan, Vernon E(ulion, Jr.) 1935— **3, 35**
Jorge, Seu 1970— **73**
Joseph, Kathie-Ann 1970(?)— **56**
Josey, E. J. 1924— **10**
Joyce, Dru 1955— **81**
Joyner, Jacqueline See Joyner-Kersee, Jackie
Joyner, Marjorie Stewart 1896–1994 **26**
Joyner, Matilda Sissieretta 1869(?)–1933 **15**
Joyner, Tom 1949(?)— **19, 90**
Joyner-Kersee, Jackie 1962— **5**
Julian, Hubert 1897–1983 **90**
Julian, Percy Lavon 1899–1975 **6**
Julien, Isaac 1960— **3**
July, William II 19(?)(?)— **27**
Juma, Calestous 1953— **57**
Just, Ernest Everett 1883–1941 **3**
Justice, David Christopher 1966— **18**
Ka Dinizulu, Israel See Ka Dinizulu, Mcwayizeni
Ka Dinizulu, Mcwayizeni 1932–1999 **29**
Kabbah, Ahmad Tejan 1932— **23**
Kabila, Joseph 1968(?)— **30**
Kabila, Laurent 1939— **20**
Kagame, Paul 1957— **54**
Kaigler, Denise 1962— **63**
Kaiser, Cecil 1916— **42**
Kalbani, Adil 1959(?)— **77**
Kamau, Johnstone See Kenyatta, Jomo
Kamau, Kwadwo Agymah 1960(?)— **28**
Kandi 1976— **83**
Kani, Karl 1968(?)— **10**
Kanouté, Fred 1977— **68**
Karenga, Maulana 1941— **10, 71**
Karim, Benjamin 1932–2005 **61**
Kariuki, J. M. 1929–1975 **67**
Kassahun, Tewodros See Afro, Teddy
Katoucha See Niane, Katoucha
Kaufman, Monica 1948(?)— **66**
Kaunda, Kenneth (David) 1924— **2**
Kay, Jackie 1961— **37**
Kay, Ulysses 1917–1995 **37**
Kayira, Legson 1942— **40**
Kearney, Janis 1953— **54**
Kearse, Amalya Lyle 1937— **12**
Kebede, Liya 1978— **59**
Keckley, Elizabeth 1818–1907 **90**
Kee, John P. 1962— **43**
Keene, John 1965— **73**
Keflezighi, Meb 1975— **49**
Keita, Salif 1949— **83**
Keith, Damon J. 1922— **16, 74**
Keith, Floyd A. 1948— **61**
Keith, Rachel Boone 1924–2007 **63**
Kelis 1979— **58**
Kelley, Cliff 1941— **75**
Kelley, Elijah 1986— **65**
Kelley, Malcolm David 1992— **59**
Kellogg, Clark 1961— **64**
Kelly, Leontine 1920— **33**
Kelly, Patrick 1954(?)–1990 **3**

Kelly, R. 1967— **18, 44, 71**
Kelly, Robert Sylvester See Kelly, R.
Kelly, Sharon Pratt See Dixon, Sharon Pratt
Kem 196(?)— **47**
Kemp, Herb 1941–2011 **94**
Kendrick, Erika 1975— **57**
Kendricks, Eddie 1939–1992 **22**
Kennard, William Earl 1957— **18**
Kennedy, Adrienne 1931— **11**
Kennedy, Florynce Rae 1916–2000 **12, 33**
Kennedy, Lelia McWilliams Robinson 1885–1931 **14**
Kennedy, Randall 1954— **40**
Kennedy-Overton, Jayne Harris 1951— **46**
Kenney, John A., Jr. 1914–2003 **48**
Kenoly, Ron 1944— **45**
Kente, Gibson 1932–2004 **52**
Kenyatta, Jomo 1891(?)–1978 **5**
Kenyatta, Robin 1942–2004 **54**
Kerekou, Ahmed (Mathieu) 1933— **1**
Kerry, Leon G. 1949(?)— **46**
Keyes, Alan L(ee) 1950— **11**
Keys, Alicia 1981— **32, 68**
Khan, Chaka 1953— **12, 50**
Khanga, Yelena 1962— **6**
Khumalo, Leleti 1970— **51**
Kibaki, Mwai 1931— **60**
Kid Cudi 1984— **83**
Kidd, Jason 1973— **86**
Kidd, Mae Street 1904–1995 **39**
Kidjo, Angelique 1960— **50**
Kiir, Salva 1951— **85**
Kikwete, Jakaya Mrisho 1950— **73**
Killens, John O. 1967–1987 **54**
Killings, Debra 196(?)— **57**
Killingsworth, Cleve, Jr. 1952— **54**
Kilpatrick, Carolyn Cheeks 1945— **16**
Kilpatrick, Kwame 1970— **34, 71**
Kimbro, Dennis (Paul) 1950— **10**
Kimbro, Henry A. 1912–1999 **25**
Kimbro, Warren 1934–2009 **76**
Kincaid, Bernard 1945— **28**
Kincaid, Jamaica 1949— **4**
King, Alonzo 19(?)(?)— **38**
King, B. B. 1925— **7**
King, Barbara 19(?)(?)— **22**
King, Bernice 1963— **4, 81**
King, Colbert I. 1939— **69**
King, Coretta Scott 1927–2006 **3, 57**
King, Dexter (Scott) 1961— **10**
King, Don 1931— **14**
King, Freddie 1934–1976 **92**
King, Gayle 1956— **19**
King, Martin Luther, III 1957— **20**
King, Martin Luther, Jr. 1929–1968 **1**
King, Martin Luther, Sr. 1899–1984 **89**
King, Oona 1967— **27**
King, Preston 1936— **28**
King, Reatha Clark 1938— **65**
King, Regina 1971— **22, 45**
King, Riley B. See King, B. B.
King, Robert Arthur 1945— **58**
King, Robert Hillary 1942— **84**
King, Teresa 1961— **80**
King, Woodie Jr. 1937— **27**

King, Yolanda (Denise) 1955— **6**
King Curtis 1934–1971 **92**
Kingston, Sean 1990— **94**
Kintaudi, Leon 1949(?)— **62**
Kintaudi, Ngoma Miezi See Kintaudi, Leon
Kirby, George 1924–1995 **14**
Kirk, Ron 1954— **11, 75**
Kitt, Eartha 1927–2008 **16, 75**
Kitt, Sandra 1947— **23**
Kittles, Rick 1976(?)— **51**
Kitwana, Bakari 19(?)(?)— **86**
Klugh, Earl 1953— **59**
K'naan 1978— **76**
Knight, Etheridge 1931–1991 **37**
Knight, Gladys 1944— **16, 66**
Knight, Gwendolyn 1913–2005 **63**
Knight, Marie 1925(?)–2009 **80**
Knight, Marion, Jr. See Knight, Suge
Knight, Suge 1966— **11, 30**
Knowles, Beyoncé See Beyoncé
Knowles, Tina 1954(?)— **61**
Knowling, Robert Jr. 1955(?)— **38**
Knox, Simmie 1935— **49**
Knuckles, Frankie 1955— **42**
Kobia, Samuel 1947— **43**
Kodjoe, Boris 1973— **34, 89**
Kolosoy, Wendo 1925–2008 **73**
Komunyakaa, Yusef 1941— **9**
Kone, Seydou See Blondy, Alpha
Kong, B. Waine 1943— **50**
Kool DJ Red Alert See Alert, Kool DJ Red
Kool Moe Dee 1963— **37**
Kool Rock Ski See Fat Boys
Koroma, Ernest Bai 1953— **84**
Kotto, Yaphet (Fredrick) 1944— **7**
Kountz, Samuel L(ee) 1930–1981 **10**
Kravitz, Lenny 1964— **10, 34**
Kravitz, Leonard See Kravitz, Lenny
KRS-One 1965— **34**
Krute, Fred See Alert, Kool DJ Red
K-Swift 1978–2008 **73**
Kufuor, John Agyekum 1938— **54, 82**
Kunjufu, Jawanza 1953— **3, 50**
Kuti, Fela Anikulapo See Fela
Kuti, Femi 1962— **47**
Kuzwayo, Ellen 1914–2006 **68**
Kwei-Armah, Kwame 1967— **84**
Kweli, Talib 1975— **93**
Kyles, Cedric See Cedric the Entertainer
La Menthe, Ferdinand Joseph See Morton, Jelly Roll
La Salle, Eriq 1962— **12**
LaBelle, Patti 1944— **13, 30**
LaChanze 1961— **93**
Lacy, Sam 1903–2003 **30, 46**
Ladd, Ernie 1938–2007 **64**
Ladner, Joyce A. 1943— **42**
Laferriere, Dany 1953— **33**
Lafontant, Jewel Stradford 1922–1997 **3, 51**
Lafontant-MANkarious, Jewel Stradford See Lafontant, Jewel Stradford
LaGuma, Alex 1925–1985 **30**
Lamming, George 1927— **35**
Lampkin, Daisy 1883(?)–1965 **19**

Lampley, Oni Faida 1959–2008 **43, 71**

Lampley, Vera *See Lampley, Oni Faida*

Lane, Charles 1953— **3**

Lane, Dick 1927–2002 **92**

Lane, Lunsford 1803–18(?)(?) **93**

Lane, Vincent 1942— **5**

Lane, William Henry 1825(?)–1852(?) **90**

Langford, Larry P. 1948— **74**

Langhart Cohen, Janet 1941— **19, 60**

Lanier, Bob 1948— **47**

Lanier, Willie 1945— **33**

Lankford, Raymond Lewis 1967— **23**

Laraque, Georges 1976— **48**

Laraque, Paul 1920–2007 **67**

Larkin, Barry 1964— **24**

Laroche, Joseph Philippe Lemercier 1889–1912 **85**

Larrieux, Amel 1973(?)— **63**

Lars, Byron 1965— **32**

Larsen, Nella 1891–1964 **10**

Laryea, Thomas Davies III 1979— **67**

Lashley, Bobby 1976— **63**

Lashley, Franklin Roberto *See Lashley, Bobby*

Lassiter, Roy 1969— **24**

Lateef, Yusef 1920— **91**

Lathan, Sanaa 1971— **27**

Latimer, Lewis H(oward) 1848–1928 **4**

Lattany, Kristin Hunter 1931–2008 **88**

Lattimore, Kenny 1970(?)— **35**

LaVette, Bettye 1946— **85**

Lavizzo-Mourey, Risa 1954— **48**

Lawal, Kase L. 19(?)(?)— **45**

Lawless, Theodore K(enneth) 1892–1971 **8**

Lawrence, Jacob (Armstead) 1917–2000 **4, 28**

Lawrence, Martin 1965— **6, 27, 60**

Lawrence, Robert Henry, Jr. 1935–1967 **16**

Lawrence-Lightfoot, Sara 1944— **10**

Laws, Hubert 1939— **90**

Lawson, James M., Jr. 1928— **90**

Lawson, Jennifer 1946— **1, 50**

Layton, William 1915–2007 **87**

Leadbelly 1885–1949 **82**

Leary, Kathryn D. 1952— **10**

Leavell, Dorothy R. 1944— **17**

Ledbetter, Hudson William *See Leadbelly*

Ledisi 197(?)— **73**

Lee, Annie Frances 1935— **22**

Lee, Barbara 1946— **25**

Lee, Bertram M., Sr. 1939–2003 **46**

Lee, Canada 1907–1952 **8**

Lee, Consuela 1926–2009 **84**

Lee, Debra L. 1954— **62**

Lee, Don Luther *See Madhubuti, Haki R.*

Lee, Eric P. 1958— **79**

Lee, Gabby *See Lincoln, Abbey*

Lee, Joe A. 1946(?)— **45**

Lee, Joie 1962(?)— **1**

Lee, Leslie 1935— **85**

Lee, Malcolm D. 1970— **75**

Lee, Raphael C. 1949— **87**

Lee, Shelton Jackson *See Lee, Spike*

Lee, Spike 1957— **5, 19, 86**

Lee-Smith, Hughie 1915— **5, 22**

Leevy, Carrol M. 1920— **42**

Lefel, Edith 1963–2003 **41**

Leffall, Lasalle, Jr. 1930— **3, 64**

Legend, John 1978— **67**

Leggs, Kingsley 196(?)— **62**

Leland, George Thomas *See Leland, Mickey*

Leland, Mickey 1944–1989 **2**

Lemmons, Kasi 1961— **20**

Lemon, Don 1966— **94**

Lennox, Betty 1976— **31**

LeNoire, Rosetta 1911–2002 **37**

Lenox, Adriane 1956— **59**

Leon, Kenny 1957(?)— **10**

León, Tania 1943— **13**

Leonard, Buck 1907— **67**

Leonard, Sugar Ray 1956— **15**

Leonard, Walter Fenner *See Leonard, Buck*

Leslie, Lisa 1972— **16, 73**

Lester, Adrian 1968— **46**

Lester, Bill 1961— **42, 85**

Lester, Julius 1939— **9**

Lesure, James 1975— **64**

LeTang, Henry 1915–2007 **66**

Letson, Al 1972— **39**

Levert, Eddie 1942— **70**

Levert, Gerald 1966–2006 **22, 59**

Lewis, Aylwin B. 1954— **51, 88**

Lewis, Butch 1946— **71**

Lewis, Byron E(ugene) 1931— **13**

Lewis, (Frederick) Carl(ton) 1961— **4**

Lewis, Daurene 194(?)— **72**

Lewis, David Levering 1936— **9**

Lewis, Delano (Eugene) 1938— **7**

Lewis, Denise 1972— **33**

Lewis, (Mary) Edmonia 1845(?)–1911(?) **10**

Lewis, Edward T. 1940— **21**

Lewis, Emmanuel 1971— **36**

Lewis, Henry 1932–1996 **38**

Lewis, John 1940— **2, 46, 83**

Lewis, Lennox 1965— **27**

Lewis, Leona 1985— **75**

Lewis, Marvin 1958— **51, 87**

Lewis, Norman 1909–1979 **39**

Lewis, Oliver 1856–1924 **56**

Lewis, Ramsey 1935— **35, 70**

Lewis, Ray 1975— **33**

Lewis, Reginald F. 1942–1993 **6**

Lewis, Ronald *See Lewis, Butch*

Lewis, Samella 1924— **25**

Lewis, Shirley Ann Redd 1937— **14**

Lewis, Terry 1956— **13**

Lewis, Thomas 1939— **19**

Lewis, William Henry 1868–1949 **89**

Lewis, William M., Jr. 1956— **40**

Lewis-Thornton, Rae 1962— **32**

Ligging, Alfred III 1965— **43**

Ligon, Glenn 1960— **82**

Lil' Bow Wow *See Bow Wow*

Lil' Kim 1975— **28**

Lil Wayne 1982— **66, 84**

Lilakoi Moon *See Bonet, Lisa*

Liles, Kevin 1968— **42**

Lincoln, Abbey 1930–2010 **3, 88**

Lincoln, C(harles) Eric 1924–2000 **38**

Lindo, Allen Pineda *See apl.de.ap*

Lindo, Delroy 1952— **18, 45**

Lindsey, Tommie 1951— **51**

Lipscomb, Mance 1895–1976 **49**

LisaRaye 1967— **27**

Lister, Marquita 1965(?) **65**

Liston, (Charles) Sonny 1928(?)–1970 **33**

Little, Benilde 1958— **21**

Little, Floyd 1942— **86**

Little, Larry 1945— **90**

Little, Malcolm *See X, Malcolm*

Little, Robert L(angdon) 1938— **2**

Little Milton 1934–2005 **36, 54**

Little Richard 1932— **15**

Little Walter 1930–1968 **36**

Little Warrior *See Barrow, Willie T.*

Littlepage, Craig 1951— **35**

LL Cool J 1968— **16, 49, 94**

Llewellyn, J. Bruce 1927–2010 **13, 85**

Lloyd, Earl 1928(?)— **26**

Lloyd, John Henry "Pop" 1884–1965 **30**

Lloyd, Reginald 1967— **64**

Locke, Alain (LeRoy) 1886–1954 **10**

Locke, Attica 1974— **85**

Locke, Eddie 1930— **44**

Lofton, James 1956— **42**

Lofton, Kenneth 1967— **12**

Lofton, Ramona 1950— **14**

Logan, Onnie Lee 1910(?)–1995 **14**

Logan, Rayford W. 1897–1982 **40**

Loguen, J. W. 1813–1872 **91**

Lomax, Louis E. 1922–1970 **90**

Lomax, Michael L. 1947— **58**

Long, Eddie L. 1953— **29, 89**

Long, Huey 1904–2009 **79**

Long, Loretta 1940— **58**

Long, Nia 1970— **17**

Long, Richard Alexander 1927— **65**

Lopes, Davey 1945— **92**

Lopes, Lisa " Left Eye" 1971–2002 **36**

Lord Pitt of Hampstead *See Pitt, David Thomas*

Lorde, Audre (Geraldine) 1934–1992 **6**

Lorenzo, Irving *See Gotti, Irv*

Loroupe, Tegla 1973— **59**

Lott, Ronnie 1959— **9**

Loueke, Lionel 1973(?)— **88**

Louis, Errol T. 1962— **8**

Louis, Joe 1914–1981 **5**

Loury, Glenn 1948— **36**

Love, Darlene 1941— **23, 92**

Love, Ed 1932(?)— **58**

Love, Laura 1960— **50**

Love, Nat 1854–1921 **9**

Love, Reggie 1982— **77**

Lovell, Whitfield 1959— **74**

Lover, Ed **10**

Loving, Alvin, Jr., 1935–2005 **35, 53**

Loving, Mildred 1939–2008 **69**

Lowe, Herbert 1962— **57**

Lowe, Sidney 1960— **64**

Lowery, Joseph E. 1924— **2**

Lowery, Myron 1946(?)— **80**

Lowry, A. Leon 1913–2005 **60**

Lucas, John 1953— **7**

Lucie, Lawrence 1907–2009 **80**

Lucien, Jon 1942–2007 **66**

Luckett, Letoya 1981— **61**

Lucy, William 1933— **50**

Lucy Foster, Autherine 1929— **35**

Ludacris, 1978— **37, 60**

Luke, Derek 1974— **61**

Lumbly, Carl 1952— **47**

Lumet, Jenny 1967— **80**

Lumpkin, Elgin Baylor *See Ginuwine*

Lumumba, Patrice 1925–1961 **33**

Luna, Donyale 1946–1979 **88**

Luper, Clara 1923–2011 **94**

Lushington, Augustus Nathaniel 1869–1939 **56**

Luthuli, Albert (John Mvumbi) 1898(?)–1967 **13**

Lyfe *See Jennings, Lyfe*

Lyle, Marcenia *See Stone, Toni*

Lyles, Lester Lawrence 1946— **31**

Lymon, Frankie 1942–1968 **22**

Lynch, Shola 1969— **61**

Lynn, Lonnie Rashid *See Common*

Lyons, Henry 1942(?)— **12**

Lyttle, Hulda Margaret 1889–1983 **14**

Maal, Baaba 1953— **66**

Maathai, Wangari 1940— **43**

Mabley, Jackie "Moms" 1897(?)–1975 **15**

Mabrey, Vicki 1957(?)— **26**

Mabry, Marcus 1967— **70**

Mabuza, Lindiwe 1938— **18**

Mabuza-Suttle, Felicia 1950— **43**

Mac, Bernie 1957–2008 **29, 61, 72**

Maceo, Antonio 1845–1896 **82**

Machado de Assis 1839–1908 **74**

Machel, Graca Simbine 1945— **16**

Machel, Samora Moises 1933–1986 **8**

Mackey, Biz 1897–1965 **82**

Mackey, Nathaniel 1947— **75**

Madhubuti, Haki R. 1942— **7, 85**

Madikizela, Nkosikazi Nobandle Nomzamo Winifred *See Mandela, Winnie*

Madison, Joseph E. 1949— **17**

Madison, Paula 1952— **37**

Madison, Romell 1952— **45**

Madlib 1973— **88**

Magan, Ayaan Hirsi *See Ali, Ayaan Hirsi*

Magloire, Paul Eugène 1907–2001 **68**

Mahal, Taj 1942— **39**

Mahlasela, Vusi 1965— **65**

Mahorn, Rick 1958— **60**

Mainor, Dorothy Leigh 1910(?)–1996 **19**

Maitreya, Sananda 1962— **85**

Majette, Denise 1955— **41**

Major, Clarence 1936— **9**

Majors, Jeff 1960(?)— **41**

Makeba, Miriam 1932–2008 **2, 50, 74**

Malco, Romany 1968— **71**

Malcolm X *See X, Malcolm*

Mallett, Conrad, Jr. 1953— **16**

Mallory, Mark 1962— **62**

Malone, Annie (Minerva Turnbo Pope) 1869–1957 **13**

Malone, Karl 1963— **18, 51, 90**

Malone, Maurice 1965— **32**

Malone, Moses 1955— **79**

Malone Jones, Vivian 1942–2005 59

Malveaux, Floyd 1940— 54

Malveaux, Julianne 1953— 32, 70

Malveaux, Suzanne 1966— 88

Mandela, Nelson 1918— 1, 14, 77

Mandela, Winnie 1934— 2, 35

Mane, Gucci 1980— 91

Manigat, Mirlande 1940— 90

Manigault, Earl "The Goat" 1943— 15

Manigault-Stallworth, Omarosa 1974— 69

Manley, Audrey Forbes 1934— 16

Manley, Edna 1900–1987 26

Manley, Ruth 1947— 34

Mann, Tamela 1966— 92

Manning, Frankie 1914–2009 78

Manuel, Jerry 1953— 94

Marable, Manning 1950— 10

March, William Carrington 1923–2002 56

Marchand, Inga See Foxy Brown

Marechera, Charles William See Marechera, Dambudzo

Marechera, Dambudzo 1952–1987 39

Marechera, Tambudzai See Marechera, Dambudzo

Mariner, Jonathan 1954(?)— 41

Marino, Eugene Antonio 1934–2000 30

Mario 1986— 71

Markham, E(dward) A(rchibald) 1939— 37

Marley, Bob 1945–1981 5

Marley, David See Marley, Ziggy

Marley, Rita 1947— 32, 70

Marley, Robert Nesta See Marley, Bob

Marley, Ziggy 1968— 41

Marrow, Queen Esther 1943(?)— 24

Marrow, Tracey See Ice-T

Marsalis, Branford 1960— 34

Marsalis, Delfeayo 1965— 41

Marsalis, Ellis 1934— 90

Marsalis, Wynton 1961— 16, 90

Marsh, Henry L., III 1934(?)— 32

Marshall, Bella 1950— 22

Marshall, Gloria See Sudarkasa, Niara

Marshall, Kerry James 1955— 59

Marshall, Paule 1929— 7, 77

Marshall, Thurgood 1908–1993 1, 44

Marshall, Valenza Pauline Burke See Marshall, Paule

Martelly, Michel 1961— 90

Martha Jean "The Queen" See Steinberg, Martha Jean

Martin, Darnell 1964— 43, 78

Martin, Helen 1909–2000 31

Martin, Jesse L. 19(?)(?)— 31

Martin, Louis Emanuel 1912–1997 16

Martin, Roberta 1907–1969 58

Martin, Roland S. 1968— 49, 84

Martin, Ruby Grant 1933–2003 49

Martin, Sara 1884–1955 38

Martinez, Pedro 1971— 81

Marvin X See X, Marvin

Mary Mary 34, 92

Mase 1977(?)— 24

Masekela, Barbara 1941— 18

Masekela, Hugh (Ramopolo) 1939— 1

Masire, Quett (Ketumile Joni) 1925— 5

Mason, Biddy 1818–1891 89

Mason, Felicia 1963(?)— 31

Mason, Herman, Jr. 1962— 83

Mason, Ronald 1949— 27

Massaquoi, Hans J. 1926— 30

Massenburg, Kedar 1964(?)— 23

Massey, Brandon 1973— 40

Massey, Walter E(ugene) 1938— 5, 45

Massie, Samuel Proctor, Jr. 1919— 29

Master Gee See Sugarhill Gang, The

Master P 1970— 21

Matejka, Adrian 1971(?)— 87

Mathabane, Johannes See Mathabane, Mark

Mathabane, Mark 1960— 5

Mathis, Greg 1960— 26

Mathis, Johnny 1935— 20

Matson, Ollie 1930–2011 93

Matthews, Benjamin 1932–2006 93

Matthews, Denise See Vanity

Matthews, Mark 1894–2005 59

Matthews Shatteen, Westina 1948— 51

Matzeliger, Jan 1852–1889 93

Mauldin, Jermaine Dupri See Dupri, Jermaine

Maupin, John E., Jr. 1946— 92

Maxey, Randall 1941— 46

Maxis, Theresa 1810–1892 62

Maxwell 1973— 20, 81

May, Derrick 1963— 41

Mayberry-Stewart, Melodie 1948— 94

Mayers, Jamal 1974— 39

Mayfield, Curtis (Lee) 1942–1999 2, 43

Mayhew, Martin R. 1965— 76

Mayhew, Richard 1924— 39

Maynard, Nancy Hicks 1946–2008 73

Maynard, Robert C(lyve) 1937–1993 7

Maynor, Dorothy 1910–1996 19

Mayo, Whitman 1930–2001 32

Mays, Benjamin E(lijah) 1894–1984 7

Mays, Leslie A. 19(?)(?)— 41

Mays, William G. 1946— 34

Mays, William Howard, Jr. See Mays, Willie

Mays, Willie 1931— 3

Mayweather, Floyd, Jr. 1977— 57

Mazrui, Ali Al'Amin 1933— 12

M'bala M'bala, Dieudonné See Dieudonné

Mbatha-Raw, Gugu 1983— 89

Mbaye, Mariétou 1948— 31

Mbeki, Govan A. 1910–2001 80

Mbeki, Thabo 1942— 14, 73

Mboup, Souleymane 1951— 10

Mbuende, Kaire Munionganda 1953— 12

MC Breed 1971–2008 75

M.C. Hammer 1963— 20, 80

MC Lyte 1971— 34

McAdoo, Bob 1951— 75

McAnulty, William E., Jr. 1947–2007 66

McBay, Henry C. 1914–1995 91

McBride, Bryant Scott 1965— 18

McBride, Chi 1961— 73

McBride, James 1957— 35, 87

McCabe, Jewell Jackson 1945— 10

McCall, H. Carl 1938(?)— 27

McCall, Nathan 1955— 8

McCann, Renetta 1957(?)— 44

McCarthy, Sandy 1972— 64

McCarty, Osceola 1908— 16

McCary, Michael S. See Boyz II Men

McCauley, Gina 1976(?)— 76

McClellan, George Marion 1860–1934 91

McClendon, Forrest 1965— 94

McClendon, Lisa 1975(?)— 61

McClinton, Marion Isaac 1954— 77

McClurkin, Donnie 1961— 25

McCoo, Marilyn 1943— 53

McCoy, Elijah 1844–1929 8

McCrary, Crystal See McCrary Anthony, Crystal

McCrary Anthony, Crystal 1969— 70

McCray, Nikki 1972— 18

McCullough, Bernard Jeffrey See Mac, Bernie

McCullough, Geraldine 1917–2008 58, 79

McDaniel, Hattie 1895–1952 5

McDaniel, Randall Cornell 1964— 81

McDaniels, Darryl See DMC

McDaniels, Ralph 19(?)(?)— 79

McDonald, Audra 1970— 20, 62

McDonald, Erroll 1954(?)— 1

McDonald, Gabrielle Kirk 1942— 20

McDougall, Gay J. 1947— 11, 43

McDuffie, Dwayne 1962— 62

McEwen, Mark 1954— 5

McFadden, Bernice L. 1966— 39

McFarlan, Tyron 1971(?)— 60

McFarland, Roland 1940— 49

McFerrin, Bobby 1950— 68

McFerrin, Robert, Jr. See McFerrin, Bobby

McFerrin, Robert, Sr. 1921–2006 94

McGee, Charles 1924— 10

McGee, James D. 1949— 74

McGee, James Madison 1940— 46

McGill, Anthony 1979— 76

McGlowan, Angela 1970— 64, 86

McGrady, Tracy 1979— 80

McGrath, Pat 1970— 72

McGriff, Fred 1963— 24

McGriff, James Harrell See McGriff, Jimmy

McGriff, Jimmy 1936–2008 72

McGruder, Aaron 1974— 28, 56

McGruder, Robert 1942— 22, 35

McGuire, George Alexander 1866–1934 80

McGuire, Raymond J. 1957(?)(—) 57

McHenry, Donald F. 1936— 83

McIntosh, Winston Hubert See Tosh, Peter

McIntyre, Natalie See Gary, Macy

McJunkin, George 1851–1922 93

McKay, Claude 1889–1948 6

McKay, Festus Claudius See McKay, Claude

McKay, Nellie Yvonne 19(?)(?)–2006 17, 57

McKee, Lonette 1952— 12

McKegney, Tony 1958— 3

McKenzie, Jaunel 1986— 73

McKenzie, Vashti M. 1947— 29

McKinney, Cynthia 1955— 11, 52, 74

McKinney, Nina Mae 1912–1967 40

McKinney Hammond, Michelle 1957— 51

McKinney-Whetstone, Diane 1954(?)— 27

McKinnon, Ike See McKinnon, Isaiah

McKinnon, Isaiah 1943— 9

McKissack, Leatrice 1930— 80

McKissick, Floyd B(ixler) 1922–1981 3

McKnight, Brian 1969— 18, 34

McLean, Jackie 1931–2006 78

McLendon, John B., Jr. 1915–1999 89

McLeod, Gus 1955(?)— 27

McMillan, Rosalynn A. 1953— 36

McMillan, Terry 1951— 4, 17, 53

McMillan, Tracy 1964— 93

McMurray, Georgia L. 1934–1992 36

McNabb, Donovan 1976— 29

McNair, Ronald 1950–1986 3, 58

McNair, Steve 1973–2009 22, 47, 79

McNeil, Lori 1964(?)— 1

McPhail, Sharon 1948— 2

McPherson, David 1968— 32

McPherson, James Alan 1943— 70

McQueen, Butterfly 1911–1995 6, 54

McQueen, Steve 1969— 84

McRae, Carmen 1920–1994 77

McRae, Hal 1945— 84

McTell, Blind Willie 1901–1959 89

McWhorter, John 1965— 35

McWorter, Free Frank 1777–1854 91

Meadows, Tim 1961— 30

Meek, Carrie (Pittman) 1926— 6, 36

Meek, Kendrick 1966— 41, 89

Meeks, Gregory 1953— 25

Meeks, James T. 1956— 92

Mehretu, Julie 1970— 85

Meles Zenawi 1955(?)— 3

Mell, Patricia 1953— 49

Mello, Breno 1931–2008 73

Melton, Frank 1949–2009 81

Melton, Harold D. 1966— 79

Memmi, Albert 1920— 37

Memphis Minnie 1897–1973 33

Menard, John Willis 1838–1893 90

Mengestu, Dinaw 1978— 66

Mengistu, Haile Mariam 1937— 65

Mensah, John 1982— 87

Mensah, Thomas 1950— 48

Mercado-Valdes, Frank 1962— 43

Meredith, James H(oward) 1933— 11

Merkerson, S. Epatha 1952— 47, 83

Mescudi, Scott Ramon Seguro See Kid Cudi

Messenger, The See Divine, Father

Metcalfe, Ralph 1910–1978 **26**

Method Man 1971— **81**

Meyer, June See Jordan, June

Mfume, Kweisi 1948— **6, 41**

Mhlaba, Raymond 1920–2005 **55**

Michaux, Solomon Lightfoot 1884–1968 **91**

Micheaux, Oscar (Devereaux) 1884–1951 **7**

Michele, Michael 1966— **31**

Mickelbury, Penny 1948— **28**

Miles, Buddy 1947–2008 **69**

Miles, George Allen, Jr. See Miles, Buddy

Milla, Roger 1952— **2**

Millender-McDonald, Juanita 1938–2007 **21, 61**

Miller, Bebe 1950— **3**

Miller, Cheryl 1964— **10, 74**

Miller, Dorie 1919–1943 **29**

Miller, Doris See Miller, Dorie

Miller, Larry G. 1950(?)— **72**

Miller, Marcus 1959— **84**

Miller, Maria 1803–1879 **19**

Miller, Omar Benson 1978— **93**

Miller, Patina 1984— **94**

Miller, Percy See Master P

Miller, Reggie 1965— **33**

Miller, Rice See Williamson, Sonny Boy

Miller, Warren F., Jr. 1943— **53**

Miller, Wentworth 1972— **75**

Miller-Travis, Vernice 1959— **64**

Millines Dziko, Trish 1957— **28**

Millner, Denene 1969(?)— **76**

Mills, Dylan Kwabena See Rascal, Dizzee

Mills, Florence 1896–1927 **22**

Mills, Joseph C. 1946— **51**

Mills, Sam 1959— **33**

Mills, Stephanie 1957— **36**

Mills, Steve 1960(?)— **47**

Milner, Ron 1938— **39**

Milton, DeLisha 1974— **31**

Minaj, Nicki 1984— **86**

Mingo, Frank L. 1939–1989 **32**

Mingus, Charles Jr. 1922–1979 **15**

Minor, DeWayne 1956— **32**

Minoso, Minnie 1925— **89**

Minott, Sugar 1956–2010 **86**

Mitchell, Arthur 1934— **2, 47**

Mitchell, Arthur Wergs 1883–1968 **91**

Mitchell, Brian Stokes 1957— **21**

Mitchell, Clarence M., Jr. 1911–1984 **88**

Mitchell, Corinne 1914–1993 **8**

Mitchell, Elvis 1958— **67**

Mitchell, Keith 1946— **82**

Mitchell, Kel 1978— **66**

Mitchell, Leona 1949— **42**

Mitchell, Loften 1919–2001 **31**

Mitchell, Nicole 1967(?)— **66**

Mitchell, Parren J. 1922–2007 **42, 66**

Mitchell, Russ 1960— **21, 73**

Mitchell, Sam 1963— **82**

Mitchell, Sharon 1962— **36**

Mitchell, Shireen 1970— **89**

Mizell, Jason See Run-DMC

Mkapa, Benjamin W. 1938— **16, 77**

Mo', Keb' 1952— **36**

Mobutu Sese Seko 1930–1997 **1, 56**

Mofolo, Thomas (Mokopu) 1876–1948 **37**

Mogae, Festus Gontebanye 1939— **19, 79**

Mohamed, Ali Mahdi See Ali Mahdi Mohamed

Mohammed, Nazr 1977— **64**

Mohammed, W. Deen 1933— **27**

Mohammed, Warith Deen See Mohammed, W. Deen

Mohlabane, Goapele See Goapele

Moi, Daniel Arap 1924— **1, 35**

Mokae, Zakes 1934–2009 **80**

Mollel, Tololwa 1952— **38**

Monáe, Janelle 1985— **86**

Mongella, Gertrude 1945— **11**

Monica 1980— **21**

Mo'Nique 1967— **35, 84**

Monk, Art 1957— **38, 73**

Monk, Thelonious (Sphere, Jr.) 1917–1982 **1**

Monroe, Bryan 1965— **71**

Monroe, Earl 1944— **89**

Monroe, Mary 19(?)(?)— **35**

Montgomery, Isaiah T. 1847–1924 **91**

Montgomery, Tim 1975— **41**

Montgomery, Wes 1923–1968 **88**

Moody, James 1925— **83**

Moody, Ronald 1900–1984 **30**

Moody-Adams, Michele 1956— **76**

Moon, Warren 1956— **8, 66**

Mooney, Paul 19(?)(?)— **37**

Moore, Alice Ruth See Dunbar-Nelson, Alice Ruth Moore

Moore, Barbara C. 1949— **49**

Moore, Bobby See Rashad, Ahmad

Moore, Chante 1970(?)— **26**

Moore, Dorothy Rudd 1940— **46**

Moore, Gwendolynne S. 1951— **55**

Moore, Harry T. 1905–1951 **29**

Moore, Jessica Care 1971— **30**

Moore, Johnny B. 1950— **38**

Moore, Juanita 1922— **83**

Moore, Kevin See Mo', Keb'

Moore, LeRoi 1961–2008 **72**

Moore, Maya 1989— **94**

Moore, Melba 1945— **21**

Moore, Minyon 19(?)(?)— **45**

Moore, Richard See bin Wahad, Dhoruba

Moore, Shemar 1970— **21**

Moore, Undine Smith 1904–1989 **28**

Moore, Wes 1978— **86**

Moorer, Lana See MC Lyte

Moorer, Michael 1967— **19**

Moose, Charles 1953— **40**

Morales, Mark 1960— See Fat Boys

Moran, Jason 1975— **89**

Morgan, Garrett (Augustus) 1877–1963 **1**

Morgan, Gertrude 1900–1986 **63**

Morgan, Irene 1917–2007 **65**

Morgan, Joe Leonard 1943— **9**

Morgan, Rose (Meta) 1912(?)— **11**

Morgan, Tracy 1968— **61**

Morganfield, McKinley See Muddy Waters

Morial, Ernest "Dutch" 1929–1989 **26**

Morial, Marc H. 1958— **20, 51**

Morón, Alonzo G. 1909–1971 **91**

Morris, Garrett 1937— **31**

Morris, Greg 1934–1996 **28**

Morris, Nathan See Boyz II Men

Morris, Raheem 1976— **77**

Morris, Wanya See Boyz II Men

Morris, William "Bill" 1938— **51**

Morris, Stevland Judkins See Wonder, Stevie

Morrison, Keith 1942— **13**

Morrison, Mary Thelma See Washington, Mary T.

Morrison, Sam 1936— **50**

Morrison, Toni 1931— **2, 15, 86**

Morrison, Vanessa 1969(?)— **84**

Morton, Azie Taylor 1936–2003 **48**

Morton, Ferdinand Q. 1881–1949 **90**

Morton, Frederick A., Jr. 1967(?)— **93**

Morton, Jelly Roll 1885(?)–1941 **29**

Morton, Joe 1947— **18**

Mos Def 1973— **30**

Moseley-Braun, Carol See Braun, Carol Moseley

Moses, Edwin 1955— **8**

Moses, Gilbert, III 1942–1995 **12**

Moses, Robert Parris 1935— **11**

Mosley, "Sugar" Shane 1971— **32**

Mosley, Tim See Timbaland

Mosley, Walter 1952— **5, 25, 68**

Moss, Bryant See Moss, Preacher

Moss, Carlton 1909–1997 **17**

Moss, J. (?)— **64**

Moss, Otis Jr. 1935— **72**

Moss, Otis, III 1971(?)— **72**

Moss, Preacher 1967— **63**

Moss, Randy 1977— **23, 90**

Moss, Shad Gregory See Lil' Bow Wow

Mossell, Gertrude Bustill 1855–1948 **40**

Mossell, Nathan Francis 1856–1946 **91**

Moten, Etta See Barnett, Etta Moten

Motlanthe, Kgalema 1949— **74**

Motley, Archibald, Jr. 1891–1981 **30**

Motley, Constance Baker 1921–2005 **10, 55**

Motley, Marion 1920–1999 **26**

Moton, Robert Russa 1867–1940 **83**

Moura, Paulo 1932–2010 **87**

Mourning, Alonzo 1970— **17, 44**

Moutoussamy-Ashe, Jeanne 1951— **7**

Mowatt, Judy 1952(?)— **38**

Mowry, Jess 1960— **7**

Mowry, Tamera 1978— **79**

Mowry, Tia 1978— **78**

Moyo, Dambisa 1970(?)— **76**

Moyo, Karega Kofi 19(?)(?)— **36**

Moyo, Lovemore 1965— **76**

Moyo, Yvette Jackson 1953— **36**

Mphalele, Es'kia (Ezekiel) 1919— **40**

Mswati III 1968— **56**

Mudimbe, V. Y. 1941— **61**

Mugabe, Robert 1924— **10, 71**

Mugo, Madeleine See Mugo, Micere Githae

Mugo, Micere Githae 1942— **32**

Muhajir, El See X, Marvin

Muhammad, Ava 1951— **31**

Muhammad, Elijah 1897–1975 **4**

Muhammad, Jabir Herbert 1929–2008 **72**

Muhammad, Khallid Abdul 1951(?)— **10, 31**

Mukoko, Jestina 1957(?)— **75**

Mullen, Harryette 1953— **34**

Mullen, Nicole C. 1967— **45**

Muluzi, Bakili 1943— **14, 76**

Mumba, Samantha 1983— **29**

Mundine, Anthony 1975— **56**

Murphy, Eddie 1961— **4, 20, 61**

Murphy, Edward Regan See Murphy, Eddie

Murphy, John H. 1916— **42**

Murphy, Laura M. 1955— **43**

Murphy McKenzie, Vashti See McKenzie, Vashti M.

Murray, Albert L. 1916— **33**

Murray, Cecil 1929— **12, 47**

Murray, Eddie 1956— **12**

Murray, Lenda 1962— **10**

Murray, Pauli 1910–1985 **38**

Murray, Tai 1982— **47**

Murrell, Sylvia Marilyn 1947— **49**

Muse, Clarence Edouard 1889–1979 **21**

Museveni, Yoweri (Kaguta) 1944(?)— **4**

Mushikiwabo, Louise 1961— **88**

Musiq 1977— **37, 84**

Mutebi, Ronald 1956— **25**

Mutola, Maria de Lurdes 1972— **12**

Mutombo, Dikembe 1966— **7**

Mutu, Wangechi 19(?)(?)— **44**

Muzorewa, Abel 1925–2010 **85**

Mwanawasa, Levy 1948–2008 **72**

Mwangi, Meja 1948— **40**

Mwinyi, Ali Hassan 1925— **1, 77**

Mya 1979— **35**

Myers, Dwight See Heavy D

Myers, Walter Dean 1937— **8, 70**

Myers, Walter Milton See Myers, Walter Dean

Myles, Kim 1974— **69**

Myrie, Mark Anthony See Banton, Buju

Nabrit, Samuel Milton 1905–2003 **47**

Nagin, Ray 1956— **42, 57, 88**

Nail, John E. 1883–1947 **92**

Najm, Faheem Rasheed See T-Pain

Nakhid, David 1964— **25**

Naki, Hamilton 1926–2005 **63**

Nance, Cynthia 1958— **71**

Nanula, Richard D. 1960— **20**

Napoleon, Benny N. 1956(?)— **23**

Nas 1973— **33**

Nascimento, Abdias do 1914–2011 **93**

Nascimento, Milton 1942— **2, 64**

Nash, Diane 1938— **72**

Nash, Joe 1919–2005 **55**

Nash, Johnny 1940— **40**

Nash, Niecy 1970— **66**

Nash, Shannon King 1971— **84**

Nash, Terius Youngdell See The-Dream
Nate Dogg 1969–2011 92
Naylor, Gloria 1950— 10, 42
Nazario, Zoe Yadira Zaldaña See Saldana, Zoe
Ndadaye, Melchior 1953–1993 7
Ndegeocello, Meshell 1968— 15, 83
Ndiaye, Iba 1928–2008 74
N'Dour, Youssou 1959— 1, 53, 79
Ndungane, Winston Njongonkulu 1941— 16
Neal, Elise 1970— 29
Neal, Larry 1937–1981 38
Neal, Mark Anthony 1965(?)— 74
Neal, Raful 1936— 44
Neale, Haydain 1970— 52
Neals, Otto 1930— 73
Nelly 1974— 32, 90
Nelson, Jill 1952— 6, 54
Nelson, Prince Rogers See Prince
Nelson, Sophia A. 1967— 93
Nelson, Stanley 1951— 92
Nelson Meigs, Andrea 1968— 48
Neto, António Agostinho 1922— 43
Nettles, Marva Deloise See Collins, Marva
Neverson, Tremaine Aldon See Songz, Trey
Neville, Aaron 1941— 21
Neville, Arthel 1962— 53
Newcombe, Don 1926— 24
Newkirk, Pamela 1957— 69
Newman, David 1933–2009 76
Newman, Lester C. 1952— 51
Newsome, Ozzie 1956— 26
Newton, Huey (Percy) 1942–1989 2
Newton, Thandie 1972— 26
Ne-Yo 1982— 65
Ngaujah, Sahr 1976— 86
Ngengi, Kamau wa See Kenyatta, Jomo
Ngilu, Charity 1952— 58
Ngubane, (Baldwin Sipho) Ben 1941— 33
Ngugi wa Thiong'o 1938— 29, 61
Ngugi, James wa Thiong'o See Ngugi wa Thiong'o
Niane, Katoucha 1960–2008 70
Nicholas, Denise 1944— 82
Nicholas, Fayard 1914–2006 20, 57, 61
Nicholas, Harold 1921— 20
Nichols, Grace See Nichols, Nichelle
Nichols, James Thomas See Bell, James "Cool Papa"
Nichols, Nichelle 1933(?)— 11
Nissel, Angela 1974— 42
Nix, Robert N. C., Jr. 1928–2003 51
Njawe, Pius 1957–2010 87
Njongonkulu, Winston Ndungane 1941— 16
Nkoli, Simon 1957–1998 60
Nkomo, Joshua 1917–1999 4, 65
Nkosi, Lewis 1936— 46
Nkrumah, Kwame 1909–1972 3
Nkunda, Laurent 1967— 75
Nkurunziza, Pierre 1963— 78
N'Namdi, George R. 1946— 17
Noah, Yannick 1960— 4, 60
Noble, Gil 1932— 76

Noble, Reginald See Redman
Noble, Ronald 1957— 46
Norman, Christina 1960(?)— 47
Norman, Jessye 1945— 5
Norman, Maidie 1912–1998 20
Norman, Pat 1939— 10
Norris, Michele 1961— 83
Norton, Eleanor Holmes 1937— 7, 93
Norton, Meredith 1970(?)— 72
Norwood, Brandy See Brandy
Norwood, William Raymond, Jr. See Ray J
Notorious B.I.G. 1972–1997 20
Nottage, Cynthia DeLores See Tucker, C. DeLores
Nottage, Lynn 1964— 66
Nour, Nawal M. 1965(?)— 56
Ntaryamira, Cyprien 1955–1994 8
Ntshona, Winston 1941— 52
Nugent, Richard Bruce 1906–1987 39
Nujoma, Samuel 1929— 10
Nunez, Elizabeth 1944(?)— 62
Nunn, Annetta 1959— 43
Nutter, Michael 1958— 69
Nuttin' but Stringz See Escobar, Tourie, and Escobar, Damien
Nyanda, Siphiwe 1950— 21
Nyerere, Julius (Kambarage) 1922— 5
Nzo, Alfred (Baphethuxolo) 1925— 15
Obadele, Imari 1930–2010 84
Obama, Barack 1961— 49, 74, 91
Obama, Michelle 1964— 61, 90
Obasanjo, Olusegun 1937— 5, 22
Obasanjo, Stella 1945–2005 32, 56
Obote, Milton 1925–2005 63
O'Brien, Soledad 1966— 88
ODB See Ol' Dirty Bastard
Odetta 1930— 37, 74
Odinga, Raila 1945— 67
Odom, Lamar 1979— 81
Oglesby, Zena 1947— 12
Ogletree, Charles, Jr. 1952— 12, 47
O'Grady, Lorraine 1934— 73
Ogunlesi, Adebayo O. 19(?)(?)— 37
Ojikutu, Bayo 1971— 66
Ojikutu, Bisola 1974— 65
Okaalet, Peter 1953— 58
Okara, Gabriel 1921— 37
Okonedo, Sophie 1969— 67
Okosuns, Sonny 1947–2008 71
Ol' Dirty Bastard 1968–2004 52
Olajuwon, Akeem See Olajuwon, Hakeem
Olajuwon, Hakeem 1963— 2, 72
Olatunji, Babatunde 1927— 36
Olden, Georg(e) 1920–1975 44
O'Leary, Hazel (Rollins) 1937— 6
Oliver, Jerry 1947— 37
Oliver, Joe "King" 1885–1938 42
Oliver, John J., Jr. 1945— 48
Oliver, Kimberly 1976— 60
Oliver, Pam 1961— 54
Olojede, Dele 1961— 59
Olopade, Olufunmilayo Falusi 1957(?)— 58
O'Neal, Rodney 1954— 88
O'Neal, Ron 1937–2004 46

O'Neal, Shaquille (Rashaun) 1972— 8, 30
O'Neal, Stanley 1951— 38, 67
O'Neil, Buck 1911–2006 19, 59
O'Neil, John Jordan See O'Neil, Buck
Ongala, Ramadhani Mtoro See Ongala, Remmy
Ongala, Remmy 1947–2010 9, 91
Onwueme, Tess Osonye 1955— 23
Onwurah, Ngozi 1966(?)— 38
Onyewu, Oguchi 1982— 60
Orange, James 1942–2008 74
O'Ree, William Eldon See O'Ree, Willie
O'Ree, Willie 1935— 5
Orlandersmith, Dael 1959— 42
Orman, Roscoe 1944— 55
Ormes, Jackie 1911–1985 73
Ortiz, David 1975— 52, 82
Osborne, Jeffrey 1948— 26
Osborne, Na'taki 1974— 54
Otis, Clarence, Jr. 1956— 55
Otis, Clyde 1924— 67
Otunga, Maurice Michael 1923–2003 55
Ouattara 1957— 43
Ouattara, Alassane 1942— 90
Ouattara, Morou 1966— 74
Ousley, Curtis See King Curtis
Ousmane, Sembène See Sembène, Ousmane
OutKast 35
Owens, Dana See Queen Latifah
Owens, Helen 1937— 48
Owens, J. C. See Owens, Jesse
Owens, Jack 1904–1997 38
Owens, James Cleveland See Owens, Jesse
Owens, Jesse 1913–1980 2
Owens, Major (Robert) 1936— 6
Owens, Terrell 1973— 53
Oyelowo, David 1976— 82
Oyono, Ferdinand 1929— 38
P. Diddy See Combs, Sean
Pace, Betty 1954— 59
Pace, Orlando 1975— 21
Packer, Daniel 1947— 56
Packer, Will 1974(?)— 71
Packer, Z. Z. 1973— 64
Page, Alan (Cedric) 1945— 7
Page, Clarence 1947— 4
Page, Greg 1958–2009 78
Page, Inman 1853–1935 82
Paige, Leroy Robert See Paige, Satchel
Paige, Rod 1933— 29
Paige, Satchel 1906–1982 7
Painter, Nell Irvin 1942— 24, 88
Palcy, Euzhan 1958— 94
Palmer, Everard 1930— 37
Palmer, Keke 1993— 68
Palmer, Rissi 1981— 65
Palmer, Violet 1964— 59
Papa Wendo See Kolosoy, Wendo
Parham, Marjorie B. 1918— 71
Parish, Robert 1953— 43
Parker, Barrington D. 1915–1993 92
Parker, Candace 1986— 74
Parker, Charlie 1920–1955 20
Parker, Jim 1934–2005 64
Parker, Kellis E. 1942–2000 30

Parker, (Lawrence) Kris(hna) See KRS-One
Parker, LarStella Irby See Parker, Star
Parker, Maceo 1943— 72
Parker, Nicole Ari 1970— 52
Parker, Ray, Jr. 1954— 85
Parker, Star 1956— 70
Parker, Tony 1982— 75
Parks, Bernard C. 1943— 17
Parks, Gordon 1912–2006 1, 35, 58
Parks, Henry Green, Jr. 1916–1989 89
Parks, Rosa 1913–2005 1, 35, 56
Parks, Suzan-Lori 1963— 34, 85
Parr, Russ 196(?)— 51
Parsons, James Benton 1911–1993 14
Parsons, Richard Dean 1948— 11, 33
Pascal-Trouillot, Ertha 1943— 3
Paterson, Basil A. 1926— 69
Paterson, David A. 1954— 59
Patillo, Melba Joy 1941— 15
Patrick, Deval 1956— 12, 61
Patterson, Floyd 1935–2006 19, 58
Patterson, Frederick Douglass 1901–1988 12
Patterson, Gilbert Earl 1939— 41
Patterson, J. O., Jr. 1935— 80
Patterson, Louise 1901–1999 25
Patterson, Mary Jane 1840–1894 54
Patterson, Orlando 1940— 4
Patterson, P(ercival) J(ames) 1936(?)— 6, 20
Patterson, Robert, Jr. See Ali, Rashied
Patton, Antwan 1975— 45
Patton, Antwan "Big Boi" 1975(?)— See OutKast
Patton, Paula 1975— 62
Paul, Chris 1985— 84
Payne, Allen 1962(?)— 13
Payne, Donald M. 1934— 2, 57
Payne, Ethel L. 1911–1991 28
Payne, Freda 1942— 58
Payne, Les 1941— 89
Payne, Ulice 1955— 42
Payne, William D. 1932— 60
Payton, Benjamin F. 1932— 23
Payton, John 1946— 48
Payton, Philip A., Jr. 1876–1917 88
Payton, Walter (Jerry) 1954–1999 11, 25
Pearman, Raven-Symone Christina See Raven
Peck, Carolyn 1966(?)— 23
Peck, Raoul 1953— 32
Peete, Calvin 1943— 11
Peete, Holly Robinson 1965— 20
Peete, Rodney 1966— 60
Pelé 1940— 7
Pena, Paul 1950–2005 58
Pendergrass, Teddy 1950–2010 22, 83
Penniman, Richard Wayne See Little Richard
Peoples, Dottie 19(?)(?)— 22
Pereira, Aristides 1923— 30
Perez, Anna 1951— 1
Perkins, Anthony 1959(?)— 24
Perkins, Edward (Joseph) 1928— 5

Perkins, James, Jr. 1953(?)— **55**
Perkins, Joe Willie See Perkins, Pinetop
Perkins, Marion 1908–1961 **38**
Perkins, Pinetop 1913— **70**
Perren, Freddie 1943–2004 **60**
Perrineau, Harold, Jr. 1968— **51**
Perrot, Kim 1967–1999 **23**
Perry, Emmitt, Jr. See Perry, Tyler
Perry, Herman 1922–1945 **89**
Perry, James 1975— **83**
Perry, Laval 195(?)— **64**
Perry, Lee "Scratch" 1936— **19**
Perry, Lincoln See Fetchit, Stepin
Perry, Lowell 1931–2001 **30**
Perry, Rainford Hugh See Perry, Lee "Scratch"
Perry, Ruth 1936— **19**
Perry, Ruth Sando 1939— **15**
Perry, Tyler 1969— **40, 54**
Perry, Warren 1942(?)— **56**
Person, Waverly 1927— **9, 51**
Peters, Lenrie 1932— **43**
Peters, Margaret 1915— **43**
Peters, Maria Philomena 1941— **12**
Peters, Matilda 1917— **43**
Petersen, Frank E. 1932— **31**
Peterson, Hannibal See Peterson, Marvin
Peterson, James 19(?)(?)— **81**
Peterson, James 1937— **38**
Peterson, Jesse Lee 1949— **81**
Peterson, Karen Carter 1969— **90**
Peterson, Marvin 1948— **27**
Peterson, Oscar 1925— **52**
Petry, Ann 1909–1997 **19**
Phifer, Mekhi 1975— **25**
Philip, M. Nourbese See Philip, Marlene Nourbese
Philip, Marlene Nourbese 1947— **32**
Phillips, Charles E., Jr. 1959— **57**
Phillips, Helen L. 1919–2005 **63**
Phillips, Joseph C. 1962— **73**
Phillips, Teresa L. 1958— **42**
Phipps, Wintley 1955— **59**
Pickens, James, Jr. 1954— **59**
Pickett, Bill 1870–1932 **11**
Pickett, Cecil 1945— **39**
Pierce, Elijah 1892–1984 **84**
Pierce, Harold 1917-1988 **75**
Pierce, Paul 1977— **71**
Pierce, Wendell 1962— **90**
Pierre, Andre 1915— **17**
Pierre, Percy Anthony 1939— **46**
Pierre-Louis, Michèle 1947— **75**
Pincham, R. Eugene, Sr. 1925–2008 **69**
Pinchback, P(inckney) B(enton) S(tewart) 1837–1921 **9**
Pinckney, Bill 1935— **42**
Pinckney, Sandra 194(?)— **56**
Pindell, Howardena 1943— **55**
Pinder, Jefferson 1970— **77**
Pinderhughes, John 1946— **47**
Pindling, Lynden 1930–2000 **81**
Pinkett, Jada See Pinkett Smith, Jada
Pinkett, Randal 1971— **61**
Pinkett Smith, Jada 1971— **10, 41**
Pinkney, Fayette 1948–2009 **80**
Pinkney, Jerry 1939— **15**
Pinkston, W. Randall 1950— **24**

Pinn, Vivian Winona 1941— **49**
Piper, Adrian 1948— **71**
Pippen, Scottie 1965— **15, 89**
Pippin, Horace 1888–1946 **9**
Pitt, David Thomas 1913–1994 **10**
Pitta (do Nascimento), Celso (Roberto) 19(?)(?)— **17**
Pitts, Byron 1960— **71**
Pitts, Derrick 1956(?)— **77**
Pitts, Leonard, Jr. 1957— **54, 85**
Pitts, Robb 1941— **84**
Pitts, Robert Lee See Pitts, Robb
Plaatje, Sol. T. 1876–1932 **80**
Player, Willa B. 1909–2003 **43**
Pleasant, Mary Ellen 1814–1904 **9**
Pleasure P 1984— **84**
Plessy, Homer Adolph 1862–1925 **31**
P.M. Dawn, **54**
Poindexter, Hildrus A. 1901–1987 **87**
Poitier, Sidney 1927— **11, 36**
Poitier, Sydney Tamiia 1973— **65**
Polite, Carlene Hatcher 1932–2009 **82**
Pollard, Fritz 1894–1986 **53**
Pollard, William L. 1945(?)— **91**
Pomare, Eleo 1937–2008 **72**
Poole, Elijah See Muhammad, Elijah
Pope.L, William 1955— **72**
Porter, Countee Leroy See Cullin, Countee
Porter, Dorothy See Wesley, Dorothy Porter
Porter, James A(mos) 1905–1970 **11**
Porter, Terry 1963— **75**
Portuondo, Omara 1930— **53**
Potter, Myrtle 1958— **40**
Pough, Terrell 1987(?)–2005 **58**
Pounder, Carol Christine Hilaria See Pounder, CCH
Pounder, CCH 1952— **72**
Poussaint, Alvin F. 1934— **5, 67**
Poussaint, Renee 1944— **78**
Powell, Adam Clayton, Jr. 1908–1972 **3**
Powell, Benny 1930–2010 **87**
Powell, Bud 1924–1966 **24**
Powell, Colin 1937— **1, 28, 75**
Powell, Debra A. 1964— **23**
Powell, Kevin 1966— **31, 74**
Powell, Maxine 1924— **8**
Powell, Michael Anthony See Powell, Mike
Powell, Michael K. 1963— **32**
Powell, Mike 1963— **7**
Powell, Renee 1946— **34**
Powell, William J. 1916–2009 **82**
Power, Will 1970— **83**
Pratt, Awadagin 1966— **31**
Pratt, Geronimo 1947— **18**
Pratt, Kyla 1986— **57**
Pratt Dixon, Sharon See Dixon, Sharon Pratt
Preer, Evelyn 1896–1932 **82**
Premice, Josephine 1926–2001 **41**
Pressley, Condace L. 1964— **41**
Preston, Billy 1946–2006 **39, 59**
Preston, William Everett See Preston, Billy
Préval, René 1943— **87**

Price, Florence 1887–1953 **37**
Price, Frederick K.C. 1932— **21**
Price, Glenda 1939— **22**
Price, Hugh B. 1941— **9, 54**
Price, Kelly 1973(?)— **23**
Price, Leontyne 1927— **1**
Price, Richard 1930(?)— **51**
Pride, Charley 1938(?)— **26**
Primus, Pearl 1919— **6**
Prince 1958— **18, 65**
Prince, Richard E. 1947— **71**
Prince, Ron 1969— **64**
Prince, Tayshaun 1980— **68**
Prince Markie Dee See Fat Boys
Prince-Bythewood, Gina 1969— **31, 77**
Pritchard, Robert Starling 1927— **21**
Procope, Ernesta 19(?)(?)— **23**
Procope, John Levy 1925–2005 **56**
Prophet, Nancy Elizabeth 1890–1960 **42**
Prothrow, Deborah Boutin See Prothrow-Stith, Deborah
Prothrow-Stith, Deborah 1954— **10**
Pryce, Trevor 1975— **89**
Pryor, Rain 1969— **65**
Pryor, Richard 1940–2005 **3, 24, 56**
Puckett, Kirby 1960–2006 **4, 58**
Puff Daddy See Combs, Sean
Pugh, Charles 197199— **81**
Purdie, Bernard 1939— **77**
Purnell, Silas 1923–2003 **59**
Puryear, Martin 1941— **42**
Putney, Martha S. 1916–2008 **75**
Quarles, Benjamin Arthur 1904–1996 **18**
Quarles, Norma 1936— **25**
Quarterman, Lloyd Albert 1918–1982 **4**
Queen Latifah 1970— **1, 16, 58**
Querino, Manuel Raimundo 1851–1923 **84**
?uestlove 1971— **74**
Quigley, Helen G. 1944–2004 **49**
Quince, Peggy A. 1948— **69**
Quirot, Ana (Fidelia) 1963— **13**
Quivers, Robin 1952— **61**
Rabb, Maurice F., Jr. 1932–2005 **58**
Rabia, Aliyah See Staton, Dakota
Radcliffe, Ted 1902–2005 **74**
Radcliffe, Theodore Roosevelt See Radcliffe, Ted
Ragin, Derek Lee 1958— **84**
Rahman, Aishah 1936— **37**
Raines, Franklin Delano 1949— **14**
Rainey, Ma 1886–1939 **33**
Ralph, Sheryl Lee 1956— **18**
Ramaphosa, (Matamela) Cyril 1952— **3**
Rambough, Lori Ann See Sommore
Ramphele, Mamphela 1947— **29**
Ramsey, Charles H. 1948— **21, 69**
Rand, A(ddison) Barry 1944— **6**
Randall, Alice 1959— **38**
Randall, Dudley 1914–2000 **8, 55**
Randle, John 1967— **87**
Randle, Theresa 1967— **16**
Randolph, A(sa) Philip 1889–1979 **3**
Randolph, Linda A. 1941— **52**
Randolph, Willie 1954— **53**

Rangel, Charles B. 1930— **3, 52, 85**
Ranglin, Ernest 1932— **78**
Rankin Don See Rhoden, Wayne
Ransome, James E. 1961— **88**
Raoul, Kwame 1964— **55**
Rapier, James T. 1837–1883 **82**
Ras Tafari See Haile Selassie
Rascal, Dizzee 1985— **82**
Rashad, Ahmad 1949— **18**
Rashad, Phylicia 1948— **21**
Raspberry, William 1935— **2**
Raven, 1985— **44**
Raven-Symone See Raven
Rawlings, Jerry (John) 1947— **9**
Rawlings-Blake, Stephanie 1970— **93**
Rawlinson, Johnnie B. 1952— **79**
Rawls, Lou 1936–2006 **17, 57**
Ray, Charlotte E. 1850–1911 **60**
Ray, Gene Anthony 1962–2003 **47**
Ray J 1981— **86**
Raymond, Usher, IV See Usher
Razaf, Andy 1895–1973 **19**
Razafkeriefo, Andreamentania Paul See Razaf, Andy
Ready, Stephanie 1975— **33**
Reagins, Tony 1967— **94**
Reagon, Bernice Johnson 1942— **7**
Reagon, Toshi 1964— **76**
Reason, Joseph Paul 1943— **19**
Record, Eugene 1940–2005 **60**
Redd, Dana 1968— **93**
Reddick, Lance 19(?)(?)— **52**
Reddick, Lawrence Dunbar 1910–1995 **20**
Redding, Ann Holmes 1951— **77**
Redding, J. Saunders 1906–1988 **26**
Redding, Louis L. 1901–1998 **26**
Redding, Otis, Jr. 1941— **16**
Redman 1970— **81**
Redman, Joshua 1969— **30**
Redmond, Eugene 1937— **23**
Redwood, John Henry 1942–2003 **78**
Reece, E. Albert 1950— **63**
Reed, A. C. 1926— **36**
Reed, Alaina See Reed Hall, Alaina
Reed, Ishmael 1938— **8**
Reed, Jimmy 1925–1976 **38**
Reed, Kasim 1969— **82**
Reed, Willis, Jr. 1942— **86**
Reed Amini, Alaina See Reed Hall, Alaina
Reed Hall, Alaina 1946–2009 **83**
Reems, Ernestine Cleveland 1932— **27**
Reese, Calvin See Reese, Pokey
Reese, Della 1931— **6, 20**
Reese, Milous J., Jr. 1904— **51**
Reese, Pokey 1973— **28**
Reese, Tracy 1964— **54**
Reeves, Dianne 1956— **32**
Reeves, Gregory 1952— **49**
Reeves, Martha 1941— **85**
Reeves, Rachel J. 1950(?)— **23**
Reeves, Triette Lipsey 1963— **27**
Regis, Cyrille 1958— **51**
Reid, Antonio "L.A." 1958(?)— **28**
Reid, Irvin D. 1941— **20**
Reid, L.A. See Reid, Antonio "L.A."
Reid, Senghor 1976— **55**

Reid, Tim 1944— 56
Reid, Vernon 1958— 34
Reivers, Corbin Bleu See Corbin Bleu
Reuben, Gloria 19(?)(?)— 15
Rev Run See Run; Run-DMC
Reverend Ike 1935–2009 79
Reynolds, Harold 1960— 77
Reynolds, Star Jones 1962(?)— 10, 27, 61
Rhames, Ving 1959— 14, 50
Rhimes, Shonda Lynn 1970— 67
Rhoden, Dwight 1962— 40
Rhoden, Wayne 1966— 70
Rhoden, William C. 1950(?)— 67
Rhodes, Jewell Parker 1954— 84
Rhodes, Ray 1950— 14
Rhone, Sylvia 1952— 2
Rhone, Trevor 1940–2009 80
Rhymes, Busta 1972— 31
Ribbs, William Theodore, Jr. See Ribbs, Willy T.
Ribbs, Willy T. 1956— 2
Ribeau, Sidney 1947(?)— 70
Ribeiro, Alfonso 1971— 17
Rice, Condoleezza 1954— 3, 28, 72
Rice, Constance LaMay 1956— 60
Rice, Emmett J. 1920–2011 94
Rice, Jerry 1962— 5, 55, 89
Rice, Jim 1953— 75
Rice, Linda Johnson 1958— 9, 41
Rice, Louise Allen 1941— 54
Rice, Norm(an Blann) 1943— 8
Rice, Susan E. 1964— 74
Richard, Dawn 1983— 92
Richard, J. R. 1950— 87
Richards, Beah 1926–2000 30
Richards, Hilda 1936— 49
Richards, Lloyd 1923(?)— 2
Richards, Sanya 1985— 66
Richardson, Desmond 1969— 39
Richardson, Donna 1962— 39
Richardson, Elaine Potter See Kincaid, Jamaica
Richardson, Julieanna 1954— 81
Richardson, LaTanya 1949— 71
Richardson, Laura 1962— 81
Richardson, Nolan 1941— 9
Richardson, Pat See Norman, Pat
Richardson, Rupert 1930–2008 67
Richardson, Salli 1967— 68
Richie, Leroy C. 1941— 18
Richie, Lionel 1949— 27, 65
Richmond, Cedric 1973— 93
Richmond, Mitchell James 1965— 19
Rideau, Iris 1940(?)— 46
Ridenhour, Carlton See Chuck D.
Ridley, John 1965— 69
Riggs, Marlon 1957–1994 5, 44
Rihanna 1988— 65
Riles, Wilson C. 1917–1999 79
Riley, Boots 1971— 89
Riley, Helen Caldwell Day 1926— 13
Riley, Rochelle 1959(?)— 50
Rillieux, Norbert 1806–1894 92
Ringgold, Faith 1930— 4, 81
Riperton, Minnie 1947–1979 32
Rivers, Doc 1961— 25, 81
Rivers, Eugene F., III 1950— 81
Rivers, Glenn See Rivers, Doc

Rivers, Kim See Roberts, Kimberly Rivers
Roach, Max 1924–2007 21, 63
Roberto, Holden 1923–2007 65
Roberts, Darryl 1962(?)— 70
Roberts, Deborah 1960— 35
Roberts, Ian See Kwei-Armah, Kwame
Roberts, James See Lover, Ed
Roberts, Kimberly Rivers 1981(?)— 72
Roberts, Kristina LaFerne See Zane
Roberts, Lillian 1928— 83
Roberts, Marcus 1963— 19
Roberts, Marthaniel See Roberts, Marcus
Roberts, Mike 1948— 57
Roberts, Robin 1960— 16, 54
Roberts, Roy S. 1939(?)— 14
Roberts, William Leonard, II See Ross, Rick
Robertson, Gil L., IV 1964— 85
Robertson, Lance See DJ Lance Rock
Robertson, Oscar 1938— 26
Robeson, Eslanda Goode 1896–1965 13
Robeson, Paul (Leroy Bustill) 1898–1976 2
Robinson, Aminah 1940— 50
Robinson, Bill "Bojangles" 1878–1949 11
Robinson, Bishop L. 1927— 66
Robinson, Cleo Parker 1948(?)— 38
Robinson, Darren 1967–1995 See Fat Boys
Robinson, David 1965— 24, 90
Robinson, Eddie G. 1919–2007 10, 61
Robinson, Eugene 1955— 77
Robinson, Fatima 19(?)(?)— 34
Robinson, Fenton 1935–1997 38
Robinson, Frank 1935— 9, 87
Robinson, Jack Roosevelt See Robinson, Jackie
Robinson, Jackie 1919–1972 6
Robinson, LaVaughn 1927–2008 69
Robinson, Luther See Robinson, Bill "Bojangles"
Robinson, Malcolm S. 1948— 44
Robinson, Matt 1937–2002 69
Robinson, Matthew, Jr. See Robinson, Matt
Robinson, Max 1939–1988 3
Robinson, Patrick 1966— 19, 71
Robinson, Rachel 1922— 16
Robinson, Randall 1941— 7, 46
Robinson, Reginald R. 1972— 53
Robinson, Sharon 1950— 22
Robinson, Shaun 19(?)(?)— 36
Robinson, Smokey 1940— 3, 49
Robinson, Spottswood W., III 1916–1998 22
Robinson, Sugar Ray 1921— 18
Robinson, Sylvia 1936— 79
Robinson, Will 1911–2008 51, 69
Robinson, William, Jr. See Robinson, Smokey
Robinson-Berry, Joan 19(?)(?)— 94
Roble, Abdi 1964— 71
Roby, Kimberla Lawson 1965— 86
Roche, Joyce M. 1947— 17

Rochester See Anderson, Eddie "Rochester"
Rochon, Lela 1965(?)— 16
Rochon, Stephen W. 1950(?)— 78
Rock, Chris 1967(?)— 3, 22, 66
Rock, The 1972— 29, 66
Rodgers, Johnathan 1946— 6, 51
Rodgers, Rod 1937–2002 36
Rodman, Dennis 1961— 12, 44
Rodney, Winston See Burning Spear
Rodrigues, Percy 1918–2007 68
Rodríguez, Arsenio 1911–1970 87
Rodriguez, Jimmy 1963(?)— 47
Rodriguez, Cheryl 1952— 64
Rogers, Alan G. 1967–2008 72
Rogers, Desirée 1959— 88
Rogers, Jimmy 1924–1997 38
Rogers, Joe 1964— 27
Rogers, Joel Augustus 1883(?)–1966 30
Rogers, John W., Jr. 1958— 5, 52
Rogers, Kelis See Kelis
Rojas, Don 1949— 33
Roker, Al 1954— 12, 49
Roker, Roxie 1929–1995 68
Rolle, Esther 1920–1998 13, 21
Rollins, Charlemae Hill 1897–1979 27
Rollins, Howard E., Jr. 1950–1996 16
Rollins, Ida Gray Nelson See Gray (Nelson Rollins), Ida
Rollins, James Calvin, III See Rollins, Jimmy
Rollins, Jimmy 1978— 70
Rollins, Sonny 1930— 37, 94
Rollins, Theodore Walter See Rollins, Sonny
Ronaldinho 1980— 69
Rooakhptah, Amunnubi See York, Dwight D.
Rose, Anika Noni 1972— 70
Rose, Derrick 1988— 82
Rose, Lionel 1948— 56
Ross, Araminta See Tubman, Harriet
Ross, Charles 1957— 27
Ross, Diana 1944— 8, 27
Ross, Don 1941— 27
Ross, Isaiah "Doc" 1925–1993 40
Ross, Rick 1976— 79
Ross, Tracee Ellis 1972— 35
Ross-Lee, Barbara 1942— 67
Rotimi, (Emmanuel Gladstone) Ola-(wale) 1938— 1
Roundtree, Dovey 1914— 80
Roundtree, Richard 1942— 27
Rouse, Cecilia 1963— 93
Rowan, Carl T(homas) 1925— 1, 30
Rowell, Victoria 1960— 13, 68
Roxanne Shante 1969— 33
Roy, Kenny 1990(?)— 51
Rubin, Chanda 1976— 37
Rucker, Darius 1966— 34, 74
Rudder, David 1953— 79
Rudolph, Maya 1972— 46
Rudolph, Wilma (Glodean) 1940— 4
Ruffin, Joseph Lee See Shakur, Yusef
Ruffin, Josephine St. Pierre 1842–1924 75

Ruffins, Kermit 1964— 85
Rugambwa, Laurean 1912–1997 20
Ruley, Ellis 1882–1959 38
Run 1964— 31, 73, 75
Run-DMC 31, 75
RuPaul 1960— 17, 91
Rusesabagina, Paul 1954— 60
Rush, Bobby 1940— 78
Rush, Bobby 1946— 26, 76
Rush, Otis 1934— 38
Rushen, Patrice 1954— 12
Rushing, Jimmy 1903–1972 37
Russell, Bill 1934— 8
Russell, Brenda 1944(?)— 52
Russell, Herman Jerome 1931(?)— 17
Russell, Nipsey 1924–2005 66
Russell, William Felton See Russell, Bill
Russell-McCloud, Patricia 1946— 17
Rust, Art, Jr. 1927–2010 83
Rustin, Bayard 1910–1987 4
RZA 1969— 80
Saar, Alison 1956— 16
Saar, Betye 1926— 80
Sabathia, Carsten Charles, Jr. See Sabathia, CC
Sabathia, CC 1980— 74
Sade 1959— 15, 92
Sadler, Joseph See Grandmaster Flash
Sadlier, Rosemary 19(?)(?)— 62
St. Jacques, Raymond 1930–1990 8
Saint James, Synthia 1949— 12
St. John, Kristoff 1966— 25
St. Julien, Marlon 1972— 29
St. Patrick, Mathew 1969— 48
Saint-Georges, Chevalier de See Boulogne, Joseph, Chevalier de Saint-Georges
Saint-Georges, Joseph Boulogne See Boulogne, Joseph, Chevalier de Saint-Georges
Saldana, Zoe 1978— 72
Salih, Al-Tayyib 1929— 37
Sallee, Charles 1911— 38
Salter, Nikkole 1979(?)— 73
Salters, Alisia See Salters, Lisa
Salters, Lisa 1966(?)— 71
Salvador, Bryce 1976— 51
Samara, Noah 1956— 15
SAMO See Basquiat, Jean-Michel
Sample, Joe 1939— 51
Sampson, Charles 1957— 13
Sampson, Edith S(purlock) 1901–1979 4
Samuel, Sealhenry Olumide See Seal
Samuelsson, Marcus 1970— 53
Sanchez, Sonia 1934— 17, 51
Sanders, Angelia 1961(?)— 86
Sanders, Barry 1968— 1, 53
Sanders, Bob 1981— 72
Sanders, Deion (Luwynn) 1967— 4, 31
Sanders, Demond See Sanders, Bob
Sanders, Dori(nda) 1935— 8
Sanders, Joseph R(ichard, Jr.) 1954— 11
Sanders, Malika 1973— 48
Sanders, Pharoah 1940— 64

Sanders, Rose M. See Touré, Faya Ora Rose
Sanders, Satch 1938— 77
Sanders, Thomas Ernest See Sanders, Satch
Sands, Diana 1934–1973 87
Sané, Pierre Gabriel 1948–1998 21
Sanford, Isabel 1917–2004 53
Sanford, John Elroy See Foxx, Redd
Sangare, Oumou 1968— 18
Sanhá Malam Bacai 1947— 84
Sankara, Thomas 1949–1987 17
Sankoh, Foday 1937–2003 74
Santamaria, Mongo 1917–2003 81
Santiago-Hudson, Ruben 1956— 85
Santos de Freitas, Antonio Carlos See Brown, Carlinhos
Sapp, Marvin 1966(?)— 74
Sapp, Rhonda LaChanze See LaChanze
Sapp, Warren 1972— 38
Saro-Wiwa, Kenule 1941–1995 39
Satcher, David 1941— 7, 57
Satchmo See Armstrong, (Daniel) Louis
Savage, Augusta Christine 1892(?)–1962 12
Savimbi, Jonas (Malheiro) 1934–2002 2, 34
Sawyer, Amos 1945— 2
Sawyer, Eugene 1934–2008 81
Sayers, Gale 1943— 28
Sayles Belton, Sharon 1952(?)— 9, 16
Sbraga, Kevin 1979(?)— 88
Scantlebury, Janna 1984(?)— 47
Scantlebury-White, Velma 1955— 64
Scarlett, Millicent 1971— 49
Schmoke, Kurt 1949— 1, 48
Schomburg, Arthur Alfonso 1874–1938 9
Schomburg, Arturo Alfonso See Schomburg, Arthur Alfonso
Schultz, Michael A. 1938— 6
Schuyler, George Samuel 1895–1977 40
Schuyler, Philippa 1931–1967 50
Scott, C. A. 1908–2000 29
Scott, Coretta See King, Coretta Scott
Scott, Cornelius Adolphus See Scott, C. A.
Scott, David 1946— 41
Scott, George 1929–2005 55
Scott, Harold Russell, Jr. 1935–2006 61
Scott, Hazel 1920–1981 66
Scott, Jill 1972— 29, 83
Scott, John T. 1940–2007 65
Scott, "Little" Jimmy 1925— 48
Scott, Milton 1956— 51
Scott, Robert C. 1947— 23
Scott, Stuart 1965— 34
Scott, Tim 1965— 87
Scott, Wendell Oliver, Sr. 1921–1990 19
Scott-Heron, Gil 1949–2011 94
Scruggs, Mary Elfrieda See Williams, Mary Lou
Scurry, Briana 1971— 27
Seacole, Mary 1805–1881 54

Seal 14, 75
Seale, Bobby 1936— 3
Seale, Robert George See Seale, Bobby
Seals, Frank See Seals, Son
Seals, Son 1942–2004 56
Sears, Leah Ward 1955— 5, 79
Sears, Stephanie 1964— 53
Sears-Collins, Leah J(eanette) See Sears, Leah Ward
Sebree, Charles 1914–1985 40
Seele, Pernessa 1954— 46
Selassie, Haile See Haile Selassie
Sembène, Ousmane 1923–2007 13, 62
Senghor, Augustin Diamacoune 1928–2007 66
Senghor, Léopold Sédar 1906–2001 12, 66
Sengstacke, John Herman Henry 1912–1997 18
Senior, Olive 1941— 37
Senna, Danzy 1970— 93
Sentamu, John 1949— 58
Sermon, Erick 1968— 81
Serrano, Andres 1951(?)— 3
Sewell, Terri 1965— 93
Shabazz, Attallah 1958— 6
Shabazz, Betty 1936–1997 7, 26
Shabazz, Ilyasah 1962— 36
Shadd, Abraham D. 1801–1882 81
Shaggy 1968— 31
Shakespeare, Robbie 1953— See Sly & Robbie
Shakur, Afeni 1947— 67
Shakur, Assata 1947— 6
Shakur, Meshell Suihailia Bashir See Ndegeocello, Meshell
Shakur, Tupac Amaru 1971–1996 14
Shakur, Yusef 1973— 85
Shange, Ntozake 1948— 8, 89
Shank, Suzanne F. 1962(?)— 77
Shannon, Randy 1966— 82
Sharper, Darren 1975— 32
Sharpton, Al 1954— 21
Shavers, Cheryl 19(?)(?)— 31
Shaw, Bernard 1940— 2, 28
Shaw, William J. 1934— 30
Sheard, Kierra "Kiki" 1987— 61
Sheffey, Asa Bundy See Hayden, Robert Earl
Sheffield, Gary Antonian 1968— 16
Shell, Art 1946— 1, 66
Shelton, Paula Young 1961— 86
Shepherd, Sherri 1970— 55
Sherrod, Clayton 1944— 17
Sherrod, Shirley 1948— 87
Shider, Garry 1953–2010 87
Shinhoster, Earl 1950(?)–2000 32
Shipp, E. R. 1955— 15
Shippen, John 1879–1968 43
Shirley, George I. 1934— 33
Shockley, Ann Allen 1927— 84
Shonibare, Yinka 1962— 58
Short, Bobby 1924–2005 52
Short, Columbus 1982— 79
Shorter, Wayne 1933— 75
Shorty, Ras, I 1941–2000 47
Showers, Reggie 1964— 30
Shropshire, Thomas B. 1925–2003 49
Shuttlesworth, Fred 1922— 47

Sidibe, Gabourey 1983— 84
Sifford, Charlie 1922— 4, 49
Sigur, Wanda 1958— 44
Siji 1971(?)— 56
Silas, Paul 1943— 24
Silva, Marina 1958— 80
Silver, Horace 1928— 26
Siméus, Dumas M. 1940— 25
Simmons, Bob 1948— 29
Simmons, E. Denise 19(?)(?)— 79
Simmons, Gary 1964— 58
Simmons, Henry 1970— 55
Simmons, Jamal 1971— 72
Simmons, Joseph See Run; Run-DMC
Simmons, Kimora Lee 1975— 51, 83
Simmons, Russell 1957(?)— 1, 30
Simmons, Ruth J. 1945— 13, 38
Simms, Margaret 1946— 94
Simone, Nina 1933–2003 15, 41
Simpson, Carole 1940— 6, 30
Simpson, Lorna 1960— 4, 36
Simpson, O. J. 1947— 15
Simpson, Valerie 1946— 21
Simpson-Hoffman, N'kenge 1975(?)— 52
Simpson-Miller, Portia 1945— 62
Sims, Howard "Sandman" 1917–2003 48
Sims, Lowery Stokes 1949— 27
Sims, Naomi 1948–2009 29, 79
Sinbad 1957(?)— 1, 16
Sinclair, Madge 1938–1995 78
Singletary, Mike 1958— 4, 76
Singleton, John 1968— 2, 30
Sinkford, Jeanne C. 1933— 13
Sir Mix-A-Lot 1963— 82
Sirleaf, Ellen Johnson 1938— 71
Sisqo 1976— 30
Sissle, Noble 1889–1975 29
Sister Souljah 1964— 11
Sisulu, Albertina 1918— 57
Sisulu, Sheila Violet Makate 1948(?)— 24
Sisulu, Walter 1912–2003 47
Sizemore, Barbara A. 1927— 26
Skerrit, Roosevelt 1972— 72
Skinner, Kiron K. 1962(?) 65
Sklarek, Norma Merrick 1928— 25
Slash 1975— 75
Slater, Rodney Earl 1955— 15
Slaughter, John Brooks 1934— 53
Sledge, Percy 1940— 39
Sleet, Moneta (J.), Jr. 1926— 5
Slice, Kimbo 1974— 73
Slick Rick 1965— 93
Slim Thug 1980— 86
Slocumb, Jonathan 19(?)(?)— 52
Sly & Robbie 34
Slyde, Jimmy 1927–2008 70
Smalls, Robert 1839–1915 82
Smaltz, Audrey 1937(?)— 12
Smiley, Rickey 1968— 59
Smiley, Tavis 1964— 20, 68
Smith, Anjela Lauren 1973— 44
Smith, Anna Deavere 1950— 6, 44
Smith, Arthur Lee, See Asante, Molefi Kete
Smith, B. See Smith, B(arbara)
Smith, B(arbara) 1949(?)— 11
Smith, Barbara 1946— 28
Smith, Bessie 1894–1937 3

Smith, Bruce 1984— 80
Smith, Bruce W. 19(?)(?)— 53
Smith, Cladys "Jabbo" 1908–1991 32
Smith, Clarence O. 1933— 21
Smith, Clifford See Method Man
Smith, Damu 1951— 54
Smith, Danyel 1966(?)— 40
Smith, DeMaurice 1964— 92
Smith, Dr. Lonnie 1942— 49
Smith, Emmitt 1969— 7, 87
Smith, Greg 1964— 28
Smith, Hezekiah Leroy Gordon See Smith, Stuff
Smith, Hilton 1912–1983 29
Smith, Ian 1970(?)— 62
Smith, Jabbo See Smith, Cladys "Jabbo"
Smith, Jaden 1998— 82
Smith, James Todd See LL Cool J
Smith, Jane E. 1946— 24
Smith, Jennifer 1947— 21
Smith, Jessie Carney 1930— 35
Smith, John L. 1938— 22
Smith, Joshua (Isaac) 1941— 10
Smith, Kemba 1971— 70
Smith, Lonnie Liston 1940— 49
Smith, Lovie 1958— 66
Smith, Malcolm A. 1956— 75
Smith, Mamie 1883–1946 32
Smith, Marie F. 1939— 70
Smith, Marvin 1910–2003 46
Smith, Mary Carter 1919— 26
Smith, Morgan 1910–1993 46
Smith, Myrna 1941–2010 92
Smith, Nate 1929— 49
Smith, Orlando See Smith, Tubby
Smith, Ozzie 1954— 77
Smith, Princella 1983— 86
Smith, Randy 1948–2009 81
Smith, Richard 1957— 51
Smith, Rick 1969— 72
Smith, Roger Guenveur 1960— 12
Smith, Shaffer Chimere See Ne-Yo
Smith, Stephen A. 1967— 69
Smith, Stuff 1909–1967 37
Smith, Tasha 1971— 73
Smith, Trevor, Jr. See Rhymes, Busta
Smith, Trixie 1895–1943 34
Smith, Tubby 1951— 18, 83
Smith, Vincent D. 1929–2003 48
Smith, Walker, Jr. See Robinson, Sugar Ray
Smith, Will 1968— 8, 18, 53
Smith, Willi (Donnell) 1948–1987 8
Smith, Willow 2000— 92
Smith, Zadie 1975— 51
Smyre, Calvin 1947— 90
Smythe Haith, Mabel 1918–2006 61
Sneed, Paula A. 1947— 18
Snipes, Wesley 1962— 3, 24, 67
Snoop Dogg 1971— 35, 84
Snow, Samuel 1923–2008 71
Snowden, Frank M., Jr. 1911–2007 67
Soglo, Nicéphore 1935— 15
Solomon, Jimmie Lee 1947(?)— 38
Somé, Malidoma Patrice 1956— 10
Somi 1979— 85
Sommore, 1966— 61
Songz, Trey 1984— 88

Sono, Jomo 1955— **86**
Sosa, Sammy 1968— **21, 44**
Soto Alejo, Federico Arístides *See Güines, Tata*
Soulchild, Musiq *See Musiq*
Souleymane, Mahamane 1940— **78**
Southern, Eileen 1920–2002 **56**
Southgate, Martha 1960(?)— **58**
Sowande, Fela 1905–1987 **39**
Sowande, Olufela Obafunmilayo *See Sowande, Fela*
Sowell, Thomas 1930— **2**
Soyinka, Wole 1934— **4, 93**
Sparks, Corinne Etta 1953— **53**
Sparks, Jordin 1989— **66**
Spaulding, Charles Clinton 1874–1952 **9**
Spearman, Leonard H. O., Sr. 1929–2008 **81**
Spears, Warren 1954–2005 **52**
Spector, Ronnie 1943— **77**
Speech 1968— **82**
Spence, Joseph 1910–1984 **49**
Spencer, Anne 1882–1975 **27**
Spencer, Michael G. 1952— **87**
Spencer, Winston Baldwin 1948— **68**
Spigner, Archie 1928— **81**
Spikes, Dolores Margaret Richard 1936— **18**
Spiller, Bill 1913–1988 **64**
Sprewell, Latrell 1970— **23**
Spriggs, William 195(?)— **67**
Stackhouse, Jerry 1974— **30**
Staley, Dawn 1970— **57**
Stallings, George A(ugustus), Jr. 1948— **6**
Stampley, Micah 1971— **54**
Stanford, John 1938— **20**
Stanford, Olivia Lee Dilworth 1914–2004 **49**
Stanton, Alysa 1963— **78**
Stanton, Robert 1940— **20**
Staples, Brent 1951— **8**
Staples, Mavis 1939(?)— **50, 88**
Staples, "Pops" 1915–2000 **32**
Staples, Roebuck *See Staples, "Pops"*
Stargell, Willie 1940(?)–2001 **29**
Staton, Candi 1940(?)— **27**
Staton, Dakota 1930(?)–2007 **62**
Staupers, Mabel K(eaton) 1890–1989 **7**
Stearnes, Norman "Turkey" 1901–1979 **31**
Steave-Dickerson, Kia 1970— **57**
Steele, Claude Mason 1946— **13**
Steele, Lawrence 1963— **28**
Steele, Michael 1958— **38, 73, 91**
Steele, Shelby 1946— **13, 82**
Steely 1962–2009 **80**
Steinberg, Martha Jean 1930(?)–2000 **28**
Stephens, Charlotte Andrews 1854–1951 **14**
Stephens, John *See Legend, John*
Stephens, Myrtle *See Potter, Myrtle*
Stevens, Yvette *See Khan, Chaka*
Stew 1961— **69**
Steward, David L. 19(?)(?)— **36**
Steward, Emanuel 1944— **18**
Stewart, Alison 1966(?)— **13**
Stewart, Ella 1893–1987 **39**

Stewart, James "Bubba," Jr. 1985— **60**
Stewart, Kordell 1972— **21**
Stewart, Mark *See Stew*
Stewart, Nzingha 1974— **89**
Stewart, Paul Wilbur 1925— **12**
Stewart, Sylvester *See Stone, Sly*
Stewart, Tonea Harris 1947— **78**
Sticky Fingaz 1970— **86**
Still, William Grant 1895–1978 **37**
Stingley, Darryl 1951–2007 **69**
Stinson, Denise L. 1954— **59**
Stith, Charles R. 1949— **73**
Stith, Tom 1939–2010 **93**
Stockman, Shawn *See Boyz II Men*
Stokes, Carl 1927–1996 **10, 73**
Stokes, Louis 1925— **3**
Stone, Angie 1965(?)— **31**
Stone, Charles Sumner, Jr. *See Stone, Chuck*
Stone, Chuck 1924— **9**
Stone, Sly 1943— **85**
Stone, Toni 1921–1996 **15**
Stoney, Michael 1969— **50**
Stott, Dorothy M. *See Stout, Renee*
Stott, Dot *See Stout, Renee*
Stoudemire, Amaré 1982— **59**
Stout, Juanita Kidd 1919–1998 **24**
Stout, Renee 1958— **63**
Stoute, Steve 1971(?)— **38**
Stoutt, H. Lavity 1929–1995 **83**
Strahan, Michael 1971— **35, 81**
Strautmanis, Michael 1969— **87**
Strawberry, Darryl 1962— **22**
Strayhorn, Billy 1915–1967 **31**
Street, John F. 1943(?)— **24**
Streeter, Sarah 1953— **45**
Stringer, C. Vivian 1948— **13, 66**
Stringer, Korey 1974–2001 **35**
Stringer, Vickie 196(?)— **58**
Stroman, Nathaniel *See Earthquake*
Strong, Barrett 1941— **89**
Stuart, Moira 1949— **82**
Studdard, Ruben 1978— **46**
Sudarkasa, Niara 1938— **4**
Sudduth, Jimmy Lee 1910–2007 **65**
Sugarhill Gang, The **79**
Sullivan, Jazmine 1987— **81**
Sullivan, Leon H(oward) 1922— **3, 30**
Sullivan, Louis (Wade) 1933— **8**
Sullivan, Maxine 1911–1987 **37**
Summer, Donna 1948— **25**
Sun Ra, 1914–1993 **60**
Sundiata, Sekou 1948–2007 **66**
Supremes, The **33**
Sutphen, Mona 1967— **77**
Sutton, Percy E. 1920–2009 **42, 82**
Swann, Lynn 1952— **28**
Swaray, Fanta Estelle *See Estelle*
Sweat, Keith 1961(?)— **19**
Sweet, Ossian 1895–1960 **68**
Swoopes, Sheryl 1971— **12, 56**
Swygert, H. Patrick 1943— **22**
Sy, Oumou 1952— **65**
Sykes, Roosevelt 1906–1984 **20**
Sykes, Wanda 1964— **48, 81**
Syler, Rene 1963— **53**
Tademy, Lalita 1948— **36**
Tafari Makonnen *See Haile Selassie*
Tait, Michael 1966— **57**

Talbert, David E. 1966(?)— **34, 93**
Talbert, Mary B. 1866–1923 **77**
Talley, André Leon 1949(?)— **56**
Tamar-kali 1973(?)— **63**
Tamia 1975— **24, 55**
Tampa Red 1904(?)–1980 **63**
Tancil, Gladys Quander 1921–2002 **59**
Tandja, Mamadou 1938— **33, 78**
Tanksley, Ann (Graves) 1934— **37**
Tanner, Henry Ossawa 1859–1937 **1**
Tate, Eleanora E. 1948— **20, 55**
Tate, Larenz 1975— **15**
Tatum, Art 1909–1956 **28**
Tatum, Beverly Daniel 1954— **42, 84**
Tatum, Elinor R. 197(?)— **78**
Tatum, Jack 1948— **87**
Tatum, Wilbert 1933–2009 **76**
Taulbert, Clifton Lemoure 1945— **19**
Taylor, Billy 1921–2010 **23, 92**
Taylor, Bo 1966–2008 **72**
Taylor, Cecil 1929— **70**
Taylor, Charles 1948— **20**
Taylor, Darren *See Taylor, Bo*
Taylor, Ephren W., II 1982— **61**
Taylor, Gardner C. 1918— **76**
Taylor, Helen (Lavon Hollingshed) 1942–2000 **30**
Taylor, Jason 1974— **70**
Taylor, Jermain 1978— **60**
Taylor, John (David Beckett) 1952— **16**
Taylor, Karin 1971— **34**
Taylor, Koko 1928–2009 **40, 80**
Taylor, Kristin Clark 1959— **8**
Taylor, Lawrence 1959— **25**
Taylor, Marshall Walter "Major" 1878–1932 **62**
Taylor, Meshach 1947(?)— **4**
Taylor, Mildred D. 1943— **26**
Taylor, Natalie 1959— **47**
Taylor, Recy 1919— **92**
Taylor, Regina 1959(?)— **9, 46**
Taylor, Robert Robinson 1868–1942 **80**
Taylor, Ron 1952–2002 **35**
Taylor, Susan C. 1957— **62**
Taylor, Susan L. 1946— **10, 86**
Taylor, Susie King 1848–1912 **13**
Teasley, Lisa 1962— **92**
Teer, Barbara Ann 1937–2008 **81**
Temptations, The **33**
Tergat, Paul 1969— **59**
Terrell, Dorothy A. 1945— **24**
Terrell, Mary (Elizabeth) Church 1863–1954 **9**
Terrell, Tammi 1945–1970 **32**
Terrell-Kearney, Kim 1965— **83**
Terrill, Saunders *See Terry, Sonny*
Terry, Clark 1920— **39**
Terry, Sonny 1911–1986 **88**
Tharpe, Rosetta 1915–1973 **65**
The Artist *See Prince*
The-Dream 1982— **74**
Thiam, Aliaune Akon *See Akon*
Thigpen, Lynne 1948–2003 **17, 41**
Thomas, Alma Woodsey 1891–1978 **14**
Thomas, Arthur Ray 1951— **52**
Thomas, Clarence 1948— **2, 39, 65**

Thomas, Claudia Lynn 1950— **64**
Thomas, Debi 1967— **26**
Thomas, Derrick 1967–2000 **25**
Thomas, Emmitt 1943— **71**
Thomas, Frank 1968— **12, 51**
Thomas, Franklin A. 1934— **5, 49**
Thomas, Irma 1941— **29**
Thomas, Isiah 1961— **7, 26, 65**
Thomas, Jefferson 1942–2010 **88**
Thomas, Michael 1967— **69**
Thomas, Mickalene 1971— **61**
Thomas, Rozonda 1971— **34, 78**
Thomas, Rufus 1917— **20**
Thomas, Sean Patrick 1970— **35**
Thomas, Stayve Jerome *See Slim Thug*
Thomas, Thurman 1966— **75**
Thomas, Todd *See Speech*
Thomas, Trisha R. 1964— **65**
Thomas, Vivien (T.) 1910–1985 **9**
Thomas-Graham, Pamela 1963(?)— **29**
Thomason, Marsha 1976— **47**
Thompson, Ahmir *See ?uestlove*
Thompson, Bennie G. 1948— **26**
Thompson, Cynthia Bramlett 1949— **50**
Thompson, Dearon *See Deezer D*
Thompson, Don 1963— **56**
Thompson, John Douglas 1964— **81**
Thompson, John W. 1949— **26**
Thompson, Kenan 1978— **52**
Thompson, Larry D. 1945— **39**
Thompson, Tazewell (Alfred, Jr.) 1954— **13**
Thompson, Tina 1975— **25, 75**
Thompson, William C. 1953(?)— **35**
Thoms, Tracie 1975— **61**
Thornton, Big Mama 1926–1984 **33**
Thornton, Yvonne S. 1947— **69**
Thrash, Dox 1893–1965 **35**
Three Mo' Tenors **35**
Thrower, Willie 1930–2002 **35**
Thugwane, Josia 1971— **21**
Thurman, Howard 1900–1981 **3**
Thurman, Wallace Henry 1902–1934 **16**
Thurmond, Nate 1941— **88**
Thurston, Baratunde 1977— **79**
Thurston, Stephen J. 1952— **49**
Till, Emmett (Louis) 1941–1955 **7**
Tillard, Conrad 1964— **47**
Tillis, Frederick 1930— **40**
Tillman, Dorothy 1947— **76**
Tillman, George, Jr. 1968— **20**
Timbaland 1971— **32**
Tinsley, Boyd 1964— **50**
Tirico, Michael *See Tirico, Mike*
Tirico, Mike 1966— **68**
Tisdale, Wayman 1964— **50**
TLC **34**
Tobias, Channing H. 1882–1961 **79**
Tobin, Patricia 1943–2008 **75**
Todman, Terence A. 1926— **55**
Tolbert, Terence 1964— **74**
Toler, Burl 1928–2009 **80**
Tolliver, Mose 1915(?)–2006 **60**
Tolliver, William (Mack) 1951— **9**
Tolson, Melvin B(eaunorus) 1898–1966 **37**
Tolton, Augustine 1854–1897 **62**
Tomlinson, LaDainian 1979— **65**

Tonex, 1978(?)— 54
Toney, James 1968— 89
Tooks, Lance 1962— 62
Toomer, Jean 1894–1967 6
Toomer, Nathan Pinchback See Toomer, Jean
Toote, Gloria E. A. 1931— 64
Torres, Gina 1969— 52
Torry, Guy 19(?)(?)— 31
Tosh, Peter 1944–1987 9
Touré, Amadou Toumani 1948(?)— 18
Touré, Askia (Muhammad Abu Bakr el) 1938— 47
Touré, Faya Ora Rose 1945— 56
Touré, Sekou 1922–1984 6
Toussaint, Allen 1938— 60
Toussaint, Lorraine 1960— 32
Townes, Jeffrey Allan See DJ Jazzy Jeff
Towns, Edolphus 1934— 19, 75
Townsend, Robert 1957— 4, 23
T-Pain 1985— 73
Trammell, Kimberly N. See Holland, Kimberly N.
Travis, Tracey T. 1962— 94
Tresvant, Ralph 1968— 57
Tribbett, Tye 1977— 81
Tribble, Israel, Jr. 1940— 8
Trotter, Donne E. 1950— 28
Trotter, Lloyd G. 1945(?)— 56
Trotter, (William) Monroe 1872–1934 9
Trotter, Tariq Luqmaan See Black Thought
Trouillot, Ertha Pascal See Pascal-Trouillot, Ertha
Troupe, Quincy 1943— 83
Trouppe, Quincy Thomas, Sr. 1912–1993 84
True, Rachel 1966— 82
Trueheart, William E. 1942— 49
Tsvangirai, Morgan 1952— 26, 72
Tubbs Jones, Stephanie 1949–2008 24, 72
Tubman, Harriet 1820(?)–1913 9
Tucker, C. Delores 1927–2005 12, 56
Tucker, Chris 1972— 13, 23, 62
Tucker, Cynthia 1955— 1561
Tucker, Rosina Budd Harvey Corrothers 1881–1987 14
Tuckson, Reed V. 1951(?)— 71
Tunie, Tamara 1959— 63
Tunnell, Emlen 1925–1975 54
Ture, Kwame See Carmichael, Stokely
Turnbull, Charles Wesley 1935— 62
Turnbull, Walter 1944— 13, 60
Turner, Big Joe 1911–1985 92
Turner, Henry McNeal 1834–1915 5
Turner, Ike 1931–2007 68
Turner, Izear See Turner, Ike
Turner, Tina 1939— 6, 27
Tutu, Desmond (Mpilo) 1931— 6, 44
Tutu, Nontombi Naomi 1960— 57
Tutuola, Amos 1920–1997 30
Tyler, Aisha N. 1970— 36
Tyner, McCoy 1938— 92
Tyree, Omar Rashad 1969— 21
Tyrese See Gibson, Tyrese
Tyson, Andre 1960— 40

Tyson, Asha 1970— 39
Tyson, Cicely 1933— 7, 51
Tyson, Mike 1966— 28, 44, 93
Tyson, Neil deGrasse 1958— 15, 65
Uggams, Leslie 1943— 23
Ukpabio, Helen 1969— 86
Ulmer, James 1942— 79
Underwood, Blair 1964— 7, 27, 76
Union, Gabrielle 1972— 31, 92
Unseld, Wes 1946— 23
Upshaw, Gene 1945–2008 18, 47, 72
Usher 1978— 23, 56
Usry, James L. 1922— 23
Ussery, Terdema Lamar, II 1958— 29
Utendahl, John 1956— 23
Valdés, Bebo 1918— 75
Valdés, Chucho 1941— 89
Valdés, Dionisio Ramón Emilio See Valdés, Bebo
Valentino, Bobby 1980— 62
Van Lierop, Robert 1939— 53
Van Peebles, Mario 1957— 2, 51
Van Peebles, Melvin 1932— 7
van Sertima, Ivan 1935— 25
Vance, Courtney B. 1960— 15, 60
VanDerZee, James (Augustus Joseph) 1886–1983 6
Vandross, Luther 1951–2005 13, 48, 59
Vanessa James and Yannick Bonheur 84
Vanity 1959— 67
Vann, Harold Moore See Muhammad, Khallid Abdul
Vanzant, Iyanla 1953— 17, 47
Vaughan, Sarah (Lois) 1924–1990 13
Vaughn, Countess 1978— 53
Vaughn, Gladys Gary 1942(?)— 47
Vaughn, Mo 1967— 16
Vaughn, Viola 1947— 70
Vaughns, Cleopatra 1940— 46
Vega, Marta Moreno 1942(?)— 61
Velez-Rodriguez, Argelia 1936— 56
Vera, Yvonne 1964— 32
Verdelle, A. J. 1960— 26
Vereen, Ben(jamin Augustus) 1946— 4
Verna, Gelsy 1961–2008 70
Verrett, Shirley 1931–2010 66, 91
Vick, Michael 1980— 39, 65, 94
Vieira, João Bernardo 1939–2009 14, 84
Villarosa, Clara 1930(?)— 85
Vincent, Marjorie Judith 1965(?)— 2
Vincent, Mark See Diesel, Vin
Vincent, Troy 1971— 91
Virgil, Ozzie 1933— 48
Von Lipsey, Roderick 1959— 11
wa Ngengi, Kamau See Kenyatta, Jomo
Waddles, Charleszetta "Mother" 1912–2001 10, 49
Waddles, Mother See Waddles, Charleszetta "Mother"
Wade, Abdoulaye 1926— 66
Wade, Dwyane 1982— 61
Wade-Gayles, Gloria Jean 1937(?)— 41
Wagner, Albert 1924–2006 78

Wagner, Annice 1937— 22
Wainwright, Joscelyn 1941— 46
Walcott, Derek 1930— 5, 94
Walcott, Louis Eugene 1933— 2, 15
Wale 1984— 92
Walker, Albertina 1929–2010 10, 58, 89
Walker, Alice 1944— 1, 43
Walker, Arthur, II 1936–2001 87
Walker, Bernita Ruth 1946— 53
Walker, Cedric "Ricky" 1953— 19
Walker, Cora T. 1922–2006 68
Walker, Dianne 1951— 57
Walker, Eamonn 1961(?)— 37
Walker, George 1922— 37
Walker, Herschel 1962— 1, 69
Walker, Hezekiah 1962— 34
Walker, John T. 1925–1989 50
Walker, Kara 1969— 16, 80
Walker, Kurt See Blow, Kurtis
Walker, Lucius, Jr. 1930–2010 88
Walker, Madame C. J. 1867–1919 7
Walker, Maggie Lena 1867(?)–1934 17
Walker, Margaret 1915–1998 29
Walker, Nellie Marian See Larsen, Nella
Walker, Rebecca 1969— 50
Walker, T. J. 1961(?)— 7
Walker, Thomas "T. J." See Walker, T. J.
Walker, Wyatt Tee 1929— 80
Wall, Orindatus S. B. 1825–1891 92
Wallace, Ben 1974— 54
Wallace, Joaquin 1965— 49
Wallace, Michele Faith 1952— 13
Wallace, Perry E. 1948— 47
Wallace, Phyllis A(nn) 1920(?)–1993 9
Wallace, Rasheed 1974— 56
Wallace, Ruby Ann See Dee, Ruby
Wallace, Sippie 1898–1986 1
Wallace, William 1939–2008 75
Waller, Fats 1904–1943 29
Waller, Thomas Wright See Waller, Fats
Walters, Richard See Slick Rick
Walters, Ronald 1938— 83
Walton, Cora See Taylor, Koko
Wambugu, Florence 1953— 42
Wamutombo, Dikembe Mutombo Mpolondo Mukamba Jean Jacque See Mutombo, Dikembe
Wanjiru, Sammy 1986–2011 94
Ward, Andre 1984— 62
Ward, Benjamin 1926–2002 68
Ward, Douglas Turner 1930— 42
Ward, Hines 1976— 84
Ward, Lloyd 1949— 21, 46
Ware, Andre 1968— 37
Ware, Carl H. 1943— 30
Ware, DeMarcus 1982— 92
Warfield, Marsha 1955— 2
Warfield, William 1920–2002 94
Warner, Malcolm-Jamal 1970— 22, 36
Warren, Michael 1946— 27
Warren, Mike See Warren, Michael
Warsame, Keinan Abdi See K'naan
Warwick, Dionne 1940— 18

Washington, Alonzo 1967— 29
Washington, Booker T(aliaferro) 1856–1915 4
Washington, Denzel 1954— 1, 16, 93
Washington, Dinah 1924–1963 22
Washington, Ebonya 1973(?)— 79
Washington, Elsie B. 1942–2009 78
Washington, Fred(er)i(cka Carolyn) 1903–1994 10
Washington, Gene 1947— 63
Washington, Grover, Jr. 1943–1999 17, 44
Washington, Harold 1922–1987 6
Washington, Harriet A. 1951— 69
Washington, Hayma 19(?)(?)— 86
Washington, Isaiah 1963— 62
Washington, James, Jr. 1909(?)–2000 38
Washington, James Melvin 1948–1997 50
Washington, Kenny 1918–1971 50
Washington, Kerry 1977— 46
Washington, Laura S. 1956(?)— 18
Washington, MaliVai 1969— 8
Washington, Mary T. 1906–2005 57
Washington, Patrice Clarke 1961— 12
Washington, Pauletta Pearson 1950— 86
Washington, Regynald G. 1954(?)— 44
Washington, Tamia Reneé See Tamia
Washington, Valores James 1903–1995 12
Washington, Walter 1915–2003 45
Washington Wylie, Mary T. See Washington, Mary T.
Wasow, Omar 1970— 15
Waters, Benny 1902–1998 26
Waters, Ethel 1895–1977 7
Waters, Maxine 1938— 3, 67
Waters, Muddy 1915–1983 34
Watkins, Donald 1948— 35
Watkins, Frances Ellen See Harper, Frances Ellen Watkins
Watkins, Gloria Jean See hooks, bell
Watkins, Joe 1953— 86
Watkins, Levi, Jr. 1945— 9
Watkins, Perry James Henry 1948–1996 12
Watkins, Shirley R. 1938— 17
Watkins, Tionne "T-Boz" 1970— See TLC
Watkins, Walter C. 1946— 24
Watley, Jody 1959— 54
Watson, Bob 1946— 25
Watson, Carlos 1970— 50
Watson, Diane 1933— 41
Watson, Johnny "Guitar" 1935–1996 18
Watt, Melvin 1945— 26
Wattleton, (Alyce) Faye 1943— 9
Watts, Andre 1946— 42
Watts, J(ulius) C(aesar), Jr. 1957— 14, 38
Watts, Reggie 1972(?)— 52
Watts, Rolonda 1959— 9
Wayans, Damien 198(?)— 78
Wayans, Damon 1961— 8, 41
Wayans, Keenen Ivory 1958— 18
Wayans, Kim 1961— 80

Wayans, Marlon 1972— **29, 82**
Wayans, Shawn 1971— **29**
Waymon, Eunice Kathleen See Simone, Nina
Weah, George 1966— **58**
Weathers, Carl 1948— **10**
Weaver, Afaa Michael 1951— **37**
Weaver, Michael S. See Weaver, Afaa Michael
Weaver, Robert C. 1907–1997 **8, 46**
Webb, Veronica 1965— **10**
Webb, Wellington 1941— **3, 81**
Webber, Chris 1973— **15, 30, 59**
Webster, Katie 1936–1999 **29**
Wedgeworth, Robert W. 1937— **42**
Weekes, Kevin 1975— **67**
Weeks, Thomas, III 1967— **70**
Weems, Carrie Mae 1953— **63**
Weems, Renita J. 1954— **44**
Wein, Joyce 1928–2005 **62**
Wek, Alek 1977— **18, 63**
Welburn, Edward T. 1950— **50**
Welch, Elisabeth 1908–2003 **52**
Welles, Rosalind See Washington, Elsie B.
Wells, Henrietta Bell 1912–2008 **69**
Wells, James Lesesne 1902–1993 **10**
Wells, Mary 1943–1992 **28**
Wells, Vernon 1978— **91**
Wells-Barnett, Ida B(ell) 1862–1931 **8**
Welsing, Frances (Luella) Cress 1935— **5**
Wendo See Kolosoy, Wendo
Wesley, Dorothy Porter 1905–1995 **19**
Wesley, Richard 1945— **73**
Wesley, Valerie Wilson 194(?)— **18**
West, Allen 1961— **89**
West, Cornel 1953— **5, 33, 80**
West, Dorothy 1907–1998 **12, 54**
West, James E. 1931— **87**
West, Kanye 1977— **52, 93**
West, Togo Dennis, Jr. 1942— **16**
Westbrook, Kelvin 1955— **50**
Westbrook, Peter 1952— **20**
Westbrooks, Bobby 1930(?)–1995 **51**
Whack, Rita Coburn 1958— **36**
Whalum, Kirk 1958— **37, 64**
Wharton, Clifton R(eginald), Jr. 1926— **7**
Wharton, Clifton Reginald, Sr. 1899–1990 **36**
Wheat, Alan Dupree 1951— **14**
Whitaker, Forest 1961— **2, 49, 67**
Whitaker, Mark 1957— **21, 47**
Whitaker, Pernell 1964— **10, 89**
Whitaker, "Sweet Pea" See Whitaker, Pernell
White, Armond 1954(?)— **80**
White, Barry 1944–2003 **13, 41**
White, Bill 1933(?)— **1, 48**
White, Charles 1918–1979 **39**
White, (Donald) Dondi 1961–1998 **34**
White, Jesse 1934— **22, 75**
White, Jessica 1984— **83**
White, John H. 1945— **27**
White, Josh 1914(?)–1969 **86**
White, Josh, Jr. 1940— **52**
White, Linda M. 1942— **45**

White, Lois Jean 1938— **20**
White, Maurice 1941— **29**
White, Michael Jai 1967— **71**
White, Michael R(eed) 1951— **5**
White, Reggie 1961–2004 **6, 50**
White, Reginald Howard See White, Reggie
White, Terri 1948— **82**
White, Walter F(rancis) 1893–1955 **4**
White, Willard 1946— **53**
White, William DeKova See White, Bill
White, Willye 1939— **67**
White-Hammond, Gloria 1951(?)— **61**
Whitehead, Colson 1969— **77**
Whitfield, Fred 1967— **23**
Whitfield, LeRoy 1969–2005 **84**
Whitfield, Lynn 1954— **18**
Whitfield, Mal 1924— **60**
Whitfield, Norman 1940–2008 **73**
Whitfield, Van 1960(?)— **34**
Whitlock, Jason 1967— **78**
Whittaker, Hudson See Tampa Red
Wideman, John Edgar 1941— **5, 87**
Wilbekin, Emil 1968— **63**
Wilbon, Michael 1958— **68**
Wilder, L. Douglas 1931— **3, 48**
Wiley, Kehinde 1977— **62**
Wiley, Ralph 1952–2004 **8, 78**
Wilkens, J. Ernest, Jr. 1923— **43**
Wilkens, Lenny 1937— **11, 88**
Wilkens, Leonard Randolph See Wilkens, Lenny
Wilkerson, Isabel 1961— **71**
Wilkerson, Robert King See King, Robert Hillary
Wilkins, David 1956— **77**
Wilkins, Dominique 1960— **74**
Wilkins, Ray 1951— **47**
Wilkins, Roger 1932— **2, 84**
Wilkins, Roy 1901–1981 **4**
Wilkins, Thomas Alphonso 1956— **71**
will.i.am 1975— **64**
Williams, Alice Faye See Shakur, Afeni
Williams, Ann Claire 1949— **82**
Williams, Anthony 1951— **21**
Williams, Anthony Charles See Tonex
Williams, Armstrong 1959— **29**
Williams, Bert 1874–1922 **18**
Williams, Billy 1938— **86**
Williams, Billy Dee 1937— **8**
Williams, Carl See Kani, Karl
Williams, Clarence 1893(?)–1965 **33**
Williams, Clarence 1967— **70**
Williams, Clarence, III 1939— **26**
Williams, Claude 1908–2004 **80**
Williams, Daniel Hale (III) 1856–1931 **2**
Williams, David Rudyard 1954— **50**
Williams, Deniece 1951— **36**
Williams, Denise 1958— **40**
Williams, Deron 1984— **92**
Williams, Doug 1955— **22**
Williams, Dudley 1938— **60**
Williams, Eddie N. 1932— **44**
Williams, Eric Eustace 1911–1981 **65**

Williams, Evelyn 1922(?)— **10**
Williams, Fannie Barrier 1855–1944 **27**
Williams, Frederick (B.) 1939–2006 **63**
Williams, George Washington 1849–1891 **18**
Williams, Gertrude See Morgan, Gertrude
Williams, Gregory (Howard) 1943— **11**
Williams, Hosea Lorenzo 1926— **15, 31**
Williams, J. Mayo 1894–1980 **83**
Williams, Joe 1918–1999 **5, 25**
Williams, John A. 1925— **27**
Williams, Juan 1954— **35, 80**
Williams, Ken 1964— **68**
Williams, Lauryn 1983— **58**
Williams, Lindsey 1966— **75**
Williams, Maggie 1954— **7, 71**
Williams, Malinda 1975— **57**
Williams, Marco 1956— **53**
Williams, Margaret Ann See Williams, Maggie
Williams, Mary Lou 1910–1981 **15**
Williams, Michael L. 1953— **86**
Williams, Michelle 1980— **73**
Williams, Montel 1956— **4, 57**
Williams, Nat D. 1907–1983 **91**
Williams, Natalie 1970— **31**
Williams, O(swald) S. 1921— **13**
Williams, Patricia 1951— **11, 54**
Williams, Paul R(evere) 1894–1980 **9**
Williams, Paulette Linda See Shange, Ntozake
Williams, Pharrell 1973— **47, 82**
Williams, Preston Warren, II 1939(?)— **64**
Williams, Rhonda Y. 1967(?)— **86**
Williams, Ricky 1977— **85**
Williams, Robert F(ranklin) 1925— **11**
Williams, Robert Peter See Guillaume, Robert
Williams, Ronald A. 1949— **57**
Williams, Roy 1968— **89**
Williams, Russell, II 1952— **70**
Williams, Samuel Arthur 1946— **21**
Williams, Saul 1972— **31**
Williams, Serena 1981— **20, 41, 73**
Williams, Sherley Anne 1944–1999 **25**
Williams, Stanley "Tookie" 1953–2005 **29, 57**
Williams, Stevie 1979— **71**
Williams, Ted 1957— **91**
Williams, Terrie M. 1954— **35**
Williams, Tony 1945–1997 **67**
Williams, Vanessa A. 1963— **32, 66**
Williams, Vanessa L. 1963— **4, 17**
Williams, Venus 1980— **17, 34, 62**
Williams, Walter E(dward) 1936— **4**
Williams, Wendy 1964— **62**
Williams, William December See Williams, Billy Dee
Williams, William T(homas) 1942— **11**
Williams, Willie L(awrence) 1943— **4**
Williamson, Fred 1938— **67**
Williamson, Lisa See Sister Souljah
Williamson, Mykelti 1957— **22**

Williamson, Sonny Boy 1899(?)–1965 **84**
Willie, Louis, Jr. 1923–2007 **68**
Willingham, Tyrone 1953— **43**
Willis, Bill 1921–2007 **68**
Willis, Cheryl See Hudson, Cheryl
Willis, Deborah 1948— **85**
Willis, Dontrelle 1982— **55**
Willis, William Karnet See Willis, Bill
Wills, Harry 1889(?)–1958 **80**
Wills, Maury 1932— **73**
Wilson, August 1945–2005 **7, 33, 55**
Wilson, Brian Courtney 19(?)(?)— **94**
Wilson, Cassandra 1955— **16**
Wilson, Chandra 1969— **57**
Wilson, Charlie 1953— **31, 77**
Wilson, Debra 1970(?)— **38**
Wilson, Donald E. 1936(?)— **88**
Wilson, Dorien 1962(?)— **55**
Wilson, Ellis 1899–1977 **39**
Wilson, Frederica 1942— **92**
Wilson, Flip 1933–1998 **21**
Wilson, Gerald 1918— **49**
Wilson, Jackie 1934–1984 **60**
Wilson, Jimmy 1946— **45**
Wilson, Margaret Bush 1919–2009 **79**
Wilson, Mary 1944 **28**
Wilson, Nancy 1937— **10**
Wilson, Natalie 1972(?)— **38**
Wilson, Phill 1956— **9**
Wilson, Stephanie 1966— **72**
Wilson, Sunnie 1908–1999 **7, 55**
Wilson, Tracey Scott 1967(?)— **77**
Wilson, William Julius 1935— **22**
Wilson, William Nathaniel See Wilson, Sunnie
Wimbley, Damon 1966— See Fat Boys
Winans, Angie 1968— **36**
Winans, Benjamin 1962— **14**
Winans, CeCe 1964— **14, 43**
Winans, David 1934–2009 **77**
Winans, Debbie 1972— **36**
Winans, Marvin L. 1958— **17**
Winans, Ronald 1956–2005 **54**
Winans, Vickie 1953(?)— **24**
Winfield, Dave 1951— **5, 91**
Winfield, David Mark See Winfield, Dave
Winfield, Paul (Edward) 1941–2004 **2, 45**
Winfrey, Oprah 1954— **2, 15, 61**
Winkfield, Jimmy 1882–1974 **42**
Winslow, Kellen 1957— **83**
Wisdom, Kimberlydawn 1956— **57**
Withers, Bill 1938— **61**
Withers, Ernest C. 1922–2007 **68, 88**
Withers-Mendes, Elisabeth 1973(?)— **64**
Witherspoon, John 1942— **38**
Witt, Edwin T. 1920— **26**
Wiwa, Ken 1968— **67**
Wofford, Chloe Anthony See Morrison, Toni
Wolfe, Ann 1971— **82**
Wolfe, George C. 1954— **6, 43**
Womack, Bobby 1944— **60, 92**
Wonder, Stevie 1950— **11, 53**

Wonder Mike *See Sugarhill Gang, The*
Woodard, Alfre 1953— **9**
Woodard, Lynette 1959— **67**
Woodbridge, Hudson *See Tampa Red*
Woodruff, Hale (Aspacio) 1900–1980 **9**
Woodruff, John 1915–2007 **68**
Woods, Abraham, Jr. 1928–2008 **74**
Woods, Eldrick *See Woods, Tiger*
Woods, Georgie 1927–2005 **57**
Woods, Granville T. 1856–1910 **5**
Woods, Jacqueline 1962— **52**
Woods, Mattiebelle 1902–2005 **63**
Woods, Scott 1971— **55**
Woods, Sylvia 1926— **34**
Woods, Teri 1968— **69**
Woods, Tiger 1975— **14, 31, 81**
Woodson, Ali Ollie 1951–2010 **89**
Woodson, Carter G(odwin) 1875–1950 **2**
Woodson, Mike 1958— **78**

Woodson, Robert L. 1937— **10**
Woodson, Rod 1965— **79**
Wooldridge, Anna Marie *See Lincoln, Abbey*
Worrill, Conrad 1941— **12**
Worthy, James 1961— **49**
Worthy, Kym 1956— **84**
Wright, Antoinette 195(?)— **60**
Wright, Bruce McMarion 1918–2005 **3, 52**
Wright, Charles H. 1918–2002 **35**
Wright, Deborah C. 1958— **25**
Wright, Jeffrey 1966— **54**
Wright, Jeremiah A., Jr. 1941— **45, 69**
Wright, Lewin 1962— **43**
Wright, Louis Tompkins 1891–1952 **4**
Wright, Nathan, Jr. 1923–2005 **56**
Wright, Rayfield 1945— **70**
Wright, Richard 1908–1960 **5**
Wright, Timothy 1947— **74**
Wyatt, Addie L. 1924— **56**
Wynn, Albert R. 1951— **25, 77**

X, Malcolm 1925–1965 **1**
X, Marvin 1944— **45**
Xuma, Madie Hall 1894–1982 **59**
Xzibit 1974— **78**
Yabby You 1946–2010 **83**
Yancy, Dorothy Cowser 1944— **42**
Yar'Adua, Umaru 1951–2010 **69, 89**
Yarbrough, Camille 1938— **40**
Yarbrough, Cedric 1971— **51**
Yayi, Boni T. 1952— **84**
Yeboah, Emmanuel Ofosu 1977— **53**
Yette, Samuel F. 1929— **63**
Yoba, (Abdul-)Malik (Kashie) 1967— **11**
York, Dwight D. 1945— **71**
York, Malachi Z. *See York, Dwight D.*
York, Vincent 1952— **40**
Young, Al 1939— **82**
Young, Andre Ramelle *See Dre, Dr.*
Young, Andrew 1932— **3, 48**
Young, Charles 1864–1922 **77**

Young, Coleman 1918–1997 **1, 20**
Young, Donald, Jr. 1989— **57**
Young, Jean Childs 1933–1994 **14**
Young, Jimmy 1948–2005 **54**
Young, Ledisi Anibade *See Ledisi*
Young, Lee 1914–2008 **72**
Young, Leonidas Raymond *See Young, Lee*
Young, Roger Arliner 1899–1964 **29**
Young, Thomas 194(?)— *See Three Mo' Tenors*
Young, Whitney M(oore), Jr. 1921–1971 **4**
Young Jeezy 1977— **63**
Youngblood, Johnny Ray 1948— **8**
Youngblood, Shay 1959— **32**
Zane 1967(?)— **71**
Zollar, Alfred 1955(?)— **40**
Zollar, Jawole Willa Jo 1950— **28**
Zook, Kristal Brent 1966(?)— **62**
Zulu, Princess Kasune 1977— **54**
Zuma, Jacob 1942— **33, 75**
Zuma, Nkosazana Dlamini 1949— **34**